HAKLUYTUS POSTHUMUS, OR PURCHAS HIS PILGRIMES : CONTAYNING A HISTORY OF THE WORLD IN SEA VOYAGES AND LANDE TRAVELLS BY ENGLISHMEN AND OTHERS

HAKLUYTUS POSTHUMUS, OR PURCHAS HIS PILGRIMES : CONTAYNING A HISTORY OF THE WORLD IN SEA VOYAGES AND LANDE TRAVELLS BY ENGLISHMEN AND OTHERS

Samuel Purchas

www.General-Books.net

Publication Data:

Title: Hakluytus Posthumus, or Purchas His Pilgrimes : Contayning a History of the World in Sea Voyages and Lande Travells by Englishmen and Others
Volume: 1
Author: Purchas, Samuel, 1577?-1626
Publisher: Glasgow : J. Maclehose
Publication date: 1905
Subjects: Voyages and travels – Collections

1

HAKLUYTUS POSTHUMUS, OR PURCHAS HIS PILGRIMES : CONTAYNING A HISTORY OF THE WORLD IN SEA VOYAGES AND LANDE TRAVELLS BY ENGLISHMEN AND OTHERS

THE TABLE

The Christian, how both Free and a King. The Christian free, rich, a King. Heroicall Kings. Q. Elizabeth and K. James Englands two great Lights. Englands blessed shade under the Jacobajan Tree.

. 5. Of the propriety which Infidels have in their lands and goods: of propriety in the Sea, and of Salomons propriety of the Sea and Shoare at Ezion Geber. 38

Christians hold in Capite. Ethnicks in Villenage. Image of God. Keyes of Religion lock from heaven not earth. Meum Tuum. vi

The Contents of the Chapters Continued. page . 6. The commendations of Navigation, as an Art worthie the care of the most Worthie; the Necessitie, Commoditie, Dignitie thereof. 45

Navigation necessary. Seas manifold serviceablenesse. Excellencie of Navigation, of the Sea and Salomon. The Tyrians. Sea-monopoly. Sea addes true great-nesse to greatest Kings. Sea-greatnesse of English and Dutch. Mariners, why unruly. Concent and consent of Elements to Navigation.

, 7, Of Ezion Geber, Eloth, and the Red Sea: that of Edom it received that name, and communicated it to the Indian Ocean, by the Phoenician Navigations frequent in those times to India. 58

Eziongeber where. Eloth Esiongeber. Red Sea named of Idumaea, that of Edom. Elath. Sinus Elani-ticus. The Phoenix true in Mystery, not in History. Sinai-desert and Ophir-voyage, mysteries of faith and free grace.

. 8. Of Ophir, divers opinions weighed and censured; whether the Compas was knowne to the old World; that the remote parts were lately inhabited, the new World but newly, and a great part thereof not yet.

Peru why and whence so named. It was not Ophir. No new thing under the Sunne, how to be understood. The Ancients had not the Compasse. Peru is not Ophir. Columbus and Cabot mistaken. Sofala is not Ophir. Discourse of the confusion of Languages; of the Ebrew and Punick. The World peopled by degrees. America but newly.

. 9. Joctans posteritie seated in the East parts of Asia, amongst them, Ophir in India ultra Gangem, where Chryse was of old, and now is the Kingdome of Pegu, and the Regions adjoynlng.

Name-search of Joctans Posterity in India. Ophirs deriva-vatives. Mesha, Sephar, Ophir. Gold-Ants and Gryphans, Emblems. Reports ancient, midle and moderne of the Gold in those parts. Store of Gold in Pegu and Sumatra, the head and foot of Ophir.

The Contents of the Chzpters Contmuet. page . lo. Of the Gold, Silver, Gemmes, Ivorie, Almug trees, Apes and Peacockes, which Salomons Fleet brought from Ophir, with divers other profitable observations inserted. 95

Excellence of Metals, superexcellence of Gold. Greatest Ethnick sums. Davids talents, Salomons Revenue, audited. Davids Husbandry, Salomons Navigation, 2. wings of Magnificence. Varietie of Indian Gemmes; which prove Ophir to be India. India yeelds store of the things brought from Ophir.

. II. Probable conjectures of the course taken in the Ophirian Voyage, and accounts given of the three yeeres time spent there: also of the course taken in like Voyages by the Romans: and the divers Ports whereto the Spices and riches of India have in divers Ages beene brought, and thence dispersed to the severall parts of Europe.108

Roman Navigations to the Indies. Arabian Gulfe. Ophirian Voyage discussed, and accounts of the time and course. D. Dees calculation. Salomons servants who. First Spice-Merchants. Severall Ports of Indian Merchandise, changing with the Empires. Succession of Ports and Staples for the Indian Spice-trade.

Ophir and the voyage to Ophir. Opinions of Ophir and Tharshish. Tarshish what and where it was, discussed. Tartessus not Tharshish. Circumnavigations of Africa. Phaenician and Spanish Antiquities. Q. Elizabeth and King James.

The Contents of the Chapters Continued. page

CHAP. II.

Mans life a Pilgrimage. The Peregrinations of Christ, and the first Encompassing the habitable or then inhabited World by the holy Apostles and first Planters of the Gospell.-135 . I. Man by sinne becomne a Worldly Pilgrime; Christs Pilgrimage in the Flesh to recover him: Mans Spiritual! Pilgrimage in and from the World. 135

Mans Creation, Fall, Recoverie by an invaluable price. Christs peregrinations. Mans pilgrimage.

Apostles preeminence. Apostles preached thorow all the World in proper sense.

Peter not Bishop of Rome. Difference of an Apostle and Bishop.

Apostles tongues and miracles. Saints, Andrew, John, James. Saints, Jacobus, Justus, Philip and Simon Zelotes.

Saints, Thomas, Barthol. Matthew. Leaden legends Counterfeits. Changelings fathered on Apostles. S. Paul his Evangelists. S. Mark.

The Apostles preached onely in the old knowne World. Alexander. Christians much fewer since the Tartars.

The Contents of the Chapters Continued. pack . 7. Of America, whether it were then peopled. '159

America new-peopled. Conquerors the conquest of Religion. Americas peopling and progresse. Multiplication of the Israelites in Egypt, and of Americans.

Apostolicall Acts and Conquest compared with greatest Captaines. Two Hirams Paralel of Tabernacle and Temple; Printing Navigation. Learning revived by printing, by navigations help preacheth to the World. Romish and Jewish Church compared. Spaine fitted against Rome. Praier for more full Conversion of the World.

CHAP. in.

Of divers other principall Voyages, and Peregrinations mentioned in holy Scripture. Of the travels and dispersions of the Jewes; and of Nationall transmigrations.179

History and Mystery of the Patriarkes Travells. Jewes Travells and dispersions. Hope of their conversion. World peopled by peregrination. National Travels.

CHAP. IIIL

Fabulous Antiquities of the Peregrinations and Navigations of Bacchus, Osiris, Hercules, the Argonauts, Cadmus, the Grascian Navie to Troy, Menelaus, Ulysses, yeneas, and others.186

Truth occasion of Fables. Travells of Bacchus, Theseus, Hercules, the Argonauts. Argonauts Arts. Cadmus. Muster of the Grecian ships against Troy. The Travells of Menelaus, Ulysses, Daedalus, Eneas.

The Contents of the Chapters Continued. page

CHAP. V.

A briefe recitall of the famous expeditions mentioned in ancient Histories, of the Assyrians, Egyptians, Scythians, Ethiopians, Persians, and others., 195

Ninus his conquests and Ninive. Semiramis invadeth India. Sesostris Pillars. Zerah. Tearcon. Cyrus. Xerxes. Rom. Emperors travels.

CHAP. VI.

The travels of the antient Philosophers and learned men briefly mentioned.

The Author a great-little Traveller. Thales his Epistle. Solon. Solon and Croesus. Travells of Philosophers. Basenesse of Flatterers. Travels of Zeno, Pythagoras, Apollonius, Histaspis, of Historians.

CHAP. VII.

Phoenician Voyages, and especially that of Hanno, a

Carthaginian Captaine. 207

Phasnician Hand. Hanno Himilco discover the South North parts.

The Navigation of Hanno a Carthaginian Captaine on the Coasts of Africa, without Hercules Fillers, which he dedicated, written in the Punick tongue in the Temple of Saturne, after translated into the Greeke, and now into the English, with briefe annotations. 210

Hanno voyage, acts and discoveries on the African-Atlantine Coast. Discourse on the Voyages of Hanno and Iambulus.

The Contents of the Chapters Continued.

CHAP. VIII.

Iambulus his Navigation to Arabia, and Ethiopia, and thence to a strange Hand, from whence he sayled to Palimbothra in India.

Description of Iambuli Insula, the people, rites, creatures, Iambulus his reports of his Indian Travels.

CHAP. IX.

Great Alexanders Life, Acts, Peregrinations and Conquests briefly related.220

Alexander. Bucephalus. Alexander the Great his Acts, Arts, Persian Expedition. Alexanders sicknesse, battels with Darius, Ammon-voyage. Darius slaine. Amazonian fable. Crueltie. Fountaine of Oile. Alexanders Ambition frustrate; danger, escape, view of the Ocean. Alexanders returne, Mariage, Feasts, Guard, mourning, rage, death.

The Voyage of Nearchus and his Fleet set forth by Alexander the Great, from the River Indus to the bottome of the Persian Gulfe.232

Journall of Nearchus his voyage from Indus to the Persian Gulfe. Nearchus his Voyage from Indus to Tigris: honoured by Alexander.

CHAP. X.

The travels of Musaeus, Thebseus, and others mentioned by Saint Ambrosc; of others also mentioned in the Ecclesiasticall Histories of Eusebius, Ruffinus, Socrates, and Sozomen.239 Indian voyages of Musaeus and Thebaeus. Epistle of Calanus. Frumentius. Conversion of Indians and Iberians. Palladius his posting.

CHAP. XI.

A briefe and generall consideration of Europe. 24.4

The Contents of the Chapters Continued. page . I. Of Europe compared with the other parts of the

World 244- . 2. The names of Europe.245

Bounds of Europe and Etymologies of the name, with their . 3. The Ouantitie and Bounds. 247

Frankes and Romanes. Quantitie, Qualitie, Conquests of Europe.

8. 4. The Oualitie and Excellencies. 248 Europes Arts and Inventions. Religion, Civility.

. 5 Of the Languages of Europe.252

Languages. The Languages of Europe. Authors excuse for Europaean promise.

CHAP. xn.

Enquiries of Languages by Edw. Brerewood, lately professor of Astronomie in Gresham Colledge. 256

Extent of the Greeke tongue in antient times. Extent of the Greeke tongue in vulgar use. Decay of the old Greeke, where and whence. How corrupted. Difference of the old and moderne Greeke. Extent of the Latine. Roman tongue spread by Roman Colonies. The Latine abolished not the vulgar Languages. African, Gallike, Spanish, Panonian and Roman tongues. Latine, not vulgarly spoken in all places o the Roman Empire. When the Latine degenerated into Italian, French Spanish. Roman Emp. when and by whom it fell. Threefold corruption of Latines. Extent of the Latine tongue, discussed. Change of the Roman and English tongues. Tongues of Italy and France. Originall of French, Walsh language of the Celtas. Spanish, c. Punike or Phoenician language, that of Canaan: Hebrew, xiii

The Contents of the Chapters Continued.

Punike, the same, or neere to Hebrew. Extent of Slavonian, The Arabike, Syriake Turkish languages where spoken. Chaldee paraphrase. Hebrew not vulgarly understood after Captivity.

CHAP. XIII.

Master Brerewoods Enquiries of the Religions professed in the World: Of Christians, Mahumetans, Jewes, and Idolaters; with other Philosophical! speculations, and divers Annotations added. 304

Almost all Europe Christian. Almost all Afrike Mahumetan or Gentiles. Christians of Egypt. Habassia and other African Lands and Hands. Scaligers errour touching Presbyter John. Christians in Asia. The Christians in America, and their poore Christianity. The World of Mahumetan professors in the World. Mahumetans in Asia. The cause. Christianitie advanced other wayes. Idolatrous Nations in Europe, Africa and Asia. Idolatry in Asia and America. Judaisme in what Regions. Traditionary and Karaim Jewes and Samaritans. Tartars not Israelites. Tar-tarians not Israelites. Saracens not of Sara. Their Circumcision. Tartars not Israelites. Esdras his allegation discussed. Jewish Fables of Inclosed Jews of the Sea. Behemoth Liviathan. Hyperbolicall Whales. Depth of the Sea more then the height of Hils. Land not levell: where highest. Declivitie of the Chanels of Rivers. Christians, Mahumetans and Gentiles how proportioned in the World. Centre of the Earth and Sea, the same. Divers sorts of Christians. Patriarke of Constantinople why so great. Opinions of Greeke Church. Tyrus gave name to the Syrians: Now subject to the Pat. of Antiochia. Georgians, Circassians, Russians, their Rites and Opinions. Greeke faith in Russia and Poland. Nestorians in the East. Muzal Patriarchal! See of Nestorians. Their opinions and rites. Patriarcke of Mozal, or Seleucia. Nestorian opinions and rites. Syriake Testament. Jacobites whence called. Their opinions and rites. Opinions of Jacobites. Of the Egyptian Cophti. Rites and xiv

The Contents of the Chapters Continued.

opinions of the Cophti, or Egyptian Christians. Alvarez taxed. Patt. BB. of the East. Monks of SS. Antony Basil. Rites and Opinions of the Ethiopian Church. Abassine Circumcision and annuall Baptisme. Armenian Church. Rites and opinion of the Armenian and Maronite Christians. Patriarch, rites and opinions of the Maronite Christians. Succession of Easterne heresies. Saracens scourge amending the posteritie. Christian, Jewish, and Mahumetan, in what Languages. Armenians. Scriptures and Liturgie in vulgar tongues, of divers sorts of Christians. Scripture-translations. Greeke, Latine, Chaldee, Syriake Liturgies. What Liturgies in the Syriake, Chaldee, Greek, or Latine tongues.

CHAP. XIIIL

Relations of divers Travellers, touching the diversities of Christian Rites and Tenents in divers parts of the World. 403 . I. Tecla Maria an Abassine, his answeres to questions touching the Religion of the Abassines and Cophti. 403

Christians divided into foure parts, Greeks, Romists, Protestants, c. Ethiopian Rites and Faith declared by Tecla Maria an Ethiopian. Difference between the Cophti Ethiopians. Their Orders how given.

. 2. Relations of the. Jacobites and Armenians, written by Leonard Bishop of Sidon, Pope Gregorie the 13. his Nuncio to the Easterne parts,.411

Jacobite rites, Patriark BB. Two Armenian Patriarks their BB.

. 3. Of Simon Sulaka a Papall Easterne Patriarke amongst the Chaldaeans: and of divers others thither sent. Of Abdesu, Aatalla, Donha his successor?. 414

Titular Patriarks obeying Rome.

The Contents of the Chapters Continued. page . 4. Of the Cophti, their Synode at Cairo, the Jesuites being the Popes Agents, and of Stephen Colinzas message to the Georgians, and two Jesuites sent to the Maronites.415

Synods of the Cophti. Georgians. Popes Messengers and gifts to the Maronites.
Errores ex libris Maronitarum excerpti 1580 sunt autem hujusmodi.418
A Jesuites collection of opinions ascribed to the Maronites.

. 5. Of the condition of life in which the Greeks now live, and of their Rites
of Fasts, Feasts, and other observations, gathered out of the booke of Christo-pheros
Angelos, a Greekish Monke and Priest. 422

Scripture mis-applied. Greekes tributes divers. Tithing of children. Greeke Rites
observed in their foure Lents. Their manner of fasting. Wed. Frid. Sat. Sunday,
Twelfdaies rites. Holy Bread and Water. Grascian giving of Orders, rites of Prayer,
Confession, c. Greekish manner of administring the Sacraments, their Excommuni-
cation. Patriarch of Alexandria drinketh poison unhurt; Jew poisoned by it. Greeke
Menkes hand-labour, habit, diver-sitie, fasts: no begging. Life of Greek-Monks,
penance, fasts, night-prayers, probation. Greekes Monk-sharing, Forgivenesse, Easter,
conceits of the Crosse. Maintenance of the Greeke Clergie.

CHAP. XV.

Collections out of Peter Stroza, Secretarie to Pope Paul the Fifth, his Treatise of
the Opinions of the Chaldsans, touching the Patriarke of Babylon, and the Nestorians
in Asia. 449

From the Patriarchall Chamber, Prayers and
Blessings be given to you. 450

Elias Patriarke of Babylon. Flattering Letter of the poore Babylonian Patriarch to
the Pope. Elias beliefe. In what things Easterne Nestorians differ from us. xvi

The Contents of the Chapters Continued. page

CHAP. XVI.

A briefe Survey of the Ecclesiasticall Politic ancient and moderne, or of the severall
Patriarchs, Archbishops and Bishops Sees thorow the Christian world: also of the
Jesuites Colledges and numbers, and of other Monasticall Orders. 456

Beginning and alteration of the number and power of Christian Patriarkes. Division
of the Easterne world; Patriarchs of Constantinople, c. One Patriarchall See made five.
Bishopricks Sc Jesuits Colledges in Italic. Catalogue of Bishoprickes and Jesuites
in Italy and Sicilia. Bishoprickes of Spaine and their Revenues, as also of Dukes,:
c. Catalogue of Bishoprickes and Jesuites in Spaine and France. Belgian, German
and Switzer Bishops and Jesuits. Catalogue of Bishoprickes and Jesuites in Europe
and India. Bishops Sees. Jesuits upstarts. Orders of Knighthood. Other disorders.
Numbers, kinds, and beginnings of Papall-religious Orders. Papall Orders.

CHAP. XVII.

A Discourse of the diversitie of Letters used by divers Nations of the world: the
Antiquitie, manifold use and varietie thereof: with exemplarie descriptions of very
many strange Alphabets.485

Letters, how ancient and usefull; by whom invented. Samaritan Letters whether
ancienter then the present Hebrew. Greeke Inscriptions in Ionike Letters. Inventers
of Letters. Diversity of Letters, and of the posture or reading of them. Phoenician,
Hebrew, Ionike, Greeke and Latine Letters compared. Hiero-glyphicall Obeliske.
Hebrew Letters. Israel-Samaritan Coines. Divers kindes of Alphabets. Divers Al-

phabets, old and new. Divers kinds of Easterne Alphabets. Malabar writing. Gotike, Saxon and English Alphabets.

PUBLISHERS' NOTE

Samuel Purchas, son of George Purchas, Yeoman, was born at Thaxted in Essex. The date of his birth is uncertain; in his Marriage Allegation, dated 2nd December, 1601, his age is given as about 27," but in the Thaxted Baptismal Register the date of his baptism is entered as 20th November, 1577." The use of the word about' points to some uncertainty in the mind of the writer, and it is probable that his baptism took place shortly after his birth, and that at the time of his marriage he was really only in his twenty-fifth year. This is confirmed by the statement on the engraved title page of his ' Pilgrimes," that at the date of its publication in 1625 he was aged forty-eight. He was educated at St. John's College, Cambridge, where he took the degree of M. A. in 1600, and afterwards proceeded to that of B. D. In 1601 he was Curate of Purleigh in Essex, where he married in December of that year Jane Lease, daughter of Vincent Lease of Westhall, Co. Suffolk, Yeoman. Both Purchas and his bride are described as household servants of Dr. Freake, Parson of Purleigh. On the 24th August, 1604, he was instituted to the Vicarage of Eastwood on the presentation of the King, and there he remained until 1614.

It was doubtless during his residence at Eastwood that he commenced to gather materials for his Pil-grimes." Eastwood is only two miles from Leigh on the Thames, and Leigh, at that time, was a flourishing seaport ' well stocked with lusty seamen." There lived, when they were not afloat, the Cockes, the Bonners, the Goodlads, and many other seafarers whose names are mentioned in the ' Pilgrimes," and there Purchas took down from ' his owne reports to myself the ' strange adventures of Andrew Battell, of Leigh, sent by the Portugals prisoner to Angola." Purchas himself was no traveller: he tells us indeed that 'least Travellers may be greatest writers Even I, which have written so much of travellers and travells, never travelled 200 miles from Thaxted in Essex where I was borne." But he made up for his want of experience as a traveller by his untiring industry. He was never able to maintain ' a Vicarian or Subordinate Scribe," but ' his own hands had to worke as well as his head to contrive these voluminous Buildings his books except in some few Transcriptions or Translations, the most also of them by his sonne S. P. that one and the same name might both father and further the whole." When it is mentioned that his Pilgrimage ' and ' Pilgrimes' together fill over five thousand folio pages of close print, his industry becomes impressive. In 1614 he was appointed Chaplain to George Abbot, Archbishop of Canterbury, and in the same year he was inducted Rector of St. Martin's, Ludgate, by the patronage of John King, 'late Lord Bishop of London, to whose bountie under God, I willingly ascribe 1 Camden's Britannia, ed. Gibson, 1695, column 341.

2 ' Pilgrimes," I. i. 74.

xrii my life, delivered from a sickly Habitation, and consequently (as also by opportunities of a London Benefice) whatsoever additions in my later editions of my Pilgrimage; these present Pilgrimes also with their peregrinations," The latter preferment ' afforded him the opportunities of bookes, conference, and manifold intelligence; and as the benefice was not the worst, so was it the best suited in the world to his content." On July nth, 1615, he was incorporated B. D. of Oxford. He died in 1626, aged 49, leaving behind him a son Samuel, and a daughter Martha, another daughter, Mary, having predeceased him in 1619.

Anthony a Wood in his Fasti Oxonienses (and most of Purchas's biographers follow him) says of his ventures that ' by the publishing of which books he brought himself into debt, but died not in prison as some have said, but in his own house (a little while after the king had promised him a deanery)." Purchas was not a rich man; he says, ' If I had not lived in great part upon Exhibition of charitable friends, and on extraordinary labours of Lecturing (as the terme is) the Pilgrime had beene a more agreeing name to me, than Purchas'; yet from his Will, which is here reprinted, it would seem that when it was drawn up on the 31st May, 1625, in the year before his death, he had considerable property to dispose of, and there is no evidence to show that in the interval his affairs had become embarrassed. The misunderstanding has probably arisen from the statement in the Preface to the ' Microcosmus," where Purchas mentions the death of his brother-in-law, Wilham Pridmore, in 1618, 'leaving Mee the cares of another Family, the

Wood's Athenae Oxonienses, ed. Bliss, 181 5, Vol. II. column 363. Page xxix.

Widdow and the Fatherlesse," and a few weeks after, the death of ' my dearest Brother (Daniel) whose intangled Booke-estate perplexed Me in a new kind of Book-ishnes, with Heterogenean toyle of Body, and unacquainted vexations of Minde, to pay manifold debts, and to provide for his foure litde Fatherlesse and Motherlesse Orphans. But as this happened seven years before his Will was made, it would appear that Purchas had overcome whatever temporary difficulties the death of his brother and brother-in-law had occasioned.

The only original portrait of Purchas now known is that on the engraved tide page of the ' Pilgrimes," the portraits by Boissard and Richardson being copies of it. The Wiir of the Rev. Thomas Purchas (brother of Samuel, and his successor in the Vicarage of

Eastwood), shows that there were in 1657 portraits both of Samuel Purchas, ' with the Coat of Arms," and of his father, but these, if still in existence, have not been traced.

Of Samuel Purchas's books the first to be published was ' Purchas His Pilgrimage or Relations of the World and the Religions observed in all Ages and Places Discovered, from the Creation unto this Present." This volume was first published in 1613, a second edition appeared in 1614, a third in 1617, and the fourth and last in 1626. This fourth edition being printed uniform in size and type with the ' Pilgrimes' is frequently bound and lettered as the Fifth Volume of that work: it is, however, a distinct work.

' Purchas his Pilgrim. Microcosmus, or the Historie of ' Transactions of the Essex Archaeological Society, 1869, Vol. IV. p. 178.

Man. Relating the Wonders of his Generation, Vanities in his Degeneration, Necessity of his Regeneration. Meditated on the Words of David. Psalm 39, 5." was published in 1619, as a thick foolscap 8vo., and has never been reprinted. ' The King's Tower, and Triumphant Arch of London," a Sermon on 2 Samuel xxii. 51, appeared in 1623.

Hakluytus Posthumus, or Purchas his Pilgrimes, Con-tayning a History of the World, in Sea Voyages, lande Travells, by Englishmen and others," was ' Imprinted at London for Henry Fetherston at ye signe of the rose in Pauls Churchyard 1625." It has an engraved title page, and also four other title pages which detail the general contents of the four volumes into which the work is divided.

In the Preface To the Reader (p. xli) Purchas says As for Master Hakluyts many yeeres Collections, and what stocke I received from him in written Papers, in the Table of Authours you shall find; whom I will thus farre honour, that though it be but Materials, and that many Bookes have not one Chapter in that kind, yet that stocke encouraged me to use my endevors in and for the rest. I was therein a Labourer also, both to get them (not without hard conditions) and to forme and frame those Materials to their due place and order in this iedifice, the which Artifice (such as it is) being mine owne." From this it may be inferred that Purchas was assisting Hakluyt to collect the materials which were left unpublished at Hakluyt's death in 1616; it accounts, too, for the bequest of Hakluyt's papers to Purchas, and for the title ' Hakluytus Posthumus' on the engraved title page of the 'Pilgrimes."

Purchas tells us that the book was four years in printing, and that ' it had not beene possible for me in London distractions to have accomplished so great a Designe, but for the opportunities of His Majestie's Colledge at Chelsie, where these foure last Summers I have retired my selfe (without Pulpit Non-residence) to this Worke." He pays a well-deserved tribute to 'Master Henry Fetherstone' in these words: 'And for the price, as I cannot set it, so I must acknowledge the adventurous courage of the Stationer Master Henry Fetherstone (like Hercules helping Atlas) so long to beare this my heavy world at such expense."

The first book of the ' Pilgrimes," which is intended as an introduction to the whole, is paged separately, as it was printed after the greater part of the other nine books. Some copies of the first book contain on page 6 a map entitled ' Hondius, his Map of the Christian World' with the Latin title ' Designatio Orbis Christiani." This map is repeated on page 115. Other copies contain on page 65 a difi erent map entitled 'Typus Orbis Terrarum," with the motto beneath 'Domini est Terra Plenitudo ejus, Orbis Terrarum Universi qui habitant in eo. Psalmo 24." Both maps are here reproduced.

The text of this edition is an exact reprint of that of 1625 with the following exceptions: the letters i, j, u, and v are used according to modern custom, contracted forms of letters have been extended, and obvious printers' errors, both of spelling and punctuation, have been corrected. The quaint headlines to the pages of the original edition, which Purchas states were partly his work, and partly ' such as pleased the Corrector," are given in the Table of Contents. References to the volumes and pages of the original text have been inserted in square brackets in the margin, following the suggestion of Professor Skeat regarding Messrs. Maclehose's edition of Hakluyt's ' Principall Navigations." The five indexes of the original edition of the ' Pilgrimes' will be superseded by a fuller index in this edition.

Glasgow, January, 1905.

Dated 31 May, 1625, Proved 21 Oct., 1626 P. C. a 137 Hek.

In the Name of God, Amen. May 31, a. d., 1625, I Samuell Purchas, Clarke, Rector of the Church of St. Martin's, neere Ludgate in London, often admonished of the present to provide for a better life and nowe in toller-able health, blessed be God, doe make and constitute and ordaine this my Last will and testament. Imprimis, I commend my soule to God my Father in the name of his Sonne Jesus my saviour, through the sanctifyinge of the Holy and Coeternall spirit, beleevinge that Christ, (God manifested in the flesh), hath died for my sinnes, risen againe for my justification, hath ascended in tryumph leadinge captivity captive, and beinge sett at the right hand of power farre above all heavens, there appeareth before God for all saints and for me, lesse than the least of all, to make intercession for us synners and in his Fathers house to take possession for us mortalls that where he is wee may bee also; and from whence I expect with hope his glorious cominge to Judgment, my soule meane while shall out of his body of death returne to God that gave it, and rest with the spiritts of just and perfect men whose names are written in the booke of life; My body also shall rest in hope of a better resurrection, whereby this vile body shalbe made like to his glorious body who hath loved me and hath given himselfe for me. O Lord I have waited for thy salvation, I live not but Christ liveth in me, and to me to live is Christe and to dye is gayne, nor desire I to live but to do his worke, and so doe service to his servants, nor feare I to dye because I serve soe mightie, soe mercifuu a Lord. Even soe come L: Jesu, come into me the worst of the worst of synners that where my synnes have abounded, thy grace may in the pardon and mortification of them super-abounde, that whensoever thou shalt come unto me, I may be ready with my loynes girded with oyle in my lampe and my lampe burninge, my soule also wakinge to enter with the Bridegroom, that what by faith I have beleeved by hope as an ancor of the soule sure and sted-faste laid hold on, I maye in his presence where is fullnes of ioye enioye in super excessive charitie. Amen Amen; the waie, the truth, the life, come L: Jesus, come quicklie, with with the spiritt of grace and power unto thy whole Church; enlarge the bounds thereof to the worlds end and now make it truly Catholike in sinceritie of truth and in extension of thy charitie unto Jewes, Turks, Infidells that thou mayest be the light to enlighten the Gentiles, and the glory of thine Israeli; Protect thy people in peace, unite the disagreeinge harts and disioynted states of Christendome, recover those which have fallen by Mahametan impiety and thy ser-vantes which groane under Turkish tyranny; Bringe out of Babilon those which are involved in the misteries of Papall impurity; Let God arise and lett his enemyes bee scattered, that Babell may be Ruined and Syon repaired; Putt into the harts of Christian princes to hate the whore and to love thy spouse, that they may be nursinge Fathers and nursinge mothers to the Israeli of God, And as wee blesse thy name for our late godly princes Q, Elizabeth and Kinge James of happy memory, soe lett this testimony of love and duty be inserted as a christian legacie, my prayer for his gratious Majestie Kinge Charles, that from the pre- sent hopes he may daily proceede In grace and godlines, still growinge noe lesse in piety then in yeares, filled with the spiritt of wisdome and understanding, the spiritt of counsell and fortitude, the spirit of knowledge of the feare of the Lord, that under him thy people of this citty and kingdome maye live in all godlynes honesty. The Lord make our gratious Queene now cominge unto his house like Rachell like Lea, which two did build the house of Israeli, that through them Create Brittaine may bee famous and Ireland may reioice, and their posteritie may swaye these scepters till the endes of time. To this Citty lett me bequeath prayers for thy mightie protection manifold bounties and deliverance from the present pestilence, and from all hardnes of hart in sacrilege, usury and other synnes, and to that litle flocke committed to thy servantes unworthy ministery, give O Lord fructifyinge grace, the ymortall seede which the mortall seedman hath sowen in their eares, still sproutinge and multiplyinge in theire harts and lives when he shall have passed the possibilitye of further mortalitye, and double thy spirit in the succeedinge Pastor. Now for the rest, thou, O Lord, art my rest, my hope, my happenes, my love, my life, thou art the husband of the widdowe, and father of the fatherles, the God of thy servantes and of their seede, and thou art the porcion of the livinge and of the dead, in confidence of whose free grace and meere mercy thy servant is bold to bequeath this legacie which thou hast written in thy testament and ratified by the death of the testator, and whereof thou ever livest the executor, that thou wilt never faile nor forsake them and that thou wilt bee their shield and their exceedinge great reward, Blessed be thy name O Lord which out of nakednes and nothinge hast created and raised unto me this estate of worldlie goodes, and though I am lesse than the least of all thy mercies, borne naked into the world at first, and onely not naked when I entered into the affairs of the world in the state of matrymonie after beinge then without porcion or purchase of either fide (sic) without house, lands, livinge, or any ritches else, but thy gracious promise to those which seeke the Kingdome of God first and his righteousnes that all these things shalbee added; yet hast thou given me house and landes with other goodes to bequeath to myne (or rather to thine) after me: my will is, (for thine is such) that all my debts be first trulie and fully satisfied and the charges of my Funerall in moderate sorte discharged, Also I bequeath five poundes to be given to the poore people of Thaxted where I first receaved light. Item I give will and bequeath to my sonne Samuell all that my messuage and tenement in the parish of Thaxted in Essex which I latelie bought of Absolon Onion, with the lands, mill and other the appurtenances nowe in the occupation of the said Absolon or his assignes conteyninge about tenn acres more or lesse. To have and to hold to him and his heires for ever. Item, I give, will and bequeath one other porcion of land of tenn acres or thereabouts lyinge neere to the former which I lately bought of my brother William Purchas, by him purchased of one

Kent alias Reynolds who formerlie had bought the same of Absolon Onyon aforesaid, unto Martha my daughter and to her heires for ever. Moreover I bequeath unto the said Martha all those landes in fower croftes or closes neere to a hamlett called Boyton end (which latelie were belonginge to my Father George Purchas of pious memory) in the parish of Thaxted aforesaid, nowe in the tenure of my brother William above mentioned and containing about tenn acres more or lesse, with all the commoditics and appurtenances thereto. To have and to hold to the said Martha and her heires for ever. Provided alwaies, and my will is that my wife Jane shall, so longe as she shall contynue a widdowe, have, hold and enioye the profittes and disposicion of the same house and landes before bequeathed to my sonne Samuell and my daughter Martha, to inhabite, sett, or lett, and to the use of the same as shall seeme best to her, payinge yearlie duringe the said terme, unto my son Samuell and to my daughter Martha other three poundes yearlie by even and equall porciones every quarter (that is to saye at Christmas, our Lady daie in March, Midsummer day and Michaelmas daie) to be paid unto each of them exceptinge such yeares or quarters of yeares as my said Sonne or daughter shall live in house with their said mother or shall receave soe much or more from her towardes or to his or her maintenance. But if my said wife Jane shall after my death be married to another husband, then my will is that she shall from thenceforth have the thirdes onely of the premised houses and landes, and that my sonne and daughter shall have present power to enter on the same tenementes landes according as is before bequeathed, and the same to have hold and enjoie to their best behoofe. Item, my will is that if one of my children die before the other seized and in possession of any part of the premisses, that the survivor shall inherite the same, except the deceased left legitimate issue, but if (which God forbidd) both my Sonne and daughter shall dye without issue, my will is that, whatsoever of the premisses shall not be alienated by them or either of them before their said death, shall descend unto Daniell Purchas the sonne of my brother William and to his heires for ever, And if the said Daniell be then dead or leave noe issue, I bequeath the same to Samuell Purchas the sonne of the said William and to his heires for ever. And if it should happen that my brother William's posterity should faile (which God forbidd) I bequeath the said landes and remainder of landes with the appurtenances unto the heires of my brother George Purchas, that is to his eldest sonne John and his heires for ever. And in defect of such yssue of my brother George, I bequeath the said landes and remainder of landes as afore said to Samuell, sonne of my brother Thomas Purchas of Eastwood, and to his heires for ever, Provided alwaie and my will is that in such succession of Daniell Purchas or any other which shall inherite the premisses or any part thereof by defect of yssue of my sonne and daughter aforesaid, the fifte parte of the profittes and rentes reasonably valued and without fraude shalbe yearlie paid at Christmas to the Vicar and Church Wardens of Thaxted aforesaid for the time beinge, successively, to be distributed to the poore of that parish at their dis-crecion, And in defect of such payment my will is that the said Vicar and churchwardens or any two of them shall and may enter and distraine on the premisses soe much as maye make satisfaction for such defect or defects from time to time and for ever. Item, I will and hereby charge my said sonne and daughter that in case of unliklynes of yssewe of their own bodies that neither of them do alienate or sell awaye any parte of the premisses with intent to frustrate the intents before mentioned of the said Daniell or the rest, except uppon such cause or necessitye or other just motive as in the feare of God and in good conscience they shall finde reasonable and meete, without indirect dealinge or fraudulent carriage herein, that as I would not abridge their libertie in case of honestie for their iust good, soe they doe not wilfully abuse it to pleasure others and needlesly or wantonly to hinder the premised intent. Item, I give and bequeath to Daniell the sonne of my brother William aforesaid, the somme of twentie marks to be paid to his Father or mother when he or they shall resume him into their tuition and maintenance, for the use and benefitt of the said Daniell. Item, I give my library and all my books, globes, mapps and chartes unto Samuell my sonne, except those bookes or workes or any part of them whereof I have beene the author, namely my Pilgrimage, Pilgrim and Pilgrimes of which he hath already had one printed coppie of each of them. The other printed bookes thereof nowe in my custody, or nowe due, or hereafter to be due uppon reckoninges from Mr. Fetherstone, I reserve and bequeath to the performance of my will, that is, one of each to my daughter Martha, Item, to my brethren George and William, and to my brother in law William Perkins to each of them one entire worke of my Pilgrimes in fower bookes nowe in their handes, and if any reckonings they or any of them have alreadye paid anye thinge for any of them, or shall pay hereafter (except the charges of bindinge) I will that the same or the worth thereof shalbe repaied to them againe. The rest of those bookes reserved as aforesaid, I bequeath to my wife to doe with as she shall thinke fitt. Alsoe I except out of the former guifte to my Sonne such English bookes of devotion as my said wife Jane shall reserve for her own use and her daughters. Item, I give and bequeath to Martha my said daughter thirtie poundes of English money to be paid her out of the said bookes by her brother for recompense and consideration of so great a guifte given to him, the same thirtie poundes to be paid to her assignes by her said brother Samuell my sonne at the daie of her marriage, or when she shall bee one and twentie yeares old, which shall first happen. Item, I give and bequeath to the said Martha my best bedd and bedd-stedd with curtaines, valence and coverlett, a paire of blanketts a paire of pillowes and pillowbeers, two paire of sheetes, a boulster, one damaske tablecloth and a dozen of napkins (all which peeces of household and naperie I will to bee of the best I have). Alsoe my best bowle ot silver guilt with the cover, one double salt of silver guilte and six guilded spoones of silver. Item, if my wife Jane shalbe married againe my will is that my said daughter Martha shall and maye demande, challenge and carry awaye the one moiety or halfe of all my goodes and moveables which shalbe left after the debtes and Funerall paid and discharged, or in defect thereof, soe much money as they shalbe valued at in equall and iust estimacion. Item, I make and ordaine my wife Jane sole Executrix of this my last will, and my brethren George, William and William Perkins aforesaid overseers, desiringe their care and assistance therein. Item, I give my seale ringe to my Sonne Samuell and my ringe with the deatheshead to my brother William. Alsoe I give to my sonne Samuell whatsoever bookes household or other goodes nowe in his possession at Cambridge. Item, my will is con-cerninge that peece of land at Monkes streete bequeathed to my daughter Martha, which I bought of my brother William, that if my sonne Samuell shall like to hold it and to contynue it to the house, that then he shall paye or cause to be paid to my daughter Martha or her assignes the somme of a hundred and tenn poundes for the same landes within six monethes after his mother's decease or marriage, which shall first happen, or else the same to remaine to Martha as above is in this my testament declared. This my last will and testament, written all with mine owne hand, was sealed, subscribed and acknowledged the daie and yeare above written in the presence of Wm. Slatyer, Theodore Heape, John Gee, Richard Wossencrofte by his marke, William Purchas, Mary Bullivant her marke, Mary Colson her marke.

DECLARATION OF PROBATE.

Probatum fuit testamentum suprascriptum Apud London, coram Magistro Thoma Eden, Legum Doctore, Surrogato venerabilis viri Domini Henrici Marten, Mili-tis, Legum etiam Doctoris, Curiae Prerogativas Cantu-aniensis Magistri custodis sive Commissarii legitime constituti, vicesimo primo die mensis Octobris Anno Domini millesimo sexcentesimo vicesimo sexto, Juramento Janae Purchas relictae dicti de-functi et executricis in hujusmodi testamento nominatae, cui commissa fuit admin-istratio omnium et singulorum bonorum, jurium et creditorum antedicti defuncti, de bene et fideliter administrand' eadem ad Sancta Dei Evangeha juratae.

Prince of Wales.

Most Excellent Prince,

Ay a poore Pilgrime salute Your High-nesse in the words of a better Samuel and. Sam. c). 20. Seer, On whom is the desire of all Israel? is it not on Thee and all thy Fathers House? In this House we admire the innumerable Royall Ancestrie, wee triumph in His Majesties present

Kin. 7. 2 1.

light, wee praise God and pray for the two hopefull Columnes, that they may be Pillars of Stabilitie and Strength in the Lords House, firmer then Salomons " 3- ' Jachin and Boaz.

Sir, having out of a Chaos of confused intelligences framed this Historicall World, by a New way of Eye-evidence; Your Princely pietie, innate clemency, and the Time it selfe (festivall both in the ordinarie season and extraordinarie preparation) emboldned my obtrusion on Your Highnesse. The Magnificence of Your Princely Court hath entertayned Men of many Nations, yea hath admitted (in Parkes and Places fitting) Beasts, Fowles, Plants of remoter Regions: and now much more, in a World of acclamations to Your joyfuu designes, a world xxxvii of Pilgrimes seemed sutable; each of which presents one or other Countrey; and all, the rarities and varieties of all. Here also Your Highnesse may refresh Your weari-nesse from State-affaires (if any of these Lines may at any time be ambitious of such lustre) in seeing at leisure and pleasure Your English Inheritance dispersed thorow the World, whereof these Twentie Bookes are the Evidence and Records: the English Martialist everywhere following armes, whiles his Countrey is blessed at home with Beati Pacifici; the Merchant coasting more Shoares and Hands for commerce, then his Progenitors have heard off, or himselfe can number; the Mariner making other Seas a Ferry, and the widest Ocean a Strait, to his discovering attempts; wherein wee joy to see Your Highnesse to succeed Your Heroike Brother, in making the furthest Indies by a New Passage neerer to Great

Britaine. Englands out of England are here presented, yea Royall Scotland, Ireland, and Princely Wales, multiplying new Scepters to His Majestie and His Heires in a New World. In all, the glorie of His Majesties happy Raigne, and thereby of the English Name and Nation, by a poore Zelote of both, is truly and amply related, beyond the conjectures of the passed Ages, to the admiration of the present, and amusing (if not amazing) of the future. In which so long a Worke humbly craveth pardon for other errors, for this presumption.

Your Highnesse most humbly devoted

SAMUEL PURCHAS

To the Reader Isdome is said to bee the Science of things The profit to Divine and humane. Divine things are J' p jh either naturall or supernaturall: these such, as the naturall man knoweth not, nor can know, because they are spiritually (with a spirituall Eye) discerned; called i. Cor. 2.14. wisedome to salvation, the proper subject of Theologie, and not the peculiar argument of this- '- 3-Worke; which notwithstanding beeing the labour of a '5 professed Divine, doth not abhorre from the same; but occasionally every where by Annotations, and in some parts professedly by special! Discourses, insinuateth both the Historic and Mystery of Godlinesse, the right use of History, and all other Learning.

Naturall things are the more proper Object, namely the ordinary Workes of God in the Creatures, preserving and disposing by Providence that which his Goodnesse and Power had created, and dispersed in the divers parts of the World, as so many members of this great Bodie. Such is the History of Men in their diversified hewes and colours, quantities and proportions; of Beasts, Fishes, Fowles, Trees, Shrubs, Herbs, Minerals, Seas, Lands, Meteors, Heavens, Starres, with their naturall affections: in which many both of the Antient and Moderne have done worthily; but if neernesse of the Object deceive me not, this surmounteth them all in two Priviledges, the veritie and varietie, especially of things in this kind remotest and rarest.

It is true, that as every member of the bodie hath somewhat eminent, whereby it is serviceable to the whole; so every Region excelleth all others in some peculiar Raritie, which may be termed extraordinary respectively, though otherwise most common and ordinary

See of the in its owne place. So Our England in the naturall

Wonders of temper, accidentall want of Wolves, artificiall Rings of

Harrison's Bels, Sheepe not at all or seldome drinking, Lands and

Description of Waters turning Wood in some parts to Stone, Wonders

Brit. . 2. of the Peke and other parts, doth not degenerate from 7 f'rf nature, but hath a peculiar nature, almost miraculous to other Countries, as the naturall Wonders of their Regions are to us: so also Irelands want of venome in Creatures, fulnesse of it, and barbarousnesse in many of her wilder

Natives, after so long trayning in Civilitie, and so ancient

Renowme for Sanctitie: and so each part is to other part in some or other part, and particular respect admirable.

What a World of Travellers have by their owne eyes observed in this kinde, is here (for the most part in their owne words transcribed or translated) delivered. What kinde of not by one professing Methodically to deliver the Historie Hiftorie this Nature according to rules of Art, nor Philosophically is to discusse and dispute; but as in way of Discourse, by each Traveller relating what in that kind he hath scene. And as David prepared materials for Salomons Temple; or (if that be too arrogant) as Alex, furnished Aristotle with Huntsmen and Observers of Creatures, to acquaint him with their diversified kinds and natures; or (if that also seeme too ambitious) as Sense by Induction of particulars yeeldeth the premisses to Reasons Syllogisticall arguing; or if we shall be yet more homely, as Pioners are employed by Enginers, and Labourers serve Masons, and Bricklayers, and these the best Surveyers and Architects: so here Purchas and his Pilgrimes minister individuall and sensible materials (as it were with Stones, Brickes and Mortar) to those universall Speculators for their Theoricall structures. And well may the Author be ranked with such Labourers (howsoever here a Master- builder also) for that he hath beene forced as much to the Hod, Barrow and Trowel, as to contemplative sur-vaying: neither in so many Labyrinthian Perambulations thorow, and Circumnavigations about the World in this and his other Workes, was ever enabled to maintaine a Vicarian or Subordinate Scribe, but his own hands to worke, aswell as his head to contrive these voluminous Buildings; except in some few Transcriptions or Translations, the most also of them by his sonne S. P. that one and the same name might both father and further the whole.

As for Master Hakluyts many yeeres Collections, and what stocke I received from him in written Papers, in the Table of Authours you shall find: whom I will thus farre honour, that though it be but Materials, and that many Bookes have not one Chapter in that kind, yet that stocke encouraged me to use my endevours in and for the rest. I was therein a Labourer also, both to get them (not without hard conditions) and to forme and frame those Materials to their due place and order in this Edifice, the whole Artifice (such as it is) being mine owne. Traduce mee not, nor let any impute to boasting what I have said of my sole working (I know there is a vae soli) but I am compelled to doe it to prevent an Objection of my promised Europaean supply to my Pilgrimage. I confesse, I was too forward to promise, because others have beene so backward to assist: which I have in former Editions signified, but to blind Eyes and deafe Eares. Whose Librarie, whose Purse hath beene opened to me, let his mouth be opened against me also: Europe otherwise could not, nor now upon any price (it is too late) can be Purchased. I would not be misconstrued to ungratitude. Many have applauded my endevours, but probitas laudatur alget. If I had not lived in great part upon Exhibition of charitable friends, and on extraordinary labours of Lecturing (as the terme is) the Pilgrime had beene a more agreeing name to me, then Purchas. Yet let my name be for ever forgotten, if I remember not his, which the Adversaries have (seeking to steale him from us after his death) by their calumnie made more memorable; I meane, my decessed Patron Doctor King, late Lord Bishop of London, to whose bountie under God, I willingly ascribe my life, delivered from a sickly Habitation, and consequently (as also by opportunities of a London Benefice) whatsoever additions in my later Editions of my Pilgrimage; these present Pilgrimes also with their peregrinations. Yet such is ordinarily the greatnesse of the Epha, and smalnesse of the Shekel, in London Cures (especially within the wals) that wee are inabled thereby to disablings for workes of that kinde, whiles we must preach in season and out of season, (I say not out of reason) that wee may live.

One wing that Reverend and bountifull hand gave in hope that some blessed hand would adde the other, to fit me for an Europaean flight, wherein not finding his hopes seconded, he promised to right me himselfe (these were his syllables) but death righted him, and I am forced to wrong the World. I speake not to accuse any, for of whom, to whom can I complaine, but to plaine and excuse my selfe, and withall to dedicate my thanke-fulnesse with the continuance of this Monument to that worthy Name. Acts 17, 21. But to returne to our Philosopher; I also have beene an Athenian with these Athenians, one delighting to tell, the others to heare some new thing. I have therefore either wholly omitted or passed dry foot things neere and common; Far fetched and deare bought are the Lettice sutable to our lips. Common and ordinarie plants I remit to the Herbarists. Europaean Rarities (except in the remoter Regions both from our habitation and knowledge, as Island, Norway, Sueden, Constantinople, the Mediterranean Hands, c.) to the Historians peculiar to each Countrey therein. My Genius delights rather in by-wayes then high-wayes, and hath therein by Tracts and Tractates of Travellers made Causies and xlii

High-wayes, every where disposing these Pilgrime-Guides, that men without feare may travell to and over the most uncouth Countries of the World: and there be shewed with others Eyes, the Rarities of Nature, and of such things also as are not against Nature, but either above it, as Miracles, or beside the ordinarie course of it, in the extraordinary Wonders, which Gods Providence hath therein effected according to his good and just pleasure. And thus much for the workes of God.

Things humane, are such as Men are, or have, or have done or suffered in the World. Here therefore the various Nations, Persons, Shapes, Colours, Habits, Rites, Religions, Complexions, Conditions, Politike and Oecon-omike Customes, Languages, Letters, Arts, Merchandises, Wares, and other remarkeable Varieties of Men and humane Affaires are by Eye-witnesses related more amply and certainly then any Collector ever hath done, or perhaps without these helpes could doe. And thus we have shewed the scope of the Author, and profitable use of the Worke: which could not but be voluminous, having a World for the subject, and a World of Witnesses for the Evidence: and yet (except where the Author or Worke it selfe permitted not) these vast Volumes are contracted, and Epitomised, that the nicer Reader might not be cloyed. Here also both Elephants may swimme in deepe voluminous Seas, and such as want either lust or leisure, may single out, as in a Library of Bookes, what Author or Voyage shall best fit to his profit or pleasure. I might adde that such a Worke may seeme necessarie to these times, wherein not many Scholers are so studious of Geographic, and of Naturall and Universall knowledge in the diversified varieties which the various Seas and Lands in the World produce, seeming as exceptions to Generall Rules, which Aristotle the best Scholer in Natures Schoole and her principall Secretarie could not so punctually and individually see in the Ocean, the Remoter Lands and New Worlds, none of which he xliii to THE READER ever saw, nor till this last Age were knowne. And for the most part, those which are studious know not either to get, or to read the Authors of this kinde, of which so few speake Latine.

As for Gentlemen, Travell is accounted an excellent Ornament to them; and therefore many of them comming to their Lands sooner then to their Wits, adventure themselves to see the Fashions of other Countries, where their soules and bodies find temptations to a twofold Whoredom, whence they see the World as Adam had knowledge of good and evill, with the losse or lessening of their estate in this English (and perhaps also in the heavenly Paradise) bring home a few smattering termes, flattering garbes. Apish crings, foppish fancies, foolish guises and disguises, the vanities of Neighbour Nations (I name not Naples) without furthering of their knowledge of God, the World, or themselves. I speake not against Travell, so usefull to usefull men, I honour the industrious of the liberall and ingenuous in arts, bloud, education: and to prevent exorbitancies of the other, which cannot travell farre, or are in danger to travell from God and themselves, at no great charge I offer a World of Travellers to their domestike entertainment, easie to be spared from their Smoke, Cup, or Butter-flie vanities and superfluities, and fit mutually to entertaine them in a better Schoole to better purposes. And for the price, as I cannot set it, so I must acknowledge the adventurous courage of the Stationer Master Henry Fetherstone (like Hercules helping Atlas) so long to beare this my heavy World at such expenses.

The Method IVTOw for the Method, I confesse, I could not be there-and order of f exact: first because I had such a confused Chaos of printed and written Bookes, which could not easily be ordered: partly because this Method by way of Voyages often repeates the same Countries and (though I have often pruned repetitions) yet, sometimes admitted for more full testimonie the same things, by divers of our xliv this Works.

Authors travelling the same parts, observed, in which my Method brings in ordinarily the Authours whole Voyage there, where that part or Countrey, in which and for which we entertaine him, principally occasioneth his memorie; and partly because in this long space of imprinting (from August 1621.) many things have comne to my hand by diligent enquiry, which were not enrolled, nor in possession to be mustered in their due file and ranke; yea, divers things have beene done since our other passages of like nature were printed off: And thus divers Dutch quarrels are related, which yet since the Impression of that part have beene composed. Yet are we not altogether without Order.

First, we have divided the World in our Method The first into the Old and New, alloting to each his owne Tome, ' ” the first Ten Books to the former, the later to the other. But the Worke growing more voluminous then was expected, we are forced to cut each of them asunder in the midst, the figures in the top and Alphabets in the bottome, and some marginall references and annotations intimating but two Tomes, which only the quantitie hath made Foure. Againe in the Elder World, that is, Asia, Africa, and Europe, we observe Antiquities and Generalities in the First Booke, one of the last printed, though first placed: universall Circumnavigations (all knowne in that kind) in the Second; which though they containe many things of America and the South Continent, yet being from and for Europe, and spending most of their time on the Asian and African Coasts, are thither referred: in the Third, Fourth, and Fifth, are Indian Voyages and Affaires of the English, with Portugall and Dutch intercourse; in which is observed a tolerable order of time from Queene Elizabeths Times to the present.

In the Second Part you have first Africa in Two Bookes The Second (the East Indie ships but touched on the Coasts) the ' ' Sixth Booke handling the Northerne parts, whatsoever of Africa is not termed Ethiopia, and the seventh the-Ethiopian part. The Eighth Booke enters into the

Continent of Asia; in the first Chapters relating the History of the Franks (as all Asia since cals the Western Christians) in the Holy Land Wars; in the later, some Pilgrimages thither and the parts adjoyning, with divers Turkish Observations. The Ninth proceedeth thorow the mayne land of Asia into Persia, Arabia, India, taking large view of those and other Asian Regions, returning by Africa with later and larger intelligence of the Easterne, Westerne and Northerne shores thereof; New view of the Turkish Dominion and Seraglio, as also of the Maldivae Hands: which and the whole Tenth Booke came later to hand, and therefore is rather a Supply to all, then any well ordered part of the Worke, being therefore printed after the rest.

Now for the New World, we begin at China, which the Ancients knew not, and take all the East and North parts of Asia from the Caspian Sea, the Arctoan Regions, all America and Terra Australis, comprehending all in that New Tide. The First of those Bookes beginning our Third Part, delivereth especially the Authors of Tartaria in the succession of about three hundred yeeres, wherein the Second succeedeth, adding also Japan, Corea and China, with the first Discoveries of the Northerne and Caspian Seas by the English. This Arctoan Region contayning Russia, Nova Zembla, the Samoyeds, Siberia, Island, Frisland, Norway, with the Neighbour Regions, Cherry Hand, Greenland, Greenland, c. the Third Booke relateth; continued in the Fourth with further Discoveries intended for a North or North-west Passage. The Fifth Booke giveth generall Relations of America, in her Mexican or Northerly, and Peruan or Southerly Moyties (with what we could find of the South Continent) their Antiquities and state before, and since the Spanish Conquest. The Sixth (which begins the Fourth Part) containeth English Voyages to America, the Great Bay especially and the Southerne Moytie to the Magellan Straits; which in the Seventh Booke are more amplified, and further enlarged with the Creatures, and Countries xlvi within Land, the Peruan Antiquities related by one of the Inca Linage, the Spanish Conquest, and other occur-rents of the Peruan America and Terra Australis. The Eighth Booke comes homeward thorow the Mexican America and Florida unto Canada, relating the French Acts and English beginnings in those parts, touching in the way homeward at the Azores. Virginia is the Argument of the Ninth Booke, in the succession and successe thereof from the Plantation 1606. to 1624. whereto Summers Hands are added. The English Plantations in New England and Newfoundland follow in the Tenth, with divers Fleets set forth by Queene Elizabeth of famous memory, with whose blessing continued and confirmed by His Majestie, wee commit you to God, and give you leave to rest at home in peace, under the shadow of your owne Vine and Fig-tree, which God for his Christs sake continue and confirme to us and our posteritie. Amen.

You have here a long Preface to a long Work, and yet you have a longer touching the utilitie thereof in the first Paragraphs of Salomons Ophir. It had not beene possible for me in London distractions to have accomplished so great a Designe, but for the opportunities of His Majesties Colledge at Chelsie, where these foure last Summers I have retired my selfe (without Pulpit Non-residence) to this Worke: which as it one way furthered, so another way it occasioned many Errata, by my absence from the Presse, as in the Bodie of the Worke, so especially in the Titles over each page; halfe of which I thinke, are mine owne, the other such as pleased the Corrector, needing correction enough, and sometimes not giving sufficient direction to the Reader; whom I intreat to accept of his Day and Night, Summer and Winter together, pardoning the one for the others sake. A Table had beene necessary, if Time and assistance to a wearie hand had permitted; I adde, if some had not committed contrary to promise. It is time to make an end of Prefacing. The Authors follow; such xlvli as have no letter annexed are Mine; such as have H. added, I borrowed from Master Hakluyts papers, and such as have H. and P. pertaine to both, beeing otherwise printed or in my possession written, wherein yet I made use of some labour of his. Let the name and glory be to any other, so as above all and in all it bee to God the Father of our Lord Jesus Christ (who hath enabled my weake bodie beyond hopes; to so great a Worke) and the profit to Thee Reader, whom in the Lord, I bid farewell.

xlviii

A Note touching the Dutch.

THe necessitie of a Historic is, as of a sworne Wit-nesse, to say the truth, all the truth (in just discretion) and nothing but the truth. This I have indevoured in the whole Worke. But, Veritas odium parit. Some perhaps will blame me for relating some Truths, specially the Dutch Zelots, in that I have related such abuses of some of that Nation in the East Indies and Greenland to the English there, as if I sought like an unseasonable and uncharitable Tale-bearer to raise discord betwixt Neighbours. I answere that no Nation is in this World so pure, but hath both officious members, and some bad members also as Diseases thereof; which to impute to the whole, were as if a man should kill himselfe for a felon in his Thumbe, or Corne in his Toe: or as if he should therfore find fault with his own body because it hath not only a head, heart and hands, but excrements also, a fundament, and other parts for evacuation; with a Palace for houses of Office, with a Citie for common Sewers, with the World which hath Devils and Hell in it. I question not, but that the English have also such, and such wee have occasionally noted. Fugitives, Apostataes, Theeves, Murtherers, c. which yet are not Nationall faults, but personall, except the Nation doth justifie such unjustice, as Troy the Rape of Helena, and the Benjamites those Beasts of Gibeah, either by impunitie or defence. Nor needed wee good Lawes, but for bad Subjects. If the Dutch have such also, in the History of both I must mention both, and yet protest before God (to whom I xlix shall answere it with the burning of bodie and soule, not these Bookes alone, if I bee perfidious) that I am not guiltie to my selfe of hatred to that Nation, yea in these Discourses I have honoured it with and before others, following them round about the World to that purpose. And for this cause I have omitted some odious

Greenland Relations, have altered and reprinted some more offensive generall speeches disgorged by the passionate loosers, with Titles on the tops of pages, intended to

Offenders, but in such unwarie termes as might by ill willers be extended to the whole Nation: yea, I had purposed to omit many things printed alreadie, rather leaving a x " then causing a Chaos, but that since the sore hath broken out by that terrible Tragedie at

Amboyna. I could have wished that such things had never beene told in Gath, nor published in the streets of Askalon, lest any enemie of our State and Religion should rejoyce. But seeing the necessities of the English

East Indian Societie have forced such a publication, my sparing purpose had beene in vaine to conceale the

Shilling where the Pound was made manifest. I might also have beene accounted partiall against mine owne

Nation. This I have done; I for the most part, doe but publish others Relations, (and Losers perhaps will speake the most) and by Annotations dispersed intimate that these are personall faults of that East Indie

Company, or some Commanders there, not of the whole Nation; and if any Marginall Notes with

Dutch Epithetes seeme to speake more, yet are they but directions to the Reader to shew what in that page or place is handled without further intent; so with my Prayers for Peace on both sides I commend both to the God of Peace.

Amen.

THE FIRST VOLUME

Purchas His Pilgrimes

Contayning the Voyages and Peregrinations made by Antient Kings, Patriarkes, Apostles, Philosophers, and others. To and thorow The Remoter Parts of the Knowne World: Enquiries also of Languages and Religions

The Voyages f Peregrinations i.

made by Antient Kings, Patriarkes, Apostles,

Philosophers, and others, to and thorow the remoter parts of the knowne World:

Enquiries also of Languages and Religions, especially of the moderne diversified

Prosessions of Christianitie

THE FIRST BOOKE

Chap. I.

A large Treatise of King Salomons Navie sent from Eziongeber to Ophir: Wherein, besides the Typicall Mysteries briefly unvailed, and many Morall Speculations observed; the voyage is largely discussed out of Divine, Ecclesiasticall and Humane Testimonies: Intended as an his-toricall Preface to the Histories following.

Ntending to present the World to the World in the most certaine view, I thought a world of Authors fitter for that purpose, then any One Author writing of the World: whose discourse might haply bee more even, facile, methodicall, and contracted to a more compendious forme; but could not avoid to be dispendious (if I may so speake) in the matter, and to suspend the Readers judgement for the authoritie. Oculatus testis unus praeestat auritis decern. I had rather heare Plaut. the meanest of Ulysses his followers relating his wanderings, then wander from the certaintie with Homer after all his readings and conjectures. Lo here then (after my Pilgrimage of the former Nature, for such as better like that course) in open Theatre presented a Shew of Discoveries on an English Stage, wherein the World is both the Spectacle and Spectator; the Actors are the Authors themselves, each I. i. 2. presenting his owne actions and passions in that kind, kindly (in generous and genuine History) acting their acts; not affectedly straining, or scenic-all-ly playing Terent. their part; the Arts indeed of the Poet, Maker, or Composer, aiming at delight more then truth (Populo ut placerent, quas fecisset Fabulas) seeking to please the vulgar with fabulous wonders, and wonder-foole fables.

And for a Prologue, behold Salomons Ophirian

Navigation, that Worthy of Men, being most worthy to bee Our Choragus, whose ayme is in this long

Worke to fetch from Ophir Materialls for the Temples structure, and to edifie Christs Church, with more full and evident knowledge of Gods Workes in the

World, both of Creation and Providence, then any one

Naturall or Humane Historian, yea (absit invidia verbo) then all hitherto in this (perhaps in any) course have done. I compare not with Aristotle, Plinie, and others in philosophicall! and learned speculation of Reason, but in evident demonstration of Sense, and herein (not to us

Lord, not to us, but to thy Name be given the glory) it exceedeth not modesty to speake thus much in behalfe of this cloud of witnesses which we bring, testifying what they have seen, that these exceed the former in certainty (relating what they have seene) and in ful- nesse (by advantage of New Worlds found in, and besides the World knowne to them) no lesse then they are exceeded in Antiquitie and learning.

For mee, I say with Agur, surely I am more foolish Prov."io. z, then any man, and have not the understanding of a ' '" 5-man in mee; Alas Master (I may proclaime to each Reader) all is borrowed: I never travelled out of this Kingdome (ingenuously I confesse, it is the totall summe of all my Travell-readings) the Centre of the Worlds good things, and Heart of her happinesse; and yet (yea thereby) have, as thou seest, conceived (where Dinahs gadding gained onely losse) and travelled- 34- 2. of a Gad, a Troup of Travellers; So said Leah, A '"- 3- " troup commeth and shee called his name Gad. And seeing we have stumbled on that Word, let it be ominous, so others read it Fceliciter, Bagad, being by the Hebrewes resolved into Ba Mazal tob, that is; Seem. Se-Good fortune commeth. I am not Leah, I take no f' " ' ' such authority on mee, but when shee hath left bearing (when better leisures, quicker wits, sounder health, profounder learning, and all abler meanes looke on) let not Jacobs Bed, for the propagation and edification of the Church, be envied to Zilpah, Leahs mayd; And let this my Service in conceiving and nursing up this Gad be accepted of all Jacobs Friends. And that it might bee accepted, I have begun (Dimidium facti qui bene cepit habet) with the most acceptable Voyages mentioned in the Old and New Testaments; the one a Type of the other; those of Solomon to Ophir, and of the Apostles about the World.

Salomon was first in time, and shall bee first here; the first in all things which usually are accounted first, Royaltie, Sanctitie, Wisdome, Wealth, Magnificence, Munificence, Politie, Exploits, Renowme: Salomon Matth. 6.29. in all his glory, is proverbiall, and He first in these by the first and greatest of testimonies; the particulars of Salomons voyage are recorded in the first, best, and more then humane Histories; Yea the things recorded, are first indeed, before other things, yea before and greater then themselves, and that which

Apoc. I. the First and Last hath said, is true of them all in typicall relation, A greater then Salomon is here. Let Salomon then, as elsewhere, so here also have the preeminence; let Salomons name as the Character of peace and happinesse, boad holy, happy, and peaceable successe to this Work; and let Thy Name, O thou Greater then Salomon, grant protection, assistance, some. part of Salomons wisdome and prosperity to our Ophirian voyage, that we may buy of thee Gold tried in the fire to make us rich in grace, so to prepare us

Jpoc. 21. lo, to that holy Jerusalem, descending out of Heaven from II, 18, 22, Qod, having the Glory of God; a Citie of pure Gold like unto cleere glasse, where the Lord God Almighty and the Lambe are the Temple, and the Glory of God doth lighten it, and the Lambe is the light thereof. Be thou, O Christ, in this our Navigation both Load-starre and Sunne, for direction of our course, and knowledge of our true height and latitude: Let our Sayles hoised up in thy Name, be filled with inspiration of thy Spirit, and aspiration of thy favour,

Ac. 27. till they arrive in the Fair-havens of humane Pleasure and Profit, thy Churches service and edifying. Divine acceptance and glory. Amen, O Amen.

Of Salomon the holy Scriptures have thus recorded. I. Kings 9. 26, 27, 28. And King Solomon made a Navie of Ships in Ezion Geber, which is beside Eloth, on the shoare of the Red Sea in the Land of Edom. And Hiram sent in the Navie his servants, Shipmen I. i. 3. that had knowledge of the Sea with the servants of Solomon. And they came to Ophir and set from thence Gold 420. Talents, and brought it to King Solomon. And Cap. 10. 11. The Navie also of Hiram, that brought Gold from Ophir brought in from Ophir great plenty of Almug trees and precious stones; 12. And the King made of the Almug trees, Pillars for the house of the Lord, for the Kings House; Harps also and Psalteries for Singers: there came no such Almug Trees, nor were scene unto this day. 13. Now the weight of Gold that came to Solomon in one yeere was 666. Talents of Gold. 15. Besides that he had of the Merchant-men, and of the trafficke of the Spice-Merchants, and of all the Kings of Arabia, and of the Governours of the Countrey. V. 21. And all King Solomons drinking Vessells were of Gold, and all the Vessells of the House of the Forrest of Lebanon were of pure Gold: none were of Silver, it was nothing accounted of in the dayes of Solomon. For the Kings Ships (the cause is added, 2. Chro. 9. 21.) went to Tarshish with the servants of Hiram: every three yeerfes once came the Ships of Tarshish, bringing Gold and Silver; Ivory, and Apes, and Peacockes. 22. And King Solomon passed all the Kings of the Earth in Riches and Wisdome. 26. And hee reigned over all the Kings, from the River, even unto the Land of the Philistines, and to the border of Egypt. 27. And the King made Silver in Jerusalem as Stones, and Cedar Trees made hee as the Sycomore Trees, that are in the Low Plaines in abundance.

The Allegoricall and Anagogicall sense or application of Solomons Ophirian Navigation.

His is an extract of Solomons Story, so much as concernes our present purpose, the authoritie whereof is Sacred, a Divine, infallible, inviolable.

and undenyable veritie; the fitter ground for many high whitak. des-and worthy consequences hereafter to be delivered. I crip. q. 5. shall here leave to the Divinitie Schooles, in more leisurely contemplation to behold the Allegoricall sense (shall I say, or application) wherein Solomon seemes to signifie Christ, his Navy the Church, (long before lively represented in that first of Ships, the Ark of Noah) which in the Sea of this variable World seekes for the golden Treasures of Wisdome and Knowledge, with (that plentiful! riches) the rich plentie of good Workes. The Servants of Hiram, the Doctors chosen m. Ep. Qut of the Gentiles, with the learned Christian Jewes (the doc Christ 1 '"vants of Solomon) imployed joyntly in this Ophirian 2. c. 40. Discovery, thence bring the rich materialls (as the

Bns horn. 24. Israelites the Egyptian spoyles for the Tabernacle, so de legend lib. these) for building and adorning the Temple (the true

Nvsensintnt " Scripture) after long absence by a troublesome

Mosis, Navigation (in the search of Authors Divine, Ecclesiasticall I. Co. 2. 14. and Humane, an Ocean of toyle) from their homes.

I. T. 3. 16. Por the naturall man, that abides at home in himselfe, and hath not travelled from his owne Wisdome and

Selfe-conceit, knowes not the things of God, nor the great

Mysteries of Godlinesse; he must leave the Land, his

Earthly Wisdome (Terraque urbesque recedant) and lanch into the deepe, there having his sayles filled with the winde, the illumination of that Spirit, which leads into all truth; the Scriptures being their Card, the faithful heart the Load-stone, Christ himselfe the Load- starre and Sunne of Truth, as before is intimated. Thus shall the Temple, and Church of God be edified, enriched, adorned, after wee have arrived at Ophir, and have scene our owne weaknesse, and taken paines in myning Gods

Treasures, and undermining our owne hearts, searching and trying our owne and Gods wayes; casting off, and purging from us all superfluous Earth, and detaining the

Gold and richer Mettall, which wee may carry and present, as the Talents gained by our Talents, in the best improvement of Gods graces, when wee shall returne to our Solomon, the Judge of quicke and dead, after our Navigation and earthly Pilgrimage ended.

But alas how many make shipwracke of Faith by the way, and either are split on the Rockes of enormous crying Sinnes, or sinke in the smaller innumerable sands of habituall Lusts, covered with the shallowes (meere shadowes) of civill Righteousnesse.

Or if you had rather adjoyne to the Allegory, the Anagogicall sense and use; this History will appeare also a Mystery and Type of Eternitie. Every Christian man is a ship, a weake vessell, in this Navie of Solomon, and dwelling in a mortall body, is within lesse then foure inches, then one inch of death. From Jerusalem the Word and Law of our Solomon first proceeded, by-preaching of Solomons and Hirams servants, the Pastors and Elect vessells to carry his Name, gathered out of Jewes and Gentiles, which guide these Ships through a stormy Sea, beginning at the Red Sea, Christs bloudy Crosse, which yeelded Water and Bloud, till they arrive at Ophir, the communion of Saints in the holy Catholike Church. Thither by the water of Baptisme first, and by the waters of Repentance, drawn out of our hearts and eyes in manifold Mortifications after; (the feare of God beginning this Wisdome, the windy lusts of concupiscence, and unstable waves of the world in vaine assailing) they attaine in the certaintie of Faith and assurance: where Col. z. seeking for Knowledge as for Silver, and searching for ' "- her as for hidden Treasures, they doe as it were labour in the Mynes for Gold, which they further purifie by experimentall practise and studie of good Workes: yet i Co. 3. 12. not in such perfection, but that to this foundation. Gold, Silver, precious Stones, some Almug trees are added for the Temples Pillars, oftentimes also of our owne. Hay and Stubble, as worse and more combustible matter joyned; the Ivory, being a dead Bone may serve for a secular Throne and worldly use; but here death is dead; I. i. 4. the Apes and Peacockes lively expresse Hypocrisie and worldly pompe, which in the best of Saints usually leave some tincture in their voyage for Heaven. In the returne to Solomon, these shall be burnt (as those were by Nebuzaradan) but he himselfe shall bee saved; Jer. 52. and the former admitted by that Prince of Peace, the Heavenly Solomon to the building of that Temple in the new Jerusalem, for charitie never falleth away. This is that holy Citie figured by that of Palestina, where all is brought to Solomon, that God may bee all in all, as the Alpha which set them forth, so the Omega, who hath made all things for himselfe, for whose will and glories sake, all things are and were created: And the Kings of Ap. 21. 24.

the Earth bring their glory and honour unto this Citie. Not that hee needs any thing, but that wee need the same, who in seeing him as hee is, doe all partake of his glory. Happy are thy men (may more truly be said I Reg. lo. 8. of this Solomons servants) happy are these thy servants which may stand in thy presence and heare thy wisdome: which may enjoy eternitie, signified by Gold, which alone of mettalls neither fire, nor rust, nor age consumeth Jpoc. 2 1. 18. (and this Citie is pure Gold) and that Inheritance of the Fi. P. Ptl. I. Saints in light, figured by Silver, the most lightsome and delightsome of mettalls to the eye. As for precious Stones, the foundations of the Wall of the Citie are garnished with all manner of them. And touching the Jpoc. 3. 12. Almuggim Trees, whereof Solomon made Pillars for the tffjii. Temple and Psalteries, every Tree which here beareth good fruit, and every one that overcommeth, will this Solomon there make a Pillar in the Temple of his God, and hee shall goe no more out. And they shall serve him Day and Night in his Temple, and hee that sitteth on the Throne shall dwell among them. These have also the Harps of God, And they sing the Song of Moses, and the Song of the Lamb, nay these are the Ps. 16. Psalteries and Harpes, which filled with all fulnesse of

God, alway resound praises thanks unto the King of Saints, and with everlasting harmony in that Angellical Quire, are tuned with Alleluiah, and Te Deum, and Holy, holy, holy, in fulnesse of joy at his right hand, Jp. 21 22, and plea'sures for evermore. Thus in divers respects are f- 3- I- 15- they both the Citie, and Temple, and Kings and Priests, and Instruments, and all these, and none of these: For I saw no Temple therein, saith that Seer, for the Lord God Almightie, and the Lambe are the Temple of it. Even God himselfe shall bee with them, and God shall bee all in all: and as hee is incomprehensible, so Eye hath not seene, nor eare hath heard, nor can the heart of man conceive what God hath prepared for them that love him: Coeli coelorum Domino, terram dedit Filus Hominem. And unmeet is it for me to attempt so high climbing.

Not so the Tropologie or Morall use, not so the History, for our learning wherein the same is written. And although the History in Nature should precede, yet because wee intend the Tropologicall sense or application of this History, as a kind of Preface or preamble to the many Histories ensuing, wee have here given it the first place.

II. The Tropologicall use of the Story; and of the lawfulnesse of Discoveries and Negotiation by Sea.

Erein therefore Solomon may become a wise guide unto us, and first by his example teach us the lawfulnesse of Navigation to remote Regions. His particular Dominion is Palestina, his subject Provinces added, extend not beyond Egypt and the River Euphrates, as is before delivered. But God which had enlarged Solomons heart with Wisdome, did not enlarge it to injustice by an overlarge conscience: and hee which renounced the price of a Dog and a Whore in his offerings, would not permit the Temple, which sanctifieth the offerings, to bee built and adorned with robbery and spoyle. It remaines then that Solomon had a right, not extraordinary as the Israelites to spoyle the Egyptians, by Divine especiall Precept; but such a right wherein Hiram was interessed also. The Ebrewes might P ilo de vita both at Gods command, who is Lord of all, and in j" ' ' Equitie demand wages ot the Egyptians tor so long- and tedious service; which had not Divine Precept and deojubenti power interposed, the same tyranny which had imposed minhtenum the one, would have denied the other. But what had f l"' '" '-the Ophirians wronged Solomon, of whom and whose jq. j. ' ' Countrey they had not heard, that thus by a numerous and strong Fleet hee should enter on their Coasts.? We must not thinke godly Solomon to be Alexanders pre-decessour, whom the Poet calls Terrarum fatale malum fidus iniquum Gentibus: whom the Pirat accused as the

Aug. deciv. greater, finding no other difference betwixt them, but 4– + a smal Ship and a great Fleet. Remota institia, quid sunt regna saith Augustine, nisi magna latrocinia, quia ipsa latrocinia quid sunt, nisi parva regna? And before

Cy. -. (Z hini Cyprian, Homicidium cum admittunt singuli, onat. 2. criiyien est, virtus vocatur cum publice geritur.

Jc. I-'. 26. Impunitatem acquirit saevitiae magnitudo. Surely Solomons right was his being a Man, which as a wise a mightie King of Men, hee might the better exercise and execute. For howsoever God hath given to every man to every Nation, a kind of proprietie in their peculiar possessions; yet there is an universall tenure in the Universe, by the Lawes of God and Nature, still remaining to each man as hee is a Man, and coftjtotroxr;?, as the common or Royall right of the King or State is neither confounded nor taken away by the private proprietie of the Subject.

I. i. 5. True it is that God, which hath made of one bloud all Nations of men for to dwell on all the face of the earth, and hath determined the times appointed, hath also determined the bounds of their habitation. But not so straitly of Negotiation. In Habitation proprietie is requisite, that every man may sit under his owne Vine, and under his owne Fig-tree, and drinke the waters out of his owne Cisterne and running waters out of his owne Well, and that they bee onely his

Prov. 5. 15, owne, and not the strangers with him. But hee that 7 hath made all Nations of one bloud, would still they should bee as fellow members one of another; (a

Deut. 23. shadow of which was in the Law, permitting to eat in the neighbours Vineyard, but not to carry forth;) and that there should still remaine mutuall Necessitie, the Mother of mutuall Commerce, that one should not bee hungry, and another drunken, but the superfluitie of one Countrey, should supply the necessities of another, in exchange for such things, which are here also

Hrg. necessary, and there abound; that thus the whole World might bee as one Body of mankind, the

Nations as so many members, the superabundance in each, concocted, distributed, retained or expelled by merchandising (as by the Naturall bodily Offices and Faculties in nourishment) whereby not without mutuall gaine One may releeve others Wants. Non omnia possumus omnes: may bee said of Arts; Nee vero Ez. zyif ii terras ferre omnes omnia possunt, may bee added of Regions, each Countrey having her owne, both Artificiall and Naturall Commodities, whereby to inrich themselves with enriching of others. Thus in old times, Tyrus chief Staple of the worlds Merchandise, and consequently chiefe Store-house of the worlds Treasures; (see the same elegantly particularly jbz. 27. 33. deciphered by the holy Ghost) as it received from all parts, so when her wares went forth out of the Seas, shee filled many people, and did enrich the Kings of the Earth, with the multitude of her riches and merchandise.

And because no one National Law could prescribe in that wherein all are interested, God himself is the Law giver, and hath written by the stile of Nature this Law in the hearts of men, called in regard of the efficient, the Law of Nature, in respect of the object, the Law of Nations, whereto all Men, Nations, Commonwealths, Kingdomes and Kings are subject. And as he hath written this Equity in mans heart by Nature, so hath he therfore encompassed the Earth with the Sea, adding so many inlets, bayes, havens and other naturall inducements and opportunities to invite men to this mutuall commerce. Therefore hath he also diversified the Windes, which in their shifting quarrels conspire to humaine trafficke. Therefore hath hee divided the Earth with so many Rivers, and made the shoares conspicuous by Capes and promontories; yea, hath admitted the Sunne and Starres in their Firg. y tt. direction and assistance unto this Generall Councell, wherein Nature within us and without us, by everlasting Canons hath decreed Communitie of Trade the

Sunt autem privata nulla natura. Cic.

Horat.

Jvignus.

Omnia reruni usurpantis erantav'tenus.

Ov. Met. I. I.

Ov. Met. I. 6.

world thorow. And thus hath she taught them who had no other instructor, with dishke and disdaine to admire at such immanity and inhumanity, Quod genus hoc hominum quaeue hunc tam barbar a morem, Per-mittit patria? hospitio prohibemur arenae! yea whereas by Nature the Earth was common Mother, and in equall community to be enjoyed of all hers.

Nam propriae telluris herum Natura nee ilium.

Nee me, nee quenquam statuit: and howsoever this case is since altered in this element, lest the idle should live on the sweate of others browes: yet the other and nobler elements still remaine in greatest part in their originall communitie, and cannot so fully bee appropriated to private possession, since the supposed Golden age is vanished, and this Iron (or golden in another sence) hath succeeded. Yea, then also the house, wife, children, and such things as are wasted or growne worse in the use, as meate, drinke, apparell, were appropriate and private chattels to the possessor, howsoever things immoveable continued the freehold of every man in the common tenure of common humanity, as still in the life of Brasilians and other Savages in the following relations is to be scene. By humaine consent and divine dispensation the Earth was divided among the Sonnes of Noah.

Communemque prius ceu lumina solis aurae.

Cautus humum longo signavit limite messor.

Thus some things became publike, that is, proper to the Kingdome, State, or Nation: other things private, as each mans possession, and that also in differing degrees, as the Commons, and Champaine Countries with us in their differing tenure from grounds inclosed, doe manifestly enough argue. But since that division of Languages and Lands; the Poet still proclaimes Natures right.

Quid prohibetis aquas? usus communis aquarum est.

Nee solem proprium Natura nee Aera fecit.

Nee tenues undas. In publica munera veni.

and another -Cunctis undamque auramque patentem.

These so farre as they have not by possession of Firg. n. 7. other men before, or otherwise by their own Nature cannot be appropriated, are Natures Commons, which both Free-holders as Men, and Coppie-holders, as other Hving creatures. Beasts, Fishes, Fowles, and creeping things according to their scverall kinds do communicate in. If any quarrell this poeticall Proofe; I answere that they were Natures Secretaries in the cases of Reason, and the Common Law of Humanitie, which having not the Law, were a Law to themselves, and in like Rom. 2. cases therefore produced as good evidence by the Planter I. i. 6. of the Gospel, and Doctor of the Gentiles. And if we will surmount Reason, and appeale to divine censure, what need we other testimonie then this of Salomon "f"- 2-in his best times, and for his best act, imitated herein f gj. (though with unlike successe) by godly Jehoshaphat? 7 ,1." These things are also written for our learning to the ends of the World, that wise, magnanimous, fortunate, peaceable and godly Kings might propound this pat-terne to their industries. Yea, more then in Salomons time is this lawfuu to Christian Kings, in regard that the Jewish Pale is downe, and the Church is Catholike, not appropriated to One people, or circumscribed in a circumcised corner, or swadled in a small Cradle, as in that infancie of the Circumcision; but open and common to the Communitie of Mankind, to which in this last Age no better meane is left then Navigation and commerce; wherein though the most aime at gaine, yet God that can raise of stones children to Abraham, and made Davids Conquests and Salomons Discoveries serviceable to the Temple, can no lesse convay the Gospel then other Wares into those parts, to whom hee hath given such rich attractives in the East and West, perhaps that this negotiation might further another, in barter and exchange of richer treasures for their temporall.

He which brought the Northerne people being then Pagans, into the Roman Empire, to make them Lords of it and Subjects to him, can of Merchants allured with Gold, make, or at least send with them, Peachers of his Sonne. And if the Devill hath sent the Moores with damnable Mahumetisme in their merchandizing quite thorow the East, to pervert so many Nations with thraldome of their states and persons, out of the frying panne of Paynim Rites, into the fire of Mahu-metrie: Shall not God be good to Israel, and gracious to the ends of the earth, so long since given in inheritance to his Sonne?

III.

The Tropologicall or Morall use enlarged and amplified; and a view taken of Mans diversified Dominion in Microcosmicall, Cosmo-politicall, and that spirituall or heavenly right, over himselfe and all things, w hich the Christian hath in and by Christ.

H Enerall Rules have exceptions. Salomon was just 1 9 and wise, well knowing the difference of ' Ezion-Geber and Ophir, and that difference of

Dominion which God (that made Man after his Image) hath given us over the Creatures, diversified both in the subject and object. E Coelo descendit yvcooi aeavtcov, was written in Adam by Creation, in Salomon by Revelation, before Nature suggested that sentence to Chilo, or the Delphian Devill (the Ape of Divinitie) had caused it to be written in Golden Letters on the Frontispice of that Temple. To know a mans selfe aright is annexed to the knowledge of God (in whom wee live, moove, and are, of whom and for whom are all things) not his essence, but his expressed Image thereof in his workes, of which, Man is in this World the principall; what hee hath received, what he hath lost, what he retaineth by Nature, and what he recovereth, and more then recovereth by grace, in and of that divine resemblance. In the first state all men had a naturall right in common over the creatures. But the Devill (the greatest Incloser) by sinne inclosed these Maninhisfall Commons of Humanitie, and altered their tenure from "" '" f f Fee Simple, to meere Vdlenage: yet so (God m justice J. ainhis remembring mercie) that some ruines remaine since naturall gifts. the fall, not only in the faculties and substance of Supernaturali bodie and soule, but in the personall rights also over 'Vf l l torpid, vegetative, and all unreasonable creatures, con- f; J tinued to him by that Charter of Reason, which in so obtained but well ordered furniture, and so well furnished order as h-j Gods free the name Kotr o'i and mundus import, could not but have gft. and called beene confounded, if both the immortall and spirituall r i mes part in himselfe, should not have exercised dominion in y holinesse. some kind over the mortall and bodily; and if in the Eph, 4. greater World, the reasonable should not have disposed f."' "fj lf of the unreasonable. As for the conformitie of mans ' J! "! will and actions to God and right, using of that right over yed nature. the creature, to the sole glory of the Creator (to whom man is subordinate, as the creature to him) this was by the cracke of our earthen Vessell in Mans Fall lost, and as a more subtile and spirituall liquor, ranne out. Yet still remaine in this defaced Image some obscure lineaments, and some embers raked up in the ashes of Mans consumption, which being by naturall diligence quickned, give lively expressions of God; and where supernaturali worke recovereth, are more then recovered, internally and inchoatively in the state of grace, externally also and eternally in that perfection of glorie.

Hence ariseth to a man a threefold tenure, more Foure kinds and more excellent then any which Littleton hath " j lj"' related; a Microcosmicall in respect of our selves; a q ' Cosmopoliticall in regard of the World; a Catholike, Spirituall, and Heavenly in relation to Christ the Head, his Bodie the Church, and that everlasting inheritance; besides that (which is the last and least of all) in reference to Politicall Law and Societie. The first I. i. 7.

costne or Pil-grime

PURCHAS HIS PILGRIMES orlginall of all dominion and right is God, who is Lord of all, whose Image as is said is imprinted on and in Man, as otherwise so in this Lordship or right; which he hath first See my Micro- nd on himselfe Microcosmically in the members of his bodie, as the Regions of this Selfe-kingdome; where the continuall Court of Conscience, the large jurisdiction of Reason (without which a man is, as suspended from the power of himselfe, termed impos sui, besides himselfe, as in drunkennesse and madnesse) the freedom of the Will (which is no longer will, then willing and cannot be constrained) the Naturall, and Vitall actions wrought within us, (and yet without us, without our owne knowledge or direction, and much lesse subject to the correction of others) the Animall also in externall and internall senses, which cannot but exercise their faculties upon their due objects: these all proclaime that the poorest Slave is Lord by divine grant, even since the fall, of no lesse then this little-World; yea, while he obeyeth others, he commands himselfe to that obedience; in which selfe-commands is the true exercise of vertue or vice. This Inheritance and Dominion is so naturall that it cannot be alienated, without confiscation of the whole to the eternall giver of whom he holds it. For even in and by his eternau Law, is this made the rule of all righteousnesse, to doe as we would be done to, to love our Neighbours as our selves; and if there were no power in and of our selves, there could neither be vertue nor vice in loving or hating our Neighbour: if no freedome of will and affections, no reward with God or man; if no government of mans selfe reserved. Martyrs of all men were the most monstrous, which for obeying God rather then man, are the most honoured and admired. Once; subjection to God is absolute; to Princes as they are called Gods, and yet die like men, with reservation; for conscience of Gods Com-mandement, where his revealed will to the contrary frees not; and yet even then we must by suffering doe the will of Superiours, thereby to shew our fidelitie in keeping Gods Proviso, though with losse, of our Wils where we love, and our lives where wee feare; shewing that we love feare him most of all, which yet were neither love, nor Pro. i6. 32.

feare, nor vertue, without this liberty of wil and power in our selves. He that ruleth his owne mind is better then hee that winneth a Citie. This is the greatest conquest, the greatest possession to be master of thy selfe. Nor is this power absolute to our selves over our selves: Wee are not our owne, wee are Gods who hath created us; our

Parents which have procreated us, our Countries which sustayneth us, our Kings which maintayneth us; our

Neighbours in common humanity: to neglect a Mans fame or life, (much more prodigally to reject them) is to robbe all these of their due in us.

But in Christians it were a deeper Sacriledge: they are i Cor. 6. 20. not their owne, they are bought with a price (the greatest 7- 23-of prices, the bloud of God) they are gained by conquest, p Christ having bound the strong man and spoiled his goods; they are given by the Father for the Sonnes Inheritance, and in Baptisme have by mutuall Covenant, given over themselves to his service. The freedome Christian which Christ hath purchased for us, doth yeeld Libertie, 't"-not Licentiousnesse; frees not from duties, to doe what wee lust, but makes us have a lust to doe our duties; sweetly inclining the Wil, and renewing the Minde to esteeme the Service of God, and of men for his sake, the greatest freedome. Hee then that is Christs, is a new Gal. 5.

Creature, to which, bondage or freedome and other worldly ' "- 7-respects, are meere respects and circumstances. For hee that is bond, is the Lords freeman, and hee that is free, is the Lords Servant. It is the Devils Sophistry, as to separate what hee hath joyned, so to confound what hee hath distinguished; and it is observable, that the Pope The Pope and the Anabaptist, which are brethren in this Iniquity, " " have first denied their Baptisme, the Scale of their Christianitie. For these many rights doe not subject us other is re-to many Masters, but subordinate our subjection in the baptised. beautie of order. Even in Politicall or Civill right One may be Lord of the Fee; another of the Soile; a third I 17 B

As is the use of some Parishes after Lamas, i c.

Sen. Epist. 9.

Ad I'ivendum multis reb. opus est, ad bene vivendum animo sano y erecto y despiciente fortunam.

I. i. 8. Laert. in Zen.

of the way by ingresse, egresse, regresse; a fourth, hath right in the same ground, in time of Faire or Market; the whole Vicinity in Commoning times; and others other wayes: all whose Rights, are subject to the Right Royall, and Sovereigne.

And if in proprietie of strictest Nature, there may bee such communitie of subordinate rights without tumultuous crossing or pernicious confusion, how much more in things more spirituall, and more easily communicable? In which respect, the Philosophers, held themselves of themselves compleate, and (in whatsoever state) sapientem seipso contentum esse, not dependant (where he is properly a man) of other men of the World: not contracting him intra cutem suam (to use Senecaes words) in this Microcosmicall happinesse, but needing the Cosmo-politicall helpe ad vivendum, not ad beate vivendum; to live at least, howsoever to live well, a sound heart and good conscience are sufficient; to the other food and raiment are necessary, to this ex te nascentia bona: the best societie is of vertuous thoughts which make men, as Scipio said, nunquam minus solos quam cum soli, nee minus otiosos quam cum otiosi sint, but vicious company (as the company of Vices) are the most horrid and desolate Wildernesse. No exile can deprive a man of this Citie, no Prison of this Societie, no Pillage of these Riches, no bondage of this Libertie, In this sence Socrates said he was Koa-fio-Kokirri all places his Countrie, all men his Countrimen; in this, Bias, when he had lost all by fortune of warre, carried all his away with him: in this Zeno, marvelled at nothing neither in Nature, whose depths cannot be searched, nor in Fortune, whose possibilitie of most licentious effects must be the glasse to view our owne fortune, and to make that light by long premeditation, which others doe by long suffering: in this, Seneca, Coelo tegitur qui non habet urnam; in this, another Seneca teacheth. Cum Orientem Occidentemque lustraveris animo, cum tot ani-malia, tantam copiam rerum quas Natura beatissime fundit, aspexeris; emittere banc Dei voce In omnia mea sunt; in this, Diogenes when Pirats exposed him to sale, professed his art was to rule men, and bad them sell him to

Xeniades, for he needed a Master; from whom when his friends would have redeemed him, he refused, saying,

Lions were Masters, and not servants of them which fed Laert. indiog.

them; in this, the Stoicks called their poorest Wiseman, rich, free, a King; in this sense Socrates with whom we began, said if his fortune would not sute and sort to him, he would make himselfe sutable to his fortune.

So long as life lasteth and humanitie continueth, they are universall possessors of the Universe, in which kind, Aristotle hath left more memorable Monuments of Contemplation, then Alexander of Conquest: Natures commons, the Sun, Stars, Heavens, Aire, are common, at least to their mindes in utmost of miseries, and with internall plentie they supply all externall defects. In this Miscro-cosmicall and Cosmopoliticall Wealth, consisted all the Philosophers estate and revenue, which they called Vertue and Moralitie: which made them Masters of themselves, and thereby of the World, the just Circle of the Centre of Humanitie, for which it was created. These things (me thinkes) I see not without pittie, nor can resemble Them more fitly then to Horses of excellent courage; but hoodwinked so, that some little transparence of light makes them more importunate to others mischiefes, and their owne prascipice (whence Philosophers have been called Tertul. Patriarchs of Heretikes) or else like Mil-horses to com-passe with this Worlds Wheele the immoveable Centre of Natures corruption, to which they are subject, no lesse then others which worke at a Querne, and stand still at their Hand-mill; by a larger circumference alway mooving, promovendo nihil, proceeding in true freedome nothing at all. If the Sonne make you free, you shall be Joh. 8. free indeed. These, to make the noblest comparison may seeme starres, children of the night, which in their Moralitie gave rayes of light that to the World made them eminent Ornaments, and may make many of us ashamed,

Tertuldcpat. saith of the Philosopher, sceca vivunt. Mai. Col. I. I. Thes. 5.

P.4. II, 12, I 3. Discip- I'wa, Scientia,

Mysterium, Impenum est arsista, Regina art'ium, quod ex verbis

Pauunis apparet 1 Cor. 2. 14.

PURCHAS HIS PILGRIMES which in the Daies Sun-shine of the Gospell love and live darknesse, and like Owles, Bats, and wild Beasts, hide our selves studiously from the Sun, flie abroad and prey in the darke, fashioning our selves to this World, have our cogitations and conversations darkened. Christ is never-thelesse to all that have eyes to see, the Sunne of Right-eousnesse, by whome wee are by Regeneration translated from the power of darknesse, and made the children of the day; that wee may know what wee worship, and whom we have beleeved, not so much talking as walking, even in this bodily prison, these liberties of the Gospell, being truly (though yet in the imperfect grouth of in-fancie) restored to our selves, to the World, yea to a more glorious state, whereof Nature could not so much as dreame; that wheras Man had lost both the former by suggestion of Evill, Devil-Angels, Christ hath exalted farre above all Heavens visible, to supply these Thrones of Dominion, which those rebellious Thrones and Dominions lost. The evidence whereof we have by Faith and Hope, our Head already having taken Liverie and Seisin, and from thence living in us, actuating and mooving us by his Spirit, preparing us in this fight of militant grace to that light of triumphant glorie.

Even these first fruits are sweet and solid; 1 have learned (saith our Apostle) in whatsoever state I am, therewith to be content. And I know both how to be abased, and I know how to abound, everie where and in all things, 1 am instructed both to be full and to be hungrie, and to abound and have need. I am able to all things through Christ strengthening me. This was the true riches not in the Chist, but in the heart, which therefore neither men nor Devils could take away. And see his Degrees in this Schoole; first eixaoov I have learned this Discipline, not in the Schoole of Nature but of Grace, for we are all taught of God: secondly, oi a this Science, I know: whereas the wisest of Philosophers professed to know but this one thing that hee knew nothing: thirdly uejlvr'imaij and without all contro- versie this is a great mysterie of godlinesse, in which the naturall man is not initiated, hee knowes not the things of God, nor can know them, for they are foolishnesse to him; but the unction of the Spirit only enters men in these mysteries (which the word signifieth) after which followes in due order, Udvra i(rxv(jo. I am able to all things, to doe, J"- i5-to suffer all things, (and therefore Lord of himselfe and of '- 5-the World) but ev rep evsvvam. ovuti fxe- lcttu) in Christ enabling; without me saith Christ, yee can doe nothing; and not 1, saith Paul but the grace of God in me: whereas those Philosophers having no stocke, but their owne, were poore Pedlers, not Royall Merchants, which would seeme to flie but wanted wings, yea life.

And as for this Christian selfe and World, and Heaven-interest, it troubles not, intermedles not, dis-turbes not Earthly possessions and powers, for the greatest is a servant of all, and hee is often poore in Luk. 22. secular sense which makes many rich, as having nothing,- '–even then when he possesseth all things. Am I not free.? y. ' have we not power saith Paul, Who when he was free from all, made himselfe the servant of all that he might gaine the more; not (as they) running quasi in incertum, and fighting quasi aerem verberans, but in this freedome and rule of thc Spirit, beating downe and subduing the i. Cor. 9. 26, bodie of flesh and mortifying his earthly members, not! ' seeking his owne but the good of others: As I please all 'g men in all things (lawfull, for of other things he saith, if I should please men, I should not be the servant of Christ) not seeking mine owne profit, Cal. i. 10. but of many, that they may bee saved. The contempt of riches and greatnesse is the most compendious way to bee rich and great (the contempt I meane, which proceeds from content, not that of the unthankfull prodigall, nor of the desperate begger) and he can never be poore that hath Christ, himselfe, and all things in present possession; God and Heaven in reversion. This, this is that which lifts up his thoughts, and so fils them with the fulnesse of God, that he neglects these baser and Ephes. 3.

truly inferior matters; and, that which others are vitiously, hee is (and it is his vertue to bee) covetous, voluptuous,

Rom. 14. 17. ambitious, but the objects are righteousnesse, joy in the Holy Ghost, and the Kingdome of Heaven.

This whole Globe of Earth and Waters, seemes great to them that are little, but to thoughts truly great and like to God, it holds its true place, price, quantitie, that is, the lowest, basest, least. Quid ei potest videri magnum in rebus humanis, cui aeternitas omnis, totiusque Mundi nota sic maegnitudo? said the Orator. Hoc est punctum, quod inter tot gentes ferro igni dividitur. O quam ridiculi sunt mortalium termini.? said Seneca.

Som. Sap. Scipio was ashamed of the Roman Empires point of

Pifi. L 2. this point: and another (haec est materia gloria nostra, hic tumultuatur humanum genus, c.) is ashamed of this stirre for earth by foolish man, not considering quota terrarum parte gaudeat, vel cum ad mensuram avaritias suas propagaverit, quam tandem portionem ejus defunctus obtineat. Horum agrorum possessione te effers, qui nulla pars sunt terras said Socrates to Alcibiades bragging of his lands, which yet in an universall Map hee could not shew: whereas the Universe it selfe is not large enough to bee the I. Co. 3. 22. Mappe of the Christians inheritance, whose are the

Heh. 2. world, and life, and death, and things present and things to come, all are theirs; the third Heaven and Paradise of God their Patrimonie; the Angels their Gard (are they not all ministring spirits sent forth for their sakes that are heires of salvation.''') the Devils, the World, Sinne, Death and Hell their triumph; Paul, Apollo, Cephas, all the Worthies, Elders, Senators

Heb. 12. Patres Conscripti of the celestiall Jerusalem, those first-borne, whose names are written in Heaven, their Kindred, Brethren, fellow Citizens, fellow members; Christ him-

Apoc. zi. selfe their head, their life; and God their portion, their exceeding great reward, their owne God amongst them, in a tenure like himselfe, eternall and unspeakably glorious. The degrees of this Scala Coeli, are men- tioned by Paul,''' All are yours, and you Christs and '' i- Cor. 3, Christ Gods, and this the descent of our right, God, ', 9- 20. Christ, all things; God gave all to his Sonne, his Sonne with all to us. Christ with his bodie is the Centre, and God the Circumference of this mysticall Corporation.

Rowze up then thy thoughts, O my Soule, let these worldly Pismires toile about their Hils, and busie Bees about their Hive; and let them in Courts and Suits, where Forum "" litibus mugit insanum, contest about the shadow " Cyprian. of the Asse. Shadowes; obscure darke shadowes are Time of ternitie. Motion of immutabilitie. Earth, of Heaven; and in a vaine shew or shadow walks he, disquieting himselfe in vaine, that heaps up riches and knowes not who shall gather them. All that I see is mine, said the Philosopher: Foolosopher! that I see not is mine, things seen are temporall, things not seen are- n- i-eternall; my faith is the evidence of things not scene, T'' my hope were not hope if scene, and my Charitie mind the things above, out of sight, where Christ my love (so Ignatius called him) sits at the right hand of the God of love, which is love. And yet if I affect shadowes, this Sunne yeelds so farre to my yet weaker and grosser bodily affects, and whiles it thus shines on my soule, by grace it makes the shadowes as mooving indices of time attend my bodie, this being the prerogative of Christian godlinesse, to have the promises of this life, and that which is to come. Sure if I were in the. starrie Heaven, with mortall eyes I could not thence 715 in such distance be able to see this small Globe, whence The sun is, I see so small the greatest starres, whence the light of the if rt hath World and King of starres (so much neerer in place, 0" 'j "-greater " in quantitie, more visible in qualitie) seemes iss times-as little, as the head that viewes it. And should this the greatest Earth which cannot there be scene, so Eclipse my lower " '-f lo 'e Moon-like borrowed beames by interposition, that all " S ' ' " should be shadow in a double night and twofold darknesse.''' No, No, I will get up thither, even farre above Rom. lo.

my selfe, farre above all Heavens, (say not in thine heart, who shall ascend into Heaven? that is to bring Christ from above) and thence with a spirituall and heavenly eye looke on earth, and not here and hence with a carnall and sensuall eye looke on Heaven (this makes the heavenly bodies little, the great light of Heaven eclipsed, not in it selfe, but to me by every interposed Moone, and the Heaven of Heavens wholy, invisible) so shall it not annoy my sense; so shall not my sense of earth annoy my reason; so shall not my reason perplexe my faith, but I shall use it as not using, as not abusing' it, to helpe and not to hinder my present Pilgrimage. I. Cor. 7. And thinke not that we speake impossibilities: of

Epaes. 2. 6. every Christian it is said, conresuscitavit consedere Rom. 6. 5. j-coelestibus in Christo Jesu; and we are crvfxcpvtoij planted together into the similitude of his resurrection by Baptisme, both in regard of the imputation and infusion. If this high Mysterie be hid, yet, as when thou hast viewed the Sunne, it makes thee uncapeable of seeing the earth, either at that time or for a space afterwards: so the soule that often by devout contemplation is accustomed to view this Sunne, neither can then equally, nor cares much to fixe his eyes on earthly delights after, but having drunke of these heavenly waters, is not very thirstie of these muddie Springs, and of troubled Ale after such generous Wines. These things I. i. 10. are indeed effected by degrees, nor can we at once leape from the Cradle to the Saddle, and I suspect the forward Herculean hands that can so soone with new-borne gripes strangle old Serpents: yet is not the Christian alway a Dwarfe, but still growes up in grace, and is ever grow-EAes. 4. ing into him which is the head, Christ. He is the Alpha and Omega, hee is Lord of all as the Son and Heire, of Man, the World and Heaven; and he with all this right is given unto us, inhabiting, purifying, quickning Mans heart by faith; whence he also is Microcosmically Master of himselfe, Cosmopolitically of the World, in

Catholike Christianitie heire of Heaven; All, of, in, by and for Christ, to whom be glory for ever. Amen.

. nil.

The Christian and Philosopher compared in that challenge to be rich, free, a King; that this hinders not but furthers Pohticall subjection: and of the happy combination of wisdome and royaltie in Salomon, as likewise in our dayes.

LI Arts are but the supply of Natures defects, to patch up her ragged and worne rents, to cover rather then to cure or recover Mans fall; even that King of Arts, the Politicall Art of Kings, is not heire by whole bloud; but the gift of God, begotten since the fall, and abundantly argues our unrulinesse otherwise, which must have Lords and Lawes to rule us. By like favour of God, least mans dissolution should bring a desolation, came in Politicall tenure and Civill state and Right amongst men. The lest possession is this, which wee call our proper, as being no part of our selves, and a small part of the smallest part of the Universe: greater is the Universe it selfe, and the greatest right thereto is that which is most universall, whereof the soule is only capable; greater then the greater World is this Little, for whom that was made, yea, for whom the Word, the maker of both was made flesh; and as in it selfe, so also to us, whom little it advantageth to winne the whole world Psal. i6. and loose our owne soules: greatest of all and Greatnesse it selfe is God, the lot of the Christians inheritance and the portion of his cup, to whom the Father hath given the Sonne, and with him all things. These things may con-curre and did in Salomon, without confusion; that the three last may also be separated from the first, and that subsist without the least knowledge of these last, is a true conclusion. And how many have much in Politicall and

Sen. de bene. I.- c. ad reges potestas pertinety ad singulos dominium, Laert.

dwui JLev TT)S 7r6 ewj, W(i)s de Twv xpwyo-vwv.

See Laert. in vit. Diog. ifj Amb. Ep. 7. where you may read Calamus whole Epistle, and in the end of this Bookc.

Cuncta cupit Crcesus, Diogenes nihilum. Eum maxime divitiis frui qui minimi divitiis indiget. A nimusoportet sejudicet divi-tem, non homi-num sermo, 3c. Cic. Ccelo tegitur qui non habet umam.

Civill possession, which are had and held of the things they have and hold, as the price of their freedom, not so much as dreaming of any other tenure but propriety, laughing at the Philosopher, and raging at the Christians farther challenge, which yet disturbes not (as not a worldly tenure) Propriety but that positive sicut erat in principio, (in the fuit of mans incorrupted nature) is now comparatively more certaine, more ample by faith, and shall be in saecula saeculorum a superlative of fullest happinesse. Even still proprietie in strictest sence, is the Subjects state and that with many subdivisions and diversifications; a higher and universall right appertaineth in each mans proprietie to the King, as Lord of all. That naked Cynike, that neither had house nor dish, not only compared himselfe with Alexander, (in emulation of his great Titles, proclayming I am Diogenes the Dogge) but even great Alexander, had he not beene Alexander, professed hee would wish to bee Diogenes. Neither feare nor desire could any whit dazzle him in that Royall lustre, but beeing questioned by Alexander, if hee feared him not, asked if hee were good or bad; beeing answered, good; and who (saith he) is afraid of good being bidden aske, he desired no-thing but the restitution of the Sunne which his interposition had taken from him; insinuating a greater riches in Natures inheritance, then in the greatest Kings beneficence; and in his owne mind, then in the Others spatious Empire. Plus erat quod hie nollot accipere, (saith Seneca) quam quod ille posset dare. Nor had Greece alone such spirits: Calanus in India was more admired of Alexander, then the King of him. Corpora, saith he in his Epistle to Alexander, transferes de loco ad locum, animas non coges facere, quod nolunt, non magis quam saxa, ligna vocem emittere. I speake not, as approuving these men in all their speeches and actions: but if they could doe so much in that twilight of Nature, how much more may Christians aspire unto, on whom, as is said before, the Sun of righteousnesse is risen."' These indeed are Children of the day, which know how to honour the King, in that feare of God, which is the beginning of wisdome; which the Cynikes, Gymnosophists and Stoikes, not having attained, dreamed in their night, and did those things rather as men talking and walking in their sleepe, then as men truly knowing what they said and did. Like these Ophyrians wee write of, which possessed much Gold, but Salomon alone knew how to bestow it on the Temple, which sanctifieth the Gold. And yet how farre did these Philosophers Dreames exceed the seeming waking and watchfull cares of Croesus and Crassus (which rather in troubled, feverous, phrenzie, or Opium sleepes were more fatally perplexed) esteeming Vertue the truest treasure; and Riches rather to consist in needing little, then holding much, and a contented mind to bee a surer Coffer, then the bottomlesse Bags of insatiate I. 1. ii. Avarice; and Natures commons of the Heavens and q gj s Elements to be greater possessions, then a few handfuls of sunt non inclosed dust; more admiring the Physicians skill, occupatione sed then the Druggists shop full of simples, or the Apothe- " "J J caries of medicines; more joying in, more enjoying (as the " " J members of the body) the publike then the private wealth, singula more the contemplation, whereby the minde reasonably mancipantur. useth all things, even those of others, without further Tuetur hoc cares, then that proprietie whereby the sense distinguisheth intumr: VU. the owner, and addes to this little owne, the great cares of up, Manud. getting, keeping, spending, and no lesse feares of loosing, adstoic yea (in many a Tantalus) of using, as if he were the PAt.. s. dtss. Gaoler rather then Owner of that wealth which hee lades J," Ep, with Irons and strangles in his Iron Chest, for no other Oonat. L 2. fault, but calling such a Mizer Master. Quibus hoc Ep. 2. sordibus emit ut fulgeat vigilat in pluma; Nee intelligit miser speciosa esse sibi supplicia, possideri magis quam possidere divitias. The wise man is like Isaac in whom Abrahams seede is called, whom he makes his heire: but these which are called rich, are sometimes like Ismael, thrust out of all; at the best, like the Sonnes of the Con- "- 5- cubines, to whom Abraham gave gifts and sent them j '- Vs. away: the Minde, as that which alone is immortall, hath

Amb. Ep. 7. handles this Theme sagely, learnedly, godly, Eivai 7d3 Tid) exeu-deplave ovatav: ai'Toirpayias Ttu disovxeid-fft prqffiv avtO-vpayidi: Laeri. in Zenone. Epictetus.

Xevdepos i(XTiv 6 Civ ws oiXe- avaykdffai itxTiv, ijfc. it may be said of a good man, and his affections as Virgil of Augustus, Victorque volentes. Per populos dat jura viamque affectat Olympo. Epict. irpocfKo.-Tartra xdfj-ov rtw Opfjitd) Tl

Sev, isc. Subducit se custodiee in qua tenetur iff ceelo rejicitur. Sen.

Joh. 14. 23. Gal 2. 2. 20, Joh. 6. Cant. I. Bern in Cant. 21. Satius est ut me trahas, ut

State of perpetuity and inheritance, the Sense in her propriety is capable onely of gifts and moveables.

From this glimpse of reason did those Philosophers the sonnes of Nature (how much more should we the Sons of the free women?) attribute libertie and a Kingdome to their Wise man. Saint Paul more fully, Justo non est lex posita. Saint Ambrose laden with the spoiles of these Egyptians, therewith adornes the Christian Tabernacle. He is a free man saith he, which doth "" what he will, and lives as he pleaseth, nor can be forced to any thing: now the wise man wils that which is good, hates the evill; not for feare but for love, obeieth the commandement; seekes not to please the uncertaine vulgar, but his minde hangs evenly in the ballance poized with the sheckle of the sanctuary; not forced by Law, but he is law to himselfe, and hath the same written not in tables of stone, but in fleshie tables of the heart,; not fearing the Law, because his debts are acquitted, and cannot therefore be arrested; not servant to any, yet making himselfe the servant of all, for their good; whose service to God doth not consume but consummate his libertie, for God's service is perfect freedome; to whom when all things are lawfull, yet nothing is lawfull that is not expedient, that edifies not; who abides founded and grounded on Christ the rocke, and therefore feares not the swelling waves, nor raging windes, fluctuates not with every blast of doctrine: is not pufl ed with prosperity, dejected with adversity, but like Joseph (which bought those that bought him, even all the land of Egypt besides, for Pharao, after himself had bin sold for a slave) abides himself in whatsoever changes of fate and state. He hath subordinated his will to Gods will, and if hee will have him doe or suffer any thing, possesse or loose either himselfe or ought he hath, it shall be his will also. This made Job abide himselfe, when he was shaken, and as it were thunder-stricken out of all at once: yea, by a sacred antipcristasis he gathered his spirits together and not onely not blasphemed, but blessed; then and therefore blessed God, who is no lesse good In taking then in giving, who hath vim qualitn loved us and given himselfe for us, before he takes ought ' f Zdo, from us, yea therefore takes this that he might give that y. (both himselfe and our selfe) to us. He that looseth his quodammodo life findes it, and hee that denieth himselfe and his in vitam ut owne will, puts off the chaines of his bondage, the slavery-.- jf ll to innumerable tyrants, impious lusts, and is thus a free forpentem ut ' man indeede, freed from the divell, the world, himselfe, reddas cur-breathing the free ayre of heaven in the lowest and rentem, y darkest dungeon, yea in the closest of prisons (his owne g-J'Ji body) closely by contemplation conveies himselfe forth to 7 fetch often walkes in the Paradise of God. Once, he loves moribas. Christ, hee lives Christ, and therefore cannot be compelled Ck. par. 5. by another, will not be compelled and mastered by Him- p ' ' ' ' selfe, longs to be more and more impelled by that Spirit j ' ' (which sweetly forceth into the desired haven) and to be drawne by the Father that he may be enabled to follow the Sonne, with whom he is unable to hold pace; and fearing because he loves, thus desires helpe, that (be it by stripes, or threates, or other tentations) his feete may be made more sure, more swift. He feares God, and therefore feares nothing. And whereas hee that com-mitteth sinne is the servant of sinne, he is thus not onely set free by Christ, but more highly dignified and made a King and Priest to God. He daily sacrificeth praiers, praises, good workes, his owne living body in reasonable service, not the bodies of dead and unreasonable beasts; hath alway the doore of the heavenly pallace, the eare of the heavenly King open to his intercessions. He is also a King over himselfe (a little world, a great conquest) over Fortune the magnified Lady of the greater World (which he frames to his owne manners; and if he cannot bend it to his will, knowes how to bend his will to it) over the Divell, the God of the World; over Death, which hee makes (as Sapores did the Roman tyrant Valerian, and Tamerlane the Turkish Bajazeth) his foot-stoolc, or stirrop to mount up to a higher and better life, and like David cuts off the head of this Gyant (which

Eph. I. ult. Pro. 14. 17. Lips. Manu-duct, . 3. d. 13.

oia-qs dpx s d UTTcu dj'oi. Ltf r.;' Zen. regnum potestas nulli obnoxia.

to his true home; prepare a place for spirit with us, hath to take possession, hath defied all the armie of Mankinde) with his owne sword: hee is (a King) over the world, which he neither loves (for his heart and treasure is in heaven) nor feares (for what can it doe at the worst, but further his heavenly happinesse) nor fashions himselfe to it, but it to himselfe, using it as not using it, not setting his heart on it, for the fashion of this world passeth away, as a Scene, where he but acts a while his part; and a strange Country thorow which he travelleth where his King is gone before to him, and leaving the earnest of his taken our earnest, our flesh, there to make intercession in the presence of God for us. Our Head is there already which cannot so farre degenerate as to neglect his body, the reall and living parts of Himselfe, the fulnesse of him that fils all in all things: This Kingdome is not meate and drinke, pompe and splendor, and much less intruding into the secrets, obtruding on the scepters of their soveraignes, but righteousnesse, peace, and joy in the holy Ghost, which the Philosophers knew not, and whatsoever they have challenged (as a Ratione Reges) yet in comparison of true Christians they were but as Kings in a Play (as Plutarch said of the Stoickes) which talked, stalked, walked on their Stage, and acted that part which in deede and in spirituall right is our reall part and inheritance. And if a Kingdome be a power subject to none, then every true Christian is a King (not in Ana-baptisticall phrenzie to cast off all yoakes of loyalty, to cast out all States and Royaltie, and like their John of Leyden to make himselfe a licentious Monarch, pressed downe meane while with so many envies, vices, miseries, but) in this, that pectore magno, Spemque metumque domat, vicio sublimior omni, Exemptus fatis: in that he obeieth his soveraigne not so much of his slavish feare, as because he loves him, and loves that God which hath given him soveraignty, and therefore as to the living image of God yeeldes obedience to him, not grudgingly or of necessitie but cheerefully, and with a willing heart, making his superiours will to be his owne (because it is Gods) will. And if he commands that which he findes countermanded by the highest Law, he rebels not, reviles not, Rex Se ec. est qui posuit metus, Et diri mala, pectoris, where he cannot be willing to doe, he will yet be willing to suffer the will of his soveraigne, Occurritque suo libens Fato, nee queritur mori. Thus is this man spiritually a King and Infra se, videt omnia, beholds all things beneath him, by suffering, overcomming; by obeying, ruling, himselfe if not others. In this sence Christ saith of the Church of Smyrna, I know thy poverty, but thou art rich: and of y poc. z. y 3. the Laodiceans which esteemed themselves rich, encreased- 3-with goods, and needing nothing, that they were wretched, and miserable, and poore, and blinde, and naked. Silver and Gold have I none, said that rich Apostle, whose pretended successours, out of a will to be rich, have fallen into tentation, and a snare, and many foolish and noisome lusts: For the love of money is the roote of all evill, Tim. 6. which while these covet after, they have erred from the faith: and instead of Apostolical, have proved Apostati-call, with Babylonicall mysteries confounding things spirituall and externall, enclosing all the commons of the Church and the Spirit, to the onely use of the Vatican; and then with the spoile of all Christians This spirituall man must judge all, and be judged of none, usurping the rights of, and right over Kings, not considering the diversity of these tenures.

But yet (to returne to our Salomon), if a man by this fiozv good a Christian wisdome becomes free, rich, a King; what shall f- ”””’ ”””” a King of men be (with addition of this wisdome) but heroicall, and if not more then a man, yet a worthy of men, and neerest to God.? This appeares in David and Salomon, two learned, no lesse then potent Kings, the one gaining greatnesse at home, the other dispersing those raies beyond their owne Orbe, to remotest Ophir. This we see in Philip and Alexander, in Cassar and Augustus. Learning is the best Jewell in a Kings Crowne, and Christian wisdome like the verticall crosse upon it; which both in Bookes (by King Alphonsus called his faithfuuest Counsellors) and in their bosomes, speakes that without feare or flattery, which servants cannot or dare not; makes them to see with their owne eyes, and not onely by experience of others; yea with the eyes of the Worthies of former times, and to converse with the Auncients of all ages: and searching into the causes of things to penetrate seasonably into aflfaires which suddenly assault others. But especially in Marine discoveries, we are not so much indebted to the power as the learning of Kings, and both together make a blessed match, and have produced to the world the best knowledge of it selfe. Salomon is example, who in the writings of Moses, being instructed of Ophyr, attempts the discovery. How little knowledge had the Greekes of Asia till Alexander emploied both Aristotle with great costs, and Himselfe also in discovery of the Lands and Seas, besides Nearchus and other his Captaines,? Julius and Augustus opened the first lights in manner to the Romans, the one in discovery of the world and the parts adjoyning, the other also unto the Indies. How little of the world hath beene discovered for want of learning by the Turke, Mogoll, Persian, Chinois, and Abassine, howsoever called great? how little are most of them all But what neede 1 forraine examples? How little in comparison hath our Nation (the Oceans darling, hugged continually in her bosome) discovered and made use of (yea they were the prey of the Easterlings and Lumbards, scarcely knowing their neighbour Seas) before the late eruption of captived learning in the former age, and more especially in the glorious Sunshine of Queene Elizabeth, and (after that Sunset, Sol occubuit nox nulla sequuta est) in the succeeding, that I say not in Ophyrian regions, exceeding times of King James? I dare not presume to speake of his Majesties learning which requires a more learned pen, and where to speake the truth would seeme flattery; nor yet of that learned Queene, who sometime brake in peeces the artlesse pictures made to represent her

(for Apelles is onely fit to paint Alexander, Homer to sing Achilles, and Virgil his Augustus.) Thus a more learned Sir F. Bacon witnesse hath said, and I will recite: that to the last yeare " f ")"- of her life duely and daily shee observed her set houres for reading: that this part of the Island never had 45. yeares of better times, and yet not through the calmenesse of the season, but through the wisedome of her regiment: the truth of religion established, the constant peace and security, the good administration of justice, the temperate use of the prerogative not slacked nor much strained, the flourishing state of learning, the convenient state of wealth and meanes both of Cowne and Subject, the habit of obedience, and moderation of discontents, notwithstanding the differences of Religion, her single life, Romes I. i. 13. alarmes, and the neighbour Countries on fire. Hence that felicity of the State, of Religion, and especially of Navigation, now in threescore yeeres continuance, growne, almost out of the cradle and swadling cloathes, to the present ripenesse amongst us. That our Virgin-mother, in her preparation to the Crowne by the Crosse and in happy exploits, another David; in care of just Judges and Justice Jehosaphat, in reformation Hezekiah, in restoring the Law that was lost Josiah, The Saxons 1-n J u-n expelled the m peace, plenty, successe, magnincence, and (the pillar Brttaineswith of all this) Navigation, another Salomon, and (with their learning. greater happinesse then his) leaving her Name without The Danes Salomons imputation of falling to Idolatry, to survive iflfier learning,,, 1 1 J had blessed the her person, and to become her heire and successour.- in them all: dying

in a good age (as is said of David) Saxons) full of daies, riches, and honour. In these times drowned all

Britaine hath recovered her eyes and spirits, and hath learned men, discovered the Westerne Babylon and her labyrinthian ' JJ j' mazes and gyres of superstition, first of all Europaean p d, that in

Kingdomes: and in maturest order casting off that K. Alfreds yoake, which igno-rance (caused by irruption of bar ' '"f hmselfe barians' into all parts of the Roman Empire had " j 'J brought in as a myst, whereby that Romish mistery priest could of iniquitie might worke unespied) had put on the understand his I 33 =

Ladu Service, and till the conquest this mist continued in great part, that Priest then being a zuonder that knew his Grammer. Al-fredi epist. ap. Asser. Men. Mat. Paris, An. 1067 Clerici adeo lit. carebant ut cateris stu-pori esset qui gram, didi-iissct.

Sir F. Drake zvas the first Generall that swam about the Globe, Candish the next.

In the question of Antichrist in his Majesties Monit. Preface, neckes and veiled hearts of our forefathers, which by the light of learning was now espied and exiled: and this freedome maintained maugre all the gates and forces of Rome and Hell. Yea, he that commanded Honour thy Mother, made her sexe honorable, and caused that a Woman had the honour over that Sisera, that Abimelech, that Holofernes; the sword of a woman prevailed, not by close advantages but in the sight of the Sun, in the worlds amphitheatre, all Europe looking on and wondring (yea the most, still giddie with that cup, enterposing against her.) This Christian Amazon overthrew those Romish both gladiatores sicarios and (as they write of the Rhinoceros) tossed those Buls (which had thought to have pushed her by their homes of deprivation and invasion, and the close fights of treason and insurrection, out of England and Ireland) to the admiration of men, the joy of Angels, and acknowledgement in all of the sword of the Lord and of Gedeon, the power of the highest perfected in her weakenesse. And (which more fits our Navigation treatise) this virago (not loosing her owne virgin-zone) by her Generall first loosed the virgin zone of the earth, and like another Sunne, twice encircled the Globe. Learning had edged her sword then, but the successour of this our Debora, like Achilles in the Poets, hath a Panoplie, a whole armor of learned devise; and like Apollo in the mids of the Muses, so have we seene him in the learned disputations of both Universities; such an Apollo whose Oracle discovered the Divels Master peece and Papall monster peece of powder treason, and brought it to poulder, by the light of his wisedome preventing those infernall lightnings and sulfurous hellish thunders: whose learned writings as the arrowes of Pythius have given the deepest and most fatall wounds to this mystie mysticall Python: whose birth hath made him a great King, whose great learning hath purchased another Kingdome, and made the Schooles to admire him in Divinitie, the Tribunall in Law, the Senate and (he Mo-Counsell table as the table of Counsaile and Map of f ' Z humaine wisedome: whose armes! but blessed are we that his learning and wisedome keepe us from their of (Ais war) as drery noise and dismall experiments; that we in the a' h f-tragedies of so many Nations are spectators, that the l " f God of peace hath with the Gospell of peace given us Jj dor a Salomon, truest type of the Prince of peace, whose there. daies are daies of peace at home, whose treaties propound wayes of peace abroad, whose sun-like raies have shined not by bare discoveries, but by rich negotiations to this our Salomons

Ophir in what part of the world soever the quarelsome wits of men have placed it. If you looke neere hand, Scotland is added, and Ireland now at last made English dispersing feares by English Cities, and plantations: If you looke further, with those which seeke for Ophir in the West Indies, there may you see English Plantations and Colonies in Virginia and other parts of both those supposed Peru's, the Northerne and Southerne America: if to Sofala on the South of Afrike, or to the East of Asia, there also have the English fleetes passed, traded (and if you thinke nothing compleate without armes) surpassed, the most advantagious assailants: that even the Indians (which yeelde commonly in martiall, alway in Neptunian affaires to the Moores) have a proverb, three Moores to a Portugall, three Portugals to an Englishman: whose happy times have exceeded Salomons and Hirams discoveries; even where no writing hath mentioned any name of Noahs Sonnes, where none of Noahs Sons ever yet inhabited, where the Sun it selfe seemes affraid of uncouth Seas, horrid lands, and marine monsters, hiding himselfe divers moneths in the yeere together, and but peeping when he doth appeare, as it were fearfully prying and compassing about with obliquer beames, there have the beames of, "! f"?. T,.,, J 1 1 J its Nezv land.

our Brittish Sunne descried, named, and exhaled profits ' The Whale from those portentuous = Dragons of the Sea (loe these fishhg.

the happiest warres against the beasts by Sea and

Land, not like Nimrods hunting of men) and sought In the new "discoveries, notwithstanding the Oceans armies

Northtvestdis- f j jg Hands affronting, till the Sea it selfe (fearing ' Hud'son' But- tot l subjection) hath embaied it selfe and locked up ton, Baffin all passages by unknowne lands. And (not to mention yr. the New Wales there discovered) England hath her

Beet. Virginia, Bermuda, New England; Scotland, a New an magn, Y)2i xg tqv of her own name; yea, Ireland by the care

See Bests voy- of the present Deputie is now multiplying also in age. America, and his Majestie hath sowne the seedes of

New Kingdomes in that New World.

Let not the severer sort censure me of presumption, if I thus embellish my ruder lines with these glorious names, wherein I communicating in the publike benefit, at once testifie my feare of God the Authour, with mine honour to these two great lights of heaven to our Britaine-World, as actors, autors, instruments, mortall images of the immortall. He alone it is qui tempus ab aevo ire jubet, and makes our King a defender of the faith, by which aeternitie flowes from time well husbanded, to resemble herein also, stabi-lisque manens dat cuncta moveri. In this tranquilitie I. i. 14. we may employ our industry in painfull and gainfull labours. I also in this peace, under Israels Salomon, can from the shore behold with safety, with delight, in this glasse let others see, the dangerous Navigations and Ophyrian expeditions of our Countrie men, view their warlike fights in the waterie plaine as from a fortified tower (so the Mogols did the battell of the English and Portugals) not only free from perill, but enjoying, some the gaines of their paines, others the sweete contemplations of their laborious actions, all of us the fruites of our labours and negotiations at home and abroad, which grow from that Jacobaean tree: whose blossomes are inscribed Beati pacifici. This Worke is the fruite of that Peace, and my Song may be, Deus nobis haec otia fecit, that I may write with Inke at leisure, and (under the shadow of this tree) you read with pleasure, what these Pilgrimes have written with hazard, if not with bloud in remote Seas and Lands.

I flatter not the present, I devote to future posterity, this monument of praise to the Almighty, who hath given us this Salomon, if not in all dimensions, (never was there, or shall be such) yet herein like, that wee enjoy under his wings (in the combustions of neighbour Countries) this our peace, plenty, learning, justice, religion, the land, the sea voyages to Ophir, the world, new worlds, and (if wee have new hearts) the communion of Saints, guard of Angels, salvation of Christ, and God himselfe the portion of our Cup, and lot of our inheritance. Blessed are the people that be in Psa. 144. ult. such a case, yea blessed are the people that have the Lord for their God, This is the day that the Lord Psa. 118. hath made, let us rejoyce and be glad in it. And if our times yeelde some exceptions also, and the Tra-ducer impute it to flattery that I bring not evils on the stage: I say that blessed and loyall Shem and Japheth hid from themselves others that which cursed Cham and Canaan quarrelled: Salomons times yeelded grievances, and we live on earth, not in heaven; there is the perfection of wisdome, holinesse, happinesse, whereof Salomons times were a compleate type: we have the truth in part, but all fulnesse is in him, in whom dwelleth all the fulnesse of the Godhead bodily. Col. i. y 2. which to expect here were Epicurisme and state-Puri-tanisme. Quis me constituit vel judicem vel indicem? Malecontent, I am no Lord of times, nor Prince of Princes (they are both Gods peculiar) I endevour to keepe me in the ofiices of my calling, to choose the good part, and in conscience towards God to acknowledge Gods workes in all, and specially in those of whom he hath said, Yee are Gods: To be an accuser is the Divels office, and they which be evill themselves will onely see evill in others.

Of the proprietie which Infidels have in their

Lands and Goods: of proprietie in the Sea, and of Salomons proprietie of the Sea and Shoare at Ezion Geber.

Hus have wee discoursed of the prerogative of Gods peculiar, the right which the true Children of the Church have in Christ and by him in all things: but what shall we say of propriety? of propriety of Infidels? Christs Kingdome is not of this world, and properly neither gives nor takes away worldly proprieties, civill and politicall interests; but addes to his subjects in these things a more sanctified use, all Tit. 1. u! t. things being pure to the pure, impure to the impure; I Tim. 4. qj, j gy j. g sanctified by the word and praier, which Infidels know not. In that interior court of conscience (which in the wicked is defiled) the just have before God a juster use, using the world as not abusing it, not being high minded, nor trusting in uncertaine I Cor. 7. riches: not setting their heart on them, though they I Tm. 6. increase, nor loosing their hearts with them in their Mat. 6. decrease or losse: not laying up to themselves trea-Luk. 12. sures on earth where rust and moth and theefe have power: not singing a requiem, soule take thine ease, thou hast laid up treasure for many yeeres, when this fooles soule it selfe is the worst thing it hath, and may be turned this night out of that secure body and secured state. But in the outward civill Court, and before Men, the Gospell alters not, removes not the land marke of the law, but as well bids Give to Cassar that which is Caesars, as to God that which is Gods. And therefore the rights of men by the royall or common lawes established (all derived from that of Nature, and consequently from God, who is Natura naturans, the creator of Nature) are in conscience of Gods com-mandement to be permitted to them. Neither without

Gods speciall command might the Israelites spoile (as they did) the Egyptians, or invade the Canaanites. It is Saint Judes note of filthy Sodomites, sleepers, . Ep. ignorant, beasts, disciples of Cham, Balaam, and Core, rock. es, clouds without water, corrupt trees twise dead, raging waves, wandring starres, to despise government: naturall bruit beasts (saith Saint Peter prophesying of Pet. z. his pretended successors) spots and blots, wels without water, clouds carried about with a tempest, to whom the blacke darknesse is reserved for ever: promising to others liberty, and are themselves the servants of corruption (in this sence the servants of servants.) Neither could the Divell devise a greater scandall to the Gospell, then that it should rob Kings of their supremacy and preheminence, subjects of their lands and state, as if to convert to Christ were to evert out of their possessions, and subvert states: which is the cause of so few Jewes converted, and so perverse conversions in America, as I have elsewhere shewed. The Gospell is not a sword to take away earth, but to destroy hell, and adds the Keyes of the Kingdome I. i. 15- of heaven, not a hammer to breake in peeces the doores of earthly Kingdomes: and least of all making instead of Keyes, Picklockes (the note of a theefe, even though he should enter at the doore and lawfully succeede lawfull Bishops) which open and shut all at pleasure; against which there is but one word of force, and that is, force it selfe and power which their faction cannot overthrow, the Romish conscience being Lesbian and leaden, or Iron and running compasse and variation, as the Needle of that See hath touched it to observe the Pope as the magneticall Pole, which Philosophers say is not that of heaven but of the earth. God hath made us men, his Sonne hath called us to be Christians, and this opinion doth turne men into Beasts, yea Christian men into wilde Beasts without all propriety, or any thing proper to humanity, which with the rights thereof extends to Infidels. Infidelspro-

These hold not Christ, nor hold of him, as joynt heires: f' '- yet are they not without all right, yea of him also they hold in another tenure, not as sonnes, but as servants (and the servant abideth not in the house for ever, but 704.8.35.36. the Sonne abideth ever: but if the Sonne make them free they are free indeede?) These hold, in a tenure of villen-age not in state of spirituall inheritance, which yet warrants a just title for the time, contra omnes gentes, against all men (as servants use their Masters goods) but being called by death to give accompt to their Lord, are dispossessed of all and themselves also for ever: whereas the children here seeme in wardship, and to receive some short allowance in the nonage of this life, but in the day of death (the birth day of true and eternall life) as at full age, enter into full possession of heaven and earth for ever. That tenure yet of godlesse men (whith are without hope, without Christ, without God in the world) is a tenure from God, though as is said in a kinde of villen-Eph. 2. 10. age; and warrants against all men, as holden of and at the Col. 1. 16. jji of the Lord Christ, by whom and for whom all things ' ' ' were created, and hee is before all things, and in him all things consist. And hee is the Head of the Body the Church. This tenure in capite is the Churches joynture; that of humane nature, from him whose all things are Eph. 2, jure creationis, remaines to forreiners, which are strangers

Col. I. ixovci the Common-wealth of Israel, and from the pri- viledges of the Holy Citie the New Jerusalem. For after the Image of God, by this Image of the invisible God were all Men created; which though it bee in part by sinne defaced, yet through the mercy of God in part remaineth in the worst of men, which still retaine an immortall reasonable spirit indued with understanding, will, and memory (resembling the unity and Trinity) animating and ruling (how imperfectly soever) the organi-call body, and with it the inferiour creatures: which dominion over the creatures is by God himselfe reckoned to the image of God; infected with sinne, and infested Gr. 1.26. y curse; but God even in the sentencing that judge-3.17.18.19. ment remembring mercy, added thornes, and thistles, and sorrow, and sweate, but tooke not away the use; yea he renewed the blessing to all the Sonnes of Noah, and enlarged their commission, indenting in mans heart this naturall right, and in the Beasts this naturall awe and subjection, by Natures owne hand writing.

Hee that then blessed them with. Replenish the earth. Gen. 11.7. 8. did confound their Babel building, and scatter them abroad from thence upon the face of all the earth, to put it in execution, and hath made of one bloud all Nations of men f- 7-26. (as is said before) to dwell on all the face of the earth, and hath determined the times and bounds of their habitation. Thus hee that gave Canaan to the Israelites is said (in a proper sense though differing manner) to have given Are Deui. z. g. ig. unto the children of Lot for a possession, the land of the Emims, and the land of the Zamzummims which hee destroyed before them: as he did that of the Horims to the children of Esau, that as the former generations entered by the Law of Nature, as first finders, so these by the law of Warre, as confounders of the former, and founders of a second state and succession, both guided by the hand of divine providence. Salomon gave Hiram 1 R'g- 9. twenty Cities in recompence of Cedars, and Firre-trees and Gold: and innumerable are the compacts and contracts mentioned in Histories, whereby the rule of Countries and States have beene made over to new Masters, or to the old in a new tenure, as Joseph bought Gen. 47. 20. all Egypt, their lands and persons to Pharaoh. But in all these workes of Men, God is a coworker; the most O "- 4-high ruleth in the Kingdomes of Men, and giveth it to whomsoever hee will, was verified both actively and passively in Nebuchadnezzar: Cyrus is called his servant, Pilates power is acknowledged by the Lord of power to be given from above, and to that Roman soveraignty (how Joh 19. n. unjust soever their conquest was) hee submitted himselfe in his birth (occasioned at Bethlehem by the decree and taxation of Augustus) in his life by paiment ot tribute, and in his death by a Roman both kinde and sentence.

Regiapotestas not! a repub. sed abipso deo, ut Catholtci doctores senti-unt. quamvis n. a rep. ccn-stituatur, non potestatem sed propr'iam au-thoritatem in regem trans-fert, 55V. Fr. a v'ut. Re led. de pot. Civii. Omne Dominium a deo est: domini est terra i5 plen-eius Dom. totius creature ISj omnis po-testas a deo. Rom. 13. Jos. Angles. Valent. parts, z. q. de dom. Rom. 13. I Pet. 2. 13. I. 1. 16.

Hence came the Lawyers Fee."vid. S. T. Smiths common wealth. I. 3. c. 10. Zee this question handled more largel' in baiting P. Alex his bull. I.2. C. I. Read also a Spanish divine Fr. a Victoria in his
PURCHAS HIS PILGRIMES

Per me reges regnant is his Proclamation, whether by-divine immediate vocation as in Moses, or mixed with Lot, or meere, or free choise, or inheritance, or conquest of warre, or exchange, or gift, or cession, or mariage, or purchase; or titles begun in unjust force, or fraud at first, yet afterward acknowledged by those whom it concerned, and approved by time, which in temporall things pro-scribeth, and prescribeth: by this King of Kings doe Kings reigne, and the powers that be are ordained of God, to which every soule must be subject, even for conscience sake, propter Deum; Whosoever therefore resisteth the power, resisteth the ordenance of God, and they that resist shall receive to themselves damnation.

This was written when all Kings were Idolaters and Infidels, nor had the World many Ages after ever heard, that Infidelitie, Heresie, or Idolatry were causes sufficient for rebellion in Subjects or invasion of Neighbours, as in the many examples of the Israelitish and Jewish Kings, which neither invaded others for Infidelitie, nor were at home deprived for Heresie, though all the neighbours were Infidells, and most of those Kings Idolaters. To usher Religion by the Sword is scarsly approved amongst Mahumetans, which permit men liberty of soule, though not of body: but to turne all the World into Timars, and Knights or Souldiers fees, is more intolerable. It was barbarous Latine to turne fides into feodum, the title of all free lands of Subjects holden in fide, in trust of performing rents, services, and other conditions annexed to the first Donation by the superior Lord: but this more barbarous Divinitie, to dispossesse Barbarians of their Inheritance, and by their want of Faith to increase our fees of Inheritance, as if all the world were holden of the Pope in Catholike fee, obtruded on us for Catholike Faith: Christ came not to destroy the Law but to fulfill it; and therefore did not disanuu by the Gospel, that naturall Commandement of Alleageance and Obedience to Princes, the Honor due to the Parents of our Countrey. Neither doth Religion make a Father or Mother, but

PROPRIETY m THE SEA

Nature; and it is said. Honour thy Father and Mother, Select, de Pot.

without annexion of qualitie good or bad. Nor could J '

Jonathan deny filiall observance, or loyall subjection to y, ',

Saul with such excuse; nor could the Keyes that came arguments con- later expel Scepters, which were of more ancient founda futcththispre- tion; nor heavenly Keyes open or shut earthly Doores: "' "' nor can Infidelitie which concerneth Divine Law, yea in Qaietanal'soi matters supernaturall, take away that right which Positive 2. q. 66. a. 8.

or Naturall Law hath given; nor exclude from just title T. Aq. 2. 2.

on Earth, which some hold poena, rather then peccatum, j- jo- f-J- in such as have not heard: nor can a pretended Vicar j ' y challenge justly, what his Lord never claimed, what hee pertotamrela.

also disclaimed: nor did hee send Souldiers but Preachers, In which he to convert the World to the Faith truly Catholike, and "' ' e therein shewed himselfe a true Salomon, a Prince of Peace, "cfuld not figured by this our Salomon who sent Ships of Merchan gwe just title dise and not of Warre to Ophir. And as for any High to the Indies, Priests Bull (whose roaring might conjure the spirits of nd conjutcth

Princes, within the circle of Pontificall censure) those 7-y dayes knew no such brutish dialect, yea wise and just i a'w. 2,35.

Salomon was so farre from fearing or desiring the Bulls Fia. ubi sup.

of Abiathar, that hee put him out of the High Priests Barbari sunt place for intermedling with the Crowne-succession, and 'lr '"lv set Zadok in his roome. And for Ophir, long before privatim. Jus inhabited (as appeareth, Gen. 10.) he did not for the autem gentium discovery thereof, then new, challenge jurisdiction or tit quod in

Soveraigntie, as Lord of that Sea or Region by him 5 ""

J J 1 1 1 111 T J-f ' occupmrtt discovered (no more then the Uphinans had beene JLords cedat. dh. fere of Israel, if they had then discovered it) but left things best. as hee found them, the Countrey appropriate to the Inhabitants, the Sea open to such as would and could in like manner adventure. Otherwise it was with him and his right in Ezion Geber, on the shoare of the Red Sea in the land of Edom. For this was peculiar (both the shoare and sea adjoyning) unto Salomon, chiefe Lord of Edom: which David had before conquered, and so it continued under the Kings of Juda till the evill Chr,. t,.

dayes of Jehoram the sonne of good Jehoshaphat, 2 Cro. z.

who made like use of this Haven, but with unlike effect.

True it is that if Man had continued in his first integritie, Meum Tuum had never proved such quarrelling Pronounes, to make warre more then Gram-maticall, in setting all the Parts of Speech together by

Rom. 5. y 6. the eares. But sinne entring into the world, yea as an 7 invading tyrant ruling, it was necessary that proprietie should prevent rapine of the idler and mightier, and incourage the industry of the just laborer, which for the sweat of his browes might earne and eate his owne

Gen. 4. bread. Thus had Cain and Abel their proper goods, he the fruits of the earth, this of his cattell, the proper Objects of their labour. And when the whole earth was filled with crueltie, God clensed the confusion of those Fence-breakers by a generall deluge. After the Floud,

Gen. 10. Noahs Posteritie had the earth divided amongst them. And in that renovation of the world, in the Golden yf. 4.32.34. Age of the Church, when they had all things common; +5 the reason was, as many as were possessours of lands sold them and brought the price: so that they had a just proprietie of those their owne possessions, and con-

Lttk. 12. 14. ferred the same to others, and after it was sold the money was their owne, and remained in their owne power. He that refused to divide the inheritance to brethren, would not dissolve and dissipate it to

Thou shalt strangers, and abolish one of the precepts of the , J Decalogue; for stealing in properest sense cannot some borderers.?, ',. 1.7-,11 1 r are reported to "ce, it there be no proprietie. Wickedly therefore hold first put doe the Anabaptists in generall, the Papists for their into the deca- owne advantage; the one by confusion, the other H Th y combustions, deprivations, and depravations of sure are bor- estates, remove the Land-marke. Nor doe others derers, that is, well to take away all Sea-markes and right of Marine theeves in proprietie.

tjlllheltout contrary wee see in Salomons Ezion Geber. gffj g Thorow other Seas hee sailed by universall and naturall decalogue. right, in this as his owne proprietie, he builded his

Fleet, prepared, victualled manned his Navie, and altogether used the Sea and Shores, and Port, as is his proper and just Inheritance.

The commendations of Navigation, as an Art worthy the care of the most Worthy; the Necessitie, Commoditie, Dignitie thereof

JWJjlan that hath the Earth for his Mother, Nurse, WM Grave, cannot find any fitter object in this World, to busie and exercise his heavenly and better parts then in the knowledge of this Earthly Globe, except in his God, and that his heavenly good and Inheritance; unto both which this is also subordinate, to the one as a Booke set forth by himselfe, and written of his Wisdome, Goodnesse, Power and Mercy; to the other as a way and passage, in which Man himselfe is a Pilgrim. Now, though I might borrow much from Ptolemey, Strabo, and others in Geographies prayse, yet will I rather fixe my selfe on Salomon and his Ophir.

If Wee should respect persons, and be mooved by authoritie, wee have in this Ophirian Navigation, the patterne of two most worthy Kings, as two witnesses beyond exception, Jewes and Gentiles conspiring; wee have Reverend Antiquitie of Time, Sanctitie of Sociall leagues, Holinesse of sacred Designes, Greatnesse of highest Majesty, Magnificence of brightest Splendour, Munificence of rarest Bountie, Wisdome of justest Temper, Provisions of maturest Prudence; all these in this Expedition of Salomon proclayming, that there is no way by Land alone to the top, of humane Felicity (wherin Salomon also was a type of a Greater) but as God hath combined the Sea and Land into one Globe, so their joynt combination and mutuall assistance is necessary to Secular happinesse and glory. The Sea covereth one halfe of this Patrimony of Man, whereof God set him in possession when he said, replenish the earth and

Gen. 7. 22. subdue it, and have dominion over the fish of the Sea, and over the fowle of the Aire, and over every living thing that mooveth upon the Earth. And when the Sea had, as it were, rebelled against rebellious Man, so that all in whose nosethrils was the breath of life, and all that was in the dry Land died, yet then did it all that time indure the yoke of Man, in that first of ships the Arke of Noah; and soone after the Goad also, when God renewed the former Covenant, and imposed the feare and dread of Man upon Gen. 9. 2. everie beast of the Earth, and upon every foule of the Aire, upon all that mooveth upon the Earth, and upon all the fishes of the Sea.

Thus should Man at once loose halfe his Inheritance, if the Art of Navigation did not inable him to manage this untamed Beast, and with the Bridle of the Winds, and Saddle of his Shipping to make him serviceable. Now for the services of the Sea, they are innumerable; it is the great Purveyor of the Worlds Commodities to our Vid. D. j4mb. use, Conveyor of the Excesse of Rivers, Uniter by Hexaem. I. 3. Xraflfique of al Nations; it presents the eye with diver-' ' 5 sified Colours and Motions, and is as it were with rich

Brooches, adorned with various Hands; it is an open field for Merchandize in Peace, a pitched field for the most dreadfull fights of Warre; yeelds diversitie of Fish and Fowle for diet. Materials for Wealth, Medicine for Health, Simples for Medicines, Pearles and other Jewels for Ornament, Amber and Ambergrise for delight, the wonders of the Lord in the Deepe for instruction, variety of Creatures for use, multiplicity of Natures for Contemplation, diversity of accidents for admiration, compendious-nesse to the way, to full bodies healthfull evacuation, to the thirsty earth fertile moysture, to distant friends pleasant meeting, to weary persons delightfull! refreshing; to studious and religious minds (a Map of Knowledge, Mystery of Temperance, Exercise of Continence, Schoole of Prayer, Meditation, Devotion, and Sobrietie: refuge to the distressed. Portage to the Merchant, passage to the Traveller, Customes to the Prince, Springs, Lakes, Rivers, to the Earth; it hath on it Tempests and Calmes to chastise the Sinnes, to exercise the faith of Sea-men; manifold affections in it selfe, to affect and stupifie the subtilest Philosopher; sustaineth moveable Fortresses for the Souldier, mayntayneth (as in our Hand) a Wall of defence and waterie Garrison to guard the State; entertaines the Sunne with vapours, the Moone with obsequiousnesse, the Starres also with a naturall Looking-glasse, the Skie with Clouds, the Aire with temperatenesse, the Soyle with supplenesse, the Rivers with Tydes, the Hils with moysture, the Valleyes with fertilitie; contayneth most diversified matter for Meteors, most multiforme shapes, most various, numerous kindes, most immense, difformed, deformed, unformed Monsters; Once (for why should I longer detayne you?) the Sea yeelds Action to the bodie, Meditation to the Minde, the World to the World, all parts thereof to each part, by this Art of Arts, Navigation.

Neither should we alone loose this halfe of Natures dowrie, without the benefit of this Art, but even the Earth it selfe would be unknowne to the Earth; here immured by high impassable Mountaynes, there inaccessible by barren way-lesse Deserts; here divided and rent in sunder with violent Rivers, there ingirt with a strait siege of Sea; heere possessed with wild devouring beasts, there inhabited with wilder man-devouring men; here covered with huge Worlds of Wood, there buried in huger spacious Lakes; here loosing it selfe in the mids of it selfe, by showres of Sand, there removed, as other Worlds I. i. i8. out of the World, in remoter Hands; here hiding her richest Mynes and Treasures in sterill Wildernesses, which cannot bee fed but from those fertile Soyles, which there are planted, as it were removed hither by helpe of Navigation. Yea, wheras otherwise we reape but the fruits of one Land, or the little little part thereof which we call our owne lands, hereby wee are inriched with the commodities of all Lands, the whole Globe is epitomised, and yeelds an Abridgement and Summarie of it

This is effected by such as saile about the Worldy as is knowne of all such as know the Sunnes selfe in each Countrle, to each man. Nor should we alone loose the full moytie of our Demesnes by Sea, and a great part of that other moytie the Land, but the Heavens also would shew us fewer starres, nor should we grow familiar with the Sunnes perambulation, to overtake him, to disapoint him of shadow, to runne beyond him, to imitate his daily journey, and make all the World an Hand, to beguile this Time-measurer in exact reckonings of Time, by adding or loosing a day to the Sunnes account. Nor could wee know the various Climates, with their differing seasons, and diversified affects and effects of the Heavens and Elements. Nor could we measure the Earths true Dimensions and Longitudes, nor know many creatures both vegetable and sensitive therein (which are our Chattels) nor her high prized Minerals and Gemmes;

nor yet could wee know and use the varietie of Fowle, or (like inferiour Gods) dispose of the winds in the Ayre, bringing constant effects, out of their varietie, and observe their Seasons to flie with them about the World, had we not these Sayle-wings of shipping; whereby we out-runne the wildest beasts, out-swimme the swiftest fish, out-flie the lightest Fowles, out-stretch the fiercest Windes, out-set the strongest Currents, out-passe most spacious Seas, and tame all Nature to the nature of Man, and make him capable of his Naturall Patrimony.

What shal I say of other men.? The holiest, the wisest, the Greatest of Men, of Kings, of Kings of Kings (Salomons example speaks all this) hereby honour God, hereby have made themselves to all Posterities honorable. Wil you have al commendations at once? Salomon the Epitome of al human worth and excellence, promised by Prophesie before his birth, named by speciall appointment of God when he was borne, founder of (that Miracle of Earth, and mysticall Mirrour of Heaven) the Temple; glorious in his other Erections, Customes, Tributes, Riches, Government, and in (that Soule of happinesse) the happy endowments of the Soule in

Visions, Wisdome and Holinesse, in his Fame exceeding Fame it selfe, his Renowme attracting all the Kings of the Earth to seeke his presence, in his Writings elected a Secretary of God to record wisdome to salvation, to all Ages and places of the World, in these things passing others, yea surpassing himselfe (even here may we say, as before is said, is a greater then 2. Chron. 8. Salomon) typing the Great Creatour and Saviour of the World; This first, and most eminent of men, is by the first, and best of Stories, set forth as the first Founder of Long and Farre Navigations, and Discoveries. As for Noahs Arke, it was intended rather to cover and secure from that tempestuous Deluge, and to recover that handful, the Seed of a New World, from the common destruction, then to discover New Worlds, or to make Voyages into any parts of the old: though if we should yeeld This the beginning of Navigation (as indeed it was, though not of Discovery) wee have hereof a greater then Salomon, God himselfe the Institutor and Author, Christs Crosse typed in the matter. Mans Baptisme in the speciall, and Salvation in the generall scope and event. But for Heathens, Josephus hath shewed that Salomon was ancienter then their Gods, not their Navigations alone; and that Carthage was conceived many yeares after Salomons death: and for Greece, Plato hath recorded that Egyptian testimony, that they in all things were children, which yet doted with age, when the Romanes were in the vigor of their youth. The Tyrians indeed were supposed Authours of this Art, but neither could they make this Voyage, but passing over Land through the Countries of others, there to build a Navie, (as in this case they did with Salomon) nor is there record or likelihood of any farre Navigation of theirs till this, yea, it is likely, that heere and hence beganne the greatnesse and supereminent lustre of their Name; the Art which they exercised at, and neere home before, being thus brought out of the Nest, and by Salomons wisedome taught such remote flights.

Thus the Author, and thus Antiquity commends Navigation: and no lesse the ends which mooved Salomon thereto, which were to get Gold, Silver, Ivory, precious Wood and Stones, and other Rarities, which gave such lustre to his State, fewel to his Magnificence, glory to his Name, Ornament to the Temple, splendour to Religion, Materials to the exercise of his Bodie and Minde, that I mention not the Customes increased, others by the Kings example, adventuring the Seas, and Merchandise quickened. This also he makes the fit Object of his Royall thoughts and unmatchable wisdome; not trusting others care, he went himselfe to Ezion-Geber, to make provisions for his Navie; yea, and not leaning to his sole Wisdome, Power, and Successe, entred into league with Hiram, and employed his Ships and Mariners, as he, which hath proclaimed to the World, vae Soli, and

Ecc. 4. esteemed two better then one, and to have better wages for their labour, and a three-fold coard not easily broken.

Jol 40, Hee was not like Behemoth, to trust that hee could draw up Jordan into his mouth, much lesse to make a Monopoly of the Ocean, as if the whole East had been created for Ezion-geber: but amidst his incomparable Designes, framed of Greatnesse, clothed with Wealth, enlived with Wisdome, attended with Successe and Glory, disdaines I. i. 19. not, yea, seekes assistants, and admits a Heathen Kings Society in this, in the Temples Negotiation; inferring that they neither mind the good of the true Temple, or the Catholike Church, which will not endure Christian compartners in the Voyage to Ophir, which impound the World in a corner, and entile a corner to the World. And as he sought not to prejudice Egypt, or any of his Neighbours, if out of their owne Ports they intended to seek the World abroad, no more did he proove injurious to the Ophirians, with whom he dealt, eyther in their Wealth, hindred, by prohibiting all others to trade with them; or (among his many cares of building) by erecting Forts against their wils, as Prisons of their Libertie, and Fetters of their Captivity.

For if to doe as we would be done to, be the Law and Prophets, this Prophet of the Law would not seeke his owne profit, by invading the publike of whole Nations remote and to him innocent, and force upon them so unwelcome knowledge of God and his people Israel, that through their injuries his Name might be bias- Rom. z. phemed amongst the Heathen: but as he might use his owne right where were no people, so in places inhabited, not to neglect the security of his own, nor to usurpe the Sovereignty of the Natives, or prevent and intervert the Rights of common humanity. God that would not (as before is intimated) the price of a Dogge or a Whore, nor the Patrociny of a lie, would not by publike Latrociny have his Temple adorned, nor suffer his House to bee built with bloud, nor the holy Citie with iniquity. Righteousnesse and Peace kisse each Jb. 2. other in Gods Kingdome, and acts of Warre though just, excluded David from the honour of building the Lords House. It followes then that Salomon was in this Ophyrian businesse, a man of peace, and thereof an example to all following Discoverers, according to that Christian Rule, as much as is possible to have Rom. 12. peace with all men.

As Salomons Justice, so his Wisdome and Prudence is exemplary, which though in him supereminent, yet found (as is alreadie observed) no meanes at home to maintaine the glory of Salomon, no meanes by Land correspondent to such Magnificence and Munificence, but addresseth himselfe by Sea and long Voyages to seek it: nor doth he esteeme others eyes enough, nor others assistance too much, but surveyes his Navie himselfe, is glad of Hirams helpe. Nay, this was not only the subject of his wisedome, but the furtherer and Purveyor, by new experiments in Minerals, Gems, Beasts, Fowles, Fishes, Serpents, Wormes, Trees, Fruits, Gums, Plants, Men;

Climates, Winds, Seasons, Seas, Lands, Soyles, Rivers, Fountaynes, Heavens, and Stars; and a World of the Worlds Varieties; of all which howsoever he had received the mayne stocke of Wisdome by Ea. i. i. zi. immediate Gift of God, yet did he frugally employ his Talent, and thriftily improove that Revenue, labouring to be more wise, and travelling in Wisdome and Know- Ecc. I. 13. ledge, and Equitie; and gave his heart to search and ' find out wisdome by all things that are done under the

Heaven, God humbling him with this sore travell, although he excelled in wisdome, all that were before him in Jerusalem. Thus Homers Ulysses in the Schooles of divers Nations Navigations is trained to that peer-lesse wisdom, thus Aristotle the chiefest of Natures Schollers, travelled with Alexanders Purse and Experience to furnish himselfe, and succeeding Ages with Naturall Science and Wisdome. And our Age which God hath blessed beyond many former, produced as Twinnes Navigation and Learning, which had beene buried together in the same Grave with the Roman Greatnesse, and now are as it were raysed againe from the dead.

Hence it is that barbarous Empires have never growne to such glory, though of more Giant-like stature, and larger Land-extension, because Learning had not fitted them for Sea attempts, nor wisdome furnished them with Navigation. Thus the Persian, the Mogoll, the Abassine, the Chinois, the Tartarian, the Turke, are called Great, but their greatnesse is like Polyphemus with one eye, they see at home like purbund men neere to them, not farre off with those eyes of Heaven, and lights of the World, the Learned knowledge, whereof is requisite to Navigation. The Chinois at home, is hereby stronger, and so is the Turke: but the other are braved by every pettie Pirat on their owne shores: the rest like Ostriches spread faire plumes, but are unable to rayse themselves from the Land: yea, their Lands also (as hath happened to the Abassine) and Sea-townes taken from them to the downfall of their estate. One Salomon left greater testimonies of greatnesse, by this his wisdome and helpe of Navigation, then many of the later Otto- mans, which possessed all Salomons Territories, and perhaps a hundred times so much added. But as God gives huge strength and vast bodies to beasts, yet makes Man by art and reason secure from them, if not wholy their Masters; so to the good of Christendome, hath hee denied Learning to those Barbarians, and skill or care of remote Navigations, which how otherwise they might infest the World, appeares by their Christian Slaves and unchristian Pirats, whereof they make use against us, and whereby their Mediterranean is guarded. But on the Arabian, the Portugals before, the English since have put a bridle into the mouth of the Ottoman ost hist. Horse, and shewed how easie it is to intercept his "'– '- ' Maritime incomes, and if not to smother him (as the Floridans serve the Whale by stopping the two holes, whereby he breath's) yet to impoverish him by diverting the riches of the Persian and Arabian Gulphes.

And hereby is evident that as we have observed in Salomons Justice, and Wisdome, so Fortitude it selfe here is exercised, hence increased: nor did Alexander thinke it enough to have overcome men, but would I. i. 20. also encounter the unknowne Ocean. Salomons riches made him eminent and secure, his Navigations rich. But besides the necessary exercise of Fortitude in the Mariner exposed and opposing himselfe to Step-dame Elements, to Shelves and Rockes from the Earth, Whirle-pooles, Currents, Billowes and Bellowes of the Sea, Tempests, Huricanos, Tufons, Water-spouts, and dreadfuu Meteors from the Aire: by Sea-fights is the safest defence of our owne (as the Oracle instructed the Graecians by Wooden-castles, to fortifie against that World of men in Xerxes his Armie) and surest offence to the Enemy. What reputation of courage, what increase of State, did the Portugals hereby attaine in Africa and Asia."' cooping up the Natives within their shoares, possessing themselves of divers petty Kingdomes, enriching themselves with the richest Trade in the World, and that maugre the force of the

Moores, of the Egyptian and Turkish Sultans? The Sea was the Work-house, and Navigation the Anvile, whereon the fortitude of a Woman, wrought the safetie of her Subjects, and hammered the terrours of that enemy, which was called, Omnium aetatum totius orbis amplissimi Imperii Monarcha. Nor need I name the Belgian United Provinces, whose Free estate like another Venus arose out of the Sea, and hath forced Mars to woe this Ladies love and amitie, when force could not ravish her; which seemes since not only to contemne that force, to neglect this love, but almost wantonly in many of hers, remembers to forget herselfe in some respects to her quondam best friends, by whose helpe this Neptunian Amazon was secured at home, by whose ayde and example, that I adde not their Name, her Fortune and Fortitude hath attempted both East and West, yea, hath taken away the name of East and West out of the World, and three times compassed the Compasse. Thus hath a little remnant of Land by Sea-assistance, swelled to this present greatnesse, and filled the remotest Indies with her Martiall and Mer-curiall Designes.

Now for Temperance, Salomon himselfe stumbled and fell at that stone; neither are Sea-men usually on Land the most temperate: Ulysses had not heard of Cyrce or the Syrenes, had hee not adventured the Sea. Yet let this be a commendation of the Marine art, how ever the Mariner be to blame. It is the excellency of the thing that makes it a strong temptation; strong and sweet wines are commended, though weake braines and distempered heads bee justly blamed for their intemperance; in the good gifts of God, beautie, wealth, and honor (as the wormes breede in best fruits) are I. Joh. 2. the lists of the lust of the flesh, the lust of the eyes and pride of life, which are not of the Father but of the world. Nor was Heaven to blame for the fall of Angels, or Paradise for that of Men; nor the Sea if her riches make mens mindes sea-sicke, wavering, inconstant, distempered, and like the Sea, subject to tempestuous temptations. Yea, if you looke neerer, you shall see, as men blame and feare death for the last fatall paines, which yet are not properly of death (which is not in possession till paine and sense be quite dispossessed) but of the remainders of life; so deale they with Navigation in this case, whereas the Sea holds them in good temper, and is a correction house to the most dissolute; but the Land makes them forget the Sea and temperance together. Salomons uxoriousnesse and idolatries were Land-beasts, not Sea-fishes: nor could his Apes and Peacocks, the vainest of his Sea wares, teach him that vanitie. The wonders of the Psal. 107. Lord in the Deepe teach many, no doubt, deepest Divinitie and profoundest Temperance, though some froth swims on the top of the Sea, and beates on every shore where the winde drives it, carried about with every blast of tentation, to the death of more in the wrongly-accused voyage of the East Indies by Bacchus and Venus, then Neptune and Mars, and all such other supposed Deities, and perhaps (I will not speake Dutch) that scurvy Sea-devill too. Coelum non animum mutant qui trans mare currunt. They carry their vices with them, which because the Sea, a Schoole of sobrietie and temperance, permits not to practise, breake out on them aland in greater furie. And as Oviedo tels of Lice, that they leave men a litle past the Azores, as they saile to the West Indies, and die and vanish by degrees, nor trouble them in the countrie, but at their returne about the same height (as if they had waited all that while for them) breede afresh; so is it with vices, which being practised most on Land, doe finde men on every shore, where people and plentie offer opportunitie. Once, Earth is predominant as in our complexions, so in our conditions.

Now for the vertues called Theologicall, Faith, Hope, and Charitie, the Sea is a great Temple not to contemplate their theorie, but really to practise them. Faith hath her greatest eclipse by interposition of Earth, as we see in the Moone; but at Sea, Coelum undique, undique pontus, no Earth is seene, only the Heaven (the walls of our fathers Palace) and the inconstant shifting Elements, which constantly put us in minde of our Pilgrimage, and how neere in a thin ship, and thinner, weaker, tenderer body we dwell to death, teaching us daily to number our dayes, and apply our hearts to wisedome. And what can more lively traine us in Hope then Sea-navigation, where the life we live is hope, where as Davids former deliverance confirmed I. Sam. 17. him against the uncircumcised Philistine, so daily deliverances from death in so few inches distance by windes and waves, which like the Beare and the Lion alway assault us, may the better traine us to the fight with Goliah himselfe, and as I have said (by death escaping death) to cut off Goliahs head with his owne sword. But the chiefest of these is Charitie, and the chiefest charitie is that which is most common; nor is there any more common then this of Navigation, where one man is not good to another man, but so many Nations as so many persons hold commerce and intercourse of I. i. 21. amitie withall; Salomon and Hiram together, and both with Ophir; the West with the East, and the remotest; parts of the world are joyned in one band of humanitie; and why not also of Christianitie? Sidon and Sion, Jew and Gentile, Christian and Ethnike, as in this typical! storie? that as there is one Lord, one Faith, one Baptisme, one Body, one Spirit, one Inheritance, one God and Father, so there may thus be one Church truly Catholike, One Pastor and one Sheepfold? And this also wee hope shall one day be the true Ophirian Navigation, when Ophir shall come into Jerusalem, as Jerusalem then went unto Ophir. Meane while, wee see a harmonie in this Sea-trade, and as it were the concent of other Creatures to this consent of the Reasonable, united by Navigation, howsoever by Rites, Languages, Customes and Countries separated. Heaven conspires with the inferior Elements, and yeelds, as it were, a Sea Card in the Sun and Stars. The Elements which every where else are at open warres, herein agree in sweetest symphonie; the Earth yeelding Shores, Capes, Bayes and Ports, as nests; the Aire windes as wings to these artificiall Sea-fowles (so esteemed at their first sight by the Americans, and by the Negros) and the Sea admitting strange Children into her Familie, and becomming a Nurse against her Nature, to the Earths generation. What shall I say more? Omne tulit punctum qui miscuit utile dulci. To the many profitable effects of Navigation, many pleasures may be added both of Reason in speculation, and of Sense in more then sensuall delight. Salomon in his Ophirian voyage furnished himselfe with Gold and Silver, and other solid commodities; with Almuggim trees also, yea with Apes and Peacocks, the one for the musicall delights of the Temple, the other domesticall and naturall. But I am plunged in an Ocean, when I goe about the Oceans praise, which goes about all things: I shall sooner drowne my selfe in these Deepes, then measure the true depth of the Seas commendations, or Navigate thorow the commodities of Navigation by commerce abroad by his owne, or by Customes at home by others employments. The Text it selfe is a Sea, and needes a better Steeresman to instruct in these Points of Salomons Compasse, which saith more for Navigation then I can, who yet to shew my love and honour of that Noble Science have adventured to say this, to pay this as Custome for the whole Worke, wherein are returned so many returnes from Sea. And now it is high time we come to the History it selfe, and historicall or litterall sense; the first in our intention, howsoever last in execution.

. VII.

I. Reg. 9. 26.

. VII.

Of Ezion Geber, Eloth, and the Red Sea: that of Edom it received that name, and communicated it to the Indian Ocean, by the Phoenician Navigations frequent in those times to India.

INd King Salomon made a Navie of Ships in Ezion Geber, which is beside Eloth, on the shoare of the Red Sea in the Land of Edom, c.

This is the first and best testimonie of a holy Navie. Noah had by Divine Wisdome and Precept built a Ship, which preserved the remainders of the Old, and beginnings I. Pet. 3.21, of the New World, a figure of that Baptisme which now saveth us by the resurrection of Jesus Christ. The Temple, a later and livelier figure of Heaven and Salvation it selfe, must bee furnished with due materialls by a whole Fleet of Ships, which shall not save alone from dangers, but crowne with fulnesse ot joy and glory; this typically then renewed by Salomon for new supplies every Trinitie of yeares; but there the Eternall Trinitie Jpoc. ii. iz, shall at once bee the Temple, the Sunne, the exceeding ' great reward, and all in all for ever. No passage was ucoiil. found for Israel out of Egypt to the Wildernesse (a type of the life by Faith) nor for abundance of the Temples riches the shadow of glory, but by the Red Sea; so meritorious is the blood of our Redeemer, which, by bloody sweat, whippings, and a thorny Crowne, welled Springs of the water of life out of all parts of his body; out of his hands and feet yeelded the foure Rivers which watered the Paradise of God; out of his pierced side and heart flowed a sea, a Red Sea of water and bloud to save, to enrich us, to purchase our Justification by Grace, and beginnings of Sanctification growing unto perfect Glory.

But as all faire things are farre from easie possession, so is it with Heaven, and all her mysteries, so is it with us in this Voyage of Salomon, to know where this

Ezion-geber was, from whence he set sayle, and to come to that Ophir, where he made his Voyage: touching both which, things otherwise enough difficult are made the harder by those mysts, which disagreeing opinions have raised in our way. The Text giveth three markes to know the first, that it was beside Eloth, on the shoare of the Red Sea, and in the Land of Edom. This third marke of Ezion-geber is delineated by Moses, Deut. 2. 8. and before in Num. 33. 35. made the two and thirtieth Station of the Israelites removing, or march in the Wildernesse. And heerein our Maps of that Chapiter, were in the former Bibles much to blame, which are in that and other respects much amended, in the Map of the Holy Land added to the last Translation. Now that it was on the shoare of the Red Sea, and not on the Mediterranean, this Text proveth: and the conceite of Goropius in this kinde that denieth Idumasa to extend J-Gonp. to the Red Sea, and averreth that this Fleet was set Becan Hts-forth from the Idumasan Mediterranean shoare, it is pj j'jvV as many other disputations of his, more full of industry then wit, of wit then learning, of learning then judgement. Strange are his conceptions, and strong his disceptations, but having weake foundations (grounded commonly on names and wordes buried under succession of rubbishes) they prove in the end (as Joseph Scaliger speaketh) but Josep. Antiq. Doctas nug, more wordy then worthy guides, which— doe but verba dare. Againe, that Josephus placeth Esiongeber at Berenice, is either a marginall note of some novice Geographer crept into the Text, or else an old error; for Berenice is on the Egyptian shore, Esiongeber on the Arabian. Josephus placeth it neere Elana: and in the Text Eloth is set a guide to Esiongeber. Now Eloth being written in the holy tongue rn N d ni) was by transmigration shifted and removed to divers pronuntiations, a thing usuall in Ebrew names, both of places and persons. Hee that seeth how John or James are transported in such unlike sounds from the Originall, in Greeke, Latine, French, Dutch, Spanish, Italian,

English, and other languages, in all so unlike and diversified, would scarcely acknowledge them brothers, or to have any kindred either to the mother tongue, or in those many sister languages: and so is it commonly with other names. . 16. Strabo calls it Aeixa, Josephus 'Kixavh, the Latins Elana, and the Gulfe or Bay neere to it is termed Elaniticus. Of this place how it lieth, and how the Ancients were deceived, you have the Relations of Don John Di Castro, from his owne eyes and learned judgement, supposed to bee the same which is now called El Tor, or Toro. Yea the Red Sea is likeliest to have received that name from Edom, as the Pamphilian, Ionian, Tyrrhene, Brittish, and other Seas are ordinarily so named of the Principall shoares they wash. Castro hath better examined the rednesse then any man, and compared the Moderne and Ancient opinions with his owne eyes. And for a Booke-traveller, I must needs applaud Master Fuller, Our Country-man, who in the last Chapter of the fourth Book of his Miscellanea Sacra, hath mustered the testimonies of the Ancients together, and ascribeth the 25, name of Red-sea to Edom, of whom Idumaea tooke name, and of him and it, this Sea. For Ptolemey's Idumea is farre short of the Ancient, which contained also Nabathaea and their Citie Petra, whence Arabia Petrea received the name; Esaus Sword, (of which his Father had prophesied) conquering to both Seas.

This Edom or Esau was that Erythras, which the Grecians mention to have given name to that Sea, by translating Edom into Erythras or Erythraeus, as Cephas into Petrus. Postellus had stumbled on this Note, which Fuller more fully and learnedly hath opened, as other things also pertaining to our purpose. That there is a rednesse in some parts of that Sea, by reason of the cleerenesse of the water, and abundance of a kind of red Corrall, branching it selfe on the transparant bottoms, Castro hath made evident, but that in a small part of that Sea; the like whereof happneth in other Seas of cleerest waters, which show white from sands, greene from weeds, particoloured with pleasant diversified hue, as Pineda citeth the testimony of Ferandez observed neere to Carthagena in America, every Stone, Shell, or whatsoever else was See Saris his in the bottom, in those liquid waves yeelding so pleasant ' y S'- 4- '" and various a tincture, as his many Navigations had no ' where else observed; and Captaine Saris in this Sea, called anciently Erythraean (which name, besides the Arabike and Persian Gulfes, contained the Indian Ocean, so named as it seemeth, from the frequent Navigations out of Eloth and Esion Geber in Edom unto India) was one night almost terrified with a glare yeelding light to discerne Letters, suspected to bee some breach, and proved nothing but Cuttle Fish in the bottome.

But to returne to our Red Sea, Agatharchides in Photius his Bibliotheca, saith it is not called Red of the pwt. Bib. colour, but 0.1Z0 Tov Svvaartovcrauto? of some man which there ruled. The Scriptures call it Siph, Suph, or Souph, trans- Co. 13 22, lated algosum, caricosum, juncosum (to which accordeth i'-Martialls Verse; Quicquid Erythraea niger invenit Indus in alga) it seemes of the abundance of Rushes and Weeds there growing. The Moores, Turkes, and Traders thereof in later times call it the Sea of Mecca: Mela mentioneth the 1 'f" colour, and the King Erythras there reigning; Plinie addes j'" j' 7-for the name. The Sunnes repercussion from the Sand and Land; Strabo cites the same out of Eratosthenes, with S(ral. 16. a tale of Ctesias of a Fountaine emptying his red-okerie waters thereinto, and the Relation of Boxus a Persian, that Erythras a Persian planted a Persian Colonie in an Hand thereof. Ouranius in Stephanus tells of the red adjoyning Mountaines: the Poets have their Perseus, and others their other conceits and deceits, which I leave to p.,, their Authors, as also Pinedas later device. The nature. Salom. li. of that Sea is better delivered in the voyages of Castro, 4.10. Midleton, Saris, Dounton, Haines, and others in these thinketh this our Navigations. But for Eloth and Esiongeber, Master " Sea to be

T- ii-r 1 01-I TXT J SO named of duller IS or opinion that Salomon in his great Wis-dome, Red Weeds wanting fit Mariners, sent to Hiram for Tyrians and growingthere-in, sojoyning Phaenicians, and that a large Colonic was sent by Hiram to

Suphandery inhabit those parts, then subject to King Salomon, by

Telubilon '" " meanes Solomon and Hiram enter into societie for

Vuuho se'red the Indian traffick by that Sea of Edom, so to get the

Herbs are his riches of the East in possession. This Colonie numerous creatures: for strong he placeth at Esiongeber the Arsenal, or fittest neither he ci, building Ships, and at Eloth the fittest Port, teth, norcanl r, o i r i t j- u j- t u u find any au Mart, and Staple for the Indian merchandise, ihus hee, thentlke Au- and very probably: adding that the Hebrew lath in the thor for them, singular, and ieloth in the plurall number, was by the Inphotum Phenicians turned into Ailath, whose singular is Aila, and Xajlr v ' plurall Ailan: thence the Greekes Ailae, Ailana, Eilane, xb Ttov. Elana, and the Latins Elana, and by inversion Laeana.

This Phoenician Colonie hee observeth to have beene of I. i. 23. most name of all other the Inhabitants thereof For the Jewish yoke was soone shaken off by the Edomites 2. Chron. 21. themselves, after Jehoshaphats death, Jehoram rebelling against God, and the Edomites against him. After that 2. Reg. zz. Azariah recovered Elath and built it. It continued not Z. Reg. 16.6. long, but Rezin King of Syria recovered Elath to Syria, The Edition and drave the Jewes from Elath, and the Syrians came of Brixianus (. q Elath, and dwelt there to this day. Thus the Jewes hath Idumai j j j Lords, and received the Customes, were runt, 15c. to expelled; but the Idumaean

Natives and Phasnicians, whichamanu- which might bee usefull to the conquerours remained, script of M. j- e Tyrians being Syrophasnicians, and speaking the ' r th Syrian language, and by their merchandising so profit- able to their Kings. Sr.. 16. This Elath was after called Albus Pagus, by Strabo called the chiefe Mart of the Nabatjeans, whence the Indian and Arabian Merchandise was carried to Petra, thence to Rhinoculura in Phsnicia neere Egypt, and thence dispersed to other places. Thus in the times before the Ptolemeys. But in Salomons time, and whiles the Jewes ruled there, they were brought to Jerusalem and to Tyrus; and after that to Myos Hormos and Arriani Peri- Berenice, i gyptian Ports on the other side of the Red plus Sea, to be thence convayed to Alexandria. Arrianus in his time mentioneth the Garrison at Albus Pagus and Custome there taken, the transporting of wares thence to Petra, notwithstanding the Egyptian flourishing.

Saint Jerom also placeth Ailat In extremis finibus Pales- '– d c, tinae, adjoyning to the Wildernesse and the Red Sea: '

Unde ex gypto in Indiam inde ad gyptum navi- gatur. Sedet autem ibi legio Romana cognomento

Decima; Et olim quidem Ailat a veteribus dicebatur, nunc vero appellatur Aila.

Ptolemev placeth Phsnicum oppidum not far from He which will T-., 1 tt A-ri "1 i. if "'Ore or

Elana; the He Astarte is a Phaenician memorial also;-;.

Plinie mentioneth Gens Tyra, and Herodotus the Syrians i on the Red Sea shoare; that I pursue no other An- read M. Ful-tiquities. These Tyrians it seemeth first began the ' sailing of the Indian Seas, and Habitation on the Arabian shoares, instructed by the Wisdome, and procured by the Friendship of Salomon with Hiram: which they continued under many State-changes, till the Mahumetan times, the Staple of those Indian Merchandises being altered after the Jewish times, with the chiefe Monarchies, Assyrian, Babylonian, Persian, Ptolem an, Roman. And this is the onely Phoenix-neast made of sweet Spices in ' p f Nature false (for God made all Fowles at first, and after ' ' """" brought to, and out of the Arke, in both sexes, male and female) but true in this Alegory, the Phasnicians of all the Nations known, being the only skilful Mariners in the Arabian and Indian seas, and from the one, by the other, bringing the Spices and Riches of the East into the West, that skill being ever communicated not by Generation, but by Industry; which made Tyrus (as Ezekiel describeth it) the Phoenix indeed of all Cities E i'k- 27- of Trade in the World. Master Fuller learnedly addeth. the Fables of Bacchus and Hercules their Indian Expedi- the fables of tions, to this of Salomon and Hiram, Hercules being Bacchus and adored of the one, and Jehova of the other, which name Hercules. by Heathens was perverted to m ayo and io(3dkxo? names q J ' J of Bacchus in Hesychius; which agreeth to Plutarchs ijjj fio and conceit, that the Jewes worshipped Bacchus on their is evident, ter-

Sabbaths, and deriveth the name Sabbatum from a-a dl eiv, and a-a acrioij a name of Bacchus, as his Priests were termed ara ol. Now for that Gulfe in which Strabo placeth Elana, and calls it therefore Elaniticus, and another towardes Egypt, I referre you to Castros following relations, which better knew those parts then Strabo Put. Sympos. could; Gaza by Strabo and Plinies reckoning seemeth 4 to bee about one hundred and fiftie of our miles or more I "j n " thence. Salomon went in Progresse

to take care halfe, the other of this his Ophirian Fleet from Jerusalem to Esion-geber, 150. almost as farre as from London to Yorke.

Asion Geber in Saint Jeroms interpretation signifieth

Hieron. Epist. ligna viri, aut lignationes viri, aut dolationes hominis, ed. Tabtol. uxakiafmo opo; whence some gather that much Timber grew there usefull for building of Ships: perhaps, and I rather beleeve, for the Timbers brought thither as to an arsenall or storeyard for that purpose. For as Woods agree not with Moses his Wildernesse, so I find little mention of Wood in all the Arabike shoare; at lest, later times have knowne none there. And Soliman the Great Turke, A. 1538. is said to have brought the materialls of the great Fleet which hee built at Sues in the Red Sea, to invade Dium and expell the Portugalls out of India, from remote Regions, Materiam ex long- inquis colligi jussit (Damianus a Goes is our Author) illamque sumptu in stimabili ad mare rubrum vehi

Com. Venrt. curavit. Comito Venetiano, who with other Venetians ' "" J i r' forced to that service out of their Ships at Alex- c l of these andria to goe to Cairo and Sues, more particularly

Deserts and relateth that Sues is in a. Desert place where no Hearb of Sues. of any sort groweth, where the Armada for India was

Satalin is in j de, and all the Timbers, Ironworkes, Tackling, ajTamher Munitions were brought from Satalia and Constantinople some saf) in by Sea to Alexandria, and thence carried on the Nile

Cilicia. by Zerme (Boats, or Rafts) to Cairo, and thence on

Camells to Sues. This Voyage is eightie miles, in which is neither habitation, nor water, nor any thing for life: they carry Nilus water on Camells when the

Carovans goe thither. In the Pagans times, it was a great Citie and full of Cisternes, and had a trench from Nilus which filled all their Cisternes, destroyed by the Mahumetans, so that now they fetch their water six miles off from brackish Wells. There the Turke built a Fleet of seventie six Vessells of all sorts, c.

Don John di Castro speakes of this Fleet of Salomon, and sayth, the Timber whereof it was made was brought from Libanon and Antilibanon (so little signe saw hee, or heard of any Trees or Wood in these parts) and saith, that from Toro all the Coast is West, and without any Port but Sues, and that therefore Cleopatras Fleet was I. I. 2+. brought by Land from Nilus, to Sues over the Isthmos. This is in 29. degrees 45. minutes, supposed Arsinoe of the Ancients, Some say, Civitas Heroum; and said to be the Turkes Arsenale for his Armada, for those Seas, the Materials being brought from Caramania: which at Castros being there, consisted of one and forty great Gallies and nine great Ships. It seemeth by Sir Henry Middletons Story following, that their strength in those Seas is weake in later times. As that whole Wildernesse yeelded nothing for mans life, but their food was Manna from Heaven, and their apparell was by heavenly power preserved, so here Salomons wisdome is freely given, and his Materials for an Ophirian Fleet, and Temple structure must be not naturally there growing. His Mariners also must be borrowed, to shew that the just live by faith, and in matters of grace, wee have nothing i. Cor. 7. 4. which wee have not received, not growing out of the naturall powers of free will, but framed out of the will freed by divine grace, agreeing to which Mystery nothing of the Temple was framed in Moriah, nor the noyse of a Hammer once heard; the Tabernacle before built also of Egyptian spoyles; and Israel inherited Cities which they builded not, and Vineyards planted by them: and lastly, Christ himselfe was crucified without the gate, that neither Jew nor Jerusalem may challenge either Monopoly or Merit, but all may bee ascribed to I 65 E meere mercle and free grace, Non nobis domine, not to us Lord, not to us but to thy Name be given the glory.

I. i.5. VIII.

Of Ophir, divers opinions weighed and censured; whether the Compasse was knowne to the old World; that the remote parts were lately inhabited, the New World but newly, and a great part thereof not yet.

His Golden Countrey is like Gold, hard to find and much quarrelled, and needes a wise Myner to bring it out of the Labyrinths of darknesse, and to try and purifie the Myners themselves and their reports. And here our best Athenians seeme Owles indeed, which dazled with Salomons splendour hide themselves affarre off, and seeke for Easterne Ophir in Peru, and the West Indies. Such conceits have transported Postellus, Goropius Becanus, Arias Montanus, Vatablus, Possevinus, Genebrard, Marinus Brixianus, Sa, Engu-binus, Avenarius, Garcia, Noble Morney, and many others by their authority. Their reason is spelled out of the Letters of Ophir and Peru, so neere of Kinne. Arias Montanus in his Phaleg is both large and little in this point, saying, both much and nothing; for from the Scriptures stiling the Ophirian Gold D- ino Paruaim, he gathereth that it was brought from the two Perues, one of which he maketh new Spain, and the other that which now is called Peru; or the Northerne and Southerne moyties of America; and that those parts were commonly traded in ancient times. He maketh the rowe of hils which runne from Panama, to the Magellan Straits to be Gen. 10. 26, Mount Sephir: for so it is said Gen. 10. speaking of 27.28,29,30. joktans Sonnes, the brother of Peleg or Phaleg; And Joktan begat Almodad, and Sheleph, and Hazarmaveth, and Jerah And Hadoram, and Uzal and Diklah, and Obal and Abimael and Sheba. And Ophir and Havilah and Jobab: all these were the sonnes of Joktan. And their dwelling was from Mesha, as thou goest unto Sephar, a Mount of the East; or as Tremellius, ad montes orientes usque.

If learned Montanus had viewed his owne Map only, hee should have seene his Ophir in the West, and not in the East: and if it be said Salomons fleet went by the East to the Westerne parts of the World, as the Philippinae and Moluccan shippes of the Spaniards use to doe, yet Moses speakes of the dwelling and habitations (not of Journeyings and Navigations) which God after the Babylonian conspiracy had alloted to the generations of men; their dwelling must then bee in regard of Moses when he wrote this in the Desert, or of the scattering from Babylon, whereof he wrote. But these parts of America, are more then halfe the Globe distant from those places Eastward, and much neerer by the West.

Againe, the name Peru or Piru is a vaine foundation, Sepharuaim.

for divers places (see Ortelius his Thesaurus Geograph.)- S- i7-"

,.,,..: r a name as like.

have like, or the same names, neyther is any part ot.

America by the Inhabitants called Peru, but this name ding but a was accidentally by the Spaniards ascribed to those begin- Sameck to nings of their Discoveries on the

South Sea, and con- P f' ' '" tinued to that great Kingdome of the Incas found by l duedby he Pizarro. Garcilasso de la Vega of the Inca bloud Royall Assyrians. by his mother, sonne to one of the Spanish Conquerors, Vega. com. borne and brought up at Cozco, chiefe City of Peru, realesl. x. c. sayth that they had no generall name for the Kingdome, Jj 5- but Tavantin Suyu, that is, the foure parts of the World; . 7. r, 13. nor acknowledge the appellation of Peru: but the first Discoverers seising on a fisherman in a River, asked him of the Countrey, and he amazed and not understanding them, answered Beru, and annon added Pelu, as if he should say, my name (if you aske me thereof) is Beru, and I was fishing in the River, Pelu being the common name of a River. The Spaniards, as if he had answered directly, corrupted a name of both those words, which they understood not, and called the Region Peru, a name

Lopez de Go-mar a Gen. hut. c. 2.

Bias Val. hut. Peru.

Acost. hut. I. 2. cap. 13.

I. i. 26. Lem. de Occul-tis Nat. mirac. I. 3. c. 4. Full. Miscel. I. 4. c. 19. Ec. I. 10.

which the Natives had never heard. The like they did in another Province, where asking a Native what was the name of the Countrey, he answered, Tectetan, Tectetan, that is, I understand you not, which they corruptly called Jucatan and Yucatan, as if the Indian had affirmed that to be the name of the Region. The like casuall names he observeth of other American places.

The Jesuite Bias Valera, in his History of Peru affirm-eth the same, that Peru is not the proper name but accidentall, which the Natives know not. Acosta acknow-ledgeth it unknowne to the Naturals, and an occasioned name from a small River, which Vega saith was called so first by those Spaniards, which there tooke the fisherman. Thus the name which they would make as old as Salomon, began but Anno 1515. at the most, and that which is extended to New Spaine, and Peru, was knowne in neither, nor in any place else of the World.

Thirdly, I answere that Peru was not inhabited, nor yet New Spaine, one thousand yeares after Salomons time; of which I shall speake more anon, and in my following Discourse of the Apostolicall peregrinations.

Fourthly, neither could so long a Voyage then have beene performed in three yeeres, beeing farre more then to have compassed the Globe, which hath cost Drake and others three yeares worke: where their worke was not in Mynes but in quicke fights.

Fiftly, this could not then be done without the Com-passe. Pineda may conceit himselfe that those times knew it, but the Phenicians have in no Story left any such memoriall; nor others of them, yet these were Salomons Sea men. Levinus Lemnius, and Master Fuller would have us beleeve that the Ancients had the Compasse within the compasse of their art, by reason of the Phaenicians Marine skill and experience, which we say might be as much as it was, by the Starres, the Monsons, the Soundings, and Shores. Another reason is, the Learning and skill of those times, whereof Salomon saith, Is there any thing whereof it may be said, this is new? it hath beene alreadie of old time which was before us. It might therefore be knowne in those times, and by barbarous invasions be after lost, and by better times restored: I answer that the times were learned before and after Salomon, but when that learning should by

Barbarian incursions be lost, I know not. The Egyptian, Assyrian, Chaldaean invasions might rather increase and disperse, then eclipse and abolish learning, being then more learned then the Greekes, who borrowed their very Letters from the Phaenicians. The Persian times are knowne, and the Greeke Learning then grew to the highest pitch, when their Empire succeeded, and in love of Learning exceeded the other. Hippocrates, Socrates, Plato, Xenophon, Aristotle, and before them Pythagoras and other Philosophers flourished before the Persian ruines, and travelled into the East for that Learning, which they brought into Greece and Italic.

The Romanes borrowed their Arts from the Greekes, neither doe we read of Learning evaporated in Barbarian flames, till the Deluges of those Savages in the Romane Empire, which yet continued both Empire and Learning in the East, till the West had in good measure recovered it selfe out of those Mysts, and the Barbarous Saracens Joseph com. had growne lovers of Learning, and our Teachers. And " '"-yet, had there beene such Barbarians which had rooted- j that skill out of the World (which is unlikely, that fiure Bookes. Marine skill beeing the best meanes to encrease their Empire, to enrich their Coff ers, to doe them other services in Warre and Peace, the ancient Conquerors using Fleets also to their purposes) yet some of the Bookes and Monuments of all Ages, from Salomons f "Yi time being left to that of the Romans, as appeareth by gcessary to Josephus so well acquainted in the Tyrian Libraries, and Moral!, Poli-other Authors of divers Nations, and by the fragments tikeaudsaving which are come to our hands, and by whole Bookes 'ff j' f of Voyages in the Indian and Mediteranean Seas, as this. j ij q Booke will declare; it cannot be but some mention of gave him so large a heart. But the Sea hath bounds. Is so had Salomons wisdom. Somewhat ivas left for John Bap tist to be greater then he, or any borne ofzco-men. 'Neither was the knowledge of the Compasse necessarie to Salomon, who without it could and did compasse the Goldofophir.

Above I 3000 miles space.

Perhaps the Whale-constellation took up this Sea 11 hale into his Chariot, some part of the way.

the act, if no description of the Art, would have remained to Posteritie.

Now for Salomons testimony, it confuteth those which make him the author and first founder of the Loadstone (which to M. Fuller and others seemeth probable) if nothing were then new; it may aswell be alleaged for many Generations before, that they also made ships at Esion-geber, to goe to Ophir for like Rarities; and against all new Inventions in any Age: which sense is also contradicted by Salomon in the same Chapter, Verse 16. Where hee saith, that hee had more wisdome then all they that had beene before him in Jerusalem: and I. Reg. 3. 12. There was none like before thee, nor after thee shall arise any like unto thee. This was then a new thing under the Sunne, this his wisdome, which brands us for Fooles, if wee make him contradict himselfe and divine Veritie.

The Scripture would goe one mile with them and shew the vanitie both of men and other creatures, and they post and force it two, applying what Salomon spake of kindes, to individuall acts and events; which might aswell enforce Platoes great yeere, and a personall revolution of each man withall his conceits, words and acts. The Magnete is no new thing, but this use of the Magnete was newly knowne two thousand yeares after Salomons death. The Argument to mee seemeth a merrie one, rather then serious, and I will answere it accordingly with a jest. The Jesuite Pineda (which out of Lemnius citeth these Arguments to prove that the Compasse is ancient) is no new thing as a Man; but as a person, as a Jesuite (a new order which beganne 1540.) as an Author which conceiteth that that great fish which tooke up Jonas carried him in three dayes quite thorow the Mediterranean, and round about the African vast Circumference (statim atque deglutitur Jonas, revertitur ccetus velocitate in-credibili ad mare Indicum Sivum Arabicum, per Medi-terraneum Gaditanum fretum, immani totius Africae circuitu, these are his owne words) these are new things under the Sunne, and this a new interpretation, which himselfe prefaceth with Papae! novam inauditam ex-ponendi rationem! These particulars are new, and yet that text is true. I wil not adde (that were too serious and severe) that all Jesuitisme is new, and their Expositions of Scriptures, Councels, Fathers for the Roman Monarchic, are all new, New-gay-no-things, Vanitie of vanities and vexation of spirit; yet to lye (the genus generalissimum of Jesuitical! tenents, as they are Jesuites; Christians is a name too old for them) is as old as the old Serpent.

But lest I be over-bold with our Author, and may seeme to passe from a new argument to an old quarrell, and from jeasting to jerking; I contayne my selfe, lest any Veterator take mee for a Novelist; and with reverence and thankes for his better paines, crave pardon for this jocoserium, and come to his third Argument out of Plautus, where in speech of sayling, hee hath these words, Hue secundus ventus nunc est, cape mode versoriam, Plauti Met–Hie Favonius serenus est, isthic Auster imbricus. ' '

Here Lemnius, Giraldus de Navigiis, and Calcagninus I. i, 27. with others men-tioned by him, doe interprete Versoria of the Compasse: whom Pineda beleeveth not, and yet saith, hee hath quod nostro Acostas reddere possimus requirenti aliquod idoneum ex antiquitate hujus aciculas testimonium: notwithstanding, hee conjectureth it to bee some pole to thrust the Vessell (if any Instrument) and acknowledgeth that the Cares and Rudder might bee Versoriae, in regard of turning the ship, and lastly concludeth it to be spoken without respect to any Nautike Instrument, interpreting Cape Versoriam to returne: and that Plautus his actor did point to the Heavens, not to any Instrument, when he said, hue secundus ventus est, hie Favonius, c. which seemeth to bee the Poets true sense.

Pineda addes, that we ought not to doubt but that Salomon knew this of the Loadstone aswel as other Stones and Herbs. I answer we have a better Loadstone and Leadstone for one then for the other; the Scripture speaking of him more as a Herbarist, then as a Lapidarie and Mariner. He alleageth, that the attractive facultie would reveale that Polare. I answere, that experience hath produced many Ages to testifie the contrarie; which knew the one, not the other. His Argument from the store of Load-stones in those Easterne parts, concludes nothing for the skill, any more then that the naked artlesse Indians in Hispaniola were better Gold-smiths then the Europaeans, because they had more Gold. His last Argument is least, from the Divine Providence which would not permit men so many Ages to be ignorant hereof. Rom. 11.33, For heere we come to an, O altitudo! O the depth 3+ of the riches both of the wisdome and knowledge of God, how unsearchable are his judgements, and his wayes past finding out For who hath knowne the minde of the Lord, or who hath beene his Counseller. f I like much better that which Pineda addes of the Ancients abilitie to sayle without kenne of the shoare, without Magneticall helpe, which Strabo, Arianus and Plinie acknowledge: and Aratus saith, that the Phaenicians followed the Load-starre (not the Load-stone) which Tully citeth also out of him. Cic. Acad. i. Arrianus mentioneth the helpe of the Monsons (as now Ego meas cog- j erme them) or seasons of the Windes, observing: a fltttotlcS stc.

dirigo non ad constant course m the Indian Ocean, which with experi-illam pawn-ence of the frequented Coast, might easily teach Hippalus lam Cym- a compendious passage thorow the Mayne, or at least t' J t"y Q further from kenne of Land. Whereupon Plinie having nocturnaphce- " the former course, addes Secuta astas propiorem nices in ahum, cursum tutioremque, c. Compendia invenit Mercator, ut ait Aratus Lib. 6. cap. 23. They also observed the flying of certain-. Birds which they caried with them. But al these could

Cynosura nothing helpe to a Peruan Voyage from the Red Sea, tamen salcan- where the knowne Starres were laid asleepe in Tethys tibus aquor, lap; where neither Birds carried with them, could instruct yr. Arat. q ivvf neere shoare, nor any Birds in the mayne Ocean were to be scene; where the Monsons and Seasons of the winde are so diversified; where without the Compasse all things are out of Compasse, and nothing but miracle or chance (which never produce Arts) could save or serve them. I have spoken of the Load-stone in another place I the begin-to which I referre the Reader, least that makes mee " f! wander and drowne, which directeth and saveth others.

Lastly, Peru could not be Ophir, if wee conceive that The sixth Salomon brought thence Ivorie; and Peacockes. For ' ' " Peacockes they read Parrots, and for Ivorie they are forced to take it up by the way in some place of Africa or India, which distraction must needs prolong the Voyage, which without such lets could not (as before is observed) in three yeares bee performed. As for such (Asse for such, I might have said) which thinke so huge and vast a tract of Land as that New World, might bee now emptie of Elephants which then it had (for it is confessed by all Classike Authors, that America never saw Elephant) as England is ridde of Wolves, wherewith it hath sometimes abounded; Why should not other kinds of Creatures bee utterly destroyed aswel as these, being more hurtfull to the Inhabitants I meane, Tigres, Leopards, and other ravenous beasts whereof America hath more then a good many. And if they should destroy Elephants for their Ivorie, what piece of Ivorie was ever found in Peru or all America, before our men came there."' If Salomons men had destroyed all, it were inhumane to intervert after-ages. The hunting of Wolves in the North of Scotland at this day, and the huntings used by many Nations, Tartars, Cafres, c. easily tell us how England was cleered of Wolves; Armies, or Multitudes in a large Ring, encircling the beasts, with Fire, Waters, Dogs, Armes, c. bringing all into a narrow Compasse, and there killing them. But in the New World that would have required another World to have done it. I adde that no Elephant could come into Peru but by Miracle, the cold and high Hilles every way encompassing, beeing impassable to that Creature, as wee shall see in our Spanish entrance with Horses. Yea, I averre further, that an

A second opinion for Hispaniola.

Colon a happier Discoverer of the new World then the old.

Third opinion for Sophala.

See inf. I. 9. c. 12.

Elephant could not live in Peru, but by Miracle. For the Hilles are cold in extremitie, and the Valleyes, till the Incas made artificiall Rivers were without water, it never rayning there, whereas the Elephant delights in places very hote and very moist. But I deserve blame to fight with Elephants in America, which is with lesse then a shadow, and to lay siege to Castles in the Aire.

These arguments have no lesse force against Columbus and Vatablus their Ophir in Hispaniola: which from the Red Sea makes a farther fetch with like or greater improbabilities. This errour was more fortunate then learned. For out of a right rule that the World is round, and that therefore men might sayle to the East by the West, Columbus first, and presently after him Sir Sebastian Cabot made their Discoveries, and stumbled on a New World by the way, whereof they had not dreamed.

Cabots Voyage was to seeke Cathay or China. Columbus his intent was for the East Indies, and finding much Gold in Hispaniola, without examining other difficulties, and falsly supposing himselfe to have attayned the East Indies, he called that Hand Ophir; which conceit Francis Vatablus received.

Now for Sofala or Cefala, many arguments are alleaged by Ortelius (who here placeth Salomons Ophir) and others. And indeed the abundance of Gold, and the excellencie thereof, as likewise of Silver, there taken out of the Mynes; Peacocks, or Parrots, whether you choose to interprete; Elephants, Apes, (Monkeyes and Baboones) excellent Woods for such uses as the Almuggim Trees were applied; all these, together with the easie Navigation from the Red Sea thither alongst the African shoare; and lastly the name it selfe may seeme to plead for a Sofalan Ophira, or Sophira (as Josephus cals it) in this place. Joaon dos Santos lived eight yeares in those parts, and alleageth many things to this purpose. He saith that neere to Massapa, is a great high Hill called Fura, in the Kingdome of Monomotapa, to which hee will not suffer the Portugals to passe lest the rich Mynes should cause their too potent Neighbour-hood. On the top of that Hill are old ruinous wals of lime and stone. Barrius saith, there are also unknowne Letters over Barrosdeci. the gate: the people ignorant of such workes, say ' they were built by Devils, thinking them impossible to men, judging others by themselves. They are five hundred and ten miles from Sofala, in one and twentie degrees of Southerly latitude. He conjectureth it to bee Ptolemeys Agysimba, the buildings being still called Simbaoni. Thomas Lopez addes, that the Moores T. Lopez ap. affirmed, that their Bookes and ancient Writings con- " "" tayned, that King Salomon fetched his Gold in his three yeares Voyage from thence.

At that time 1502. there were warres, but formerly the Moores of Mecca and Zidem, used to carrie two Millions of Mitigals (which are about eight shillings a piece) yeerely from thence. But to returne to Santos, hee alleageth a Tradition of the Natives, that these Mynes and Buildings belonged to the Queene of Saba, and that others ascribe them to Salomon, making this Fura or Afura to be Ophir, See the place, and his pleading of this I fra Tom. point, wherein I could be perswaded to be of his minde, if- S- '5+9-that Moses did not place Ophir Eastward, Gen. 10. 30. Who (it is likely) gave name to this golden Region.

There are that seeke for Tarshish at Carthage, and some A fourth and I have knowne which place Ophir neere Gambra. Of this fif " ' " """' minde was Captaine Jobson, which travelled up that River, nine hundred and sixtie miles, and heard such golden reports of the In-land Countreyes, as this Worke will from him deliver to you. And indeed I doe easily perswade my selfe, that the richest Mynes of Gold in the World are in Africa; especially in the heart of the Land from the Line to the Tropike of Capricorne. (See our Relations out of Bermudez, Jobson, Battell and others) and I cannot but wonder, that so many have sent so many, and spent so much in remoter Voyages to the East and West, and neglected Africa in the midst; which perhaps might proove as much richer as neerer, then both the Indies. But Rectum est index sui obliqui: if wee shew Ophir to bee in the East Indies, it cannot be in

J sixth America or Africa, unlesse we be of Acostas opinion, who

T"! howsoever he thinketh that Salomons Gold, c. came

J from the East Indies, yet conjectureth that Ophir and

Tharsis signifie no certayne Regions, but are taken in a generall sense, as the word India is with us, applied to all remoter Countreyes. Ophir might be any of the former, remote farre from the Red Sea.

But I can tell that India received his name from the

River Indus, still called Sinde, (which hath also foiled all our Geographers hitherto, making it to passe thorow lnf. l. c. 6. Cambaya, which Sir Thomas Roes Voyage will confute, that it is lesse marvell if Ophir trouble us so much) and because the Countreyes beyond India, were so meanly knowne by their true names, and Indus came from so remote Regions, they continued and extended that name to them: and (as even now you heard) Colon by misprision called America, India, not dreaming of a Westerne, but

See. 12. for supposing that by the West, he had arrived in the

Jcost. opinion. Eastern India. Now, why Ophir should be so dilated, I see no such reason. Tarshish we shall better examine

Other after. And for others opinions of Ophir to be an Hand in opinions. j gj gg Y Qd Urphe, or Ormus in the Persian, they are not worth examining: beeing not able to yeeld

Gold, and the other Commodities which Salomon sought.

The truth of Ophir must as from a deepe Myne bee

"drawne out of Moses, Gen. lo. Wherein although wee cannot approve the opinion of those which conceive Moses in that Chapter, to have set downe the just number of

Languages and Nations, as if there were seventie two of each, and neither more nor fewer; yet it must needs be granted, and the Text plainly averreth. These are the

Families of the sonnes of Noah after their generations, in

Gen. lo. 31. their Nations, and by these were the Nations divided in 3 the Earth after the Floud: and particularly of the Sonnes of Shem (here questioned) These are the sonnes of Shem, after their families, after their tongues, in their lands, after their Nations. So that wee gather that the first originalls of Nations are there mentioned, such especially as concerned his Ecclesiasticall story, or was necessary I. i. 29, for the Church to take knowledge of For neither were they all differing Nations and Languages which hee mentioneth, nor are all Nations or Languages there mentioned. For eleven of them are the sons of Canaan, which all peopled that little region, which Israel after by Joshuas conduct possessed: al which also spake one language, or else Abraham the Patriarks must have learned many tongues in their frequent perambulations; which some thinke the same which the Israelites spake, judge it evident in the History of the first Spies, and of Rahabs entertaining of the later Spies; and that it is called by the Prophet, The Language of Canaan, Es. 19. 18, and carried thence into Egypt before by the Patriarks, to whom Joseph spake first by an Interpreter, but in reavealing himselfe, hee with his owne mouth (that is, in their tongue) spake unto them, when the Interpreter and all others were excluded. And in the whole story of the Old Testament, no difference of language is notified in all the commerce and cohabitations of all sorts of both Nations. Priscian saith, Prise.

Lingua Poenorum Chaldaeae vel Hebraeae similis: and fj'- o-T-r–rn 1 TT1 Jer. i. Arnod.

Samt Jerom, Pceniquasi Phceni, quorum Imgua Hebraeas- pjt j magna ex parte confinis est. Saint Augustine often jug de verb. saith as much; and divers wordes of the language con- Dom. s. 35. firme it. As for a Shiboleth, and Siboleth, or some 'ont. lit. Pet I. difference of Dialect (which wee see with us almost in jg 6 tifr every Shire) wee make not that a difference of, but Ber. Aldrete in the Language. And so it seemeth it was in the first Anteg. I 2, c Ages, before Conquest and Commerce brought in so many new wordes to the Punike language. The Punike Scaigin Scene in Plautus his Poenolus, by Scaliger, M. Selden prokgom. ult. and others is found a kind of Hebrew, after all those ' "selden ages and changes. I will not herein contend with M. jg D. S. pro-Fuller and others which have written contrary. But Ugom. c. 2.

either they were the same, or not much differing: and The Spies (which I principally ayme at) all these eleven Nations having such J j s2imq language at lest in the Patriarkes times, tio7in Egypt ' "ot unlike the Hebrew, which was so little altered, had no meanes after such alterations of time and place. to learn Now because that Countrey was given to Abrahams tongues. posteritie, Moses is more exact in bounding the places, ' ' ' ' ' intimating the peoples, then in all Joktans posterity (which it seemeth peopled one hundred times so much Countrey) as not pertaining to Israels Inheritance, and not much to their neighborhood or knowledge. And if Salomon imployed above eight score thousands in continuall workes so many yeeres for the Temple, how many shall we thinke imployed themselves in that Babylonian structure, which occasioned that diversifying of languages; and which is therefore likely to have happened long after Pelegs birth, by which time the world could not likely be so peopled.? Neither may wee deny more then ordinary multiplication in those first Ages after the Floud: though we grant a good space after Pelegs birth, for how else could such a multitude have assembled so soone to such a purpose Wee see the like admirable increase of the Israelites in Egypt, in despite of bloudy butchery and slavery, which yet asked above two hundred yeeres, from seventie persons. And can any man thinke that where a World was multiplied, that the Fathers had no more Sonnes then are there mentioned."' especially seeing of Sems line, Gen. ii. it is said they begat other sonnes: and of them are expressed five generations, of the other but two or three, and most of them omitted, except such as most concerned Israel in neighbourhood or other affaires. How could Jocktan yeeld thirteene Nations then, when Peleg gives name to none, till of Abraham, six generations after, some were derived? I suppose therefore that Moses there names not all Nations, as writing not a Story of the World, but those principally which by vicinitie or Inheritance, or future commerce (as this Ophir and his brethren) it behooved the Israelites to take notice of; especially Him, who was to alter Moses his Tabernacle into so glorious a Temple, and to bee so lively a figure of a greater then Moses and Salomon both. Nor is it likely but that there was a greater confusion of languages, then into so many as can bee gathered in the tenth of Genesis; or that all there mentioned differed in tongue from each other; for so Shem, Cham, and Japheth should never have understood each other, nor their posteritie. It is probable therefore, that God multiplying the World in so short a space (which, as I said, I rather thinke to have hapned some good while after Pelegs birth, then at that very time) almost to a miracle, most men of most families were there, and their languages also miraculously multiplied; (The Jewish tradition is that it hapned a little before Pelegs death, as Genebrard observeth out of them) but being a conspiracy against God, many others were not there and retained their ancient Ebrew; especially the pious and religious Patriarkes. Such perhaps was Peleg him-selfe, then a man of yeeres, and therefore his name given him of that division in others. For if any thinke that Pelegs name intimates the building of Babel at his birth, we see that Abraham, Sarah, and Jacob had their names changed in their riper yeeres.

This division of languages caused that dispersion, Therefore is the name of it called Babel (or Confusion) because the Lord did there confound the language of all the Earth: and from thence did the Lord scatter them abroad upon the face of all the Earth. Yet cannot we say that presently this was wholly executed; but even then so many as spake one language, dwelt together in one Region: Other Persons and Families in other Regions, which then were thinly planted, and in processe of time more fully peopled, and Colonies also derived to people remoter Regions. For although Man, (that is Mankind) hath a right to all the Earth, yet heere there was a very great part of the Earth unpeopled in Moses time, yea to these dayes of Ours. And if we marke I. i. 30. all the Heads of Families mentioned by Moses, wee shall see none, which at that time had inhabited so farre as this our Britaine: but how much neerer the Regions were to the Arkes resting, and Babels confusion, so much sooner were they peopled. Sure it is that some Ages after, the best and most frequent Habitations, and neerest those parts were but meanly peopled, as appeareth by Abraham, Isaac, and Jacob, Lot, Laban, and their children wandring and remooving from place to place with their great Flockes and Herds, as if Grounds and Pastures had then even in the Regions of Syria and Canaan beene of small value. Compare Abrahams time with Joshua, and you shall see a great difference, more Cities and Villages seeming then builded, then before were Families of note, and that in foure hundred yeeres space. Ammon, Moab, Ishmael, all the Families of the sonnes of Keturah, and that of Edom, with innumerable other were not in rerum natura, neither the language (which it seemes by mixture with others was altered) nor the Nation.

Yea how poore a thing was our Britaine in Caesars time, either for the numbers or civilitie How thinly is all the Northerne America, from thirtie degrees upwards towardes the Pole inhabited."' a world of Continent by no probabilitie, containing in the whole so many people as some one small Region in Asia or Europe. All Virginia, New England, and New-found-land, cannot have (notwithstanding such commodious habitations and innumerable commodities) so many Inhabitants, so farre as my industry can search, as this one Citie with the Suburbs containeth, though we adde all even to the Pole, and take one hundred miles within Land alongst the Coast all the way; which easily argueth the later peopling thereof Neither is there any thing Jmerica in all America which doth not indeed proclaime it a newly inhabit- y j World. For as in the Old World, first there was " simplicitie of Herdmen, Shepheards, and Husbandmen; and after that Trades, Merchandise, Riches, Cities, King-domes, more curious Rites Civill and Religious, and some Monuments of them (which those which had, esteemed others for the want therof Barbarians Savages, as a wilder kind of men) and this Civilitie, Cities, Populations and Kingdomes began in Assyria, Chaldaa, Egypt, and other places neerer the first confusion, and ' ' after proceeded to Greece (whom the Egyptians called children, as is before said, for their later Civilitie, Arts, and Histories) and thence to Italy, which was long swadled in Roman rusticitie, and later attained to politer Sciences; and thence into France (as wee now call it) and after that into Britaine, and later into Germany, all by Roman Conquests and imparting Arts with their Armes: so may wee judge of the New World, wherein two Empires were growne great, civill, rich, and potent, after their manner, as our Mexican and Inca stories will shew in due place. This their great-nesse produced stories of their Acts by Quippos, Pic- 5 Amta tures and other Monuments, which derived to posteritie f" the knowledge or former times and acts. By which we 2.. c. flyy may gather that the Northerne America was first peopled, Vega his Inca and that probably from the Easterne or Northerne parts story. l. j. cat,. of Asia; and communicated people to the Southerne parts, the Northerne Antiquities of Mexico, being ancienter then those of Peru. Those first stories also (see them in the Picture-Booke, and in Vega and Acosta following) how raw and infantly beginnings and proceedings doe they shew."' What barbarisme Yet neither containing memorialls of one thousand yeeres: So that allow six hundreth yeeres to meere breedings and barbarous infancy, with creeping in dispersions, as out of the cradle of American humanity amongst them, till they were fuller of People and Townes, where one wit whetts another to new devices, yet we scarcely come to the times of Christ and his Apostles. I may adde, that till about one thousand two hundred yeeres after Christ, neither of those Empires were worthy the I 8i F names of pettie Kingdomes, and even then had scarcely crept out of the shell.

Now for Hands in the Seas betwixt Asia and them, as also along the North Sea, as they cal it, on the Easterne shoare of America, in the North and South parts thereof also, these Relations will shew you Worlds of them not yet peopled. The Southerne Continent is yet but saluted on the shoares and Hands, of which we may no lesse conjecture much emptinesse. For the ful-nesse of the Continent disburthens it selfe into Hands; and fulnesse of the first peopled parts, Asia, Africa, and Europe, made them seeke to root out one another by the Sword, or to possesse vacant places by Sea or Land, which either chance or industry had found. But except Deucalion and Pyrrha had sowne stones to procreate Men, or Cadmus his sowne teeth had procreated Armies, or the Clouds had rained Peoples, as they are said to doe Frogs, I know not how wise and learned men (by their leaves inconsiderately enough) fill China and America with people in those dayes before Moses and Abraham, and find great commerce and knowledge of the New World, when the Old was but yesterday begun. So necessary to Humane and Divine knowledge is Geo-graphie and History, the two

Eyes with which wee see the World, without which our greatest Clerkes are not the wisest men, but in this part blind and not able to see farre oflt. If any deride this as paradoxicall and new, I say againe, that in America alone, so much hath beene discovered, and whereof knowledge from ey-witnesses hath come to my hand, partly in the Continent, partly in Hands, as much (and in great part as commodious for mans use) as all Europe, is either wholly unhabited, or so thinly inhabited, that men roague rather then dwell there, and so as it would feed and sustaine a hundreth, perhaps a thousand times as much people by due husbandry.

Joctans Posteritie seated in the East parts of Asia, i. i. 31. amongst them, Ophir in India ultra Gangem, where Chryse was of old, and now is the king-dome of Pegu, and the Regions adjoyning.

Frica fell to Chams part, with some adjoyning Regions of Asia; Asia it selfe in greatest part to Shem, and Europe with Asia Minor, and the

Northerne parts of Asia to Japheth. Their very names have left memorialls of them, as Arias Montanus, Junius, Montanipha-

Broughton, and others have observed, to whose Com– """"g- mentaries I referre the Reader. But for Joctans sonnes, ' p-,"

we find in and neere to India, the prints of all their names. . i.

Elmodad had left his name in the Hill Emodus, whence the Indian Rivers flow, and Comedus, the greatest Hills of Asia, elsewhere called Taurus, and by divers names as it runneth thorow divers Countries, from the one end of Asia to the other: also in the Themeotae or

Thetmontas in Sarmatia. Of Sheleph are the Mountaines

Sariphi, whence Oxus floweth. Seilon is a famous Hand in these dayes. Of Hazarmaveth, Sarmatia; of Jerah,

Aria and Arachosia; of Hadoram the Ori, Oritas, Oxi- dracae; also the Adraistae, Andresti, Adrestae: Of Uzal,

Muziris, Musopalle, Ozoana, Oxus, Udia, or Odiae a

Citie, and Udezza a Kingdome, in India; Auzacia, a

Citie extra Imaum, and Auxacitis. Of Diklah, Delly,

Dankalee, Tacola and Tagola; also Dela, Dekaka, the

Laos, Bacola, Bengala, and (by conversion of D into R, not unusuall) Rhacan and Arracan, Orixa; Dandagula and Dasdala. Of Obal, the Bolitae and Cabolitae neere

Paraponisus; of Abimael the Mount Imaus, and the

Massi in India mentioned by Curtius.

Now for Sheba and Havilah; Cush had Seba and Gen. 10. Havilah, and his sonne Raamah had also Sheba; all mentioned in the same Chapter: and Jokshan Abrahams Sonne by Keturah, begat Sheba. Chush his two sonnes, Gen. 25.

were Authors of the Sabaeans in Arabia, so famous for the Merchandise of Myrrhe and Frankinsence; some

Job. I. 15. distinguish the Sabasi in Arabia deserta (whose posteritie robbed Job) from the richer Sabaeans of Sheba in Arabia I. Reg, 10. Fcelix, whence that rich Queene called of the South (that Countrey is called Alieman, that is, the South, to this day) came to visit Salomon. Abrahams Sheba had his habitation Eastward in the Northerly parts of Arabia

Gal 4. deserta; as if his kindred by the flesh, the sonnes of

Keturah and Hagar (the carnall Israelites, and such which insist on Justification by their owne Workes of the Law) should never have to doe with Canaans fertilitie and

Rom. 14. 17. felicitie, the type of Heaven, Righteousnesse, Peace and

Gal. 4. jqy j j g Holy Ghost; but distract themselves in wandring errors, a disconsolate miserable estate, as those Arabians do to this day.

Joktans Sheba was Author of the Sabae beyond Ganges; of Sabana, Sahara, Sobanus; and now Siam, Champa, Camboia, are famous in these parts.

Havila of Chus is hee which planted that Countrey, at the entrance of Susiana in Persia, commended, Gen. 2. for the Gold. And of him also might Abila in Syria, and Avalites, a Bay and Port on the Red Sea, and the Avalitas populi, which thence removed into Ethiopia, and the Chalybes among the Troglodytae bare names.

Joctans Havila might give name to the He Sundiva, the Gulfe Tavai, to Ava, Martavan, Cavelan also, and Cublan all Kingdomes lately subject to the King of Pegu. The Avares in the Northerne parts might bee a deduction from him, Chaberis also and the Avaslai a Bactrian Nation, by some called Savadii, and the Auchastae, where Hipanis springeth; the Abii and Indian Abali, and Zebas; Abarimon also in Scythia, and Jesual, a Kingdome in these daies. Of Jobab came the Jabadii, the Ibi, or 'I oi (an Indian Nation) the Sobi, and Sarmatian Ibiones; Jacubel also in the Kingdome of Pegu, the He Java, Jamba, and in old times Barebe and Bepinga.

Some impression of the name of Ophir is left in Ophar, Ortelh Thes.

a Sarmatian River, and the Opharitas, and in those names " ""

.,,,, '-rii 1 J 1 Taurus.

of the Hil Taurus, Paropamisus, Fharphariades, otherwise Pariades, Parthenasis, Partao, Chaboras, Oscobar, Pariedrus, Para; Choatra, Parthaus, Tapurius, Opuro-carra, Bepyrrus, Parsuetus, Paryadres. I might adde the renowmed Indian Hand Taprobane, the Prasii, Hip-puros, the Citie Paraca, Palibothra, Perimula, Doperura, Sobura, Cottobora, Sippara, Mapura, Caspira, Brachme, Brachmanae, Opotura, Pharitras, and other names in Ptolomey, and the Pharasii in Curtius. Also the Hippuri in Plinie, to omit Porus the great King of India, whom Alexander subdued. And many places of principall note in India in these dayes have such a termination, as Fetipore Jounpore, Sinpore, Merepore, and the like, of more certaintie then the occasionall and yesterday name of Peru.

Thus have wee brought arguments of names, to find all Joctans posterity in the way to India, or the Inland Indian Countries, where it is likely they first seated themselves, and afterwardes spread themselves both to the Northerne Sarmatians, and Sythians, and to the Sea Coast Southerly after the Floud, some feare whereof did not a little terrific the first Ages. At this day Tippara, Serepore on Ganges, Caplan, the place where they find the Rubies, Saphires, and Spinells, six dayes journey from Ava, Pegu it selfe, and the Bramas, which founded the New Citie, and which still people the Kingdomes of Prom, Melintay, Calam, Bacam, Miriam; and Pur-dabin, Purbola at the Spring, and Benpurbat the entrance of Ganges to the Sea; the Straits of Cingopura, with divers other places in those Regions where wee place Ophir, have some footprints left of that name after so I. i. 32. many Ages. Their Brachmanes, Probar their chiefe God, Talipoies their Priests might be added for sound. But words are windie, sounding and not sound, wordy not worthy arguments, except things agreeing make the truth evident. For accidentally names are the same

Ptoll. J. Tab.

4-Asue.

2 Reg. 17.22.

Esay 36 If c.

Hee nameth Mesa and Se-phar as better knotvne, ifs but the entrf of their further population, ad montes orientis usque, as Tre-melhus translates.

In divers Countries, as if any man lust to observe in a Geographicall Dictionary, hee shall easily see.

These are onely probabilities which are to be weighed with the words of Moses, And their dwelling was from Mesha, as thou goest unto Sephar, a Mount of the East; ad montes Orientis usque, Tremelius reades it: Josephus interpreteth from Assyria to a River of India called Cophene. Sepher is, if ye receive Mon-tanus, the Peruan Andes, the Mountaines of the West in the Worlds situation from Babylon, and the place where Moses wrote; Ptolemie mentions Sipphara not farre from Euphrates: Postellus makes it Imaus, Saint Hierom placeth it in India: Sepharuaim of the Assyrians (which is perhaps Ptolomies Sipphara, is often mentioned, and confirmeth well that opinion of Josephus. From Mesa therefore which taketh his beginning East from those parts where Moses wrote, being also part of that hill Taurus, whereto we have found all Joktans Sonnes neighbouring (afterwards called Mount Masius, in Mesopotamia) to Sephar, another part of that great hill Taurus, both Eastward, and thence also in processe of time to further Easterly Mountaines, the remotest Easterne parts of Taurus, did Joktans Posterity spread and disperse themselves; one of the most Easterly whereof we finde this questioned Ophir. Or if any like rather to finde them more Easterly, Plinie mentions the Masuae and Mesae in India, and there also is Ptolomies Sapara and Sippara, agreeing with Sephar: Sarpedon also and Sariph are hils so called, parts of Taurus.

It remaines then to see whether the Commodities of those parts, and the Voyage thither be correspondent to the Scriptures description. For the Commodities, we will give both auncient, middle, and moderne testimonies (with this difference, that the auncient and middle are not so particular nor directly expressing and notifying places and things as the last) the rather because this hath beene the stumbling stone to Ortelius, and others, to make them seeke for Ophir elsewhere. The

Ophirian Voyage (it is probable) comprehended all the gulfe of Bengala from Zeilan to Sumatra, on both sides: but the Region of Ophir we make to be all from Ganges to Menan, and most properly the large Kingdome of Tab. Jsiaw

Pegu, from whence it is likely in processe of time, the ' "

Southerly parts, even to Sumatra inclusively was peopled before Salomons time.

In India beyond Ganges, Ptolomie placeth both Argentea and Aurea Regio. Super Argenteam autem regionem, in qua multa dicuntur esse metalla non signata, superjacet Aurea Regio, Besyngitis appropinquans, quae ipsa metalla auri quam plurima habet. Arrianus in his Peri-plus, or Treatise of the sailing about the Erythraean Sea (which as is said before contained the Indian) speaking of Ganges and the rising and falling thereof like Nilus, placeth XP Golden Region, neere to it, and addes the reports of golden Mines in those parts. Xeyerai T6 Koi pvaopvyia irepi Tot9 TO'7ro9 eivai. Marcianus mentions this golden Chersonessus also. Long before them Hero- f e xjj evrss dotus in his Thalia relatmg the Tributes paid to the Persian xpv v Monarch, saith, The Indians as they are more in number "" "jj 'jj then other men, so their tribute is greater, 360. talents iari of Gold: and then addeth the reports of Ants, not so bigge as Dogges, but bigger then Foxes, which cast up antheaps full of golden sands. Arrianus cites Nearchus Heml. Thai. and Megasthenes (whom Strabo produceth also) for these "– 3-Ants, which I thinke rather to be an Embleme then a Story. For as Salomon sends the Sluggard to schoole to the Pismire, to learne of that little creature great industry and providence, so Salomons and other Princes Mines could not be better expressed then in such an alegory; living in darkenesse, and as it were buried alive, and bearing excessive burthens, yet baited with poore diet and wages. And thus Georgius Fabritius, Indi suos P t'- reb. Metallicos fxopii. r)K. ai appellarunt, unde fabulis locus, c.- '- The like fable they had of monstrous Griffons, thereby expressing the miserable monstrosity of covetousnesse.

Plinie hath (speaking of the Indian Nations) Fertilissimi sunt auri Dardae, Setae vero argenti. Sed omnium in India prope, non modo in hoc tractu, potentiam clari-tatemque antecedunt Prasii, amphsma urbe ditissimaque Palibotra: unde quidem ipsam gentem Pahbotros vocant, imo vero tractum universum a Gange. Regi eorum peditum sexcenta M. equitum triginta M. elephantorum novem M. per omnes dies stipendiantur, c. These Plut. Alexand. Prasii placed neere Ganges, Plutarch cals Praesii, Curtius Pharasii, Diodorus Tabraesii, all which names they which know any thing in Ebrew can tell how easily they may be derived from Ophir, passing the Greeke termination after other changes. And Palabothra, or Palimbothra is by Arrianus placed at the confluence of the Rivers " Erannaboa Erannoboa and Ganges, Strabo speakes of the sailing perhaps ts nozv Ganges to Palibothra against the streame, and saith Strab."i iq. Ganges descends from the Mountaines and from the plaines takes an Eastward course; then passing by Palibothra a very great Citie, enters the Sea with one channell, although it be the greatest of the Indian Rivers. Master Fitch our Country man spent five moneths in passing downe Ganges (he might have done it sooner) Sanba! stands and mentions Serrepore, which (as Sanbal ' by the first where Jetmi syllable) may seeme to be the same by the situation, fl w5 an- j. g j j j gj- syllable; and tels of the Gold Mines in the way. Diodorus Siculus, speaking of India saith, Z).5.7.3.10. Nascitur in ea ingens argenti aurique vis, non parum quoque aeris, ferrique orichalci. Another Diodorus in his Geographicall Verses saith of the Indians Gold-mining: I. i. 33.1 Tcov 0' olfxev " pva-olo ixetoxkevovai yeueoXrjv ' axjiiov euyvaulitTrja-i a-)((uvovte fxakexijcriu and after ')(jpv(Tol. o yevebXrjv Aai a i v 'YTraw re (pepei, Oetog re Meyaocro? Aa potUTOi irotajuwv ', utto S oupeo? 'Hjucosoio Opvviieuoi Trpopeoucriv eiri VayyrjtL a- (aprju. Mea..:. c.8. Pomponius Mela mentions those Ants, More Gry-phorum keeping the Gold, cum summa pernicie attin- gentium. He, Solinus, and Plinie mention Chryse and Plin. l.6. z. Argyre so plentifull of Mettals, that men reported the "- ' "t'- 54-soyle was Gold and Silver: so hyperbolicall reports were raised of their store.

But as the ancients knew not these parts of India so well as later times, wee will produce later testimonies. And generally it is esteemed in the remotest East parts, that

Gold by reason of the plenty hath not his true Seeto. z. Li. and natural preasminence above Silver Cwhich ordinarilv i' f' is twelve to one) but lower by much, in some places i pao-' 7qa more, in some lesse, as the following Relations will better acquaint you. So Marco Polo saith that in the Province of Cardandan, they give one ounce of Gold Cardandan for five of Silver: Gold being exceeding plentifull, " which many brought thorow the Desarts to change as ' aforesaid, the wayes being unpassible for others. I omit the golden Monument he mentions in Mien. In Tholo-man hee saith, is great quantity of Gold. The former place is somewhat Northerly, this Easterly from the necke of the Chersonessus. Nicolo de Conti mentions Bcls of Gold commonly sold in those parts, still in use in Pegu to put in mens yards. Odoardo Barbosa mentions store of Gold at Queda, and in the Kingdome of Pam, in this Chersonessus. But I am too suddenly slipt into later times: Long before these. Saint Isidore V.. 14.3. mentioneth Chryse and Argyre plentifull of Gold and Silver, and those golden Mountaines quos adire propter Dracones Gryphas, immensorum hominum monstra, impossibile est. lian hath a long discourse of those- Han de Gryphons out of Ctesias, keeping the Gold in vast '- + Deserts; of which I noted before, as of the Phenix ' and the Ants, that a Mysterie rather then Historie is intended, either shewing the barrennesse of Misers producing no good fruites in the mids of golden abundance, but rather ready to devoure all which came in their clutches; or else intimating the difficulty to get Gold, and manifold dangers in respect of the neighbouring inhabitants, of famine in those Deserts. Rabanus

See the Glosse 15 Lyran. in I. reg. 9.

See my Pilgrimage Lins-choten. Fitch, Balbi, all which have written of these parts, lian de

Barthema.

Frederik. See L 10.

Fitch.

Maurus, and long after him Nicolas Lyra relate these Beasts perillous to such as seeke the Gold in these parts. And indeede for wilde Beasts, both Lizards, Tygres, and others, I thinke no places more infested then those in and neere Pegu: for which cause the Country and people are forced to build their houses above ground, that they may goe up to them on Ladders, Barros tels of one Tygre which in Malacca seised on a peece of wood to which three slaves were chained, and carried all away, leaping therewith over a high wall also. Neither are the Tygres of other Countries comparable to these in these parts, being another kinde, called Thoes, or some other kinde, rather than true Tygres, of which are many in Afrike and America. But leaving the testimonies of auncient and midle times, wee will come to later dayes.

Ludovico Barthema in his third Booke of India, c. 16. much extolleth Pegu for riches (he wrote sixe score yeeres agoe) especially for Jewels, and he saith the King had a Million of Gold in revenue: and note that the Bramas Empire or Monarchy was not then begun. Barthema also mentions the Gold in Somatra. Barbosas testimony is before. Caesar Fredericke which was at Pegu, neere sixty yeeres since in the Bramas reigne in Pegu, saith that the King had divers Magazines full of Gold and Silver, every day increased without diminishing. He is Lord also of the Mines of Rubies, Saphires, and Spinels. He mentions also Colosses, or prodigious and more then Gyantly statues of Gold and Silver, the foote as bigge as a mans body: innumerable Varelles or Idou Temples covered with leafe Gold, with other things which I omit. Master Fitch, besides the Gold Mines at Patenaw as he descended the Ganges, relates the like golden stories of Pegu (where hee was 1586.) as Fredericke hath related, of houses of the King full of Gold, of guilded Idoll houses and statues. The Merchandise in Pegu, saith he, is Gold, Silver, Rubies, Saphires, Spinels, Muske, c. neither is their money of those mettals, but of a kinde of Brasse called Gansa, Gansa is a wherewith Gold and Silver are bought, sometimes deerer, '"'" f., 11 CI Brasse and sometimes cheaper, no lesse then other wares, bo also saith Fredericke, saying that every man may stampe that money at his pleasure, and therewith buy Gold and Silver, as aforesaid. Gasparo Balbi a Venetian Balbi began

Jeweller was there a little before Fitch, and relateth his journey likewise of the statues, Magazens of Gold, Silver, Ganza, pj j"

Jewels, Cloathes, Muske, c. under severall Treasurers, 1583. W and concludeth, that this King, for Gold, Silver, and staid till

Jewels, is the richest Kinsf in the world, except the 1586.

?:. ' which space

Kmgofchma. was a combat

But the Jesuites Letters have best opened these Mines betwixt the of the King of Pegu. N. Pimenta writes; Fernandus Kings of Ava also from Syripore 1599. 16. Kal. Feb. of the state o "- "", Pegu; that the Kings father a Braman had subjected twelve y il'lf Kingdomes to his scepter, viz. the Kingdome of Cavelan, j, lame. whence come the best Rubies and Saphires: Ava, which hath Mines of Cyprian Brasse, Lead, and Silver: the Kingdome of Bacan which hath many Mines of Gold: the Kingdome of Tangoma, abounding with Copper, Muske, Pepper, Silke, Gold, Silver, (all which are also had, saith he, in the rest of the Kingdomes of the Peguan Empire) Cablan abounding with Gemmes, c. Hee proceeds to relate the miserable ruine destruction I- i. 34- of that Kingdome, which then had lately happened, not yet recovered, as you may reade at large in him, and in my Pilgrimage. The former King of Pegu is reported to have cast 366. combalengas of Gold, each containing 180. pound weight, which none knowes what is become of them. This King had 67. Idou-statues of Gold, adorned with all kinde of Gemmes. He killed 200. Eunuches lest they might disclose his treasures. Andreas Boves, another Jesuite, related the miserable death of the King (in his Letters from Sirian in Pegu, March P. P. l. s. c. 28. 1000.) slaine by the King of Tangu, to whom he had yeelded himselfe, who neglecting Silver, and things of smaller value, onely with Gold and Gemmes laded

One Copy sixe or seven hundred Elephants, and as many Horses. Hc LT oo " Arracan tooke his leavings, gleaning so ' much Silver as was valued at three Millions besides Ordnance 3300. Peeces.

Now for trade of Gold out of the adjoyning parts, I could adde hither out of Fernand Mendez Pinto which He places Ca- travelled from Timplan in Calaminhan (the Emperour twixt Pe u whereof, he saith, hath seven and twenty Kingdomes and Chitia Subject to him) to Pegu, An. 1546. then possessed by the neeretoprom. Braman Conquerour. Hee reporteth that the Bramans Monarchy had anciently contained thirteene Kingdomes; and that abundance of Gemmes, Gold, Silver, and innumerable riches are in the Calaminhan Empire; in which is no money of Gold, or Silver, but they trade by weight of Gates, Tadis, Maazes, and Conderins. Hee also reporteth that the Lake Chiama containeth in circuit sixty Jaons, each of which is three leagues, alongst which are many Mines of Silver, Copper, Tin, and Leade, which they carry in Cafilas of Elephants, and Badas (I thinke hee meaneth Rhinocerots) to the Kingdomes of Sornau, to wit, Siam, Passiloco, Savady, Tangu, Prom, Calaminham, and returne therefore much Gold, and Diamonds, and Rubies. As for the Mines of Gold neere the Lake Pinator whence the River of Camboia runneth, yeelding yeerely two and twenty Millions of Gold, and a rocke of Diamants there also, I referre you Peregrin. F. to the Author, which placeth them further then our ' limits.

Pinto c. 39. But if we adde Sumatra (which the most thinke to be

Taprobone, in which Ophirs name is evidently seene still) we have the tradition of the people, the Gold also (Bonferrus a Franciscan hath related that the Peguan tradi-Peguans are descended of Salomons servants sent to '""' these Mynes; but I know not whether the Natives have any such tradition, perhaps it is the Friers conjecture) as appeareth by the following testimonies. And if wee adde the next Neighbour on the West, which now possesseth the Easterne parts of Ganges, and the

Kingdome of Bengala, I thinke wee shall utterly take away Ortelius his scruple (Sed hanc Chersonesum auri The cause why divitem olim fuisse, nemo veterum, quod sciam auctor rtehusre- est) neque nunc etiam esse, ex recentioribus palam est:) opi io of

Onely remember that in the Ophirian Voyage, we take josephus.

not onely the Chersonesus, but all the Countrey from

Ganges, and thence to Sumatra, placing Pegu in the centre as the Ophir of Ophir, or Ophir in most proper sence; annexing the rest, with all the Choromandell coast also, as being subject to one and the same trade and Navigation, all on the shoares of the gulfe of

Bengala. I like Master Dees simihtude, which sets the feete of his Ophirian compasse, one in Zeilan, the other in Sumatra, the head I place in Pegu. This head is caput caenae, the true Ophir, the other parts of the compasse, the parts compassed and traded in, in this

Ophirian Voyage. From Ganges to Menan are divers

Chersonesi, or rather Hands, in regard of the Rivers which come from the Lake Chiamay; and from Bengala to Menan is the Peguan Chersonesus, which perhaps is the true Chryse and Aurea (for that Malaccan Cher- sonessus hath never beene renowned in latter times for any great quantity of Gold that I have read or learnd, not yet altogether destitute, as we have shewed; but not sufficient for Salomons Ophir) from which as first peopled, the Inhabitants of Sumatra might (as is said) be a Colony.

Whether it were so or no, I dispute not, nor whether it or Zeilan be the true Taprobant; nor whether it were anciently an Hand, and since separated by the Seas irruption: that it is well stored with Golden Mines needes no question, and therefore fit to be saluted by Salomons Navie, then in their Ophirian Voyage, and by us here in our Ophirian Discovery. Of Sumatra, Odoardo Barbosa witnesseth that there are many Gold Mines, vi son molte minere d'Oro: and speaking of Menancabo one of the Kingdomes in the South part of that great Hand saith, qui e il principal fonte dell'oro,

c. there is the principall originall of the Gold of that Hand, as well of the Minerals, as of that which is gathered neere the brinkes of Rivers. He wrote An. 1516. and was one of Magelans companions in his Voyage about the World. Long before him Nicolo di Conti testified of Sumatra, that in it is abundance of Gold. Andrew Thevet mentions the gold Mines: but wee have later and better testimonies from our owne men. Captaine Davis was in that Hand, Anno 1599. Seelnf. paii. and mentions not onely the King of Achens store, but the Mines of Gold and other commodities of that Hand: and the Brasse Mines to be also rich in Gold; and (which maketh most to our purpose) a tradition of the Natives that Salomons Ophirian voyage for Gold was to that Countrey. Sir James Lancasters Voyage, and divers other English Voyages will ratifie Sumatras Gold. But what neede we better testimony then the Letter of that King to our King, which this story See Inf. pa. yeeldeth to your view, and worth your reading. To 468. y 532. j j. Q Walter Paytons testimony of the Gold of Passaman in this Hand I referre you. Likewise for the next adjoyning parts on this side, I will trouble you onely with two testimonies, one of Master Fitch, I. i. 35. who travelling downe the River Ganges, at Patenaw observed the golden Mines, where saith he, they digge deepe pits and wash the earth thence taken in great boles, and so finde the Gold: the other of Captaine Hawkins, who bare the name of the English Embas-sadour in the Mogols Court, and speaking of six severall treasuries of that King, relates the particulars of that one of Agra, which stands on Jemni or Gemini, Inf. 217 y a River tributary to Ganges, where his Gold, Silver, " ' and Jewels may seeme to our poorer World, beyond credit. But I had rather point you to the place, then here trouble you with transcribing. And thus have we used a threefold argument, one of names, a second of situation, a third of the principall commodities returned, to prove that Ophir was in these parts, and have before shewed that it could be in none other alleadged. But Gold and Gemmes have such a lustre, and Salomons other rarities were so precious, that wee may I hope be pardoned to take longer view on them, both for our better knowledge in such things, and for better confirmation of the Ophirian Pegu, and the Regions adjacent.

Of the Gold, Silver, Gemmes, Ivory, Almug-trees, Apes and Peacockes, which Salomons Fleet brought from Ophir, with divers other profitable observations inserted.

Etals are our Mothers hidden treasures, by mens covetousnesse often occasions of her violent ravishments, and no better to her then a

Viperous Issue, or as Wormes, or Colike passions in her entrals. In themselves, and in divine Ordinance, they are many wayes profitable for medicine against diseases, armour against enemies, ornaments for peace, engines for Warre, Instruments for daily labour, utensils for daily food, and in money-emploiment, they are All things. Of all Metals Gold hath preeminence, as likest the Sun in purity of substance, glory of splendour, powerfull attraction, longest endurance (in despite of

Age and Fire) most operative influence, and of base '- i–9- Idolaters most adored. How it is found in Grains, 12. 3. TV.

Pippins, or Powder, this Booke elsewhere sheweth. ' y And although Silver bee a durable metall, and well y. induring both times and flames, yet herein is it short Seebrerewood of Gold: and notwithstanding the colour is more light- ' umms c.

2022 Pollux some, and the sound more delightsome, yet Gold hath g Takn-in great proportion alway beene preferred. Jullius turn Hes. in Pollux citeth Menander, and Hesychius Polemarchus, xpv ovi y which make this proportion ten fold, which the Romans p)'f "' ' also observed in their agreement with the ietolians, ' '. ' " that if they paid in Gold, one peece should counter- TMia, vaile ten of Silver. The old Greekes and Persians seeme to have observed the like rate. Plinie mentions at the first coyning, the proportions of fifteene; and neere that, to wit, fourteene and a halfe, is observed in the Constitutions of Arcadius and Honorius. Herodotus makes one Talent of Gold equall to thirtccnc of Silvcr. In Galbas timc it was twclve and a halfe. But China and some parts of the East Indies, by reason of plenty of Gold, and small store of Silver, have diversly undervalued the Gold. The most generall, which Plato also approved, and In Plinies time was currant, and is most usuall in these parts, is ordinarily twelve for one, as an ounce of Silver five shillings, of Gold three pounds.

The purest Gold, and which is as much as may be, purified from all other mixture, is called Obryzum, a Gorop. Pine, word procreated in the Mints, not of Ophirian parent-y age (Obrlzum quasi Ophirlzum) and such are (as they say) the Darike coines and our Edward Nobles; not above the nintie sixth part being of other mixture. They say (saith Master Brerewood) that it may be so farre refined that onely the three hundred eighty fourth Tal. lmafol. part shall be of other mettall. The Greeke coines of 44; Philip and Alexander admitted a fiftieth part of Silver,

Hter. tn Jer. Romans forty eight, now observed In Turkish, Job. 21. 2. Hungarian, Spanish, and Venetian coines: those of y 28 16. Rome, Luques, Mlllaine have alloy thirty two, French ic r. 29.4. Crownes sixteene, Italian nine, c. The Talmudists mention seven kindes of Gold, or observe seven names by which Gold is named in Scripture: Saint Jerom also Intimateth the same, and Pineda hath long discourses of them, which I omit. The Scripture seemeth to ascribe a prerogative to the Gold of Ophir, before Salomons time, in Job, and in Davids dales, wherby It may seeme that the Voyage to Ophir for Gold was in use long before Salomon, and some thinke that a great part of Davids Gold consecrated to the Temple, was by his care fetched thence. For above his other preparations, mentioned i. Chron. 22. 14, which were a hundreth thousand talents of Gold, and a thousand thousand talents of Silver, in the nine and twentieth chapter, he out of his proper goods giveth 3000. other talents of Gold, of the Gold of Ophir, and 7000. talents of refined Silver: the Princes offered also 5000. talents of Gold, and loooo drams, and of Silver loooo. talents, c.

This is diversly summed by divers Expositors differing in their computation of a Talent. Master Dee and Master Brerewood have seemed to have given the best construction, derived from Moses himselfe, Exod. 38. 25, 26. which Rabbi Salomon and Lyra, had observed before them; that a Talent containeth 3000. Shekles, 6003550. which is 375 li. a Talent of Silver, and a Talent of halfe a shekel Gold, allowing twelvefold proportion, is 4500. li. Accord- ' Pp ing to which just reckoning Salomons foure hundreth, rro twenty Talents of Gold brought from Ophir, came to shekels: so one million eight hundred ninety thousand pounds. 600000 Davids 3000. Talents of Gold of Ophir, i. Chron. 29. 4. 3Joj -aforesaid, was thirteene millions and five hundreth thou- sequenth a sand in English money. His Silver then offered (7000. talent is 6000 Talents) is two millions 625000. li. The off ering of halfe shekels. the

Princes (5000. Talents of Gold) was two and twenty t– 3-J millions five hundreth and seven thousand 500. pounds: and their ten thousand Talents of Silver came to three millions and seven hundred fiftie thousand pounds. Salomon had also given him by the Queene i. i?, 10.10. of Sheba 120. Talents, that is five hundreth and fortie thousand pounds. As much was sent him by Hiram. Now the whole Furniture of the Tabernacle was twentie nine Talents of Gold, and 730. Shekles; in Exod. T,.2. our money, one hundreth thirtie and one thousand, 5-five hundreth ninety and five pounds; the silver was 100. talents, and 1775. shekles, that is, thirtie seven thousand, seven hundreth and twentie one pounds seventeene shillings six pence. Thus hath Master Brerewood cast up these summes. Now for this Ophirian I 97 e

Gold, Salomon is said, 2. Chron. 8. i8. to have had from Ophir foure hundred and fiftie talents, thirtie more then I. Reg. 9. are mentioned, which thirtie Talents, it seemeth were spent in wages or other charges, and came not to the Kings Coffers.

But a great scruple remaineth about the 100000. talents of Gold, mentioned before out of i. Chron. 22. 14. which amount to foure hundreth and fiftie millions of English pounds; and the million of Silver talents to three hundreth seventie five millions of pounds: summes stupendious and prodigious beyond all that the Persian, Greeke, or Roman Empires ever saw at one time, after greater and longer conquests then Davids; and such, as even Salomons wealth had beene by much overtopped by Davids; which agreeth 2. C5r(?. I. not either to the History, or to the Mystery, that 12. Heavens peace glory should be surmounted by mili- tant Faith and Grace. Alexander the richest Conquerour, left but eighteene millions and seven hundreth and 50000. pound of money at his death: and in conquest of Darius, had gotten but thirtie two millions 750000. pound: and Cyrus out of the conquest of Asia gathered but 125. millions, which yet is the greatest sum (except that of Sardonapalus mentioned by Ctesias, an Author not much to bee credited) which any Ethnick story mentioneth. Wee must therefore find another acceptation of the word there translated Talent, which is taken sometimes for a lumpe of mettall in forme of a Cake, or else that name Talent is sometimes taken for a small summe, as out of Pollux and Homer, M. Brerewoods paines have observed; who also having cast up the particulars, findeth that such summes could not have beene spent on the Temple, had the Walls and Pavements beene of massie Silver, the Roofe and all the Linings of the Walls and the Furniture of solid Gold. Salomons yeerely revenue (as some interpret, 2 Chron. 9. 13.) was six hundreth sixty six talents of Gold, besides his Customes, and the rich Presents of Gold and Silver sent him from the Kings of Arabia and the

Governours: that lackes but three pounds of three millions in our reckoning. Some would make up this great summe of the Ophirian Gold, and Hirams, and the Queene of Shebas gifts, which all lacke but six talents; as if it were not an Annuall, but Casuall

Revenue, which I cannot approve. Some interpret it of ordinary tributes levied of his Subjects; some of the posteritie of the Chanaanites (a thing unhkely) and some of forraine voyages, making him to send every yeere a Fleet, though none of those Fleets returned till the third yeere. Villalpandus makes it but one Vilal. To. z.

returne from Ophir, the first, of foure hundreth and Explan. p. z.

twenty Talents, the second, of foure hundreth and ' i,. jj omht fiftie, the third, of six hundreth sixty six of Gold, home much besides Silver and other goods. And, as for Salomons more then entire Revenues, hee with great paines in the auditing, o- raiseth them higher then the Persians, then Alexanders, then those of the Roman Empire: arising from his

Customes, his Gifts and Presents, Taxations, Tributes, provisions of Corne, c. That of the King of Tyrus he reckoneth a tribute, and out of Eupolemus alleageth that the Tyrians were tributaries. Wee may here also remember, that there is no mention of the summe of the Silver which they brought from Ophir, which is likely was farre more then the Gold, insomuch that it i. Chron. 9.

was reputed as Stones, and was of none account in the 7 J g' dayes of Salomon.,,. u'cln. 9.

To mee it seemeth that the sixe hundreth sixtie sixe 23, 24. Talents of Gold is spoken onely of forraine Gold, partly by Ophirian and other merchandising Trades, and partly by Presents; of which the two principall, Hiram, and the Queene of the South are expressed: but it is added of others. That all the Kings of the Earth sought the presence of Salomon, and brought every man his Present, vessells of Silver, and vessells of Gold, and Raiment, Harnesse and. Spices, Horses and Mules, a rate yeere by yeere. Grant then a Fleet yeerely set forth, which came not home till the third yeere, one succeeding another (as in the Spanish Fleets to Peru, and ours to the Indies, of which is a yeerely returne, yet not of the same) and these yeerely Presents, there could not be lesse then six hundreth sixty six Talents: besides perhaps, tenne or twelve times as much in Silver, and all the Spices, Horses, Mules, Customes of Merchants, Tributes of the Edomites, Moabites, and Vassalls, Vili p. ubi Taxes on his Israelitish Subjects, Revenues out of his sup. ratseth Pastures and innumerable Cattell and husbandry of e ti ues 0 Qj. Q j g Lands (wee will not adde, with some, Chimistry; Israel to izo. v i i -n i j n l talents each that might have saved his Uphirian paines) and all the

Tribe, y as riches left him by Inheritance from his Father. Now much of–j e six hundreth sixtie six Talents is to be under- hos ub'ec Stood of Strangers, appeareth in that exception. Vers. 14.

tion I dispute where none but forraine Incombes are mentioned. And not, it agreeth hereby most lively is both the calling of the Gentiles with Canaans figured, of which the 72. Psalme was by the Spirit of 7romistofa'll ' purposely indited in correspondence of this type,

Caanan to nd the Christian Truth; as also the glory of the Israel) which heavenly Jerusalem, which ariseth not out of the workes together make of righteousnesse which we have done, but ot tree gifts, 262 'for" ' ' y ""g y"

Roinanducats: honour of the Nations into it. Rev. 21. where in vision besides Silver that glorious Citie is represented, and correspondent and all other to Salomons type. The Citie was of pure Gold, and projits which foundations and gates of precious stones, but there he brought. 11 r c-i together above s no mention at all of Silver.

Assuerus, Another question ariseth out of Davids 3000. Talents

Jlexander, the of Gold of Ophir, whether hee practised the Ophirian Roman Em- Yoyapre also: and some suppose that hee had made tire with faire ',., 1 1 1 t' 1 probabilities seven voyages thither, which reckoning 420. lalents I. i. 37. a time, makes much about that summe of three thousand

Whether Da- Talents. For my part, I thinke David a greater Warrior v dj nttleets Merchant, allowing the greatest summes before t, ' questioned to be reserved and consecrated out of the yig 11' spoiles, as himselfe confesseth, In my trouble I have

D. Dee. prepared for the house of the Lord 100000. Talents of Gold, c. and more plainly, i. Chronicles i8. ii. considering also that it was long before his State could be setled at home, and fitted abroad to attend such Navigations; which likewise have neither ground in the Sacred Story (for the Gold of Ophir is proverbiall, usually in Scripture for fine and pure Gold) nor agree with the type, David one way, Salomon another resembling Christ, and their times the state of the Church; likewise that David had much care of husbanding his estate to the best, thrift being the Jewell of Magnificence, i. chron. 27. as appeareth in the particular enumeration of the Officers 2 5 26, 27, for his Rents, Store-houses, Husbandmen in the Field, ' 9 3. Vineyards, Olive-trees, Sycamores and Oyle, Herds in Sharon, and in the Vallies, Camells, Asses, Flockes; it is no marvell if such industry acquired such substance in such continuance of time, and that hee said I have of mine own proper goods of Gold and Silver which I have given to the house of my God, over and above all that I have prepared (to wit, in consecrated spoyles) for the holy House three thousand Talents of Gold of Ophir, c. This example of David sheweth that Two remark-it is no impeachment, yea the true advancement of t ' jj'- Honour for Princes to use all frugall husbandry and JJ g g ". meanes of thriving at home; as that other of Salomon, handry on to adde helpe of Discoveries and Trade abroad (both in Land, and a Royall manner by their just Officers) that Magnificence ig on by may stand firme on both legs: the want whereof hath denied that wealth (not to speake of power) these many Ages to many Kings out of farre farre greater meanes (besides other inconveniences to themselves and their Subjects) which David, Salomon, and other Kings in the old World had. Once these examples so moved that good King Tehoshaphat, that hee built Cities o Chron xj.

, 1 1 J T-l 1 J J CU 11,12. C5 20

Store at home, and had many Hockes, and made bhips also to goe to Tarshish, and they made the Ships in Ezion-Geber, the same Port where Salomon made his Navall provisions; but joyning therein with Ahaziah King of Israel, who did very wickedly (So much worse before God is an Ahaziah then a Hiram, the one an honest minded Gentile, the other a schismaticall Idolatrous Israelite) that the Lord broke the workes, and the Ships were not able to goe to Tarshish.

We have beene very long in this metall Discourse: yet how much longer was Salomon in his three yeeres Voyage, and how much longer the most of men, which make their whole life a voyage to Ophir for Gold and Silver, thorow so many diversified Seas of Arts, force, frauds to get those metalls which procreated neerest Hell, carry these eager seekers thither altogether. That the Silver was more by farre then the Gold, was before proved; but the quantitie is not expressed, as not D. Dec. agreeing with Salomons either Litterall Story, or Mysticall

Glory. Some thinke that there was in every voyage 24. times as much Silver as Gold; both because they conceive that Nature hath given so much more thereof in quantitie, as the qualitie and price is undervalued; and because all Stories Ancient and Moderne magnifie India for store of Silver; and so prodigious prodigality, I. Kings 20 to give Silver in Jerusalem as stones, must have a deep 7 fountain for such a flowing streame, besides those other

Silver Hooks and Brooks mentioned in Salomons History. But we still leave these precious, specious Gemmes. objects to take view of Gemmes.

And herein American Peru, and Sofala are beggarly in comparison of those parts of India, where we have placed Ophir, as the former testimonies well weighed with whatsoever can be brought for the other, will easily and superabundantly convince. In Northerne America are some Turkesses, in the Southerne are saide to bee (which others question) Emeralds, in both Pearles, but not comparable to the Orientall: these Bezars are twice so good; in Spices to make comparison hath no spice of knowledge. And first for the first of gemmes, Plin. I. 37. Diamants, Pliny saith. Maximum in rebus humanis non- 4 solum inter gemmas, precium habet Adamas, unus modo in metallis repertus. Some have conceited it to dull the Loadstones attraction, and to resist all force of Hammer, which experience hath found contrary. The Kingdomes of Narsinga, Biznagar, Orissa, Masulipatan, and all the Countries on the Choromandel Coast, are the most famous for Rockes of Diamants, and now also Soccodanna (where they dive for them as for Pearles) See C. Saris. Decan, Delli, and Agra, Tarriam also in the Tract of +"" Malacca, and Java. Here then is the Worlds Centre "' P"'-of Diamants, both for the most and best. Garcias ab Horto writes, that he hath seene one of one hundreth and forty Mangels (that is seven hundreth Graines) another of one hundreth and twentie, and hath heard I. i. 38. of one two hundreth and fiftie, and a credible man Garc. abhorto told him that hee saw one as big as a small Hens Egge ' ' ' ' in Bisnager. This soyle is so diamantine, that where you have digged and taken them now, in two yeeres space you may dig and find others. Neither is it poyson, as some affirm, but he hath knowne the whole stone, and the powder, taken without hurt.

The Heaven-coloured Sapphire, with some obtaineth Exod. 24. 10. the second place, because of the likenesse thereof under Epiphan. hbel the feet of the Almightie when hee spake to Moses; j 'i T"' or which are store in Zeilan, and the most true, hard fine as Barbosa testifieth. But M. Fitch and M. Fredericke have before told you of Mynes of them in Pegu; and these saith Garcias and Linschoten, are esteemed the finest, and are in great plenty. So is there Linschot, cap. also of the Rubie, a stone of greater value, none in 86. the world exceeding that King in excellencie and varietie of Gems, as appeareth by generall voyce. Of Rubies, the Carbuncle is esteemed the best, the Ballas next, the Spinell in the third place, of fiery colour: there are besides. White, Carnation, halfe White, halfe Red Rubies, others halfe Sapphires, halfe Rubies, and one thousand other sorts, if wee beleeve Linschoten. Garcias ascribeth this to the generation of the Ruby, which at first is whitish, and groweth unto rednesse in processe of time: and because the Sapphire and Rubie grow Gar. cap. 49.

in one Rocke, they are found sometimes such participles as is delivered, Sapphire-rubies, called Nilacandi. The Granado and Hyacinth are also reckoned by some amongst the Rubies, calling the yellowish Rubie the Hyacynth, and the blackish a Granado. These are plentifull in Cananor, Calecut, and Cambaia (neerer Westward, and in the way to the Gulfe of Bengala) in Zeilan also, as Nicolo di Conti and Andrea Corsali affirme; Pimenta his testimony of Cavelan and Cablan, two gemme Kingdomes you had before. The Jaspar is found in much plenty in Cambaia; Chrysolites, and

Amatists, there and in Zeilan and in Balagate (the Apennine of the Great Indian Chersonesus) where they have also the Alaquera or Quequi, which stayeth the issue of bloud presently. Pegu, Brama, Zeilan, yeeld the Cats-eye and Agat, of which the Indians conceive the owner shall increase in wealth; and Garcias saith, Hee hath tried that no fire can burne a linnen Cloth pressed to the eye of it. The Armenian Stones are found also in Balagate, the Loadstone in Zeilan, neere to which is the fishing for Pearles, but the best of the world are in the Persian Gulfe neere Ormuz: The Alambie in Cambaia. The Bezar Stones are at Pahan neere Malaca, and Cambaia, taken out of the maw of a Sheepe or Goat. The Berills are in Pegu and Zeilan. The Topaz is almost like a Diamant, and is digged out of the Earth in many places of India. There are White Sapphires and Rubies hardly knowne from Litis, c. 87. Diamants. In Cambaia also is found plentie of the Stone Alambre. There are found in Zeilan also the Topaz, Jagongas and Marucha, whose names I can better give you then the understanding. There are also many sorts of Stones (you reade Linschoten) as well Precious Stones as against poyson and other diseases of many properties and vertues: but I have onely mentioned those that are daily bought and sold, and are commonly knowne. The Emeralds I mention not, though said to bee in these parts, because some doubt of them, and in other parts are found better, wherewith the Venetians have made good gaine at Pegu in exchange for Rubies: those also of Peru are suspected. For gemmes (wee now conclude) no part of the world but India, could fit Salomons turne; wherein, if Aarons brest- plate were so glorious in the Tabernacle, to how precious height will Salomons Temple elevate our thoughts?

and consequently both manifest and magnifie the Indian-
Ophirian Voyage, these being found either naturall in the
Peguan Ophir, or by trade there or in the way from
Ophir by the Westerne parts of India, part of the
Persian Gulfe, and the shores of Arabia and Ethiopia.
Of which, Arabia is said to yeeld the Hemathite, Topaz, Pmedadereb.
Sardonyke, Onyx, Molochite, Myrrhite, Corall, Andro- 5 om. L. c.
made, Iris; Ethiopia, the Chrysolite, Chrysolamp, Qfi ji
Heliotrope, Hyacinth, Hemathite, Chrysoprase; the store of Jewells
Persian gulfe from Babylonia the Sagda, Sardy, and and their rkh- the best Pearles:
gypt in ordinary trade, the Galactite, " '
Emerald, and iegyptilla: some of which you had before ' " 55- particularly mentioned in India, and likely enough should j. ji g. lo.
there find most of the rest with many other unknowne, 12.
if India were as much frequented with Philosophers from hence as Merchants.

Wee are next to consider the Almug Trees, whereof fj " l J were made Pillars for the House of the Lord, and for M the Kings House, Harpes also and Psalteries for Singers: 9. u Jos. i. there came no such Almug Trees, nor were seene unto 8. c 2 this day. Josephus Interprets Pine Trees, but saith, 7-J nv-they differed from the usuall, resembling the Timber g j,-j of the Figge Tree to the eye, but that they were whiter Hak'l. hand, and brighter. There is mention of Algum Trees in amongst whose Lebanon, 2. Chron 2. 8. which some thinke to bee ff y f " the same with the former, and the word onely altered by transposition of letters; others, that that trans- much use of it, position intimates no lesse specificall difference in the although much wood then in the word, though otherwise having some ' ' f f. ' likenesse to those of Lebanon, but of greater excellency. D. Dee hath written a laborious Treatise almost wholly cited.

of this Ophirian argument (the same yeere in which I was borne, A, 1577. of seventie sheets of paper) howsoever intituled, Of Famous and Rich Discoveries; of which I have a written Copie, and could willingly but for the length have published it; which may appeare in this, that he hath ten sheets of paper about these Almug trees, more profitable to the leasurely Schouer, then commodious to be inserted to so voluminous a Worke, as this Library of ours. Hee there, as Commissioner for Salomons Timbers, like a learned, both Architect and Planter, hath summoned a Jury of twelve I. i. 39. sorts of Trees (mentioned by divers Interpreters) to examine or to bee examined rather, which of them were the Almugs here mentioned. I should bring you into a Wood to relate his labours in this kind; the kinds are, the Deale, Boxe, Cedar, Cypresse, Ebonie, Ash, Juni-The Spanish per. Larch, Olive, Pine, Oke and Sandall Trees: all Bible reads which with their severall qualities and fitnesse for Royall and Sacred buildings hee examineth by best testimonies, and concludeth nothing absolutely, but inclineth to Josephus, who either by some Monuments in writing might have learned, or in some remainders to his time in Instruments Musicall, or other profane or sacred memo-rialls, might probably bee thought to have seene thereof. Plin. I. 13. r. I easily beleeve that these Pines or Thynes (Thyina) or 16. whatsoever other Trees, were both odoriferous to the Sent, of beauteous aspect to the Eye, of fittest temper to refract Qfth ' T sounds to the Eare, smooth to the Touch, and of long con-andofele- tinuance and strong substance for building, therein to bee phantsyseem. serviceable to all senses. Of which sorts it is evident out Terry . 9. c. of Ancient and Moderne Writers, and out of the fouow- ' 'f ing Relations, that India hath the best in the World.

their Apes as d,,. l i-i l bis: as Grey- ' living Creatures remaine to our search, Ulephants, hounds ib. 7,. Apes, Peacockes; of which I need say little, saying so See also San- much in our following Histories, and having said so much tosy Jobson, already. Elephants come neerest Men in understanding, others in this Apes in forme (Simia quam similis turpissima bestia nobis worke. said Ennius) and Peacocks for their beauty, as Parrots also,

Birds of Paradise, and many other Indian Fowles might be desired. The greatest Elephants are found in all this our Ophirian Tract, from Zeilin to Pegu; those esteemed to have a naturall preeminence, and these had of late a Politicall, the King of Pegu stiling himselfe, The King of White Elephants, and keeping them Royally attended, his Subjects and Tributary Kings also (it is Gasper Balby his report) kneeling to them. Once all India is plentifull of them, and therefore of Ivory; this Countrey also neere Ganges is stored with the Abada or Rhinocerote, whose Home is (in Bengala, by reason of certaine Hearbs hee there feeds on) a good Counter-poyson. Indian Asse-horne in these parts is also used for Bucklers, and drinking Cups, and esteemed a great Jewell, as Master Finch affirmeth, infra Pag. 436.

For Peacocks or Parrats, translate which you will, heere Peacocks tvild, are not onely so many of both, that they flie wild, as the 'JJg- ' following Relations shew, but for excellency beyond ff c those of other parts; as the Apes also are for their beauty and strength. See Sir T. Roe, Master Finch, and others Journalls, or rather talke with our

Indian Merchants, which usually trade and travell those parts, some of which in the Mogolls Countrey, carrying with them an English Grey-hound, one of the company shot at a great white shee Ape on a Tree, and wounded her, whereby shee with her Cub fell downe: they set on the Grey-hound, and this Ape before seeking shifts for her Cub, seeing the These Apes Grey-hound come, layd it aside and encountred the Grey- ' '" ' ' hound so fiercely about the necke, that hee dyed within a few houres, the company with their weapons comming in, and killing the Ape (as themselves related to mee) and carrying away the young one. The Countrey people, in I know not what superstition forbeare to kill them, whereby they multiply exceedingly. Heere by the way may bee observed, that it appertaineth to Royall Magnifi-cencie, and disagreeth not to humane Excellency, to procure rarities of living Creatures, and to keepe them as testimonies of our admiration of Gods various Workes,

Plin. I. 6. cap.

As covetous rich men are ever needy 3 greedy, so India hath ever sivallowcd in Trade the worlds Treasure, and yet is the Treasury of the World I. i. 40.

and exercise of the Minds Contemplation, the Bodies pleasure, with the right Humane over Sensitive Creatures: which Nature taught Alexander; yea Motezuma and the Incas in that wilder World; and Divine Grace our Salomon, as these Scriptures manifest. The imitation of whose Wisdome hath whetted my Studies almost to curiositie to give to the World a world of Rarities in that kind, as any occasion offered it selfe in these voluminous Voyages.

Probable conjectures of the Course taken in the Ophirian Voyage, and accounts given of the three yeeres time spent therein: also of the Course taken in like Voyages by the Romans: and the divers Ports whereto the Spices and riches of India have in divers Ages beene brought, and thence dispersed to the several! parts of Europe.

Ee have now undertaken a hard taske, where we tell not but spell a Voyage, and from reasonable conjectures grounded on other experiments, gather what is most likely in this of Salomons, D. Dee hath written 23. sheets of paper in examining the miles, the dayes, the way, the employments of the time, and mustering of Men and Ships employed in this service. I cannot presume either of so much learning in my Selfe, or so much patience in the Reader. Yet I shall bee bold both to follow him, and to adde somewhat for further light. Pliny writes, that in his time this Voyage from Egypt to India was made every yeer. Every yeer India consumed H-S 500. (which Jacobus Delachampius in his notes summeth to 1200000 Crownes) of the Roman Empires Treasure yeerely, yeelding merchandises therefore in returne sold at a hundreth times so much. Their course, hee saith, was from Alexandria twelve dayes by Nilus to

Coptus, thence by Camells over Land to Berenice, two hundreth fiftie eight miles (travelling most part by night by reason of the heate) in twelve dayes more.

From Berenice on the Red Sea, they beginne to set forth at Midsummer, or about the beginning of Dogge- dayes, and in thirtie dayes come to Ocelis in Arabia, (or to Canaan or Muza, if they goe not to India, but for Arabian Frankincense and Odours) and from Ocelis in fortie dayes they arrived at the first Indian Port

Muziris. Remember that in this Course they both tooke Muziris is by benefit of the Monson, and went the neerest way: for so some thought to a little before hee mentioneth another Course by the j-f"J; J

Shoare, Secuta atas propiorem cursum, c. donee com- his Periplus it pendia invenit
Mercator, Lucroque India admota est. is placed more

Quippe omnibus annis navigatur. Hee mentions the Southerly, on
Voyage of Onesicritus and Nearchus from India to fjj t!
Tigris, in the bottome of the Persian Gulfe, which helde Qg st. D.

them till the seventh moneth. So much was Navigation Dee thinkes it improved in
Plinies time. Their Pepper they tooke in Surat.

on the Malabar Coast, and returned in December the same yeere. The names which
then they gave to places were quite differing from the Antients; and the like Indian
mutations have continued to our times.

The course to Taprobane had accidentally come to their knowledge a little before,
found in Alexanders time to bee an Hand by Onesicritus, mentioned by Megasthenes.
Foyage of The Antients deemed it another World. The Sea is Onesicritus full of
shoalds, the North-starre is not seene there, and ""pf li f '; they observed their course,
by sending out Birds which yo age to they carry with them and followed their flight.
But in Taprobana. the Empire of Claudius, Annius Plocanus having farmed the
Customes of the Red Sea, one of his Retainers or Free-men sayling on the Arabian
Coast, was by a Libertus, Northerne storme carried alongst the Carmanian shoare to
Hippuros a Port therein, and was kindly used by the King, who admiring his Roman
Relations, sent foure Embassadours backe with him. These related amongst other
things that the side of the Hand which lieth

That is toward India, is loooo. furlongs, and that they had 1250, miles, trade with
the Seres. I will not recite Nearchus out whtch cannot f Arrianus nor Ptolemey and
Marianus, which can agree to Letlan,.1,. jcii i ij r but Sumatra: " advantage us in
regard or the lesse Knowledge or the Easterly the former, and lesse certainty of the
later passing the situation also ignorance of Transcribers, aad above one thousand
yeares ultra montes darknesse. Yet herein is Ptolemey profitable, where his commerce
with Longitudes and Latitudes are false, that by his order Seres agree to of position
and successive setting downe of places some Sumatra. knowledge may arise. But the
length of the way is Jrrian. I. 8. better knowne by later Writers,

John di Barros hath set downe the coasting distances, from the Bab or Mouth of
the Red Sea to Cape Nigraes, the Southerly part of our Peguan Ophir, whose Portugall
leagues (allowing for each three English miles, and a fifth part of a mile) come to
57694 and from that Cape to Singapura is 1008. miles more. From the Bab or Mouth
of the Red Sea to the bottom, is by Inf. to. I. J. Comito Venetiano, in Ramusio
reckoned 1441. miles, f-6. and in his returne 1514. the breadth in some places two
hundreth, the way full of shoalds, so that it cannot bee sailed neere the shoare but by
day. So troublesome is this Sea, and so difficult to bee sayled, that Don John di Castro
(whose voyage followeth at large) spent no lesse then three moneths in the way from
Cosir. the Straits to Sues, from the nine and twentieth of

January, 1541. to the seven and twentieth of April; and returning the eight and
twentieth of April, arrived at the Bab the eighteenth of July; So that here the way is
to be weighed by the qualitie as well as the quantitie. Hieronimo da Santo Stephano
in Ramusio, spent from Cosir to Aden fiftie dayes, almost three hundreth miles
Southward from Sues, and therefore so much lesse way.

We must here note also that neither the ships, nor their furniture; the shipmen also nor their furniture of skill, could in Salomons dayes, be any way comparable to these later times: and that if three moneths were spent by the Portugall Navie from Sues to the Bab, we may at least allow so much time to these Ophirians. For if these had more haste, the other had more skill and better ships. Neither may we thinke that they durst there saile but by day in Salomons fleete, and therefore were likely to make it longer. The lesse vessels and many men, would require also oftner stales for water and refreshing, besides the seventh dayes rest, which Salomons servants according to the law, and especially in a Voyage for adorning the Temple, built in honor of the legall worship, must not breake. Being out of the Straits into the Ocean, they were neither willing nor able (as appeares by the mentioned Voyage of Onesicritus and Nearchus) to adventure the sailing beyond ken of Land. And therefore also Ptolemie in his longitudes and latitudes, abates of Marinus and the Mariners reckonings one third part, because of the crooking in their coasting, as every Bay and point enforced them. And that compendious way mentioned by Plinie was then new in his time, when shipping and the Mariners art had beene by frequent experience much improved, and from the swadling bands in Salomons time growne to some virility. So that except forced by distresse of weather we cannot make the Ophirian course but within ken of shoare all the way. Now then if it were the seventh moneth, as we have read in Plinie, before Alexanders fleet could arrive in Tigrus from Indus, in which Arrianus reporteth that there were Phaenician, Egyptian and Cyprian, besides his best Graecian Mariners, they all being then his subjects: we can allow no lesse to Salomons fleete before it could touch the neerest Indian Port, being no lesse way. And howsoever it may be objected that triumphall devotions, and tempests, and fights, and reparations of the Fleete, I. i. 41. tooke up much of Nearchus his time: I answere, that this Ophirian fleet was neither warranted from enemies nor tempests, was likely also to spend time in reparations, and in provisions, and in devotions, specially that which was peculiar to them, the Sabbaths.

And although single ships in the Arabike gulfe, and in the Ocean might even then make quicker way then this mentioned, yet in that of Castro, of Nearchus, and this of Salomon, where care was to keepe a whole fleet together for mutuall helpe and common security, the greater body must needes have slower motion. Thus then allowing three moneths to the Red Sea, and six moneths from thence to India, we shall follow Comito Venetiano, who reckons the one 1514. miles from the Straits to Sues inward, and thence outward to Diu 2023. to which adde the coasting about to the Ormuzian strait, and comming to any Port in India, as namely Muziris, or any in the Malabar coast, it could not much lesse then double the length of the way, and therefore the time. By this proportion we should spend the three yeeres in going and returning, if we adde that spacious way from Muziris to our neerest Port in Ophir: and so should both their labour and ours be vaine, and nothing should be done. Barros himselfe (to make this more evident) hath reckoned short of the way which Salomons Fleet must make in bouts and windings by the shoare, for which he makes no allowance. D. Dee is sparing in this calculation, and yet makes it from Ezion Geber to Cape Negraes 9155. miles; of which we deduct for the Arabike gulfe but 1514. and leave 7641. remaining. We therefore in regard of the manifold dangers and shelfes of that Gulfe, allow to it eighty dayes, of which deducting eleven Sabbaths, there remaine sixtie nine, to which (one with another) we allow one and twenty miles a day, somewhat more, as much as can conveniently in that Sea be allowed to a Fleet sailing together. And this allowance is so large, that Castro was eighty eight dayes (and that in the daies of better Navigation) in the way which we allow to sixtie nine. Now in the Ocean, where they might make better use of the Monson and Tides, as freed from the dangers which attend the Gulfe, wee will allow thirty two miles a day one with another (the Sabbaoths deducted) which by the yeeres end will bring us to our Port at Pegu, or some other the neerest to Cape

Negraes, where we may harbour our Fleete. For to Cape Negraes it selfe (deducting the one and forty Sabbaths remaining of the yeere) 7641. miles are proportioned in each daies equall saihng, in requisite and direct way, one and thirty miles and-gvr which being very far from any safe Port, must needs make it two thirty miles the day to bring us thither, allowing nothing for New Moone, or any other Jewish solemnitie, or other occa-sionall stay whatsoever: nor for those bords, gibes and fetching turnes (which Mariners, and specially coast-winders must make) and consequently much superfluous way, which alone (besides force of stormes) would make this thirty two to be above forty miles a day ordinary way, broken and whole, one with another.

And if this seeme to any man a small thing, let him Thirt- two consider the weakenesse of Navigation then, both in skill p and shipping: the Phaenicians before this time not l 'JJ acquainted with those Indian Seas, but onely with the g g y with Mediterranean, as probably may be thought; their using another: for the Care more then the saile, and not daring to saile by hatthatfrac-night when they could not see shoare, their necessary " Ji Jgyin occasions of stay sometimes for watering and provisions, going from sometimes by foule weather detained, sometimes for re- Cape'Negraes parations of some of the Fleet occasionally needing helpe, either to the that all the Fleet may keepe together, sometimes for trade 7, t s. tft by the way, sometimes for healthfull disport, recreation ' and joy: and (which is of principall observation in those Port. Seas) for expectation of the Monson, or season of the winde, which there keepes an even course, as out of the following Voyages you shall see. All which laid together, it will not seeme miserably and unjustly done to have allowed the proportion before mentioned. If you read t 2 c i-the first Discoveries on the coast of Africke by the 2 j ' g Portugals, and see how little they discovered in a whole age had passed Summer, when their skill was not inferiour to these before they Phaenicians, and experience more, you will thinke me f l ' ll g liberall if not prodigall in this allowance. Captaine Q p y q Hawkins in the Hector (a ship not the worst of saile, Hope. I 113 H and which before had beene twice at the Indies) was from the first of Aprill 1607. till August 24. 1608. ere he could arrive at the Barre of Surat, in the neerest part of the Indies, almost seventeene moneths space, where no Jewish Sabbath, nor shore-creeping enforced their stay. The Dragon at the same time was longer in her way to Sumatra, and I beleeve many of our later Voyages doe not much exceede this proportion. It seemeth therefore

Sum. total, to me probable in a round reckoning to allow but one yeere little more or lesse on the Voyage, a second in the stay at their severall ports, and in the mines of

Gold and Silver, and for further provisions of Almug trees, Ivory, Apes and Peacocks; and a third yeere in their returne.

D. Dees Doctor Dee allowes fiftie miles a day of requisite way, reckoning, j-j. jg 1200. miles every foure weekes, resting the Sabbath, and forty miles a day within the Gulfe or Red Sea: the miles he computeth 9155., and the whole Voyage to be performed in seven moneths and six and twenty dayes outward, and as much homeward; one fortnight of rest after their landing before they fell to their Mine-workes, to be spent in mind-workes of devout thankful-nesse, prayers and festivall rejoycing; as much before their shipping for returne, the rest in their workes and purveying of commodities. So that for what I allow a yeere, to each of these he alloweth the space of eight I. i. 42. moneths or there abouts: the third yeere he bestoweth on their businesse, rest, and triumph at home, care of their family and state preparations for the next returne, as trimming the ships (in these times the wormes which in those Seas breede in ships, and eate them, compell us to sheath them) and other provisions. He alloweth 4500. workemen for the mines, not all at once working, but in courses, some resting by turnes, others working, and then those succeeding to their workes whiles they againe rested (the workes and yeeldings whereof hee diligently examineth) three hundred for the Almug trees, for Elephants teeth twenty, for Apes and Peacockes ten: one hundred Officers: in all 5040. To this businesse he holdeth requisite fiftie tall ships, to each ship thirty Mariners, in all 1500. which with the former number make up 6540. men. Thus he and more then thus with much curiositie of minerall and navall learning, which cannot here be expressed without that libertie of long discourse, which neither the vulgar reader could understand, nor others perhaps (except some few) finde leisure to reade. Otherwise I would have inserted it.

I honour his great industry, but cannot conceive that that age yeelded such great ships to carrie so manie, nor that they could one day with another make so much way, nor that Salomon would permit so long a stay as a whole yeere, but rather presse new men. As for the Phaenician Mariners, upon this occasion it is likely that they setled their dwelling at or neere Ezion Geber, as all antiquitie mentioning Phaenicians in the Red Sea, seemeth to argue. And for the servants of Salomon, Salomons ser-they were the posteritie of the people that were left of qz ' l the Amorites, Hittites, Perizzites, Hivites, and Jebusites, Urlelites. which were not of the children of Israel. Their children i Reg. 9. 20. that were left after them in the land, whom the children 21. 22. of Israel also were not able utterly to destroy; upon those did Salomon levie a tribute of bond service unto this day. But of the children of Israel did Salomon make no bondmen. Thus the holy writ but a few verses before the mention of this Ophirian Navie. Of these it is said 2 Chro. 2. 17. And Salomon numbered all the strangers that were in the land of Israel after the numbring wherewith David his father had numbred them, and they were found an hundred and fiftie thousand and three thousand and six hundred. And hee set 70000. i eg. 5. 14. of them to be bearers of burthens, and 80000. to be hewers in the Mountaines, and 3600. overseers to set the people aworke. If Salomon would not ease them by courses neerer home (for they were the Israelites which served by those courses, not these strangers) I cannot here ease them; and if he would not employ the Israelites in the neerer quarries and Forrests, neither would he send them to remoter Mines, a more dangerous and difficult worke. Now some of those hewers in the Mountaines were fittest for this hewing and mining in the Mountains for Mettals, to which that place may also be intended and extended. Officers to Ophir and men of command he might have out of Israel, but for the Oare by Sea and Ore at land, these were likely to be the servants of Salomon mentioned in the text: the rather because that name ever after continued to them, as you may read even after the return from the captivitie in Ezra 2. 55. Nehem. 7. 60. This hath beene omitted by others handling this argument, and therefore I am the fuller in it. Viualpand. Besides, it is as likely (which others also observe, and

Pineda, tffr. before is mentioned, agreeth to the 666. talents of Gold yeerely) that Salomon after the Temple buildings were ended, emploied Fleetes yeerely to Ophir, one under another, that each should make their voiage in three yeers, but of them every yeere one should returne: which agrees not with D. Dees speculation of a yeers stay. Neither is it probable that in seven or eight moneths so much Gold and Silver could be gotten by so unexpert miners. Nor doth D. Dee consider the Monsons of those Seas which are by six moneths regulated, and not by eight. Nor may we thinke but that many of Salomons servants setled some abode in the Countrie, so long (at lest if we will permit courses, which I will not much quarrell amongst them) as Salomon used the voiage; by whom the Ivorie, Apes, and Peacockes might be procured, and Gems also without any speciall allowance of men each third yeere to that purpose; except as the Fleet in comming or going might touch by the way at each good mart, for which Doctor Dees time of eight moneths seemes also too short. Yet if any approve, and lust to follow him, I have no Empire First Mer- opinions.

divers Marts Ophirian voiage which brought the riches of the for Spices. East to Ezion Geber, occasioneth a quaere of the voiages of Spices, and the manifold shiftings of the Marts Ports thereof in former times, in a worke of voiages not unfit for consideration. The first mention of Merchants Gen. 37. 23. is of Ishmaelites and Midianites, which travelled in a Caravan together with Camels carrying spicerie, balme, and Mirrhe to Egypt. These inhabited not far from Ezion Geber, or the shoares of the red Sea. Whither their Spicerie came out of the Southerne parts of Arabia, or further out of India brought into some Arabian port, is not easie to determin. Their Balme they might have at Gilead by the way, though Arabia yeelds of that also, Jer. zi. I3 as the Myrrhe likewise; what Spicerie the first men- ' tioned is, is not so easie to decide. Jobs mentioning the gold of Ophir, and other passages in that Booke may cause conjecture of an Indian trade in his dales. Suidas. But this is easily gathered out of Histories that the great Monarchs endevoured to make themselves Lords of India for the riches aforesaid. Semiramis is said to have invaded India, to have beene repelled by Stauro-bates, which I can beleeve, though not so prodigal of faith as to accept the report of three Millions of foot, See Full. and five hundred thousand horse in her army; no more then that she was the founder of Babylon. But both Ninus or Ninive (which her husband Ninus had made the seate of the Assyrian Empire) standing upon Lycus which floweth into Tigris; and Babylon seat of the I- i- 43- Chaldasan Empire on Euphrates, Seleucia also Bagdet of later building not farre from thence, have in their times beene fitting seats to receive either by land or sea, or both, the Indian riches, thence to be dispersed to other Marts and thorow the world. The Persians were Lords of India, as both the Scripture Herodotus Este. 8. 9. affirme, Alexander advanced the Macedonian Empire thither also; whose Empire after his death being rent into foure parts, Seleucus possessed Babylonia, and Ptolemeus Egypt, which by the red Sea made most Egyptians. advantage of the Spicerie. jo, Antiq. I.

Sesostris (whom Josephus esteemeth to be Shishak, 8. c.

2 Chro. 12. the King of Egypt which tooke away great Strab. I. 16. part of these Ophirian treasures) is by Strabo reported the first which subdued Ethiopia and Troglodytica: at the straits of Dira (where the red Sea is but sixtie furlongs or seven miles and a halfe broad) left Monuments of his exploits, a pillar engraven with hiero-glyphikes: he passed thence into Arabia and thorow all Asia. His westerne expedition I omit (Lucan singeth, Venit ad occasum mundique extrema Sesostris) but it is like that being in the time of Salomon and his 2 Chro. 35. emulous enemie, that the glory of Salomons Ophirian ' ' arts had whetted him to this Asian and Indian expedi-Pl. I. 6. c. 29. tion. Pliny mentions the Tyrians in this coast, and the Diod. Sic. I. port Daneon whence Sesostris first of all thought to ' J- 3 bring a Navigable River to Delta of Nilus 62. miles.

9-; echo long after (hee which slew King Josias) is said to have sought to make a marriage betwixt the Red Sea and Nilus (the cause is evident, the Arabian, Ethiopian and Indian commerce to be joyned with the Mediterranean) and to have sent Phasne-cians from that Sea upon discoverie round about Africa; in which voiage they spent two yeeres. Cambyses conquered Egypt, and built Cambisu a Citie on the red Sea. Darius the Persian pursued Nechos project, thinking Some make to perfect a trench from the River to the Sea, but was Psammeticusa deterred by those which said that Sea was higher then lhis end" gyp ' therfore would drown it. Yet did this project outlive the Persian Empire in Egypt, for Ptolemie made a trench 100. foot broad and 30. deepe, 37. miles and 400. paces, as far as the Bitter fountaines, and then brake off fearing an inundation, the red Sea being found three cubits higher then the land of Egypt. Some (saith Plinie) say the feare was, lest Nilus should be corrupted by the Sea water. Yet by three waies did rsinee or they then passe to Arsinoe built by Ptolemasus Phila-r ' ' ' delphus. The Trench still continues, as Furerus a inf. 12, c German (which saw it in his way to Mount Sinai from Cairo) testifieth.

Coptus way was found by King Ptolomie, and the Egyptian Exchequer thereby so advanced, that that in Auletes time, a King nothing frugall, the prodigall Father of prodigious Cleopatra (Strabo cites it out of 5v7. . 17. an Oration of Cicero) the royal revenues came to 12500. talents, which is of English coine by M. Brerewoods reckoning, two millions, three hundreth forty three thousand seven hundreth fifty pounds. And if that he, saith Strabo, which carelesly and negligently administred his Kingdome had so much revenue, what may we thinke of the present Roman government, the Indian and Trogloditicall Merchandises being added."' For whereas afore scarsly 20. ships adventured out of the Straits, now very great fleets are set forth to India and Ethiopia; whence precious Merchandises are brought to Egypt and thence transported to other places, with the benefit of double custome for importation and exportation. But those precious wares have heavie imposts, because of the Monopolies, onely Alexandria receiving and dispersing them. Thus Strabo, who calleth Alex- Alexandria. andria efxiropelov meyiarov t oikovmevr the greatest Mart in the World. How gainfull this trade was, and what course they held in this voiage in Plinies time, you have heard out of him alreadie.

Alexandria being orewhelmed with a Saracen Deluge, See Leo y by Schismaticall Chaliphas beganne at last to hold up Sandys. head againe, and whiles the Mamalukes Empire lasted, was the chiefe Mart for the Spices brought to Mecca, and thence carried to Alexandria, the Trade whereof was in the Venetians hand, and enriched their Signiorie very much, till the Portugals in our Grandfathers dayes found the way by Sea into the Indies, whereby both the Moores and Venetians were impoverished. This See inf. I. 2. Trade set Henrie that Noble Prince of Portugall on f- i- 2. worke to begin that, which was so long before it produced any fruit. Yea, this Indian Trade set Columbus, and after him Cabot on worke to find the way to the Indies by the West; which their industrious simplicitie

God rewarded with a New World by them discovered. Rham. vol. I. But to returne to our Romans, Rhamusio cites out of fol- 371 the Roman Law, the Customes for the Indian goods set downe in the Reigne of Marcus and Commodus: viz. Cinamon, Pepper long, and white, Cloves, Costus, Cancamo, Spikenard, Cassia, Frankincense, Xilocassia, Myrrhe, Amomum, Ginger, Malabathrum, Ammoniake, Galbanum, Laser, Agolochum, Gumme Arabike, Carda-mome, Carpesium, Silkes, Parthian and Babylonian Workes, Ivorie, Ebonie, all sorts of precious Stones, Pearles, Sardonix, Ceravnia, Hiacinth, Emerald, Diamond, Saphire, Callimo, Berill, Cilindre, Indian and Sarmatian Clothes, c. which I have mentioned that we may see the Trade then, and now are much alike.

Strabo and Plinie (before this greatnesse of Alexandria, Dioscurias. as it may seeme) extoll Dioscurias in the bottome of pt' V' the Euxine or Blacke Sea, where people of seventie Languages, or as Timosthenes affirmed, three hundred severall Nations resorted; and after that the Romans used one hundred and thirtie Interpreters in their businesses. In Plinies time this Babylon was waste. I imagine that when the Persian Empire possessed India and Asia Minor, this Dioscurias was the Staple of Indian Commodities: brought partly by the Persian Gulfe as farre as Tigris would permit, the rest by land, which is no great way. Or, as some thinke, and I, 1. 44. not without cause, those Seas being so infested with Pirats, as appeares in Plinie, and the Arabs being alway Robbers; they carried their goods up the Indus (as many still doe from Tatta to Lahor) and thence by Caravan over the Candahar and other Hils, the River Oxus, and over the Caspian Sea to the River Cyrus, and so to Dioscurias.

When the Seleucidas succeeded in those parts, it is like that the Trade continued, though weaker, till the Romans drew all to Alexandria: especially the Parthian Empire not permitting such Commerce to their Roman Enemies, as neither the Persians after.

That Barbarous myst of so many Nations which overcame the Roman Empire, buried this Trade in darknesse, till the Saracens grew to some height, and Bagdet was made the chiefe Seate of their Caliph, builded on Tigris, and commodious to attract the Trade of the East, and disperse it to the West. A great part of this Trade after the declination of Bagdet, the East beeing infected Bagdet. with Mahumetan follies, honoured also with colour of Religion, was conveyed by the Arabian Moores, and Moorish Indians to Mecca (the sinke of that Superstition) Mecca. by the Red Sea, Judda, and Ziden being their Ports, and thence was much of it carried to Damasco, and thence to Aleppo, which Trade hath continued to our dayes; and another part to Cairo, hereby flourishing, and thence to Alexandria as aforesaid: which is still used also, but much empaired, and almost forsaken by the Europaean Navigations" into India. This caused

Whiles the Tartarian Empire flourished, these Indian ' ' " "

Wares were carried much (as you may reade in Polo) f S ' "l TV,.,. r- y 1-1 gals from the to Mangi or Lhma; to Cathay, many also carried to Moores the

Boghar in Bactria, and to Samarcand, and thence to Mamalukes, other parts. Also in those troublesome times when "' the Tartars had overrunne all, and when Boghar was ' l'"

f. J, Ti ivyri T Since from m esteeme tor trade, the Indian Merchandises were q.

shipped on the Caspian Sea by Oxus, and thence con- andtkedutch.

vayed to Astracan, on the River Rha, or Volga, and- Galvam so to Novogrode, and thence partly over-land, partly r i ' by water to Caffa, or Theodosia, where the Genowayes jstracan.

fetched it (who then were of great power in these parts) Novogrode.

and dispersed it in Christian Ports; the Venetians and Caffa.

Genowayes being Corrivals in this Trade, as in other things, and in those dayes very great. Much also passed to Trapezond, that Citie so flourishing that it became Trapezond.

an Empire, a Title too heavie for it, and the ruine both of Constantinople the Mother thus weakened, and of it selfe.

Ormuz was famous by this Trade, and Moha in the Ormus.

Red Sea, but both have their course to Aleppo; of o '-

London.

Lib. cap. ult.

Jnastas. Sinai tai lib. I 2. Hexam. Pined de reb. Salom.

Acosta de Nat. Novi orb. I. I. c. 13, 14.

which our Travellers shall in due time tell you in the following Discourses. And now we see London an Indian Mart, and Turkie it selfe from hence served with Pepper, and other Indian Commodities, as Master Mun Deputie of that Company in his following Tractate will shew you.

Thus much of the Ports made famous by Indian Spicerie and Merchandize. Anastasius Sinaita affirmeth, that Salomons Fleet made a returne every yeere, which of the same Fleet cannot bee understood. Pineda yeelds to this, but he makes us more labour about Tharsis, to which, now wee are returned from Ophir, he enforceth us to a new Voyage, and to finde Tharsis in Spaine. Josephus Acosta also hath made a scruple both of Ophir and Tharsis, and makes them to signifie no particular set place, but generall and remote, as India doth now with us signifie all the Easterne World in vulgar appellation. Yet doth he acknowledge the substance of that wee have spoken, and professeth to agree with Josephus, so that with him wee shall have but a Grammer quarrell. We will adde a word of the Phaenicians which here are expressed to have beene Solomons Mariners, and of their ancient Navigation, and so shall we make an end of our Ophirian Voyage, which to some Readers will perhaps seeme much longer then three yeeres.

Of Tharsis or Tharshish, whether it bee the same with Ophir, and both, some indefinite remoter Countrey; whether it be the Sea, or Tartessus, or any place in Spaine. Of the ancient Navigations about Africa, and of the Phsnician Antiquities.

Earned Acosta having alleaged Reasons sufficient Jcost. denat. for confuting that Opinion of Peru to be Ophir,- O– ' an upstart name, unknowne to the Natives; and " ' ' ' whence neither Ivorie nor such precious Gemmes could be brought, and whither Solomons Navie in those times ignorant of the Load-stone, could not come to fetch them; the Easterne India being fitter then the West for Solomons purposes: he concludeth, Ego sane Ophir

Tharsis in divinis Uteris saepius non certum aliquem definitumque locum sonare suspicor, sed generale potius esse vocabulum, idemque efficere apud Hebraeos, quod apud nos vulgo Indiarum vocem. He conceiveth, that as India is a name given to any remote, rich, and strange

Region very much differing from ours, as to Mexico, I. i 45.

Brasil, Malaca, c. So likewise Ophir and Tharsis; and as for Tharsis, it signifieth either the maine Sea, or most remote and strange Regions. Thus he con- jectureth.

For Ophir we have before found it, the proper name of a man and of a Region de-nominated of him; but withal have acknowledged the Ophirian voyage to comprehend more then the Region of Ophir, including the other Indian Ports wherat they touched and traded in that voyage, especially the two Hands now called Seilan and Sumatra, and all places on the Coast within the Gulfe of Bengala, which might fit their purpose. It is usuall now to call an Indian Voyage, not only to Iacatra. Bantam, or Banda, but thereto also they reckon their touching at Soldanha, on the maine of Afrike, or at the River of Saint

Augustine in the great Hand of St. Laurence, and the Hands of Comoro, or Socatra, or wheresoever they arrive on the Abash or Mohan shoare in the Red Sea, or in any Arabike Port, or in the Persian Gulfe before they come to India: and there also Surat, Diul, Calicut, or wheresoever they touch besides on this side or beyond that principal Port where they make their Voyage, as they terme it, that is, where they take in their chiefe ladings. Of which, the following Relations will give you many instances. So the Straits Voyages, intimate not the meere sayling to or thorow the Straits of Gibraltar, in vulgar appellation, but all Voyages within those Straits whether to Venice, or Ligorne, or Zant, or Constanstinople, or Scanderone, or Alexandria, or in one Voyage to visit many or all of these Ports, is yet called but a Straits Voyage. We may yeeld thus much therefore to Acosta, The bounds of that Ophir, was a proper Countrey (as India also is) Ophir. extending from Ganges to Menan, and betwixt the Lake

Chiamay, and the Gulfe or Sea of Bengala; but as it happened, that India being the remotest knowne Region, gave name in old times to all later Discoveries beyond it, and in after times accidentally to the New World, which the first finders mistooke for Easterne India; so also the Voyage to Ophir, accidentally might give name to all those Remote parts, and comprehend all the farre Ports, which by occasion of the Voyage to Ophir they visited, lying in the way thither, or somewhat wide or beyond. And as there is a Region truly and properly called India, even al that which extends from Indus (whence it is so named) to Ganges; which name by others ignorance of the proper names of Regions, was extended further both beyond Ganges, and to all remote Regions; so was there a true Ophir, named of Ophir the sonne of Joktan, which occasioned other remote Countreyes to beare that appellation, at least in this Voyage thither.

But for Tharsis or Tarshish, or Tharshish; we see Acosta himselfe in his finall upshot, to make an aut of it, Aut immensum mare, aut regiones semotissimas valde peregrinas accipl solere. So that his former Proposition admits now another, that either it is the maine Ocean (which I take to be the true sense) or some remote

Region. Some are of opinion that the Voyage to Ophir, Ribera, and that to Tharsis differed, because the Scripture saith, P da, iffc according to our Translation, For the King had at Sea a i. Reg.10.22.

Navie of Tharshish, with the Navie of Hiram once in 2. Ciron. 9.

three yeeres, came the Navie of Tharshish, bringing Gold.

and Silver, Ivorie, and Apes and Peacockes. j ip g f fg

Tremellius hath it. Nam classis Oceani pro rege cum Thanhhh' c.

classe Chirami erat: semel ternis annis veniebat classis ex every three

Oceano afferens aurum, c. The Vulgar, Latine and r res once.-.,,",., o,. came the ships

Septuagmt, Navis Tharsis erat regi balomom m man cum r rj.

navibus Chiram. shish.

Saint Jerome in many places examineth this Tharshish, as in Es. 2. Melius est Tharsis vel mare vel pelagus absolute ponere, and alledgeth Jonas his fleeing to Tharsis, who from Joppe could not come to India by Sea.

Most of the late Writers agree with Tremellius, that R'tbera in Tharsis is the Ocean; and make that a difl erence betwixt "- ' Tharshish and O"' Jam which signifies the Sea, as the Red g ' Sea, or Mediterranean, and withall those lesse collections Forerius in of waters as the Dead Sea, the Sea of Galilee, and that Es. 2. Brazen Vessell for the largenesse, called a Sea, 2 King. 25. j- " '" 16. whereas Tharshish is only the Maine or large Sea. j ' ' i R. Mose Hadarsan citeth foure significations, Tarsus a jrca. Leo Citie of Cilicia, Carthage, India, and the Sea. This place Jud. 3. cannot admit Tarsus nor Carthage, beeing in another Sea,. f, ' '. to which Esiongeber, on the Red Sea had not beene the 'zt Port to have sailed from, but Joppe or Tyrus, or some R. Mos. Had. other Haven in the Mediterranean. Now if any thinke in Ps. 71. them two Voyages from two severall Ports, the Scripture is plaine, where it is said, Jehoshaphat made ships of Tharshish to goe to Ophir for Gold; but they went not, for the ships were broken at Esiongeber. And lest any might thinke that they were called ships of Tharshish, because the materials came from Cilicia, it is more full, 2 Chron. 20. 35. And after this did Jehoshaphat King i.;?.22.4.8, of Judah, joyne himselfe with Ahaziah King of Israel, who did very wickedly. And he joyned himselfe with him to make ships to go to Tarshish, and they made the ships in Esiongeber. Then Eliezer prophesied, c. and the ships were broken that they could not goe to Tarshish. Note also that the vulgar translateth in one place Sea, in the other Tharsis, Post de Some hence gather it to be a Region in India, as that

Ori n. Rabbi, and Jerome also doth in some sort averre, with

Josephus, and many late Writers, But because no such Region in India can be found, hence so many opinions. Postellus placeth Ophir in the Golden Region where Malaca standeth, but makes Tharsis to extend further, even to the South Sea; or the Peruan Coast, so that Ophir and Peru are divorced for a marriage Chal. 2. with Tharsis. The Chaldee will have it Africa, and

Parap. Emanuel Saa in Angola; Acosta no certaine place; Rib'injon i Rit)era will have them two Voyages, and not the same I. i. 46. to Ophir and Tharsis; Pineda and Goropius bring us to Tartessus in Spaine. But I embrace the opinion of Cornelius Cornelii. Villalpandus (and heerein Ribera also agreeth) which say that of Tarshish the Sonne of Javan, Gen. 10. 4. Cilicia tooke name at first, still continued to Tarsus (where Saint Paul was borne, famous in old times by Straboes report for the Universitie and other Antiquities) and the Inhabitants therof, and the adjoyning Regions being famous at Sea, might cause that great Sea (as the Scrip- Jos. 15. 12. ture cals it, in comparison of the lesser Seas in Judaea) to be called Tarshish, a name then easily by the Jewes derived to all great Seas, whether Mediterranean or Ocean.

Now that which makes Interpreters to question some place in India, or elsewhere, is the phrase of going to and comming from Tarshish, and bringing goods from thence, a kind of speech which to Pineda seemeth ridiculous, if thereby be not meant some certaine place on Land. Wee see at this day the Hill Atlas in Afrike, hath given name to that huge huge Ocean, extending even to the New

Worlds of the South and West. The Straits betwixt Spaine and Afrike, give name with our Mariners to all the Midland Sea within and beyond them. Indus gave name to India, and all the Ocean adjoyning; and the South Sea (the greatest of knowne Seas) is so termed, because Vasques Balboa first saw it lying to the South from him; neither can the Westerne Scite, take away that name Del Sur to this day. Is it then any marvell, that Tarshish the Cilician Sea next adjoyning to Judaea, should give name to all the deeper and larger parts of the Mediterranean, which they had occasion after to take notice of, and to other Seas from the Red Sea forward more wide and spacious. Pineda himselfe confesseth, that Tartessus which hee would have to be Tharsis, gave name not only to Boetica, but to all Spaine. And is it any more ridiculous or absurd to say, the King had a Navie of Tharshish at Sea, then that which our vulgar Mariners say, the Straits fleet is now at Sea, or the Straits fleet is come from Sea, speaking of our Merchants ships, which keep company together in the Seas for feare of Algier Pirats? Do not they cal them Straits Merchandise? and say, that such such goods are brought out of the Straits, or caried to the Straits, that are sent thorow those Seas, and brought by those Seas to or from any Port therein? And as usuall a Phrase it is, which Pineda judgeth so absurde, that a Mariner being asked whither he goeth, should answere to Sea, or that Gold, Silver, Ivorie, Pea-cockes and Apes should be said to be brought from Sea: For our Mariners (which learne not their Idiome of Scholers) use to say, when all their money is spent, they will goe to Sea and get more; that they brought this or that from Sea, that shortly they are to goe to Sea, or have lately come from Sea, without naming any Port; that such a man hath got all his goods by Sea, great wealth hath come to him by Sea; hee hath had great losse by Sea, and other like phrases of Sea-men (for so also are they called, in opposition to Land-men, in regard of their Trade and course of life, though the habitation of both be

Jonas I.

H'Ieron. in Jon. I.

By some un-discreet and vain Cutters or Printers fiatterie, or ignorance insensible of divine mysteries, in the forefront of a great Booke, some tvords of this Psalme proper to on Land.) This then may be the sense: Salomon had at Sea a Navie at Tharshish, that is, ships built for long voyages at Sea: as we call men of Warre, or ships of Warre; which are built for that purpose. And how easie is the construction, Jehoshaphat made ships of Tharshish to goe to Ophir, in these words, a Sea-navie, or ship of the Sea, to goe to Ophir; that is, not such Fisher-boates, as they saw in the Sea of Galilee, or such small Barkes as they used in Palaestina to trade from Port to Port, but a Navie Royall of strong ships able to brooke long Voyages in the Ocean.

I also thinke that in regard of the length of those Voyages, in which they were two thirds of the time at Sea (after our account) and three whole yeeres in each Voyage from their Land-home, in a kind of eminence, they were in these Voyages said to goe to Tharshish or to Sea. And so Jonas likewise minding to flie from that Land whither he was sent, was hurried in the strength of temptation, a quite contrarie way, whether that ship intended Tarsus in Cilicia, or whithersoever it went, he chusing rather a certaintie of flight then of scite, or setling himselfe any where, as Saint Jerome saith of him, Non ad certum fugere cupiebat locum, sed mare ingrediens, quo-cunque pergere festinabat. Et magis hoc convenit fugitivo timido, non locum fugae otiose eligere, sed primam occasionem arripere navigandi. Likewise in that Psalme which mystically and fully is true of Christ in the calling of the Gentiles; typically and in part verified in Solomon (wickedly and Antichristianly since applied to the Pope in many passages of the last Councell oflateran under Julius the Second, and Leo the Tenth) it is said, The Kings of Tharshish and of the lies shall bring presents, the Kings of Sheba and Seba shall offer gifts; it is plaine by the Historic of Solomon in Scripture, and by joyning of Tharshish and Sheba together, that no Tartes-sus, nor Angola, nor Peru, are intended; and that Maritime Kings are meant (Tremellius reades Reges Oceani accolas) which ruled in Hands (which is also added) or

Coasts and Ports neere the Sea (sure as Hiram then Christ are was, and all remote Maritime Provinces the Scripture 'ffj fjj" f" 1 1 1 1 r L majesties pic- cals Hands) which used also (as m those parts or the. q

East Indies, almost all the Kings are at this day gentes servient Merchants) trade by Sea, and perhaps enjoyed the ei, c zvhich Title of the adjoyning Seas (as his Majestic is King f.;; j of the Bnttish Ocean, and another Pacihcus his Vx- Scripture decessor added it to his Royall Title, Ego Edgarus andhismajes-Anglorum Basileus, omniumque Regum, Insularum, tiefrom Oceanique Britanniam circumjacentis, cunctarumque ' J' " ' Nationum, quas infra eam includuntur, Imperator p Dominus. Such were the Kings of Tharshish, whose Customes from the Sea, and Trade by it, made them have their ships of Tharshish, wealth from Tharshish: as in later dayes, the Kings of Aden, Ormus and Malacca; and still of Fartaque, Socatra, Calicut, Cochin, Zeilan, Achen, and many others included in the circuit of our Ophirian Voyage are; and might therefore justly be called I. i- 47- Kings of Tharshish: from all which no doubt either in the course of this Ophirian Voyage and Trade, or otherwise sent by speciall Messengers, Solomon had presents, as in I. Reg. lo. 24. 25. is expressed.

Pineda himselfe citeth out of Straboes third Booke of the Gaditans (which is Tartessus, or with him Tharshish) plerique mare incolunt, pauci domi desident: and in this respect Tyrus may by the Prophet be called filia Thar-sis, daughter of the Sea, as seated in it, ruling on it, and living of it. The Chaldee Paraphrase hath the Kings of Tharsis, and the Hands of the great Ocean Sea; which may bee understood of the Indian Sea: and not as Goropius and Pineda would urge us, of Spaine. Pineda citeth Anastasius Sinaita, that Tharsis is Hes-peria Regionis Occidentalis; and Forerius Eugubinus to assist Goropius: whose authoritie shall so farre moove as their reason is weightie.

As for Goropius, his fifth, sixth and seventh Bookes of his Hispanica are principally spent on Tharshish the Sonne of Javan, which he writes Tarsccs, as signifying I 129 I in that which he makes the first of Languages (the Dutch tongue mother of ours) one that dares adventure the Seas, or one which tarries in the Seas: therefore also sirnamed Atlas or Atlant, quasi Hat-lant, or Hate-land, Him he makes with his brother EHsha the peoplers of Spaine, and saith, that of his skill in Astronomie and invention of the Sphere, he was fabled to beare the Heavens; and to have named his daughters with names of starres; to have sailed also to Ophir, so called as over the videst Sea, as Peru of a peere there built; and other like collections hee hath very wittie, learned and pleasant, not solid enough to convince, nor so contemptible as very easie to be confuted. Pineda hath written many sheets of paper to honour his Spanish home with Salomons Voyages for the Temples structure, wherein his error amoris and not amor erroris may plead his excuse, according to that of the Poet, Nescio qua natale solum dulcedine cunctos Ducit, imme-mores non sinit esse sui. I cannot but marvell, that two so learned men are so strongly carried by so weake reasons as the likenesse of words in Tharsis and Tar-tessus, when Geographers tell us of, and themselves confesse, Tarsus in Cihcia, Tarsis in Syria, Tarsius in Pannonia, and a River of that name in Troas, with I know not how many others; and besides, Tartessus being a Phaenicean Colonie might of Tharshish or the Ocean receive the name (whether we intend Gades or Cadiz thereby, or the whole Bcetike Province as seated in, or on the Sea or Coast, and living by Maritime Arts.

But of names of places wee have before spoken how casuall and accidentall they are. Even Tartarus the Strab. 1. 3. name of Hell is neere the former, Strabo ghesseth that Homer called it so of this Tartessus in the remotest West; which Hellish kindred of termes, me thinks, should not be very gratefull to Spanish eares. Etimo-logists may easily runne mad if they bee permitted libertie; neither is any argument sound from the sound of syllables without other credible Witnesses. Therefore Pineda addeth the frequent Circumnavigation of Africa in those dayes; of which he citeth one out of Herodotus, of the Phaenicians long after this sent by Neco, which makes against him; for Herodotus both doubted of it, as a matter seeming to him incredible, that they should saile beyond the Sunnes course, and therefore could not be frequent; for that Navigation would have Circumnavi-made both Tropikes familiar: he also saith in hunc f!!" modum Africa primum est agnita: if that were the first ' ' Voyage, Salomons were none, or at least his Title is false, De frequenti celebri a mari Arabico in His- Herod I. 4. paniam navigations

They wintered also by the way, and stayed the growing and ripening of Corne, which argueth no people, at lest no Trade in those parts. His next testimonie is of Setaspes, who having defloured the Daughter of Zopyrus should therefore have beene crucified, but by his mothers intreatie Xerxes pardoned him upon condition of this African Circumnavigation; which argueth the rarenesse of the attempt, as did the sequell also: for having sailed out of the Straits, and coasted some parts of Afrike, he returned (in despaire) and said he could saile no further, his ship beeing detained that it could not goe forwards. As for Darius sending to Indus, it is not to this purpose. The fragments of Spanish ships in the Arabike Gulfe is mentioned by Plinie, as a wonder in PUn. l. z. c. S'. Caius Caesars time; and that of Hanno agreeth not with the Historie which is extant of his Voyage, and more credible: and for Eudoxus fleeing the tyranny of Lathyrus, and comming to Gades by that Circumnavigation it was not for Trade, but at a dead lift, to save his life. Another is said by Antipater to have sailed from Spaine to Ethiopia, which might be to the neerest Blackes before he came to that which now is called Guinnee.

And these are all which are brought for that frequenti celebri navigatione, that of Neco and of

Eudoxusj and a Spanish wracke, being all that all Ages could yeeld unto Plinies time; and all also long after Salomon: and of these that of Eudoxus which is the

Strab. I. 2. most likely is farre otherwise told by Strabo, and at large refuted. As for the long tale of Semiramis out of Suidas, it was to India by the Indian Ocean (if it were at all) and not to Spaine. And out of Silius his Verse, Et celebre Oceano atque alternis aestibus Hispal, to gather the Baetike Navigations to India, round about Africa, or to Mexico Peru, argueth the Author to be Hispalensis; a Bastike wit, ravished with I know not what beatike fancies: as that also that Salomons

Psal. 72. raigning from Sea to Sea, must be from the Red Sea to the Gaditan, as if from Esion-geber to Joppe, were not from Sea to Sea.

From hence he turneth to the Phaenician Navigations, ri i 481 which to mention here is more to our purpose (they being Salomons Mariners to Ophir) then to his of Tartessus. Plinie and Mela applaud the Phenicians for invention of Letters, Astronomie, navau and militarie Sciences. Cains posteritie first in the old World, Chams in this, florished in Arts and humaine Sciences. Joshuahs conquest caused many of them, as Procopius and others affirme, to flee into remoter Regions, specially the Maritime parts of Africa. Commerce added Spaine, and whatsoever was fitting to that purpose of trade, Navigation and riches, especially to the Phenicians, both before and after Carthage. Their comming in and thorow Spaine is acknowledged by Varro also (in Uni-versam Hispaniam pervenisse) and they were the first discoverers of the Fortunate Ilands in Straboes opinion, and before Homers age held the best places in Africk and Spaine, tiu the Romans dispossessed them. Carthage in Africa is knowne a Phasnicean Colonie to schoole boies, and Plinie saith, that all the Bastike coast was of Phasnicean originall, or of the Paeni, which in authors are often confounded with the former, of whom they proceeded, and as Saint Jerom observeth, are called

Paeni quasi Phaeni, still in great part retaining that language; as is also the name Carthaginian, of whom Polybius testifieth that they possessed all Spaine, from the Strait to the Pyrenasan hils. But he that will view a Map of the Tyrian greatnesse and the auncient Phas-nicean Navigations, Traffiques and Discoveries, let him read the 27. of Ezekiel, with some good commentarie; and from the best evidence it shall appeare that all the best parts and Ports in Asia, Afrike and Europe were then familiar to this Daughter of Tharshish. The Baetike by Strabo are reputed the most learned of the Spaniards using Grammer, Poesie, Antiquities, and Lawes as they said 6000. yeeres old; which agreeth with their Phaenician originall. To hunt the Legends of Bacchus, Osiris, I here purpose not, as having little truth, and no mention at all of Spaine: nor is that more credible of the Pheniceans besieged by Nabuchodonosor, and relieved from their Phasnicean Colonies in Spaine, and his revenge upon them therefore invading the Spaniards. Aldrete a learned Spaniard rejects both, however Megastenes otherwhere found fabulous, may make somewhat for them.

Yet I beleeve their commerce and Phasnician originall, and great trafficke; their Mines also of Gold and Silver: but such as yeelded more to the Phasnicians and Carthaginians then all the New World hath hitherto to the Spaniard, or many yeeres after Goropius his hitherto, added by Pineda, Credat Jud us apella. Yea still Pineda brings testimonies to prove it no lesse rich in Mines; which makes me not a little marvell at their wisedome to be at such cost to fetch so farre off that which they have so plentifull at home; and that as the throate which swalloweth all the meate and nothing staies there (it would cause suffocation) so the Spaniards before Columbus his time were so poore and quiet accordingly; and that at that time there appeared so little monie or credit, that the Queene pawned her Jewels to borrow a small summe of 2000. Duckets, or litde more; and that since, Spaine hath (except soone after the returne of the Indian Fleete) so little coine stirring but base monies. Shall we thinke them miserable, miser-like, rich-poore, or is it that their Mines seeme wholly recollected in their mindes? they being, if you beleeve Pineda, a Nation opum tarn contemtrix quam lucratrix, ingenio acuto (hoc quorundam exterorum ineptissima invidia suspiciosum callidum vocat, saith he) ad magnas res nato (hoc sor-dida aliorum socordia superbiam tumorem.) I envie not their happinesse to them so much chanted by this Spaniard, I wish that they were so contented therewith, that they disturbed not the quiet of others; and that as they have their Navies of Tharshish yeerely bringing Gold and Silver (as for Apes and Peacockes they neede not goe so farre for them) so they would doe as Salomon, live in peace with their neighbours and build the Temple at home: which had they done, much of this our paper Navie of Tharshish had not beene, neither had their Gaditane Tartessus become a pray to Her Navie of Tarshish, who in her daies was filia Tarshish indeede, not Venus orta Mari, but Cui conjur ati venere ad classica venti, who defended her owne at home, by home invading, by hunting her enemies round about the World. Let us leave the Spaniards magnifying the present riches of their Mines, as that of Guadalcanal, one of the best in the world by the Kings Treasurer reported in a Letter to our Author, dated 1607. and another of Francisco Tesada his Sonne, so farre extolling the Spanish (hee names divers) beyond those of Potossi, that whereas a quintall (that is 1600. ounces) of Potosi Ore, or earth digged up, yeeldes but an ounce and halfe of pure Silver, most of the Spanish yeelde ten ounces of a quintall, some more to 15. 30. 60. Markes, each of eight ounces. It is fit in a long tractate, and as it were another Voyage to Ophir, to end with Mines: and fitter in Salomons Ophir to end with honorable mention of our Salomon, who without any Hirams helpe, sent her servants to Ophir and Peru too, and round about the universe to repaire that Temple, and to defend the Faith, which a greater then Salomon had by her in England restored from Babylonish captivitie: which the greatest powers on earth sought in vaine to hinder, she sailing further by her servants, raigning longer in her owne person, more glorious in her last daies, then Salomon, and leaving a peaceable Salomon to succeede her; yea to exceede, with addition of another Kingdome; (not a Rehoboam, to loose the greatest part of the former.) Him God defend to defend his faith long amongst us, with Salomons vertue and Ophirian magnificence. Amen.

Chap. II. I. i. 49-

Mans life a Pilgrimage. The Peregrinations of Christ, and the first Encompassing the habitable or then inhabited World by the holy Apostles and first planters of the Gospell.

Man by sinne becomne a Worldly Pilgrime; Christs Pilgrimage in the flesh to recover him: Mans spirituall Pilgrimage in and from the World.

OD which in the beginning had made the World, and endowed Man with the Naturall inheritance thereof, whom also hee made another, a living and little World, yea, a compendious Image of God the World together: did in the fulnesse of time send his owne Sonne Gal. 4. (by whom hee had made the World and Man) to be made a Man in the World, that he might make new and recreate the World and Man, now lost vanishing to perdition. Which salvation first accomplished in the infinit worth and worthinesse of his person and passion,

He committed to faithfull witnesses, giving them charge Marke i6. to go ' into all the world and preach the Gospel to every '5 creature, that by those Ministerial conduits (in the co- operation of his Spirit) his amiable and imitable Example might, as the loadstarre of Christians be proposed; his saving vertue as heavenly influence infused; his all-covering and al-curing merits imputed to his beleeving members by spirituall grace to prepare them to super-caelestiall Glory, whither Hee is before ascended as our Priest to make intercession, and as a King in humane flesh to take possession for Us, by him made Kings and Priests unto God.

Thus have we one Author of the World, of Man, of Peregrinations by men in and about the World. The first he made by his omnipotent Word, he commanded and in sixe dayes this huge Fabrike was both made and furnished. The second is vouchsafed greater indulgence, in preparation premised as of consultation, Let us make "Gen. 1.26. Man; in the worke doing"j as of a Master-peece, he y 2. 7. 22. formed, and builded; in the exemplar or prototype in our owne image, after our likenesse: in his bountifuu portion, the Sea and earth with all their appurtenances, subjected to his regall possession, the heavens with their reall influence and royall furniture to his wise un-erring contemplation.

Thus at first; but the first became last, by setting the last first, and preferring the Creature to the Creator, and therefore is justly turned out of Paradise to wander, a Pilgrime over the world: But therefore did his Creator (for medicines are of contraries) preferre this Creature to himselfe, by infinitenesse of humilitie to make satisfaction for his unspeakable pride; and hee which had before made Man after his image, makes himselfe after mans image, to recover that which was lost. Q (pixavopcoma! O amanda admiranda dignatio! propicious, unspeakeable, superadmirable bounty! The World he made that he might give it Man. Man he made such as might be capable of the world, and gave him now a double world, adding to the former greater, this lesser of Mans selfe.

And when both these were lost, by wilfull Treason and voluntary actuall rebellion, that he might forgive the

Traitor He gave the Prince, who to Himselfe forgave not the demerits of his servant; nor was content to regive the forfaited world of creatures, but added a world supercelestiall, where fallen regained Man might supply the roomes of fallen forlorne Angels: yea Hee restored Folly and lost Man to himselfe in a surer and nobler possession: '"' ' " f

Ctlvlb V lt 111 and for the complement of Bounty he gave to this lost Creature the Creators selfe: dedit se in meritum, dabit cretures taken se in prasmium. In this unity given God hath observed by a higher a Trinity of giving. Hee gave his Sonne unto us, doth 11 "' " give his Spirit into us, reserveth Himselfe for us to be craftlnesse! our exceeding great reward, our crown of glory who envying diadem of beautie in that glory where we " shall see him as man his Para-he is, and God shall be all in all unto us. Nor was j ' fj '" this a six daies worke, but he which made the world andgodtyea, and man in sixe daies, vouchsafed to be made Man, kft those indured to converse with sinners more then halfe sixtie Thrones and yeeres; and not with a word commanded this new Ppn ipaltties creation to be made, but the Word was commanded (and ' dixit" multa gessit mira petulit dura) God over Thrones to bee all blessed forever was made obedient' to the death, even bygodsmerde the death of the Crosse, and was made a curse for us, recovered and to redeeme us from the Curse, and to make us heires "' X? of blessednesse. they had made

This was indeede the greatest of all peregrinations, sinful, when the word was made flesh and (leaving in a sort y '- 5- i-his heavenly Country, and his Fathers house) dwelt f " ' 5-amongst us. The next remote peregrination was his g Qq. 15. ascension from the lower parts of the Earth (where also Ber. de his life was a certaine uncertaine pilgrimage, farre"" above h- Feo. all heavens, to leade captivitie captive, and give gifts to ' Men. And he gav6 some Apostles, and some Prophets, j-j j ' oj and some Evangelists, and some Pastors and Teachers, jo. i. By whom in the worke of the Ministery is effected a " Eph. i.,. double remote Peregrination; one in us, when we travel ' from our selves, that each man might say to his corrupt corrupting flesh (as that traveller to his quondam Mis-tresse", seeking after his returne to renew her dissolute acquaintance, and saying, when she saw him strange as if he knew her not, Ego sum? Tis I: At ego non sum ego, answered he, I am not I now) I travell in birth till Christ be formed in me, and, I live not but Christ lives in me, that I may deny my selfe and take up my crosse and follow him. The other is when wee put off our earthly tabernacle, and departing from this house of clay, whose foundation is in the dust, arrive in the faire havens of Heaven, in the quire of Angels and triumphant societie of the Heavenly first borne. And thus is Mans whole life a Pilgrimage, either from God as Cains, or from himselfe as Abels, and all the Saints which confessed themselves Pilgrims on the earth, and Heb. w. ig. to seeke another Country that is, a heavenly. Unto Ps. 39. 12. this spirituall and celestiall peregrination, was subordinated that bodily, of those first Evangelists unto all Nations thorow the World to plant the Church and settle it on ' Mat. z. her foundation, which also in their 'itimes was effected Mark. ib. ult. according to the Prophesie and precept of our Saviour, whose peregrinations, if wee had all the particulars, were alone sufficient to yeelde a large Volumne of Voyages.

Christ indeede vouchsafed, even in literall sense, to honour peregrinations in his owne person, whose blessed

Mother soone after his conception travelled from

Nazareth in Galilee, into the hill Countries of Judaea, to her cousin Elizabeth, and after her returne is by 'Luk. 2. Cassars Edict brought back that in"" an Inne at Bethlehem,

"Mat. 2. this Pilgrime might in a Pilgrimage bee borne, the Gov- ernour of his people Israel, that is of spirituall Pilgrimes.

And there from a remote place by Pilgrimes of the East is he visited; and how soone is his infancy forced to an Egyptian peregrination how restlesse and manifold were his after-peregrinations in Galilee, Samaria, the

Wildernesses and Cities of Judaea in the Coasts of Tyre

Mat. 9.35. and Sidon, in Decapolis by Sea, by Land, 'going about all the Cities and Villages, teaching and preaching, and healing every disease among the people, till the Heavens received him into a certaine rest. But my Pen is unworthy to follow his foot-prints.

How Apostles differed from Bishops: their preaching the Gospell to all Nations.

I Is Apostles as they differed from others in im- " Belkr-mediate vocation, to Evangelicall Ministery, and "-" l infallible revelation of the Evangelicall mysterie; touching the so in the unbounded limits of their Mission unto all Pope and the world: whereas other ordinary commissions and Bishops suc-callings are (though of God, yet) by Men; nor have "j' l"figf priviledge of unerring illumination; and must take heede yf y Tortip. to the severall flockes over which the holy Ghost hath"" set 248. and hozv them overseers: whence also Episcopall Churches are improperly called Cathedrall, and sees, from their sitting" or teaching fpP"

y 1 11 Called Otlt (that being the preachmg posture or the ancients both jp ig. z. Jewes and Christians) in their speciall places of charge, Acts zo. z'i.

Well therefore did Saint Gregorie" Bishop of Rome f f o evio-Ko-hold the title Oecumenicall incompetible to a Bishop, and " Uat. z. z. Antichristian: and as ill have his Successors in that See 5.1. Luk. swelled over all Episcopall bankes into Titles, and 4- 20. universalitie Apostolicall. J h '

The Apostles were not all in all places, and sometimes d i i,. as in consideration of divine blessing upon Pauls Minis- andirat. l. z. tery amongst the Gentiles, " as of Peters amongst the in principw. Jewes, they did especially employ themselves where '- ' 7-they saw their labours most fruitfuu, in which respect some setled their longer abode in certayne Cities, and some scarsly departed from Jerusalem, whiles others of them went forth and preached every where, and the Mar. 6. o. Gospell was in all the world (not vertually, but actually) 2CV. 1.6,23. and was fruitfull, and was preached unto every creature under Heaven, that is in Saint Matthewes phrase, to" all Mat. 28. Nations, or to all sorts of men. After which Embassage

Rom. II. 12.

Sulp. Sever.

Idem Bed. in Mat. 13. I. i. 51.

Bell. de Rom. Pont. I. 3.4. Lessus de An-tich. d. 8.

Rom. II. 12.

""Luk. 2. I.

dnoypap dai wacav TT i' 6ikovfj. evriv.

Acts 2. 5.

accomplished, the Temple as Christ had prophesied, and all the Legall Ceremonies, which dyed in the death of our Saviour, received a more solemne then honourable Funerall, by the revenging Romane; Divine Providence ordering that' The fall of the Jewes should bee the riches of the World, and the diminishing of them the riches of the Genetiles; and preventing the revolting of weaklings, which seeing those things to remaine, which the Prophets had built, and God had ordayned, might in a Judaizing retire, embrace the shadow for the bodie, and preferre the dazeling lustre of carnall shewes to the synceritie of faith and spirituall truth: Nimirum id Domino '' ordinante dispositum ut legis servitus (saith Sulpitius) a libertate fidei atque Ecclesis tolleretur.

And that this was accordingly in the Apostles daies effected, we have not onely generall testimonies of the Ancients, but the particular Regions and peoples mentioned and acknowledged elsewhere by that genera-tion, which in the question of Antichrist hence raise a demonstration, (no lesse still serves them, their Geese are all Swans) that he is not yet comne, because the Gospel is not yet preached thorow the World. Neither doe we seeke advantages of the word World, as it is used in opposition to the narrow limits of Judaea, where the Church in her nonage was impounded, and as it were swadled in that cradle of her Infancy (so you even now read the fall"" of the Jewes the riches of the World.) Nor in a Roman challenge, wherein Rome pretends her selfe Head of the World, in the stile of her quondam Emperours (succeeded and exceeded therein by her Moderne Prelate) one of which decreed in the Edict above intimated, That'' all the World should bee taxed; which World was no more then the Roman Empire, as since also the petty Councells Papall are called Oecu-menicall (even that of Trent) and the Church of Christ, in a strange Babylonian contradiction, Catholike-Roman: Nor yet in a figurative Hyperbole, as that seemes spoken of the Jewes at Jerusalem of every Nation under Heaven, which heard the Apostles in their severall Languages, uttering the great things of God. But their sound P went over all the Earth, and their words to Rom. lo. is. the ends of the World, is true of the heavenly Bodies, and these heavenly Messengers; Neither can any of the World bee shewed then inhabited, that is, no Nation of the World, whereof wee have not plaine History, or apparant probability, that the Gospel had there sounded before that generation of the Apostles passed. Whereof as wee have alleadged Divine both prophecie before, and testimonie after the fulfilling: so our Ecclesiasticall Authors are herein plentifull. Thus doth Saint Chry-sostome '' interprete that prophecie of our Saviour, CArys. in Matthew 24. to have beene fulfilled before the destruc- Mat. hom.-js. tion of Jerusalem, and proves it by the fore-alleadged places, Romans 10. 18, Colossians i. 6. and 23. So Theophilact"" after him. So Saint Hilarie' Cum ' Tkeoph. in universis fuerit cognitio Sacramenti coelestis invecta,- f+ tum Hierusalem occasus finis incumbent: Then q ' '' shall bee the end of Jerusalem, when the knowledge of the heavenly Mysterie hath beene carried to all men. So Tertullian, Beda, Euthimius, Lyranus, Tostatus, 'Temlde Jansenius, Barradius, and others cited by the Reverend '-". J" and learned Bishop Downam, to whom I referre the j)Q, jg' Reader. And how else had they executed their com- Antich. part. mission to all Nations, if this mission had not succeeded."' 2. ad Lessii. For if by succession of after Popes or Bishops; then ' '– f' " ought that gift of tongues to have continued or beene J restored, and that of immediate revelation, whereby the Hleron. Am-glory of the Worlds conversion might be Gods peculiar, bros. Theod. and not diminished by the arts (nor by the acts and Ignatius l c. labours alone) of Men." Ad quid enim necessariae p "' linguas gentium nisi ad conversionem gentium."' And x Qg g, Genebrard" accordingly affirmes that whiles the Apostles Chron. An. lived, in thirtie yeeres space at most, the Gospell (which 4+-hee calls the Faith of the Romans) was divulged thorow the World, even all the most remote Nations and barbarous. Hereof he citeth witnesses (besides the

Acts 8. I. y II. 19.

Acts 10. 13.

Gal. 2. 6, 7.

Acts 6.1. y I. Pet. 11. Jo. 7. 35. V'td. Jos. Seal. Annot hi Euseh. p. 124. y Can. Lag. pag. 278.

Sctf. cont. Serar. trib.

Acts 6. 9.

former) Clement Alexand. Justin Martyr, Irenaeus, Origen, Cyprian, and the Prophecie of Esay. c. 66.

. III.

The peregrination of Saint Peter.

E see the persecution which began against

Stephen proceeded to the dispersion of the

Disciples into the Regions of Judaea and

Samaria, and Phaenice, Cyprus, and Antioch (where they first heard the name Christians:) Peter also warned by vision, breakes the partition wall, and preacheth to

Cornelius and other Gentiles, unto whom soone after

Paul and Barnabas receive larger commission. Saint

Peter also (as Ecclesiasticall writers testifie) besides

Palestina, Syria, and the Regions adjoyning to Judaea, preached the Gospell in Antiochia, and after in Rome (in both which places they constitute and celebrate his Episcopall Chaire) in Pontus, Galatia, Cappadocia,

Asia, Bithynia, to whom is inscribed his former Epistle, that is, to the dispersion of the Jewes, in those Regions, he being principally the Apostle of'= the Circumcision.

For the Jewes were divided into three sorts, the

Hebrewes (which were the inhabitants of Palestina) and the scattered strangers, which were either Hellenists,

Siacnropd EXXriwjv, or Suxa-Tropd Ba uxwj o?, the remainders of the Babylonish deportation which still continued in those parts, when others returned, and from thence were occasionally dispersed afterwards. The Metropolis of these was Babylon, of the former Alexandria. Of this sort were the Italian, Egyptian and Grecian Jewes, which used the Greeke tongue in their Synagogues, in which also they read the Scriptures translated by the seventie two Interpreters: yea they were ignorant of the Hebrew, as Scaliger affirmes of Josephus and

Philo, two of their most learned: they had a Synagogue at Jerusalem, (called of the Alexandrians) of which were those Disputers against Stephen. Of the Baby-

Ionian dispersion were the Jewes in Asia, to whom Saint Peter wrote that Epistle from Babylon. And although Baroniuss and our Rhemists out of divers Baron, torn. Ancients labour to proove by Babylon in that place of J" p ' i, Peter, to bee ment Rome, that some Scripture might y; j ' ' testifie his beeing there at least (though little could Annot. onthose thence be inferred a 25. yeeres Episcopality, and lesse, words the Apostohke succession, and least of all an approbation H'- iji alu-of later novelties successively hatched in the last and teth'you.) worst ages (yea the current of the Jesuites argue (not Bellarm. de say onely) that Rome is the mysticall and Apocalypticall- P- era Babylon, and cry out upon us for unhonest partiality, p z that there acknowledge it, here in Peter disclaime it, not considering what a hooke they swallow with this baite: yet because that Epistle of Saint Peter' is ' See this delivered in litterall and not mysticall forme, like the Z rls ' ' Apocalyps, and because that opinion ot ir'eters hve and j ainold. Ch. twenty yeeres Bishopricke delivered by Eusebius, is 6. manifestly repugnant to the Scriptures; and because that some of the Romanists" themselves differ from ' Onuph in the received opinion as incredible, as ' Onuphrius and P '- "- 3-Genebrard, and Marianus Scotus also alleadgeth out V J '. of Methodius that Peter preached at Babylon, to which 2. Baby hee also addeth Corinth and almost all Italic, and hniam verba because the Ancients'" received that conceit of Papias, pr dicatioms a man of no great judgement, as appeared by the!, f J J; Millenary fancie derived from his tradition: though I Ec. Lz'. ca. will not meddle with that controversie, whether Peter were ever at Rome, or no, the negative whereof in whole bookes Velenus and Bernard have written, yet " Uricus I cannot beleeve but that he wrote that of and in the f' enus his Chaldaea Babylonia. The rather because that was the "Jifl-Fishei Metropolis of the Asian dispersion (as is said) that his answer, it wel agrees with the prime Apostle to execute his printed at Apostolicall mission to remote and many Nations, " erpe especially to the Circumcision (whose peculiar Apostle I q j he was) in all Countries where they were scattered, as appeares by his care of the Hellenists and Alexandria

"Nicep. Cal. Ec. hist. I. 2.

' Metaph. in 29. Jun.

' Onupi. ad Pla. in Vita Petri.

In Ckoropis-copos sive co-adjutores suos instituit. pere-grinatione deinde per iotamferi Eu-ropam sus-cepta.

'Hier. de script. Eccles. in verba., Clemens. Iren. I. t,. c.

Eus. Chron. y hist. I. 3. c. 19. ""Iren. ubi sup.

Rufin. pre-fat. recognit Clem, ad Gaudent.

' Epipha. hoer. 27- their Mother Citie, where he placed, as Authors affirme, Saint Marke the first Bishop; and because Ecclesiasticall writers affirme that he preached ubique fere terrarum, almost all the world over (so p Nicephorus) breviter in totius Asias Europae oris, omnibusque adeo qui in dispersione erant Judaeis Graecis c. ' Metaphrastes affirmeth that after the Church of Rome and many others set in order, Saint Peter went to Carthage in Africa. "" Onuphrius acknowledging his Roman See, yet will have him a Non resident (if not an Apostle rather) not to abide there, but findes him in that five and twenty yeeres space at Jerusalem, after that at Antioch, seven yeers together, whence he came to Rome and reformed that Church, constituted Linus and

Cletus his " Suffragans or Coadjutors; and travelling thence thorow the most part of Europe, at his returne to Rome, was there crucified.

Thus in a larger sense of the word Bishop, might Peter bee stiled Bishop of Rome, as having care to oversee that as a principall Church, not neglecting meane while his Apostleship, to which properly belonged the care of all Churches. And hence is that diff erent reckoning of the Roman Bishops, ' Hierom reckoning Peter the first, Linus second, Cletus the third, Clemens the fourth. But Irenaeus" nameth Linus the first Bishop, Cletus the second,: c. The like diff erence is in the See of Antioche twixt Hierom and Eusebius, the one beginning with Euodius, the other with Peter, which sheweth their opinion that Peter preached in both places as an Apostle, not as Bishop in proper sense. So Irenasus, the two Apostles (Peter and Paul) having founded the Roman Church, committed the Bishoply charge thereof to Linus: and Rufinus that Linus and Cletus were Bishops while Peter lived, that they might have the care of the Bishoply charge (Episcopatus curam) and he might doe Apostolatus Officium, the dutie of the Apostleship: Epiphanius, in Roma fuerunt primi Petrus Paulus Apostoli iidem ac

Episcopi, deinde Linus, c. Peter and Paul were both

Apostles and Bishops in Rome; and after other wordes of doubt touching Clemens his being Bishop in the times of Linus and Cletus, all of them living in the same times while Peter and Paul were Bishops, saith, propter a quod Apostoli saepe ad alias terras ablega- bantur propter Christi praedicationem, non potuit autem urbs Romae esse sine Episcopo. That the Apostles went often into other Countries to preach Christ, in So Damasus which meane while Rome could not bee without a in Pontif. saith

Bishop. For the Apostolicall function enjoyned an tf '! Pf r- r. t,- ' AJ dained Linus universall; the Episcopall, a particular charge. And Qlg as the greater Office includes the lesse, as the Office presentialiter of the Lord Chancellour, or Lord Cheefe Justice, or any omne minis-

Councellor of State, containeth the authority of a Justice J ' '- of peace in each shire, with larger extension and g hij rent.

intension of power, and a diocesan Bishop the Minis jnd Gene- teriall function in any pastorall charge in his Diocesse, brard. An. which the Parson or Curate must yeelde to him being fth of Linus 111 1 J. 3 y Lletus, eos present, and pleased to supply and execute: so, ana p.

more then so, the Apostolicall comprehends the Epis- episcopos sive copall com- mission, as lesse: and the Apostles were in coadjutores this respect Bishops whereso- ever they came, not by f "!"- ordmary constitution, but by a higher and extraordinary q function: to whom other Bishops are successours not ,, coepis-in the Apostleship strictly taken, but as Bishop to copus sub. Apostles, as Justices of peace in their limits to the Petroapostolo 1.1 r ' J r Ti- extenora higher Commissions either ordinary as ot Itinerant-

Justices, or extraordinarie by speciall commission on-, o. Cletus speciall occasions constituted, in part, not in all their coepiscopus authoritie. successit after

We shall launch into a Whirle-poole if we proceede. j 7 o of to declare Peters Successors (as some call the Bishops p pg ' of Rome) the Fathers themselves dis- agreeing in their Post Petrum, Catalogues. So farre off were they from making Papall imkum Petro, succession an essentiall either Note of the Church, or "Qll g ground and rule of Faith. But for their preaching the, f y- Gospell thorow the World, all Bishops are all Apostles eccles. I successours, these in their limited, those in an universall Commission; which either they performed, or not: if they did not, it was disobedience, as in Sauls expedition against Amalek: if they could not, it was impotence, and the command of preaching to all Nations, impleadeth defect in the Commander, who is the wisdome of God, and the power of God. His wisdome appeared also together with his power in giving them tongues, and not onely healthfuu constitution of body, but miraculous transportation and power, Natures defects not hindring the effects of Grace, as appeareth in the story of Philip and the Eunuch, Acts 8. of Pauls surviving a stoning, John the scalding in Oyle, and others other difficulties, mentioned in part, both in Divine and Ecclesiasticall History. Neither have Miracles and tongues necessary to such a conversion, ever since happened, nor have we promise that they ever shall. Nor was it ever meeter that the New King should be proclaimed, then when having led captivitie captive, he ascended on high, and tooke possession of his supercaelestiall throne: the Apostles herein doing that, for the heavenly Salomon with spirituall magnificence, which Nathan, Zadock and others had done for the typicall Salomon, by Davids appointment. The universall Ceremonies being the same in the whole Church, and such as no generall Councell could determine, argue the unitie of the spirit in the Apostolicall preaching, Thus as we have partly shewed in all, and particularly shewed in Peter for his part, we will declare of the rest.

Of Saint Andrew, John, the two Jacobi, Philip, and Simon Zelotes.

Dorat.

Synops.

Ap, Huron.

Catol scrip.

Eccl.

Ndrew the brother of Saint Peter, as Dorotheus and Sophronius testifie preached to the Scythians, Sogdians, and Sacae, and to the inner or Savage Ethiopians; was buried at Patrae in Achaia, being crucified by TEgcclS Governour of the Edesens. Nicephorus "writeth that he travelled into Cappadocia, "Nk. hist. Ec. Galatia, and Bithynia, and thence to the Countrey of- ' 39-the Anthropophagi, or Man-eaters, and to the Wildernesses of the Scythians, to both the Euxine Seas, and to the Southerne and Northerne Coasts, as also to Byzantium now called Constantinople, where hee ordained Stachys Bishop: after which, hee went thorow Thrace, Macedonia, Thessalia, and Achaia. That hee was sent to the Scythians, Baronius prooveth out of Origen, ' and Orig. inge.

Eusebius; and out of Nazianzene " his descent into i- r J T7 Euseb. hist. I.

(jrascia and ilpirus.

"Greg. Naz.

SAint John his banishment into Pathmos, and Epistles Orat. in to the seven Churches of Asia (which Tertuuian ' cals f'" "-

Joannis alumnas Ecclesias) are extant in his owne Writ cont Man ings. Irenaeus and many other mention his labours iren. l. x. cx.

at Ephesus, Prochorus, (his supposed Disciple) hath Prochor. in written a Historie of his Asian Peregrination, his actions f""'– ' "- at Ephesus, his passions at Rome, whither hee was sent, " ' ' and in other places, but his authoritie is no better then of a Counterfeit, as Baronius 'hath also branded him, 'Baron, to. i. Of this nature we find many counterfeit Gospels and ' Journals, or Histories of the Apostles acts, censured by the Ancients, the Devill then labouring to sowe his tares in the Apostolicall Historie, which in after Ages, Antiquitie might countenance with venerable authoritie. Metaphrastes relateth his acts in Phrygia Metaph. in and Hierapolis: That he preached in other Regions. eptem.

of the East, Baronus 'affirmeth, especially to the Relat. exep.

Parthians, to whome his first Epistle was inscribed in Jesuit, an.

ancient Copies: that hee converted the Bassorae, is still 555 holden by Tradition amongst them.

J Ames the brother of John was put to death by Herod to please the Jewes, ""a wicked Generation not pleas- " Act. 12. ing God, and contrary to all men. It is reported of some, that before his death he travelled as farre as

Spaine, and there preached the Gospel, at least to the " Bar. Mart, dispersed Jewes, Baronius in his Martyrologe "produceth Jul. 25. Booke of suspected faith attributed to Isidore, testi- fying his preaching to the Nations of Spaine, and of the Westerne Regions; and the Breviarie of Toledo, in which are these Verses, Regens Joannes dextra solus Asiam, Et laeva frater positus Hispaniam, c. the testimonies also of Beda, Turpinus and others. All the " Annal. to. i. Churches in Spaine, hee saith, hold the same opinion. an. 44. Yet is he uncertaine, and so leaves his Reader, because of that untimely timelinesse of his death. It is not likely that the Apostleship and office of preaching to all Nations, and the name of the Sonne of Thunder was given to him by Him, which as easily infuseth. the vertue as imposeth the name, and foreknew the tribtibusln imes and seasons of his life and death, but that the dispersione sequell was answerable.

constituth. His hastie death argues his forward courage, as of catalog. j jj which stood in the forefront of the battle. That ?? r5. ojo- preached to the dispersed tribes Phath many authors: the. bynopsts.,.,,. i ir t l o-

Mermannii that his bodie was brought rrom Jerusalem to bpame, tkeatrum, l c. the Romane Martyrologe, and the Popes Callistus and

"Euseb. hist. Innocentius are cited bv Baronius. l.2. c. nd.

n Abd. l."d. 'T He other James called Alphaei and Oblias, and ' Hier. de- JL Justus, and the brother of our Lord (either because script. Eccles. g s the sonne of Joseph by a former wife, according 1. 1. 54. Eusebius,"! or because his Mother was sister to the . 20. c. 8 Blessed Virgin, as Saint Jerome' rather thinketh) was ' Talmud. a man famous for Sanctitie and Devotion amongst the Bab. de Idol. Jewes by the testimonie of Josephus, which imputeth ' k-'hi h" " to his cruell and unjust murther, the terrible desolation which soone after befell that Nation. And the Talmud

Sohieroni. both of 'Jerusalem and Babylon, mention him as a but Euseb. I. worker of Miracles in the Name of Jesus. 2. c. 12. hath Hegesippus a man neere the Apostles times, saith TJteris'jpos- " Suscepit Ecclesiam Hierosolymae post Apostolos tohs. frater Domini Jacobus cognomento Justus Sec. Of which wordes this seemes the sense, That whereas the Apostles by common consent in a just Aristocratic had governed the Church of Christ, residing at Jerusalem, untill the time of their dispersion to divers parts of the World, (which as Eusebius" citeth out of Apouonius, "Euseb. hist. was the twelfth yeere after Christs Passion) they then ' 5–i7-betaking them to their severall Provinces, jointly agreed to leave James the Just at Jerusalem for the regiment of the Church both there, and as from other places of the World occasions were offered thorow the Universe. For as Jerusalem was farre" the famousest of "" Phi.. c the Cities of the East, not of Judaea alone, in other i- ongedariss. respects, as Plinie hath honoured it; so in Religion, " f ' ' ' it was by better testimonie called the Holy Citie, and mo g the Citie of the great King, whose Tabernacle was in ymat. Salem and his dwelling in Sion; not in the time of Ps.76. the Law, but of the Gospel also; the Law of the Lord went out of Sion, as Esay had prophesied, and " . 2. 3. the Word of the Lord from Jerusalem. This was the Staple of Christian Merchandize, Emporium" fidei Cl. Espenc. Christians (saith Espencasus) the Mart and Mother '"- ' "- + of the Christian Faith, which therefore alway needed some grave Father to be the principall Factor in her Holy affaires: Hierusalem was before her destruction, the Center of Christianitie, whence all the lines of Apos-tolicall Missions were diffused and thither againe reduced; the Ocean, whence all the Ecclesiasticke" streames of " Ec. i. 7. the Evangelicall waters of life issued, and whither they againe returned; Once it was the Senate-house of Christian Councels and Counsailes for all Provinces of Christianitie, the confluence of others, but specially of the Jewish dispersions, which from all Countries comming to the Legal Feasts, might there freight themselves home with Festivall wares of Evangelicall commodities. Necessarie it was therefore that some Apostolicall Senator and principall Apostle should there reside, with whom in all difficulties to consult, not so much as Bishop (in proper sense) of that Citie, as of the Jewes, yea and as opportunitie served, of other

Nations thorow the whole World. This was that James which wrote the Epistle bearing his name, whom Paul

Gal. I. 19. mentioneth to the Galatians', and the Acts often,

Jet. 15. especially in the fifteenth Chapter, where you see him

The other president of the first Councell (if not the only in strictest general Loun r r a i r u eels were sense termed (jenerall) or the Apostles, arter their rather of the Provinciall dispersions assembled at Jerusalem. For in Roman, then his sentence the Councell concludes; and if the Apostles the untversall Fathers concurre) had committed to him being bledb Roman " Apostle, the government of Jerusalem, to whom Emperors might the Presidentship of Councels in that place apper-o b taine, rather then to this Apostolicall Bishop and Bishoply

Apostle, to whom the Lord first committed his throne Ep. har.". on earth, as Epiphanius testifieth.? As a Deputie or As the Pre- President resides in one Citie, though his government sidentoftorke j g j q. there confined, but extends to the whole Kingdome Province "the Region, so was it with this Apostles Bishoprike at Fice-roy of Jerusalem, from that high Pinacle to oversee and provide Goa for all the for the affaires of the Catholike and Universall Church. Indies ISc. From that high pinacle (in another sense also) was he cast downe, stoned, and at last with a Fullers Club brained by the Jewes, which were soone in a terrible desolation called to accounts for this and other Apostolicall and Propheticall bloud, yea of the high Prophet and Apostle of our salvation, which yet the Jewes attributed to this Martyrdome of James, as lately and neerely preceding. His Successour was Simeon his brother, in that See of Jerusalem, not Simon called the Cananite, Bar. p. Tfiz,. one of the twelve, as Baronius " hath also observed. to. I

SAint Philip is recorded to have preached in Asia Superior, and (as the Romane Martyrologe saith) J '- ' almost all Scythia. Baronius" supposeth the testimonie

Mart r. Isidore, and the Toletan Breviarie, that Philip converted the Galls, is falsly written for Galatians, which yet, if Nieeph.1.2. Nicephorus Relations'be true, needs no such correction. 8 T o " Simon was called Cananite, as Nicephorus saith, for his birth at Cana, whose marriage was there celebrated when Christ turned water into Wine, and for the fervour of his Zeale, hee was sirnamed Zelotes. His preaching peregrinations he relateth thorow Egypt, Cyrene, Africa, Mauritania, and all Libya even to the Westerne Ocean, yea, to our Britaine Hands. Hee preached last in Phrygia, and at Hierapolis was crucified.

Of Saint Thomas, Bartholomew, Matthew, Jude, Matthias: and of counterfeit Writings in the Apostles names.

Aint Thomas called Didymus, preached to the Parthians, as' Origen, and after him "Eusebius ""Origen. in have written: Gregorie Nazianzene addeth the Get.. iffc.

Indians: Chrysostome saith, he whited the blacke Ethio- " " '- ' 3-plans, Theodoref reciteth the Parthians, Persians, Medes, o' y. kom. Brachmans, Indians and the adjoyning Nations: Nice- ad Arian. phorus'hath the same, and addes the Hand Taprobane, ""Chrys. kom. which is now called (in the opinion of the most) Samotra:- l' f 'j in Hieroms Catalogue is added out of Sophronius, the (p ' q Germanes (of India) Hircans and Bactrians, and his death "A'V. . 2. c. at Calamina. On the Coast of Choromandel, where the 4-River Ganges is swallowed of the Sea called the Gulfe of Bengala, are divers Christians from old times called S. Thomas Christians. Some of the Jesuits have added China also to the labors of S. Thomas. Of these Christians, both in Narsinga, and Cranganor on that Sea where Indus falleth, and in divers parts of the Indies you may read in Osorius'Maffaeus and others. His Osor. dereb. Feast day is celebrated at Malipur, (so they now call vz, jr ',-the Citie where he lyes buried) not by the Christians i j alone, but the Ethnikes also of those parts. The Eunuch of Candace"" converted by Saint Philip, is amongst the "Acls. Ethiopians in Prester Johns Countries honoured for Plantation of the Gospel in those parts of Africa; but Dor, Synops. by Dorotheus " said to have preached in all the Erythrean injine.

PURCHAS HIS PILGRIMES

Coast, and the Hand Taprobana, before ascribed to Saint Thomas, and in Arabia Foelix.

Chrp. horn. OAint Bartholomew (saith Chrysostome y) passed into de 12. Apost. O Armenia Major, and instructed the Lycaones; Sophro- f" "" nius' addes the Albani- ans, and the Indians termed For-

Hier'on de tunate; Origen saith the hither India; Socrates, India script. Ec. next to Ethiopia, Eusebius testifieth, that Pantaenus a oc. l. I. e. Stoike Philosopher and Rector of the Schoole or Uni- 5; versitie at Alexandria, was ordained Preacher of the

Q 5- Qospel to the Easterne Nations, and pierced to the

Regions of the Indians. For there were at that time

"In the time many "= zealous imitators of the Apostles: of whom was f " rehus i-g Pantaenus, which preached to the Indians, amongst whom he is reported to have found the Gospel of S.

Matthew, in the hands of some Christians, which" had received the faith by S. Bartholomew, and left them the said Gospel in Hebrew, reserved till that time. Nice-

Nic. l. z. c. phorus' adjoyneth S. Bartholomew, to S. Philip in his 39 Plantations of the Gospel in Syria and Asia Superior, and after at Hierapolis, where he was crucified with

Philip, but delivered, and yet againe at Urbanopolis in

Cilicia, died that ignominious death and glorious Martyr-

Hier. ubi dome. This Hebrew Gospel of Saint Matthew, Saint

P Hierome, both saw and copied out. It was reserved in the Library of Caesarea.

SAint Matthew travelled into Ethiopia, that namely which adhereth to India, as Socrates writeth. Nice-g";. phorus addeth the Anthropophagi, and tels I know not what Legends, rejected also by Baronius. For such was the indulgent providence of God, not to burthen the faith of the Church with voluminous Histories of Apostolicall Acts thorow the whole World, which scarsly (as Saint Johnzi. John hath of our Lord) the whole World could have contained. Unto the faith of all, not to the curiositie of some, was written enough by those holy Penmen, the Secretaries of the Holy Ghost in holy Scripture. But the Devill impiously provident, hence tooke occasion to Counterfeits burthen the Church with so many unworthy Legends, '"

both presently after their times forged in their names, and since by Upstarts devised and obtruded on the

Credulous world, as Lives, (lies) of the Saints, Histories, yea, Misse-stories, Hisse-stories, by the old Serpent hissed and buzzed amongst superstitious men (missing worthily the right, and deceived with lyes, because they had not received the love of the truth; to make way to the succeeding mysterie of Iniquitie; out of which Babylonian Mint, wee have lately that babbling and fabling Abdias, by Lazius his Midwifery borne after so many Ages, an Abortive indeed, or Changeling, as the wiser' of themselves confesse. Hee can tell you 'Baron. Isc insteed of Saint Matthewes life, many Ethiopian Fables, and intertayne you in a (Fooles) Paradise situate above the highest Mountains, with such delicacies, as shew that

Adams children are still in love with the forbidden fruit, and will lose, or at least adventure the true Paradise to find a false. Inopes nos copia fecit. Their abundant labours and travels which Came, Saw, Overcame, each so large portions of the World, left them no leisure to write

Annales (whence some have found leisure to write Aniles, olde wives Tales) and makes the conversion of the World an object of our faith, rather in beleeving the prediction and testimony thereof in the Scripture, then of humane credit, where the Apostles and Martyrs of their golden

Actions and Passions, have found such Leaden Legends V'wes and and woodden workmen. Makers or Poets, rather then f."- ""'; Tx-' 1-11 1 1 Tj platne no lesse

Historians: which here once spoken may bee applied to fj. gj the rest, of whose great workes so little is recorded. d. Harding,

Saint Augustine' complaines of such Apocrypha Scrip I3c.

tures amongst the Manichees, a nescio quibus sutoribus 'J ' fabularum sub Apostolorum nomine Scriptas: and re. 'j J 'j fuseth the like testimonies of John and Andrew produced j,-. yg.

by the Marcionites. S. Hierom " nameth five Apocrypha I. i. 56.

Bookes falsly attributed to Peter; his Acts, his Gospel, '" "'- his Praedication, his Apocalipse, his Judgement. Some " '

"Cm. Alex, also mention" Itinerarium Petri, which perhaps is the same trom. I. 6. i Clements Recognitions, another counterfeit. In Pauls name was published a Gospel, Apocalypse, his Revelations, his Ascent to Heaven (which the Gnostiks "Epiph. hcer. used, as saith Epiphanius) his Acts, third Epistles to the Corinthians, and to the Thessalonians, and one to the

Baron an 4.4. Laodiceans. John is made a Father of other Revelations, to. I, and of the Virgins Departure. Saint Andrewes Gospel,

Saint Thomas his Gospel and Apocalypse. Saint Bartholomews Gospel, Saint Matthews Booke of Christs Infancy, received by the Valentinians, are condemned Gel. in by pqelasius. Neither did Matthias, Philip, and Thad-decret. de lib. Jgeus want their Gospels, hereticall births injuriously laid ' ' at their doores: nor Barnabas also, nor Marke, no nor

Judas, the Traitor, which the Caians acknowledged, as Theodoret and Epiphanius have written, lettice sutable to such polluted lips. Wee might adde the Acts (so inscribed) of Andrew, of Thomas, of Philip, of Paul and Thecla Johns Circuit. Yea the Colledge Apostolicall was made to father like Bastards, as the Doctrine of the Apostles, the Lots of the Apostles, the Praise of the Apostles, besides other Acts of the Aposdes, and the manglings of the truly Apostolicall Pages by Addition, or Subtraction. What shall I say Our Blessed Lord escaped not hereticall Impostures in his Name, as the Booke De magia ad Petrum Paulum. And I thinke him rather prodigall then liberall, or just of his faith which subscribes " Euseh. I. I. to that story' of Abagarus. But it were endlesse no- 3 lesse then needlesse, to intangle our selves in this dia- bolicall Maze and hereticall labyrinth of sacred forgeries, in that and after Ages, the Envious mans super seminations to bewitch unstable soules, not contented with Gods dimensum and provident allowance. If therefore of Saint Matth. 13. Matthewes Ethiopian peregrinations, if of Saint Matthias in-Ethiopia also (for a great part of Asia, and the greatest Sophron. if of Africa were stiled by that name) if of Judas Thaddeus f. 4.0 preaching in Mesopotamia, Arabia, Idumaea, and the

Regions adjacent, we have so little recorded, it is no great marvell. It may be sufficient to understanding Readers, that wee have out of the best Authors extant, named the most Countries of the then knowne world. And if every Region and People bee not mentioned, impute it to the want of History of their several! Acts, who sought rather to write Christs Passions in the hearts, then their owne Actions in the bookes, of Men; to produce deeds not wordes, and monuments of Divine, not their owne glory. Few places can be named in Asia or Africa, which wee have not mentioned in their peregination and preaching: and faire probabilitie is for those not mentioned by consequence of reason, which at lest can prove nothing to the contrary; and more then probability is the Divine testimony before observed.

Of Saint Paul: of Apostolicall Assistants: some doubts discussed.

S for Saint Paul, the Doctor of the Gentiles, he flew like a swift Fowle over the World: wee have his owne testimony of his Preaching in Arabia, his returne to Damascus, and journey after"" three ""Gal. i. yeers to Jerusalem, thence to the Regions of Syria and Cilicia; yea that hee (not sprinkled, but) filled Jerusalem to Illyricum with the Gospel; of his preaching in Italy and Rome, of his purpose for Spaine, which some say 'Mermannii hee fulfilled afterwards, adding thereto Portugall, France, Theat. Con-Britaine, the Orchades, the Hands and Regions adjoyning ' " ' S " ' to the Sea, and his returne by Germany into Italy, " where Bed. Aug. hee suffered Martyrdome, being by Nero beheaded. I Sa-ip(. Ntceph. force no mans credit, as neither to that of Joseph of ' ' ' Arimathea his preaching to the Britons, nor Saint Denis his Conversion of the Galles, at least in all things written of them. But for the Acts of Paul, as the Apostle of the Gentiles, the Scripture is more ample then of any the rest, the greater parts of Saint Lukes History, being of Pauls Acts.

What should wee adde the labours of Evangelists, Assistants, and Co-workemen with the Apostles in those first Plantations, sent by them in several missions to Vid. dehis divers places? Such were Barnabas' Silas, Philip the Synol Mer– O"' Silvaiius, Timothee, Titus, and others: some of man. Baron, which were after Bishops (as is anciently beleeved) of yc. particular Churches. Epaenetus Saint Sauls disciple is said to have beene Bishop of Carthage. Andronicus another of them in Pannonia, now called Hungary, Amplyas at Odyssa, Urbanus in Macedonia, Jason at Tarsus, Trophimus at Aries, Crescens at Vienna, Aristo-bulus in Britaine, Asyncritus in Hyrcania, Hermes in Dalmatia, and others in other places; a Catalogue of whom in Mermannius his Theatre you may see at leasure. Saint Marke disciple of Saint Peter having preached to Libya, Marmarica, Ammonica, Pentapolis, and Egypt ordained Bishops in the new planted Churches, Eutro-pius another of Saint Peters disciples, is said to have preached in France: Mansuetus another of them, to some parts of Germany, as Symon of Cyrene, to other parts. But it were too tedious, to bring hither all that Authors have written of the seventy disciples, and other Apostolicall Assistants, who spent and were spent, consumed and consummated their course in and for the Gospel. 1.1. 57. But here some may say, that wee have not named all

Countries of the World, and of those named there is in Authors much varietie of report, in judicious Readers much scruple to credit. I answere that it were a farre harder taske to prove that any Countrey, not here mentioned, was neglected in this Ministry. Neither did the Geography of those times extend their survey much further, then that wee have here in their Journalls expressed: although it much extended it selfe beyond the truth. Besides, who can wonder that the Apostles found not Pen-men, to record their Evangelicall conquests thorow the World, seeking to establish a Kingdome Spirituall and Internall, contemning the worlds glory, and of vaine-glorious worldlings contemned, when the great Conquerours, which sought to subdue the World by force, and plant Empires by Armes, have left so obscure notice of their exploits, though dedicated to humane applause and admiration? Of the Egyptian Conqueror Sesostris, Lucan sings, Venit ad occasum mundique extrema Sosostris, Et Pharios currus regum servicibus egit! Of Nabucho-donosor the Scripture witnesseth, that his greatnesse Dan. 22. reached to Heaven, and his Dominion to the end of the Earth; Yet have they neither Journalls nor Annalls of their great Acts left to posterity, not so much as the names of their subdued Provinces, not so much as wee have here produced of the Apostles. Nay, what is left to memory of the long-lived Assyrian Monarchy, but shadowes, glimpses, fables? Who hath left in Register the names of the one hundred twenty seven Provinces, Ester 8. 9. subject to the Persian Monarchy from India to Ethiopia? Nay, how little and how uncertaine is remaining of the Greeke Alexander his Expedition, although then undertaken, when Greece had arrived at the height of humane learning, and by him that was himselfe a famous Scholler of the most famous of Philosophers? Did not hee deplore his owne unhappinesse in this kind, Ck. pro treading on the Tombe of Achilles? And had not " P'-Curtius and Arrianus long long after his death, written of him (I question not the certainty) how little should wee have of Great Alexander? Great in his Acts and Arts, greater in his Attempts, greatest in the unbounded Ambition of Greatest Renoume to latest posterity; yet how much more is left of the Acts of Humble Apostles, then of Ambitious Alexander? And now his Conquests are obliterated and I. i. 58. forgotten, how are theirs written not in Bookes and Lines, but in the minds and lives of Men, so great a part of the World still remaining the Volume of their Expeditions in their Christian profession?

And how much more did so, till the unbeleefe and unthankfulnesse of wicked men, provoked Divine Justice to remove his golden Candlestick from so many Nations thorow the World, which for contempt of Christian Truth, were againe abandoned to Ethnicke superstitions? Thus had God dealt with the Jewes before; thus after with the Christians in Africa almost generally in a great part of Europe, and in a great great part of Asia by Mahumetan madnesse, in which what that Arabian Canker-worme had left, the Tartarian Caterpiller did almost utterly devoure. Thus in Marco Polo, in Rubruquius, in Odoricus and Mandivile, yee may read of Christian Nations dispersed quite thorow Asia 1200. yeeres and more after Christ, overwhelmed with that Tartarian deluge, where the Name of Christians in the remotest parts is extinct, till Navigation in the last Age revived it. And had not Navigation and Peregrination opened a window, no Geographer had let us know the names of Nations, which Christians of the West found, professing the same Christ in the unknowne Regions of the East, at once scene to bee, and to be Christian. Yea, how little of the remote North and East of Europe and Asia, or of the South of Africa, was knowne to Plinie, Ptolomey, and other ancient Geographers, where their Christian light hath shined to us with the first notice of themselves."' I inferre not, that the Gospells lightning kindled an Evangelicall flame, and obtained Episcopall entertainment in every place where the Apostles preached: nor that every Lord, Tribe, and Family heard this Divine Message; nor that each Country was filled with the Gospel, or any with an universall profession in the first Planta-The reason of tions, or in their times. The name Paganus which the name signifiing a Pesant or Rustike, for this cause was altered Pagan or-q Panime or Ethnike, because Religion could not, but aymm. j i mq diffuse her bright beames and lines of light, from her Episcopall City Centre (that also not wholly Christian) to those ruder parts of her remoter Rom. 10. 18. circumference. This I say, that their sound went into all the Earth, and their words unto the Ends of the World, in some Countries and Nations more fully, in some more obscurely, in all by fame at lest, if not by the Apostles presence, as the Spirit permitted utterance, that some of all might be converted.

. VII.

Of America, whether it were then peopled.

Nd if any more scrupulous doubt of the New World, and of many places where no foot print of Christianity is extant, I answere, (besides what S. r. i.8. before in our Ophirian Tractate is spoken) not onely that time eates up her owne Children, and that none can prove that Christ hath not beene there preached in former times, because these are thereof ignorant; (for a deluge of opposing persecutions, another of ecclipsing superstitions and heresies, a third of warre and invasions, extinguishing both the Religion and People also hath succeeded, in some the most renowmed Churches of the World: and what then may time have done in unknowne places?) But who can tell that America, and many parts of Asia, Afrike and Europe were then peopled with Men, the Subjects capable of this Preaching.? Nay, may wee not in probabilitie think the contrary? how great a part of the World is yet without habitation? how great a part of the World is yet unknowne All the South Continent is in manner such, and yet in reason conjectured to bee very See Bmr-large, and as it were another New World; Also Fernand "" Book of de Quiros saith hee hath discovered eight hundred leagues ' of shoare. Neither is it probable but that so temperate i parts are inhabited (which in part, so farre as is knowne i. c. i8. on the Shoares and adjacent Hands, is apparant) nor is their likelihood of Christianity, where the Nations every way adjoyning are Ethnike, that I say not Savage on the parts of Asia and America: and both these and they seeme latelier peopled then the Apostles dayes. In the new Straits beyond the Magellane, the stupidity of the Fowles argued they knew not the face of Men, which they not at all dreaded. And many many Hands not yet inhabited, this ensuing Discourse will manifest. Yea in large Tracts of the Continent of Groenland, other parts unto New-found-land, it is found that eyther there are no people, or they but for some time in the Summer, and for some purpose, as of hunting or fishing, not certaine and setled dwellers: a name scarcely fitting to the people in Virginia and Florida. Even in our old World it self, how new are the eldest Monuments Antiquities, in al the North, Norway, Sweden, Finland, Lapland, the Samoyeds, Tartars, yea the Northermost Russes, Lithuranians, Livonians, Poles; how new their Arts, their Acts, their Lawes, Government, Civility and Fame."' Which therefore must needs as the World increased, bee evacuated from Countries neerer the Sunne, by necessitie inforced to harder Climates. Of Island our story will shew, it was but yesterday inhabited. See my Pig. The Scythians and Sarmatians of the ancient are more . 4. c. 10. Southerly; and well may we reject the fables of Hyperboreans, and I knowe not what devised Northerne Peoples I. i. 59. and Monsters, the Creatures and Colonies of idle busie braines. These Northerne people, scarsely worthie the name of a People, did God use when the sinnes of the Roman Empire were full, to punish their pride by so base instruments, in Gottish, Vandall, Hunnish, Saxon, Franke, and other names, in judgement remembring mercy to the chastised Children, and to the chastising Rod, not therefore cast into the fire, except to refine them, but by conquering Christian Nations, themselves disposed by divine hand to become a Christian Conquest, and to submit themselves to that God, to that Religion, whose looser Professors they overcame with an overwhelming inundation.

How unsearchable are thy wayes, O God, and thy judgements passing knowledge, which of Stones raisest children to Abraham, and bringest Lions into the Sheep-fold in hope of prey and spoyle, where thy discipline transformes them into Lambes."' and persecuting Saul turnes a Prophet."'

The remotest Northerne and Southerne parts o As Canaan America are yet thinly inhabited, and in great part not i ' at all, as before is observed, whereas Mexicana, and othingso Peruviana were abundantly peopled at the Spaniards populous as in first arrivall, with the Hands adjacent. Two great Em- Joshuas. pires were there erected, one in Mexico, the other of Jcosta the Ingas in Cusco; but neither of them ancient. Nor " ' let any impute this to their illiterate barbarousnesse. 1 J 'gj For they had meanes to preserve memorie of their acts f i owne by computation no lesse certaine then ours, though histories, about more troublesome: and thereby is the Mexican Epocha,- 9oo-J ' or first beginning, then beginning to bee a People, the ' " ". Devill imitating the Israelites in their Exodus towards Qj o and the Countries which they after possessed, apparant to of the stocke oj have beene above seven hundred yeeres after Christ: Ingas, be-as that of the Ingas some hundreds later. For it is fjjlfter"' most likely that America was first peopled from the North j, joo of Asia and Europe in her neerer and Northerne parts, which were whence by secret instinct, and hopefull allurements they before most were inticed to remove neerer the Sunne, and from the '-Mexican to passe to the Peruvian Continent. Neither can probable reason be given of peopling America but from thence, as by the Discourses of Acosta and Master Brerewood appeareth: neither did those Northerne parts receive Inhabitants till the Regions of the World neerer Noas Arke, and of more commodious habitation were first peopled, whence the East and South parts were soone after Noas time replenished: the colder and worse successively, and the extreme North by later compulsion and necessitie, the better being peopled before: and there exceeding their just proportion, they emptied themselves partly by returning into the South by Conquests to over-runne civiller Nations, and partly were forced to seeke further, as vicinitie of Seas and Lands aflfoorded, till America was also peopled. For (besides that those Northerne parts were as fertile in the wombe, as barren in the soyle, numerous beyond due food) those rough, cold mountainous habitations I i6i L

yeelded like constitution of body and unquietnesse of mind strong and able to indure, bold and forward to adventure greatest difficulties, still pressing (where worse then the present could hardly befall) and following their hopes till neerer propinquitie to the Sunne, Climates more temperate, richer Soyle, consent of Elements and Aliments bred content to their mindes and more prosperous concent of Fortunes, which softned their rigid dispositions, and by degrees disposed them to thinke on mechanicall and politike Arts, further to humanize their society, and to polish their cohabitation with Politic, This we see soone done in Egypt, and Babylonia presently after the Floud: but how long before the Persians were civilized? how long after before the Macedonians, or Romans? yea, how long before there were Romans?

Nature infused the first cares of necessary being, which being by the fertile habitation and industrious culture richly supplied, in the settled standing the Milke of humane wits yeelded the flower or creame of Arts for flourish and beautie, which unsettled and discontented estates weary of the present, and pressing still forwards cannot produce; neither can a rolling stone gather mosse.

And thus we finde the Germans now a civill Nation, which many ages after Christ were barbarous. Yea, where more feritie and savage rudenesse then this our

Britaine yeelded not long before the birth of our Saviour, for their painting, naked-nesse, and other rude demeanours worse then the Virginians now, and like some more barbarous Americans? What hath America savouring of Antiquitie? what besides the former, not savouring

"j si Cradle, and later transmigration?

. I. c. z. ' Those memorials which they have of the Floud might

Feg. torn. 2. passe with them by Tradition even from the Arke it ii. 7. c. 13. selfe thorow all their removes and transmigrations. And y.?- H54- no lesse might be said of that Ticsiviracocha mentioned

Nav. in Bra. Y Acosta, (whom Vega observeth to have many things c. 16. not so truly) like to Our Men, and preached amongst them many good lessons with httle effect, and after many miracles amongst them was slaine; whose picture some of the Spaniards had scene, resembling those ot our Saints. Vega tells another and more likely storie of Viracochas apparition in that habite, which no doubt was the Devill. The like is recorded by Lerius, of a tradition amongst the Brasilians, that innumerable Moones before, there came a Mair or Stranger, clothed after the Christian manner, and bearded, which preached unto them the knowledge of God, but none would beleeve him: after whom another came which delivered them a Sword, since which time they had used to slay and eate one another. These things, as they may be true, so may they be the New actions of the old Serpent ambitious of Deitie, or may by Tradition flit with them thorow all their habitations; or if any shall thinke it there happened (which I cannot beleeve) yet are they I. i. 60. rather to interpret it of the Apostles (so further confirmeth our opinion) then of any other, seeing no such men could there have accesse, and their speach be understood, but by miraculous dispensation. As for the Rocke in Brasill called Etooca (where, as Master Knivet Kn'wets Jour-affirmeth, Saint Thomas preached) converted out of ' " Wood into Stone, the Fishes being his auditors, who seeth not a Frierly supersemination in the report."' wee reade in Theophrastus or Aristotle, or whosoever else be Authour of that Booke De Mirabilibus Auscultat, of a fertile desart Hand found by the Carthaginians, abounding with Woods and Rivers navigable, and other bounties of Nature, distant many dayes sailing from the African Continent: some of the Carthaginians intended there to inhabite, but were repelled, and all men prohibited on paine of death, lest the Soveraigne power and weale publike of Carthage might thence be endam-maged. This is by some interpreted of the West-Indies, or some Hands thereof; which if it be so, confirmes our opinion that those parts were not then inhabited. Nor P- Pilg. I. 8. did any civilitie appeare in America to argue civill Pro– genitors, but that which was ot later memorie. Plato's Atlantis wee have elsewhere shewed to be allegoricall, at least no historicall truth: nor any likelihood in other ancient Navigations mentioned in Plutarch, Diodorus and others to point at these parts.

If the multitudes of people found there by the first Spaniards seeme to pleade for a longer habitation then that we allow; let it be observed that a thousand and foure hundred yeeres (for the first Discoverie was 1492. after Christ) might well fill a world with people, especially considering their Polygamie, or many Women, their simple Diet, and that which attended the same, health-full Constitution and long Life (in some places admirable) their easie course of life contented with a little, not fearing to exceed their meanes and maintenance by numerous issue; where Nature yeelded home-spunne or rather womb-spunne attire, and the Mother Earth with little importunitie or labour yeelded food sufficient; where Plagues, Morraines, Famine, were scarse heard of; where Covetousnesse the root of all evill had so little worke; Ambition scarsely knew to diversifie titles of honor; and warre (the inchanted circle of death, compendium of misery. Epitome of mischiefe, a Hell upon Earth) had not Iron, Steele, Lead, not Engines, Stratagems, Ordnance, not any humane Arts of in-humanitie to fill those parts of the World with empti-nesse, and there to erect Theaters of Desolation and Destruction. Nor did Nature yeeld many devouring Beasts, but reserved all her savagenesse to the Men.

To let passe the peopling of the World before and after the Flood, in no great time, we see that in Egypt in the midst of heavy burthens, inhumane butcherie, and intolerable tyrannie, the Israelites were multiplied, in the ='G.46.27. space of two hundred and ten yeeres, from seventy

Ex. 11.17- persons to above two miluons, as may be ghessed, in "Num. 1.46. j gj. g gj-e 600000. men, besides children, and m'm ie-i besides the females also as appeareth in the ' second 6 "'"' ' ' numbring by Moses, and in the third by him and

Eleazar, when all those but Caleb and Joshua were dead. Allowing therefore the male children not much lesse, as that third numbring evinceth, and the females in probabihtie as many as the males (the rather for that Pharaohs cruell Edict touched not them) you cannot but find above 2000000. Now this their encrease w as by naturall meanes though by singular providence, and therefore might as well happen in America, those impediments removed, and many other furtherances annexed, in libertie, plenty, and largenesse of Territorie, all elements conspiring to multiplication. Neither can any thing but Divine providence (which none can denie in America, and had many more easie and visible meanes, fewer lets then in Egypt) be alledged for the one more then the other. This I may say, that if any list to examine the proportion, and suppose like providence, in that time of 1400. yeeres may follow a more numerous inundation of people, then ever America (perhaps the whole World) may probably be supposed at once to have numbred, although large deductions be allowed both for ordinary mortality and some more dismal accidents. Neither is it likely that the first plantations were so few (if voluntarily seeking, not by accident forced to those habitations) as 70. persons twice told: nor that America at once or from one place received her first Colonies, as by the divers languages, statures, habits of men may appeare, although time, custome, accident, be allowed no litle power in these things. This we see amongst our selves, where one Dutch or Teutonike Distrib. de hath yeelded not onely a distinction of higher and lower, Europ eor. but the English, Danish, Sweden, Norwegian, Islandish, l- "f; Nordalbing, Frisian (besides the subdiversified dialects j,"f Qq which each of these multiplieth) Languages, Peoples, mog. part. 2. Rites, so much differing, and the elder both tongues . c. 8. and customes (as in our Saxon) by Variation and succession after a few Centuries in manner extinguished. So vaine a thing is Man. Let me conclude this discourse of multiplication in America, by an American

A casta. I. i. cap. 2 1. y . 4– 34- c. I, A few Herses also and mares left by the River of Plate so en-creased, that since they have slaine them only for their tailes, to sell to the Negros. Of Conies strange en-crease, see I. 2. c. I. 2. I. i. 6i.

example of cattell transported out of Europe thither, especially Kine, which as they beare no more at a burthen then a woman, nor oftner, so are they shorter-lived usually by two third parts: yet have they so increased there, that one man the Bishop of Venezuela had above 16000. yea they have growne wilde, their numbers exceeding the care of owners, and every man at pleasure killing them for their hides. And one man, the Deane of Conception, had of one Kow living 26. yeeres, in her life time the increase of 800. Sic canibus catulos similes

These Indians which respected in generation little else but sensuality, and in manner of life resembled brute beasts rather then civill (that I say not Christian) Men, enjoying like priviledges of Nature in other things, might in this also.

i VIII.

The glorie of Apostolicall Conquests: the hopes of enlarging the Church in this last Age, by knowledge of Arts and Languages through the benefit of Printing and Navigation.

Et me conclude this Discourse of Apostolicall Peregrinations with consideration, with collau-dation, with admiration even to extasie and astonishment, of Their (shall I say or Gods.?) Exploits, and renowmed Acts. Little are the Acts of Great Alexander, Pompeius Magnus, Fabius Maximus, and other Greats and Grandes of the World, who by Armes and Arts military, by Fire, Sword, Famine, Massacres forced the bodies (the least part) of Men to a compulsive subjection, shaken off with the first oppor-tunitie. But how shall I adorne your noble Conquests, Yee Divine Apostolicall Worthies.? who walking in the flesh, not warring after the flesh, without, yea, against the force of carnall weapons, pulled downe strong holds, cast downe imaginations, and every high thing that exalted it selfe against the knowledge of God, and brought into captivitle every thought to the obedience of Christ? Herein they used not assistance of other z. Chotwo. Nations by confederation, nor mustered multitudes in 3 4 5 pressed and trained bands of their owne; nor received supportation by Subsidies, nor made invasion by force, nor obtained an unwilling conquest of Bodies (the shell without the kernel) nor entertayned close intelligence, nor wrought by close Treasons, nor divided to them selves the spoiles; nor erected Forts, established Garrisons, imposed taxations, transplanted inhabitants, depressed Nobles, shared new Provinces into Timars, tithed Children, planted Colonies; nor had their counsels of Warre at home, or warlike customes abroad, Engines, Stratagems, Combats, Sieges, Skirmishes, pitched Fields, Ships, Horses, Chariots, Tents, Trumpets, Munition, nor that worst Baggage of Armies, Crying, Spoyling, Sacking, Wounding, Mayming, Killing with Multiformities of Crueltes, as if the nethermost Hels had mustered and evaporated the most and worst of Her Fumes and Furies into Our world, which might therefore take, that they might destroy, the shapes of Men, by humane inhumanitie. But a few poore Fishermen, and Tent-makers overthrow the Worlds Wisemen, in the most flourishing times of worldly learning, subdue the Scepters of greatest Kings and Monarchs, ruine the gates of Hell, undermine the deepnesse of Satan, supplant the pro-foundest, suttlest, mightiest of Satanicall combinations Ap. 2. with the whole World of Men against a handfull; and maugre their united Forces, preaching a Crucified God, and teaching the Crosse as the first Principle of Christian Learning, to overcome the edge of the Sword with suffering it, to stop the mouthes of Lions with their flesh, to quench the violence of fire with their bloud; to forsake all Goods, good Name, Wife, Life, Childe, to deny themselves, to plucke out their right eyes, to cut off their right hands, to pray for their persecutors, to recompence hatred with love, and overcome evill with goodnesse, looking for no other reward then what the World can neither looke on, nor for; they invade with innocence, and with Saving overcome, the World; and whiles it most resisteth, persecuteth, overcommeth, incline it to willing-nesse, calmenesse, subjection; write their conquests not in the bloud of the Conquered but of the Conquerors; erect Trophees, not in Obeliskes, Pyramides, Arches, by others industry, but in their owne Funerals, Crucifyings, Stonings, Martyrdomes; solemnize Triumphs not with their owne Armies, not with captived troupes, attending in greatest pompe the sublime Triumphall Chariot, but by being led forth with out-cries, shoutes, clamours, to the basest and most ignominious deaths. Those of whom the World was not worthy, reputed unworthy of the World; have the Panegyrikes of their prayses, written not by the pens of Parasites or Poets, nor in the lines, (as is said) but in the lives of men; the Christian World (as before is observed) remayning not written, but reall 2, Co;-. 6. lo. Annalls of the Apostles Acts, who being poore made many rich, and having nothing possessed all things.

Tkeod. Orat. The Solaecismes of Fishermen dissolved the Syllo-gismes of Philosophers, and where but a few of any Nation could be wonne, to professe themselves the Disciples of any Philosophicall Sect, though graced and admired by the World, yet the World becomes Christian in despite of the Worlds disgraces and persecutions: nor could the immane-cruelties ot some, or superfine subtleties of other, subvert, nay they converted men to the Gospel; the seed, the fatning of the Church was the Bloud of her slaine Martyrs; all ages, sexes, sorts of men, even women, even children, even women-children, out-braving the greatest, the fiercest, the wisest of Satanicall instruments, by suffering, conquering, and at once overcomming the Devill, the World, Themselves. Even so O Father, because it pleased thee.

And be not angry Reader, if the passed present unto my contemplation future things; and if the consideration of divine assistance in Tongues, Revelations,

Miracles, immediately conferred for the first Plantation of Christianitie, occasion my thoughts to a more serious survay of future hopes in the propagation and reformation thereof In the first foundation of IMosaicall '- 3i– 6. Rites, God raysed Bezaleel, and Aholiab with others, 5-3-by divine instinct inabled to curious workmanship, fitting that Oeconomie of the Tabernacle, whiles that Jewish Church was as it were rocked in the Cradle, and God vouchsafed to dwell amongst those Tent-dwellers in a Tent. But after that State was setled, I– and the Church flourished in the Reigne of David and Salomon. God did not againe infuse Sciences by Miracle, or by miraculous disposition (as before the Egyptians were spoyled) provided materials to that Worke; but furnished Salomons wisdome, with helpe of the two Hirams, the one a cunning workman in Gold, Silver, 2. Ciron. 2. Brasse, Iron, Stone, Timber, to grave any manner of H-graving, and to find out every device, the sonne of a Tyrian, by an Israelitish woman; the other his Master, the King of Tirus, a man furnished with a Navy of ships and store of Mariners, by whose meanes the Temple and Court might be provided of necessaries from remotest Ophir, aswell as the neerer Lebanon. I implore not, I importune not any unwilling assent or follower of my apprehension and application hereof to what I now propound in like differing states of the Christian Church, Omnia contingebant illis in figura. This was i. Cor, lo. ii. likewise founded, and as it were a Tabernacle built for IZl"! at " "' Christ by the Apostles, men wholy enabled by immediate isc vov graces and gifts of the Spirit to so divine a Worke. A ""''''''' Tabernacle I call the Church, not only as being yet militant, and therefore abiding in Tents, but in comparison and respectively to that externall spendour which followed long after the Apostles times, when Kings became her Nursing Fathers and Queenes her Nursing Mothers, subjected their Crowne to the Crosse, shining in the highest top thereof Albeit therefore in puritie of doctrine and manners the Apostolicall times had their spirituall preeminence (as the Tabernacle also exceeded the Temple in the ordinary Cloud, Pillar of fire, Manna, Miracles, syncerest worship by Moses, and the like.) Yet when the World became Christian, and the Crosse became the Imperiall Banner the Church, before persecuted, now revived under Constantine, Jovianus, Theodosius, and other Religious Monarchs, and Kings, seemed to renew the Golden revolutions and setled returnes of Christian Davids and Salomons; and they which before had not a Smith in Israel, scarsly a Bishop or Temple to be scene, had Temples, Schooles, Bishops, Councels, whence Religion was propagated and established in the severall Realmes and Nations of Christianity; not now by Miracles as before by the Apostles, but by the Ministery of Bishops and Priests of ordinary cauing and gifts; and hee himselfe was now the greatest Miracle that beleeved not, the whole World beleeving and wondering at infidelitie as a Monster.

And as the Temple and state or Religion declining was repaired and reformed by godly Kings, as Joash, Hezekiah, Josiah; and Zealous Priests such as Jehoiada; after the ruines thereof was rebuilded by Princes and Priests, Zorobabel and Joshua, Nehemiah and Ezra: so hath God stirred up good Kings Pastors in the declining age of the Church, as Charles the Great, King Alfred and many others in Histories mentioned; after the deportation thereof into Mysticall Babylon, when shee seemed in her truest members fled out of the Worlds easier view into the Wildernesse, hath God raysed up the Kings of England, Sweden, Denmarke, and other Christian Princes, States, and Potentates with Religious Bishops and Ministers to repaire the desolations of Sion, and restore Jerusalem with the Temple, if not to her first splendour, yet from her late Captivity, where Psal. 37. 4. she had smal pleasure to sing the Lords song in a strange land, babble her holies in the unknown Language ot Babylon. As therefore the first Plantation of the Tabernacle was by miracle and immediate instinct; the erection of the Temple, and succeeding reparations were by the art and humane industry of such Heroike spirits as God raysed up and sanctified in every age: so the Christian Church planted by Apostles, hath beene since watered by faithfull Pastors, exalted by pious Emperours, depressed by Heretikes and Persecutors, captived by Popes, and in her diversified changes and chances, rather ex-pecteth extraordinary blessing upon the ordinary helpes, functions, and graces, then meanes meerly extraordinary and miraculous. Amongst all which helpes by humane industry, none (in my mind) have further prevailed then those two, the Arts of Arts, Printing and Navigation, both in manner given at once to the World by divine goodnesse, this for supply of matter, that other of forme, to this Spirituall Reedification of Gods Sanctuary. And as Hirams Art improoving natural wit by diligent industry, succeeded the infused Sciences of Bezaleel and Aholiab; so to that Apostolicall gift of Tongues, in the foundation of the Church hath succeeded for reformation thereof, the principall Tongues and Languages of Nations Ebrew, Greeke, Latina, Syriake, Arabike, and the rest, partly refined, partly renewed by humane Industrie, through the benefit of Printing, For how were the learned and remoter Tongues buried and unknowne in these parts, till that Art brought in plentie, facilitie and cheapnesse of Bookes, whereby Languages became the Keyes, Bookes the Treasuries and Storehouses of Science; whiles by those men found access into these; and Printing yeelded admittance to both in plentie and varietie? And thus was unvailed that mystery of Iniquity in the age before us, which had captived so many Ages in worse then Egyptian darknesse. This mystery at first arose in a myst from the bottomlesse pit, in a time of barbarous ignorance, occasioned by irruption of Barbarians into all parts of Christendome, successively like wild Bores out of the Forrest, rooting up Gods Vineyard, and preparing a way to the Romish Foxes to spoile the Vines, to corrupt and devoure the fruits thereof,

The Goths, Vandals, Hunnes, Herules, Lombards, Saracens, in Spaine, Afrike and Italy; the Frankes, and after them the Saracens, Danes, and Normans in France, and the places adjoyning; the Picts, Saxons and Angles, and after them the Danes, in these parts; the Avares, Saracens, Tartars, Turkes in the East and South; with other deluges of Ethnikes hating learning, burning 1. i. 63. Libraries, killing learned men, in these and other parts seconded with factions, treasons, and civill uncivill combustions of Christians amongst themselves, made easie way first, and strong confirmation after to the Papacy apprehending all opportunities to advance it selfe, first in spirituall things, after also in temporall.

But what illiterate ignorance little discerned, not much withstood, renewed litera-ture hath exposed to the view of all, and by revived Arts hath discerned the Arts or that painted Jezabel, whose fouler wrinkles, her Jeza-belicall, Jesuiticall Parasites still labour with renewed and refined Arts also to playster and fill up a fresh; but hereby whet the industry of others to improove their Arts and industry on the otherside, in more eagre search and diligent inquisition to take those wise in their craftinesse, and to let men see that the materials of this later Babylon in the West are turfes of earth, which humane wits have baked into brickes, and with slime of Policy, have raysed to so superadmirable a frame and structure.

And lest so great a blessing procured by Printing, should rest and rust amongst our selves in this Westerne corner of the World, God hath added that other Art of Ofihh im- Navigation, as that other Hirams assistance to Salomon, provement of and of Nehemiah to Ezra, the Prince and Priest, learning Nazngation- power combined. This Art was before obscure and Chapter " rude, but by the industry of the Portugals lifted up to higher attempts, with care of their Kings (employing Astronomic to her better furniture) enabled to new Discoveries in Africa, and after that in all the East, whose example the Spaniard following happily encountred a

New World, and first of all men unlosed the Virgin Zone of the Earth, encompassing the whole Compasse of this vast Globe. And thus hath God given oppor-tunitie by Navigation into all parts, that in the Sun-set and Evening of the World, the Sunne of righteousnesse might arise out of our West to illuminate the East, and fill both Hemispheres with his brightnes: that what the Apostles, by extraordinary dispensation sent, by extraordinary providence protected conducted into all parts, by extraordinary gift of Tongues were able to preach to all sorts of men; this latter Age following those glorious Fathers and Founders (though farre off, non passibus aequis) might attempt and in some sort attaine by helpes of these two Artes, Printing and Navigation, that Christ may bee salvation" to the ends of =, 2. y 22. the Earth, and all Nations may serve him; that according to the Scripture innumerable numbers of all Nations and Luke 2. Kindreds, and peoples, and Tongues, may be clothed f' ' ' " 9-with the white robes of the Lambe. I am no Prophet, nor Sonne of a Prophet, instructed in future revelations, but one with all others praying, thy Kingdome come; neither dare I take upon me the revelation of the Revelation in that Prophecie of the holy Jerusalem descending out of Heaven from God, newly measured with a golden Reed, to apply it to the reformation of the Church in the last times; which howsoever some have interpreted only of her glorious and celestiall estate, others have included the terrestriall also, after the calling of the Jewes (which Saint Paul cals life trom the dead, as if it were the Resurrection of the World, and consequently in spirituall respects, a new Heaven and new Earth) alleadging many Arguments, seeming altogether to this purpose not improbable. And least of all, will I, lesse then the least of all, take upon me the reducing of the Jewes into I know not what externall pompe and policie, and exalt them in splendour above all other Nations and Monarchs (the very stumblmg stone of their downfall; this dreame of a glorious Messias, pro-

Forbis Brigki-man, Bernard, tsfc. if! Jpoc. Rom. II. 15. Psal. 19. Rom. 10. Jug. Epj-So. vid. Prosp. de lib. orbit. Syb. Or. I. 3.

Bellar. Les-sius, l3c. Fid. J cost, de Proc. Ind. sal. I. 4. c. 2. y de temp, novis. I. i. f. 17. 18. Collect on Good Friday. Except in the quondam Roman Empire tfs the Countries next adjoyning, viz the Swedens, Poles, ISorzve-gians, Dunes, Russes, and other Nor theme people most of them lately added to the Church; y the Abas-sines on the South Ij some handfuls on the East; Christianity hath rather bin dispersed in Nations then publikely and generally professed. God voicing them to crucifie the Lord of glory, whose Kingdome is not of this World, though prefigured by-types, and painted in shadowes of Secular glorie) T meddle not with Secular States, but pray for the conversion and spirituall regeneration of all men. And Nature it selfe preacheth thus daily: if the Sunne daily, shal not the Sunne of righteousnesse once, enlighten all the World? It is the Holy Ghosts resemblance. If the Fathers' of old did expect a further conversion of Nations by the Gospel; if the Sybilline Oracles promise as much; if the Papists make this a demonstration that Antichrist is not yet come, because the Gospel is not yet preached to all men, which they hope hereafter shall bee effected; if the Prophecies of the glorious state of the Church mentioned in Esay and Zacharie, shadowed in Ezekiels Temple, and destruction of Gog and Magog, renued in the Revelation, seeme not yet to have taken their full effect, but to promise some better future estate, as even those many Ancients also conceited, whose full sayle and forward gale carried them beyond the Truth into the Millenary Errour: if our Church prayeth for all Jewes, Turkes, and Infidels, that they may be one sheep-fold under one Pastor: then I may also with the Streame bee carried into expectation of that dilating the Churches Pale, and a more Catholike enlarging of her bounds, specially in those parts of the World, where though we grant the Gospel preached by the Apostles, yet little fruit in comparison followed in many Countries; nor any generall conversion of Nations, except of the Romane Empire with the adjoyning Regions, and some few, scarce a few Provinces annexed, hath hitherto happened. And how litde to the rest of the World is all that which is called Christendome, or that also which in any setled flourishing estate of a Church hath ever yet beene Christian Pardon therefore this Charitie extended to all men, to pray and hope for the remotest of Nations no more remote from Christ in Nature or promise, then our selves.

And (to returne to our Navigation) the present Navi- S' p ' gations, Missions, Preachings, of Jesuites and Friers in f" .;- the Heathen Nations of the World, seeme to present j d i j unto my minde that state of the dispersed Jewes before mj Charitie Christs comming in the flesh. He came to his owne, then of my and his owne received him not, which yet by their Scrip- f j J f tures. Synagogues, Rites, in their many many dispersions,-j j 5 j had unwitting prepared a way unto him amongst the Gentiles. Let none contemne this figure of the Jewish " The greatest Church (which yeelds' in most objections of Popery "' f touching Visibility, Succession, Antiquity, Universality, "paphturlwn Consent, Pontificall Priviledges, and most of their vulgar from the and popular flourishes, reall and experimentall resolutions, autharity, l3c. bv paraleline the Tew and Romanist; this bein inferiour of the Church, . 'r D '.-ri-1 f '9 be with m evidence, superiour m arrogance) it herein also " fairer shew l see them like; and those later Pharises, compassing Sea surer ground and Land to make Proselites, by preaching some Christian applyed to the verities amongst their Traditionary chaffe, become f!""',., Apparitors and Harbengers of a future purity, which J"J f J yet themselves crucifie as Hereticall. Spaine hath as is said, in Navigation best deserved (in leading the way to others, some of which have since in the Art equalled, "English and in attempts perhaps exceeded her) and by divine Provi–Oa J. dence hath beene bountifully rewarded in the East and West, both overshadowed under her wings: is also one of the ten homes (as the current of our Interpreters Jpoci-j. it,, agree) which together with the beast receive power as ' Kings, out of the ruines of the Romane Empire; of which it is prophesied that the ten homes shall hate the z. Reg.(). zz. Whore, and shall make her desolate and naked and shall eate her flesh and burne her with fire. For God hath put into their hearts to fulfill his will, c. God put into their hearts to be thus truly Catholike, and able to discerne the whoredoms and many witchcrafts of their mother Jezabel, the mother of fornications of jpoc. 17. 5. the Earth; enable them to see that Catholike-Roman Exploits of is the Language of Babel, where men but babble, and P" "-the word (like Esau and Jacob striving in the wombe) supplants the next preceding; that the now-Roman is but new-Roman, and therefore Catholike no more in time then place, no more in sound apprehension of truth, then in round comprehension of the Universe. And that God which hath given them to chase the relikes of the Moores out of Europe, to chastise them in Afrik Asia, to find that New World of America, with her two armes of Navigation from Lisbone and Sivill yeerely, to embrace the whole

Globe, and to have greater opor-tunities for so Catholike a worke then yet is granted to any other Nation; put into their hearts with other Princes and Christian Nations to fulfill this his will against that Whore; which the Prophesie enforceth to beleeve shall bee done, and their King in our Fathers dayes gave instance how easie. I ring not, sound not an alarme, nor strike up a march for warre, I determine not the particular way or instruments of that desolation. Jpoc. 17. 6. I delight not in imprecations, nor to that Whore drunken with the bloud of Saints and IVIartyrs wish any bloudy Apoc. e. reward of my selfe: but God himselfe hath foretold Vid. Prafat. devouring her flesh and burning her, and enjoyned also,

S' ' ' " "P double. Which howsoever it shall bee effected, I doe not prescribe, nor doe I single out that Nation to this purpose, but joyne them with others in my Prayers for the execution of that Prophecie, both to goe out of Babylon, and to goe against it in just reformation, that it may bee no more found at all; at least by making her naked of that protection which thence she receiveth, and redemand-ing their owne, may detayne the over-flowings of Euphrates that the way of the Kings of the East may bee prepared to exterminate Babylon out of the World. And is it not better thus to pray for them that they may have an honorable part in that Prophesie, that Babylon may further fall by their falling from them, then that they should fall with her or to reckon up the bloudy effects of their Inquisition in Europe, and their inhumanity in America, and number them amongst the

Kings of the Earth, who shall bewayle and lament Romes ruines; or to those Ship-masters, Ship-companies, Saylers and Traders by Sea, and Merchants of the Earth weeping for her desolations? Once, I say not that they of all men have the most eminent oportunity to subvert Babylon by their Italian neighbourhood and Territories; I pray that they endevour to convert the Easterne and Westerne Indians making that best use of their Navigations, giving them Gold refined and truly spirituall for their temporall. And though they now of all Nations seeme most enamoured of that Roman (therein truly Catholike, that is, common) Harlot, yet Hee which hath Prov. 21. i. the heart of Kings in his hand as the rivers of water,- 'z- 29- i9-can turne it, when and whithersoever he will: can effect this also by others, without, yea against them: can reward (as sometime hee did Nebuchadnezzar for his service done at Tyrus, with the land of Egypt for the wages E. 27. y of his Armie, and the Israelites at their departure with A 12 Egyptian spoiles) can reward I say both those which at his command go out of, or when his Providence shall dispose, against this Babylon (which for captiving the people of God is called Egypt, for filthinesse Sodom, for the Staple of Spiritual Merchandise, is also resembled to Tyrus) with the spoyles of the Spirituall Egyptians, with the Turks destruction (which litterally possesse Egypt) with the riches of the Gentiles brought to the Church, besides their own and the Churches liberty. And as Jerusalem (to return to our similitude) being demolished by the Romans, the Church became truely Catholike, not looking any more to walls of a Temple, to carnall Sacrifices, to the petty pinfold of one Nation, to one City, as the Mart Mother of Christian Religion ' ' 'j;-and discipline (how much had the Apostles to doe whiles 1Uapog Jerusalem stood, to withhold Christians from Judaizing?) Apoc.2o. so is it to bee hoped and prayed, that this Mysticall p- 9- " Babylon, which now by usurpation challengeth to bee ', J', ivyi 1 r 1 r 1 -I i i Ep. ad Gal.

Mistresse and Mother or the Church, arrivmg at that-T p y prophecied irrecoverable downefall, Catholike-Roman Heb. iff. I 177 M (universall-particular) may no more bee heard, but true I. i. 65. Catholicisme recovering her venerable and primary Anti-quitie, may v ithout distracted faction, in free and unanimous consent, extend her Demesnes of Universalitie as farre as the Earth hath Men, and the light of her truth may shine together with the Sun-beames, round about the habitable World: that as Salomon by Hirams Mariners fetched materials, Gold, Gemmes, Almuggim Trees, to the Temples structure, v hich by the others Hirams Art were brought and wrought into due forme; so the Heavenly Salomon, the Lord Jesus, may by this his gift of Navigation supply those remote Fields, white unto the Harvest, with plentie of labourers, to bring into the Societie of the True Church those rude Ethnikes, of them to frame Pillars in the house of God, vessels of sanctimony in the sanctuary finer then Prov. 8. the Gold of Ophir, enlightened with spirituall wisdome and understanding of Holy things, richer then Rubies, and the most incomparable Jewels: that these may by the art of Hiram, the Son of an Isralitish woman by a Tyrian Father, that is by the Ministery of Pastors and Doctors, learned in divine and humane Literature be instructed, baptised, edified and disciplined; that in the places where yet is no Christian, nay no Humane or Hos. I. 10. Civill people, it may be said unto them, yee are the Sonnes of the living God; that there may be one Pastor and one sheepfold, one Salvation, Redeemer, and Advocate, to Jew and Gentile, Jesus Christ the light ot the Gentiles and the glory of his people Israel: whom my Discourse having now obtained to embrace, shall here confine it selfe with a Nunc Dimittis, and end with Amen, to that Amen, in whom all the promises of God are yea and Amen. Even so. Amen Lord Jesus.

Chap. III. I. I 66.

Of divers other principall Voyages, and Peregrinations mentioned in holy Scripture. Of the travels and dispersions of the Jewes; and of Nationall transmigrations.

Aving premised the two former Tractates, as the two Eyes of Peregrinations most faire Face, I shall bee as briefe in the following, as I have in them beene tedious and discursive. The first voyage of Mankind was out of Paradise Paradise. into the cursed parts of the Earth, thence with sweat and labour to get his living. Caines restlesse wandrings, and yet still dwelling in the land of Nod, that is of agitation and vexation, never being still (there is no peace saith my God, to the wicked) and Henochs contrary walking with God, I need not men- Esdras. 57. tion. And I have already mentioned the first Ship and 3i-voyage by water, Noahs Arke, and the first early Peregrination after to the Plaine of Shinar, where Babels Babel. building was with mutuall babbling or confusion of Languages confounded; which gave occasions to the dispersion of Mankind over the Earth, that is, to the planting and peopling of the World, of which I have given account somewhat largely before, in the first Booke of my Pilgrimage. Abram is called out of Ur of the Abram and Chaldees, and travels with Lot to Haran first, and after Lot. into Canaan: thence Famine forced him into Egipt; after hee sets forth for the recovery of Lot in a Martiall Expedition against foure Kings, returning by Melchi-sedek King of Salem. Abraham after many tent- Abraham and wandrings comes to Gerar, and after Isaacs birth and ” ”='-blessed hopes conceived of him, is sent on the most difficult journey to Moriah: at Hebron he burieth his Wife and fellow Traveller: sends his servant to Mesopotamia for Rebekah: and having sent his multiplied issue by

Keturah unto the East Countrey (as before Ishmael) hee ended his earthly Pilgrimage. Isaac inherites the promises, and yet travelleth of them by travelling, not founding Cities but dwelling in Tabernacles, as did Jacob also, before and after his long service in Padan Aram, till at last hee descended into Egipt, whither God had Jacob sent Joseph in a former Peregrination. These both dyed JoeA. in Faith, and gave charge, the one for his dead body, the other for his bones to travell to Canaan the type of their hopes. Moses Out of gipt God called his Sonne, now multiplied j4 rott. into an armle as is before observed: which yet are not presently in Canaan after the passage of the Red Sea, Isrars Pere- but are Pilgrims fortie yeeres in the Wildernesse. Wee grination iti Iso after wee have escaped the bondage of hellish Pharao, VJitkfoithi " " vanquished in the Red Sea of Christ Map. blood, whereinto wee are baptised, must live the life of Faith, passing thorow the wildernesse of this World, having no more sustenance to our soules from our meere Naturall powers, then there their Plowing and Hus-bandrie yeelded their bodies: but as their food and rayment, were the effects of Gods grace, and not humane Tit. 3. 5. labour; so not by the workes of righteousnesse, which wee have done, but according to his mercy hee saveth us: Exoti. 13. and by his Word and Spirit as a Pillar of cloud by Day, and of fire by Night travelleth with us, till Joshua, the true Jesus (for Moses brings not into Canaan, nor can the Law justifie) set us in possession of the heavenly Canaan, where Jericho is battered not by warhke Engines, but by the power of faith in the Word and Covenant of God; and the Houses which our workes builded not, and Vineyards which our merits planted not, even the Thrones which Angels lost, are made ours for ever by free Grace and meere Mercy. This is that rest, into which none but Travellers can enter, and that by crowding so Mntth. 7. hard into that narrow gate, that they must leave them- Matt. 16. selves behind; nor take possession of, but by losse of 24. life it selfe, passing that Jordan which floweth the way of all flesh into the Dead Sea, before they can live with God.

Nor need men thinke much to travell, where God himselfe was a Mysticall Traveller in the Tabernacle, till Salomon built him an House adorned by Ophirian Navigations. Saul before this had travelled to seeke SW. Davu. lost Asses, and stumbled on an earthly Kingdome: David by keeping of Sheepe and following the Ewes with young was initiated, and after by many many travels trained to the Mysteries of Royaltie, which with diversified travels he exercised all his dayes. Jero- Jeroboam. boams travels to gipt taught him those calvish devotions, which made Israeli travell into many Assyrian Plantations; and Judah also was carried captive to Capthnde. Babilon, restored by a travell from thence to Jerusalem under Zorobabel, Ezra, and Nehemiah; a mysterie of that mystie deportation of the Christian Church, by ignorance and superstition, and her reformation by Godly Princes and Pastors. Hirams Mission, the Queene of Shebas Visitation, Jonahs Journey to Ninive, intimate the calung of the Gentiles, whose First-fruits were the Wise-men of the East, which came so farre a voyage Matth. 2. to salute the New-borne King of the Jewes. J oh. i.

The Devill also is a Traveller, and continually com-passeth the Earth to and fro, and goeth about as a roaring i. Pet. 5, Lyon seeking whom to devoure; travelling of mischiefe, and conceiving lies. Such were the Assyrian, Syrian, Persian, Babilonian,

Egyptian, other travels of the Churches Enemies; theirs also which in blind zeale compassed Sea and Land to make Pharisaical Proselites. In Mordecais time, you see in the Booke of Esther the I. i. (il, Jewish dispersions thorow all the one hundred and-" twenty seven Persian Provinces, even from India to Ethiopia, long after the returne under Zorobabel, which multiplied no doubt in Ages following accordingly.

But why looke I for Travellers and Voyages there, Deut. 16. where the Church was tied to one place, to travell thither three times a yeere, and therefore ordinarily not to bee farre from thence? The Babylonian and Alexandrian I dispersions, after the Captivity we have already men- I tioned; whereby the World was strewed with Jewes, (not to mention the Israelites) as Apparitors to the Mes- sias, and preparers thereof to Christianitie in the Apostles preaching. Then indeed the Jewes were Travellers from all parts to Jerusalem, as men were more reli- Act. 2. 5,9, giously affected, There dwelled at Jerusalem Jewes, lo, II. devout men out of every Nation under Heaven, which ' being of Jewish Parentage, were by the place of their birth, Parthians, Medes, and Elamites, Mesopotamians, Cappadocians, of Pontus and Asia, Phrygia and Pam-philia, Egypt, and of the parts of Libya about Cyrene, Strangers of Rome, Jewes and Proselytes, Cretes and Arabians. Matt. 27. This was after that imprecation of theirs. His bloud bee on us and on our children: so did God seeke to overcome their evill with his goodnesse: but when they Act.-J. IS I-), which had before persecuted the servants, and crucified the Lord of glory himselfe, now resisted the holy Ghost, being uncircumcised in hearts and eares, and judged themselves unworthy of eternall life; God let out his Vineyard to other Husbandmen, and the fall of the Jewes Deut. 28. became the riches of the World. Then came the wrath of God on them to the utmost, and they became a travelling Nation indeed, travelling now above 1500. yeeres from being a Nation; and Moses his prophecie was verified in their scattering from one end of the World Jos. de Bel. to the other. Eleven hundred thousand are said to have Jud. l.-j. c. z. perished in Jerusalem alone (where Christ had been crucified) besides all other slaughters in all other parts of Judaea, in that fatall warre under Vespasian and Titus: 97000. were sold to be distracted slaves thorow the Gal. Arcan. world, Galatinus saith 200000. thirty of them for one . 4. 21. piece of Silver, which had given thirty pieces for him which came to make them free. Yet had not the Land spued out all her Lihabitants, but grew so queasie and full of qualmes, that the remainders in Adrians time enter- tained Bencochab for their Messias, who with 200000. Jewes in his Army, is said to have rebelled and bred such combustions, that this Sonne of the Starre (so his name soundeth) was after called Barchosba, the Sonne of Lying. It were prodigious, not hyperbohcall alone, to tell what See my Pil-the Jewes tell of their following slaughters: 700000. grimage I. 2. slaine in Egypt, and in Judaea, so many as passeth all ' ' ' modesty to relate after them. Dion Nicgeus tells of fifty Dion Adrian. Castles and nine hundred and eighty of their best Townes rased, 580000. slaine, besides innumerable multitudes which perished by famine, fire, diseases, and other Baggage of Invading Campes.

i lius Adrianus banished the Jewes from Cyprus and Judasa, erected a new City instead of Jerusalem, called of his owne name ielia, and set Images of Swine over the Gates as Porters to keepe out the Jewes, yea prohibited by Edict the Jewes to looke toward it from any high place. Trajan before was instigated by their rebellion,

to destroy Jewes destruc-many thousands of them in Egypt, Cyrene and Meso- ' '"
potamia. And ever since, those which are contrary to all men, have found all men
contrary to them; and have lived (if such slavery and basenesse be a life) like Cain,
wandring over the World, branded wth Shame and Jetves dispcr-Scorne. Spaine,
England, France, Germany, Poland, Italy, " "-Turkie, all the Indies as farre as China
have had them Inhabitants; have had indeed, for many have given them terrible
expulsions, the rest using cruell and unkind hos-pitalitie, so that they are strangers
where they dwell, and Travellers where they reside, still continuing in the throwes of
travell both of misery and mischiefe. But I have handled this matter more fully in my
Pilgrimage, See my Pil. L and both Benjamin Tudelensis a Travelling Jew, and other
2. r. 21. Travellers in the following Relations, will give you strange travells of theirs
thorow Asia, Africa, and Europe; in all their dispersions to this day retaining their
bloud, name, rites, as disposed by a higher and most mercifull providence, which in
his time will shew mercy on them, to see him by the eye of Faith, whom by the hand
of Cruelty they had crucified, and all Israel Rom. II. 26. shall be saved, and returne
to the Church by a more generall Conversion then hath yet beene seene; and Rom.
II. 15. as their rejection hath proved the reconciling of the World, so the receiving of
them shall be life from the dead.

All times are in Gods hand, but hee which hath promised is able to performe: and
perhaps if Rome the Spirituall! Babylon bee captived and ruined, which hath obtruded
so long on them the monsters of Image worship, Tran-substantiation, worshipping of
so many Saints, with other seemings of refined Ethnicisme, and imposeth on Converts
the losse of all their substance; the way shall bee made more plaine for them: which
wee hope is growing to some ripenesse in this Age, when about so many yeeres have
passed since the calling of the Gentiles, as from Jacobs Family in Egypt, growing to
the face and proportion of a People and Nation, unto their destruction: and full out
as many as were from Josephs death in Egypt, to the destruction of the Temple under
Titus, and more then from Moses his Exodus, to that other Exodus and extermination
under Adrian. We are no Prophets, and must learne by event the certainty of Gods
(before secret) counsells. In meane while let us pray. Hallowed be thy Name, thy
Kingdome come, that this Gal. 4. 19. travelling Nation may one day travell in birth
of Christ Luc. 15. 17. till he be formed in them, and with the prodigall Sonne, 18.
may travell from their wandrings, and at once returne to I. i. 68. their Father and to
themselves, that we may all meet in the unity of Faith, and Gods will may bee done
in Earth, as it is done in Heaven, there being but one Shepheard and one Sheepefold,
Amen. As the Jewish Nation hath been litterally Travellers, so the Christian Church is
alway travelling spiritually to her home, and from her selfe; and the Jewish deportation
to Babylon, was a figure of the Antichristian Captivity in Romish and To. I.. 8. Popish
superstition, of which wee have taken occasion c- 6. to speake more fully elsewhere.

As at first the World was peopled by peregrination successively from Noahs Arke,
and Babels Tower: so in the worldly vicissitude of all things, a world of peregrinations
have happened in the World, and that of worlds of men together, in Nationall invasions,
plantings, sup-plantings, Colonies and new alterations of the face of the world in each
part thereof Thus the Israelites D "- 2- 9' supplanted the Canaanites dwelt in their
rooms; as did ' ' the Moabites to the giantly Emims, the Edomites to the Horims, the

Ammonites to the Zamzummims, and other Nations to others. To recite these were to recite all Stories in manner of the World: Lazius de Migra-tionibus Gentium, and others have in part undertaken it. For even in Palestina alone how many successions have beene, of Canaanites, Israelites, Assyrians (after called Samaritans) and Jewes together."' Of those which the Romans placed or permitted, of Saracens, of Frankes, or Westerne Christians in so many millions as two hundred yeers space sent out of Christendome thither; of Dru-sians, Syrians, a very Babylon of Nations (none and all) ever since This Britaine of ours, besides those which first gave it name (whose remainders still enjoy Wales) hath admitted Romane sprinklings and Colonies, and after that a generall deluge of Saxons, Juttes, and Angles; tempests and stormes out of Denmarke and Norway, and lastly the Norman mixture and combination. Neither is there any Region of ancient Note, which hath not sustained chance and change in this kind. But wee mind not such neere peregrinations, as these usually were, but longer Voyages and remoter Travells. And such also we have already mentioned in Sesostris the Egyptian, in Varro dhtln-the Phoenicians, in the Assyrians, under Semiramis to guhhed Rek-India, besides Eudoxus and other privater persons; and '"" of tunes such are the Fables or outworne Stories of Ethnike J kz Antiquity, touching the Atlantines, Osiris, Bacchus, Her- v, ttopikov: cules, Perseus, Daedalus; and those which retaine some,":, "' 11 11 1 r 1 A "" f Obscure, more truth, though obscure enough, or the Argonauts, Histori-Ulysses, Menelaus, ienasas, Hanno, Himilco, lambolus, call.

and others; some of which shall follow in the following Relations. That of Alexander is more renowmed, and first opened the East to the West, and to Europe gave the Eyes of Geography and History, to take view of India and the Regions adjacent. And here is the first solid foot-print of History in this kind, though heere also Travellers have beene as farre from the truth, as from their homes, and have too often travelled of Vanitie and Lies.

Chap. nil.

Fabulous Antiquities of the Peregrinations and Navigations of Bacchus, Osiris, Hercules, the Argonauts, Cadmus, the Grecian Navie to Troy, Menelaus, Ulysses, ieneas, and others.

T is not the fable or falshood which wee seeke in fabulous Antiquities, but that truth which lieth buried under poeticall rubbish. For nothing but nothing can rise of nothing. Some truth therefore gave occasion to those fables, as Thamars and Dinahs beautie occasioned their ravishment; the Devill (a Lier from the beginning) lusting to defloure that beautie, and then like Ammon adding a second force, in hatred turning her as much as he may out of the World. Hence the fables of Poets, Idolatries of Ethnikes, dotages of Rabbins, phrensies of Heretikes, phancies and Ly-legends of Papists: to all which, when Histories cannot make them good. Mysteries are sought to cover their badnesse, and bald nakednesse; and were they never so bad before (like the shearing of a Friar, or vailing of a Novice Nunne) suddenly they are heereby become errant honest persons, nay venerable and religious. And thus hath that Impostor, not only insinuated and procured admission and credit to lies, but thence hath raised the very Faith Jom 4. of Infidels, which worship they know not what; and obtruded I know not what Pias fraudes, and religious Lies, forsooth, upon unchristian and Anti-christian Christians; to whom because they received not the love of the truth 2- Thess. z. to be saved, God hath sent the efficacy of error, that they might beleeve a lie. This is the Devils triumph, and Mans madnesse; out of which confusion, if wee cannot try out the pure truth, yet those Divine Relations and Revelations premised, will appeare more lovely and admirable from these Ethnike Fables.

I may here mention Saturnes Travells into Latium, being ejected Heaven: Joves fabled five encompassings of the World; Apollos daily circuit; Mercuries frequent Messages to all parts, who was also the Travellers God, and had his Statues in High-wayes; Junos jealous wand-rings; Bacchus and Hercules were renowmed by the Travells of Poets for their Peregrinations, perhaps (as before is ' """ ' observed) no other but Salomon and Hirams Ophirian Voyage. Bacchus (they tell) was the sonne of Jupiter I. i. 69. and Proserpina, who being torne in pieces by the Titans, Jupiter gave his heart to Semele to drinke, and thereby conceived of this other Bacchus; whereupon jealous Juno H gm. Fab. transformed into the shape of Beroe Semeles nurse, 1, 7; perswaded her to desire Jupiters company in Majesticall """ '" appearance, as hee accompanied Juno, which was her destruction; the babe taken out and sewed in Jupiters thigh, and after put to Nysus to nurse, whereupon he was named Dyonisius. I should distract you to tell the disagreeing tales of Poets touching his birth and life (for lies never agree) as also his Miracles, which ever make up the greatest part of a Legend. Tigres, Ounces and Panthers, with Pans, Nymphs, Sileni, Cobals, and Satyrs were his companions and attendants. Hee was drawne in a Chariot by Tigres, and held a Thyrsus in his hand for a Scepter (which was a Speare or Javelin, adorned with the Leaves of Vines and Ivie) and marched thus madly both to India in the East, and to Spaine in the West, which of Pan was called Pania, whence Spania and Hispania have beene derived. A learned Spaniard saith, that in the eight hundred and tenth yeere, before the

Oros. l. i. c. c). building of Rome, Bacchus invaded India, moistned it with bloud, filled it with slaughters, polluted it with lusts, which before had beene subject to none, and lived content and quiet in it selfe. Some apply that of Noah to him, and make him the Inventor of Wine, Hony, and Sacrifices: say also that hee reigned at Nysa a

Citie in Arabia; some adde other Kingdomes, and that hee had Mercurius Trismegistus his Counsellor; and leaving Hercules his Egyptian Lieutenant, Antaeus in

Lybia, Busiris in Phoenicia, conquered all the East, built

Nysa, and erected Pillars in the Easterne Ocean, as did

Hercules on the Westerne. His story is also confounded with that of Osiris, this being the name which the

Her. Euterpe. Egyptians gave him, as Herodotus affirmeth. And

Diod. Sk. l. i. Diodorus relateth his Epitaph in hierogliphicall Letters ' ' in these words, I am Osyris the King, which travelled thorow au the world to the Indian Deserts. Ovid also singeth;

Te memorant Gange, totoque Oriente subactis

Primitias magno seposuisse Jovi. Cinnama tu primus captivaque thura dedisti Deque triumphato viscera tosta bove. S(j-ab. I. I. His journey they describe first thorow Ethiopia, and

Eurip. e. j. gj Arabia, and so to Persia, Media, Bactria, and India: after his returne, to Hellespont, Lidia, Phrygia, Thrace, Greece, and whither travelling witts please. Wee shall lose our selves to follow him further; as they doe which with worst prophanesse celebrate his drunken Holies daily. Theseus iff Theseus and Hercules lived in one time, of which

Hercules. Theseus is famous for his Acts in Crete, Thebes, Thessaly, with the Amazons, and his descent into Hell, with other his Voyages and Navigations: But farre farre more famous is Hercules for his Travells, and for his twelve Labours, his Peregrination being another Labor added to each of them. The Nemaean Lion, Lernaean Hydra, Phrygian Bore, Arcadian Hart, Augean

Stable, Cretan Bull, Thracian Diomede, with his man-eating Horses, Celtike, Alexia, Alpine passage, Italian Tenths, Stymphalide Birds, Amazonian Belt, Atlantike Dragon, Balearian Geryon, Lybyan Antaeus, Egyptian Busiris, Lydian service to Omphale, Thessalian Centaure, and Tartarean Cerberus, proclaime his travells over and under the World; as his Pillars; to the end of the World, and his helping Atlas, that the World travelled on him, Neither travelled hee by Land alone, but by water also hee navigated with those famous Argonauts, The Argo-which make us another Voyage to find them, nauts.

Hyginus hath registred their names: Jason a Thes- Hygin. Fab. salian, Orpheus a Thracian, Asterion of Peline, Polyphemus of Larissa, Iphictus, Admetus, Eurytus Echion, Ethalides, Coeneus, Mopsus the Soothsayer, Pirithous, Menaetius, Eurydamas, Amponitus, Eribotes, Ameleon, Eurytion, Ixition, Oileus, Clytius and Iphitus, Peleus and Telamon, Butes, Phaleros, Tiphys the Master of the Ship, Argus the Shipmaker, Philiasus, Hercules and Hylas his companion, Nauplius, Idmon, Castor and Pollux, Lynceus (which could see things hidden underground, and in the darke) and Idas, Periclymenus, Amphidamus and Cepheus, Ancaeus, Lycurgi, Augaeus, Asterion and Amphion, Euphemus (which could runne dry-foot on the water) Ancasus Neptuni, Erginus, Meleager, Laocoon, Iphictus Thestii, Iphitus Naubo Zetes and Calais (sonnes of Aquilo with winged heads and feet, which chased away the Harpyes) Focus and Priasus, Eurymedon, Palaemonius, Actor, Thersanon, Hippal-cinnos, Asclepius, Atriach, Mileus, Iolaus, Deucalion, Philoctetes, Ceneus sonne of Coronis, Acastus, voluntary companion to Jason. These with their Countries and Parentage Hygynus hath recorded. Their Voyage was to Colchos, but many of them came not thither. Hylas was stollne by the Nymphs in Massia, whom Hercules and Polyphemus seeking, were left behind. Tiphys died by the way, Ancaeus son of Neptune succeeded in his Masters place. Idmon was slain by a

Bore; Butes threw himselte Into the Sea, allured by the Syrens Musick, In their return also Euribates was slain in Libya, Mopsus died in Africa of a Serpents byting.

Now for the Voyage of the Argonauts, they say that Pelias Jasons Uncle was commanded by Oracle to sacrifice to Neptune, to which if any came with one shooe on, the other off, then his death should not bee farre off. Jason came thither, and wading thorow the River Euhenus, left one of his shooes in the mire, which he stayed not to take out, for feare of comming late to the Holies. Pelias seeing this, asked Jason what hee would doe, if hee had a prophecie that any man should kill him. I would send him, said hee, To fetch the Golden Fleece. This was the Fleece of the Ram (which some say was the name of a Ship having a Ram on the Beake, I. i. 70. that had carried Phryxus to Colchos, who sacrificed the Ram to Jupiter, and hanged up the Fleece in the Grove of Mars) and thus Pelias out of his owne mouth sentenced him. Argus made the Ship which of him was called Argos, which they say was the first ship of long fashion. These first came to Lemnos, where they were so kindely entertained, that Jason by Hypsipila the Queene had two sons, and staied till Hercules chode them away., i f " Next they came to Cyzicus, in Propontis, which liberally deliverance of sted them; and being gone thence, by foule weather Hesionefrom they were put backe in the night, where Cyzicus mis-thewhale, the taking them for enemies was slaine in fight. Thence hllmgofking sailed to Bebrycia, where Amycus the King chal-iakil oftrov l g d them to a single encounter at whorlebats, in in their return which Pouux slew him. Lycus a neighbour King was for breaking glad hereof and gave the Argonauts entertainment, where his promise of jphis or Tiphis died, and Idmon was slaine. cuks l ' Phineus the Son of Agenor a Thrasian was blinded by Harpyes. Jupiter for revealing the gods secrets, and the Harpyes set to take the meate from his mouth. The Argonauts consulting with him of their future successe, must first free him of this punishment, which Zetes and Calais did, chasing them to the Strophades. Phineus shewed them how to passe the Symplegades, following the way which a Dove sent forth of the Ship, shewed them. Thence they came to the He Dia where the Birds Stymphalides shot quils which killed men, whom by Phineus his precepts they feared away with sounds (such as the Curetes make) and used thereto shields also and speares. Thus being entred the Euxine Sea to Dia, they found poore, naked, shipwracked, the Sons of Phrixus, Argus, Phron-tides, Melas and Cylindrius, which travelling to their Grandfather Athamas there encountered that misfortune. Jason entertained them, and they brought him to Colchos by the River Thermodoon; and comming neere Colchos caused the ship to be hidden, and came to their Mother, Chalciope sister of Medea, to whom they related Diod. maketh Jasons kindenesse, and the cause of his comming. She f " brings Medea to Jason, who as soone as she saw him,,. j J knew that it was the same whom in her dreame she had Hecate. I. scene and loved, and promiseth him all furtherance.

ieeta had learned by Oracle that hee should so long reigne as the Fleece which Phrixus had consecrated, remained in Mars his Temple. He therefore imposeth on Jason to yoak the bras-footed firebreathing buls to the plow, and to sow the Dragons teeth out of the Helmet, whence armed men should suddenly be produced and kill each other. This he did by Medeas helpe, and likewise cast the Dragon into a sleepe which guarded the Fleece, and so tooke it away, i eta hearing that Jason and his Daughter Medea were gone, sent his son Absyrtus in a ship with souldiers after him, who pursued him to Tmceus Istria in the Adriaticke Sea, where Alcinous compounded saith that they their quarrel so little to Absyrtus his liking, that follow- ' "Jf ' " ' ing him to Minervas He, Jason slew him, and his followers crossed over builded there a Citie called of his name Absoris. Some land to the tell of the Syrtes which the Argonauts passing carried Ocean, and their ship on their shoulders twelve dales. But the f f b' 'h .-11 1 11 r I- Lades into the varieties are inextricable and innumerable. Arter his fy its. returne, by Medeas helpe he made away his Unckle Ody. n.

Sirab. I. I. speaking of the Poets Argonauts salth in qui-busdam cum historia con-sen tit, qua" dam etiam assingit, moremferuans 15 communem 15 fuum. Cum historia consentit, quando j letam nominat iff Jasonem tif J go i5c. Greciannavie against Troy.

Pelias (to whom she had promised to restore his youth) and gave his Kingdome to Acastus his sonne, which had accompanied him to Colchos. The exile of Medea and the rest of the tale you may have amongst the Poets. I am more then wearie with relating so much. This voyage was so admired of Antiquitie that this Argo which Homer calleth iraa-iixexova-a, was not onely praised to the stars by the Poets, but placed amongst the stars by their Minerva, and the constellation famous to these times. The Argonauts after this instituted the Olympian games. The Poets are full of such Chymasras, mixed lye-truths, not sparing any of their Gods or Heroes. Jupiter having stolne Europa transformed into a Bull, or as some say in a ship of that name, or having a bull in the Beke, Cadmus and Thasus her brethren were sent by Agenor their father to seeke her. The Phenician Navie is divided betwixt them. Thasus having long sought in vaine, returned not, but in the gaean Sea built a Citie of his name. Cadmus built Thebes, and after that! But what and why doe I while you in these uncertainties Yet have I touched a little of his storie who is famed the first inventer of the Grsecian Letters, and of Historic. But we will turne your eyes to the most fabled of all Poeticall fables, and in a peece of an houre with a swift pen will dispatch ten yeeres worke with looo. ships.

The Princes in the Trojan siege and their ships are these: Agamemnon brought from Micenae one hundred ships: Menelaus his brother from thence also 60. Phaenix of Argos 50. Achilles of Scyros 60. Automedon his Chariot driver 10. Patroclus of Phthia 10. Ajax ot Salamine 12. Teucer his brother as many, Ulisses of Ithaca 12. Diomedes of Argos 30. Stenelus of Argos 25. Ajax the Locrian 20. Nestor the Pylian 90. Thrasymedes his brother 15. Antilochus sonne of Nestor 20. Eurypylus of Orchomene 40. Macaon of Attica 20. Podalyrius his brother 9. Tlepolemusof Mycenae 9. Idomeneus of Crete 40. Meriones from thence as many, Eumelus of Perr- hebia 8. Philoctetes of Melibaea 7. Peneleus of Bceotia 12. Pithus a Baeotian also as many, and his brother Chronius 9. Arcestlaus 10. Prothasnor 8. ladmenus of Argos 30. Ascalaphus 30. Schedius 30, and Epistrophus his brother 10. Elephenor, Calchodontis and Imenaretes (all likewise of Argos) 30. The sonne of Menaeus from Athens 50. Agapenor from Arcada 60. Amphimachus of Elea 10. Eurychus of Argos 15. Amarunceus of Mycenae 19. Polysenes from jetolia 40, Meges the Dulichian 60. Thoas 15. Podarces his brother 10. Prothous the Magnesian 40. Cycnus the Argive 12. Nireus from thence 16. Antiphus the Thessalian 20. Polyboetes the Argive 20. Leophites of Sicyon 19. You see the particulars amount farre above the thousand usually named. The Voyage was too short, and the Siege too long for this place.

Menelaus having recovered his eye-sore faire Helena, I. i. 71. is said to have beene eight yeeres wandering the world, Travels of and Ulysses longer. Menelaus his errour was about " " Cyprus, Phaenicia, gypt, and the neighbouring Ethiopians and Arabians (so Strabo expoundeth Homers Strab. I. i. Erembos in his first Booke, and in his sixteenth, yet there addes also the Troglodites) he produceth some which place the Sidonians in the Persian Gulfe, I know not how justly. Homers Verses, where Menelaus relateth his travels to Telemachus are: "- l vtTpov, oivlKrjvre, Kai Aiyutrriov?, e7raxr)6ei9

AioioTra 9' ikOfxtiv, koi 'Zisonoug Koi 'E 0e3oi'?, Ka Ai vtjv.

Cypres, Phasnicia, JEgypt having past,

Th' Ethiops, Sidons, 'Erembs, I went at last. And Libya

Aristonicus the Grammarian, and after him Eustathius, Traveh oj interpret it of sailing round about Africa, as is said of 'Ulysses. Eudoxus and others before (Trepn-rxevcrag tov QKeavov Sia rovg Taseipcou ue iot rrjg Ivsikrj) a thing to mee altogether un-probable, and easier to be sailed by the Poet or his Commenters in an Inkie Sea with a quill Mast, then by the ruder Sea-men of those times. Menelaus his errours I 193 N we see continued more then eight yeares, yea are not yet ended, but breede new travels in Grammarians braines. Tantae molis erat infame reducere scortum.

Ulysses returning from Troy, came to the Ciconae, the Lotophagi, and after that to Polyphemus the Giant, with one eye in his forehead, thence to olus, to the Lestrygonae, to- naria infamous by Circes charmes, to Avernus, to the Syrenes, to Scylla, Sicilia, Charybdis, to ieaea, to the Phaeaces, and at last to Ithaca. The like fables Grammer-schoole boyes can tell you of ienaeas out of Virgil, and other Poets. I am weary of travelling in such a loose sandy soile, where so few footeprints and paths of truth are to be found. And for ienaeas his travels, I will present you them in another fashion as Hondius hath in his Map described them.

I might adde D dalus his flight from Athens, his sleight for Pasiphae in Crete, his acts in Sicilia, his arts every where in his travels. As for his, and his sonne I. i. 72. Icarus his flying, the truth is found in taking away the first letter, except you flye to Mysteries. And this is the salve too ordinary in all the Poets fables, Perseus, the Atlantines, and others, which I forbeare to relate.

See of d these Other fabulous Relations of Travellers we have, hi Photius his meerely fained, as that of Heliodorus his iethiopike

Heliof" ' History, Achilles Tatius, Iamblichus, all in Love-stories;

Jchiles are Lucius Patrensis his Metamorphoses (whence Lucian had extant. his Lucius, and thence Apuleius his Asinus) Antonius

Diogenes his Thule, and other like, they are not fabulous

Histories but Parables, Mysticall Fables and Poems in

Historicall forme, as Utopia and Arcadia; that I adde not more then a good many others amongst us of worse note, which idle wits have made both Mothers and

Daughters of Idlenesse, or fruitlesse foolish businesse without braine or heart.

I have more mind to give you a History, though even here wee cannot secure Quicquid Grascia mendax Audet in Historia. Some things are uncertaine in the best, yet better a tattered truth then nothing.

The Philosophers and Wisemen of Greece were Travellers for knowledge (of which some travelled with knowledge also, and have left Geographicall Monuments) Merchants for gaine, and mightie Potentates for Dominion and Glory. The Merchants had their reward in that which they sought, the other for better knowledge of times, deserve more leisurely view.

Chap. V.

A briefe recitall of the famous expeditions mentioned in ancient Histories, of the Assyrians, Egyptians, Scythians, Ethiopians, Persians, and others.

S these last have bin told by Poets as fables, that is truths eeked and wrought upon by their wits for greater delight, so the stories of the first Assyrian Monarchic and Egyptian Dynasties have little more solidity. Ninus by the Greeke and iv . Latine stories is renowned for his ambitious marches, and travels thorow all Asia from the Red to the Euxine Sea, and thorow Scythia to the Bactrians. P- Oros. . i. Hee conquered (saith Diodorus) the Armenians and their.+-. King Barchanes, Pharnus also King of Media and all Asia from Tanais to Nilus, the Egyptians, Phaenicians, Syrians, Cilicians, Pamphiha, Lycia, Caria, Phrygia, Misia, Lydia, Troas, Propontis, Bythinia, Cappadocia, the Barbarians upon Pontus, Cadusians, Tapyrans, Hyrcans, Dranges, Derbici, Carmani, Coronei, Rhomni, Vorcani, Parthians, Persians, Susians, Caspians, and many others. Ariaeus the Arabian King was his Collegue in armes in these expeditions. After which he built Ninus or Ninive, Ninive the wals one hundred foot high, broade enough for three builded. Carts to passe together on the tops, with 1500. Turrets 200. foote high, the squares unequall the two longer 150. furlongs, the two shorter 90. Hee made a second expedition against the Bactrians, and then maried Semir- Semiramis.

The Scripture more truly ascribeth Babylon to Nimrod, Ninive to Ashur.

Theutamo. Memnon.

Jos. Scal. Notee ad Euseb. Chron.

amis a Syrian, which he tooke from her husband Menon, who hanged himselfe in foolish griefe.

Semiramis succeeded, and exceeded his exploits: She invaded Ethiopia, and whereas (if you beleeve Ctesias) Ninus had with him in his last expedition against Zoro-astres the Bactrian 1700000. footmen and 200000. horsemen with 10600. hooked chariots: She builded (as they say) Babylon, with a stupendious Garden in Chaona, and Pallace at Ecbatana, cut out highwaies in Persia, passed thorow Egypt to Libya to the Oracle of Jupiter Ammon, subjected Ethiopia, and made three yeers provision to invade Staurobates King of India, slew 300000. Beeves of their Hides to frame counterfeit Elephants, and with 3000000. (it is Ctesias also which taleth it) of Footmen, and 500000. Horsemen, and 2000. Ships, with Elephantine counterfeits carried on Camels, shee made that Indian invasion, where Staurobates encountered her with greater numbers, threatning to crucifie her. On Indus was the Navall fight, wherein the Indians had the worse, and lost 1000. Ships, but in the Field the Assyrian Armie was overthrowne. Thus they proceed in the Assyrian Empire for 1300. yeeres together, and say that at the warres of Troy, Theutamo the twentieth from Ninus re- lieved Priamus with 20000. Men, and 200. Chariots under the conduct of Memnon. As for Sardanapalus the thirtieth and last of them, the truth is, as in the former, a certaine uncertainty. Eusebius reckoneth the time of Semiramis to have beene the same with Abraham, so that Moses, whom Josephus, Clemens, Africanus, Tatianus, made to be 850. yeeres before the Trojan warre, is by his more probable reckoning made much later, yet, as hee saith, ancienter then the Greekish Antiquities, and their Gods also: being borne, as Scaliger calculateth out of his Positions 394. yeeres before the destruction of Troy. Now what pettie Kinges the World had in the best peopled parts in Abrahams time, the fourth Chapter of Genesis sheweth, even of those Regions; which some therefore make but Vice-roys under the

Assyrian, very daringly. Ninus his numbers savour of Nimrods Babel, which after Ages could make swel with such vanities. It may be a question (I thinke the negative out of question) whether the World had then so many soules so soone after the Flood, as those Indian and Assyrian Armies are said to containe.

The like may bee said of Vexores the Egyptian Kings Expedition, which conquered to Pontus, and Tanaus the Scythian, which conquered him and almost all Asia, as some say before Ninus. Vexores by Genebrard is supposed to bee Osiris, the first Pharao. And for Sesostris wee have already in part acknowledged his greatnesse, and withall his latenesse in the time of Rehoboam the Sonne of Salomon. He is said to have had in his Army 600000. Footmen, and 24000. Horse, 8020. Chariots of Warre, in the Red Sea foure hundred Ships. Hee conquered beyond Ganges, the Medes, the Scythians unto Tanais, and the rest of Asia. Into Europe he passed as farre as Thrace, and left Pillars as Monuments for his victories, engraven with the representation of a mans Privities, if they were valiant; of a womans, if effeminate.

Not long after was that Expedition of Zerah the Ethiopian with a million of men, overthrowne by King Asa; as that of the Queene of Sheba (some thinke shee raigned over Arabia and Ethiopia) to Salomon a little before. Tiglath Pileser King of Assyria tooke Damascus, and Shalmaneser carried away the tenne Tribes into Assyria and Media, and placed Babilonians, Cutheans and others in their roomes. Senacherib soone after invaded Judah, but Tirhakah King of Ethiopia came out against him. This Tirhakah is thought to bee that Tearcon, which Strabo mentioneth, where hee denieth that India had beene invaded by any but Bacchus and Hercules before Alexander, denying that of Semiramis, and alleadging Megasthenes both to that purpose, and that Sesostris the Egyptian, and Tearcon the Ethiopian pierced into Europe, yea that Nabucodonosor, or Navocodrosor (more celebrated by the Chaldaeans then Hercules) came

Vexores the Eg- ptian. Tanaus. I. i. 73-
Sesostris.
Died. sic. I. I.
Zerah the thiopian.
2. Chron. 9. 14.
2. Kin. 16.6 17-
Thearcon. Strab. . 15. Megasthenes his testimony of old Expeditions.
hlabuchodono-sor.
Idanthrysus.
Cyrus.
Dan. 2.
Cambyses. Darius.
Xerxes. Her. I. 7.

to the Straits or Hercules his Pillars; as did also Tear-con: also that Idanthyrsus the Scythian pierced as farre as Egypt; but none of them went (saith hee) to India. Megasthenes acknowledgeth that Cyrus came neere the Indians, in his Expedition against the Massagets, but not thither. As for Nabucodonosors Asian and Egyptian Expeditions, and his Dominion in manner over the World wee have divine testimony in Daniells Tree and Golden Image; of Cyrus also, whose Conquests are knowne, and large Peregrinations from the West parts of Asia, where hee captived CrœSus and subdued his, with the adjoyning Dominions, and all the Regions thence thorow

Syria, Armenia, Media, Persia, to the Massagets and Scythians. His Sonne Cambyses added gypt, and that foolish Expedition against the Ethiopians. Darius with 800000. men invaded the Scythians. Xerxes, as Herodotus hath recorded, invaded Greece with 1700000. Footmen, 80000. Horsemen, 20000. Chariot Men, one thousand two hundred and eight saile of Ships. Ctesias (which useth elsewhere to say the most) hath but 800000. men besides Chariots, and one thousand Ships. As for other Scythian and Amazonian invasions, with others of other Nations, for their uncertaintie I omit them. The Greeks also had their many, both Expeditions and defensive Warres against the Persians before Alexanders time. Themistocles, Xenophon, and many others of them are renowmed, tam marte quam Mercurio. And thus the Persian Empire hath brought us to Alexander, which succeeded it, of whose Expedition wee shall anon take speciall and more leisurely view.

As for the later Empires of Carthage and Rome, to tell of their Travellers and Travells would prove a History of their States, and all their famous Captaines, especially the Romans when they began to spread their wings farre from their Italian nest, and flowed out of Europaean Bankes into Africa and Asia. The Scipios in the Carthaginian warres, Lucullus in Africa, and after in the Mith-ridatike war; Great Pompey in his Europasan, Asian, and fatall African Voyages Expeditions; Greater Julius, whose travels procreated a Monarchy; Covetous Crassus, Cruell Antonius, Flourishing Augustus, Seely Claudius, Triumphant Vespasian, Gentle Titus, Proud Domitian, Glorious Trajan, Witty Adrian, in manner all the rest of their Emperors forced, or forcing on their Frontiers, whose very Imperial progresse in their own State, were great voyages peregrinations; yea their Empires (as before is observed) was called by the ambitious title Su. c. z. z. of the World: For better knowledge whereof I have here presented the Map thereof. Severe Severus died at Yorke, Christian Constantine arose a bright Sunne to the World out of our North; Apostate Julian travelled also and brought forth an incarnate Devill, which after many peregrinations perished in the East, and left the Empire to Good Jovian. To set downe the Emperours travells would be to give you the Imperiall History from Julius, till the times that the World fell in travell with Barbarian travellers, Goths, Vandals, Herules, Hunnes, Avares, Frankes, Saxons, Lumbards, Saracens, which shared amongst them that vast Empire: especially the travell of the Imperiall Seat from Rome to Constantinople giving the occasion both to a mysticall conception of Antichrist (which may seeme borne long after by Phocas midwifery, and growing up till Gregory the seventh, when the Devill was loosed from the bottom-lesse pit, and in Christian names restored in great part the Ethnike Gentilisme) and to those inundations of Barbarians and Barbarisme, which like a smoake from the bottomlesse pit prepared the Papall way. Pipine, and especiall Charles the Great were great Travellers also, and unwitting much furthered the growth of that Monster, which after swallowed up the Imperiall Eagle, and left but the feathers and shadow remaining. The Danes and Normanes were unwelcome Travellers, which perfected that, which others had begun: especiall the Normanes by their warres and greatnesse in Italy, growing out of the ruines of the Easterne Empire, and by that conspiracy of Urban and Boamund, which seeking to fish in troubled waters devised the Expeditions of the I. i. 74. Franks to the Hierosolymitan warre, which set the world in travell 200. yeers together, the Mahumetans of the South and East, and the

Christians of the North and West making Palestina the stage of fury slaughter. After these the Tartars filled the world with innumerable armies mischiefes, especially all Asia one halfe of Europe. But these are later things, and some of them follow in our Relations. For the Parthians, and later Persian Dynasty, and Saracenicall travells over, and both spirituall and temporall conquests thorow the world, and the Ottoman, Sophian, Mogoll, and other branches from that root, I have bin a large relater in my Pilgrimage.

Chap. VI.

The travells of the antient Philosophers and learned men briefly mentioned.

Ow let us examine the Voyages of Philosophers and Learned men, into remote parts for Wisdome and Learning. Diogenes Laertius maketh two kinds of Philosophy, the one Ionike, the other Italike: this began from Pythagoras, the other from Thales, both which, with many of their Successors were great Travellers. As for Thales, his Epistle to Pherecydes a Syrian (another travelling Philosopher) is yet extant in Laertius, in which he mentions his Solons travels, in these words: For neither are I and Solon the Athenian so foolish and mad, that when we have sailed to Crete pierced into Egypt, there to conferre with the Priests and Astronomers, we would not with like care saile to thee. For Solon will come also if you thinke good. For thou being holden with liking of that place seldome passest into Ionia; neither art moved with desire of Strangers: but as I hope thou onely appliest thy selfe to writing. But wee which write nothing, travell thorow Greece and Asia.

Thus have you one testimony of two Grandees, Thales I- i- 75- and Solon. This later, in his return from Egypt visited Cyprus, and after went to Croesus, who adorning him-selfe in greatest glory pompe, asked Solon if ever he had seene goodlier spectacle? Yes, said he, Cockes, Phesants, and Peacockes. Croesus being after by Cyrus sentenced to the fire, cried, O Solon, Solon, Solon, and being demanded the reason, answered, That Solon had told him, that no man might be accounted happy before his death: wherein Cyrus reading the mutabilitie of his owne fortunes, gave him his life and a competent estate. Thence Solon went into Cilicia, and built Solos.

To Croesus is an Epistle also of Anacharsis, another travelling Philosopher, borne in Scythia, and brother to the Scythian King, making some mention of his Travells in these woods: I, O King of Lidians, came into Greece to learne their Manners, Studies, and Instructions; and need not Gold, esteeming it enough to returne to the Scythians a better man, and more learned. Yet I will come to thee to Sardis, much esteeming thy friendship and familiaritie. Hee was Laer. I. z. Solons guest at Athens, whither he came in the fortie seventh Olympiad. Socrates the first bringer in of Ethikes or Morall Philosophy, was a Traveller also, and followed the warres by Land and Sea. Xenophon Xenophon. his Scholler, was both in Arts, and Armes, and Travells

Least Travellers may be greatest Writers. Even I which have written so much of travellers travells, never travelled 200. miles from

Thaxted in Essex, where I was borne: herein like a whetstone, which being blunt causeth sharpnesse; or a Candlestick holding many Candles, without which it selfe is unseene in the darke; and as the Compasse is of little compasse and motion, yet teacheth to compasse the World; or as the Pole-star is lest moved of all, most of all moving guiding the

Traveller. Envy not a marginall roome to him, who hath used

Volumes so spacious to thee; in which, how little is the travell of the greatest Traveller; or how could a great Traveller have travelled of so much.

famous, and hath left Monuments thereof written by himselfe. His voyage to Delphos, and thence to Cyrus, and after his Persian journey to Agesilaus King of Sparta, and with him against the Thebans, and after that to Helis and Corinth, are recorded by Laertius. In his daies Ctesias a Traveller and Historian lived, which writ the Persian, Assyrian and Indian Stories, but often travells from truth,

Arutippus. Aristippus was a Cyrenian by birth, by studies an Athenian, as were many others of his Countrymen, by base flattery a trencher-worme to Dionysius the Sicilian Tyrant. Ptolemeus an Ethiopian was his Schouer, and Antipater a Cyrenean. Epitemedes, Paraebates, Hegesias, Anniceris were also Cyrenaik. es, holding voluptuous opinions, as also Theodorus and another Aristippus, magnifying sensuall pleasures. The Ecclesiastike Histories of Socrates and Sozomen, mention the travells of Empedocles, which threw himselfe into the Sicilian Crateres, and of Democritus Cous which spent eightie yeeres in travelling thorow divers Countries. Meropius also, and Merodorus are mentioned with others. But ? lato. wee will come to men better knowne: Plato is famous

Laert. L 3. t i Philosophy and Travelling. Hee travelled to Euclide at Megara, to Theodorus the Mathematician, into Italy to the Pythagoreans, Philolaus and Eurytus,

Euripides, thence to Egypt to the Priests (and with him Euripides also) and intended to visit the Persian Magi, but was prohibited by the Asian warres. Returning to Athens hee set up the Academie. Thrice hee travelled in warfare to Tanagra, to Corinth, to Delos. Thrice also hee sayled into Sicilia. First to see it, at which time Dionysius the Tyrant displeased with his free speech, caused him to bee sold in gina; but being freed, Dionysius writ to him not to reproach him. Plato answered, Hee had not so much leisure as to thinke on Dionysius. He sailed thither to the younger Dionysius twice. His Disciples were Speusippus the Athenian, Xenocrates of Chalcedon, Aristotle the Stagirite, Dion of Syracuse, Amyctus of Heraclea, Timolaus of Cyzicus,

Heraclides of Pontus, and others of other Countries, his Schoole yeelding a prettie Geographicall Map of

Countries. Bion was borne neere Boristhanes, but Bion.

added honor to his Country by his studies. He was sold for a Slave, and bought by an Orator which made him his heire: he sold al went to Athens. After his studies there, he lived at Rhodes. Lacydes the Lacydes.

chiefe of the New Academie, was a Cyrenaean. Carneades Cameades.

was also of the same nation. Clitomachus was a Cartha- Clitomachus.

ginian, his true name was Asdrubal. He went to

Athens, there became the scholler of Carneades his successor. Menippus was a Phenician by birth, Menippm.

lived a Cynik at Thebes.

Aristotle was borne the first yeere of the 99. Olympiad: Aristotle.

at seventeene yeers he became Platoes Scholler, and so continued twentie yeeres. After that hee went to

Mitylene, and when Alexander was fifteene yeeres old, to King Philip, in the second yeere of the 109. Olympiad, and having commended the care ot young Alexander to his Cousin Callisthenes, in the second of the iii. Calisthenes.

returned to Athens, and taught in Lyceo thirteene yeeres, and then went to Chalcis and there died. Cahsthenes travelled with Alexander, till the Persian Conquest had made him swell beyond the measure of a man, and some Greeke Foolosophers (Philosophers I dare not call them; but amongst the Muses some have alway beene

Hedge-whores, and the learning of some in all Ages hath licked the trenchers, and fly-blowed the sores of great men; with the basest of vices. Flattery, kissing the hinder parts, sucking the Emerodes, feeding on their So the Bar- excrements, themselves the excrements of Mankind: f f ", 1-111 J 3 A ine tleventh.

but whither hath passion transported mee.-') Agis an j. j.-ian. I. 4.

Argive, and Cleo a Sicilian, some adde Anaxarchus also,

Et caetera urbium suarum Purgamenta (saith Curtius) Q. Curtis.. S.

would needs open Heaven to Alexander, and preferre him to Hercules, Bacchus, Castor and Pollux: Alexander Put. Alex.

stood behind the hangings, whiles Cleo made a speech to persuade the Persian Rites, and with them to deifie and incense their Kings. Which being gravely refuted by Callisthenes (for to him especially was the speech directed, that they which went before others in learning, should in this innovation also) that it was not for him and Cleo to make Gods, or for the Kings honor to bee beholden to them for his Divinitie, which could not give a Kingdome on Earth to him, and much lesse Heaven: Alexander concealed his malice, till upon occasion of torturing some, which had conspired his death, he tortured also even to death Callisthenes, giving him that recompence for saving his life, when having slaine Clytus in a drunken rage, hee would have I. i. 76. added in a sullen and mad penance his owne death, and was by Callisthenes wisedome reclaimed. This was his preparation to the Indian Expedition.

Many other learned men followed Alexander, and writ his story, viz. Marsyas, Pellaeus, Hecatasus Abderita, Aristobulus, Clitarchus, Anaximenes, Onesicritus, Nearchus, Ptolemasus Lagi after King of Egypt, Antipater another of Alexanders Captaines, and an Historian, Aristus, Asclepiades; Vossius addes Archelaus, Strattis, Eumenes, Diodorus, whose stories wee have cited by Arrianus, Strabo, Plutarch, c. But then the World travelled of Travellers of all sorts, learned and unlearned.

Laeri. L 7. Zeno was a Cyprian, by birth of Phasnician parentage, and at Athens began the Stoike Sect, whither hee came with Purple out of Phenicia to sell, and suffered ship-wracke in the Piraeum, upon which occasion solacing

L. 1.8. himselfe with a booke, hee followed Crates. Cleanthes was his successor, after him Sphaerus a Bosphoran, which travelled also to Alexandria to Ptolemeus Philo-pater. Heraclites the Ephesian was a travelling Philosopher, of whose acquaintance Darius Histaspis was ambitious and writ to him about it. But of all the Philosophers none were more famous, then the first

Pythagoras, founder of that name Pythagoras, either in travells with, or for Science. He was borne at Samos, thence passed to Lesbos, and there heard Pherecydes the Syrian. Returning to Samos, Polycrates the famous Minion of Fortune, commended him to Amasis King of Egypt. Hee learned the Egyptian Mysteries and Language, and travelled thence with Epimenedes into Crete, and after that into Italy to Croton, and there began the Italike Philosophy before mentioned. But who can tell his travells.? Iamblichus his Scholler, saith that PUn. l. zo. c. x. Pythogoras learned his Philosophy, partly of the Orphics, "" f""-partly of the Egyptian Priests, partly of the Chaldees and Magi. Learned Plinie saith of him, that to learne Zoroastres his Magia, Pythagoras navigavit, exilio verius quam peregrinatione suscepta. Hee (doe you beleeve it i) had beene iethalides the sonne of Mercury, and after that had beene Euphorbus in the warres of Troy, who being dead, his soule passed into Hermotinus, and travelled to Branchidae to Apollos Temple, after whose death a new transmigration befell him into Pyrrbus a Delian Fisherman, and at last you have Pythagoras. It seemeth hee had beene also in India, where the Brachmanes or Bramenes to this day observe the Rites and Opinions which the Westerne World ascribe to Pythagoras, as not eating of things which have had Hfe, transmigration of soules, and the like. Histaspis, the Father of Darius the King, is reported to have travelled into India and learned their Magike and Philosophy, which the Magi in Persia after professed. Philostratus hath written a long Legend of Apollonius Tyanaeus his Pilgrimage to the Brachmanes in India, to Babylon, iegypt, and Arabia, to Nysa, to Taxilla, to larchas the principal! Indian Brachmane, to his Egyptian and Ethiopian Gymnosophists, c. But incredulus odi. I reckon him an Hospitall Beggar, with whom I will have nothing to doe. Pyrrho an Athenian Philosopher Scholler of Anaxarchus, is said to have travelled both to the Persian Magi, and Indian Gymnosophists, and learned of them that hee could learne nothing, nay

Strab. lib. 15. Curt. 10. Fr. Elian."c. Amb. Ep. 7, Diod. Sic. I. 4. c, 9.

See Vossius of Polybius, 5 Pythias. De hist, grcec. Herod. I. 4. Scyllax sent by the Persian to discover the Grecian Coast, before that famous invasion.

learned not so much, but doubted of that also. India also yeelded some travelling Philosophers to the Graecians, of whom the most famous is that Calanus which followed Alexander to Pasargadas, some say to Babylon, and there burned himselfe, an end sutable to his severe profession beyond the Stoikes austeritie. An Epistle of his is registred at large by Saint Ambrose. Archimedes also travelled into Egypt and left famous Monuments of his Art in many parts of the World. But wee have beene too long in travell of this argument. More are wee beholden to the travells of Historians, such as Herodotus, Megasthenes, Diodorus Siculus, Strabo, Polybius, and many others which travelled into Italy, Egypt, Ethiopia, Greece, Asia, and divers parts of the World, that they might give the World unto posteritie. Herein also they deserve mention, which then were counted fablers, as Pythias Massiliensis, whom Strabo and others reject: yet his reports of short nights, c. are now knowne truths. Some have written of travelling and sailing by the Coasts, as Arrianus his Circumnavigation of the Red or Indian Sea, and of the Blacke or Euxine Sea; the 'irepi-nyr (Ti; Trepiifkov of Marcianus Heracleotes, published in Greeke by David Hoeschelius, rare Jewells for knowledge of antient Geography, but not so fitting our common Reader, The like wee may say of Scyllax Caryandensis, mentioned by Herodotus, Artemidorus the Ephesian, Dicearchus Mesenius, Isidorus, Conracasnus. The Learned know where to read them: the Vulgar would not regard them if they were here; Time having devoured the very names by them mentioned, and not the Cities and Ports alone. Yet for a taste wee will give you a Voyage of two of the Antients. And first that of Hanno.

Chap. VII.

Phcenician Voyages, and especially that of Hanno, a Carthaginian Captaine.

Iodorus Siculus reporteth of the Phoenicians (of whose Navigations in the Indian and African Ocean, and Spanish Plantations we have spoken before) that sayling to divers Marts, they planted many Colonies in Africa, and some also in the West parts of Europe: that they sailed also out of the Straits into the Ocean, and built on the Europasan Continent the Citie Gadira (or Cadiz) and therein erected a sumptuous Temple to Hercules, which to his dayes was holden in great reputation of Sanctitie, the Rites therein observed after the Phcenician manner, wherein many famous Roman Commanders after their great exploits, have paid to this God their vowed Holies. The Phoenicians sailing alongst the Lybian shore in the Ocean, were many dayes carried with tempests unto an Hand very great and fertile, with pleasant Champaines and Mountaines, goodly Woods, Gardens, Houses, Fountaines, wholsome Ayre, seeming to be the dwelling rather of Gods then Men. The Tyrrheni (which were strong by Sea) would have sent a Colonic thither, but were forbidden by the Carthaginians, which feared lest their Citizens allured by the goodnesse of the Countrey should betake themselves thither: and besides, they would reserve it for a place of refuge, if any adversitie should happen to their Citie. Aristotle also in his Booke Tre oi Oavfxacrlcov akovcrudrcov hath some such thing of Carthaginian Merchants, which sailed from Spaine into the Westerne Ocean; but I thinke both may bee applied rather to some one of the Hands of the Canaries, or Cape Verd, or Saint Thomas, or to some part of the African Continent, which they might thinke (not sailing further) to be an Hand, or to

D. Sic. l. c."j. Sup. c. I.12.

Gadira or Cadiz, built by the Pheeni-

Goodly Hand.

Galvano, O vie do and others apply it to the American Antiles.

Gerardi 10. vos. de histor, Gne. I. 4.

Plin. l. z. c. zy. some fiction, then to America. Aristotle in that Treatise mentioneth Hanno, which Vossius thinketh rather to be the worke of the younger Aristotle, called Ponticus (Laertius mentions eight Aristotles) then of that great Oracle of learning and miracle of Nature. But of Hannos Periplus (as it was falsly termed) many Authors have made mention. Plinie so speaketh of it, as if hee had sailed about Africa, in these words, Et Hanno, Carthaginis potentia florente, circumvectus a Gadibus ad finem Arabiae, navigationem eam prodidit scripto; sicut ad extera Europas noscenda missus eodem tempore Himilco. By which words it is apparent that Hanno and Himilco in those flourishing times of Carthage, Himilco. were sent by publike decree upon discoveries, Himilco to the Coasts of France, Britaine, and other parts of Europe; Hanno Southwards to coast around the African shores. The like testimony he hath in his fifth Booke, L. 5. f. I. Fuere Hannonis Carthaginiensium Ducis commen-tarii, Punicis rebus florentissimis, explorare ambitum 'aliaquis- Africe jussi: quem secuti plerique e nostris, ad alia demfab. quaedam fabulosa, urbes multas ab eo conditas ibi prodidere, quarum nee memoria ulla, nee vestigium extat. Whereby wee see that

Plinie doubted of the truth of Hannos relations: yea it was a Proverbe, as Athenaeus, which Casaubon in his Notes upon him, with Vossius also have observed; Siquid ejusmodi Juba refert, gaudeat Lybicis libris Hannonis ac erroribus: as good a testi-Qa Bavium monie of Juba and Hanno for Historians as Virgils of non odit, amet gavius and Maevius for Poets. Yet, as I will not alto-Mtevi " gether cleare him, so I thinke that ignorance of those places in those times made him seeme the more fabulous, as Marco Polo and others did till our Grandfathers dales: which appeareth in that they make that a circumnavigation about Africk, which reached not one quarter of the way from the Pillars of Hercules, to the p' ' 'm v' Arabian Gulfe. Artemidorus the Ephesian doth mention sitorb l. 3. ' Mela also with Solinus. Mela came neere the c. 10. truth, which saith that Hanno sailed a great part of the coast, and returned for want of provision, not of Sea- Hanno Car-roome. He, and Solinus and Plinie have cited much S "", out of him, which perhaps might receive a better inter- Qceani ostia pretation then Antiquity could give, as appeareth by exisset, mag-Ramusios annotations on that Voyage, and by helpe of nam partem a Portugall Pilot expert in those coasts, comparing i! JJ ' lll Hannos with the present Navigations. We will first., give you the Text and then the Commentarie. But meatu defe-first we will adde out of Galvano touching Himilco, cis e, 'c that hee is said to have sailed to Gotland and Thule, within 24. degrees of the Pole, where the day in June is two and twenty houres, and to have spent in that discovery two yeeres: I know not what good proofe he hath of that Relation. Plinie whom he citeth, saith that the Northerne Ocean was sailed for the most part by the procurement of Augustus, to the Cimbrian Promontory, and the Scythian coast, and that from the East when Seleucus and Antiochus reigned, the North Sea above the Caspian was sailed, and called by their names Seleucida and Antiochida, But that he joyneth the Caspian with the Ocean, makes it lesse Pl. l. z. c.6-j. credible, being contrary to later experience. No better credit hath that report of Nepos touching Indians which had for trade sailed out of India and comne about by the Northerne Ocean, and by tempest were brought into Germany, presented by the King of the Suevians to Quintus Metellus Celer then proconsul! of Gallia, which haply were of some Nation in the Baltike Sea, by tempest loosing themselves, and not finding any which could understand their language, were by some smattering Grammarians or trusty travellers (which by daring ignorance would adventure on applause for skill in Geography) or else by the Giver (which thought the mention of the Indian name would much commend his present) obtruded on the no lesse I. i. 78. ignorant Spectators, for Indians: a thing easily said, and not easily disproved, where none had seene any Indian. But now to Hanno. The Navigation

PURCHAS HIS PILGRIMES

The Navigation of Hanno a Carthaginian Cap-taine on the Coasts of Africa, without Hercules Fillers, which he dedicated, written in the Punick tongue in the Temple of Saturne, after translated into the Greeke, and now into the English, with briefe annotations.

He Carthaginians determined that Hanno should saile without Hercules Pillars, there build Cities of the Liby-phinicians. He set saile with threescore Ships of fiftie Oares a peece, conducting with him a great multitude of men and women, to the number of thirty thousand, with victuals and all other necessaries. We arrived at the

Pillars, and passed them, and having sailed without them two daies, we built the first Citie, Thymiate- calling it Thymiaterium. It had round about it very num. large Champaignes. After turning toward the West, we came to a promontorie of Africa, called Soloente, covered all over with woods. And having here built a Temple to Neptune, we sailed halfe a day towards the East, till we arrived at a Fen, which is situated not farre from the Sea, very full of great and long Canes: and there were in it feeding Elephants, many other creatures. Then having gone about a daies saile beyond that Fenne we built Cities on the Sea Coast, calling them by their proper names Murus, Caricus, Gitta, Acra, Melitta and Arambis. Departing from thence we came to the great River Lixus which descends from Africa: By it there were certaine men called Lixitae, feeders of Cattell, tending their flockes; with whom wee continued so long, that they became verie familiar. Moreover up in the Countrie above them the Negros inhabited, who will not traffique with any, and their Countrie is verie barbarous and full of wilde Beasts, and environed with high Mountaines, from which as they say, issues the River Lixus, and round about the Mountains inhabit men of divers shapes, which have their abiding in Canes; they runne swifter then horses, as the Lixians report: from thence taking some Interpreters, we sailed by a desart Countrie towards the South two daies. And then wee vered one day towards the East, where in the bottome of a Gulfe we found a like Hand, that was five furlongs in compasse, which we inhabited, naming it Cerne, and by the way that we had sailed we judged that that Hand was opposite to Carthage, for the Navigation from Carthage to the Pillars, and from thence to Cerne seemed equall. Parting from thence, and sailing by a great River called Crete, we arrived at a Lake, which had in it three Hands greater then Cerne. From whence sailing the space of a day, we came to the further part of the Lake: there we saw very high Mountaines which overlooked all the Lake: where were savage people cloathed in beasts skins, who chased us away with stones, not suffering us to land: sailing from thence we came to another great and large streame full of Crocodiles, and River-horses, From thence turning backe againe, wee returned to Cerne. Sailing then twelve daies Southerly, not going farre from the coast, which was peopled with Negros, who upon sight of us fled away, and spake so, as the Lixitas that were with us understood them not. The last day we arrived at a Mountaine full of great trees, the wood whereof was odoriferous and of various colours. Having now coasted two daies by this Mountaine, wee found a deepe and troublesome race of Sea; on the side whereof towards the land was a plaine, where by night we saw fires kindled on every side, distant one from the other some more some lesse. Having watered here, we sailed by the land five daies, so that we arrived in a great Bay, which our Interpreters said, was called Hesperus his home. In this there was a great Hand, and in the Hand a Lake, which seemed a Sea, and in this there was another Hand; where having landed, by day we saw nothing but woods, but in the night many fires were kindled, and we heard

Phifes and the noise and sound of Gimbals and Drum-mes, and besides infinite shouts; so that wee were exceedingly afraid, and our Diviners commanded us to abandon the Hand: then swiftly sailing from thence, we passed by a Countrie smelling of Spices: from which some fierie Rivers fall into the Sea, and the land is so hot that men are not able to goe in it; therefore being somewhat affrighted we suddenly hoised out our sailes, and running along in the maine the space of foure daies, we saw by night the Country full of flames, and in the middest an exceeding high fire, greater then all the rest, which seemed to reach unto the Starres: but wee saw this after in the day time, which was a very loftie Mountaine, called Oewv oyr ixa that is, the Chariot of the Gods. But having sailed three daies by fierie Rivers, we arrived in a Gulfe called Notuceras, that is, the South home: in the inner part thereof there was a little Hand like unto the first, which had a Lake in it, and in that there was another Hand full of Savage men, but the women were more; they had their bodies all over hairie, and of our Interpreters they were called Gorgones: we pursued the men but could take none, for they fled into precipices and defended themselves with stones; but we tooke three of the women, which did nothing but bite and scratch those that led them, and would not follow them. Therefore they killed them and flead them, and brought their skins to Carthage: and because victuals failed us, we sailed no further.

I. i. 79. TT appeares that Hannos wisdome for discoverie in Some make X that infancie of Navigation about 2000 yeeres since, Hanno at least thought small Vessels fittest by which he might keepe as atincient as,,, i-" i r ji-

Philip the neere the shoare, the edgmg whereor caused nim to Father of saile East or West, as the Land trended. The Cartha-Alexander: ginians being of Phoenician originall from Tyrus, and Vossiusthinkes Lyt)ian habitation and Empire, called their Cities Lybi-Captaine pha nician: of which Thymiaterium seemes to the Portu-which was sent gall Pilot in Ramusio, to be Azamor in 32. and a halfe, where runneth a spacious Plaine to Morocco. The against Promontory Soloente seemeth Cape Cantin in 7 2. de- ' i' '" grees. After which the coast runneth in much East- Tragus or hh ward, and the abundance of Rivers cause the great shadoto Jus-Fenne mentioned; beyond which they built those Cities, t' ne) I. 22. the same, or neere to those now in the Kingdome of 'y '" " " Morocco, Azasi, Goz, Aman, Mogador, Testhua, c. pj- g After they passe the Cape Ger, and encounter the River 16. saith of Lixus, where the Poets fables place Hercules his Antasus anotherhanm and the Hesperides Gardens. The Pilot thought it thathezoas the River of Sus, which runnes into the Sea at Messa tamtnzl ons in 29. degr. 30. min. Beyond that begins Mount Atlas the lesse, which runneth Eastward quite thorow Barbary, and to which the Romans came, the sands prohibiting their approach to the greater Atlas. After this Hanno commeth to Cape Non, Cape Bojador and Cape Blanke; and then turning to the East, comes to the He Argin, which hee called Cerne: and thought to be as farre from the Straits in the course of their sailing, as it was betwixt those Straits and Carthage. For as for the height, it is plaine that they neither used compasse, nor observed degrees. And for Ptolemeis degrees, they are almost every where false or uncertaine, rather from his conjecture, then the Mariners calculation, and in transcribing made worse in so many barbarous and ignorant ages: his places are of more use in shewing their bearing East or West, North or South, short, or beyond, or wide, then for exact gradations.

The Hands of Cape Verd in 13. are Hannos Hesperides (the Canaries or Fortunate Hands he could not see, creeping neere the shore) and for River Horses and Crocodiles, they are no rarities in Africke. From Cape Verd the race of the Sea might seeme terrible to their small Vessels, where the River of Saint Mary and Rio Grande in 15. degrees, hath troubled waters. Such fires as hee mentioneth are scene to this day of those which saile on the coast of Senega and Guinea, because the Negros eate litde in the day time for heate, but at night have their fires without doores and there refresh themselves: many of which a farre off present such lights See Jobsons at Sea; the merry Negros to fray away wilde Beasts and voyage and expresse their mirth, making such musicke with Inf. I 7. ' shouts and cries. Sierra Leona is that chariot of the Gods in 8. degrees, the continuall thunders and lightnings at some times of the yeere presenting such a fierie spectacle as Hanno reporteth: yet augmented for greater wonder, as also are his fiery Rivers, that whereas the world talked of a fiery Zone, not habitable through heate, he might lye a little to save his credit from imputation of a greater liei, if he had reported the temperature neere the line. The like humour of inclining to vulgar fancies appeareth in his tales of the Gorgones. And for the monstrous womens hairy skins, they might be of the Baboones or Pongos of those parts, some of which as Jobson and Battell our Countrimen which travelled those parts will tell you, are greater then women, the Pongos nothing in manner differing from their shape. These were, as is probable within foure degrees of the line. The Hand is thought to be that of Fernando Poo: but my learned friend Master Hoelstin a German, which is now preparing a learned treasury of Geographicall antiquities to the Presse, sup-poseth that hee passed not the Cape Tres puntas or that de Palmas.

VOYAGES OF laMBULUS

Chap. VIII.

lambulus his Navigation to Arabia, and Ethiopia, and thence to a strange Hand, from whence hee sailed to Palimbothra in India.

F Hannos Voyage and Relations seemed incredible, much more may that of lam-bulus, recorded by Diodorus. In D. Sic. I. 2. what age hee lived is uncertaine, and as uncertaine what Hand it was that hee is said to come to, which may seeme to some to be Zeilan or Java, I rather thinke Sumatra. That it is wholly fabulous I cannot thinke, but that all is true therein, I were worthy also to have my tongue slit, if I should affirme. Hee did mixe fables to the truth, to make his storie more plausible, and imitating the Poets; and without annotations the truth may easily be knowne from the fables of Platoes Republike and common women, and strange creatures, with other tales. But, if you will, thus the storie lyeth.

lambulus was learned from his child-hood and after his Fathers death (who was a Merchant) he exercised also Merchandizing. Passing through Arabia to buy Spices, he was taken by theeves, with the associates of his journie: at first with one of his fellow slaves, he was appointed to bee a Keeper of Cattle: but after that, together with him hee was taken by certaine lambulus Ethiopians, and convayed beyond the maritime Ethiopia. " ' ' Seeing that they were strangers, they were taken for an expiation of that Country. The Ethiopians that inhabited those parts had a custome, which they had I. i. 80. anciently received from the Oracle of their Gods, and observed it twenty Ages, that is sixe hundred yeeres (for an Age is finished in thirtie yeeres.) They had a little vessell prepared able to endure the tempests of the Sea, which two men might easily steere. They put into it six months victuals for two men: bringing the men aboord, they commanded them to direct their vessell towards the South according to the answere of the Oracle: and told them that they should come to a goodly Hand and courteous people, that lived happily.

And by that meanes, if they safely arrived in the Iland their Countrey should bee in peace and prosperity sixe hundred yeeres. But if, being terrified through the length of the Sea they should returne backe, they should bring, as impious and debauched persons, great miseries to all their Nation. They report that the (Ethiopians feasted divers dayes by the Sea-side, and kept their holies, wishing them a lucky Voyage, and that the accustomed expiation were accomplished. After foure moneths sayle and many a storme, they were carried lamhuli to an Hand of round forme, five thousand furlongs in insula. compasse. When they drew neere to the Iland, some of the Inhabitants sent forth a Boat to meete them.

Others running to them wondred at these new come strangers: and entertayned them very kindly and courteously: imparting to them such things as they had.

Inhabitants The men of this Iland are not like to ours, either descrtbed.- their bodies or manners, yet all have the same forme, but they exceed us foure Cubits in stature. They wind

So doe the their bones this way and that way as they please, like alios now. gjj g eg Their bodies are stronger and nimbler then ours. For if they have taken any thing into their hands, no man can pull it out of their fingers. They have no haires, except on their head, eye-browes, eye-lids, and chinne: on the other parts of their bodies they are so smooth, that there doth not appeare the least downe.

They are faire, comely, and have wel shaped bodies, the holes of their eares are much wider then ours, also their tongue differs from us. For their tongue hath

Cloven somewhat peculiar by Nature or Art. Nature hath

Lk- k given them a cloven tongue, which is divided in the bleme. bottome, so that it seemes double from the root. So

VOYAGES OF laMBULUS they use a divers speech: and doe not only speake with the voice of men, but imitate the singing of Birds. But that which seemes most notable, they speake at one time perfitly with two men, both answering and discoursing. For with one part of their tongue they speake to one, and with the other to the other. The aire is very cleere all the yeere long, as the Poet hath Temperate written, That the Peare doth ripen upon the Peare, and ' the Apple upon the Apple, and the Grape upon the Grape, and the fig upon the fig. Also they say the day and night are always equall. About noone, when the Sunne is over their heads it maketh no shadow. They live according to their kindreds and societies: which yet exceed not foure hundred. They dwell in Medowes, the earth bringing forth plentifully fruits freely without any tillage. For the goodnesse of the Hand and temperature of the ayre make the earth of its owne accord wonderfull fertill.

There grow many Reeds, bearing plentifuu fruit like This Reed is to a white Vetch; when they have gathered these, j "-they steepe them in water, till each of them be swolne ;;4";' ' to the quantity of a Doves Egge. Afterwards of these wheate. beaten they make bread, of a wonderfull sweetnesse. There are also in that Hand great Springs of water, whereof some flow forth very hot for the use of Baths, and curing Diseases; and some are cold, very sweet and wholsome. They respect all kind of Learning, especially Astrologie. They use Letters whereof they have eight Their Letters. and twentie, according to the value of signification, yet but seven Characters: each whereof is varied foure wayes. They live very long, namely one hundred and fifty yeeres, and for the most part without any sicknesse. If any have a Fever or be sicke in his bodie, they enforce him to dye according to their Law. They write not China forme by the side, as we doe, but from the top in a straight " '" '" line to the bottome. They have a custome to live to ' " ' a certaine age, which being finished, they diversly of their owne accord kill themselves. They have a double

Common women.

Fabulous creatures.

plant: upon which whosoever lyeth downe is brought into a sweet sleepe and dyeth. The women marry not, but are common to all. In like manner the Males are brought up, and common to all. They often take away the children from the Mothers, that they might not know them, whereby it commeth to passe, that there is no ambition amongst them, or factious affection, but they live peaceably without jarring.

There are small creatures in the Hand, whose bloud is of an admirable nature and vertue. Their bodies are round, and like to Tortoises, two streakes crossing one another on the middle of them: in the extremity of each of which is an eare and an eye: so that they see with foure eyes, and heare with so many eares: they have but one belly wherein they convey that which they eate. They have many feet round about, wherewith they goe both wayes. The bloud of this beast is affirmed to be of a wonderfull efficacie. For any bodie cut with gashes, while it breathes, sprinkled with this bloud presently cleaves together. And in like manner, if a hand bee cut off, or any other member, whiles life lasts, the parts will bee joyned together, if it bee applied to the wound while it is fresh. Every Family nourisheth great Birds of a divers nature, wherewith they trie what their sonnes will be. For setting their children on these Fowles, if they be not affrighted while they are carried through the Aire, they bring them up, but if they faint through feare or cowardlinesse, they cast them downe as unworthy to live any longer, and unprofitable for any exercise.

The eldest of every Family, as King commands the rest, who all obey him. When hee is one hundred and fiftie yeeres old, they take away his life according to their Law: and the eldest next him takes the Principality. The Sea wherewith the Hand is environed is very tempestuous, and causeth great waves, the water is fresh. ome truths of The Beare and many starres which appeare to us are not the Countrey. scene of them. There are seven Hands of the like great-

VOYAGES OF laMBULUS nesse, like distance betweene, and of the same people and Lawes. Although the earth doth bring forth food of its owne accord abundantly for all, yet they use it moderately. They desire plaine dishes, seeking only nourishment: they eate their flesh rosted and boiled: they reject the Cookes art, and all kind of sawces as unprofitable. They reverence the Gods, and that which containeth all things, and the Sunne, and the other heavenly Creatures. They take fishes and Birds of divers sorts. There grow of their owne accord fruitfuu Trees, Olives, and Vines, from which they draw great plentie of Oile and Wine. The Hand produceth great Serpents, but harmelesse: whose flesh they eate, which is extra-ordinarie sweet. They make their clothes of soft and shining downe, taken out of the middest of Canes: wherewith their Purple garments died with Sea Oysters are made. There are many kinds of creatures and such as will hardly be beleeved: they observe a certaine order of life, and eat but of one kind of meat in a day; for one day they eate fish, on another Birds, and then beasts; sometimes they feed only of oile. They are addicted to divers exercises: some serve, some fish, others exercise their Trades, others are busied about other necessarie affaires. Some (except the old men) minister in common, or serve one another by turnes. On their Holies and Feast dayes they sing Hymnes in commendation of their Gods, and chiefly of the Sunne, to whom they dedicate themselves and their Hand. They burie their dead on the shore, heaping sand upon the carkasse when the Sea flowes, that with the flowing and increasing of the water, the place may be made greater. They report that the Reeds from which they gather fruit, increase and decrease according to the Moone. The sweet and wholsome water retaines the heate of the Fountaines, unlesse it be mingled with cold water or wine.

Iambulus and he which came with him tarried in the Iamhulus his Hand seven yeeres, and at length were forced to depart at ' f' "-their wils, as wicked persons, and accustomed to evill conditions. Therefore preparing their Boat and victualling it, they were compelled to depart. In foure monethes they came to a King of India, through sandie and shallow places of the Sea. The other perished in a tempest: Iam-bulus was driven into a certaine Village, and carried by the Inhabitants to the King into the Citie Palibothra farre distant from the Sea. The King loved Graecians, and greatly esteemed their Learning; hee gave him many things, and first sent him safely into Persia, and then into Greece. Afterward Iambulus writ these things, and many things concerning India before unknowne to others.

Chap. IX.

Great Alexanders Life, Acts, Peregrinations and Conquests briefly related.

Ing Alexander, as they report, derived his Pedigree by the Father from Hercules, by the mother from acus; from the one descended his Father Philip, and from the other his Mother Olympia. Shee the first night of her Nuptials dreamed that she saw Lightning enter into her Wombe, and thence a great flame presently kindled. Philip also not long after seemed in his sleepe to scale his wives belly, the Scale engraven with a Lion. By these Aristander the Diviner foretold that shee was with childe, because a Seale useth not to be set on emptie things: also that shee should bring forth a child, who should have the nature and spirit of a Lion. But when a while after Philip in the night saw through a cranie of the doore a Dragon lying by her, it abated his love to her, fearing Magicall Charmes, or the familiaritie of some Deitie. Notwithstanding Olympias counselled Alexander that he would assume a minde worthy of his father. Others say, that shee said Alexander would make her (by challenging Hii birth, to bee Jupiters sonne) hatefull to Juno. On the Ides of August she was delivered of Alexander, who although he

Alexanders Pediff-ee.

were of a goodly feature, yet he bowed his necke somewhat to the left side, and a certaine whitenesse mixed with red beautified his face. Also such an odour issued both Hisfragt-an-out of his mouth, and members, that his inner clothes did " breath forth a wonderfull fragrant savour. Which as it perhaps proceeded out of the temperature of his hot bodie, so surely he was by his naturall hotnesse given to Wine and anger. While he was young, he refrained himselfe His youthfull from pleasures more then beseemed one of his yeeres, "' Sf ' '-manifesting his couragious minde, who when his equals in yeeres asked, if he would willingly contend in the Olympian Games willingly, saith he, if I were to contend with Kings. He greatly excelled in swiftnesse of foot. Hee alwayes meditated upon some great and extraordinary thing, that he might purchase fame. Therefore the Persian Ambassadors not a little marvelled at the courage of the young man: seeing he questioned no triviall, or childish thing of them, but the situation of I. i. 82. Countries and dangers of passages, and power of the King of Persia. He did seeme to bee angry at his Fathers victories; What said he, will my Father leave for me to doe, if hee atchieve all noble exploits

About those times, Philip bought Bucephalus for thirtie Bucephalus. three Talents a very fierce Horse; stomackfull, un-managed, and abiding no Rider. Now when hee would suffer none to backe him, Alexander was angry with them, who could not through feare or ignorance tame the Horse, and offered himselfe to breake him. To whom his Father, if thou dost not, for thy boasting, what punishment wilt thou have then he answered, I will pay for the Horse. Philip smiling set the price: He seeing him mooved with his shadow, turned his head to the Sunne; then letting goe his Cloke, laying hold with his hands upon his mane, mounted him, still blowing and trampling the sands under his feet. Letting goe the reines, and crying out aloud, hee spurred him and made him runne. Then holding in the reines hee easily turned His arts. him. While the people shouted, his Father weeping for joy, kissed him when he aghted, saying my Sonne, Macedonia cannot containe thee, thou must seeke a King-dome competent. Afterward Philip noticing the disposition of Alexander, that hee would rather bee induced to vertue by gentlenesse then rough dealing committed him to Aristotle to be instructed in the precepts of Philosophic. Wherein and in Physicke he so profited, that sometimes he helped his sicke friends. He learned Homers Iliads of Aristotle: calling it the Souldiers Knap-sacke, laying it with his Dagger alwayes under his Pillow. His first mar- When he was seventeene yeeres old, his Father warring tiall acts. against the Byzantines, hee swayed the Scepter of Mace-don. And when the Megarians rebelled, he discomfited them in battle, and expelling the Barbarians, called their Citie Alexandropolis. Hee first also broke through against the sacred band of the Thebans. Wherefore the Macedonians called him King; and Philip Emperour.

Not long after Philip being slaine, Alexander beeing twentie yeeres old beganne to reigne, the Barbarians revolting, many supposed that they were to bee appeased with clemencie and mildnesse. Then Alexander, we must not (saith he) maintayne our Dominions with gentlenesse, but force and magnanimitie, lest if we seeme to abate of our loftie courage, we be scorned of others: And gathering his troupes together, he repressed the mutinie of the Barbarians, chased away the King of the Tribaui, overthrew the Thebans, sacked the Citie; and levelled it to the ground. He sold thirtie thousand of the Citizens: sixe thousand that remained kild themselves. In the meane while, the Graecians hearing that the Persians would shortly invade them, elected Alexander Isthmus neere to be their Leader. Who assoone as hee came to Isthmos, Corinth. where their Generall Parliament was assembled, went to

Diogenes, whom hee found sitting in. the Sunne. Then courteously saluting him, he demanded if he wanted any thing t But he answered only this, stand aside out of the Sunne. Alexander admiring the constancie of the man, departing said, if I were not Alexander, I would be Diogenes. Thence he went to Delphos, to consult Diogenes. with the Oracle about his expedition. It was an unluckie P '-day wherein it was not lawfull to give Oracles. Alexander notwithstanding, going in haste to the Temple, began almost by force to draw along the Priest of the Oracle with him. My Sonne, said the Priest, thou art unconquerable. Hee beeing joyfuu at these words said, I have no need of any other Oracle. And returning to the Campe, where abode the Army of thirtie thousand footmen, and five thousand horsemen, hee did not goe aboard the ship before he had distributed all his Chattels, Lands, and Lordships amongst his friends. He to Perdicas asking, what will you leave for your selfe answered, only Hope.

Having sailed over the Hellespont, he went to Ilium. His expedition And then visited Achilles Sepulchre, and adorned his S ' lcTSI Otis

Statue with Garlands. Saying, O thou most happie, who hadst so faithfull a companion, living; and dead, so great a Poet to renowme thee.

In the meane while, the Chiefetaines of Darius, the King of Persia hastening to passe over Granicum with a great power, Alexander met them at the banks of the same River: and getting the higher ground, as soone as he had marshalled his bands, joyned battle with the Barbarians. The fight waxing hot on both sides, Rhesaces Spithri-dates, Darius his Captains, one with a Speare, the other with a Battle-axe, with a ful careere encountred Alexander, who was easie to be known by reason of his Target, and the Plume on his Helmet, beeing a great bush of white feathers. Avoyding nimbly the one, he strooke Rhesaces with his Speare and with his Sword made at the other, who without delay, tooke away his Helmet, with his Battle-axe to his haire, but while he lifted up his hand for another blow, he was strooke through with a Lance Clitus saveth by Clytus. Alexander having vanquished the Com- ' ', Ills tctofi manders, put the rest to flight. In which flight twentie thousand of the Barbarians (two thousand Horsemen) were slaine. But Alexander lacked not above thirtie foure Souldiers.

Having gotten this victorie, he tooke the strong Citie Sardis, with other Townes, Miletus and Halicarnassus. Having determined to try the upshot with King Darius, if he would joyne battle with him, he tooke Phaenicia and Cilicia. From thence marching to Pamphilia, he subdued the Pisidans and Phrygians. After taking Gordium, where had beene of old King Midas his Pallace, he overcame the Paphlagonians, and Cappadocians. But King I. i. 83. Darius relying on the number of his forces (for he had an Army of sixe hundred thousand) remooved his Campe from Susis. His Diviners had flattered him in the Interpretation of a Dreame of the shining of Alexanders Armie, and Alexander ministring to him, who entring into Belus his Temple, was taken out of his sight. He thought basely of him also for staying so long in Cilicia. There was Alexander detained in great danger of his life, having washed himselfe in a cold River, and fallen into a sudden sicknesse. When other Physicians gave him over, Philip an Acarnanian promised to recover him in a short space: and although there came a Letter from Parmenio, warning him to take heed of Philips Treason, who was corrupted by King Darius, yet he dranke up the potion boldly, and with all delivered the Letter to Philip. He read it very heavily, but bad Alexander to be of good cheere. In the meane time, while the potion entred into his bowels, the King lay almost dead. But such was the efficacie of the medicine, that he presently recovered his former health. Second battle. Darius approching, Alexander getting the higher Alexanders ground, ordered his battle, and after a great slaughter ' put the Barbarians to flight: ten thousand were slaine, and many more taken. Alexander himselfe was wounded.

Alexander got the Tent, Money, rich Stuff e, Chariot, and Bow of Darius, all adorned with Gold. Moreover, Darius his Mother, Wife, and two Daughters Virgins were taken with the rest. To whom hee said, compassionating their fortune, seeing them weeping and lamenting, that Darius was alive, and that they should have no hurt. And indeed (herein was Alexander King of himselfe) they suffered no hardship or dishonor, but lived unseene of any, as it were in sacred Cloysters, or Virginall Closets. Alexander did so refraine from them and all others, that he used to say in jeast, that the Persian Damsels were eye-sores. He was also very His temper- temperate in his diet, for betweene every cup, hee '"

accustomed to spend a long time in discourse.

Having divided the spoyles, his next Exploit was the dominion of the Sea, and overcomming Cyprus, he Cyprus. subdued all Phasnicia, except Tyre, which hee besieged Tyrus. seven monethes with Mounts, Engines, and two hundred Gallies, and at length after divers skirmishes tooke it by assault. But when he had added Gaza and Egypt to his Conquests, he resolved to visit the Temple of Jupiter Ammon. A very difficult Journey and dreadfull, by Amnions reason of the want of water, and store of sands: yet '-his good fortune prevayled, showres making the sands firmer, and Crowes guiding him, he came thither without any harme; Whereas Cambyses his Armie had beene buried in the sands. Entring the Temple he saluted the chiefe of them, who answered. All haile, O Sonne of Jupiter, which he received so joyfully, that ever after hee carried himselfe more haughtily. In Egypt hee Alexandria founded Alexandria a Greeke Colonie. builded.

After this the Ambassadours of the King of Persia Embassage came to him with Letters, proffering ten thousand- " lianus. Talents, and all Mesopotamia, and his Daughter in marriage, and Darius himselfe to become his friend and associate, if he would cease from Warre: such conditions, that if I were Alexander, said Parmenio, I would accept them: so would I said Alexander, if I were Parmenio. He bad them tell Darius, that he should receive all courtesie of the Graecians, if he would come to them, if he would not, let him know that we, wil he, nill he, i d wil come to him speedily. Then going out of Egypt jj' " into Phaenicia, he took all the Country between Euphrates,. ' and the second time removed his Campe against Darius, with Darius. I 225 p

Alexanders victorie.

Babylon taken.

Busce.

Persepohs burden.

And now the Armies came in sight each of other, wherein Darius had a Million of men. The battle was fought not at Arbela, but at Gausanela. The Bactrian Horsemen running upon the Macedonians provoked Alexander to fight, who encouraged his men and praying to Jupiter that he would give him aide and victory, an Eagle is reported to have been shewed him by Aristander his Diviner flying above him over his head, and thence directing her flight against the Persians, which filled the Macedonians with hopes and cheerefull courage. Forcible was the impression, and Alexander pierced into the midst of the enemies Campe, where beholding Darius well guarded in the midst of his troupes, he gave a terrible assault and routed them, many beeing slaine.

Darius was of a tall stature, comely face. Kingly countenance, and sate aloft in a Chariot covered with Gold, which Darius leaving, leaped upon a barren mare, seeking to save his life by flight. The dignitie of this victory altogether overthrew the Persian Empire, and made Alexander King of Asia. Then he tooke Babylon and Susis, the royall Citie where he found fortie thousand Talents of silver, with royall houshold-stuffe, and of Hermionike Purple kept one hundred and ninety yeeres still fresh to the value of five thousand Talents.

Now did Alexander advance into Persia, whither Darius had fled. There he found asmuch silver as before in Susis, and asmuch royall furniture and goods as laded ten thousand yokes of Mules, and five thousand Camels. Hee tarried foure moneths in his wintering Lodgings. And, as the report is, when he feasted under the golden roofe of the Kings Hall, he said. That he had obtained the fruit of his labours, seeing he so magnificently banqueted in the Palace of proud Xerxes. Thais an Athenian, a beautifull Strumpet, being present, enticed the King with her flatteries, and said, I were the happiest woman of Greece, if I might in this our mirth fire Xerxes Pallace, who sometime burnt my Athens. The King smiling, the Harlot fired the House.

The King bewitched with wine and her allurements, the rest fiirthering the flame, suffered such a goodly building to be consumed to ashes. Alexander was naturally munificent, and kept a kinde of stately magnificence in giving: which he did illustrate with infinite testimonies of his bountie, lesse esteeming those that I. i. 84. refused then these that craved. About this time Darius had now the third time gathered an Army. Alexander in eleven dayes passed with great Journies 3200. furlongs, conducting his Armie through rough places, that wanted water, so that the whole Armie well neere languished with thirst: a certaine common Souldier brought a Helmet full of water to Alexander; who looking upon all of them panting for heate and thirst, gave it him againe untouched: thinking it unfitting that he alone should cherish himselfe, and the others faint; whose continencie the Souldiers admiring, resolved to undergoe any trouble, as long as they followed such a Leader. Then after a few dayes, the Armie of King Darius beeing gathered together, did flee assoone as they came in sight of the Macedonians. The Persians being thus discomfited, the Macedonians pursuing them, found King Darius in his Chariot stricken through with many wounds, and almost dead, speaking some few things. But when Alexander came thither by chance, hee tooke Darius slain very bitterly his ignoble death, and casting his coate h. ” " f upon his carcasse, and adding the Royall Ensignes, he " ’ ’ gave charge to carrie it honourably to his Mother. Bessus, the Murtherer, Alexander caused to be tied to two trees brought by force together, which rent him in sunder.

Darius being overthrowne, he brought into his sub- Hynania sub-jection Hyrcania, and all the Cities adjoyning to the ’ "’ ’ Caspian Sea. After going into Parthia, hee attired himselfe in a habit, being a meane betweene a Persian and a Mede, that he might accustome the Macedonians the more willingly to adore him.

Passing over the River Orexartes, which he thought

Scythian expedition.

Jmazonian tale.

Philotas and Clitus slaine.

to be Tanais, hee warred on the Scythians, and chased them one hundred furlongs. Thither Clitarchus, Poly-critus, Onesicritus, Antigenes and Hister say, the Amazon came to him; which Chares, Isangelus, Ptolemaeus, Anticlides, Philon, Philippus, Hecatasus, Phihppus Chalcidensis, and Duris the Samian, say was a devised Fable: and this appeareth to be true by Alexander himselfe, who writing to Antipater an exact Relation of all things, mentions the Scythian Kings offer of his Daughter in marriage, but hath nothing at all of the Amazon. It is said that Lysimachus, when hee heard Onesicritus reading that Relation, smiled and said. Where was I then

At length beholding the beautie and noble demeanour of Roxanes, Darius his Daughter, hee married her, that so he might perpetually tie the Barbarians to him; whom hee did also so reverence, that he did not but solemnely enter in to her. But when hee proceeded to bring the rest of Asia to his obedience, he caused Philotas Parmenio his sonne a man of eminent place to be slaine. Also a little while after being drunke, he strucke Clitus through with a Lance, a man of a noble courage, which had freed him from Spithridates Battle-axe: yet he presently repented, and snatching the Lance out of Clitus his wound, would have turned it into himselfe; but was restrained by the standers by, and had died with griefe, but that Aristander the Diviner, and the Philosophers Callisthenes and Anaxarchus persuaded him to patience. Callisthenes was as ill repaid as Clitus, which before we have mentioned.

After this, Alexander sets forth towards India, and there perceiving his Army by reason of the greatnesse of pillage to bee slow and dull, hee burned up the baggage of the Macedonian Campe. After which he became an inexorable and severe punisher of faults, and a terrour to his owne. He killed Menander, one of his greatest Familiars for neglecting his charge: And slew Orsodates having rebelled with his owne hands. He carried Baby- lonians (or Chaldasans) with him, whom hee used in superstitious expiations.

Neere the River Oxus, Proxenus found a Fountayne of Oyle and fat liquor, re-sembling Oyle in colour and taste, whereas that Region knoweth not Olives. This Alexander tooke as a divine Miracle in his favour. The Diviners tooke it for a token of a difficult but glorious Warre. Hee tooke two strong Rockes in his way, which seemed impregnable. When the Macedonians refused to passe thorow the River to lay siege to Nysa, he tooke his shield and was readie to swimme over himselfe. But their Embassage for peace staid him. To Taxiles an Indian King, hee gave a thousand Talents of silver.

After that he warred upon Porus King of a great part of India (some thinke Rahanni to be his Successour, and those parts which the Reisboots now hold in the parts, which whiles they please, acknowledge the Mogoll, to have been subject to him.) Hydaspes ranne betwixt both their Tents, and Porus by his Elephants (furnished also with twentie thousand foot, and two thousand horse) hindered the passage of Alexander, who therefore raised continuall alarmes, noyses and tumults in his Tents, and got over the River with great difficultie, tooke the Indian Charets, and foure hundred of their Horsemen. In eight houres fight Porus lost the field and himselfe. Hee was foure Cubits and a handbreadth high, and rode upon an Elephant, which fought valiantly for his Rider: and finding himselfe spent, kneeled downe gently to prevent his fall. Alexander asked his Captive Porus what he would have done if he had taken him:

and Porus answered that he would have done that which should have beseemed the Majestie of either of them: because this savoured of no barbarousnesse, he restored him to his Kingdome, adding a Region of a free State there subdued, in which were fifteene Nations and 5000. Cities, besides Villages. In this battle with Porus, or soone after it Bucephalus died, being thirtie yeeres old: Bucephalia.

for whose death Alexander did so grieve, that he built a Citie upon Hydaspes, calling it by his name, as another I. i. 85. also to his Dogge Peritas. The Souldiers now being wearie of the trouble of daily warre, when they understood that he determined to goe to the inmost parts of India, refused to passe over Ganges. For they heard that Ganges was thirty two furlongs broad and a hundred fathome deepe, and the bankes covered with troupes of Horsemen, Elephants and Footmen; viz. 80000. Horsemen 200000. Footmen, 8000. Charets, and 6000. Elephants trained to the warres, by the Gandaritan and Persian Kings. Wherefore Alexander seeing his desires could not obtaine their wished end, kept himselfe very sorrowfull in his Tent, and threatned that they should receive no recompense for that they had done, unlesse they would passe over Ganges: at length over-come by the entreaties and teares of his Souldiers, he desisted from his intended Journey. But longing to see the Ocean, gathering ships together he came thither by the Rivers. Where taking many Cities he was almost slaine by the Malli, valiant men of India. For when hee had lept into the Citie from the wall (which he first ascended) he was oppressed with such a multitude of the Barbarians, that unlesse the Macedonians had speedily succoured him being grievously wounded with an Arrow and a blow with a Club upon the necke, here he had in his rashnesse finished his dayes. But being freed from the perill of death, he overthrew Cities and many places, seven monethes being so spent. At last hee came to the Ocean with his Armie. Then contemplating the shoares, and finishing his holies, he intreated the Gods that no man ever after should goe beyond his bounds: he also bad Nearchus tarrie about India, with a Navy. He went on foot to Oritus. But he was so distressed with the barrennesse of the Countrey, heate and diseases, that of a 120000. Footmen, and 15000. Horsemen, scarcely the fourth part lived. After sixtie dayes hee came to Ged-rosia, where being honourably entertained by the Kings and Officers which had prepared against his comming, hee forgot all his passed troubles: so that he spent his time day and night in drinking, banqueting, singing and I. i. 86. daliance with women. After this Nearchus returning, presently he sailed downe Euphrates: and passing over Arabia and Lybia, purposed to goe to Hercules Pillars by the Mediterranean Sea. But because his armie was very impatient, being consumed by the tediousnesse of the way, having sent backe Nearchus to defend the Sea coasts, he returned into Persia. And bestowing his money among all his women (for that was the Kings custome, as often as they entered Persia) he celebrated the Nuptials of his companions at Susis. He also maried Statyra the other daughter of Darius. Making then a costly banquet to his companions, he had 9000. Guests, and gave every one of them a golden cup. He opened the Sepulchre of Cyrus, whose Epitaph was this, Whosoever thou art, and whence soever thou commest (for I know thou wilt come) I am Cyrus which wan the Empire to the Persians. Envie me not this little earth, which covers my body. Calanus also here burned himselfe, having taken familiar leave of all, and told the King he would shortly see him againe at Babylon. He also paid the debts of his souldiers, which came to 10000. talents, lacking onely 130. He found 30000. Persian youths which hee had given order to be trained and instructed of manly growth and comely presence, which gave plausible testimonies of their admirable activity. This caused emulation to the Macedonians, which murmuring, he chose his guard of the Persians. Wereupon the Macedonians being grieved went to him, intreating him not to reject them as unprofitable; for they did confesse that they had beene ingratefull, and desired pardon. At length Alexander pittying their teares and habit, sent them away abundantly rewarded with gifts. He entertained others according to their dignity. But when he went toward Ecbatana of Media, he gave himselfe to plaies and spectacles, and about that time a fever tooke away Ephestion, whose losse heetooke

Hydaspes, perhaps that which now is called Bhat.

SO to heart that nothing could please him. Therefore to appease his griefe, he went to warre as to a manhunting: And so raced out all the Nation of the Cossaei, as it were offering them in sacrifice to Ephestio his ghost. Those things being finished, he was admonished by some of the Chaldeans, that hee should not come to Babylon. But he went notwithstanding, where he was againe troubled with many Diviners, and not onely suspected all his servants but all his gods and deities. At length to recreate himselfe he went a little into a bathe, where he began exceedingly to sweate: And being carried to bed, after a few daies the Fever increasing, hee gave directions to his Princes concerning the Empire, and died. But before his body was buried, it lay a great while in hot places. And seeing it remained sound and uncorrupted, by this all suspition of poison was taken away. We will end this Relation of Alexander with Nearchus his Voyage by him set forth.

The Voyage of Nearchus and his Fleet set forth by Alexander the Great, from the River Indus to the bottome of the Persian Gulfe.

IN this History of Voyages I thinke it not a misse to give some accounts briefly of the Fleete which Alexander set forth from Indus to the Persian Gulfe, commanded by Nearchus, gathered out of the eighth Booke of Arrianus, who had taken it out of Nearchus his owne discourse thereof. I had the whole Relation at large by me translated, as those also of Arrianus his sailing about both the Erythraean and Euxine Seas: but Time hath so altered the Names, ports and peoples, that I dare not give you them at large. This briefly was thus:

Alexander provided his ships in Hydaspes (a River which runneth into Indus) and manned them with Phe-nicians, Cypriots, Egyptians, men best skilled in Marine affaires. He chose also for Captains the Greek Ilanders of Ionia and Hellespont, divers others; amongst the rest Nearchus which writ this Navigation, of Cretan ancestry, an Amphipolitan by habitation, whom he made Generall of the Fleet. After things set in order, he sacrificed to the Gods of his Country and to such others as the Diviners prescribed, to Neptune, Oceanus, the Sea Nymphes, and to the River Hydaspes, and to Acesines, which floweth thereinto. He instituted also musicall and gymnicall Games (prizes for maisteries) also, distributing the remainders of the sacrifices to the Armie. A hundred and 20000. souldiers followed Alexander, who himselfe went with the ships downe Hydaspes. He had 800. ships, some long, some of burthen. Being afraid to adventure so long a Sea Voyage, as from Indus to the Persian Gulfe, lest his glorious lustre of victory and Fortune hitherto attending him might so be drowned; the

Monson serving (the Etesiae then ceasing which there blew in Summer) he committed the Fleet to Nearchus, which put forth to Sea on the twentieth day of Boedro-mion, in the eleventh yeere of King Alexanders reigne. Nearchus sacrificed also before his departure, to Jupiter the Saviour, and likewise instituted Games; on that day of his departure he came to a great river called Stura, River Stura. about 100 furlongs, and staied there two daies. On the third day hee came to another River called Caumana thirty furlongs further, where the water began to be salt, and the tide ascended. Thence he sailed twenty furlongs to Coreatis within the River. Moving thence they saw the white frothy surge at the mouth of the River, and in a ditch or channell made of five furlongs, he anchored his fleet when the tyde came 150. furlongs, thence he came to i. i. 87. the He Crocala, neere to the which are the Indian ik Crocala. Arrhabes. Thence he removed, having mount Irus on the right hand, and the He Halitenea on the left, to a Port Ik Hnlitenea. which he called Alexanders Port, before which is Bubarta Ik Bubarta. a small Hand. There he staid foure and twenty daies, and gathered Sea Mice and Oysters wonderful! great. The winde ceasing, he went sixtie furlongs neere the He Doma, where they were forced to goe twenty fur- Ik Doma.

Saranga. Sacalasis. Morontobor'u.

End of India. The Orita.

JII their sailing is with Oares and by shoare.

Was not this age thinke you like to saile to Peru or His-paniola?

Ships a rarity.

longs within land for fresh water: Having passed 300. furlongs the next day, they came to the Region Saranga, and fetched water eight furlongs within land. Departing thence hee came to Sacalasis, and passing two rockes so neere that the ships edged on them as they passed by, after 300. furlongs he anchored in Morontoboris, a round, deepe and safe harbour with a narrow entrance, called the Womens Port, The next day he left an Hand to Sea ward of him and yet so neere the shoare that the Sea seemed a Gut or narrow ditch. That day he sailed sixtie furlongs. On that shoare was a wood and shadie Hand. The next day he sailed thorow a narrow channell, the ebbe having left a great part dry, and having passed 120. furlongs he came to the mouth of the River Arabius, where is a great and safe harbour. They fetched water sixtie furlongs up the River in a Lake. At the harbour is an Hand full of Oisters and all sorts of fish. This River confineth India; the next Regions are possessed by the Oritse; their first anchoring on the Orite-shoare was Pagali, having sailed 200. furlongs neere a craggie rocke. The next day 300. furlongs to Bacana: and because the shoare was rockie, hee was forced to anchor farre from land. In this way three ships were lost in a storme, but the persons were saved being neere the shoare.

He sailed thence two hundred furlongs to Comala: and there went on shoare and set up tents to refresh his people wearied with their long Navigation, and desiring to have some rest. Here Leonnatus, to whom Alexander had given Commission for the Oritae, overthrew them in a great battell and slew 6000. The weatherbeaten ships being repaired, and ten daies provisions being taken in, and those sailers which were weary of the Sea, being left with Leonnatus, some of his company supplying their roomes: the Fleete proceeded 500. furlongs, and anchored at the River Thomeros. The Inhabitants dwelt in small cottages, and wondered at the Navie as a strange Noveltie:

they came to the shoare with lances of six cubits sharpned and burned at the ends, easily chased by those which were sent on shoare against them, which also tooke some, which had hard and sharpe nailes wherewith they killed fish, and cut softer wood (for they had no use of Iron) the harder they cut with stones: their garments were beasts or fishes skins. Here Nearchus staid five dayes, and repaired his Navie. Proceeding three hundred furlongs he came to Malana, the utmost border of the Oritae, who for the most part dwell up within the land and use Indian attire and armes, but differ in language and customes. Nearchus had sailed now looo. furlongs from Indus mouth to the Arrhabius, and 1600. by the Oritae. Now also their shadowes fell Southward, and at noone they had no shadow. The Starres also differed in their height and appearance. After the Oritas are the Gedrosi The Gedrost. amongst whom Alexander found more difficulty then in all the rest of India. Nearchus having sailed 600. furlongs came to Bagisara, a convenient harbour: the Towne Pasira is sixtie furlongs up from the Sea. Next day he passed by a high overhanging Rocke, which runneth farre into the Sea: and digging Wels had store of water, but brackish: sailing other six hundred furlongs hee came to Calime where Cornina lieth one hundred furlongs into the Sea, an Hand whose Inhabitants sent Nearchus sheepe, whose flesh tasted like Sea-fowles, they being fed with fishes, there being no grasse there. Next day they sailed two hundred furlongs to Carbis, the towne Cysa was thirty furlongs from Sea. Here were small Fisher-boates, but the Fishermen at sight of the Fleete ran away. He passed next a high and craggy Cape, reaching one hundred and fifty furlongs into the Sea, unto Mosarna a safe harbour. There he tooke Hydracces a Gedrosian Pilot for Carmania. The way from hence to the Persian Gulfe is not so evill as the former.

Having sailed 750. furlongs he came to the Balomon shoare, and after 400. furlongs to Barna, a towne where were Gardens of Myrtle and divers flowers, culture of trees, and more civilitie of the men. 400. furlongs further

The Ichtkyo-phagi.

Manners of the Ichthyophagi.

Fish-fed beasts.

Whales. I. i. 88.

How dijj'ers this from a Greenland Whale-t'oiage?

he came to Dendrobosa, where they fish in small Boats, not rowing like the Greekes, but like diggers beating the waters on both sides. After 800. furlongs he came to Cyiza a desert shore, and five hundred furlongs from thence to the borders of the Ichthyophagi or Fish-eaters. They invaded the Towne to get Corne which now failed them; but found little, except meale of rosted fishes, of which they make Bread. Thence he went to Bagia a rocke sacred to the Sunne, thence to Talmena a good port, 1000. furlongs from Bagia. Thence to Canasis a desert Citie 400. furlongs thence, 750. furlongs to Mount Canate: thence 800. furlongs to Taii; thence to Dagasira 300. furlongs, thence 1300. furlongs to the utmost confines of the Ichthyophagi, in great want of provision: Here was a Cape running farre into the Sea. The coast of the Ichthyophagi is about loooo. furlongs, where all feede on fish, yet are there few fishermen, but the Ebbe leaves the fish on shoare, some have nets which reach two furlongs, made of Palme-tree leaves. The softer fish they eate raw: the greater and harder they roast in the Sunne, and then beate them into powder and make a kinde of bread thereof, some sprinkle the powder with wheate meale. Their Beasts have no other foode, for there is no grasse. There is store of Crabs, Oysters, and shel-fish; Salt also and Oyle produced by the soile it selfe; some sowe a little Corne. Their houses are made of Whales bones. The Whales casting much water into the aire, the people wondred what it was, and hearing that they were fishes, the Oares fell out of their hands with feare: But after being hartned, the ships went neere together, and with great shouts and noise of Oares and sound of Trumpets feared the Whales, and made them sinke into the deepe. The prodigious tales of the He Nosala sacred to the Sunne, on which, if any went ashoare he should never be scene after, Nearchus proved false by his owne experiment: as also another tale went thereof that a Nymph there dwelt, which lay with men that came thither, and after turned them into fishes.

After he was come to Carmania, he anchored before a Thecarmani Cape where the Persian gulfe goeth inward then sailed Persiangulfe no longer to the West, but betwixt the West and North, '- ' ' for most Northerly. Being come to Padichorus he sailed thence 800. furl, to the rock Maceta, of a daies sailing, whence Cinamon and Spices are carried to the Assyrians.

After 700. furl, he came to Neapotanum and 100. furl.

further to the River Anenus; the Region is called

Armozia, cultivated and fertile, except of Olives. Here Jrmozta, nozv they went ashoare desirous to rest from their labour, and ma.

there found a Graecian which told them that Alexanders

Campe was not farre off, five daies journey from the Sea.

Here Nearchus repaired his Navie, and meane while sent to the King, after went himselfe, he and his by their changed weatherbeaten countenances and growne haire, being not knowne by those whom Alexander had sent to him. Some had made Alexander beleeve his Fleet was f i S lost, which finding otherwise, hee wept for joy, swearing ' J' ' h V SP by the Grecian Jupiter, and by the Lybian Ammon, that he more joyed in those tidings then in the Empire of all Asia.

After this hee instituted Musical and Gymnicke Games, and pompe to Jupiter Servator, to Hercules, to Apollo the chaser away of evill, and to Neptune, with the other

Sea-Gods. Especially Nearchus was eminent and glorious, the whole army casting flowers and garlands on him.

Alexander after this would have sent another to bring the Fleet to Susae, which Nearchus envying to any other, intreated that the whole glory might be entire to himselfe, and was sent backe. After sacrifice to Jupiter the savior, Nearchus exhibited a Gymnicke game (for trying of masteries, which we call prizes) and set saile. He passed by a Legend ofery-small Hand called Organa, and another lesse called 'J "f Oaracta, 300. rurlongs rrom the place whence he set rorth, Arabkke where were many Vines, Palmes, and Fruits. Here they Gulfe to this said was the Sepulcher of Erythrus, or King Red, which Persian, such gave name to this red Sea. The Hand was 800. furlongs p f long, of which having sailed two hundred, he saw another supersticious Hand forty furlongs long sacred to Neptune, and reported traditions.

to be inaccessible. At their departing three ships stucke fast by reason of the Tide, which at the next floud were afloate againe. After forty furlongs sailing hee anchored in another Hand 300. furlongs from the Continent; thence to the He Pylora, in which is Dodon a towne which hath nothing but fish and water. After 300. furlongs sailing, he came to a Cape running farre into the Sea, thence 300. furlongs to the He Cataea sacred to Mercury and Venus, whither dedicated Goates and Sheepe are yeerely sent which there grew wilde. Hitherto the Carmani extend about 3700. furlongs by the shoare. These live like the Persians their neighbours. Thence Nearchus sailed to the He Caicandros, forty furlongs, and thence to an inhabited Hand where Pearles are Beginning of found, fifty f. Thence to Mount Ochus, and thence to the Persians. Apostane, 450. f. and after 400. f. to a Bay celebrated with many Villages; thence 600. f. to the mouth of the River Oreon: thence 800. f. to River Sitacus. All this course was on the Persian shoare, shelvie for the most part and fenny. Thither Alexander had sent provision of Corne, and they staied one and twenty dales to refresh themselves, and repaire their Navie. Sailing thence 750. f. he came to Hieratis by the River Heratemis, the next day to the River Padargus, where is a fertile place called Mesambria a peninsula: 200. furlongs to Taornus to the great River, above whose entrance 200. furlongs are the Persian Kings Palaces. In this way he saw a Whale dead fifty cubits long, with Oisters growing on the skin. Dolphins also bigger then those in our Seas. He proceeded 200. furlongs to the River Rhogonis fifty furlongs to the River Brizana: thence to Arosis the bigest River in all his course, the end of the Persian borders, that Beginning of shoare containing 4400. furlongs. There begin the the Susians. Susians, and within land the Uzians, as the Mardi to the Persians, and the Cossasi to the Medes.

Having sailed on the Susian shoare 500. furlongs, he came to Cataderbis, a fishie Lake, neere which is the He Margastana: then he passed sholds which scarsely MUSieUS AND THEB US admitted ships single, discerned by stakes or poles purposely fixed there, the mirie ground taking a man up to the waste. In such way he sailed 500, furlongs. Thereafter in a night and day he sailed 900. f. to the mouth of Euphrates, neere Diridotis a Village of the Babylonians, a Euphrates and Mart for the Spices of Arabia. From thence to Babylon, Babylonians. Nearchus saith, are 3300. f Nearchus hearing that Alexander was going to Susae, sailed backe toward Pasitigris, that sailing up the streame he might meete him, having the Susians on the left hand, and the Lake into which Tigris runneth 600. f. from the River it selfe, at Aginis a towne of the Susians. Having sailed 150. f. he staid till the returne of his Messengers from the King. At last both armies were joined with incredible joy, and Alexander exhibited divers kinds of game with sacrifices, much honour was done to Nearchus; Alexander also crowned him and Leonnatus with a crown of gold. Alexander sent others on the right hand to discover all the coasts of Arabia. And thus Europe must acknowledge Alexander the chiefe Easterne discoverer, as the Roman armes first opened to us the West. We will adde a little out of Ecclesiasticall writers.

Chap. X.

The Travels of Musaeus, Thebseus and others mentioned by Saint Ambrose; of others also mentioned in the Ecclesiasticall Histories of Eusebius, Ruffinus, Socrates and Sozomen.

Usaeus Bishop of the Dolens related to the Authour of the Tractate De Moribus Brachmanorum (supposed to be Saint Ambroses) that hee intending to goe into India to see the Brachmans, had travelled thorow almost all the Region Serica, in which hee said there were Trees (which broughti fourth not only leaves, but very fine wooll also, of which they make Garments called Serica; and that

Edit. Paris. 1614.

This Tractate is in the Vatican, Florentine, and Mil-Ian Libraries attributed to Saint Ambrose. Others doubt zchether thatfaiherbee the Author, or Palladius, d c. Gotten Trees or Shrubs. Serica is Aereby is knoione to be far short of China, neere zvhich Alexander never

Aromata. Muziris.

Perhaps the Maldivas

Thebceus in many things a fabler.

there was a memorable Pillar of stone thus inscribed; I Alexander came hitherto; and that having passed thorow many Countreyes, he came at last to Ariana neere the River Indus, and by the intolerable heat was inforced to returne into Europe, not having seene the Brachmans. He reported that he had heard of Thebaeus a certaine Scholer which went into India to see and conferre with Indian Philosophers called Brachmans and Gymnosophists: but hee was there captived. For shipping himselfe with certaine Merchants in the Red Sea, he first came to the Towne of the Adulites, or the Bay Adulicus, after that to the Promontory Aromata, and a Mart of the Troglodytes, and hence to places of the Assumites, and many dayes after to Muziris the Mart of all India on this side Ganges, and having stayed a while there, he passed over to the He Taprobane. This is governed by foure Princes, one of which is the chiefe, whom the others obey, and to him are subject a thousand Hands, as he reported, of the Arabian and Persian Seas, and those which they call Mammolas. The Hand hath five Rivers very great, the temperature such that at the same time the same Trees produced blossomes and fruits some greene, some ripe. The men live on Fruits, Rice and Milke, and the chiefe men eate Mutton and Goats flesh on solemne dayes. He was taken as a Spie and kept six yeeres in Prison, but the Governour which had so used a Roman Citizen, was by the Emperors command flayed. He reporteth true and false things blended, and amongst others of the Brachmans thus. They live naked in the Regions adjoyning to the River Ganges; they have no beasts, tillage, use of Iron, nor any kinde of Instrument to doe any worke: they have an excellent Aire and temperate Climate. They alway worship God, of whom they professe a distinct knowledge, both of his Providence and Divinity. They alwayes pray, but in their Prayer looke not to the East, but directly to Heaven. They eate (as the beasts) what they find on the ground, leaves, and herbes; they have the herbe Inula and the Tree

MUSieUS AND THEBieUS

Acanthus, The men live on the further side of Ganges, on the Ocean Coasts, the women on this side, to whom their Husbands use to have recourse in July and August.

For those moneths seeme colder there, because the This is not

Sunne then comes neerer to us, and when they have " "J continued fortie dayes with their wives, they returne jji f j. ij j.

home. When a woman hath had a child or two, her in those places

Husband forbeareth her altopct er And if in five yeeres neere the hih a woman hath no child, shee is divorced. And thus their V tiaiagate, number is but small. The

River is passed over with heat and cold great difficultie by reason of the tyrannic of Ondonitus, asbyfaireand which infesteth those places, and of a certaine beast so foule weather, great that hee devoureth a whole Elephant. This beast " "' ", 1 T) L J c-in the same IS not scene when the ijrachmans time or passage is. pygpl., lt gf

There are Dragons also reported to be seventie Cubits the Stcnne on long, I saw one whose skin was two and fortie foot: one side, and

Ants as great as a mans span. Scorpions a Cubit long, Summer on the c. If this Scholler Thebaeus be worthy credit. There,,.-,,

T-. r TTT r time, to are m the same Tractate added out or the Writers of which perhaps Alexanders life many speeches and discourses of the is here alluded. Brachmans, which I forbeare here to insert. They indeed- b. Ep. I. z. are in many points admirable, if some Greekes have not I' 'j rather made experiment of their wits and facultie in Philo-sophicall discourses, then delivered a true Historic; at least mixed truth and seeming together, as wee see here in this Bishop and his Thebasus. Those Gymnosophists (as Megasthenes also related) condemned Calanus, which followed Alexander, whose Epistle is extant in a worke of Saint Ambrose lesse suspected, which I have here also inserted, out of Saint Ambrose his seventh Epistle.

Calanus to Alexander. Thy friends perswade thee to lay hands and violence on an Indian Philosopher; not so much as dreaming of our workes. For thou maist remoove our bodies from place to place, but thou shalt not compell our minds to doe that which they are not willing, any more then thou canst make Stones or Trees to speake. A great fire causeth burning smart I 241 Q ' Euseb. de. vit Const. I. 4. c. 50. Indian Embassadors to Constantine, as before to Augustus. I. i. 90.

oc, hist. Eccles. I. 1. c. 15. Sozom. hist. Ec. . 2. f. 23.

to living bodies, and worketh corruption: but we are above this, for we are burned alive. No King or Prince can extort from us to doe what we have not determined: Nor are wee like the Philosophers of Greece, which have studied words insteed of deeds, to get themselves a name and reputation. With us things are companions to words, and words to the things, our deeds quicke and speeches short, we have a blessed libertie in vertue.

Eusebius " in the Life of Constantine mentioneth an Indian Embassie sent to him with rich Presents of almost all kind of Gemmes, and beasts differing from ours, with Pictures and Statues, whereby the Indians acknowledged him Emperour, and King of all unto the remotest Coast of the Ocean, that as the Britaines, in the furthest West obeyed him at first, so now at last the Indians in the extremest East.

Socrates and Sozomene in their Ecclesiasticall Histories have related how in Constantines dayes Christian Religion entred the Inner India, which (as some thinke) till that time had not heard of Christ. Meropius a Philosopher of Tyre being desirous to see India (provoked by the Example of Metrodorus the Philosopher, which before that had travelled thorow that Region) sailed thither with two boyes of his Kindred skilful! in the Greeke Tongue. When he had satisfied his desire, and was now readie to returne, the league betwixt the Indians and Roman Empire was broken, and the Philosopher with all his company were taken and slaine, the two youths excepted, which were presented to the Indian King. The King tooke liking of them, and made one of them named Aedesius his Cup-bearer, and Frumentius (so was the other named) his Secretary. Soone after the King dyed and gave them liberty. The Queene seing the young King a child, desired their care and assistance till he were growne to manhood. They yeelded and Frumentius managed the government, who enquiring amongst the Roman Merchants which came thither, whether there were any Christians amongst them, gave

MUSieUS AND THEB US them a place by themselves to serve God after the Christian manner, and in processe of time builded a Church to pray in. These Christians instructing some of the Indians in the mysteries of the faith, added them to their societie. When the King was come to mans estate, Frumentius and iedesius deliver up their accounts, and desire leave to returne to their Countrey, the King and his mother earnestly (but in vaine) intreating their stay.

-(desius went to Tyre to see his friends, Frumentius S. Athanaslus went to Alexandria, and acquainted Athanasius, then (" Fruniea-newly Bishop with the premisses, and the hopes of Indian- inrif conversion, desiring him to send a Bishop and Clergie thither. Athanasius considering well the businesse, con-secrateth Frumentius Bishop, saying he had no man fitter for that purpose, who thus honoured returneth and preacheth the faith to the Indians, builds many Churches, and by the grace of God worketh many Miracles, healing both bodies and soules of many. Ruffinus writeth, that hee heard these things of iedesius himselfe, who also at Tyre obtayned the dignity of Priesthood. The Iberians con-Iberians (now called Georgians) were at the same time ' ' " ' converted by meanes of a Captive Christian woman, which by Miracles perswaded the King and people to receive the faith of Christ, which sent Embassadors to Constantine to enter into league, and to obtayn a Bishop Clergie, which the same Ruffinus reporteth, he heard of Bacurius a great man of that Nation. Before we leave Socrates, it is meet in this Argument of Travels, to mention his report of Palladius, a man of so strong constitution and Palkdius his admirable abilitie, that he in three dayes could ride from swiftnesse and Constantinople to the Confines betwixt the Persian and '" J f" Roman Empires, and returne thither againe to his Master '" ' ' '" ' ' Theodosius the Emperour in three other dales. Yea, he swiftly posted to all parts of the World to which he was sent, insomuch that one said of him. This man by his swiftnesse makes the Romane Empire, as large as it is, to be very narrow. The Persian King was amazed to heare these things reported of him.

' ' This was intended the beginning of our promised Eiiropaanpil-grimage: but no man assisted the Pilgrime, zvhich forced him to leave off, and in token of his intents to give this taste thereof The fourth time it is now on the Presse.

Jo. 2. lo. Gen. 15. I. i. Ccr. 15.2 Dedit se in meritumy dabit se in premium. Ber. I. i.91.

Chap. XL A briefe and generall consideration of Europe.

Of Europe compared with the other parts of the World.

Hree parts of the World have beene three times visited by our more laborious then learned Muse: the Fourth for whose sake that triple-worke received so often survay, hath seemed forgotten, Asia, Africa, and America, have first bin discovered to our Reader, not as enjoying the first and best place, but offering their readie service and best attendance unto Europe; the least in quantity, and last in discourse, but greatest in those things which for greatnesse and goodnesse deserve the most applause and admiration. Our method hath not observed that Feast-masters rule, at the beginning to set forth good Wine, and when men have well drunke, then that which is worse; but we have kept the good Wine untill now: following His example, who in the first Creation made Man last; in humane and reasonable designes, allots the last execution, to the first intentions; in Religions Mysteries sends the Gospel after the Law, gives Heaven after Earth, and reserves Himselfe for the last service, to be our exceeding great reward; when God shall be all in all unto his servants. Him I beseech that here also he will turne our water into Wine, that we may be able to give Feastivall entertainment unto our Guests, that as Europe excels the other parts of the World, so my Muse may here exceed her wonted selfe, and present it unto you in ornaments of Art, Industry and Syncerity, befitting such a Subject. Hard were our hap to suffer shipwracke in the Haven; to faile in the last Act would marre the Comaedie; to be a stranger at home, and like the Lapwing to flie most and cry lowdest, being farthest from the Nest, were to travell of vanitie, and bring forth folly, or with the wilde Prodigall in the Gospell to be Luke 15. 17. still travelling from himselfe. We are now in manner Jx6'S'"'-y. at home, when most remote, never out of European limits, and therefore need not feare (as before) burning or frozen Zones, huge Oceans, new Constellations, un-knowne Lands, unpassable Deserts, uncouth Monsters, Savage beasts, more beastly and monstrous men. We need not follow the out-worne foot-prints of rare un-certaine Travellers, where Truth herselfe is suspicious in such forren disguised habit, nor need wee doubt to want guides, except the store become a sore, and plentie troublesome. Only we may feare in this taske frequent Cen-surers, not rigid Catoes, or severer judicious Judges, but capricious Novices, which having comne to their Lands sooner then their wits, would think the World might condemne them of ill-spent time, if they should not spend an indigested censure on the Bookish Travels of others. But I should be like them if I should feare them, shallow and emptie. However, I have adventured on this European Stage: wherein we are first to consider the more generall Occurrences, and after that the particular Regions. Of the former sort are the Names, Bounds, Excellencies, Languages.

The Names of Europe.

He Ancients have differed much, nor is the question yet agreed on, about the limits of Europe, some comprehending Africa under this division f "- de ling. (making but two parts of the World) others adding the " '- ' same to Asia. Thus Varro divides the Universe into Heaven and Earth, this into Asia and Europe, allowing to that the Southerne parts, to this the Northerne. So Silius sings of Afrike,

Aut ingens Asiae latus, aut pars tertia rerum.

Luc. I. 9.

Sal. Bel. Jug. Jug. C. D. I. 16. c. 17. O70S. I.2. C.2. Paulap. Juson. hoc. in Pane. yr. Her. L 4. Horn. Iliad.

Moschus. Lycoph. Theocr. Apol-lod. Horat. Ovid. Senec. Manil ar'c. Euseb. Chron. L 2.

Lucan otherwise,

Si ventos Coelumque sequaris

Gor. Orig. I. 9. zer. by transposition Eur, astereus of Tcrucs.

Pars erit Europae, neque enim plus littora Nili Quam Scythicus Tanais primis a Gadibus absint.

This opinion is alleadged by Salust, Saint Augustine, Orosius, Paulinus, followed by Isocrates and others. But the most attribute to Europe only a third, and that the least part in their partition of the elder World.

No lesse contention hath beene about the Etymology of the Name, which Herodotus saith is unknowne. Others fetch from I know not what Europa, the daughter of Agenor, ravished by Jupiter in forme of a Bull. The Truth should indeed be ravished by our Poets, if the Fable bee received; for she was transported from Phoenicia, a Region of Asia into Africa; others say into Cyprus; and if wee agree to others that it was into Creta, yet Kjo Te? aei y ova-rai, unlikely it is a small Hand for a small stay (for shee was after that carried into Afrike) could give name to so great a part of the World. Nor have wee much more satisfaction in Europus, the sonne of one Himerus King of some part (can you tell where?) of Europe. Europs raigned over the Sicyonians, saith Pausanias: at that time when Abram was borne, if wee follow Eusebius, and may bee the likelier Author of this name. Some ascribe it to the goodlinesse of the Europaean Tract, as being beautiful! to the sight. Becanus derives it from ver, which signi-fieth great or excellent, and hop, a multitude; rather chasing a Dutch then Greeke Etymologie, that people inhabiting Europe sooner (as hee conceives) then this. And in another booke noted by himselfe for a second Impression, he liketh better that it should be composed of E, i. marriage; ur excellent; hop, hope; alluding to that prophecie of Noah, that Japheth should dwell in the tents of Shem, whose posterity being divorced, the Church of the Gentiles in Japhets progenie should succeed in a more stable and everlasting marriage. Ptolemey better thinkes it might bee called Celtica, almost every Region thereof being antiently either wholly or in part, peopled with the Celtae: which Ortelius, Paulus Merula, and others have shewed in the particulars. Some have called Europe Tyria, of that Tyriam maiden aforesaid ravished by a Bull (a Bull-formed, or as others, a Bull-signed ship; after Palephatus, a man whose name was Bull; a Band of Souldiers say others bearing a Bull in their Banner; the Mythologians can tell you more, if this bee not too much:) Some have of Japhet called it Japetia. The Abasines and Easterne Inhabitants of Asia call the Europasans Franks, which name I suppose was occasioned by their Expeditions and Conquests in the Holy Land, and the Countries adjoyning by the Westerne Forces, in the composition whereof the French were a principall Bee of this 1. ingredient; that I mention not a French Councell to-1-2.3."2 4-further it, and the Crowne of Jerusalem falling to God-frie of Buuen his heires to reward it: whence it hapned that the Europaeans then were, and ever since I. i. 92. are by the Saracens and Easterne Asians called Frankes; as perhappes for the same cause the Turkes call those of the Popish Faith, stiling those of the Greekish Religion Romaeans, of their chiefe Citie Constantinople, otherwise named New Rome.

. III.

The Quantitie, and Bounds.

He quantitie of Europe is much larger, especially towards the North, then Ptolemey and the elder Geographers have written. At Wardhouse, and the North Cape, the longest day is reckoned two moneths and seven houres, in 71. degrees 30. minutes, whereas at the Hill Calpe, one of Hercules Pillars, and at Cabo Maini in Morea (accounted the most Southerne parts in 36. degrees) the day is but fourteene houres and an halfe at the longest. Much difference hath beene about the Easterne Confines. Plato, Aristotle, Herodotus, and others extend it to the River Phasis, or that Isthmus betwixt the Euxine and Caspian Seas; Dionysius, Arrianus, Diodorus, Polybius, Iornandes, adde nothing to the River Tanais: which Ortelius passeth over and takes in both Volga and all the Muscovites and Tartarian Hords, as farre as the River Ob. Ptolemey imagineth a Une from Tanais Northwards; which well agrees to the method of our History, as including the most part of the Russian Empire. All the other parts are bounded and washed by the Sea, Palus Maeotis, the Euxine, and Egean on the East inclining to the South; the Mediterranean on the South, on the West and North the Ocean. Bertius numbers 2400. Italian miles in the latitude, and 3000. in the longitude.

The Qualitie and Excellencies.

He Qualitie of Europe exceeds her Quantitie, in this the least, in that the best of the World. For how many both Seas and Deserts take up spacious Regions in Asia, Africa, and America? whereas in Europe neither watry Fens, nor unstable Bogs, nor Inland Seas, nor unwholsome Ay res, nor wild Woods, with their wilder Savage Inhabitants, nor snow-covered Hills, nor stiffling Frosts, nor long long Nights, nor craggy Rocks, nor barren Sands, nor any other effect of Angry Nature, where she seemes in some, or other parts thereof the hardest step-mother, can prohibite all habitation and humane societie. In the most parts Nature hath shewed her selfe a naturall and kind Mother; the providence of God, and industry of Man, as it were conspiring the Europasan good. Which of the Sisters are comparable in a temperate aire." which in a soile so generally fertile, so diversified in Hills and Dales, so goodly Medowes, cheerefiill Vineyards, rich Fields, fat Pastures, shadie Woods, delightfull Gardens, varietie of Creatures on it, of Metalls and Mineralls in it, of Plants and Fruits growing out of it? Which so watered with Fountaines, Brookes, Rivers, Bathes, Lakes out of her owne bowells? such sweet Dewes and comfortable Showers from Heaven? so frequent insinuations of the Sea, both for commerce with others, and proper Marine commodities? Which so peopled with resolute courages, able bodies, well qualified mindes? so fortified with Castles, edified with Townes, crowned with Cities? And if in some of these things Asia, Afrike, and America piac. may seeme equall, or in any thing superiour, yet even therein also they are inferiour, by just and equall inequalitie made Tributaries and Servants to Europe: the first captived by Alexander, the first and second by the Romans, the last and the most commodious places of the first, with all the Sea Trade, by Spanish and Portugall Discoveries and Conquests; first, second, last, All and more then they all, since and still made open and obnoxious to the English and Dutch, which have discovered new Northerne Worlds, and in their thrice-worthy Marine Armes have so often imbraced the inferiour Globe. Asia yeerely sends us her Spices, Silkes, Gemmes; Africa her Gold and Ivory; America receiveth severer Customers and Tax-Masters, almost every where admitting Europasan Colonies.

If I speake of Arts and Inventions (which are Mans properest goods, immortall Inheritance to our mortalitie) what have the rest of the world comparable.? First the Liberall Arts are most liberall to us, having long since forsaken their Seminaries in Asia and Afrike, and here erected Colledges and Universities. And if one Athens in the East (the antient Europaean glory) now by Turkish Barbarisme be infected, how many many Christian Athenses have wee in the West for it. As for Mechanicall Sciences, I could reckon our Ancestors inventions now lost, as that malleable Glasse in the dayes of Tiberias; that oleum vinum found in olde Sepulchers still burning:, after i coo. K ', ", yeeres; 1 could glory or Archimedes his ingenuous igpgyditis 6 Engines; but miserum est ist hue verbum pessimum, repartis.

habuisse non habere. I can recite later inventions the Daughters of wonder. What eye doth not almost loose it selfe in beholding the many artificiall Mazes and I. i. 93. Labyrinths in our Watches, the great heavenly Orbes and motions imitated in so small a modell? What eares but Europaean, have heard so many Musicall Inventions for the Chamber, the Field, the Church? as for Bells, Europe alone beares the bel, and heares the Musicall consort thereof in the Steeples diversified, yea thence descending to Birds and Squirells."' Where hath the taste beene feasted with such varieties for delight, for health."' are not Distillations, the Arts also of Candying and Preserving meere Europasan? If I should descend lower, who invented the Stirrop to ascend, the Saddle to ride the Horse."' Who devised so many kindes of motions by Clock-workes, besides Clockes and Dialls to measure Time, the measurer of all things.? Who invented wild Fires that scorne the waters force and violence? Who out of ragges to bring such varieties of Paper for Mans manifold use.? Who so many kinds of Mills Who ever dream't of a perpetuall Motion by Art, or De quadratura circuli, or innumerable other Mathematicall, and Chymicall devises.? And what hath Mars in the World elsewhere to parallel with our Ordnance, and all sorts of Gunnes? or the Muses with our Printing.? Alas, China yeelds babes and babies in both compared with us and ours: the rest of the World have them borrowed of us or not at all. And for the Art Military, the exactest Science, Discipline, Weapons, Stratagems, Engines, Resolution, Successe herein, have honoured Europe with the Macedonian and Roman spoiles of the World: and even still the Turkish puissance is here seated; the English, Dutch, French, Italian, Spanish courages have not degenerated from those Ancestors, which tamed and shooke in pieces that Tamer and Terror of the World, the Roman Monarchy.

But what speake I of Men, Arts, Armes? Nature hath yeelded her selfe to Europaean Industry. Who ever found out that Loadstone and Compasse, that findes out and compasseth the World? Who ever tooke possession of the huge Ocean, and made procession round about the vast Earth? Who ever discovered new Constellations, saluted the Frozen Poles, subjected the Burning Zones? And who else by the Art of Navigation have seemed to imitate Him, which laies the beames of his Chambers in the Waters, and walketh on the wings Ps. 104. 3. of the Wind? And is this all? Is Europe onely a fruitfull Field, a well watered Garden, a pleasant Paradise in Nature? A continued Citie for habitation? Queene of the World for power? A Schoole of Arts Liberall, Shop of Mechanicall, Tents of Military, Arsenall of Weapons and Shipping? And is shee but Nurse to Nature, Mistresse to Arts, Mother of resolute Courages and ingenious dispositions? Nay these are the least of Her praises, or His rather, who hath given Europe more then Eagles wings, and lifted her up above the Starres. I speake it not in Poeticall fiction, or Hyperbolicall phrase, but Christian Sincerity. Europe is taught the way to scale Heaven, not by Mathematicall principles, but by Divine veritie. Jesus Christ is their way, their truth, their life; who hath long since given a Bill of Divorce to ingratefuu Asia where hee was borne, and Africa the place of his flight and refuge, and is become almost wholly and onely Europaean. For little doe wee find of this name in Asia, lesse in Africa, and nothing at all in America, but later Europaean gleanings. Here are his Scriptures, Oratories, Sacraments, Ministers, Mysteries. Here that Mysticall Babylon, and that Papacie (if that bee any glory) which challengeth both the Bishopricke See Boz. c. i and Empire of the World; and here the victory over that Beast (this indeed is glory) by Christian Reformation according to the Scriptures. God himselfe is our portion, and the lot of Europes Inheritance, which hath made Nature an indulgent Mother to her, hath bowed the Heavens over her in the kindest influence, hath trenched the Seas about her in most commodious affluence, hath furrowed in her delightfull, profitable confluence of Streames, hath tempered the Ayre about her, fructified the Soyle on her, enriched the Mines under her, diversified his Creatures to serve her, and multiplied Inhabitants to enjoy her; hath given them so goodly composition of body, so good disposition of mind, so free condition of life, so happy successe in affaires; all these annexed as attendants to that true happinesse in Religions truth, which brings us to God againe, that hee may bee both Alpha and Omega in all our good. Even in Civilitie also Europe is the youngest of the Three, but as Benjamin, the best beloved, made heire to the Rest, exchanging the Pristine Bar-barisme, and Incivilitie (which Authors blame in our Ancestors) with Asia and Africa, for that Civilitie of Manners, and Glory of Acts and Arts, which they (as neerer the Arkes resting place) sooner enjoyed, by Mohumetan pestilence long since becomne barbarous; the best of the one fitly called Barbaria, and the best Moniments of the other being but names, ruines, car-kasses, and sepulchrall Moniments of her quandam Excellencies.

Of the Languages of Europe.

S for their particular manners, dispositions, cus-tomes, wee shall in due place observe: their Mother Tongues and Originall Languages I

Jos. Seal.

opusc. d'latv'iba de Eur op. ling 'apmerula. tvi–i–i . 2.. i. f. 8. will here out of Scaliger (our Europaean Mithridates) relate. Of these he now reckons in Europe eleven, seven of smaller note, foure of greater, which yeeld I. i. 94. many Dialects, seeming differing languages out of them. These are the Greeke, Latin, Dutch, and Slavon', from whence by inflexion, trajection, mutation, and mixture, are derived many others. Thus the Slavon hath Daughters or Dialects, the Russian, Polonian, Bohemian, Illyrian, Dalmatian, and Windish tongues; some of these also not a little in themselves diversified. They use two sorts of letters, the Russian depraved from the Greeke, with some barbarous additions; and the Dalmatian of Saint Hieroms invention, much unlike the former. The Dutch hath three principall Idiomes, Teutonisme, Saxonisme, and Danisme. The first containes both the High and Low Dutch; the second, the Nord-albing, Frisland and English Dialects; the third Danish, Sweden, and the Norwegian, Mother of that of the Islanders. The Latin hath propagated the Italian, Spanish and French, The Greeke in so many Lands and Hands so farre distant, cannot but be much different.

The smaller languages yet Originall, without commerce and derivation from others are, the Epirotike, or Albanian in the Mountaines of Epirus: Secondly the Cosaks or Tartarian: Thirdly, the Hungarian, which the Hunnes and Avares brought thither out of Asia: Fourthly, that of Finnemark, which yeelds also the Lappian: Fiftly the Irish, which is used likewise of the Redshankes: Sixtly the Welsh or Brittish (the same with that of the ancient Galles, as Master Camden hath proved) spoken diversely in Wales, Cornwall, and little Britaine: Seventhly, the Biscaine, the remainder of the old Spanish, in use on both sides the Pyrenaean Hills. These were all in Ecclesiasticall affaires subjected to the Constantino-politan and Roman Bishops, and used five sorts of letters, the Greeke, Latin, and Gottish, besides those two formerly mentioned. The Greeke principally possesseth the South East, the Latin with her Daughters, the South; the Dutch, the North-west parts of Europe; and the North-east, the Slavon.

And thus have we given a taste, of that which sometimes was intended, an Europaean Feast: in which if I seeme to have broken promise, I have not done it alone; and povertie cleeres mee of perfidie. If yet my rashnesse bee accused, in promising upon hopes of others assistance, let him that hath relieved those wants throw the first stone at the Promiser. How ever, I will rather confesse the Action then stand Sute. Nor doe I now beg helpes in that kind; it is too late. My body is worne and old before and beyond my yeeres; and to have borne so long two such burthens as a Pulpit and Presse, that is, Heaven and Earth, would perhaps have tired my quarrelling Plaintiffe too, to have ascended the one (idque Londini) twice or thrice a weeke ordinarily, and descended the other with so frequent successions, and long continuations. Hercules and Atlas were both weary of one burthen: Patience yet and pardon! for I have paid here a great part of my debt. I have given thee the Christian Sects, and Europes Ecclesiastike part, with her other Secular parts also in great part both in Maps and History presented, especially there where shee was lest knowne: and if not so fully as the former in my Pilgrimage, yet Poore men are welcome pay-masters when they come with parts each weeke or moneth, or with day-labour-set-offs; though they cannot at once discharge the whole debt. Indeed my Genius most leads mee to remotest and lest knowne things, that where few others can give intelligence, I may supply the Intelligencers place. Of neere and knowne things, Scribimus indocti Sevenarfs of doctique poemata passim. I have given thee Arctoa fie World. Regio, the Polare World; and Antarctica, the Southerne Continent; and both Americas; besides Asia, Africa, and Europe knowne to the Antients, Yea I have given thee an Asia in Asia, and an Africa in Africa never knowne to the Ancients; as likewise I may affirme of the Northerne Parts of Europe. Coetera quis nescit " Who cannot dull and deafe thine eares with French, Dutch, Spanish, Italian affaires Neither are we destitute of some intelligence and sleighter knowledge of Spaine, France, and Germany, Italy and other parts, which you will find handled in one or other place of this Worke, as much as concerneth our Travelling purpose. As for Spaine, the Kings Title is a sufficient Lecture, which some thus expresse: P. By the Grace of God King of Castile, Lions, Arragon, both Sicills, Jerusalem, Portugall, Navarre, Granada, Toledo, Valencia, Galicia, Majorca and Minorca, Sivil, Sardinia, Corduba, Corsica, Murcia, Jaen, Algarbia,

Algeria, Gibraltar, Canary Hands, East and West Indies, of the Hands and Continent of the Ocean; Archduke of Austria, Duke of Burgundy, Loraine, Brabant, Lun-burg, Luxemburg, Geldres, Millaine, c. Earle of Habs-purg, Flanders, Tirol, Barcelona, Artois, Hannalt, Holand, Zeland, Namur, Zutphen, c. Marquesse of the Empire, Lord of Biscay, Friezland, Mecklin, Utreck, Over-Isell, Gruningen. Ruler in Asia and in Africa. This doth more fully present the present Spaine to your view, then to tell the Scituation, Mountaines and Rivers; of which every Map and Traveller can informe you. France also is not to be now measured by the antient Geographicall limits, but by the present Royall, so much being most properly France, as is comprehended in that most compact, best seated, well peopled, and goodliest of Kingdomes. The parts you shall see in the Diocesse hereafter following. Germany in largest sense by some is bounded by Rhene, Vistula, the Danow and the Ocean, is divided into Kingdomes, Dukedomes, Counties, and Cap. ult. Marquisates. The Kingdomes are Denmarke, Norway, Sweden, Boheme. The rest concerning Germany and other parts of Europe I teach not here; I point at rather these things, and therefore will returne to Our former discourse of languages, and therein produce a better Linguist and Artist then my selfe. Our learned Countryman, Master Brerewood in his laborious Travells and Industrious Enquiries of Languages and Religions.

Chapter XII.

Of the ant'ient largenesse of the Greeke tongue. Strabo. I. 8. non longe a principio.

Senec. Consol. ad Helu. c. 6. PH. I. 5. f. 29. hoc rat. in Panegerk. long. p05t. med. Lucian. in Dialog, de Amarib. non longe. ab Init.

Chapter XII.

Enquiries of Languages by Edw. Brerewood, lately Professor of Astronomy in Gresham Colledge.

Reece, as it was anciently knowne by the name of Hellas, was inclosed betwixt the Bay of Ambracia, with the River Arachthus, that falleth into it on the West, and the River Peneneus on the North, and the Sea on other parts. So that Acarnania and Thessalie, were toward the Continent the utmost Regions of Greece. But yet, not the Countries onely contained within those limits, but also the Kingdomes of Macedon, and Epirus; being the next adjoyning Provinces (Macedon toward the North, Epirus toward the West) had anciently the Greeke tongue for their vulgar language: for although it belonged originally to Hellas alone, yet in time it became vulgar to these also.

Secondly, it was the language of all the Isles in the gaean Sea; of all those Hands I say, that are betwixt Greece and Asia, both of the many small ones, that lie betweene Candie and Negropont, named Cyclades (there are of them fiftie three) and of all above Negropont also, as farre as the Strait of Constantinople.

Thirdly, of the Iies of Candie, Scarpanto, Rhodes, and a part of Cyprus and of all the small Hands along the Coast of Asia, from Candie to Syria.

Fourthly, not only of all the West part of Asia the lesse, (now called Anatolia, and corruptly Natolia) lying toward the iegaean Sea, as being very thicke planted with Greeke Colonies: of which, some one, Miletus by name, is registred by Seneca, to have beene the Mother of seventie five, by Plinie, of eightie Cities; But on the North side also toward the Euxine Sea, as farre (saith Isocrates) at Sinope, and on the South side respecting

Afrique, as farre (saith Lucian) as the Chelidonlan Iies, which are over against the confines of Lycia with Pam-phylia. And yet although within these limits onely, Greeke was generally spoken, on the Maritime Coast of Asia, yet beyond them, on both the shoares Eastward, were many Greeke Cities (though not without Barbarous Cities among them). And specially I find the North coast of Asia, even as farre as Trebizond, to have beene exceedingly well stored with them. But, it may bee further observed likewise out of Histories, that not onely all the Maritime part of Anatolia could understand and speake the Greeke tongue, but most of the Inland people also, both by reason of the great traffike, which those rich Countries had for the most part with Grecians, and for that on all sides the East onely excepted, they were invironed with them. Yet neverthelesse, it is worthy observing, that albeit the Greeke tongue prevailed so farre in the Regions of Anatolia, as to bee in a manner generall, yet for all that it never became vulgar, nor extinguished the vulgar languages of those Countries. For it is not onely particularly observed of the Galatians, Hieron. in by Hierome, that beside the Greeke tongue, they had P-:-also their pecuhar language like that or Irier: and Q i t; of the Carians by Strabo, that in their language were strab. I. 14. found many Greeke wordes, which doth manifestly import " Ub. citato it to have beene a severall tongue: but it is directly ' J- 'Ye recorded by Strabo (out of Ephorus) that of sixteene 2. severall Nations, inhabiting that Tract, only three were Grecians, and all the rest (whose names are there registred) barbarous; and yet are not omitted the Cap-padocians, Galatians, Lydians, Maeonians, Cataonians, no small Provinces of that Region. Even as it is also observed by Plinie and others, that the twentie two Plm.. j. cz. languages, whereof Mithridates King of Pontus is re- '– membred to have beene so skilfull, as to speake them (p 17. without an Interpreter, were the languages of so many 17. Nations subject to himselfe, whose dominion yet wee know to have beene contained, for the greatest part, I 257 R within Anatolia. And although all these bee evident testimonies, that the Greeke tongue was not the vulgar or native language of those parts, yet, among all none is more effectuall, then that remembrance in the second Chapter of the Acts, where divers of those Regions, Act. 2. 9. (St" as Cappadocia, Pontus, Asia, Phrygia, and Pamphylia, lo are brought in for instances of differing languages.

Fiftly, Of the greatest part of the Maritime Coast of Thrace, not onely from Helle-spont to Byzantium Dousa. Itin. (which was that part of Constantinople, in the East Constat! tinopo- corner of the Citie, where the Serraile of the Great ht. pag. zi,. 'j' j. j standeth) but above it, all along to the out-lets of Danubius. And yet beyond them also; I find many Greeke Cities to have been planted along c- Jax Can- that Coast (Scylax of Carianda is my Author, with if'jl ajd " others) as farre as the Strait of Caffa, and VerelGetic. specially in Taurica. Yea, and beyond that Strait also c. 5. Eastward, along all the Sea Coast of Circassia, and

Mengrelia, to the River of Phasis, and thence compassing to Trebizond, I find mention of many scattered Greeke Cities: that is, (to speake briefly) in all the circum-ferences of the Euxine Sea.

Sixtly, (from the East and North to turne toward the West) it was the language of all the West and South Hands, that lie along the Coast of Greece, from Candie to Corfu, which also was one of them, and withall of that fertile Sicily, in which one Hand, I have I. i. 96. observed in good Histories, above thirtie Greeke Colonies to have beene planted, and some of them goodly Cities, specially Agrigentum and Syracusa, which later Strab. I. 6. in Strabo hath recorded to have been one hundred and medio. eighty furlongs, that is, of our miles two and twenty and a halfe in circuit.

Seventhly, not onely of all the Maritime Coast of Italie, that lyeth on the Tyrrhene Sea, from the River Garigliano, (Liris it was formerly called) to Leucopetra, the most Southerly point of Itahe, for all that shoare being neere about two hundred and fortie miles, was inhabited with Greeke Colonies: And thence forward, of all that end of Italie, that lyeth towardes the Ionian Sea, about the great Bayes of Squilacci and Taranto (which was so thicke set with great and goodly Cities of Graecians, that it gained the name of Magna Graecia) but, beyond that also, of a great part of Apulia, lying towards the Adriatique Sea. Neither did these Maritime parts onely, but as it seemeth the Inland people also towards that end of Italie, speake the Greeke tongue. For I have seene a few old Coynes of the Brutians, and more may bee seene in Goltzius having Goltz. in Greeke Inscriptions, wherein I observe they are named ' mismat. pemol with an ae, and two tt, and not as the Romane i rj, i, Writers terme them, Brutii. And I have seene one 24. piece also of Pandosia, an Inland Citie of those parts, with the like. Neither was the vulgar use of the Greeke Tongue, utterly extinct in some of those parts of Italie, till of late: for Galateus a learned man of that Countrey Galat. in de-hath left written, that when he was a Boy (and he "" P- ' ' '-lived about one hundred and twentie yeeres agoe) they ""' spake Greeke in Callipollis, a City on the East shoare of the Bay of Taranto: But yet it continued in Ecclesi-asticall use in some other parts of that Region of Italie much later, for Gabriel Barrius that but lived about Bar. I. z,. de forty yeeres since, hath left recorded, that the Church J tt t t-Cala-of Rossano (an Archiepiscopall Citie in the upper Calabria) retayned the Greeke Tongue and Ceremony till his time, and then became Latine. Nay, to descend yet a little neerer the present time, Angelus Rocca Rocca Tract. that writ but about twentie yeeres agoe, hath observed, " f ' ' that hee found in some parts of Calabria, and Apulia, some remaynders of the Greeke speech to bee still retayned. strab. L 4.

Eightly, and lastly, that shoare of France, that lyeth mn long, a towards the Mediter-raine Sea, from Rodanus to Italie, princip. was possessed with Graecians, for Massilia was a Colonie ""f ' " of the Phoceans, and from it many other Colonies were- " derived, and placed along that shoare, as farre as Nicaea, P.. 3.5.

in the beginning of Italic, which also was one of them.

And yet beside all these forenamed, 1 could reckon up very many other dispersed Colonies of the Greekes both in Europe, and Asia, and some in Afrique, for although I remember not, that I have read in any

History, any Colonies of the Grecians to have beene planted in Afrique, any where from the greater Syrtis

Westward, except one in Cirta, a City of Numidia, placed there by Micipsa the Sonne of Masinissa, as is mentioned

Strab. I. 17. in Strabo: yet thence Eastward it is certaine some were: for the great Cities of Cyrene and Alexandria, were

"Locojam both Greeke. And it is evident, not onely in " Strabo citato. Ptolemie, but in Mela, and other Latine Writers,

Z'- J ' that most of the Cities of that part carried Greeke

Jfn. Mela.111 o tt 1 1 j- 1 . i. r. 8. names. And lastly. Saint Hierome hath directly re-

Hieronin. loco corded, that Lybia, which is properly that part ot supra citato. Afrique adjoyning to-Egypt, was full of Greeke Cities. These were the places, where the Greeke Tongue was natively and vulgarly spoken, either originally, or by reason of Colonies. But yet for other causes, it became much more large and generall. One was the love of Philosophie, and the Liberall Arts written in a manner onely in Greeke. Another, the exceeding great Trade and Traffique of Grascians, in which, above all Nations, except perhaps the old Phaenicians (to whom yet they seeme not to have beene inferiour) they imployed themselves, A third, beyond all these, because those great Princes, among whom all that Alexander the Great had conquered, was divided, were Graecians, which for many reasons, could not but exceedingly spread the Greeke Tongue, in all those parts where they were Governours: among whom, even one alone, Seleucus Jppian. I. de by name, is registred by Appian, to have founded in Bellis Syriac. g p j. g under his government, at least sixty Cities, all of them carrying Greek names, or else named after his Father, his Wives, or himselfe. And yet was there a fourth cause, that in the aftertime greatly furthered this inlargement of the Greeke Tongue, namely the imployment of Grascians in the government of the Provinces, after the Translation of the Imperiall seate to Constantinople. For these causes I say, together with the mixture of Greeke Colonies, dispersed in many places (in which fruitfulnesse of Colonies, the Graecians farre passed the Romanes) the Greeke Tongue spread very farre, especially towards the East. In so much, that all the Orient (which yet must be understood with limitation, namely the Orientall part of the Roman Empire, or to speake in the Phrase of those times, the Diocesse of the Orient, which contayned Syria, Palestine, Cilicia, and part of Mesopotamia and of Arabia) is said by Hierome, to have spoken Greeke: Hiero. ubi which also Isidore, specially observeth, in iegypt, and pe-lsidor. Syria, to have beene the Dorique Dialect. And this f ' ' ' great glorie, the Greeke Tongue held in the Apostles time, and long after, in the Easterne parts, till by the inundation of the Saracens of Arabia, it came to ruine in those Provinces, about six hundred and forty yeeres after the birth of our Saviour, namely, in the time of the Emperor Heraclius (the Arabians bringing in their language together with their victories, into all the Regions they i. i. gy. j subdued) even as the Latine Tongue is supposed to have perished by the inundation and mixture of the Gothes, and other barbarous Nations in the West.

BUt at this day, the Greeke Tongue is very much Of the decay decayed, not only as touching the largenesse, Kf he and vulgarnesse of it, but also in the purenesse TIJ and elegancie of the Language. For as touching the tongue, and of former. First, in Italie, France, and other places to the present the West, the naturall Languages of the Countries "' ' " have usurped upon it. Secondly, in the skirts of- ' P-Greece it selfe, namely in Epirus, and that part of Macedon, that lyeth towards the Adriatique Sea, the Sclavonique Tongue hath extinguished it. Thirdly, in Anatolia, the Turkish Tongue hath for a great part suppressed it. And lastly, in the more Eastward, and South parts, as in that part of Cilicia, that is beyond the River Piramus, in Syria, Palestine, iegypt and Lybia, the Arabian Tongue hath abolished it: Abolished it I say, namely, as touching any vulgar use, for, as touching Ecclesiasticall use, many Christians of those

parts still retayne it in their Lyturgies. So that, the parts in which the Greeke Tongue is spoken at this day, are (in few words) but these. First Greece it selfe (excepting Epirus, and the West part of Macedon.) Secondly, the lies of the Egean Sea. Thirdly, Candie, and the lies Eastward of Candie, along the Coast of Asia to Cyprus (although in Cyprus, divers other Languages are spoken, beside the Greeke) and likewise the lies Westward of Candia, along the Coasts of Greece, and Epirus, to Corfu. And lastly, a good part of Anatolia.

But as I said, the Greeke Tongue, is not onely thus restrained, in comparison of the ancient extention that it had, but it is also much degenerated and impaired, as touching the purenesse of speech, being over-growne with barbarousnesse: But yet not without some rellish of the ancient elegancie. Neither is it altogether so much declined from the ancient Greeke, Bellon. obser- as the Italian is departed from the Latine, as Bellonius vat. I. I. e."). y2, x! x also observed, and by conferring of divers Epistles uicogt c. present Language, which you may find in Crusius his Turcograecia, with the ancient Tongue, may be put out of question which corruption yet, certainly hath not befallen that Language, through any inundation of barbarous people, as is supposed to have altered the Latine Tongue, for although I know Greece to have beene over-runne and wasted, by the Gothes, yet I finde not in Histories, any remembrance of their habitation, or long continuance in Greece, and of their coalition into one people with the Grascians, without which, I conceive not, how the Tongue could be greatly altered by them. And yet certaine it is, that long before the

Turkes came among them, their Language was growne to' the corruption wherein now it is, for that, in the Writings of Cedrenus, Nicetas, and some other late Greekes (although long before the Turkes invasion) there is found, notwithstanding they were learned men, a strong rellish of this barbarousnesse: Insomuch that the learned Grae-cians themselves, acknowledge it to bee very ancient, and are utterly ignorant, when it began in their Gerkch. in Language: which is to me a certaine argument, that it P" had no violent nor sudden beginning, by the mixture corrac I 7. of other forreine Nations among them, but hath gotten p, 89. into their Language, by the ordinarie change, which time and many common occasions that attend on time, are wont to bring to all Languages in the World, for which reason, the corruption of speech grow-ing upon them, by little and little, the change hath beene unsensible. Yet it cannot be denied (and ' some of the Graecians Zjgomdosin themselves confesse so much) that beside many Romane Ep"- words, which from the Translation of the Imperiall Seate ' ' " " to Constantinople, began to creepe into their Language, as we may observe in divers Greeke Writers of good Antiquitie, some Italian words also, and Slavonian, and Arabique, and Turkish, and of other Nations, are gotten into their Language, by reason of the great Traffique and Commerce, which those people exercise with the Grecians. For which cause, as Bellonius hath Bell. obser. I. observed, it is more altered in the Maritime parts, and- '" 3-such other places of forreigne concourse, then in the inner Region. But yet, the greatest part of the corruption of that Language, hath beene bred at home, and proceeded from no other cause, then their owne negligence, or affectation. As first (for example) by mutilation of some words, pronouncing and writing h. v Vide Cms. for lurjsev va for "iva c. Secondly, by compaction of " ' 44-severall words into one, as Trodse for ttoo else?, araa-r-nbrj ' g" for ek ra (xrridrf c.

Thirdly, by confusion of sound, as 399. c. making no difference in the pronouncing of three vowels, namely n, h and two Dipthongues ei and 01, all

Burran. in Coroii. pre-tiosa. Gerlach. apud Cms. I. 7. Turcog. p. 489.

Bellon. observ. I. z. c. III.

Li. 98. Burdovitx in Epist. ad Chitra, apud ilium in li. de statu Eccle-siar. . 47. Vide Chitra. loco citato, c Turcograc. Crus. p. i. y = 415. tsr'r. Of the ancient largenesse of the Roman tongue in the time of the Roman Empire. Chap. 3.

which five they pronounce by one Letter i, as o Koi, ee'ikwv, crryjorj Xvirt, they pronounce icos, icon, stithi, lipi. Fourthly, by Translation of accents, from the syllables to which in ancient pronouncing they belonged, to others. And all those foure kinds of corruption, are very common in their Language: for which reasons, and for some others, which may be observed in Crusius, Burrana, c. the Greeke Tongue, is become much altered (even in the proper and native words of the Language) from what anciently it was. Yet never-thelesse it is recorded by some, that have taken diligent observation of that Tongue, in the severall parts of Greece, that there be yet in Morea, (Peloponesus) betwixt Napoli and Monembasia (Nauplia and Epidaurus, they were called) some fourteene Townes, the Inhabitants whereof are called Zacones (for Lacones) that speake yet the ancient Greeke Tongue, but farre out of Grammer Rule: yet, they understand those that speake Grammatically, but understand not the vulgar Greeke. As Bellonius likewise remembreth another place, neere Heraclea in Anatolia, that yet retayneth the pure Greeke, for their vulgar Language. But the few places beeing excepted, it is certaine, that the difference is become so great, betwixt the present and the ancient Greeke that their Lyturgie, which is yet read in the ancient Greeke Tongue, namely that of Basil, on the Sabbaths and solemne dayes, and that of Chrysostome on common dayes, is not understood (or but little of it) by the vulgar people, as learned men that have beene in those parts, have related to others, and to my selfe: which may be also more evidently prooved to be true by this, because the skilfuu in the learned Greeke cannot understand the vulgar.

THe ordinary bounds ot the Romane Empire were, on the East part Euphrates, and sometimes Tigris: On the North the Rivers of Rhene and of Danubius, and the Euxine Sea: On the West the

Ocean: On the South the Cataracts of Nilus in the utmost border of Egypt, and in Afrique the Moun-taine Atlas, Which, beginning in the West, on the shoare of the Ocean, over against the Canarie Hands, runneth Eastward almost to gypt, being in few places distant from the Mediterrane Sea, more then two hundred miles. These I say, were the ordinary bounds of that Empire in the Continent: for although the Romanes passed these bounds sometimes, specially toward the East and North, yet they kept little of what they wanne, but within those bounds mentioned, the Empire was firmely established. But heere, in our great He of Britaine, the Picts wall was the limit of it, passing by New-castle and Carleil from Tinmouth on the East Sea, to Solway Frith on the West, being first Spartian. in begun by the Emperour Adrian, and after finished or ' fwm 6 rather repaired, by Septimius Severus.

To this greatnesse of Dominion Rome at last arrived from her small beginnings. And small her beginnings were indeed, considering the huge Dominion to which shee attained. For first, the Circuit of the Citie wall, at the first building of it, by Romulus in Mount Palatine, could not bee fully one mile: for the Hill it selfe, as is observed by Andrea Fulvio, a Citizen nd. Fuh, and Antiquarie of Rome, hath no more in circuit: And,- that Romulus bounded the Pomerium of the Citie ntiq. Rom. (which extended somewhat beyond the wall) with the- 3-foot of that Hill in compasse Gellius hath left Gell. 1. i. c. registred. Secondly, the Territorie and Liberties of ' Rome, as Strabo hath remembred, extended at the first, trab. I. i. where it stretched farthest scarce six miles from the Citie. And thirdly, the first Inhabitants of Rome, as I find recorded in Dionysius of Halicarnassus, were not " y- ' Z-in number above 3300. at the most. Yet, with Time, ' ' and fortunate successe, Rome so increased,! that in Antiq. Rom. Aurelianus his time, the circuit of the Citie wall was fiftie yopisc in miles, as Vopiscus hath recorded: And the Dominion, ' '-grew to the largenesse above mentioned, contayning above 3000. miles in length, and about 1200. in breadth: and lastly the number of free Citizens, even in the time of Marius, that is, long before forreigne Cities and Countries, began to be received into participation of that freedome, was found to be 463000. as Euseb. in Eusebius hath remembred: of free Citizens I say (for Ciro. ad onely came into Cense) but if I should adde their Oymp. 174.- gg children, and servants, that is, generally all Lipstusde the Inhabitants, "a learned man hath esteemed them, mag. Rom. without great likelihood of truth, to have beene lie' ' ' no lesse, then three or foure Millions.

Beyond these bounds therefore of the Roman Empire (to speake to the point in hand) the Roman tongue could not bee in any common use, as neither, to speake of our Kings Dominions in Ireland, Scotland, nor Northumberland, as being no subjects of the Roman Empire. And that within these bounds it stretched farre and wide (in such manner as I will afterward declare) two principall causes there were. One was the multitude of Colonies, which partly to represse rebellion in the subdued Provinces, partly to resist forreigne Invasions partly to reward the ancient Souldiers, partly to abate the redundance of the City, and relieve the poorer sort, were sent forth to inhabit in all the Provinces of the Empire: Another was the Donation of Romane freedome, or Communication of the right and benefit of Romane Citizens, to very many of the Provinciall, both Cities and Regions. For first, all Italic obtained that freedome in the time of Sylla and Marius, at the compounding of the Italian Warre, as App'ian. 1. I. Appian hath recorded: All Italie I say, as then it was Civil, longe called, and bounded, with the Rivers of Rubicon and ante med. nus, that is, the narrower part of Italie lying betwixt the Adriatique and the Tyrrhene Seas. Secondly, Julius Caesar in like sort infranchised the rest of Italie, that is, the border part, named then Gallia Cisalpina, as is Dion. 1. remembred by Dion. But not long after, the forreigne Provinces also, began to bee infranchised, France being indued with the liberty of Roman Citizens by Galba, as I find in Tacitus; Spain by Vespasian, as it is in Plinie. Tacit. I. i.

And at last, by Antonius Pius, all without exception, pll T that were subject to the Empire of Rome, as appeareth by the testimonie of Ulpian in the Digests. The Digest. I. i.

benefit of which Romane freedome, they that would j l-f ' " use, could not with honestie doe it, remayning ignorant Leg In Orbe of the Romane Tongue. Romano.

These two as I have said, were the principall causes of inlarging that Language: yet other there were also of great importance, to further it. For first, concerning

Ambassages, Suites, Appeales, or whatsoever other busi-nesse of the Provincials, or Forreignes, nothing was allowed to be handled, or spoken in the Senate at Rome, but in the Latine Tongue. Secondly, the Lawes whereby the Provinces were governed, were all written in that Language, as beeing in all of them, excepting onely Municipall Cities, the ordinary Roman Law. Thirdly, the 'Praetors of the Provinces, were 'Digest. I. z. not allowed to deliver their Judgements, save in that j. Language: and wee reade in Dion Cassius, of a principall D g ' man of Greece, that by Claudius was put from the order i. i. g. of Judges, for being ignorant of the Latine Tongue: Dion. l. t,-. and to the same effect in Valerius Maximus, that the f al. Max. I. Romane Magistrates would not give audience to the ' Grascians, (lesse therefore I take it to the Barbarous Nations) save in the Latine Tongue. Fourthly, the generall Schooles, erected in sundry Cities of the Provinces, whereof wee finde mention in Tacitus, Hierome, Tacit. I. 3. and others (in which the Roman Tongue was the ordinary ""' '-.

. litcfott, tti hip, and allowed speech, as is usual in Universities till this Rusticum. day) was no small furtherance to that Language. And, Tom. i. to conclude that the Romans had generally (at least in the after-times, when Rome was become a Monarchie, and in the flourish of the Empire) great care to inlarge their Tongue, together with their Dominion, is by Augustine in his Bookes de Civit. Dei, specially re- Aug. de Ci. membred. I said it was so in after times, for certainly, Dei,. i(). c. j.

that the Romanes were not very anciently possessed with that humour of spreading their Language, appeareth by L'w. hist. Ro. Livie, in whom we find recorded, that it was granted ' 4- ' the Cumanes, for a favour, at their Suit, that they might pubhkely use the Roman Tongue, not fully one hundred and fortie yeeres before the beginning of the Emperours: And yet was Cuma but about one hundred miles distant from Rome, and at that time the Romanes had conquered all Italie, Sicilie, Sardinia, and a great part of Spaine.

But yet in all the Provinces of the Empire, the Romane Tongue found not alike acceptance, and successe, but most inlarged and spread it selfe toward the North and West, and South bounds: for first, that in all the Villei. I. 2. Regions of Pannonia, it was knowne, Velleius is mine Author: Secondly, that it was spoken in France and Strab. I. 3. Spaine, Strabo: Thirdly, that in Afrique, Apuleius: And 4-'. it seemeth the Sermons of Cyprian and Augustine, yet Florid. " extant (of Augustine it is manifest) that they preached to the people in Latine. But in the East parts of the Empire, as in Greece, and Asia, and so likewise in Afrique, from the greater Syrtis Eastward, I cannot in my reading find that the Roman tongue ever grew into any common use. And the reason of it seemes to be, for that in those parts of the Empire it became most frequent, where the most, and greatest Romane Colonies, were planted. And therefore over all Italy, it became in a manner vulgar, wherein I have observed in Histories, and in Registers of ancient Inscriptions, to have beene planted by the Romanes at severall times above one hundred and fiftie Colonies: as in Afrique also neere sixtie (namely fiftie seven) in Spaine nine and twentie, in France, as it stretched to Rhene twentie sixe, and so in Illyricum, and other North parts of the Empire, betweene the Adriatique Sea, and Danubius verie many. And yet I doubt not, but in all these parts, more there were, then any Historic or ancient Inscription that now remaynes hath remembred.

And contrariwise in those Countries, where fewest Colonies were planted, the Latine Tongue grew nothing so common: as for example heere in Britaine, there were but foure: i Yorke, 2 Chester, 3 Caeruske in i Eboracum.

Monmouth-shire, and 4 Maldon in Essex (for London, Debuna.

although recorded for one by Onuphrius, was none, as Camalodu- is manifest by his owne Author, in the place that num Onuphr.

himselfe alleadgeth) and therefore we find in the British in Imp. Rom.

Tongue which yet remaineth in Wales, but little rellish ' T "– (to account of) or relikes of the Latine. And, for this Q p - cause also partly the East Provinces of the Empire, citato. ' savoured little or nothing of the Roman Tongue. For first in Afrique beyond the greater Syrtis, I find never a Romane Colonie: for Onuphrius, that hath recorded' ' Vide. Digest.

Indicia Cyrenensium for one, alleadging Ulpian for- 5- i-

Author, was deceived by some faultie Copie of the '."" ''' 'S-

T T-' 1 1 1 ri. sciendum Pan-

JJigests. l or the corrected Copies have Zernensium, drell. id. and for Indicia, is to be read In Dacia, as is rightly Comment. observed (for in it the Citie of Zerne was) by Pancirellus. "'- Z '-Secondly, in Egypt, there were but two: and to be briefe, ' "" Syria onely excepted, which had about twentie Romane Colonies, but most of them late planted, especially by Septimius Severus, and his Sonne Bassianus, to strengthen that side of the Empire against the Parthians (and yet I finde not that in Syria, the Romane Tongue, ever obtained any vulgar use) the rest, had but verie few, in proportion to the largenesse of those Regions.

Of which little estimation, and use of the Roman Tongue, in the East parts, beside the want of Colonies fore-mentioned, and to omit their love to their owne Languages, which they held to be more civill then the Romane, another great cause was the Greeke, which they had in farre greater account, both for Learning sake (insomuch that Cicero confesseth, Graeca (saith he) Cicer. inorat. leguntur in omnibus fere gentibus, Latina suis finibus, P"- " hia exiguis sane, continentur) and for Traffique, to both ' which, the Graecians, above all Nations of the World were anciently given: to omit, both the excellencie of the Tongue it selfe, for sound and copiousnesse, and that it had forestalled the Romane in those parts. And certainly, in how little regard the Romane Tongue was had in respect of the Greeke in the Easterne Countries, may appeare by this, that all the learned men of those parts, whereof most lived in the flourish of the Romane

Empire, have written in Greeke, and not in Latine: as

Philo, Josephus, Ignatius, Justine Martyr, Clemens

Alexandrinus, Origen, Eusebius, Athanasius, Basil,

Gregorie Nyssene, and Nazianzene, Cirill of Alexandria, and of Jerusalem, Epiphanius, Synetius, Ptolemie Strabo,

Porphyrie, and verie many others, so that of all the

Writers that lived in Asia, or in Afrique, beyond the greater Syrtis, I thinke wee have not one Author in the Latine Tongue: and yet more evidently may it appeare by another instance, that I finde in the third

Consil. Ephe- Generall Councell held at Ephesus, where the Letters sin. Tom. 2. q (- g Bishop of Rome, having beene read by his Legates, cap. 13. E tt.- j. j Latine Tongue, it was requested by all the Bishops, ri. i. 100.1 that they might be translated into Greeke, to the end they might be understood. It is manifest therefore, that the Romane Tongue was neither vulgar, nor familiar in the East, when the learned men gathered out of all

That the parts of the East understood it not.

Roman 1 ongue abolished not r r 1 t the vulgar C weake impression therefore of the Romane languages, in J Language in the East, and large entertainment of theforreme j.- j g West, and other parts of the Empire, and of thtRoman causes of both, I have said enough. But in what

Empire. Sort, and how farre it prevailed, namely, whether so

Chap. 4. farre, as to extinguish the ancient vulgar Languages of

Galat de Sttu- Qse parts, and it selfe, in stead of them, to become the apigta. p. 2X wq and vulgar Tongue, as Galateus hath pronounced

Viv. I. de touching the Punique, and Vives with many others of traden. dis the Gallique and Spanish, I am next to consider. ciplin. = ad Y x X. therefore, it is certainly observed, that there are

Def li Q Y' fourteene Mother Tongues in Europe (beside c, 7. the Latine) which remaine, not onely not abolished, but little or nothing altered, or impaired by the Romanes.

And those are the i Irish, spoken in Ireland, and a good part of Scotland: the 2 Brittish, in Wales, Cornwaile, and

Brittaine of France: the 3 Cantabrian neere the Ocean 3 '- '"

about the Pyrene Hils, both in France and Spaine: j ' '- de the 4 Arabique, in the steepie Mountaines of Granata, fj f"

named Alpuxarras: the 5 Finnique, in Finland, and Cosm. part.2.

Lapland: the 6 Dutch, in Germany, Belgia, Denmarke, . 2. c. 8,

Norway, and Suedia: the old 7 Cauchian, (I take it to 5 5- o ' be that, for in that part the Cauchi inhabited) in East " '

Frisland, for"" although to strangers they speake Dutch, "Onel. in.

yet among themselves they use a peculiar Language of. ": their owne: the 8 Slavonish, in Polonia, Bohemia,

Moscovia, Russia, and many other Regions (whereof I will after intreate in due place) although with notable difference of Dialect, as also the Brittish and Dutch, in the Countries mentioned have: the old 9 Illyrian, in the He of Veggia, on the East side of Istria in the day of Liburnia: the 10 Greeke, in Greece, and the Hands about it, and part of Macedon, and of Thrace: the old II Epirotique" in the Mountaine of Epirus: the 12 "Sca.oc

Hungarian in the greatest part of that Kingdome: the "" '""

13 lazygian, in the North side of Hungaria betwixt ibert. in.

Danubius and Tibiscus, utterly differing from the ' "' P-

Hungarian Language: And lastly, the 14 Tarturian, ' "S- of the Precopenses, betweene the Rivers of Tanaas and

Borysthenes, neere Meotis and the Euxine Sea, for, of the English, Italian, Spanish, and French, as being derivations, or rather degenerations, the first of the

Dutch, and the other three of the Latine, seeing I now speake onely of Originall or Mother Languages, I must be silent: And of all these fourteene it is certaine, except the Arabique, which is knowne to have entred since, and perhaps the Hungarian, about which there is difference among Antiquaries, that they were in Europe in time of the Romane Empire, and sixe or seven of them, within the Limits of the Empire.

And indeed, how hard a matter it is, utterly to abolish a vulgar Language, in a populous Countrey, where the Conquerers are in number farre inferiour to the Native Inhabitants, whatsoever Art be practized to bring it about, may well appeare by the vaine attempt of our Norman Conquerour: who although hee compelled the English, to teach their young children in the Schooles nothing but French, and set downe all the Lawes of the Land in French, and inforced all pleadings at the Law to be performed in that Language (which custome continued till King Edward the Third his dayes: who disanulled it) purposing thereby to have conquered the Language together with the Land, and to have made all French: yet, the number of English farre exceeding the Normans, all was but labour lost, and obtained no further effect, then the mingling of a few French words with the English. And even such also was the successe of the Frankes among the Gaules, of the Gothes among the Italians and Spaniards, and may be observed, to be short in all such conquests, where the Conquerors (beeing yet in number farre inferiour) mingle themselves with the Native Inhabitants. So that, in those Countries onely the mutation of Languages hath ensued upon Conquests, where either the ancient Inhabitants have beene destroyed or driven forth, as wee see in our Countrey to have followed of the Saxons victories against the Brittaines, or else at least in such sort diminished, that in number they remained inferiour, or but little superiour to the Conquerours, whose reputation and authoritie might prevaile more then a small excesse of multitude. But (that I digresse no further) because certaine Countries are specially alleaged, in which the Romane Tongue is supposed most to have prevailed, I will restraine my discourse to them alone.

And first, that both the Punique and Gallique Tongues, remained in the time of Alexander Severus the Emperour (about two hundred and thirtie yeeres after our Saviours birth) appeareth by Ulpian, who lived at that time, and was with the Emperour of principall reputation, teaching, that Fidei commissa might bee left, not onely in Latine, Digest.!."Sfz. or Greeke, but in the Punique or Gallique, or any other K vulgar Language, Till that time therefore, it seemeth evident, that the Romane Tongue had not swallowed up these vulgar Languages, and it selfe become vulgar in stead of them. But to insist a little in either severally. First, touching the Punique, Aurelius Victor hath re- Aur. Victor. corded of Septimius Severus, that he was, Latinis literis P ""-sufficienter instructus, but Punica eloquentia promptior, quippe genitus apud Leptim provintiae Africae. Of which Emperors sister also dwelling at Leptis (it is the Citie wee now call Tripoly in Barbaric) and comming to see I. i. loi. him, Spartianus hath left written, that shee so badly Spartian. in spake the Latine tongue (yet was Leptis a Roman ' "-P"-Colony) that the Emperour blushed at it. Secondly jntonin. in long after that, Hierome hath recorded of his time, itimrario. that the Africans had somewhat altered their language Hieron. in from the Phcenicians: the language therefore then re- P-J '- 1 r 1, 111 r 1 Lom. tptst. ad mamed, tor else how could hee pronounce or the pre- Calat. infine sent difference Thirdly, Augustine (somewhat younger then Hierom, though living at the same time) writeth not onely that "hee knew divers Nations in Afrike, August, de that spake the Punike tongue, but also more particularly P I-'; in "another place, mentioning a knowne Punike pro- id'sermz verb, he would speake it (he said) in the Latine, be- deverb. Apost. cause all his Auditors (for Hippo where hee preached was a Roman Colony) understood not the Punike tongue: And some other' passages could I alleadge out " Id. Expos in of Augustine, for the direct confirmation of this point, ' " ' if these were not evident and effectuall enough. Lastly, y J ' J" Leo Africanus, a man of late time, and good reputa- Leo i. Africa. tion, affirmeth, that there remaine yet in Barbary, very L. i. descript. many descended of the old Inhabitants, that speake the Africa. cap. African tongue, whereby it is apparent that it was never jfi-l f i extinguished by the Romanes.

Secondly, touching the antient Gallike tongue, that it also remained, and was not abolished by the Romane in the time of Strabo, who flourished under Tiberius princip. I 273 s

Tacit, in Julio Agricola.

Lamprid. in Alexand. Severo, longe post med.

Strab. I. 4. long. antemed.

"Vel. Pater-cul. I. I.

Plin. l. i. c. df.

Vid. Annot. ad August de Civ. Dei. I. 19. c. 7. Id. I. z-de tradend. Discip.

Caesars government, it appeareth in the fourth Book of his Geography, writing that the Aquitani differed altogether in language from the other Gaules, and they somewhat among themselves. Nor after that in Tacitus his time, noting that the language of France differed little from that of Brittaine. No, nor long after that in Alexander Severus his time, for beside the authoritie of UJpian before alleadged out of the Digestes, it is manifest by Lampridius also, who in the life of the said Alexander, remembreth of a Druide woman, that when hee was passing along, in his Expedition against the Germaines through France, cried out after him in the Gallike tongue (what needed that observation of the Gallike tongue, if it were the Romane?) Goe thy way, quoth shee, and looke not for the victory, and trust not thy Souldiers. And though Strabo bee alleadged by some, to prove the vulgarnesse of the Latine tongue in France, yet is it manifest, that he speaketh not of all the Gaules, but of certaine onely, in the Province of Narbona, about Rhodanus, for which part of France there was speciall reason, both for the more ancient and ordinary conversing of the Romanes, in that Region above all the rest: for of all the seventeene Provinces of France, that of Narbona was first reduced into the forme of a Province: And the Citie of Narbona it selfe, being a Mart Towne of exceeding trafhke in those dayes, was the first forraine Colonic that the Romanes planted out of Italy, Carthage onely excepted: And yet furthermore, as Pliny hath recorded, many towns there were in that Province, infranchized, and indued with the libertie and right of the Latines. And yet for all this, Strabo saith not, that the Roman tongue was the native or vulgar language in that part, but that for the more part they spake it.

Thirdly, concerning the Spanish tongue: Howsoever Vives writ, that the languages of France and Spaine were utterly extinguished by the Romanes, and that the Latine was become ' Vernacula Hispaniae, as also Galliae Italiae; and some others of the same Nation vaunt, Marin. Skul. that had not the barbarous Nations corrupted it, the Reo. Hts-Latine tongue would have beene at this day, as pure, in Spaine, as it was in Rome it selfe in Tullies time: yet neverthelesse manifest it is, that the Spanish tongue was never utterly suppressed by the Latine. For to omit that of Strabo, that there were divers languages Stra. l.-. in the parts of Spaine, as also in 'another place, that q P j-prin-the speech of Aquitaine was liker the language of the "i J 'i Spaniards, then of the other Gaules: It is a common princip. consent of the best Historians and Antiquaries of Spaine, ' Marian, de that the Cantabrian tongue, which yet remaineth in the- "P-North part of Spaine (and hath no relish in a manner V" ' o-; at all or the Roman) was either the ancient, or at least reb. His-one of the ancient languages of Spaine. And although pan. I. 4. c. 'Strabo hath recorded, that the Romane tongue was uhim."Altb. spoken in Spaine, yet hee speaketh not indefinitely, but ' pf ' addeth a limitation, namely, about Baetis. And that in c. Veil'. that part of Spaine, the Romane tongue so prevailed, Patenul. I. z. the reason is easie to be assigned by that wee finde in Pliny. Namely, that in Baetica, were eight Roman Colonies, eight Municipall Cities, and twentie nine others indued with the right and libertie of the Latines.

Lastly, to speake of the Pannonian tongue (Pannonia contained Hungarie, Austria, Stiria, and Carinthia) it is certaine that the Roman did not extinguish it: For first, Paterculus (who is the onely Author that I know alleadged for that purpose) saith not, that it was become the language of the Countrey, for how could it, being but even then newly conquered by Tiberius Cassar."' but onely that in the time of Augustus, by Tiberius his meanes the knowledge of the Romane tongue was spread in all Pannonia. And secondly, Tacitus after Tiberius Tacit, de his time hath recorded, that the Osi in Germany might ""rib. Germ. be knowne to be no Germanes, by the Pannonian tongue, P P P'-which a little before in the same booke, he plainely Lib eod. acknowledged to be spoken even then in Pannonia. parum a

And as for these reasons, it may well seeme that the ""

Roman tongue became not the vulgar language in any of these parts of the Empire, which are yet specially instanced, for the large vulgarity of it: So have 1 other reasons to persuade mee, that it was not in those parts, nor in any other forraine Countries subject to the Empire, 1. i. I02. either generally or perfectly spoken. Not generally (I say) because it is hard to conceive, that any whole Countries, specially because so large as the mentioned are, should generally speake two languages, their owne Native and the Romane. Secondly, there was not any Law at all of the Romanes, to inforce the subdued Nations, either to use vulgarly the Romane tongue, or not to use their owne native languages (and very ex-treame and unreasonable had such Lords beene, as should compell men by Lawes, both to doe, and to speake onely what pleased them.) Neither do I see any other necessitie, or any provocation to bring them to it, except for some speciall sorts of men, as Merchants, and Citizens, for their better traffick and trade. Lawyers for the knowledge and practise of the Romane Lawes, which carried force throughout the Empire (except priviledged places) Schollers for learning, Souldiers, for their better conversing with the Romane Legions, and with the Latines, Travellers, Gentlemen, Officers, or such other, as might have occasion of affaires and dealing with the Romans. But it soundeth altogether unlike a truth, that the poore scattered people abroad in the Country, dwelling either in solitarie places, or in the small Townes and Villages, either generally spake it, or could possibly attaine unto it. An example whereof, for the better evidence may at this day bee noted; in those parts of Greece, which are subject to the Dominions of Bellon. Obser- the Turks and Venetians: for as Bellonius hath observed, vat, I. i. f. 4. g people that dwell in the principall Townes and Cities, subject to the Turke, by reason of their trade, speake both the Greeke and Turkish tongues, as they also that are under the Venetians, both the Greeke and Italian, but the Countrey people under both governments, speake onely Greeke. So likewise in Sardinia, as is recorded by others, the good Townes by reason of the Spanish Gesner. in Government and Trade, speake also the Spanish tongue, Mtthr. inlin-but the Countrey people the naturall Sardinian language ' onely: And, the like by our owne experience wee know Rocca de Dia-to bee true, in the Provinces subject to our King, namely, lect. in Ling. both in Wales and Ireland. It seemeth therefore that ' ' the Romane tongue was never generally spoken in any j, of the Roman Provinces forth of Italy. descrit. di

And certainely much lesse can I perswade my selte, Sardigna. that it was spoken abroad in the Provinces perfectly. First, because it seemes unpossible for forraine Nations, specially for the rude and common people, to attaine the right pronouncing of it, who, as wee know doe ordinarily much mistake the true pronouncing of their native language: for which very cause, wee see the Chaldee tongue to have degenerated into the Syriake among the Jewes, although they had conversed seventie yeeres together among the Chaldeans. And moreover, by daily experience wee see in many, with what labour and difficulty, even in the very Schooles, and in the most docible part of their age, the right speaking of the Latine tongue is attained. And to conclude, it appeareth by Augustine in sundry places, that the Roman tongue was f ide August. unperfect among the Africans (even in the Colonies) as Enarrat. pronuncing ossum for os, floriet for florebit, dolus for q 'T dolor, and such like, insomuch that hee confesseth, hee je doctrin. was faine sometimes to use words that were no Latine, Chris, c. 13. to the end they might understand him. dr'Tract j in loan.

THe common opinion, which supposeth that these Of the begin-
Nations in the flourish of the Romane Empire, "'gofthe spake vulgarly and rightly the Latine tongue, is, that nmh and the mixture of the Northerne barbarous Nations among anish lan- the ancient Inhabitants, was the cause of changing guages.

the Latine tonge into the languages, which now they Ghap. 5. speake, the languages becomming mingled, as the Nations themselves were. Who, while they were inforced to attemper and frame their speech, one to the understanding of another, for else they could not mutually expresse their mindes (which is the end for which Nature hath given speech to men) they degenerated both, and so came to this medly wherein now wee finde them.

Which opinion if it were true, the Italian tongue, must of necessitie have it beginning about the 480. yeere of our Saviour: Because, at that time, the Barbarous Nations began first to inhabite Italy, under Odoacer, for although they had entred and wasted Italy long before, as first, the Gothes under Alaricus, about the yeare 414: Then the

Hunnes together with the Gothes, and the Heruli, and the Gepidi, and other Northerne people under Attila, about An. 450. Then the Wandales under Gensericus, crossing the Sea out of Afrike, about An. 456. (to omit some other invasions of those barbarous Nations, because they prospered not) yet none of these, setled themselves to stay and inhabite Italy, till the Heruli, as I said under Odoacer, about An. 480. or a little before entred and possessed it neere hand twenty yeeres, Hee being (proclaimed by the Romanes themselves) King of Italy, about sixteene yeeres, and his people becomming inhabiters of the Countrey. But, they also, within twenty yeeres after their entrance, were in a manner rooted out of Italy, by Theodoricus King of Gothes, who allotted them onely a part of Piemont above Turin to inhabite: for Theodoricus being by Zeno then Emperour, invested with the title of King of Italy, and having overcome Odoacer, somewhat afore the yeere 500. ruled peaceably a long time, as King of Italy, and certaine others of the Gothes Nation succeeded after him in the same government, the Gothes in the meane space, growing into one with the Italians, for the space neere hand of sixtie yeeres together. And although after that, the Dominion of Italy was by Narses againe recovered to the Empire in the time of Justinian, and many of the Gothes expelled Italy, yet farre more of them remained, Italy in that long time being growne well with their seed and posteritie. The Heruli therefore, with their associates I. i. 103.

were the first, and the Gothes the second of the barbarous

Nations that inhabited Italy. The third and the last, were the Longbards, who comming into Italy about the yeere 570. and long time obtaining the Dominion and possession, in a manner of all Italy, namely above two hundred yeeres, and during the succession of twenty

Kings or more, were never expelled forth of Italy, although at last their Dominion was sore broken by Pipin

King of France, and after more defaced by his sonne

Charles the Great, who first restrained and confined it to that part, which to this day, of them retaineth the name of Lombardy, and shortly after utterly extinguished it, carrying away their last King captive into France. Now although divers Antiquaries of Italy there bee, which Blond in referre the beginning of the Italian tongue, and the-! " ' change of the Latine into it, to these third Inhabitants i archia Tri- of Italy the Longbards, by reason of their long and visana.

perfect coalition into one with the Italian people: yet Tinto. delk certainely, the Italian tongue was more antient then so, o '– ' ' '-r i i erona l. z. c. z.

ror besides that there remames yet to bee scene (as men c i worthy of credit report) in the King of France his Ups. depro-

Library at Paris, an Instrument written in the Italian nuntlat Ling.

tongue, in the time of Justinian the first, which was lat. cap. T,.2 before the comming of the Longbards into Italy: another Q ' g. f.

evidence more vulgar, to this effect, is to be found in c. 18.

Paulus Diaconus his Miscellane History: where wee read Paul. Diacon.

that in the Emperour Mauritius his time, about the yeer "-"

590. when the Longbards had indeed entred, and wasted ' J' jly

Gallia Cisalpina, but had not invaded the Roman diction in Italy, that by the acclamation of the word Torna,

Torna, (plaine Italian) which a Roman Souldier spake to one of his fellowes afore, (whose beast had overturned his burthen) the whole Army (marching in the darke) began to cry out, Torna, Torna, and so fell to flying away.

But the French tongue, if that afore mentioned were the cause of it, began a little before, in the time of Valentinian the third, when in a manner all the West part of the Empire fell away (and among the rest, our Coun-trey of England, being first forsaken of the Romans themselves, by reason of grievous warres at their owne doores, and not long after conquered and possessed by the Saxons, whose posteritie (for the most part wee are) namely, about the yeere 450: France being then subdued and peaceably possessed by the Franks and Burgundians, Nations of Germany: the Burgundians occupying the Eastward and outward parts of it, toward the River of Rhene, and the Franks all the inner Region. For although France before that had beene invaded by the Wandali, Suevi, and Alani, and after by the Gothes, who having obtained Aquitayn for their Seat and Habitation, by the grant of the Emperour Honorius, expelled the former into Spaine, about An. 410: yet notwithstanding, till the Conquest made by the Franks and Burgundians, it was not generally, nor for any long time mingled with strangers, which after that Conquest began to spread over France, and to become native Inhabitants of the Countrey.

But of all, the Spanish tongue for this cause must necessarily bee most antient: for the Wandali and Alani, being expelled France, about the yeere 410, beganne then to invade and to inhabite Spaine, which they held and possessed many yeeres, till the Gothes being expelled by the Franks and Burgundians, out of France into Spaine, expelled them out of Spaine into Afrike (the Barbarous Nations thus like nailes driving out one another) and not onely them, but with them all the remnants of the Roman Garrisons and government, and so becomming the entire Lords and quiet possessours of all the Countrey, from whom also the Kings of Spaine that now are be descended. Notwithstanding, even they also within lesse then three hundred yeeres after, were driven by the Saracens of Afrike, into the Northerne and mountainous parts of Spaine, namely Asturia, Biscay, and

Guipuscoa, till after a long course of time, by little and little they recovered it out of their hands againe, which was at last fully accomplished by Ferdinand, not past one hundred and twenty yeeres agoe, there having passed in the meane time, from the Moores first entrance of Spaine at Gibraltar, till their last possession in Granada, about seven hundred and seventy yeeres.

Whereby you may see also, when the Roman tongue began to degenerate in Afrike (if that also, as is supposed spake vulgarly the Latine tongue, and if the mixture of barbarous people were cause of the decay, and corruption of it) namely, about the yeere 430. for about that time, the Wandali and Alani, partly wearied with the Gottish warre in Spaine, and partly invited by the Governour Bonifacius entred Afrike, under the leading of Gensericus, a part whereof for a time, they held quietly, for the Emperour Valentinianus gift: But shortly after, in the same Emperours time, when all the West Provinces in a manner fell utterly away from the Empire, they also tooke Carthage; and all the Province about it, from the Romans. And although the dominion of Afrike was regained by Bellizarius to the Empire almost 100. yeeres after, in Justinians time, yet in the time of the Emperour Leontius (almost 700. yeeres after our Saviours birth) it was lost againe, being anew conquered, and possessed by the Sarracens of Arabia (and to this day remaineth in their hands) bringing together with their victories, the language also, and religion (Mahumatanisme) into all that coast of Afrike, even from Egypt to the Strait of Gibraltar, above 2000. miles in length.

About which time also, namely during the government of Valentinian the third, Bulgaria, Servia, Boscina, Hun-garie, Austria, Stiria, Carinthia, Bavaria and Suevia (that is, all the North-border of the Empire, along the River I. i. 104. Danubius) and some part of Thrace, was spoiled and possessed by the Hunnes, who yet principally planted themselves in the lower Pannonia, whence it obtained the name of Hungarie.

Out of which discourse you may observe these two points. First, what the Countries were, in which those wandring and warring Nations, after many transmigrations from place to place, fixed at last their finall residence and habitation. Namely the Hunnes in Pannonia, the Wan-dales in Afrique, the East Gothes and Longbards in Italie, the West Gothes in Aquitaine and Spaine, which being both originally but one Nation, gained these names of East and West Gothes, from the position of these Countries which they conquered and inhabited, the other barbarous Nations of obscurer names, being partly consumed with the warre, and partly passing into the more famous appellations. And Secondly, you may observe, that the maine dissolution of the Empire, especially in Europe and Afrique, fell in the time of Valentinian the third, about the yeere 450. being caused by the barbarous Nations of the North (as after did the like dissolution of the same Empire in Asia, by the Arabians in the time of Heraclius, about the yeere 640.) and together with the ruine of the Empire in the West by the inundation of the foresaid barbarous Nations, the Latine tongue in all the Countries where it was vulgarly spoken (if it were rightly spoken any where in the West) became corrupted.

Wherefore if the Spanish, French and Italian tongues, proceeded from this cause, as a great number of learned men, suppose they did, you see what the antiquity of them is: But to deliver plainly my opinion, having searched as farre as I could, into the originals of those languages, and having pondered what in my reading, and in my reason I found touching them, I am of another minde (as some learned men also are) namely, that all those tongues are more ancient, and have not sprung from the corruption of the Latine tongue, by the inundation and mixture of barbarous people in these Provinces, but from the first unperfect impression receiving of it, in those forraine Countries. Which unperfectnesse notwithstanding of the Roman tongue in those parts, although it had, as I take it beginning from this evill framing of forraine tongues, to the right pronouncing of the Latine, yet I withall easily beleeve, and acknowledge that it was greatly increased, by the mixture and coalition of the barbarous Nations. So that me thinkes, I have observed three degrees of corruption in the Roman tongue, by the degeneration whereof these languages are supposed to have received their beginning. The first of them was in Rome it selfe, where towards the latter end of the Common-wealth, and after, in the time of the Empire, the infinite multitude of servants (which exceedingly exceeded the number of free borne Citizens) together with the unspeakeable confluence of strangers, from all Provinces, did much impaire the purenesse of their language, and as Isidore hath observed, brought huor. Origin.

many barbarismes and solaecismes into it. Insomuch, that- 9- '- Tertullian in his time, when as yet none of the barbarous Tertul. in Nations had by invasion touched Italic (for he lived '-'-under Septimius Severus government) chargeth the "' ' ' Romans to have renounced the language of their fathers. The Second step, was the unperfect impression (that I touched before) made of the Roman tongue abroad in the forraine Provinces among strangers, whose tongues could not perfectly frame to speake it aright. And certainly, if the Italians themselves, as is remembred by Cicero, failed Cicer. 1.1. de of the right and perfect Roman pronunciation, I see not " '-how the tongues of strange Nations, such as the Gaules and Spaniards were, should exactly utter it. And the Third, was that mixture of many barbarous people (to which others attribute the beginning of the languages in question) which made the Latine, that was before unperfect, yet more corrupt then they found it, both for words and for pronouncing: So that, I rather thinke the barbarous people to have beene a cause of increasing the corruption, and of further alteration and departure of those languages from the Roman, then of beginning them. And me thinkes I have very good reasons so to be perswaded, beside all the arguments above men- Irenic. Exeg. Germ. I. i. c. '3,1. Lazius. I. lo. de Migj-ation. Gent. Gorop. Origin. Antwerp. I. 7. Gesner. in Mithridate. Rhenan lib. z. Rer. Germ. Leunclav. in Pandect Tur-ric. 71.6 Jlii multi.

Objections touching the extent of the Latine tongue and the beginning of the mentioned Languages with their solutions. Chap. 6. I. i. 105. Plutar. in quest, platonic. qua St. 9.

tioned, which I produced, both for the remaining of the vulgar languages, and for the unperfect speaking of the Roman tongue in the Provinces. First, because the Gothes, Wandales, Longbards, as also the Franks and Burgundians' language was, by the consent of learned men, the Germane tongue, which hath but small affinitie or agreement with either the Italian, French or Spanish tongues. Secondly, because among all the auncient writers (and they are many) which have written of the miserable changes made in these West parts of the World, by those infinite swarmes of barbarous people, I finde not one, that mentioneth the change of any of these languages to have beene caused by them: which me thinkes some ancient writers among so many learned, as those times, and those very Countries, abounded withall, and whose writings yet remaine, would certainly have recorded. But though we finde mention in sundry ancient writers, of changing these languages into the Roman (whom yet I understand of that unperfect change before touched) yet nothing is found of any rechanging of those languages from the Roman, into the state wherein now they are. But it is become a question onely of some late searchers of Antiquity, but of such, as determine in this point, without either sound reason or good countenance of Antiquitie.

THese reasons perhaps (joyned with the other above alleadged, whereby I ende-voured to prove that the Latine tongue perfectly spoken, was never the vulgar language of the Roman Provinces) may perswade you as they have done mee, that the barbarous Nations of the North, were not the first corrupters of the Latine tongue, in the Provinces subject to Rome, nor the beginners of the Italian, French and Spanish tongues: yet some difficulties I finde (I confesse) in writers touching these points, which when I have resolved my opinion will appeare the more credible.

One is out of Plutarch in his Platonique questions, affirming that in his time all men in a manner spake the Latine tongue.

Another, before touched, that Strabo recordeth the Strab. I. 3. Roman tongue to have beene spoken in Spaine and ' + France, and Apuleius in Africke, which also may appeare P"- i" by sundry places in Augustine, whose Sermons seeme (as " "' Cyprians also) to have bin made to the people in that language.

A third, how it falleth if these vulgar tongues of adulterate latin be so ancient, that nothing is found written in any of them of any great antiquity?

A fourth, how in Rome and Latium, where the Latine tongue was out of question, native, the latine could so degenerate, as at this day is found in the Italian tongue, except by some forraine corruption?

To the first of these I answere, either, that as Divines are wont to interpret many generall propositions; Plutarch is to be understood de generibus singulorum, not de singulis generum: So that the Latine tongue was spoken almost in every Nation, but not of every one in any forraine Nation: Or else, that they spake the Latine indeede, but yet unperfectly and corruptly as their tongues would frame to utter it.

To the second I answere: first, that Strabo speaketh not generally of France or Spaine, but with limitation to certaine parts of both, the Province of Narbon in France, and the Tract about Boetis in Spaine. Secondly, that although they speake it, yet it followeth not, that they speake it perfectly and aright (except perhaps in the Colonies) so that I will not deny but it might be spoken abroad in the Provinces, yet I say it was spoken corruptly, according as the peoples tongues would fashion to it, namely in such sort, that although the matter and body of the words, were for the most part Latine, yet the forme, and sound of them varied from the right pronouncing: which speech notwithstanding was named Latin, partly for the reason now touched, and partly because they learned it from the Romanes or Latines, as

Nitha. de disserts. filior. Ludov. Piil. i.

Antonin. in Itinerario. Plin. lun. in Epi. I. ad Caninium. "Plin. Sec. Hist. nat. I. 5. r. 4.

Velleius 1. i. Appian. I. de Bel. Punicis in fine. Enarr. Ps. 138.

' L. 2. de doc. Chr. f. 13. Tract. 7. in Ioannem.

Tschud. De-script. Alpino" cap. 36. Genebr. I. 4. Chr. Secul. 11.

the Spaniards called their language Romance, till this day, which yet we know to differ much from the right Roman tongue; and as Nithardus (Nephew to Charles the Great) in his Historie of the dissension of the sonnes of Ludovicus Pius called the French then usuall (whereof hee setteth downe examples) the Romane Tongue, which yet hath no more agreement with the Latine then the French hath that is now in use. Thirdly, to the objection of Cyprians and Augustines preaching in Latine, I answere that both Hippo, whereof Augustine was Bishop, and Carthage, whereof Cyprian was Archbishop, were Roman Colonies, consisting for the most part of the progenie of Romans, for which sort of Cities, there was speciall reason. Although neither in the Colonies themselves (as it seemeth) the Roman tongue was altogether uncorrupt, both for that I alleadged before out of Sparti-anus of Severus his sister dwelling at Leptis, and for that which I remembred out of Augustine for Hippo, where they spake "" Ossum and Floriet, and Dolus, for Os and Florebit and dolor (and yet were both Leptis and Hippo Roman Colonies:) And yet it appeareth further by Augustine, that in their translations of the Scriptures, and in the Psalmes sung in their Churches, they had these corruptions, where yet (as it is like) their most corrupt and vulgar Latine had not place.

To the third I answere, that two reasons of it may be assigned: One, that learned men would rather write in the learned and grammaticall, then in the vulgar and provinciall Latine. Another, that the workes of unlearned men would hardly continue till our times, seeing even of the learned ancient writings, but few of infinite, have remained. Furthermore, it is observed of the Germaine tongue, by Tschudas and of the French by Genebrard, that it is very little above 400. yeeres, since bookes began to be written in both those languages, and yet it is out of all doubt, that the tongues are much ancienter.

To the fourth I say, that there is no language, which of ordinary course is not subject to change, although there were no forraine occasion at all: which the very fancies of men, weary of old words (as of old things) is able enough to worke, which may be well proved by observations and instances of former changes, in this very tongue (the Latine) whereof I now dispute. For Quin- Quintil. Just. tilian recordeth, that the Verses of the Salii which were "– i-said to be composed by Numa could hardly be under- ' ' stood of their Priests, in the latter time of the Commonwealth, for the absolutenesse of the speech. And Festus fest. in Die-in his booke de verborum significatione, who lived in ""- " Augustus Caesars time, hath left in observation, that the ' "" Latine speech, which (saith he) is so named of Latium, was then in such manner changed, that scarsly any part of it remained in knowledge. The Lawes also of the Roman Kings, and of the Decemviri, (called the Lawes of the twelve Tables) collected and published in their owne Fu. Urshi. words by Fulvius Ursinus are no lesse evident testimonies, "" ' "ton. if they be compared with the later Latine, of the great j f i c alteration of that language. nlfuscmsult'

Furthermore, Polybius hath also recorded, that the i. i. io6. articles of league, betwixt the people of Rome and of Polyb. I. 3. Carthage, made presently after the expulsion of the Kings from Rome, could very hardly in his time be understood, by reason of the old forsaken words, by any of the best skilled Antiquaries in Rome. In which time notwithstanding, they received very few strangers into their Citie, which mixture might cause such alteration, and the difference of time was but about three hundred and fifty yeeres. And yet to adde one instance more, of a shorter revolution of time, and a cleerer evidence of the change, that the Roman tongue was subject to, and that, when no-S 'j f! ' forraine cause thereof can be alleadged: there remaineth p. " i """ at this day (as it is certainly recorded) in the Capitall at c. 18. A-ci–Rome, though much defaced by the injury of time, a ' f"- Cit. tad. Pillar (they call it Columnam rostratam, that is, decked " Tractat. de with beakes of ships) dedicated to the memory of Duillius yulrh Ital a Roman Consull, upon a navale victory obtained against cap. 7. c c.

the Carthaginians, in the first Punicke warre, not past one hundred and fifty yeeres before Ciceroes time, when the Roman tongue ascended to the highest flourish of Ele-gancie, that ever it obtained: And thus the words of the Pillar are (those that may be read) as I finde them observed, with the later Latine under them.

Exemet. Leciones. Macistratos. Castreis. Exfociont. Exemit. Legiones. Magi-
stratus. Castris. Effugiunt. Pucnandod. Cepet. Enque. Navebos. Marid. Consol.
Pugnando. Cepit. Inque. Navibus. Mari. Consul. Primos. Ornavet. Navebous.
Claseis. Paenicas. Sumas. Primus. Ornavit. Navibus. Classes. Punicas. Summas.
Cartaciniensis. Dictatored. Altod. Socicis. Triresmos. Carthaginiensis. Dictatore.
Alto. Sociis. Triremes. Naveis. Captom. Numei. Navaled. Praedad. Poplo, c.
Naves. Captum. Nummi. Navali. Praeda. Populo, c.

Where you see in many words, e. for i, c. for g. o. for u. and sometime for e. and
d. superfluously added to the end of many words. But (to let forraigne tongues passe)
of the great alteration that time is wont to work in languages, our own tongue may
afford us examples evident enough: wherein since the times neere after, and about the
Conquest, the change hath beene so great, as I my selfe have seene some evidences
made in the time of King Henry the first, whereof I was able to understand but few
words. To which purpose also, a certaine remembrance is to be found in Houn-sheds
Chronicle, in the end of the Conquerours raigne, in a Charter given by him to the Citie
of London.

Of the ancient T)Ut if the discourse of these points of Antiquitie, in Languages
of JQ) handling whereof I have declared, that while the F ance inp Roman Empire
flourished, it never abolished the vulgar Jfrtque. languages, in France, or Spaine, or
Afrique, howsoever

Chap. 7. in Italie. If that discourse I say, move in you perhaps a desire to know
what the ancient vulgar languages of those parts were: I will also in that point, out of
my reading and search into Antiquitie, give you tlie best satisfaction that I can.

And first for Italic: Certaine it is, that many were the ancient tongues in the severall
Provinces of it, tongues I say, not dialects, for they were many more. In Apulia,
the Mesapian tongue: In Tuscanie and Umbria, the Hetruscan, both of them utterly
perished: Yet in the booke of ancient Inscriptions, set forth by Inscrip. vet. Gruter
and Scaliger, there be some few Moniments "?-H3-H4-registred of these languages,
but not understood now of any man. In Calabria both the higher and lower, and farre
along the miritime coast of the Tyrrhene Sea, the Greeke. In Latium (now Campagna
di Roma) the Latine. In Lombardie, and Liguria, the old tongue of France whatsoever
it was. Of which last three, the two former are utterly ceased to be vulgar: and the
third, no where to be found in Italie, but to be sought for in some other Countrie. And
although, beside these five, wee finde mention, in ancient writings of the Sabine, the
Oscan, the Tusculan, and some other tongues in Italie, yet were they no other then
differing dialects of some of the former languages, as by good observations, out of
Varro, Festus, Servius, Paul. Diaconus, and others, might be easily prooved.

Secondly, of France what the ancient tongue was, hath bin much disputed, and
yet remaineth somewhat uncertaine: Some thinking it to have beene the Ger-maine,
others the Greeke, and some the Walsh tongue. But, if the meaning of these resolvers
be, that one language, whatsoever it were, was vulgar in all France, they are verie
farre wide. Caesar and Strabo having Casarl. x. de both recorded, that there were
divers languages spoken Bella Gallic in the divers parts. But, to omit the speech
of Aqui- '- taine, which Strabo writeth to have had much affinitie princip. with the
Spanish: And, of that part (in Cassar called Belgia) that at the River of Rhene confined

with Ger-manie, which for that neighbourhood, might partake much of the Germaine tongue: To omit those I say, I 289 T

Cas. I. z,. de Bello Gallic, long, post med. Varro ap. Hieron. in. prof at. I. 2. Comment epist. adgalat. 6 aptid Li-dor um li. 15. Orig. cap. i. I. i. 107. Cas. I. de Bello Gallico. Tacit. I. de Mor. Germa-nor. prope finem. Sueton. in Caligula c. 47. Hottom. in Fran, cogall. c. 2.

Perion I. de Cognat Ling. Gal. y Graca Paste II. I. de 12. Ling. Tschud in Descr. Rhet. Alp. c. 28. Gorop. in. Francicis. Isac. in Glos-sario. Prisco. gal.

Lhuid in Desert. Britan. Camden in Britannia. Strab. I. 4.

the maine question is, about the language of the Celtae, which as inhabiting the middle part of France, were least of all infected with any forraine mixture. And certainely, that it was not the Greeke, appeareth out of Caesar, written to Q. Cicero, (then besieged by the Gaules) in Greeke, lest the Gaules should intercept his Letters. And secondly, no lesse evidently by Varro, written of the Massilians that they spake three languages, the Roman, the Greeke, and the Gallique tongue: And thirdly, the remnants of that tongue, may serve for instance, whereof many old words are found dispersed in ancient writers, that have no affinitie at all with the Greeke. The Greeke therefore, was not the ancient native language of the Gaules; Neither was it the Ger-maine: for else it had beene but an odde relation and reason of Caesars, that Ariovistus a German Prince, had lived so long in Gallia, that he spake the Gallique tongue: And that of Tacitus, that the Gallique tongue proved the Gothines to be no Germaines: And that of Suetonius, that Caligula compelled many of the Gaules to learne the Germaine tongue. But Hottoman (of all that I have read) speaking most distinctly, touching the originall and composition of the French tongue, divideth it as now it is spoken, equally into two parts, of which he supposcth the one (and I thinke it is rather the greater part) to have originall from the Latine tongue: and the other halfe, to be made up, by the German and Greeke, and Brittish or Walsh words, each almost in equall measure. Of the deduction of the French words from the Greeke, you may read Perionius, Postell, and others: Of those from the Germaine, Tschadus, Goropius, Isacius, c. Of the Walsh, Lhuid, Camden, c. Which last in-deede for good reason, seemeth to have beene the native language of the ancient Celtae, rather then either the Greeke or Dutch tongues: for of the Greeke words found in that language, the neighbourhood of the Massilians, and their Colonies, inhabiting the maritime coast of Province, together with the ready acceptance of that language in France (mentioned by Strabo) may be the cause: As likewise of the Germaine words, the Franks and Burgundions conquest, and possession of France, may be assigned for a good reason: But of the Brittish words none at all can be justly given, save, that they are the remnants of the ancient language. Secondly, Tacit, in Julio it seemeth to be so by Tacitus, written, that the speech S. ' "-of the Gaules, little differed from that of the Brittaines. And thirdly, by Caesar, recording, that it was the custome of the Gaules that were studious of the Druides discipline, often to passe over into Brittaine to be there instructed: wherefore seeing there was no use of bookes among them, as is in the same place affirmed by Caesar, C– 6- de it is apparent that they spake the same language. ' '-

Thirdly, the Spanish tongue as now it is, consisteth of the old Spanish, Latine, Gottish, and Arabique (as there is good reason it should, Spaine having beene so long in the possessions of the Romans, Gothes, and Moores) of which, the Latine is the greatest part (next it the Arabique) and therefore they themselves call their language Romance. And certainely I have seene an Epistle written by a Spaniard, whereof every word was both good Latine and good Spanish, and an example of the like is to be seene in Merula. But the language of erul. m-Valentia and Catalonia, and part of Portugall, is much J f' g'"' ' tempered with the French also. Now the ancient and most generall language of Spaine, spoken over the Country before the Romaines conquest, seemeth to me out of question, to have beene the Cantabrian tongue, that namely which yet they speake in Biscay, Guipuscoa, Navarre, and Asturia, that is to say, in the northerne and mountainous parts of Spaine, neere the Ocean, with which the Vasconian tongue also in Aquitaine, neere the Pyrene hils, hath as there is good reason (for out of those parts of Spaine the inhabitants of Gascoigne came) much affinitie and agreement. And my reason for this opinion is, that in that part of Spaine, the people have ever continued without mixture of any forraine Nation, as being never subdued by the Carthaginians, nor by the Moores, no, nor by the Romans (for all their long warring in Spaine) before Augustus Caesars time, and for the hiuinesse, and barenesse, and unpleasantnesse of the Countrie, having nothing in it, to invite strangers to dwell among them. For which cause, the most ancient Nations and languages are for the most part preserved in such Countries: as by Thucyd. I. I. Thucydides is specially observed, of the Attiques, and paiil. aprincip. Orcadians, in Greece, dwelling in barren soiles: Of which Nations the first, for their Antiquitie, vaunted of themselves that they were a. vt6-) ovi;, and the second, Trpoa-exTjvoi as if they had beene bred immediately of the Earth, or borne before the Moone. Another example whereof wee may see in Spaine it selfe, for in the steepy Mountaines of Granata, named Alpuxarras, the progeny of the Moores yet retaine the Arabique tongue (for the Spaniards call it Araviga) which all the other remnants of the Moores in the plainer Region had utterly forgotten and received the Castilian (till their late expulsion out of Spaine) for their vulgar language. The like whereof, is also to be scene in the old Epirotike speech and Nation, which yet continueth in the mountainous part of Epirus, being (for the tongue) utterly extinguished in all the Country beside. And (to let forraine instances goe) in the Brittaines or Welsh-men in the hilly part of our owne Countrey. What the reason thereof may bee, I will not stand now curiously to enquire: whether that being inured to labour, to watching, to sundry distemperatures of the aire, and much other hardnesse (for otherwise their living will not bee gotten out of such barren ground) they prove upon occasion good and able Souldiers."' Or, that the craggy Rockes and Hills (like fortresses of Natures owne erecting) are easily defended from forraine invaders.? Or that their unpleasant and fruitlesse soile, hath nothing to invite strangers to desire it? Or that wanting riches, they want also the ordinary com-

panions of riches, that is proud and audacious hearts, to provoke with their injuries other Nations to be revenged on them, either by the conquest or desolation of their Countries? But whatsoever the cause maybe, certainely in effect so it is, that the most ancient Nations and Languages, are for the most part to bee found in such unpleasant and fruitksse Regions: Insomuch that the Byscaynes, who gave mee occasion of l– '-this digression, vaunt of themselves among the Spaniards, jf'"' " J' "' that they are the right Hidalgos (that is Gentlemen) as J ' " ' some also report of the Welshmen here in Brittaine to Gesner in say of themselves, which yet I that am their neighbour Mithruate. in (to confesse a truth) never heard them say. fi""!-

Now lastly, touching the Punike tongue, as I am not Rocchadedia- of Galateus his opinion, that it was utterly extinguished kct. in Ling.

by the Romanes: So neither can I bee of the phantasie Arabica.

(for it is no better) that many other learned men are:!-, namely, that it was the Arabike, that is to say the same li","jrab"

language, that is vulgar in Afrike at this day. For it Mas. ingram.

is well knowne to the skilfull in Histories, that the Syriaca. prop.

Punikes were of another off-springs (not of Arabian "'-S 'W.

j u v J. 1 J 1 de ration. Lin- racej and that it is not yet a thousand yeeres, since that.

tongue was by the Arabians, together with their victories Schidler.

brought into Afrike. And as certaine also it is, that in Lex. Pen- the remnants of the Africans progeny, as Leo Afri i' of o in voce canus hath recorded, hath a different language from the 7? P,

AL-1 T i-r-i 1 Mart.

Arabike. But the runike tongue seemeth to mee out Caleott. de of question, to have bin the Chananitish or old Hebrew doct. promis- language, though I doubt not somewhat altered from the f– originall pronuntiation, as is wont in tract of time to befall J" jk-

Colonies planted among strangers farre from home. For j Descrip.

first Carthage it selfe, the Queene of the Cities of Afrike Jfr. cap. de (and well might she be termed so, that contained in ' H- Afi (' circuit 24. miles, as Florus in his abridgement of Livie P- P ' "- hath recorded, and by the utter wall 360. furlongs, that sl ab. Lij.

is 45. miles) as it is in Strabo: And held out in emula- Plin. . 15.

tion with Rome, as is noted by Pliny, 120. yeeres, and- 8.

to conclude (before the second Punike warre) had in

Strab. li. citato. Mela. I. i. c. j, Liv. li. 32. Plin. l. c. ig. Appia. I. de. Bel. Punicis in principio. Curtius. I. 4. 1 JHiplures.

Jrias Mont, lib. Chanaan. c. 8.

Postel. in de-script. Syri. c. de yria Nominib.

subjection all the Coast of the Mediterrane Sea, from the bottome of the greater Syrtis in Afrike, to the River Ebro (Iberus) in Spaine, which is about 2000. miles of length, that the same Carthage I say, and divers other Cities of Afrike (of which Pliny nameth Utica and Leptis, as being the principall) were Colonies of the Phoenicians, and namely of the Tyrians, is not onely by Strabo, Mela, Livie, Plinie, Appian, and many other certaine Authors, acknowledged, and by none denied, but also the very names of Poeni Punici, being but variations or mutilations of the name Phoenicii import so much, and lastly their language assureth it. For Hierome writing that their language was growne somewhat different from the Phoenician tongue, doth manifestly in these words imply, it had beene the same.

And what were the Phoenicians but Chanaanites. f" The Phoenicians I say, of whose exceeding merchandizing wee read so much in antient Histories, what were they but Chanaanites, whose very name signifieth oivikT, in the Greek signifieth the

Palme, for as touching the deduction of the name Phoenicia, either from p5S by Montanus, or from M S " ais by Postellus, signifying the delicacy of the Inhabitants by the first, and their observation or adoration of the fire, by the second, they are but late sprung fantasies, and have not any ground of reason at all: for as much, as in all the Hebrew writings of the Bible, that country is never termed by any name sounding toward Phenicia, but in the Greeke onely. But in many old coynes that I have seene, I have noted the Palme Tree, as the speclall cognisance of Phoenicia, (as I have also the Olive branch, and Conies to be of Spaine: the Horse of Mauritania: the Elephant, or the spoile of the Elephant of Afrike: the Camell of Arabia: the Crocodile, or the Bird Ibis, of Egypt: and divers other specialties for other Countries:) And namely I have scene sundry old Coynes of the Emperour Vespatian, of severall devices and imagery, stamped for a memoriall of his conquest of Judaea, and taking of Jerusalem (for the Inscription is in every of them, Judaea capta) in each of them, I especially observed a woman sitting in a sad and mournefull fashion, with her backe to a Palme tree: wherein, I make no doubt, but the desolate woman signifieth Judasa, and the Palme, Phoenicia, even as Phoenicia is immediately toward the North, at the backe of Judaea.

Merchants? for, the very sarne Nation, that the Graecians called Phasnicians (poivike?) and the Romans in imitation of that name Poenos Punicos, for the exceeding store of good Palmes, wherewith that Countrey abounded: Insomuch that in Monuments of Antiquitie, the Palme Tree is observed for the Ensigne of Phoenicia: the same Nation I say, called themselves, and by the Israelites their next neighbours, were called Chanaanites. And that they were indeed no other, I am able easily to prove. For first, the same woman that in Mathew is Matia. i.2z. named a Canaanite, is in Marke called a Syropoenician. Mark. 7. 26. 2. Where mention is made in Josua, of the Kings of Jos. 5. i. Canaan, they are in the Septuagints translation named, aa-txek rrj (poivuri. 3. To put it out of question. All that Coast, from Sidon to Azzah (that was Gaza) neere to Gerar, is registred by Moses, to have beene possessed G. 10.19, by the posteritie of Chanaan: Of which coast the more Northrene part above the promontory of Carmel, or rather from the river Chorseus (Kison the J ewes called it) that neere the promontory of Carmell, entreth the Sea to the Citie of Orthosia, above Sidon Northward, is by Strabo, Pliny, Ptolomy and others, referred to Strai. I. 16. Phoenicia (although Strabo extend that name, along all ong. ante the Maritime Coast of Palestina also, to the confines of Y' ' "' gypt, as Dionysius Periegetes also doth, placing Joppa Pio'iem. Tab and Gaza, and Elath in Phoenicia) which very tract to 4. Jsu. have been the severall possessions of Zidon, and Cheth, Dionys. Jlex. and Girgashi and Harki, and Arvade, and Chamathi, six Penegest. of the eleven sonnes of Canaan (the other five inhabiting more to the South in Palestina) they that are skilfull in the ancient Chorography of the Holy Land cannot be ignorant. Seeing therefore out of this part of the Land of Canaan, (for in this part Tyrus was) the Carthaginians, and other Colonies of the Phoenicians in Afrike came, it is out of all doubt, that they were of the Chananites ug- Expos. progeny: and for such in very deed, and no other, ' ' 'Pf' they reputed and professed themselves to be: for '"' "' " as Augustine hath left recorded, who was borne and lived among them, the Countrey people of the Punikes, when they were asked touching themselves what they were, they would make answer that they were Channai, meaning, as Augustine himselfe doth interprete them Canaanites.

Certain therfore it is, that the native Punike language was the Chanaanitish tongue: but that I added for explication this clause (or the old Hebrew, meaning by the old Hebrew, that which was vulgarly spoken among the J ewes before the captivity) you will perhaps I. i. 109. suspect my credit, and bee offended, for I am not ignorant how superstitiously Divines for the most part are affected toward the Hebrew tongue: yet when I had set down the Africans language to have been the Canaanitish tongue, I thought good to adde for plainesse sake (or the old Hebrew) because I take them indeed to bee the very same language, and that Abraham and his posterity brought it not out of Chaldaea, but learned it in the land of Chanaan. Neither is this opinion of Postel. lib. de mine, a meere paradox and fantasie, but I have three Phcenic. lit. or foure of the best skilled in the language and anti- ';1 quities of that Nation, that the later times could afford Anas Monta. r-j aj-i u i,,.

L. Chanaan o the same mmde: And certamly, by Isaiah it is c. 9. Gene- called in direct termes, the language of Chanaan: And brard. I. i. is moreover manifest, that the names of the places Chron. an. Cities of Chanaan (the old names I meane by which Zcarsladfest. ' l ere called before the Israelites dwelt in them, as indict. Sarra. is to be seene in the whole course of the Bookes of y in ep. ad Moses and of Joshuah) were Hebrew names: touching Ubert. l ad hj h point, although I could produce other forceable Isa iq 18 reasons, such as might (except my fantasie delude mee) vexe the best wit in the world to give them just solution, yet I will adde no more, both to avoid prolixity, and because I shall have in another place fitter occasion.

But to speake particularly of the Punike tongue, which hath brought us into this discourse, and which I proved before to bee the Canaanitish language: it is not onely in one place pronounced by Augustine "S- " " (who knew it well, no man better) to have neere j-Jlemng. affinitie with the Hebrew tongue, which also the Punike wordes dispersed in the writings of Augustine, and others (as many as come to my remembrance) prove to be true. But more effectually in another Jug.. z. place, to agree with it in very many, yea almost in p"J'J-" every word. Which speech, seeing they could in no j sort have from the Israelites, being not of Abrahams posteritie (both because no such transmigration of them is remembred in the holy Histories, and for that the Punike Colonies, are specially mentioned to have beene deduced from Tyre, which never came into the possession of the Israelites) but from the Canaanites, whose off-spring they were: It followeth thereupon that the language of the Canaanites, was either the very same, or exceeding neere the Hebrew. And certainly, touching the difference that was betweene the Hebrew and the Punike, I make no doubt, but the great distance from their primitive habitation, and their conversation with strangers among whom they were planted, and together with both the length of time, which is wont to bring alteration to all the Languages in the World, were the causes of it. And although that Punike speech in Plautusj which is the onely continued speech of that Paut. in language, that to my knowledge remaineth extant in Pa "uo. Jet. any Author, have no such great convenience with the Hebrew tongue, yet I assure my selfe the faults and corruptions that have crept into it by many transcriptions, to have beene the cause of so great difference,

As in the Punike tongue Salus three, Augustin. in expos, inchoat. epist. ad Roman. Heb. la ld. Edom, bloud. Enar. Psalm. 136. Heb. Qiri- Mamon, lucre, De Sermon. Dom. in Mont. 1. 2. c. 14. Heb. "ll XJ- Bal. the Lord. Qusest. in Judic. cap. 16. Heb. ps?!- Samen, Heaven. Ibid. Heb. D"'72"ld. Messe, to annoint. Tract. 15. in Joan. Heb. ntd'JQ- Alma, a Virgine. Hieron. in c. 7. Isai. Heb. Piyy y. Gadir. a fence or wall. Plinie. 1. 4. c. 22. "m, and some other that diligence might observe.

Of the largene sse of the Slat'onish, Turkish, iff yirabike languages. C. 8.

Gesner. in Mithrid. in Ling. Illy-ricca. Boccha in Append de dialect, in Illyrica.

Postell. de hng. Dalmat. Rocch. in Biblioth. Vatcan. p. 161. y alii. 'Roccha. lib. citato pag. i68.

by reason whereof it is much changed from what at first it was when Plautus writ it, about one thousand eight hundred yeeres agoe: And specially because in transcribing thereof there would bee so much the lesse care taken, as the language was lesse understood by the Writers, and by the Readers, and so the escapes lesse subject to observation and controlement.

MAny are the Nations that have for their vulgar Language, the Slavonish Tongue in Europe, and some in Asia. Among which the principall in Europe are the Slavonians themselves inhabiting Dalmatia and Liburnia, the West Macedonians, the Epirotes, the Bosinates, Servians, Russians, Bulgarians, Moldavians, Podolians, Russians, Muscovites, Bohemians, Polonians, Silesians. And in Asia the Circassians, Mangrellians, and Gazarites. These I say are the principall, but they are not all: for Gesner and Roccha reckon up the names of sixtie Nations, that have the Slavonian tongue for their vulgar language. So, that it is knowne to be vulgarly spoken over all the East parts of Europe (in more then a third part of the whole) even to the utmost bounds of it the Rivers of Droyna and Tanais; Greece and Hungary, and Walachia only excepted. Indeed the Regions of Servia, Bosina, Bulgaria, Rascia, Moldavia, Russia and Moscovia, namely all the Nations of the Easterne parts, which celebrate their divine service after the Greeke Ceremony, and professe Ecclesi-asticall obedience to the Patriarch of Constantinople, writ in a divers sort of Character from that of the Dalmatians, Croatians, Istrians, Polonians, Bohemians, Silesians and other Nations toward the West (both which sorts of Characters are to bee seene in Postels Booke of the Orientall languages) of which, this last is called the Dalmatian or Illyrian Character, and was of Hieromes divising, that other bearing for the most part much resemblance with the Greeke, is termed the Servian Character, and was of Cyrills invention: for which cause, as Roccha hath remembred, they terme the language written in that Character Chiurilizza. Idpag. iyi.

But yet notwithstanding the difference of Characters in the writing of these Nations, they speake all of them (the difference of dialect excepted) the same language.

But yet is not the Slavonike tongue (to answere your question) for all this large extent, the vulgar language of the Turkish Empire. For of the Turks Dominion onely Epirus, the West part of Macedon, Bosina, Servia, Li. no. Bulgaria, Rascia, and part of Thrace, and that hee hath in Dalmatia and Croacia (beside the Mengrelli in Asia) speake vulgarly the Slavonian tongue. But no where for the more precise limitation, neither in Asia nor in Europe is that language spoken more Southward, then the North Parallel of forty degrees: some part of Epirus onely excepted: I meane it is not spoken as the vulgar language of any Nation more Southward. For else, being acceptable and usuall, as it is in the Great Turkes Serrail at Constantinople, and familiar with most of the Turkish Souldiers, by reason of their Garrisons and other great imployment in those parts toward the confines of Christian Princes, all which parts as before I said (Hungarie and Walachia excepted) speake that language: for these reasons I say, it is spoken by divers particular men in many places of the Turkish Dominion, and the Janizares and Officers for the most part can speake it, and many others also of the better sort, but yet the generall and vulgar language of his Dominion (excepting those places afore mentioned) it is not.

But in Anatolia, although the old languages still remaine, being for the most part corrupt Greeke, as also in Armenia they have their peculiar language, yet is the Turkish tongue very frequent prevaileth in them both: which being originally none other then Mkhov. I. i. the Tartarian tongue, as Michovius, and others have ' Sarmatta. observed, yet partaketh much, both of the Armenian jg iaie "in Persian, by reason of the Turkes long continuance ling. Tunica.

in both those Regions, before they setled the Seat of their Dominion, and themselves among the Grecians, for which cause it is not without mixture of Greeke also, but chiefly and above all other of the Arabike, both by reason of their Religion written in that language, and their training up in Schooles unto it, as their learned tongue. And yet although the Turkish bee well understood both in Natolia and Armenia, yet hath it neither extinguished the vulgar languages of those parts, neither obtained to it selfe (for ought I can by my reading find) any peculiar Province at all, wherein it is become the sole native and vulgar language, but is only a common scattered tongue, which appeareth to be so much the more evidently true, because the very Cities that have been successively the Seats of the Ottaman Sultans; namely, Iconium (now Cogna) in Lycaonia, then Prusa in Bithynia; thirdly, Adrianople in Thrace; and lastly, Constantinople, are yet knowne to retaine their old native language, the Greeke tongue: Although the Turkish tongue also bee common in them all, as it is likewise in all other Greeke Cities both of Greece and Asia.

But in the East part of Cilicia beyond the River

Pyramus, as in all Syria also, and Mesopotamia and

Palestina, and Arabia and gypt, and thence Westward in all the long tract of Afrike, that extendeth from gypt to the Strait of Gibralter, I say, in all that lieth betwixt the Mountaine Atlas, and the Mediterrane

Sea (now termed Barbary) excepting Marocco, and here and there some scattered remnants of the old Africans

Postell in in the Inland parts, the Arabike tongue is become the prafat Gram- y jg j. language, although somewhat corrupted and

Ludovlc. Res:, varied in dialect, as among so many several! Nations it . 8. de Fids- is unpossible but it should bee. And although I bee situd. Rer. ad farre from their opinion, which write (too overlash- lj i'f gly) that the Arabian tongue is in use in two third

Observatj. x. P ts of the inhabited world, or in more, yet I finde that c. 12. it extendeth very farre, and specially where the Religion of Mahumed is professed. For which cause (over and besides the parts above mentioned, in which it is, as I said, become the native language) in all the Northerne part of the Turkish Empire also, I meane that part that lyeth on the North side of the Mediterrane Sea, as likewise among the Mahumetan Tartars, it is thought not the Vulgar tongue, yet familiar with very many, both because all their Religion is written in that language, and for that every boy that goeth to schoole is taught it, as in our Schooles they are taught Latine and Greeke: Insomuch, that all the Turkes write their owne language in Arabike Characters. So that you see of the Sfd- the common languages of the Turkish Empire, to be ake and He- the Slavonish, the Greeke, the Turkish, and Arabike brew tongues.

tongues, serving severally for the parts that I men- f '9-. illr Masius in tioned berore., .

prcefat. Li ram-mat. Syric. THe Syriacke tongue is certainely thought to have Sixt. Senen. had beginning, in the time of the Captivitie of the o-Jewes in Babylon, while they were mingled among the oce Thar-" Chaldeans. In which long revolution of seventy yeeres, gum. Canin. in the vulgar sort of the Jewes forgot their owne language, prafat. Justi-and began to speake the Chaldee: But yet pronounc- '- y '-" ing it amisse, and framing it somewhat to their owne "" "'n Countrey fashion, in notation of Points, Affixes, Con- zoreta. in jugations, and some other properties of their ancient Apparat. ad speech, it became a mixt language of Hebrew and Bibl. Reg. Chaldee: a great part Chaldee for the substance of the. f '? wordes, but more Hebrew for the fashion, and so igxic. Syro-degenerating much from both: The old and right chalda'uum. Hebrew remaining after that time onely among the Genebrard. I. learned men, and being taught in Schooles, as among ' CJironog.

L 1 J ' ad An. 3690.

US the learned tongues are accustomed to bee. And Bellarm. I. z.

yet, after the time of our Saviour, this language began de verba Dei much more to alter and to depart further, both from-4- 'S- the Chaldee and Hebrew, as receiving much mixture of ' " "-

Greeke, some of Romane and Arabike wordes, as in i oictione the Talmud (named of Jerusalem) gathered by R. Bibia.

Jochanan, about three hundred yeeres after Christ, is apparent, being farre fuller of them, then those parts of the Chaldee paraphrase on the holy Scriptures, which 1. i. III. were made by R. Jonathan, a little before Christ, and by R. Aquila, whome they call Onkelos not long after. But yet certaine it is, both for the great difference of the wordes themselves, which are in the Syriake tongue for the most part Chaldee, and for the diver-sitie of those adherents of wordes, which they call praefixa, and suffixa, as also for the differing sound of some vowels, and sundry other considerations: Certaine it is I say that the unlearned Jewes, whose vulgar speech the Syriake then was, could not understand their nitdIS mttidPi, that is their lectures of Moses and the Prophets, used in their Synagogues in the Hebrew tongue. And that seemeth to have beene the originall reason, both of the pubuke speeches and declarations of learned men to the people, usuall in their Synagogues on the Sabboaths, after the readings of the "Jet. 13. 15. Law and of the Prophets, whereof in the New Testament wee finde some mention, and also of the translation of Jonathan and Onkelos, and others made into their vulgar language, for that the difference betwixt the Hebrew and the Chaldee was so great, that the tongue of the one Nation could not bee understood by the other. First, the tongues themselves, which yet remaine with us may bee evident demonstrations, of which wee see that one may bee skilfull in the Hebrew, and yet not understand the Chaldee, and therefore neither could they, whose speech the Chaldee then was (although much degenerated) understand the 'Nehem. ca. Hebrew. Secondly, wee find that when przra, at the V. 7. 8. 9. returne from the Captivitie, read the Booke of the Law before the people, others were faine to interprete that which was read unto them. And thirdly, the answere made to Rabshakeh, by the Officers of King Hezekiah ' Reg. 1. 2. ca. may put it out of question, willing him ' to speake 18. f. 26. y. Q i-hej in the Chaldee tongue, that the common people of Jerusalem (in whose hearing it was) might not understand what was spoken. But yet it might bee, that as at this day the Jewes use to doe, so also in Christs time of conversing on the Earth, they might also read the Chaldee Targamin (and certainely some"" 'Junius in learned men affirme they did so) together with the Bell rm. Cont. Hebrew lectures of Moses and the Prophets; for ' ' ' certaine it is, that Jonathan Ben Uziel, had before the birth of our Saviour translated, not the Prophets onely into Chaldee, (for it is his Paraphrase that wee have at this day on the Prophets, and the Language which wee now call the Syriake, was but the Jewish Chaldee, although in the after times, by the mixture of Greeke, and many other forraine wordes it became somewhat changed, from what in the times afore, and about our Saviours Incarnation it had beene) but the Pentateuch also: at least, if it bee true which Sixtus Sixt. Senens. hath recorded, namely, that such is the Tradition Bibhoth. among the Jewes, and which Galatine writeth, that him-f. f' ot'" selfe hath scene that translation of Jonathans, beside editio." that of Onkelos, the beginning of both which hee Galatin. de setteth downe, differing one from another in the first- rcan. wordes. Which (namely, touching the publike reading ' j ' ' of the Chaldee Targamin, either together with the Hebrew Text, or instead of it) I may as well conceive to bee true, as that the forraine 'Jewes, dwelling Vid. Sal-in Alexandria and others parts of iegypt, in Asia also, "' '"" P' and other Greeke Provinces abroad, used publikely in sctimra'Pro-stead of the Hebrew, which now they understood not, Ugom. 3. in the Septuagints Greeke translation, as is evident in Tomo. i, y Tertullian: And of some others of them in the Con- interpretat. stitutions of 'Justinian. Which Jewes for that very l f' f i, cause, are sundry times m the " Acts of the Apostles . i jpoig.

For of that part of the Chaldee Paraphrase, which we have in geiico. ca. 19.

the Complutense, and King Philips Bibles, on the Bookes of Moses, Novell, 146.

Onkelos is the Author: of that on Josuah, the Judges, the Booke of "" ct. S. i. y the Kings and of the Prophets, Jonathan. Of that on Ruth, 9.29. 11.

Hester, Job, the Psalmes, and the Bookes of Salomon, R. Joseph 20. Caecus.

Scalig. in Chron. Euseb. ad Annum MD-CCXXXIF. i J un. contra. Bellarm. Con-irov. I. . 2. c. 15,. 21. l Drus. Pra-toritor. I. 5. Annot. ad. Act. Ap. 6. I.

termed EXXiiio-ra). For by that name, in the judgement of learned men, the naturall Graecians are not meant, which are alwayes named EXX; ve9, not EXXivto-Tat, But, the Jewes dispersed among the Gentiles, that used to read the Greeke Scriptures in their Synogogues.

And here shall be the period of my first Enquiry touching the Languages, and beginning of the second, concerning the sorts of Religions abroad in the World. In discoursing whereof you must bee content to accept of Moderne Authors, because I am to intreate of Moderne Matters: And if 1 hap to step awry where I see no path, and can discerne but few steps afore mee, you must pardon it. And yet this one thing I will promise you, that if either they that should direct mee, mislead mee not, or (where my reason suspects that my guides wander, and I am mislead) if my circumspect observing, or diligent enquiring, may preserve mee from errour, I will not depart a haire from the way of Truth.

I. i. 112.

Of the sundry parts of the World inhabited by Christians

Chap. 10. Michov. de Sarmatia. I. 2. c. 3. Boem. de Morib. gent. I. 3. c. 7. Boter. Relat. Par. 3.. I.

Chap. XIII.

Master Brerewoods Enquiries of the Religions professed in the World: Of Christians, Ma-humetans, Jewes and Idolaters: with other Philosophical! speculations, and divers Annotations added.

LI Europe is possessed by Christians, except the utmost corners of it, toward the East and the North, for the small company of Mahumetans, inhabiting their peculiar Villages about Wilna in Litunia, or the scattered remnants of Idolaters in the same Province, and in Samogitia, are not worthy mentioning. But toward the North, Lappia, Scricsinia, Biarmia, Corelia, and the North part of Finmarke (all which together passe commonly under the name of Lapland, and make a Ttegler. in Region about nine hundred miles in circuit) are in- 5 "' '– ' ' habited by Idolaters: and toward the East, all the zflzrs. Kegion betwixt Tanais and Borysthenes, along Maeotis tract, de. and the Euxine Sea (the true native Countrey of the Lapepiis. ancient Gothes) being more then twice as large as the: hqv. I. 2. former, and withall much better peopled, is inhabited f"um ter by the Tartars, called Crimasi or Prascopitae, who are Como. 1. 4. c. all Mahumetans, excepting onely a small remainder of 37. Boter. Christians in some parts of Taurica. Relation pa.

But, in all the Turkes Dominion that hee hath in g ' If Europe, inclosed after a peninsular figure, betweene Danubius and the Sea, and containing in circuit about 2300. miles (for Moldavia, Walachia, and Transilvania, I reckon not for the parts of his Dominion) namely, from above Buda, on Danubius side, and from Ragusa on the Sea Eastward, to the utmost bounds of Europe, as also in the lies of the gaean Sea, Christians are mingled with Mahumetans. All which Dominion yet of the Turkes in Europe, though so much in circuit as I said, is neverthelesse (measured by squares) no greater then Spaine, the Continent of it being no way answerable to the Circumference: both, because it runneth farre out in sharpe angles, toward the West and South, namely in Hungary and Moraea, and is beside in Greece in many places extraordinarily indented with the Sea. And in his Dominion of the Turks in Europe, such is notwithstanding the mixture of Mahumetans with Christians, that the Christians make two third Boter. Relat. parts at least of the Inhabitants: for the Turke, so P- ' 4- that the Christians pay him his yeerely tribute (which f atruno' is one fourth part of their increase, and a Saltanie for Georgevitz. de every poll) and speake nothing against the Religion Affliction. and Sect of Mahumet, permitteth them the liberty of Christian, sub their religion. And even in Greece it selfe, although j J l" " more dissolute then any Region of Europe subject to the Turke (as having bin anciently more wasted with intestine discord, and longest groaned under the Turks I 305 u

Chitr s de statu Eccle-sior. non longe ab initio. Coiyat hath more.

Gerlach in epist. ad Cms. Turcogrcecia. I. pag. Concil. Carthag. 4. y Conci. African, sev. Carth. 6.

Martin. Po-lon. Suppat. An. 475. Vict. I. de Persecut. Van-dalec.

Of the Chris-tianitie of Africa, see Santos y Griniaysrelat. inf. I. 9. c. 12.

Pigafer. hist. Regni Con-gens. I. 2. c. z.

oppression) there remaine yet neverthelesse in Constantinople, the very Seat of the Turkish Empire, above twenty Churches of Christians, and in the Citie of Salonichi (Thessalonica) above thirty, whereas in the later this Mahumetans have but three, beside very many Churches abroad in the Province under suffragan Bishops, of whom the Metropolitan of Salonichi, hath no lesse then ten belonging to his Jurisdiction, as there are also recorded yet to remaine under the Metropolitans of Philippi, one hundred and fifty Churches: of Athens, as many: Of Corinth one hundred, together with sundry suffragan Bishops under each of them.

But in Afrike, all the Regions in a manner, that Christian Religion had gained from Idolatry, Mahu-metanisme hath regained from Christianitie: Insomuch, that not onely the North part of Afrike, lying along the Mediterrane Sea, namely, betwixt it and the Mountaine Atlas, even from Spaine to-Egypt, where Christianitie sometime exceedingly flourished, as there wee reade Synodes of above two hundred Bishops to have been gathered, and three hundred Catholike Bishops to have been there expelled by Gensericus King of the Wandales: And in some one Province alone, ' Zengitana by name (it is that wherein Carthage stood) to have beene one hundred sixty foure Bishops under one Metropolitan: Not onely that North part of Afrike I say, is at this present utterly void of Christians, excepting a few Townes belonging to the King of Spaine (of which onely Septa and Tanger are Episcopall Cities:) but even in all the vast Continent of Afrike, being about thrice as large as Europe, there is not any Region entirely possessed by Christians, but the Kingdome of Habassia, no, nor yet (which is more lamentable) any other where Christians are mingled, either with Mahumetans, but onely gypt: or where with Idolaters, but the Kingdomes of " Conga and Angola: which two about one hundred twenty yeeres agoe, ann. 1491. began first to receive Christianitie: All the rest of Afrike, being entirely governed and possessed I" these parts by Pagans or Mahumetans. To which, if I should adde Christianity is those i Yi places in Afrike afore mentioned, neere the

Strait of Gibraltar, which the Kings of Portugall and

Castile have conquered from the Moores, with the other few dispersed fortresses, which the Portugalls hold in other places on the Coast of Afrike (altogether even betwixt Spaine and India are but eleven or twelve) I know not where to finde even among all the native Inhabitants of Afrike, any Christians more. For, as for the large Region of Nubia, which had from the

Apostles time (as is thought) professed the Christian

Faith, it hath againe above one hundred yeeres since forsaken it, and embraced instead of it, partly Ma- i. i. 113.

humetanisme, and partly Idolatry, and that by the most miserable occasion that might befall, namely famine of the word of God through lacke of Ministers: for as Alvarez hath recorded, at his being in the King Alvarex. hist.

of Habassia his Court, there were Embassadours out thiopic of Nubia, to intreate him for a supply of Ministers, to- '37- instruct their Nation, and repaire Christianitie gone to ruine among them: but were rejected.

And yet are the Christians of i gypt, namely those of the native Inhabitants, but verie few in respect of that infinitenesse of people, wherewith Egypt doth, and ever did abound, as being esteemed not to passe 50000. Boter. Reat And, as touching the Kingdome of Habassia, neither '-'-3-f-is it all Christians but a great part of Gentiles, namely gieTtto toward the West, and South bounds of it, and some Thom. a Jes. part Mahumetans, toward the East border: neither so de Convers. large and spacious, as many mens relations have made g i-i-1 par. it thought to be. For although I cannot assent to Bol'er"Relat them, who assigne to that great Kingdome, but about. i.. 3. r. 662. leagues of compasse, by which reckoning (suppose de Abassia. they were Spanish leagues) it should be little larger then Germany (for I know full well, by infallible observations, that sparing limitation of others, to be untrue) yet, neither can I yeelde to them, who esteeme

Horat.

Malaguz. ncl discorse de i. cinque mass'ini Signori.

See hereof later and better intelligence I. 7. c. 7. y 8. Abassia is reduced now to a small circuit.

Boter. loco proxm. citato. Sommar. dei regni Oriental, apud Ramos, vol. i.

pag- 32+-Boter. Relat. p. I. . 3. c. Loango. An. ichi.

I doe not think it now to con-taine halfe so many Christians which yet are but halfe Christians) as any one of those foure. The Author alloweth too much., as Piga-fetta also, 15 in these times, it is little, except in misery. Better relations of these parts are since our authors death published by it greater, then the vaste dominions of the Emperours of Turkie or of Tartaric, c. Or, to them, that extend it from the one Tropique to the other, and from the red Sea, almost to the West Ocean. For first, certaine it is (that I may speake a little of the limits of this Kingdome) that it attaineth not to the red Sea (Eastward) neither within the straits of Babel mandel, nor without: for within those straits, along the Bay of Arabia, there is a continuall ledge of Mountains, known to be inhabited with Moores, betwixt that Bay, and the dominion of Habassia: So that, onely one Port there is, along all that coast (Ercoco by name) where those Mountaines open to the Sea, that at this present belongeth to it. Neither without those Straits doth it any where approach to the Ocean. All that coast, as farre as Mozanbique, being well knowne to be inhabited with Arabians.

And as touching the west limits of Habassia, I cannot finde by any certaine historie or relation (unskilfuu men may rumour what they will, and I know also that the common Charts represent it otherwise) I cannot finde I say, that it stretcheth beyond the River Nilus, so farre commeth it short of the West Ocean. For it is knowne, that all the West banke of Nilus, from the River of Zaire to the confines of Nubia, is possessed by the Anzichi, being an idolatrous and man-eating Nation, and subject to a great Prince of their owne; thus then it is with the bredth of the Empire of Habassia, betwixt

East and West. And now to speake of the length of it, lying North and South, neither doth it approach Northward on Nilus side, further then the South end of the Isle of Meroe (Meroe it selfe is inhabited by Mahumetans, and the deadly enemies of the King of Habassia) nor on the Sea side further then about the port of Suachem. And toward the South, although the bounds of that Kingdome be not perfectly knowne, yet that it approacheth nothing neere the circle of Capricorne, as hath bin supposed, is most manifest, because the great Kingdomes of Moenhemage, and Beno- Gadignus, and motapa, and some others, are scituate betwixt Habassia ""'" f " and that circle. But, as neere as I am able to conjecture, j. i having made the best search that I can, in the itineraries c. ult. and relations, that are extant of those parts, the South limit of that Empire, passeth not the South parallell of six or seven degrees at the most, where it confineth with Moenhemage. So that to make a respective estimate of the largenesse of that dominion, by comparing it with our knowne regions of Europe, it seemeth equall to Germany and France, and Spaine, and Italic laid together: Equall I say in dimension of ground, but nothing neere equall in habitation or multitude ot people, which the distemperature of that climate, and the dry barrennesse of the ground, in many regions of it, will not allow. For which cause the torride parts of Afrique are by Piso in Strabo resembled to a Libbards S, trab. . 2. skinne, the distance of whose spots, represent the disper-sednesse of habitations or townes in Afrique. But if I should absolutely set downe the circuit of that whole dominion, I esteeme the limitation of Pigasetta, nere Pigafett. de about the truth, namely, that it hath in circumference?- '"'? 4000. miles (about 1500. in length, and about 600. '- in breadth) being inclosed with Mahumetans on the North, and East, and with Idolaters, on the West and South.

Such then as I have declared, is the condition of Christians in the continent of Afrique: but the Inhabitants of the Isles along the West coast of Afrique, as namely Madera; the Canaries, the Isles of Cabo verde, and of S. Thomas, and some other of lesse importance, are by the Portugals and Castilians instruction, become Christian: but on the East side of,,. -. y: it rj,,. Faul. l enct.

Arrique, exceptmg onely Zocotora, there is no Christian ,, Isle. 3-. 3.

Even such is the state of Christians in the firme land, o."z. l. z.

and the adjacent Isles of Afrique. And it is not much V Russian better in Asia, for excepting first the Empire of Russia Christianity.

Jacob a Vit-riaco Hist. 07-ient. c. 7.

I. i. 1.4.

Since the Tartarian times Christianitie is neere extirpate out of Asia.

Paul. Venct. I. 1. c. 8.

(and yet of it, a great part is Idolatrous, namely the region betweene the Rivers of Pechora and Ob, and some part of Permia) secondly, the regions of Circassia, and Mengrelia, lying along Moeotis and the Euxine Sea, from Tanais Eastward as farre as the River Phasis. Thirdly, the Province of Georgia, and fourthly the Mountaine Libanus in Syria (and yet the last of these is of the Turkes Dominion) excepting these few I say, there is not any region in all Asia, where Christians live severall, without mixture, either of Mahumetans or of Pagans, for although Vitriacus a man well experienced in some parts of the orient (as being Bishop of Aeon and the Popes Legate in the East, at what time Palestina and Syria were in the hands of Christians) hath left registred, that the Christians of the Easterlie parts of Asia, exceeded in multitude the Christians of the Greeke and Latine Churches: yet in his time (for he writ almost foure hundred yeeres agoe) Christianitie began to decline, and since his time, it hath proceeded infinitely to decay, in all those parts of Asia: first, by the inundation of the Idolatrous Tartars, who subdued all those Regions, and after by the intertayning of Mahumetanisme in many of them. The time was indeede, (and but about foure hundred yeeres agoe) when the King of Tenduc, whom the histories of those times name Presbyter Johannes a Christian, but a Nestorian Prince, ruled farre and wide in the Northeast part of Asia: as having under his dominion, beside Tenduc, (which was his owne native and peculiar King-dome) all the neighbouring Provinces, which were at that time for a great part. Christian: but after that his Empire was brought to ruine, and he subdued by Chingis a rebell of his owne Dominion (and the first founder of the Tartarian Empire) which happened about the yeere 1190, the state of Christian Religion became in short time strangely altered in those parts, for I finde in Marcus Paulus who lived within fiftie yeeres after Vitriacus, and was a man of more experience in those parts then he, as having spent seventeene yeeres together in Tartaric, partly in the Emperours Court, and partly in travailing over those Regions, about the Emperours affaires, that except the Province of Tenduc, which as I said was the Kingdome of Presbyter Johns residence (for it was the Prince of that Kingdome, which is rightly and usually, by the ancienter Historians named Pres-byter John, howsoever the mistaking fantasies of many, have transported it out of Asia into Africke and by errour bestowed it on the King of Habassia) except that Province of Tenduc I say, wherof Marcus Paulus con-fesseth the greater part, to have professed the Christian Religion at his being in Tartarie, the rest of the Inhabitants, being partly Mahumetans, and partly Idolaters: in all the other Provinces of those parts beside, that, hee a n His observeth the Christians to bee but few, as namely in the tor. Orient. Kingdomes of Tanguth, of Chinchintales, of Succuir, c. 78. Otho. of "Caraiam, of Cassar, of Carcham, of Ergimuli, of Phnsingens. Corguth, of Egrigaia, and in the other Regions of ij'Jii ' Tartarie mentioning no Christians at all. Two Cities L. i. c. A. i onely I finde in him excepted, the one was Cingiangifu "L. i. r, 47 in Mangi, (that is China) where hee noteth, that many " L. i. r. 48 Christians dwelt, and the other ' Quinsay, in which later f' " ' yet, (although the greatest Citie in the world) he hath g " j . recorded to bee found but one Church of Christians. L. i. csz But these places excepted before mentioned, I can finde L- i– 63 no certaine relation, neither in Paul Venetus, nor any it" ' ' ' other, of any Christians of the native Inhabitants, in all

For Scaligers imagination, that it was the King of the Habas- Scaliger. de sines, that inlarged his Dominion so farre, in the North-east of Asia, Emendat. till he was driven into Africk by the Tartars, hath neither any foun- tempor. I. 7. dation at all in historic, nor probabilitie in reason. Namely that a Annot. incom-King in Africke should subdue the most distant parts of all Asia from put, Ethiop. him, and there hold residence all the Regions betwixt belonging to other Princes. Moreover it is certainly knowne of Presbyter John of Asia, that hee was a Nestorian, whereas hee of Habassia was, and still is, a Jacobite. Besides, it hath beene recorded from time to time, of the Christians of Habassia, that they were circumcised, which of those of the East, was never reported by any, c. Scaliger him-selfe in his later edition, hath altered his conceit.

the East of Asia, but Idolatrie keepeth still her olde possession, and overspreadeth all.

But yet indeede, in the more Southerly parts of Asia (especially in those where Christianitie was first planted, and had taken deepest roote) as Natolia, Syria, Palestine, Chaldaea, Ossyria, Mesopotamia, Armenia, Media, Persia, the North part of Arabia, and the South of India, Christians are not onely to be found, but in certaine of those Regions, as in Natolia, Armenia, Syria, Mesopotamia, somewhat thicke mingled with Mahumetans: as they are also in the South of India not farre from the Promontorie of Comoriin, in some reasonable number, in the Kingdome of Contan, of Cranganor, and of Choro-mandel, but mingled with Idolaters. But yet, is not this mixture of Christians with them of other Religions, in any part of Asia, after the proportion of their mixture in Europe (where I observed the Christians to make the prevayling number) but they are farre inferiour to the multitude of the Mahumetans, and of the Idolaters, among whom they are mingled, and yet touching their number, decrease every day, in all the parts aforesaid, India onely excepted. Where since the Portugals held Goa (which they have erected into an Archbishopricke) and entertayned Malabar, and some other parts of India, what with commerce, and what with amitie, the number of Christians is greatly multiplied, in sundrie places of that Region, but yet not so, as to compare in any sort with the Mahumetans, and much lesse with the Idolaters among whom they live.

Thus it is with Christians in the firme land of Asia: but in the Hands about Asia, Christianitie is as yet but a tender plant: for although it hath made some entrance into the Isles called Philippinas, namely into thirty of them, for so many onely of iiooo. termed by that name, are subject to the King of Spain, (Th. Jes. de Conu. gent. 1. i. c. i.) by the industry of the Castilians, as also by the preaching of the Portugals, into Ormuz in the Bay of Persia, and into Ceilan in the Sea of India, and some few other of the infinite multitude of Islands, dispersed in that Easterne Sea, yet hath it hitherto found in all those places, rather some faire beginning, then any great proceeding. Onely in Japonia Christianity hath obtained (notwithstanding many hinderances and oppositions) more prosperous successe. Insomuch that many yeeres since, there were recorded to have beene by estimation, about "200000. Christians in Japonia. Li. 115.

Lastly, in America, there be foure large regions, and P- (those of the most fruitful! and populous part of it, J' ' possessed and governed by the Spaniards, that is, Nueva ap. 30.

Espana, Castilla del Oro (otherwise termed Nuebo Reino) Ordatjudcem

Peru, and part of Brasil, the first three, by the Castilians, (ippella Jcsu- and the fourth, by the Portugals, all which together, may J 'y " ' by estimation, make a Region as large as Europe. In ij- gi which, as also in the Islands, specially in the greater ling their owne Islands of Hispaniola, Cuba, Jamaica, and Puerto-rico, exploits.

the Christian Region is so largely spred, that one hath " ' '. presumed, to equall in a manner, the Christians of fjnit'i hath

America, to those of the Latine Church in Europe: there gone

And another, hath left recorded, that within a few backward. See yeeres after the entrance of the Gospell among them,- 5– 2- there were no lesse then seven Millions, or as others jmlndzh–reported foureteene Millions, that in the Sacrament of ic. in Chro.

Baptisme had given their names to Christ. But especi (fit. An.

ally in the Kingdome of Mexico (or Nueva Espanna).

Christian Religion obtained that plentiful! and prosperous chr ad An successe, that we finde recorded of sundry of the chr. 1558.

Preachers, emploied about the conversion of that people, Vid. epist.

that they baptised each one of them, above 100000. Petri Gauden.

and that in few yeeres: Insomuch that (as is storied by Seduliiadvi-Surius) it is to be found among the records of Charles the tam. S. Fran- fift, that some old Priest hath baptised 700000. another m.. 219, y 300000. and certaine others very great multitudes. But '- ": yet, what maner of Christians many of those proselites f a ' ' were, I am loath to remember, or report (and it may. ' be by this time, they are better affected and instructed,. Ynd Occi- then they were) for certainly, Oviedo, and Benzo, men dent. l. ij. c.

Benz. hist. that had long lived, and were well experienced In those Nov. Orbis. parts, have left recorded, the first of = Cuba, that there Seeto 2 scarce any one, or but very few, that willingly became 5. c. 3. 6- . Christians, and both Oviedo of them, and Benzo of the 7.12.6- Christians of Nueva Espanna, that they had nothing . 8. f. 4.6'r. almost belonging to Christianitie, but onely the bare name of Christians, being so utterly mindelesse, and carelesse of Christian religion, that they remembred not any thing of the convenant and profession they made in their baptisme: Onely they kept in minde, the name they received then, which very name also, they forgot soone after. But all the rest of America, except the regions afore mentioned, which compared to the parts possessed by the Castilians and Portugals (to make estimation by the Maps that we have of those regions, for the North and West coasts of America, are not yet perfectly discovered) may be as six to one, is possessed by Idolaters.

I. i. 116. Of the parts of the luorld possessed by Mahumetans. Ch. II. The Religious of the World brought to foare heads or general! kinds.

Mathia Mi-chov. de Sar-mat. I. 2. C. 3.

HAving declared the amplitude of Christianitie, I will proceed to shew the state of other Religions in the World, and with all, what parts of it, the Pro-fessours of those Religions doe severally inhabit; and lastly, what proportion they may have each to other, and all of them to Christians. To indevour therefore your satisfaction in this behalfe. There are foure sorts or sects of Religion, observed in the sundrie Regions of the World, Namely, Idolatry, Mahumetanisme, Judaisme, and Christianitie. Of Christians I have alreadie spoken: now therefore will I relate for your better contentment, of the other three; and first of Mahumetans.

Mahumetans then possesse in Europe, as I said before (having in that part but small mixture of Christians) all the Region betwixt Tanais and Boristhenes (Don and Nieper they are now called) being about a twentieth part of Europe: beside some Villages in Lituania about Wilna, where the use of their Religion is by the King of Poland permitted them, for in Greece, Macedon, Thrace,

Bulgaria, Rascia, Servia, Bosina, Epirus, the greatest part of Hungaria, and some part of Dalmatia (which may be together about one fourteenth part of Europe) although the government be wholy the Turkes, yet Mahumetans scarcely passe one third part of the Inhabitants.

But in Afrique, Mahumetanisme is spread exceeding farre; for, first to consider the maritime Coast: It pos-sesseth all the shoare of the Atlantique Ocean, from Cape Blanco " to the Strait of Gibralter, being about i loo. miles. They reach Secondly, on the shoare of the Mediterraine, all from that "', ow Strait to Egypt, about 2400. miles, excepting onely on J 5 the one Coast, and on the other, some seven Townes, jobson infra. in the possession of the Spaniards. Thirdly, on the East . 9. c. 13. as side of Afrike, all the Coast of the Bay of Arabia, even i emse on the from Suez to Cape Gardafu, about 1600. miles, excepting osofala.

1-r f-r 1 - 1 x , Santos I. Q. c.

onely one rort (Ercoco) bemg or the Dommion of the xz, further King of Habassia. And thence (doubling that Cape) then our Southward, all the shoare of the i thiopique Sea, as ' "' f farre as Mozambique (that is over against the middest "" ' of Madagascar) about 1800. miles. And in all the Coasts of Afrike hitherto mentioned, being altogether about 7000. miles (that is, by some excesse more then halfe the circumference of Afrike) the Professors of Mahumeds Religion, have both possession and dominion, together with the " Maritime parts, of the great He of Paul Venet. Madagascar, and many other Hands along the Coast of '- 3– 39-

And yet, even beyond Mozambique also as farre as to the Cape das Corrientes, it is under the Circle of Capricorne) although they have there no rule, yet they are found mingled with Idolaters. But yet nevertelesse, observed it is, that along the East shoare of Afrike, namely from Suachem to Mozambique (being towards 3000. miles of the mentioned Coast) Mahumetans pos-sesse onely the Margent of the Land, on the Sea shoare, and have gotten but little footing in the Inland parts, except in the Kingdomes of Dangali and Adel, confining together, the first within and the second without the

Strait of Babel Mandel, which yet are but small Provinces. And this also (to extenuate their number) is also true, that from the Kingdome of Adel, and Cape Guardafu, to Mozambique, there is found among the Mahumetans, some mixture of Idolaters, although the Dominion be onely in the Mahumetans hands.

But yet on the North and West parts of Afrike, it is farre otherwise, and farre worse: Mahumetanisme having over-spread all the maine Land of Afrike, be- tweene the Mediterrane Sea, and the great River Niger: and along the course of Nilus, as farre as the He of

Meroe, which lieth also about the same parallel with the

River Niger, and is possessed by Mahumetans. And

Leo Afric. I. yet beyond Niger also, it hath invaded and obtained, all x. c. derelig. the Kingdoms of the Nigrites that border on that River.

' " ' So that all Barbarie and Biled-elgerid, and Libya deserta, and the Region of Negroes, are become of that Religion.

Excepting first some Maritime parts toward the Atlan- tique Sea, namely from Cape Blanco Southward, which are inhabited by Gentiles. Secondly, the Kingdome of

Borno, and some part of Nubia: And thirdly, certaine scattered multitudes of the olde African Progenie, that still retaine their ancient Gentilisme, and are found in divers places heere and there in the Mountaines and wilder parts of Barbarie, of Biled-elgerid, and of Libya.

These I say, being excepted, all Afrike beside, from the Mediterraine Sea, somewhat more Southward then the River Niger, is over-spread with Mahumetans: which The Mogol (adding these before mentioned, along the East Coast as great a of Ethiopia) may by estimation, take up foure nine Prince as parts of Afrique.

n '"" And yet in Asia, Mahumatisme is farther spred, being lutiis' eausi imbraced and maintained chiefly, by foure mightie Commanders Nations, namely, the Arabians, Persians, Turkes, and and best Soul- Tartars. Arabia was indeed the Nest, that bred and ' "hajt" fostered that uncleane Bird, and had it beene the Cage Zetans: V'ea o, for ever to enclose it, it had beene but too much his sonnes, dr'c. space and libertie, for Arabia is m circuit above 4000.

miles, and except a small mixture of Christians in Eltor See of these a Port Towne toward the inmost Angle of the Bay of ' ' ' '"- "- Arabia; and Petra (Krac now it is called) a mid-land Towne; and two Monasteries about the Hill of Sinai, all is possessed with Mahumetans. But from Arabia that poyson hath in such sort dispersed it selfe through the veines of Asia, that neere the one halfe, is at this day corrupted by it. For although it hath not hitherto attained to the North Coast of Asia, which is partly inhabited by Christians, namely, from the River of Dwyna to Pechora, and partly by Idolaters from Pechora to the East Ocean: nor yet to the East Coast, which from the most Northerly part of Tartary, to the most Southerly part of India (except some few places in the Kingdome Boter. Rel of Siam) Idolaters in like sort generally obtaine: yet " 3–z–' neverthelesse, it is as I said, namely, that a very great ometant. part of Asia is infected with that pestilence. For first, I-i- n?- all the Southerly Coast of Asia, from the Bay of Arabia to the River Indus, is possessed by Mahumetans: and if we proceed further along that shoare, even beyond the River of Indus also, the great Kingdomes of Cam-baya and Bengala, for a great part of them, and about one fourth part of the Inhabitants of Malabar, are observed to be Mahumetans. And secondly, to consider the Inland parts: all from the Westerly bounds of Asia, namely the River Tanais, with the Euxine, gsean, and Mediterrane Seas, as farre Eastward, as the Moun-taine Imaus (which is more then halfe the length of Asia, is possessed by them: Except, first the Kirgessi Guagin. neere Imaus, who are Idolaters: and secondly, the f'– ' ' ' mixture of Christians among them, who yet have very! " f. ' small proportion (for their multitude) to Mahumetans, in any Province, of all the mentioned vast circuit, for howsoever Burchardus about 320. yeeres agoe, hath left recorded of those parts of Asia, that there were to be found in them thirtie Christians for one Mahumetan, (Descr. ter. sanct. pag. 2. c. 2. 9.) yet certainly, that in these present times the excesse of multitude is growne 'Paul. Venet. I. c.

42-43-"Id. I. I. c. 38. 40. 47. 62, 63. 64.

Nicalde conci. Viagi-nelle Indie. Barbofap Ramus. Vol. I. de V'taggi. p. 313-318.

319-
Boter. Relat.
Mahometan.
See a perfecter
Relation of the
Maldiva I.
9. cap. vit.

great on the Mahumetans side in respect of Christians, the experience of many putteth out of question. And if we shall proceed yet further Eastward in the In-land parts of Asia, and passe in our speculation, beyond the Mountaine Imaus, even there also sundry Provinces are observed, as 'Peim, Cotam, Lop, where Mahumetans are the maine and sole Inhabitants, and many more, Cassar, Carcham, Chinchintilus, Tanguth, Ergimul, Cerguth, Tenduc, c. where they are mingled among Idolaters, which may for a great part, countervail those Regions of Asia, which Christians and Idolaters take up on this side that Mountaine. So that, in my estimation, having about these points conferred Historic with Geographic in the most circumspect and considerate manner that I was able, about nine parts of twentie of Asia are possessed by Mahumetans.

Thus then is Mahumetanisme spread over the one halfe almost of the firme Land of Asia. And yet moreover in the Hands also that are about Asia, that Religion hath found large entertainment. For not onely a good part of the small 'lies of Malidivia, namely those of them that are inhabited (for they are above 7000. in all, and most without habitation) are possessed with Mahumetans, but moreover, all the Ports of the He of Ceilan (except Colombo which the Portugals have), the Sea Coasts of Sumatra, the Port of Java, with the He of Sunda, the Ports of Banda, of Borneo and of Gilolo, with some of the Hands Malucos, are in the hands of Mahumetans.

Of the great spreading and inlargement of which Religion, if the causes were demanded of me, I should make answere, that beside the Justice of Almightie God, punishing by that violent and wicked Sect, the sinnes of Christians (for we see that by the Conquests of the Arabians, and Turkes, it hath chiefly seised on those Regions, where Christianitie in ancient time most flourished, both in Afrike and Asia, and partly in Europe) one cause I say, of the large spreading of their Religion, is the large spreading of their victories. For it hath ever beene the condition of the conquered, to follow for the most part the Religion"" of the Con-querours, A second, their peremptorie restraint (even on the paine of death) of all disputation touching their Religion, and calling any point of it into question. A third, their suppression of the studie of Philosophy, by the light whereof, the grossenesse and vanitie of many parts of their Religion might bee discovered, which is inhibited to be taught in their Universities, and so hath beene, about these foure hundred yeeres, whereas till then, it greatly flourished among them, in Cordova, in Fez, in Maroccho, in Bagded, and other Cities. And yet, as Bellonius and others write, the Turkes fall now againe, to those studies afresh." A fourth cause may

"Christian Religion (to shew the power and wisdome of Christ) hath contrari-wise conquered the Conquerours. And by this meanes the Goths, Hunnes, Vandals, Frankes, Saxons, Normans, Danes, and other Heathen Conquerours of Christians, have yet beene conquered by their Religion: A grace denyed Saracenicall Conquests, because almost all the Nations which now are Mahumetan, were before in part or wholly Christians, but rather in Faith then Workes: to which succeeded the Saracenicall Religion without the Church, and Papall Superstition within, the one professing moralitie of Workes without Faith in him which is, the way, the truth and life; the Other, on that fundamental! Faith of the Trinitie Incarnation, c. building their hay and stubble of Wil-worships and merits of Workes: the one wholly excluding Christianitie, the other corrupting it; both in steed of that great mysterie of godlinesse, our Justification by faith in Christ, obtruding mans moralitie, and a righteousnesse of our owne, even therefore unrighteousnesse.

Bellon. Obser. 1. 3, c. 30. Georgiovitz. 1. 2. de Ritib. Turcar, cap. de Scholis.

"See Withers his Seraglio, 1. 9. The Saracens at the first were so farre from rejecting Philosophie and Arts, that within the first hundred yeeres after the Hegira, they there most flourished, and Abilqualid Jacob Almansor (whose Captaines conquered Spaine) erected and endowed eightie two Colledges for Arts, as many Hospitals, and above five hundred Mesquits. Himselfe bestowed every Thursday in hearing disputations, and in his Librarie which contayned five and fiftie thousand Bookes. And after the Barbarian Deluge Christians recovered lost learning by helpe of Arabs.

well be assigned, the sensuall libertie allowed by it, namely to have many Wives, and the like promise of sensuall pleasures, to succeed after this life (to the Religious observers of it) in Paradise wherewith men for the greatest part, as beeing of things wherewith their sense is affected, and whereof they have had certaine experience, are more allured and perswaded, then with promises of spirituall delights, presented only to their hopes, and for which present and sensible pleasures must in the meane time be forsaken.

I. i. 118. Of the sundrie Regions of the IVorld inhabited by Idolaters. Chap.

Boetn. de Morib. gent.

I. 3- ' 7-Boter. relat. p. 3. I. I. e. Lituania.

NOw touching Idolaters, they possesse in Europe, a Region as I before observed, about 900. miles in circuit (although the ordinary Geographicall Charts represent it (but falsly) more then twice so large, containing Lappia, Corelia, Biarmia, Scricsinia, and the North part of Finmarch. All which together, may by estimation make about one sixtieth part of Europe, or a little more, more I meane in magnitude rather then in multitude, for it is indeed a little greater then so. Beside which Provinces, there are also to bee found in divers places of Lituania, and Samagotia, some scattered remnants of Idolaters.

But in Afrike their multitude is very great, for from Cape Blanco on the Coast of Libya, the most Westerly point of all Afrike (being about the North latitude of twenty degrees) even all the Coast of Afrike Southward, to the Cape of Buena Esperanza: And thence turning by the backe of Afrike, as farre as the Cape of Mozambique, being (over against the middest of Madagascar) in the South latitude of fifteene degrees: all this Coast I say, being not much lesse, then halfe the Circumference of Afrike, is inhabited by Idolaters. Onely, on the East side, from Mozambique to Cape de Corrientes (which is the South latitude of twentie foure degrees) they are mingled with Mahumetans: And on the West side, in the Kingdome of Congo, and the North part of Angola, with Christians: But yet in both these places of their mixture, Idolaters are the greater multitude.

But now, if we consider the Inland Region of Afrike, all betweene the River Nilus, and the West Sea of Ethiopia, from about the North parallel of ten degrees, to the South parallel of six or seven degrees, but from that parallel of sixe or seven degrees, even all Ethiopia Southward, on both the sides of Nilus, from the East Sea of Ethiopia, to the West, even to the most Southerly point of all Afrike, the Cape of Buona Speranza, is possessed by Idolaters: excepting onely some part of Congo and Angola afore mentioned, toward the West Sea, inhabited by Christians, and the utmost shoare of the East Sea, from Mozambique Northward, which is replenished with Mahumetans: And yet, beside all the Regions before mentioned, even all the Kingdome of Pfiorno, and a great part of Nubia is possessed by Leo African. them; to speake nothing of the infinite multitudes of ' 7; the "'ancient Africans, dispersed in sundry Tracts of ij J-ez' ' Barbary, of Biled-elgerid, and of Libya Deserta, which isf. thiop. still continue in their ancient Paganisme. So that (over c. 30. and beside these last) very neere about halfe Afrike, 'Leojfncl.

J L TJ 1 . c. de vims IS possessed by Idolaters. r.

And yet in Asia Idolaters abound more then in Afrike, even as Asia is larger then Afrike for the Continent, and for the people, better inhabited; for of Asia also, very neere about the one halfe, or rather a little more is possessed by Idolaters. For first, if we consider the Maritime parts, all from the River of Pechora, Eastward to the Ocean, and then turning downward, to the most Southerly point of India (and of all Asia) the Cape of Cincapura, and from that point returning Westward, by the South Coast, to the Out-lets of the River Indus, all that Maritime Tract I say, is entirely possessed by Idolaters. Saving onely, that in the neerer part of India, betweene Indus and Ganges, there is among them some mixture both of Mahumetans and Christians: and in the further part, the Citie and Terri-I 321 X torie of Malacca, is held by Portugals, and some part of the Sea Coast of the Kingdome of Siam, by Moores. So that by this account, a good deale more then halfe the circumference of Asia, is possessed by Idolaters. And, although in the In-land parts their proportion be somewhat lesse, then in the Maritime, yet if we consider well, the whole dimension of Asia, we shall find by good estimation, as before I said, that the one halfe, or rather a little more, is replenished with Idolaters: for the better declaring of which point, you may understand, Strab. . 2. that as Strabo and Ptolomie, have observed, of the Ptol. tn tab. JVIountaine Taurus, that beginning in the West parts ' ' 'of Asia (in the Confines of Lycia and Pamphilia over against the Chelidonian lies) it runneth Eastward even to the Ocean, keeping betweene the parallels of thirty and forty degrees, and so deviding the North part of Asia from the South. Even so must we observe of Vid. Ptol. in the Mountaine Imaus that beginning on the shoare Tab. orbis f Y North Ocean, it runneth along through the Merc'in tab " iddest of Asia to the South, keeping still about the gener. Asia. Same Meridian, namely about the longitude of 130. degrees, and crossing (at right Angles in a manner) the Mountaine Taurus devideth the East part of Asia from the West, Imaus therfore in this sort dividing Asia into two parts, not much unequall, divideth also in a manner, betweene the Idolaters and Mahumetans of Asia, for although the hither part of Asia, West of Imaus, and possessed of Mahumetans, take up more in the longitude of the Earth, namely East and West: yet the further part East of Imaus, spreadeth more in latitude. North and South, which may make some recompence toward that excesse.

But, if withall we subtract those parts of the hither Asia, that are covered with the Persian and Caspian Seas, beside large parts of the Euxine and Mediterrane, the further Asia (I thinke) wil fully equall it. Now, although many Mahumetans be also found on the other side of Imaus, toward the North-east of Asia, both severall in sundry Provinces, and otherwise mingled with Idolaters or Christians, or with both, as before was partly observed: Yet many more whole Regions of Idolaters (to countervail those Mahumetans) are found on this side Imaus, both toward the South, in the Kingdomes of the neerer India, and toward the North, betwixt Imaus and the River Pechora, all which Coast of Asia I-i. 119. is inhabited by Idolaters. And lastly, in the middest betwixt both, the Kirgessi, and some other of their Neighbour Nations. And not onely in the firme land of Asia, is Idolatry thus spread: but in those many thousand Hands that lie dispersed in the vast Ocean, on the East and South-east parts of Asia: 'which Pa. Fen. l. over against China, are recorded upon the report of 3– 8. Mariners, long practised in those Seas, to be 7448. and about "India, to be 27000. And which might for ".3.42. their largenesse, if they were all layed together, make a Continent as large as three foure parts of Europe. In those Hands I say, Idolatrie over-spreadeth all, excepting onely those few, which I before observed, to bee possessed by the Spaniards, and by the Arabians.

Finally, of all other parts of the Earth yet discovered. Idolatry spreadeth farthest in America, which being but little lesse, then the Easterne Continent (that wee terme the old World) is at least six parts of seven, inhabited with Heathenish and idolatrous people. For, except the Regions above mentioned, possessed namely by the Portugals, and Castilians (and yet the inner, and wilder tracts even of those, remaine still for a great part, in their ancient Paganisme) and many notwithstanding their Baptisme, withall worship Idols, together with some Tha. Jes. de later Converts made in the Region about and above the C'o. gent. I. Bay of California, of whom as yet. Histories make so '- little report, that of their number I can make no estimate: And lastly, two or three Fortresses, held by the Spaniards, on the Coast of Florida, with the English Colonies in Virginia, and the French in Canada, these I say being excepted, all the rest of America (being as

Curdi. See I.

Of the J ewes dispersed in several! parts of the World Chap. 13. Boter. relat p. I. I. z. c. de Gindei.

I said about six seventh parts) remaineth in their old Idolatry.

And thus have I declared the three principall Sects as touching Religion, that are at this present found in the several parts of the World, with their particular Regions. But beside these, observed there are, two or three irregular Nations, being for their Religion mingled as it were of some of the former Sects. As first, in Asia, the Curdi, inhabiting in the Mountainous Countrey above Mozal, betweene Armenia and Mesopotamia. Secondly, the Drusi, dwelling in Syria, about the skirts of Libanus, the Religion of which Nations (such as it is) partaketh somewhat, both of Mahumetanisme and Christianitie. And thirdly, the Morduites, in Europe, possessing the middle Confines betwixt the Precopite Tartars, and the Muscovites, that are in a manner as touching their Religion, mingled of all three Sects: for they are both baptised like Christians, and circumcised like Mahume-tans, and withall worship Idols.

NOw will I intreat a little, of the Professors of the fourth sort and Sect of Religion, that is found in the World, namely of Judaisme, for, although the Jewes have not for their Mansion, any peculiar Countrey, but are dispersed abroad among forreigne Nations, for their ancient Idolatries, and their later unthankfulnesse, in rejecting their Saviour the Sonne of God: So that even in Jerusalem, there be not to be found at this time, an hundred housholds of Jewes (Onely of all the Townes of Palestina, Tiberias (which Amurath the great Turke gave to Alvarez Mendez a Jew) and Staffiletto, are somewhat peopled with them.) Neither have they at this present, for any thing that is certainly knowne, any other Region in the World, severall to themselves: Yet because there bee some Provinces, wherein they are observed specially to abound, as others also, whence they are excluded and banished, I will consider a little of their present condition. The first Country of Christendome, whence the Jewes were expelled, without hope of returne, was our Countrey of England, whence they were banished, Anno 1290. by-King Edward the first. Not long after they were likewise banished France, Anno 1307. by Philippus Pulcher: Onely of all the Countreyes of France, in the Jurisdiction of Avignon (the Popes state) some are remayning.

Out of Spaine, Anno 1492. by Ferdinand, and shortly after out of Portugall, Anno 1497. by Emanuel. Out of the Kingdome of Naples and Sicilie, Anno 1539. by Charles the fift. In other Regions of Europe they are found, and in some of them in great numbers, as in Germanic, Boheme, Polonia, Lituania, Russia, and part of Italic, specially Venice and Rome. In Greece also a great multitude, wherein two Cities (beside all them of other places) Constantinople and Thessalonica are esteemed to bee about sixteene hundred thousand Jewes. As also they are to be found by plentifull numbers, in many parts of the Turkes Dominion, both in Asia and Afrike.

And for Asia, specially in Aleppo, in Tripoli, in Damascus, in Rhodes, and almost in everie Citie of great Trade and Traffique in the Turkish Empire: As likewise in divers parts of the Persian government, in Arabia also, and lastly in India (namely about Cranganor) and in some other more remote Regions. And, to come to Afrike, they are not only found in the Cities of Alexandria, and Cair in gypt, but, as in many other Regions and places of Afrike, so principally, in the Cities of Fez, and Tremisen: and specially, in the Hilles of Sensava, and Demen in the Kingdome of Maroccho, many of which last, are by Leo Africanus specially noted Leo African. to bee of that Sect, which the Jewes name Karraim, 2. r. 3. 6.

For of the Jewes, as touching their Religion, there be in these times three sects. The first which is the greatest of them, is named D' DS'n who beside the holy Scriptures, imbrace the Talmud also for Authenticall, and for that cause they are also termed D"'""Tl)a n The second are called a"'Nlp which receive onely the Scriptures. And the third Dins that is, the Samaritans (at this day but very few) which, of all the holy Scriptures, admit onely the Pentateuch or Bookes of Moses: of them all see my Pilgrimage Lib. 2.

I. i. 120. and by the other Jewes of Afrique, are reputed no better then Heretiques.

But yet, beside these, and such like dispersions of the Jewish Nation, that may be elsewhere in the world, there is a phantasie of many learned men, not unworthy some diligent consideration, that the Tartars of Scythia, who about the yeere 1200. or a little before, became first knowne abroad in the world by that name, and hold at this day a great part of Asia, in subjection: That Postel. De- those Tartars, I say, are of the Israelites progeny: script. Syrice. Namely of the ten Tribes, which by Salmanazar, and T ' rt ' some of his predecessours, were carried captive into . I. Boter. Assyria. Which although it be as 1 said no other then Relat. p. I. . a vaine and cappricious phantasie, yet, hath it, not onely 2. c. vitima found acceptance and entertainment, with sundry learned Tariar! a 3 " understanding men: but reason and authoritie are . 3. . 2. c. produced, or pretended to establish it for a truth. For de Gindei. first, It is alleadged that the word Tatari, or Totari Leunclav in (for SO indeede they are rightly called, as learned men Pandect. Hist, observe, and not Tartari) signifieth in the Syriaque and- Heb Hebrew tongues, a Residue or Remainder, such as these inxn Syr. Tartars are supposed to be of the Ten Tribes. Secondly, because (as the Patrons of this phantasie say) they have alwaies embraced (the ancient character of Judaisme) Circumcision. And thirdly, the authoritie of supposed z. Esd. 'i,. v. Esdras (the verie spring I take it, whence hath flowed 41. 42. 43. this streame of opinion) is alleadged. Namely, that ++ ' ' the Ten Tribes tooke this course to themselves, that they would leave the multitude of the heathen, and goe forth into a farther Countrie, where never mankinde dwelt. That they might there keepe their statutes, which they never kept in their owne land. And that they entred in at the narrow passages of the River Euphrates. The most high shewing them signes, and staying the Springs of the floud, till they were passed over. And, that their journey was great, even of a yeere and a halfe, and the region is called Arsareth.

But to the first of these arguments, I may answere, that the Tartars obtained that name, neither from Hebrew nor Syriaque originall, and appellation, but from the River Tartar, saith Leunclavius, and others. Or else Leundav. in from the Region, saith Haitho, where the principall of J;: " ' them anciently dwelled. Secondly, that the name nin Bomd'e or insn in the Hebrew or Syriaque signification, import- Mo?-ib. gent. ing a residue or remainder, can but full ill (as it seemes) . c. lo. be applied to the Tartars in relation of the Israelites, f ' ti. lib. de whom they exceedingly surpasse in multitude, as over- ' spreading halfe the vast continent of Asia, or thereabout. For all the Nations of Asia, from the great Rivers of Wolgha and Oby, Eastward, and from the Caspian Sea, the River Oxus, the Countries of India and China, Northward, are contained under the Appellation of Tartars: and yet without these bounds manie Tartars there are, both toward the West and South. And what if the innumerable people of so manie Nations, as are knowne to inhabit and overspread the huge continent of America, be also of the same of-spring."' Certainly, if I be not greatly deceived, they are no other. For first, that their originall must be derived from Asia is apparent, because (as he that readeth the relations and histories of those Countries of America may easily observe) they have no rellish nor resemblance at all, of the Arts, or learning, or civilitie of Europe: And their colour testifieth, they are not of the Africans progenie (there being not found in all that large Continent, any blacke men, except a few about the River of Saint Martha, in a small Countrie called Quarequa, which by force and violence of some tempest, are supposed to have beene transported thither, from the parts of Guinie or Ethiopia.) Therefore it seemeth, that they had their originall from

Asia. Which yet will appeare more credible, if it be observed, which by the Spaniards Discoveries is well known to be true, namely, that the West side of America respecting Asia, is exceeding much better peopled then the opposite or East side, that respecteth toward Europe. And, as for these reasons it is verie likely, that America received her first inhabitants, from the East border of Asia: So it is altogether unlike, that it received them from any other part of all that border, save from Tartarie. Because, in America there is not to be discerned, any token or indication at all, of the arts or industrie of China, or India, or Cataia, or anie other civill Region, along all that border of Asia: But in their grosse ignorance of letters, and of arts, in their Idolatrie, and the specialties of it, in their incivilitie, and many barbarous properties, they resemble the old and rude Tartars, above all the Nations of the Earth. Which opinion of mine, touching the Americans descending from the Tartars, rather then from any other Nation in that border of Asia, after the neere vicinitie of Asia to America, this reason above all other, may best establish and perswade: Because it is certaine, that that North-east part of Asia possessed by the Tartars, is if not continent with the West side of America, which yet remaineth somewhat doubtfull: but certainly, and without all doubt, it is the least disjoyned by Sea, of all that coast of Asia, for that those parts of Asia and America, are continent one with the other, or at most, disjoyned but by some narrow channell of the Ocean, the ravenous and harmelesse beasts, wherewith America is stored, as Beares, Lions, Tigers, Wolves, Foxes, c. (which men as is likely, would never to their owne harme transport out of the one continent to the other) may import. For from Noahs Arke, which rested after the I. i. 121. deluge, in Asia, all those beasts must of necessitie fetch their beginning, seeing they could not proceede by the course of nature, as the unperfect sort of living creatures doe, of Putrifaction: or if they might have Putrifaction for their parentage, or receive their originall (by any other new sort of generation) of the earth without speciall procreation of their owne kinde, then I see no necessitie why they should by Gods speciall appointment, be so carefully preserved in Noahs Arke (as they were) in time of the deluge. Wherefore, seeing it is certaine, that those ravenous beasts of America, are the progenie of those of the same kinde in Asia, and that men, as is likely, conveighed them not (to their owne prejudice) from the one continent to the other, it carrieth a great likelihood and appearance of truth, that if they joyne not together, yet are they neere neighbours, and but little disjoyned each from other, for even to this day, in the Isles of Cuba, Jamaica, Hispaniola, Burichena, and all the rest, which are so farre removed from the firme Land, that these beasts cannot swimme from it to them, the Spaniards record that none of these are found.

Wherefore it seemeth (to digresse no farther) that the

Nation of the Tartarians, spreading so exceeding farre, Josep. Amta as it doth, cannot certainly be the posterity of those datura captive Israehtes.

Neither (to answer the second objection) doth their circumcision in any sort inforce it: for, neither was circumcision, among the Tartars ancienter then Mahu- metanisme, but was received among them together with it, as Michovius hath remembred, so that to this day, Michov. de it is not intertained (for ought I can finde in Historie) Satmana.. i.

among those Tartarians, which have not received Ma- S i', rr,, o.,."., Tj 1 Of these Tar- numetanisme, but remame m their ancient Idolatrie, as tars See To. z.

for the most part, both the Tartars of Cataia, beyond . i y 2 In the Mountaine Imaus towards the East Ocean, and the b-Polo, Tartars of Sarmatia, towards the North, on both sides f f'y "' the River of Oby, doe. Neither if it should be granted, that circumcision had beene ancienter among them then Mahumetanisme, were that an argument of any importance, to prove them to be of the Israelites progenie. Because it is certainely knowne, that the ceremony and custome of circumcision hath beene and still is usuall Diodor. Sic. I. among many Nations, of whom there was never any 'tf,. i' 'f' suspition, that they descended rrom the Israelites, tor circum-Diodorus hath recorded of the Colchians, Philo Judaeus, cision. and Strabo, of the Egyptians, Herodotus of both those Strab. I. 16. Nations, and of the Ethiopians besides, that they used "" o-1--i-i y TT parum. amed.

Circumcision, and that that custome among the Egyptians '. j and Ethiopians, did seeme very ancient, even as it is long. post. med.

""Diodor. Sic. . 3. c. 3. Agatharchid. I. de Mar. Ruhr. c. 49. ap. Phot, in Bibliotheca Cyprian I. de circumcision, in principio. Nicepk. Cal-list. l. c. 35. Jeretn. 9. 26. Hieron. in Comment loci jam citati. Epiphan. Panar. I. i. h r. 30.

By Sozomcn I. 6. c. 38.

also by both those Nations retained till this day. And yet, beside these Countries already mentioned, the like is also recorded of the Troglodites by Strabo, and by "" others: Of the Phasnicians, and Arabians, by Cyprian and Nicephorus. And (to leave this accumulating of humaine testimonies) it is not obscurely acknowledged by the Prophet Jeremie, to have beene usuall (beside the Israelites) with the Egyptians, Edomites, Ammonites, Moabites, and the inhabitants of the desert, that is the Ismaelites, or Sarracens of Arabia: Of which Nations, Hierome also (to whom those regions were well knowne (as Epiphanius also of the most of them) hath left testified, that they retained circumcision, even in his time. Touching some of which, although it may be probably conjectured, that they received it (in some sort) from the Israelites: if not as their progenie (which yet in some sense may be said of the inhabitants of the desert, being the posteritie of Ismael the Sonne of Abraham: and likewise of the Edomites, being the seede of Esau, the sonne of Isaac) yet at least, by imitation of Abrahams familie, to whom also in bloud they were

For, that the Ismaelites and Sarracens are the same Nation, is manifest by Hierome, and Sozomen, and others, which being anciently termed Scenitas (as Ammianus hath observed) namely of the Graecians, airb Tuiv ffk-qvwv, because they dwelled in tents (for such to be the manner of their habitation, is not onely affirmed by Hierome Comment, in Isai ca. 21. Sozomen. Histor. 1 6. c. 38. Ammian. 1. 22. post. med. but signified, and not obscurely, by David Psal. 120. 5. vid. etiam Jerem, 49. 28. 29. lamenting his dwelling in the tents of "I P by which name Arabia deserta is termed in the Hebrew) were of their dwelling in the desert, by the Arabians themselves named Sarracens (for Sarra signifieth a desert, and Sakan to inhabit, in the Arabique tongue) or else, if not of their place, yet at least (as learned men certainely thinke, Scaliger in Animadv. Euseb. pa. 17. an. 88. Fuller. Miscellan. Theolog. 1, 2. c. 12. of their property, they might obtain that name of Sarracens, namely, because they lived much by rapine (for that the word Saracke in Arabique doth import) to which above all nations they ever were, and still are addicted. For the deduction of the name

Sarracens, from Sara, as if they claimed descent from her, being indeede Hagarens (the progeny of Hagar) is a meere fancy and fable. They claime it not.

allied, as the Ammonites and Moabites, the posteritie of Lot, Abrahams brothers sonne, and who had lived long in his familiaritie and familie. Although I say of these Nations it may be conjectured, that their cere-monie of circumcision was taken up, by imitation of the Israelites: yet that the same rite, or custome was also derived originally from them to the whole Nation of the Arabians (which was exceeding great) or to the-Egyptians, or other neighbouring Provinces, I know not why any should conceive, or if they doe, yet appeareth it to be otherwise, because they circumcised not in the eight day, which is the inviolable custome of the Israelites: but the Egyptians in the foureteenth yeere, as is recorded by Ambrose, and the Arabians in Ambr. l. z. d. the thirteenth (and some of them both sexes,) as learned h-men have recorded. Even as the ' Turkes also at this ' " '- day, who received the rite of circumcision from the Sard. dcr'ut Arabians, are knowne to circumcise in the eight or gent. l. x. cio. twelfth, or fifteenth yeere, or sooner or later, as oppor- Belkn. tunitie may serve. Of these Nations I say, how circum- g cj– cision should proceede from the Israelites to them, I vitr. I. z. de cannot conceive: no more then I can of the great Ritib Turcar. Nation of the Anzichi, on the West side of Nilus Cinum-beyond Nubia, or of the inhabitants of lucatan in ff7 221 America, whereof the first yet are, and the second (till pigafiu'de they came under the government of the Spaniards) were Re. Cong. meere Idolaters, for of these also, the second had, and- '- 5-the first still have circumcision in use.," '

And although these instances, utterly dissolve the loange force of this reason, touching the Tartarians circumcision (though it were admitted to have beene anciently in use among them, as being usuall with many other Nations, of whom no suspition at all can be conceived, to be of the Israelites progenie) yet this may furthermore declare them, not to be of that race, because namely, nothing else was to be found among them, that might savour of Israel. For first, they were meere Idolaters, and without knowledge of the true God, as

"Paul. Venet. I. 3. c. 47. Ha'ith. I. de Tartar, c. i.

Vicent. Spec. Historialis I. 32. r. 6. Paul. Venet. I. c. 55. Guiliel de Rubri. Itin. Tartar, c. 9.

Sigism. com. Rer. Moscov. Guil. de Ru-bricislttnerer. Tartar. I. 5. Boem. de Morib. gen tium. l. z. c. io. Hero dot. I. 4. lian. de Animalib. I. 10. c. 17. Esd. 2. 13.

Vers. 39. ' Vers. 41.

is recorded by Marcus Paulus, by Haitho, and others. Secondly, they had no remembrance of the Law at all. Thirdly, they neither observed the Sabboath, nor other rites and ceremonies of the Israelites: but touching their Matrimonies, married without impeachment the verie "" wives, and sisters of their Fathers: and touching their feeding, abstained not at all from uncleane Beasts, but fed on the flesh of Horses, Dogges, Cats, and dead Carrion, and drunke their bloud, all utterly forborne and forbidden among the Israelites. Fourthly, they have no records, nor regard of their ancestors and linage, from whom, or by whom, they are descended, whereof Israelites were ever curious. Fifthly, they have no affinitie of language at all, with either the Hebrew or Chaldee tongues, neither had any use of those Letters, nor of any other, till together with Mahumetan Religion, the Arabique characters came in use among some of them. Neither (in a word) doe I finde any thing at all, wherein the Tartarians savored of Israelites; for touching their abstinence from Swines flesh, which we finde recorded of them, neither is it generall among them, but peculiar to those that are Mahumetans: Nor if it were so, were that any good argument, because we know that the ancient Scythians, and iegyptians, and Arabians did, and almost all Mahumetans at this day doe the same, which yet are well knowne to be in no sort descended from the Israelites.

Now touching the authoritie of forged- Esdras, which hath stirred up as it seemeth this vapourous fantasie, in the braines of new fangled antiquaries: neither doth that which he writeth of the ten Tribes, agree at all with the Tartars: nor, if it did, could yet the circumstances of that historie agree with the truth. It agrees not with the Tartars I say, for whereas they are noted in that Revelation, to be a peaceable people, and that they 'left the multitude of the heathen, that they might keepe their statutes, which they never kept in their owne land: neither of both those properties hath any convenience or agreement at all with the Tartarians. For how are they a peaceable people, that with their warres have troubled and overturned almost all Asia, and sundry Countries of Europe, and hold a great part of the former in subjection to this day? Or how kept they the statutes of the Israelites, that were meere Idolaters, and utterly ignorant of all Jewish Lawes and Ceremonies? And touching the Historie it selfe of the Israelites departure out of Assyria, as it is set downe in that Apocriphall Esdras (howsoever it might otherwise agree with the Tartars) there is no wise or considerate man, I thinke, that can bring his understanding to give credit to it. For first it contradicteth the undoubted canonicall histories of the Chronicles, and of the Kings, in both which i Chro. t. zs. it is recorded of them, that they were carried away into 2 '"- 7-23-Ashur, and disposed in severall parts of the Empire namely Calach, and Chabor, and Hara, and Gozan, unto this day; which limitation of time (unto this day) must at least of necessitie import, the time wherein that Historie (of their remaining in Ashur) recorded in the bookes of the Kings, of the Chronicles was written. Of which later, either Esdras himselfe was the Author, as in the judgement "of learned men he is reputed, and ""R-Dav. therefore could not (as it seemeth) be the Author of 'T' ' that Apocryphall Historie: or, at least, if Esdras were sententia seni- ovum apud If ftpn be Cholchi, and "mm Iberia, j. ' ft Armenia, so called Sixi. Senens. for the mountainousnesse of it) "jn Gauzania in Media, then al Biblioih. confined together, bounded the North side of the Assyrian Empire, Sanct l. i. which stretched Northward, but to that Isthume betweene the Euxine the Caspian Seas: So that, the Israelites were by that meanes, seated farthest off from their owne Country, and placed in the parts of the Empire most wast desolate of inhabitants, as the confines of warring Nations usually are. But if Calach be Calacine, and Chabor the hill Chaboras (being part of Taurus, and severing Assyria, from Armenia, and Media) and Hara the other hilly parts in the North side of Assyria, as seemeth more agreeable to the observations of Benjamin Tudelensis, for about those parts, hee found in his travaile, the greatest multitudes of the Israelites, then in the places alleadged, I would understand by Ashur, not the Empire or Dominion, but the peculiar Kingdome of Assyria.

Abukns. in not the Author, yet, that the Author (whosoever he was) praf. Paralt-i vcd and writ that historie of the Chronicles, after the thn- " returne of the Jewes from the captivitie, or in the end of it (that is in Esdras time) is evident by the end of the Book: where Cyrus his benignitie, for restoring the Jewes, and his Proclamation for their returne to Jerusalem is recorded, and that in the verie same words, wherein Esdras in the beginning of his owne booke hath registred them. At that time therefore, it is evident, that the Israelites were not departed out of the Josepa. Jfitic. dominions of Ashur. No nor long after that in Josephus . II. r. j js time, who hath recorded that even then the ten

Tribes remained beyond Euphrates, and were there growne into innumerable mul-titudes: neither yet manie hundred yeeres after Josephus was dead; for R. Benjamin I. i. 123. a Jew, that lived but about 440. yeeres ago, and travailed diligently those parts of the world, and many other to Benjamin in visite his dispersed Countrimen, hath in his Itinerary Ittner. p. 57. Yq observed, not onely, that he found exceeding farre. " g ' greater multitudes of the Israelites, to be then remain-78.80.81.86. ing in those Provinces of the ancient Dominion of P g- 75- Ashur then he found in other places, possessing large f7- Regions, and ' many Cities, so that in the Cities of some Pae ' ead ' ' ' Region 300000. Jewes were by him numbred, observing specially, that in the parts of Media, many thousand Israelites of the progeny of them that Salma-naser led into captivity, were then remaining, but withall, he setteth downe particularly and precisely, the very places of those Regions, where certaine of the Tribes were seated and there growne into great multitudes: as Pag. 77. namely, in " one place, the Tribes of Ruben, Gad, and "Pag. 87. Manasse: And in ' another, the foure Tribes of Dan, Asher, Zebulon, and Nephtali.

But yet if there were neither authoritie of holy Scripture, nor experience to refell this fable, and the fancies that have sprung of it: yet ordinary reason, at least of men that are not ignorant of Geography and are meanly skilled in the affaires of the world, may easily discerne the futilitie of it. For first, what neede was there of such a miracle, as to "stay the course of z Esdr. 13.

Euphrates, for the Israelites passage from Assyria, or d hemost

Media toward Tartary, the River lying farre to the Jf J

West, both of the one Region and of the other, and signes and no way crossing or impeaching their journey, which lay stated the

Northward betweene that River and the Caspian Sea? '" '" f

Or, how might those poore captive Israelites, disarmed- tuuhn' as they were, and dispersed in sundry Provinces of the were passed

Assyrian Empire, and being under the oversight over. vers.

government of Assyrian Presidents, be able to leave the places, where by the Kings commandement they were to inhabite? Or, if the Israelites were able by force to depart, and free themselves from the dominion of the

King of Ashur, yet were they so wise also, as to for- They tooke this sake the places where they were peaceably setled, and ' ' .,1 11-J.1 J themselves that venture their small remamders upon perils and uncer-, tainties, namely, to finde out a place where never man- kave the mul- kinde dwelt? Or, if their stomacke served them so titude of the well, and their wit so ill, as in such manner to forsake hen.

Assyria, yet were they also able to make themselves " ' way (even a way as hee saith, of eighteene moneths passage) through the fierce and mighty Nations of

Scythia, whom neither the conquerors of the Israelites, the Assyrians I meane, nor the Persians (and I might adde also the Grecians and the Romans) were never able to subdue, but were in the aftertimes subdued by them? for that the parts of Scythia should be without Inhabitants (and in Scythia it must be where they would finde that Country where never mankinde dwelt, or else And goe forth it is not in Tartary) is scarse credible, as whereof we o a Country reade in histories, to have contended with gypt for Ziankindt antiquitie of habitation, and to have prevailed, and for dwelt, v. 41.

the abundance of people, to be termed Hominum

Officina. Insomuch that the greatest occasion of swarming abroad of those Nations of Scythia, and of their overwhelming of Asia and Europe, with Justin, hist.

their infinite multitudes and Colonies, is in histories ' princip.

recorded, to be lacke of roome for habitation in their owne Countries.

And lastly, to make an end of this tedious discourse, with the end of their imagined tedious journey: what ancient Geographer or Historian is there (set our Esdras aside) that ever remembred of such a Region as Arsa-reth, where they are said to have seated themselves. True it is indeede that I finde the Citie of Arsaratha Beros. I. 3. mentioned both in Berosus fragments, and in Ptolomie Ptole. Georg. placed neere the issue of the River Araxes into the in Tab Caspian Sea: and, it was perhaps one of the Israelitish Jsice. Colonies, planted in the confines of the Empire of

Assyria: for it may well be that Arsaratha, is but n' 'ikid T'3?, or ri""nn'a5 in, that is the Citie, or the bill of the remainder, or perhaps nns'u: y x (the last letter of the first word cut off in the Greeke pronunciation for sounds sake) the Land of the remainder: but the tale of eighteene months journey, will no more agree with this Citie, then the Region of Arsareth doth, with Geography or History.

So that me thinkes this forged storie of the Israelites voiage and habitation, in such remote regions where never mankinde dwelt, savoureth of the same phantas-""Esd. 6.42. ticall and Talmudicall spirit, that ""another tale of the same author doth, touching the collection of all the waters, into a seaventh part of the earth, the other six "Cap. eod. being left uncovered: or" a third, of (the Elephant- 5 and the Whale) Behemoth and Leviathan: namely, that

God appointed the Sea to one of them, and the Land to the other, because they were so great that the Sea could not hold them both: for else belike, if the Sea had beene large enough, we might have gone a fishing for Elephants. For how is the Sea gathered into a seaventh part of the earth, whose expansion is not onely by the most skilfull Philosophers esteemed, but found by experience of navigations hitherto made, to overspred as neerely as may be discerned, about halfe the compasse of the Earth Or being of that breadth, and withall of the depth, that it is knowne to be, how should it not be spacious enough, to receive Elephants and Whales together? The dimensions of the Elephant, even of the greatest sort of Indian Elephants, (and the earth breedeth none so large as those of India) are, saith lianus, nine cubits of height (the length in that Han de beast is equall to the height) and five of breadth, the ' l- I-greatest that have beene seene in Europe, being ob- Ipj ' qizj served to be farre lesse. The dimension of the Whale in Description. indeede is farre greater (five times saith P lianus then

Elephant. cs. the largest sort of Elephants.) But yet his ordinary dimension is but six and thirty cubits long;, and eipfht ' P-1- cubits high, as Rondeletius hath observed. But admit y, notwithstanding some of them to be fiftie cubits, of which p lian. Li6. length, Nearchus in Arrianus is said to have measured- one in the East Ocean; nay, to be six hundred foot f' 'lt J' ' g long, and three hundred and sixtie foot thicke, as "Juba c" in Plinie related to be found in the Bay of Arabia Arrian. de (where yet, as it is well knowne by the soundings of- indicis. Navigators, that Sea is not by a good deale three! ' " hundred and sixtie foote deepe.) Or, let them be more ri"Ti24l yet, even foure Acres long (that is nine hundred and Jp. Plin. I. sixtie foot) as Plinie hath related of some in the Sea 32. c. 2. of India. For, although the two last reports be in truth '–9–3-no better then fancies and fables, which the impudence of some, hath made the ignorance of others to beleeve, yet I will exclude none, but onely Basil, as intollerably Basilin Hex-hyperbolicall, affirming namely that Whales are equall f" "-Homil. to the greatest mountaines, and their backs when they 7 shew above the water, like to Islands, But admitting all the rest I say, what proportion have those dimensions of the Whale and the Elephant, to the huge bredth and depth of the Ocean

For if I may without offence intersert a short Philo-sophicall speculation: the depth of the Sea (to speake Fabian apud nothing of the breadth, which every common Map doth– represent) is determined by Fabianus in Plinie, by Meteor7"i Cleomedes, to be fifteene furlongs, that is, one mile and c. 10. ' 337 Y seven eight parts: Or else, equall to the height of the greatest Mountaines, to whose height, and the deepe-

Pluiarch in nesse of the Sea, the Geometricians (as Plutarch hath

Vita jemilu recorded) anciently assigned equall dimensions. Or yet rather (if you will any thing respect my opinion) it is a great deale more. For, as for the shallow speculation

Scalig. de Sub- of Scaliger, and others, of the shallownesse of the Sea, tihtate Exerc. determining the height of Hils, farre to surpasse the h J J v deepenesse of the Sea: And that in very few places, ce Thermis. I. It attameth one hundred passes or depth, is mdeede . c. Alii, true in the narrow Channels and Straits of the Sea:

But in the free and large Ocean, it is by the experience of Navigators knowne to be as false as the Gospell is true. Indeede touching the height of Mountaines, I finde it pronounced by the great Mathematician Eratos-

Theon. hicom- thenes in Theon, that the highest sort of them, passe ment. Magna! Qt in perpendicular erectnesse ten furlongs (that is one 'plolomti' " " fourth part) of which height also, it is

Plin. l. 2. observed in Plinie, that Dicasarchus by Dioptricall Instru- 63. ments, found the Hill Pelius in Thessalie to be, and

Plutarch, he. in Plutarch, that Xenagoras (another Mathematician) supra citato, observed the height of Olympus, in the same Region, saving, that in this later, there is an addition of twenty passes, for the whole number of passes, is 1270.

Neither doe I finde any greater perpendicular height

Cleomed. I. i, attributed to Mountaines, by any ancient writer, Cleo-

Meteor. c. io. niedes excepted: who assigneth to the height of Hils, as he doth also to the depth of the Sea, fifteene fur-

Alhazen de longs. (For Alhazen I omit, because he onely restraineth

Crepuscl. the height of hils, as namely, not to exceede eight miles, propos. I. without determining what their height should be). But yet, all these, are to be understood, I take it, with relation to the Mountanes in and about Greece, with which themselves were acquainted, which may in no sort compare with the huge Mountaines of vast Continents, such as are the Alpes in Europe, Atlas in Afrique,

Caucasus in India, the Andes in Peru, and such other.

But, whatsoever the height of Hils may be above the common superficies of the Earth, it seemeth to me after good consideration, that the depth of the Sea is a great deale more. For declaration of which point, I require to be supposed, first, that the Earth at the first forming of it, was in the superficies, regular, and sphericall: which the Holy Scripture directs us to beleeve, because the water covered and compassed all the face of the Earth: And secondly, that the face of the Land is in largenesse and expansion, at least equall to that of the Sea: And thirdly, that the unevennesse and irregularitie, which is now seene in the superficies of the Earth was caused (as is noted in Damascen) either, by taking some Damascen. I. parts out of the upper face of the Earth in sundry- fi places, to make it more hollow, and laying them in ' other places, to make it more convexe: Or else (which in effect is equivolent to that) by raising up some, and depressing others to make roome and receit for the Sea: that mutation being wrought by the power of that word. Let the waters be gathered into one place, that Genes, i. 9. the dry land may appeare. For, as for the fancy of Aquinas, Dionysius, Catharinus, and some other Divines; Aquin. in namely, that that gathering of waters, and discovery of- f– 1-the Earth, was made, not by any mutation in the Earth, n " ' I,, but by a violent accumulation ot the waters, or heaping Cathann. tff them up on high, it is too unreasonable. Because it is AH. in Com-utterly against the nature of water, being a flexible "- ' P- ' ponderous body, so to consist, and stay it selfe, " ' not fall to the lower parts about it, where in nature there is nothing at all to hinder it. Or, if it be hindered and restrained supernaturally, by the hand and bridle of the almighty, lest it should overwhelme and drowne the Land, it must follow thereof, that God in the very institution of nature, imposed a perpetual! violence upon nature: And this withall, that at the Deluge, there had beene no necessity at all, to breake up the springs of the deepe, and to open the Cataracts of Heaven, and powre down water continually, so many dayes and nights together upon the Earth, seeing, the onely withdrawing of that hand, or letting goe of that bridle, which restrained the water, would presently have overwhelmed all.

But to come to the Point. It seemeth upon the former suppositions (of which, the holy Scripture estab-lisheth the first. Experience of Travellers, and Navigators the second, and Reason the third) that in making estimation of the depth of the Sea, are not to reckon and consider onely, the height of the Hils, above the common superficies of the Earth, unto which the extraordinary depths or whirlpooles, that are found in the Sea, doe properly answere (descending beneath the ordinary bottome of the Sea, as the Hils ascend above the I. i. 125. ordinary face of the Land) but, the advantage or height of al the dry land above the Superficies of the Sea. Because the whole Masse of the Earth, that now appeareth above the waters, beeing taken as it were out of the place, which the waters now possesse, must be equall to the place out of which it was taken, and consequently it seemeth, that the height or elevation of the one, should answere the depth or descending of the other. And therefore as I said, in estimating the deepnesse of the Sea, wee are not to consider onely the erection of the Hils, above the ordinary Land, but the advantage of all the dry Land above the Sea. Which later, I meane the height of the ordinary maine Land, (even excluding the Hils) is in my opinion more in large Continents above the Sea, then that of the Hils, is above the Land.

For first, that the plaine and common face of the dry Land, is not levell, or equally distant from the Centre, but hath great declivitie and descent toward the Sea, and acclivitie or rising toward the Mid-land parts, although it appeare not so to the common view of the Eye, is to reason notwithstanding manifest. Because as it is found in that part of the Earth, which the Sea covereth that it descendeth lower, and lower toward the middest of the Sea (for the Sea which touching the upper face of it, is knowne to be levell by nature, and evenly distant from the Centre, is withall observed to waxe deeper and deeper, the farther one sayleth from the shoare toward the Maine) Even so, in that part which is uncovered, the coursings and streamings of Rivers on all sides from the mid-land parts toward the Sea, whose propertie we know is to slide from the higher to the lower, evidently declare so much.

And although I am not able precisely to determine, what the ordinarie declivitie of the earth may be, yet, if that bee convenient in the workes of Nature, which is required in the workes of Art, that imitateth Nature, it will be found true that before I said: Namely, that in great Continents, through which Rivers have long Courses, some of one thousand or two thousand miles the height of the ordinarie Midland, above the face of the Sea, is more, then of the Hilles above the common face of the earth, for Pliny in the derivation of water, PUn. . 31. requireth one cubit of declining, in two hundred and–

By which rule of the proceeding of the Rivers by the proclivitie of the earth, ever sliding from the higher ground to the lower, till they come to the Sea, is evident to be discerned, that in Continents, those Regions are the higher Land from which Rivers streame, and those the lower ground, to which they proceed, and consequently, that of all, those are the highest which receiving no forreine Rivers, to which they give passage through them, doe send forth the longest Rivers on all sides to the Regions round about them. By which observation is to be discerned, that Helvetia and Rhetia, sending forth the longest Rivers of Europe, which on all sides descend from them and their Confines, Danubius toward the East, Rhene North, Rhodanus West, beside Ticinus, Addua, and others, that fall into Padus South, are the highest Land of Europe, As the Region of Pamer, and Kir-gessi, with some other neere the crossing of the great Mountaines Taurus and Imaus above India, whence are directed, the greatest and longest Rivers of Asia, Indus and Ganges toward the South, Oxus and Jaxartus toward the West, Oechardes North, Cantan East, is prooved by the same reason, to be the highest part of Afrike and Asia, and in my opinion of all the Earth. And as the Region also about the Springs of Nilus, from which beside Nilus, that runneth towardes the North, are sent forth, the River of Magnice, towardes the South, of Zaire West, of Coavo and Zuama East, being (Niger excepted) the greatest Rivers of Afrike, is by the same reason, prooved to bee, the highest part of that Continent.

Columell. de Re Rustica. L 5. c. 1. Vitruv. Archi-tectur. I. 8. f. 7. Pa Had. de re Rustica. I. 9. ; . 11.

Philand. in Vitruv. I. 8. c, i.

fortie foot of proceeding (for he saith, unum cubitum in binos Actus, and Actus as may be observed in Columella, and others in a dimension of one hundred and twentie foot long) Vitruvius and Palladius in their conduction of waters, require indeed somewhat lesse, namely, that in proceeding of two hundred foot forward there should be allowed one foot of descending downward, which yet in the course of one thousand miles (as Danubius or Wolgha, or Indus, c. have so much or more) will make five miles of descent in perpendicular account: And in the course of two thousand or more (as Nilus and Niger, and the River of Amazons have) ten mile or more of like descent.

And although I know well enough, that water being (as it is) heavie and flexible, will slide away at any inequalitie, and therefore am altogether perswaded, that this rule of Vitruvius touching conveyance of waters, is not to be taken as a rule of necessitie, to bee observed in the deriving of them, as if water could not runne without that advantage (for in that respect the Conveyors of waters of these times content themselves even with one inch in sixe hundred foot, as Philander also on Vitruvius, hath observed) but is rather to be understood as a rule of commodity, namely with relation to the expedition and wholesomenesse of the water so conveyed, lest resting too long in the pipes it should contract from them some unwholesome qualitie, or else through the slacknesse ot motion, or long closenesse, or banishment from the Aire, it might gather some aptnesse and disposition to putrifie. Although I say, such excesse of advantage as in the artificiall conveyance of waters the forenamed Authors require, be not of necessitie exacted, in the naturall derivation of them: yet neverthelesse certaine it is, that the descent of Rivers, being as it is continual, and the course of some of them very long, and in many places swift, and here, and there headlong and furious, the difference of height or advantage, cannot but bee great, betwixt the Springs of Rivers and their Out-lets, betwixt their first rising out of the Earth, and their falling into the Sea.

Unto which declivitie of the Land, seeing the deepnesse of the Sea doth in proportion answer (as I before declared) and not onely to the height of Hils. It remayneth that we esteeme and determine that deepnesse to be a great I. i. 126. deale more, then it hath beene hitherto by Philosophers commonly reputed. And although the deepnesse of the Sardinian Sea, (which indeed Aristotle acknowledgeth Arist. Met. I. for the deepest part of the Mediterranean) be specially– recorded by Posidonius in Strabo, to have beene found Strab. L i. but one thousand fadomes (opyfxa?) which is but a mile WP and one fift part: yet what may the depth in that narrow Sea be, compared to the hollow deepnesse of the vast Ocean? Or rather (to turne this instance to our advantage) if in so narrow a Sea as the Mediterrane is (whose breadth attaineth not where it is largest, sixe hundred miles) the depth bee so great, what may wee esteeme the deepnesse of the huge Ocean to be, that is in many places above five times as broad? especially, seeing that the broader that Seas are, if they be withall entire, and free from Hands, they are answerably observed to be the deeper.

But whether have I bin carried by these Elephants and Whales? to what heights and depths, of Mountaines and Seas: I pray you pardon me, for I see I have digressed, that is, transgressed, now I returne into the way againe.

NOw, if out of the former long discourse, I should 0th quan- collect a short summe, and estimate the proportion f dpro- with respect to the whole Earth, that each one of the p. y forementioned Religions, have to the other. It being first Earth, posses-supposed, which upon exact consideration and calculation, sed by the will be found to swerve very little from the truth, that everall sorts the proportions of Europe, Afrike, Asia, and America, are igjif fj as one, three, foure, and seven. And that the professors religions.

of the forementioned Religions, possesse the severall Ch. 14. portions and proportions, of each of them, which is before

Postel. in Prof. Gram. Jrabic. Lud. Regius de Vicessitud. Rerum. I. 8. i7i fine.

set downe: It will be found I say upon these suppositions (which the best Geographic, and Histories doe perswade me to be true) that Christians possesse, neere about a sixt part of the knowne inhabited Earth: Mahu-metans, a fift part (not as 'some have exceedingly over-lashed, halfe the World or more) and Idolaters, two thirds, but little lesse. So that if we divide the knowne

Regions of the World, into thirtie equall parts, the Christians part is as five, the Mahumetans as sixe, and the Idolaters as nineteene, for the poore dispersed and distressed Christians, which are found in Asia and Afrike, mingled among Mahumetans and Idolaters, 1 receive not into this account, both because they are but thinne dispersed, in respect of the multitudes of Mahumetans and Idolaters in those Regions among whom they live (beeing withall under their dominion) and because also, many Mahumetans, are found mingled among Christians in Europe, to recompence and countervaile a great part of that number.

Such therefore may be the generall proportion of Christians to Mahumetans and Idolaters, in the Continents of the Earth hitherto discovered, namely, in this our neighbour Continent of the East comprehending Europe, Afrike, and Asia, and in that other Continent of the West, called America, and in the Hands belonging to them both. But if the South or Antarctique Continent, be so large, as I am verily perswaded it is (even no lesse, then that of the East before mentioned, which contayneth Europe, Afrike and Asia together) then will the Idolaters be found to surpasse all the other Religions, in exceeding great proportion, for that the Inhabitants of that South Continent are Idolaters, there is no question at all (as I take it) to be made, both because in the parts hitherto knowne, as namely in the Region of Beach, over against Java, they were found to be so: And also, because they are knowne to be no other then Idolaters, that inhabite all those parts of the other Continents, that neighbour most towards them, from whom it is likely, they should have received the change of their Religion, if any were: for first, in Asia, both India, and the Hands of the Indian Sea, whereof some lie close on the South Continent. Secondly, in Afrike, the Regions about the Cape of Buona Speranza. And thirdly, in America, the Countries that border on Magaglians Strait, which are the neerest Neighbours to the foresaid Continent of the South, are knowne to be all over-spread with Idolaters.

Now that the South Continent is no lesse then I before esteemed it, namely, then that of Asia, Afrike, and Europe altogether, although I might be probably induced to beleeve so, because it is well knowne, both (touching Latitude) to approach in some parts neere the Equator, and (touching Longitude) to runne along in a continuall circuite about the Earth, fronting both the other Continents: Yet have I also another reason of more certaine importance, to perswade me: Namely, because it is well knowne, that the land to the North side of the Line, in the other Continents (the old and new world) yet altogether is at least foure times as large as that part of them which lieth to the South.

Now, for as much as it is certaine, first by Archimedes Arch'm. de his rule, that the face of the Sea, is in all parts naturally l ' dentib,

Aquce I. I.

For touching the first of these suppositions. It is the propertie Propos. 2. of water, ever to fall that way, where it findeth declivitie. Wherefore, if the water, in the upper face of it, were higher in one place then in another it would necessarily fall from the higher position to the lower, because it is heavie and flexible, and hath nothing in the open and free Sea, to let or hinder it: And consequently, would never rest setled and stable, till the face of it were levelled, in an even distance from the Centre.

And touching the second, if the Earth were unequally poysed on opposite sides of the centre, then must it follow, that the least and lighter masse of the Earth should presse downe as forcibly, as the greater and weightier, because it attaineth the centre as well as it. But if it be granted, which reason doth inforce, that the weightier part of the Earth should presse downward, with greater force, and with more right challenge the centre, then the lighter part: it must follow, that the lighter masse or side of the Earth, must yeeld and give place to the weightier, so farre, till the centre of that whole masse of the Earth take possession of the centre of the world (for level, or equally distant from the center of the water, for which equalitie, it hath obtained the name of-quor,

""Farro. I. 6. and Aqua, as Grammarians say " And secondly, by the ff 'J'f: Philosophers knowne rule, that the Earth, is equally poysed " x 'c T"' owne centre. And thirdly, that y Jlii. the center of the Earth and of the water are al one (both of them being indeed no other then the centre of the World) which though some phantastical heads have called into question, yet no sound Philosopher ever doubted of: It followeth thereupon, that the I. i. 127. earth should in answerable measure and proportion, lift it selfe and appeare above the face of the Sea, on the South side of the Line, as it doth on the North. And consequently, that what is wanting in the South parts of the two foresaid Continents towards the countervailing of the North parts (which is about three five parts of both the other Continents layed together) must of necessity be supplied in the continents of the South. And yet I omit all the Land that may bee about the Artique Pole, beyond the Scythian or Sarmatian Sea, which must be also counterpoysed in that Antarctike continent, for nothing comes within the compasse of my understanding, to till then, one side will be still heavier then the other) and so the opposite halfes of the Earth, in respect of heavinesse, be brought on all sides, about the centre, unto a perfect equilibration.

And the third may be established, by manifest demonstration. Because, a clod of Earth, suffered to fall from any point of the Aire, wheresoever on the face of the Sea (the same doth water, falling on even and plalne Land) when all is calme, and the Aire not troubled with winds, nor the Sea with waves, will descend by a perpendicular line, on the face of the water. In such sort I say, that the line by which it falleth maketh exactly equall and right Angles on all sides, with the face of the water whereon it falleth. Therefore it is manifest, that the Earth so falling, tendeth directly to the centre of the water. Because no straight line insisteth perpendicularly, on the face or circumference of any special bodie (as the water is) except only those that proceed directly to the centre of the Sphere: But certaine it is, that the Earth is withall directly carried toward its owne centre, therefore there is but one common centre of the Water and of the Earth.

be hereto replyed, except any would perhaps imagine, that either the Sea on the South side of the Equator, is very shallow, or that the land of that continent may be much higher above the face of the Sea, then the land of the other two (and so equall in masse, though lesse in circuit) or that the Earth on the South side of the Equator, should be of a more ponderous disposition, then on the North, in which cases, some compensation of weightinesse, may be made for the want of extention. But of these three, the experience of Saylers evidently repelleth the first: who in equall distance from the Land, observe an equall deepnesse of the Sea, in both South and North Latitude. And neither is there any experience, nor good reason that can be alleadged to establish either of the later: which, but that I have alreadie too much offended by digressions, I could prove I doubt not against all exception. ' But this for a conclusion to this discourse, I dare pronounce touching that South continent, that it will certainly be found (in the after-times, when it shall bee better discovered) much larger then any Globe or Map hitherto extant, hath represented it.

Such therefore (as I have declared) is the generall state of Christianitie at this present in the World, and the proportion of it to other Religions. But because you require yet further to bee specially informed of the divers sorts and sects of Christians that are abroad in the World, and withall of their divers Regions and Religions, at least of those princi-pall Characters of their Religion, wherein they specially differ each from other, I will here set downe my second period, touching the generall differences of Religions, and of the severall parts of the World where they are maintayned: and will now proceed to that particular consideration touching the Sects of Christianitie, and indeavour to give you the best satisfaction that my poore reading, and observation may inable me to performe.

Of the divers 'T He Sects therefore of Christians, that carrie name

Zfczitia report at this present in the World, beside in the World Protestants and Romans in the West, of whom I and of their will be silent, because you know their condition better several! Regi then my selfe. are i the Grecians, 2 Melchites or ons And first Syrians, 7 Georgians, 4 Moscovites and Russians, c ofthegrecmns,-. i t i 11 a-i r c 1

Chap i: Nestorians, 6 Indians tearmed the Christians or baint

Thomas, 7 Jacobites, 8 Cophites, 9 Armenians, 10 Habassines, and 11 Maronites. Of which eleven Sects, there be three Principall, namely the Grecians, Jacobites and

Nestorians, with which the rest have, for the most part, either some dependance and derivation, or neerer convenience and agreement.

The Grecians acknowledg obedience to the Patriarch of Constantinople, under whose Jurisdiction are in Asia, Bellon. Obser. the Christians of Natolia (excepting Armenia the lesse, . c. 35. j j Cilicia) of Circassia, of Mengrelia, and of Russia: As in Europe also, the Christians of Greece, Macedon, Epirus, Thrace, Bulgaria, Rascia, Servia, Bosina, Wala-chia, Moldavia, Podolia, and Moscovia: together with all the Hands of the Egean Sea, and others about Greece, as farre as Corfu, beside a good part of the large dominion of Polonia, and those parts of Dalmatia, and of Croatia, that are subject to the Turkish dominion.

Of which great extendment of the Greeke Patriarchs Jurisdiction, if you demand the reason: I have observed sundry occasions, from whence it hath proceeded. For I. i. 128. first, his originall or Primitive authoritie assigned, or rather confirmed to him (as Bishop of the Imperiall Concil. Chal- Citie) by the Councell of Chalcedon; contained all cedonens. Provinces of Thrace, and Anatolia (Isauria, and

Cilicia only excepted, which belonged to the Patriarke of Antiochia) and they were in all no lesse then twentie eight Romane Provinces. Secondly, the voluntary submission of the Grecians, upon their separation from the Latine Church greatly increased it: for thereby not onely Greece, Macedon, Epirus, Candie, and the lies about Greece (in all seven Provinces) came under his obedience; but also Sicilie, and the East point of Italy, named Calabria, revolted from the Bishop of Rome, and for a long time pertained to the Patriarke of Constantinople, as appeareth in the Novell of Leo l ovell. Leon. Sophus, touching the order and precedence of Metro- ordine politans, belonging to that Patriarchy. And by the iji "-l l ii'i like ordination set downe by Andronicus Paloeologus, juris Orlen-in Curopalates, where wee find the Metropolitans of talis. Curo-Syracusa, and Catana in Sicilie, of Rhegium, Severiana, palat. de Offic Rosia, and Hydruntum in Calabria, registred among the gp' "' Metropolitans of that Jurisdiction. Thirdly, it was propefinem. inlarged by the conversion of the North Regions to the Christian Religion, performed by his Suffragans and Ministers, even from Thrace to Russia, and the Cromer de-Scythian Sea (the like whereof was the principall "" P- J '-cause, that so farre inlarged the Bishop of Rome his; J ' Jurisdiction in the West parts of Europe.) And i. i. Guagi fourthly, by the Turkes conquests made upon the Descript. c Westerne Countries, subject before to the Bishop of o ' """- Rome: all which, while partly the former Bishops and Pastors fled, to avoid the Turkes oppression (like the hireling that forsaketh the flocke, when he seeth the wolfe comming) and partly, while the Patriarke of Constantinople, to supply that default, was faine to provide them of new ministers, they have beene by little and little brought and trayned to the Greeke Religion.

Now as touching the proper Characters of their Religion, I must for the better designing and remembring of them, set before mee some instance or patterne to compare it, and other sects of Religion withall: And that is most fit to be the Romane Church, both because their differences with that Church specially, are in Writers most observed. So that, by that meanes my discourse may bee the shorter, and yet no lesse perspicuous to you, that know the opinions of the Romane Church so well. The principall Characters then of the 'uin. on 1. Concil. Florent. Sess. i8. y seque-tib. Jerem. Patriarch. Constant, in Resp. I. ad Germanos. c. i.

2. Concil. Florent. prope Initium. Re-spons. Grcec. ad car din. Guisan. Quest. 9.

3. Resp. ead gracor. g. 5. Jerem. Patr. Resp. I. c. I, 4. Jerem. Resp. ead.

5. Possevin. de Rebus Mosco-vice pag. 43.

6. Id. I. cita. p. 40.

7. Jerem. Re-spons. cap. 2 i. k. Tom. unionis inter novel. Constantin. Porphyrogen. in Tomo. i. Jur. Orien-talis. lib. 2. Zonar. Annal. Tom. 3. in Imp. Leonis philosophi.

9. Resp. Gra-cor ad Guisan. Qu st. S. Possevin. de reb. Moscov. p. W- 10. Possev. I. citat. . 41.

Grecian Religion (for none but the principall you require) and to mention every slender difference of Ceremonies, would be but tedious and fruitlesse (and is beside without my compasse) are these that follow.

1. That the Holy Ghost proceedeth from the Father onely, not from the Sonne.

2. That there is no Purgatory fire.

3. That they celebrate the Sacrament of the Eucharist in both kinds.

4. And in leavened bread, and thinke it cannot bee effectually consecrated in bread unleavened.

5. That they reject extreame Unction. 6. And Confirmation.

7. That they deny the soules of holy men to enjoy the blissefull vision of God, or the soules of wicked men to bee tormented in Hell, before the Day of Judgement. Th. a Jes. de Conv. gent. 1. 6. c. i.

8. That they admit Priests marriages, namely, so that they may keepe their wives married before their Ordination, but must not marry after Ordination.

9. That they prohibite utterly the fourth marriage, as a thing intolerable. Insomuch, that (as we find recorded) their Patriarkes have for that cause excommunicated some of their Emperors, although they had no issue left of their three former marriages.

10. That they reject the religious use of massie Images, or Statues, admitting yet Pictures or plaine Images in their Churches.

11. That they solemnize Saturday (the old Sabbath) festivally, and eat therein flesh, forbidding as unlaw-full, to fast any Saturday in the yeere, except Easter Eve.

12. That they observe foure Lents in the yeere.

13. That they eat not of any thing strangled, nor of bloud.

14. And lastly, that they deny the Bishop of Romes Primacy, and (reputing him and his Church for Schis-matikes) exclude them from their communion: And so have done, as I find in Leo the ninth his Epistles, and in

Sigebert, above these five hundred yeeres. And if you desire to see more differences of the Greeke and Romane Church, you may see them (but they are of lesse importance then those I have related in Possevines Booke of the matters of Moscovia.

SYrians are the same, that in some Histories are termed Melchites: being esteemed for their number, the greatest sect of Christians in the Orient. The first, being properly the name of their Nation: And the second noting the propertie of their Religion, Surians they were named (to let vaine fancies goe) of the Citie of Tyre, which in the ancient language of the Phoenicians, was called "nij?: and certainly, that Tyre was anciently called Sarra, is recorded by the

Roman Writers: and it is also acknowledged by

Vitriacus, Niger, Postell and others, that the place of Tyre, (for the Citie was utterly ruined three hundred yeeres ago) is still called the Port of Sur, which name it seemeth to have obtained, either because it was built on a Rocke, for so Buchardus that viewed the place hath

For Postels fantasie deriving Suria from fti Tm is meerely vaine, and being never so named in the Hebrew tongue, but alw ayes D ls, by which name also it seemeth anciently to have been knowne, even among the Grecians, for dpifioi mentioned in Homer, are no other, as Possidonius in Strabo expounds him, then the Syrians: Strabo himselfe also recording in other places, that the Syrians were called apdMo in his time: And that the naturall Inhabitants of Syria, so called themselves. Yet neverthelesse they were vulgarly knowne by the name of Si pot among the Grascians, because the Citie of "Tii?, being the maine Mart Towne of all those parts, was the place where they had their Trade and Commerce with those Aramites. But when the Phoenician tongue began to degenerate into Chaldee, then the name of Ti3? was converted into Tur, the later 3? being turned into t2 1 in sound made 1. As they that observe the differences of the Hebrew and Chaldee, and the transitions of the first into the latter know to be ordinary,

Paste, in Descript. Syrice. p. 30, Strab. I. 16. in fine. Stra. I. 13, non long, ante finem. Slrab. I. post. med. Burchard. descr. term Sanctcs. Fid. Scaliger ad Test, in dictione Sarra. y Guidon. Fabric, in Grammatic. Chaldcea, l c.

y 42, Villa-mont. en Vorag. I. 2. c. 21. l Alii.

12. Possevin. I. citato. p. i z.

13. Nilus Episco. Thes-sal. de Pri-matu Papa Barlaam de primatu Papa y Alii. Leo. 9, epist. I. ad Episcop. Con-stantinop. y Acridan. Isin pluribus aliis. Sigebert. in Chronica ad An. 1054. Possev. dereb. Mosco. . 38. y seqnentib. Of the Syrians or Melchites. Chap. 16. Botar. Relat. pa. 3. . 2, ca. de Melchiti. I. i. 129. Gellius. l. 14. c. 6. Fes-tus in Dictione sarra. Vitria. histor. Oriental, c.

Niger in com-meritar. 4. Asia. Pastel, in descript. Syria, pag. 50.

Hierom. inlib. de Nominib. Hebraicis.

""Plin. loc. citato.

Niceph. Calist. Histor. Ecclesiast. I. i8. c. 52. Ub. c.

1.2. 3. 4. 5. Jacob a Vit-riaco. Hist. Orient f. 75.

observed) which Ti5t in the Phcenician tongue signifies: or else as Hierom derives it, of the straitnesse and scarce-nesse of roome, as being seated in a small Hand (but nineteene miles in circuit, as Pliny noteth) a small Territory for such a City: or perhaps, because it was the strongest fortresse (for that also nii: importeth) of all those Regions, as being founded on a Rocke, environed with the Sea (for it was before Alexanders time = seven hundred paces distant from the firme land) mightily strengthened by fortification of Art, populous as being the Metropolis of Phcenicia, and exceeding rich, as sometime the citie of greatest traffike in the world.

Of this Citie then, both the Region and Inhabitants ot Suria obtained their names: but Melchitae as I said they were termed, meerely in respect of their Religion, wherein namely they altogether followed the examples and decrees of the Emperours. For whereas after the Councell of Chalcedon, infinite perplexitie and trouble began to arise in the East parts, principally about the opinion of Eutyches and Dioscorus, of one onely nature in Christ, which that Councell had condemned, but notwithstanding found many that maintained it, and rejected the Councell in those Easterne Countries: And thereupon the Emperour Leo began to exact (as divers other of his Successours afterward did) the suffrages and subscriptions of the Easterne Bishops, for the better establishment of the Councell. Then began they that embraced and approved the authority of that Councell, because they followed the Emperours decrees made in behalfe of it, to be termed by their adversaries Melchitse, of Melchi, saith Nicephorus (rather s b) which in the speech of Syria signifieth a King: as one would say. Of the Kings Religion) whereas they that opposed themselves to the Councell, were distracted into no lesse then twelve severall Sects, and not long after into more, as the same Nicephorus hath recorded.

Now although the Syrians or Melchites, are for their Religion meerely of the Graecians opinions. As: 1. That the Holy Ghost proceedeth onely from the Father.

2. That they celebrate Divine Service as solemnly on the Sabbath, as on the Lords day.

3. That they keepe that day festivall, eating therein flesh, and fast no Saturday in the yeere but Easter Eve.

4. That their Priests and Deacons contract not Mar- 4- VUkmont. riage, being already in Orders, but yet retaine their wives ' ' 'oycg-1- 2. before married.

5. That the fourth Matrimony is utterly unlawfull.

6. That they communicate the Eucharist in both S. j. F'Ula- il (g mon. loco citato.

7. That they acknowledge not Purgatory.

8. That they observe foure Lents in the yeere, c. And in a word, although they bee meerely of the same Religion Vitriac. loco and communion with the Grecians: yet are they not of "-the jurisdiction of the Patriarke of Constantinople, but of itlm Tom the Archbishop of Damascus, by the title of the Patriarch, c. i. of Antiochia. For Antiochia it selfe (where yet the name Bamugart. of Christians was first heard in the world, and was long Peregrin. I. z. knowne by the name oi Qeovirokii) lying at this present in a ' ' ' manner wast, or broken and dispersed into small Villages, of which onely one, of about sixtie Houses, with a small Bellon. Temple belonging to the Christians, the Patriarchall Seat "rh ' ' j' was translated thence to Damascus (where, as is reported, j. Eccksiar. are above one thousand Houses of Christians) and there pag. 5. Boter. remaineth. For although' the Patriarkes of the Maronites,- P- 3-and of the Jacobites, whereof the former keepeth residence 'j ' ' ' f in Libanus, and the latter in Mesopotamia, intitle them- Qj. Tuno. selves Patriarckes of Antiochia, and by the Christians of grar. I. 4. . their owne sects bee so acknowledged: yet doe the 296. ex rela-Melchites, who retaine the ancient Religion of Syria, l " p '-acknowledge none for Patriarke, but the Archbishop of Boter. loco Damascus, reputing both the other for Schismatickes, jam citato. as having departed from the obedience and communion of 'Boter. Relat. the true Patriarke. And yet besides all these, a fourth;-; , r 1 T 1 1 11-1 del rairiarcna there is or the Popes designation, that usurpeth the title i fi ji of the Patriarke of Antioch. For ever since the Latines stantinopoli. I

Of the Georgians, C'tr- ccss'ians 13 Metigrellians Chap. 17.

Folaierra7i. I. II. c. de sect. Syri. Prateol. de sectis. haret. in Verba. Georgiani. iff alii.

Mela. I. I. e. 2. Plin. l. S. c. i-.

Paul. Venet. 1. c. 14.

Chitra. de statu. Eccle-siar. p. 23. y 50. y Alii.

surprised Constantinople (which was about the ye ere 1200.) and held the possession of the East Empire, about seventie yeeres, all which time the Patriarkes of Constantinople, were consecrated by the Pope: As also, since the holy Land, and the Provinces about it, were in the hands of the Christian Princes of the West, which began to be about An. iioo, and so continued about eightie yeeres, during which seeson the Patriarkes of Antiochia also and of Jerusalem, were of the Popes consecration: Ever since then I say, the Church of Rome hath, and doth still create successively, imaginary or titular Patriarkes (without jurisdiction) of Constantinople, Antiochia, Jerusalem, and Alexandria, so loth is the Pope to loose the remembrance of any Superioritie or Title: that hee hath once compassed.

THe Georgians inhabite the Countrey, that was anciently named Iberia, betwixt the Euxine and the Caspian Sea: inclosed with Shervan (Media) East: with Mengrelia (Colchis) West: with Turcomania (Armenia the Greater) South: And with Albania (Zuiria) North. The vulgar opinion of Historians is, that they have obtained the name of Georgians, from their devotion to Saint George, whom they principally honour for their Patron: and whose Image they alwayes beare in their Military Ensignes. But yet (as I take it) this vulgar opinion is but vulgar errour: because I find mention made of the Nations of the Georgians in those parts, both in Mela and Pliny, afore Saint George was borne whosoever he was. Touching the properties of whose Religion, this may be sufficient to observe for all: That "" it is the same, both in substance and ceremonies with that of the Graecians, "who yet are in no sort subject (neither ever were) to the Patriarke of Constantinople: but all their Bishops (being eighteene) professe absolute obedience to their owne Metropolitan, without any other higher depen-dance or relation. Who yet keepeth residence farre off, m the Monastry of Saint Katherine, in the Hill of Sinai.

Prateo. de Haeret. sect, verbo Georgiani. Bernard. Lucem-burg. in Catalog. Haeret. in Georgiani.

Next these, I must speake a little of their next neighbours, the Mengrelians and Circassians (Colchi and Zychi) they were anciently called) seated betweene the Georgians, and the River Tanais, along the Coast of Masotis and the Euxine Sea, as being also Christians of the Greeke com- ellon. munion, and beside of the Patriarke of Constantinople j f Michov' ' his obedience, and converted by his Ministers Cyrillus de Sarmati'a. and Methodius to the Christian Religion. Which . i. c 7. Religion notwithstanding at this present is exercised l terianodelk among them, not without some depravation and mixture J ' j of strange fantasies, for the Circassians baptise not their Fabrica del children till the eight yeere, and enter not into the Church Mondo Trat. (the Gentlemen especially) till the sixtieth (or as others 2- oter. par. say, till the fortieth) yeere, but heare Divine Service " ' ' standing without the Temple, that is to say, till through age, they grow unable to continue their Rapines and Robberies, to which sinne that Nation is exceedingly addicted. So dividing their life betwixt Sinne and Devotion, dedicating their youth to Rapine, and their old age to Repentance.

THe Muscovites and Russians, as they were converted Qfthe Mus-to Christianitie by the Grecians Zonar. Annal, Tom. covites y 3. Cromer, de reb. Polon. 1. 3. so have they ever since J i "-continued of the Greeke Communion and Religion. ' '"

1. Denying the Holy Ghost to proceed from the Sonne.

2. Rejecting Purgatory, but yet praying for the Dead.

3. Beleeving that the holy men enjoy not the presence of God afore the Resurrection.

4. Celebrating the Sacrament of the Eucharist, with loan. Metropolitan. Russ. in ep. ad Episcop. Rom. apud. Sigismund. de Rebus. Muscov. p. 31. Guagin. descrip. Muscov, c. 2. Sacran. de errorib. Ruthenor. c. 2. 2. Sigism. 1. citat. p. 41. Sacran. de Relig. Ruthenor. c. 2. Searga. Polon. 1. 3. c. 2. 3. Searga. Polon. 1. 3. c. 2. Guaguin descript. Moscov. c. 2. 4. loan. Metropol. Russ. ubi supra p. 32. Guagin. descr. Muscov. ca. 2.

leavened bread, and requiring warme water to mingle with the wine.

5. And communicating in both kindes; 6. But mingling both together in the Chalice, and distributing it together with a spoone.

7. And receiving children after seven yeeres old to the Communion, saying, that at that age they begin to sin against God.

8. Omitting Confirmation by the Bishop.

9. Denying the speciall efficacie of extreame unction.

10. Excluding the fourth marriage as utterly unlawfull; whereas they approve not the second, as perfectly lawfuu, but onely permit it, but tolerate not thc third, except on very important considerations.

11. Dissolving marriage by divorcement, upon every light occasion or displeasure.

12. Admitting neither Deacons nor Priests to Orders, except they be married: but yet prohibiting marriage to them being actually in Orders.

13. Rejecting carved or massie Images, but admitting the painted.

14. Reputing it unlawfull to fast on Saturdaies.

15. Or, to eate of that which is strangled, or of bloud.

16. Observing foure Lents in the yeere.

17. Refusing to communicate with the Roman Church.

And (to conclude) excepting the difference in distributing of the Eucharist, and exacting of marriage to their Priests and Deacons, there is not any materiall dit- 5. Sigism. loc. citato, pag. 40. 6. Sigism. loc. citato p. 40. Guaguin. loc. citato. 7. Guaguin. Ibid. 8. loan. Metropol. Russ. ubi supra. apud. Sigism. p. 31. Guagin. loc. citato. Sacran. de errorib. Ruthenor. c. 2. 9. Sacran. loc, citato. 10. Sigism. lib. alleg. pag. 47. Possevin. de Rebus Moscov. pag. 2. Guaguin. Descript. Moscov. cap. 2. 11. Sacran. de errorib. Ruthenor. c. 2. 12. Sigism. lib. citat. p. 28. Searga. de uno pastor 1. 3. c. 2. Possevin. de Reb. Moscov. p. i. Guaguin. loc. citat. 13. Possev. lib. allegato. p. 44. 14. loan. Metropol. Russ. ubi. supr. p. 31. Guaguin. loc. allegato. 15. Possev. in Moscovia. pag. 42. Sacran. de error. Ruthen. cap. 2. 16. Guaguin. loc. citat. 17. Sigism. lib. citato, pag. 33. Boter. Relat. par. 3. 1. I. c. de Moscovia.

ference in points of Religion, that I find betwixt them and the Grecians. With whom, they not onely maintaine Communion, but were also, and that not long since (and I. i. 131- of right still ought to bee) of the same Jurisdiction and Government, for "their chiefe Metropolitan or Primate ""Possevln. (who is the Archbishop of Mosco) was wont to be- o ' " '-confirmed by the Patriarch of Constantinople, but is Quamln now, and hath beene about some sixtie yeeres, nominated desmp. Mos-and appointed by the Prince (the Emperour of Russia) ov. cap. 2. and upon that nomination, consecrated by two or three of his owne Suffragans: Of whom even all sorts together, Bishops and Archbishops, there are but "eleven, in al ""Possevin. loco that large Dominion of the Emperour of Russia. proxime citato

Thus is it with those sorts of Christians hitherto related Uosco'. pag. z'i. touching their Religion, and Governours. All which (as you may easily perceive) are of the same communion, and in effect of the same Religion with the Grecians: And beside these, some large parts of the King of Polonia Boter. Rel. his Dominion, for Podolia, and for the most part "Russia P- i– i- Nigra, or Rubra as some call it (the larger Russia subject."- ' ' S-for the greater part to the Duke of Moscovia, they Mmov. ca'p. z. tearme Russia alba) are of the Greeke Religion. And although the Bishops of South Russia, subject namely to the King of Polonia, submitted themselves almost twentie yeeres agoe (An. 1594) to the Bishop of Rome, as Baron. Tom. 7. Annal. in fine. Possevin. in Appar-sacr. in Rutheni. have recorded, yet was it not without speciall reservation of the Greeke Religion and Rites, as is manifest by the Articles of condition extant, ap. Th, a Jes. de Conv. gent. 1. 6. pag. 3. cap. i. pag. 328. seq. tendered by them to the Church of Rome, and accepted, before they would accept of the union. So that it was not any revolting from the Greeke Religion, but onely (in effect) from the jurisdiction of the Greeke Patriarch, to the Pope, and that also with sundrie limita- "Sigism. de tions. And in ' Wilna (the Metropolis of Lituania) 'b. Moscov, although the Archbishop professe obedience to the Pope, Qj S Jocq yet are there also in that Citie, as Sigismund hath jam citato.

observed, more Temples of the Greeke Religion (there bee thirtie of them) then of the Roman. ' Epist. ad Chitrae. de Relig. Russor. So that if wee should collect and put together all the Christian regions hitherto in-treated of: which are all of the Greeke communion: And compare them with the parts professing the Roman Religion, wee should finde the Greeke farre to exceede, if wee except the Roman new and forraine purchases, made in the West and East Indies.

Of the Nes- 'HT He Nestorians, who have purchased that name by tonans. Chap. J. j jj. ancient imitation, and maintayning of Nestorius ' his heresie, inhabite (though every where mingled with

Mahumetans, or with Pagans) a great part of the Orient, for besides the Countreys of Babylon, and Assiria, and Mesopotamia, and Parthia, and Media, wherein very many of them are found, that Sect is spread and scattered farre and wide in the East, both Northerly to Cataya, and Southerly to India. So that in Marcus Paulus his Guil. de historic of the East Regions, and in ' others, wee finde Ruhr. Itin. mention of them, and of no sect of Christians but them, Paul Fenet i Y many parts and Provinces of Tartarie: As namely . c. 38. 2. in I Cassar, 2 Samarchan, 3 Carcham, 4 Chinchintales, . eod. cap. 39. 5 Tanguth, 6 Succhuir, 7 Ergimul, 8 Tenduch, 9 Caraiam, 3. fz. 44. r.

jq Mangi, c. Insomuch, that beyond the River Tigris y 0 6- Eastward, there is not any other Sect of Christians to 48. 7. c. 62. be found, for ought I can reade, except onely the 8. c. 64. . 2. Portugals, and the converts made by them in India, c. 39. . eod. and the late migration of the Armenians into Persia. c. I. t5 64. r- reason of which large spreading and prevayling Paul. Diacon. Sect SO farre in the Orient, if you enquire I finde Hisior. Miscel. to that purpose, recorded by Paulus Diaconus of Cosrhoes B. 18. the King of Persia, that hee for the mortall hatred hee bare the Emperour Heraclius, by whom hee had beene sore afflicted with a grievous warre, inforced all the Christians of the Persian Empire to Nestorianisme permitting no Catholickes to remayne in all his Dominions. By whose preaching, the Christian Religion being farre there inlarged and propagated into the East (as it seemes both because those of the Persian Dominion, were more Eastwardly then other Christians, and because it is certaine that all of them till this day acknowledge obedience to the Nestorian Patriarch in Mesopotamia, which Countrey was then part of the Persian Dominion:) It is no wonder if sowing their owne Tares and Christs wheat together, they propagated with the Gospell also their owne heresie. Shortly after which time, the Sarracens of Arabia (Mahumetans) conquering Persia, and bringing their Religion, together with their victories into all that large Dominion, there remayned but little outward meanes and slender hope of their repayre and reformation from any sound part of the Church (from which they were more now then afore divided) except what affliction and time, and the grace of God might worke and repayre in them.

Now touching their Ecclesiasticall government: The Sand, de Fisi. Patriarch of the Nestorians, to whom all those of the j "" ' '–'-East parts acknowledge obedience (a number of whose " Suffragan Bishops and Metropolitans, you have reckoned . i, c. 15. up in Sanders booke de Visibili Monarchia, and whom Brocard Des. they call lacelich, saith Paulus Venetus Brochardus, T rr. sanct.

and others, but mistake it (or else they of the p ad. Histor.

East pronounce it amisse) for Catholick, as is observed Tuix. 3.

by Leunclavius) hath his seat in the Citie of Muzal, "Aubret.

on the River Tygris in Mesopotamia, or in the Patri Iff "' archall Monasterie of Saint Ermes fast by Muzal. Th. Or "' 5.

a Jes. 1. 7. pag. 3. c. 4. In which Citie, though subject Mas. inortel.

to Mahumetans, it is recorded, that the Nestorians inthesnur. in retayne yet fifteene temples, being esteemed about fortie ' " 'f- thousand Soules. Th. a Jes. 1. 7. par. i. c. 4. and the ' 5-

Jacobits three. Which Citie of Muzal, I either take sti-ab. l. 6.

with Masius and Ortelius, to bee the same, that anciently hnganteued.

was called Selutia (and in Plinie Seleutia Parthorum) I-i. 132- both because Seleutia was, as Strabo saith, the Metropolis Q rj.- of Assyria, even as Musal is recorded to bee And ,. also, because I finde the Ecclesiasticall jurisdiction of 21.8.

Condi. 'Nicen. Ariih. I- 3– 33- y 34

Scal. adchron. Euseb. A. M. D. CCXIII Ben in Itine-rar. in Medio. See more exact relations of Bag. I. g. c. 9. 13c. My Pilgrimage I. 3. f. 2.

Strabo. I. 16. Plin. I. 6. c. 26.

Ptol. Geoe;. I. 6. C. 18. y 20. Dion. hist. I. 40. Plin. I. 6. c. 26. ""Boter. relat. par. 3. . 2. C. de Nestoriani. The. a Jes. de confers, gent I. 7. par. I. c. 3. 4-Vitriac. hist. Orient c. 3 i. Tit. de bell. sac. . 21.

those parts committed by the fathers of the Nicene Councell, to the Bishop of Seleucia, assigning him with all, the name of Catholicke, and the next place of Session in Councels after the Bishop of Jerusalem, which name and authoritie in those parts, the Bishop of Mosal now hath. Or if Seleucia were some other Citie, now destroyed, as for certaine reasons I am induced rather to thinke, yet at least the Patriarchall Seate was from Seleucia translated to ""Muzal, for the opinion of Scahger, namely, that Seleucia was the same, that is now called Bagded, or new Babylon, my observations in Geographie and Historic, will not suffer mee to approove. First, because Seleucia is remembred by Strabo to be three hundred furlongs (seven and thirtie miles and one or two) Plinie saith, a great deale more, distant from Babylon, whereas Bagded is built close by the ruines of it. Secondly, because I find the position of Seleucia in Ptolemie to be two third parts of a degree, more North then that of Babylon, whereas Bagded is more South. Thirdly, because in Dion, and others, Seleucia is named for a Citie of Mesopotamia, which Bagded is not, but in the province of Babylon, as being beneath the confluence of Tigris and Euphrates.

The Bishop of Muzal then, is Patriarch of the Nes-torians. But yet at this present, if the Relations of these times be true, there is a distraction of that Sect: which began about sixtie yeeres agoe, in the time of Pope Julius the Third: the Nestorians in the North part of Mesopotamia (about the Citie of Caramit)

"Muzal, the Patriarchall seate of the Nestorians, is either a remainder of the ancient Ninive, as Vitriacus, and Tyrius (who therefore in his Historie calleth the Inhabitants of that Citie Ninivites) have recorded: Or at least, built neere the Ruines of it: Namely, over against it, on the other side of the River Tigris, as by Benjamin, who diligently viewed the place, is observed, for Ninive (which hee noteth to be dissolved into scattered Villages and Castles) stood on the East banke of Tigris, on Assyria side: whereas Muzal is seated on the West banke on Mesopotamia side, beeing yet both joyned together, by a Bridge made over Tigris.

submitting themselves to another Patriarch of the Popes erecting (that revolting from the Bishop of Muzal, taking also on him, the title of the Patriarch of Muzal, which the Pope bestowed on him) having first rendred and professed obedience to the See of Rome, in which obedience it is said, that those Nestorians about Caramit doe still continue.

Now touching the specialties of these Nestorians Religion, in relation to the Roman: they beleeve.

First, that there are two persons in our Saviour, Vitnac. hht. as well as two natures, but yet confesse, that Christ " "- '- from the first instant of his Conception, was perfect God and perfect man Th. a Jes. Ibid.

Secondly, that the blessed Virgin ought not to 2 Id. loco. be tearmed Oeorrcof, which yet now in some sort they " ' qualifie, confessing her to be the Mother of God Bot. relat. the Son, but yet refusing to tearme her the Mother of Z" '- 3– 2-Coa ' ' '

Thirdly, that Nestorius condemned in the third and J, p. ' fourth generall Councels, and Diodorus Tarsensis, and . 7. c. z. Theodorus Mopsuestensis, condemned for

Nestorianisme 3 Bot. loco. in the fifth, were holy men: Rejecting for their sake, pro: mocimo. the third generall Councell held at Ephesus, and all other Councels after it, and specially detesting (the mall of Nestorianisme) Cyrill of Alexandria, Th. a Jes. Ibid.

Fourthly, they celebrate the Sacrament of the Eucharist, Fimackist. with leavened bread. fj"- 78-

Fiftly, they communicate in both kinds. Fovas-es I 2

Sixtly, they use not auricular confession. r. 23.

Seventhly, nor confirmation. t Vill. lo. citat.

Eightly, they contract Marriage in the second degree E. t.-j. Mak. r: T-k T Tk- l est. profess.

or consanguinitie. In. a Jes. Ibid.

Ninthly, their Priests after the death of their first Hoth. l et.

wives, have the libertie of the second or third or oftner Patrum. p.

Marriage. Th. a Jes. Ibid. " 'v

Tenthly, they have not the Image of the Crucifixe jf brk Itlncr on their Crosses. Tartar. ex-.

Of the Indians or Christians of Saint Thomas. Chap. 20.

"Sommar. d. popoli Orient, ap. Ramus. Vol. I. de Fiaggi, p. 332-

Barhosa eod. Vol. p. 312. Bot. rel. p. 3. . z. c. della nova Chris-tianita d' India.

Bot. rel. p. 3. . z. c. della vecchlachrist. d' India Th. a Jes. de conver. gent. l. j. pa. i. c. 4. I- 1- I33-

Th. ajes. de conv. gent. li. part. I. c. 4.

Plin. loco proximo citato.

Apudramus. vol. I. de f iaggi-p-l' Z.

THe Christians of India, vulgarly named the Christians of Saint Thomas, because by his preaching they are supposed to have beene converted to Christian Religion (and his bodie as is thought, remayneth among them, buried in the Citie of Maliapar on the Coast of Choro-mandel) inhabit in the neerer part of India: namely, in that great Promontory, whose base lying betweene the Outlets of the Rivers Indus and Ganges, stretcheth out the sides farre toward the South (well nigh 1000. miles) till meeting in the point of Comori, they make, together with the base line forementioned (betwixt Cambaya and Bengala) the figure almost of an Equilaterall Triangle. In the more Southerly part of this great Promontory, I say neerer to Cape Comori, about the Cities of Coulan and Cranganor on the West side, and about Maliapar and Negapatan, on the East side, doe these Christians of Saint Thomas dwell, being esteemed afore the Portugals frequented those parts, about "15000. or ' 16000. Families, or after anothers account 70000. persons: but on the West Coast, the farre greater number of them is found, and especially their habitation is thickest, about Angamale, "15. miles from the Citie Cochin Northward, where their Archbishop keepeth residence.

Now as touching their government: Their Archbishop till twentie yeeres since or little more, acknowledged obedience to the Patriarch of Mozal, by the name of

For Mozal as I said before, is either Seleucia, or succeeded into the dignitie of it. And Seleucia is recorded to have bin inhabited. by the Citizens of Babylon, whereof it was a Colony: And such a Colony, as in short time it exhausted Babylon it selfe, of all the Inhabitants, passing, by reason of the more commodious situation, to dwell at Seleucia. So that Seleucia being Inhabited by the Babylonians, and so becomming in stead of Babylon, the princlpall Citie of the Provinces of Babylonia, and Assyria, the Citie obtayned the name of Babylon of her Inhabitants (as well as Seleucia, of her Founder) as Plinie hath recorded: And the Patriarch of it, the title of the Patriarch of Babylon. And although Barbosa note, that subordination of the Christians of India, to be to the Patriarch of Armenia (which no doubt he received from the Indians relation, the Patriarch of Babylon, as by those Christians of India he is stil tearmed. certainly that the Patriarch of Mozal, challengeth their obedience, as being of his Plin. I. 6. c. Jurisdiction, appeareth by the profession of Abil-Isu, 26. a Patriarch of Mozal, of Pope Pius the Fourth his Investing (Anno 1562.) as is to bee seene in "Sanders Sand. znsib. Booke de visibili Monarchia. But then, the Archbishop ionarch. l.- j. of these Indians, revolting from his former Patriarch, submitted himselfe by the Portugals perswasion, to the Bishop of Rome, retayning notwithstanding, the ancient Religion of his Countrey, which was also permitted by the Pope. In so much, that in a Synod held in Goa, for that purpose, hee would not suffer any alteration to bee made of their ancient Rites or Religion, as one that lived in those parts at that time hath recorded. But that Bishop being dead, his successour in another Synod, held by the Archbishop at Goa, at 'Diamper, 'Possevin. in not farre from Maliapur, Anno i cqq. made profession, PP rat. sacro together with his burtragans, and Priests, both or the concilium. Roman obedience and Religion, renouncing in such direct sort, the Patriarch of Mozal, and Nestorianisme, that they delivered up all their Bookes, to the censure of the Archbishop of Goa, and suffered their Lyturgie, in the points that rellished of Nestorianisme to bee altered, even in such sort as now it is to be seene in the last Edition of Bibliotheca veterum Patrum. Bibuoth. vet.

But before this alteration of their Religion was pro- '"f " " cured by the Portugals, those Christians of India were- 'r among whom he was) yet certaine it is, that he meaneth no other, then this Patriarch of Mozal: because those Armenians which he meaneth, are by himselfe observed to have for their vulgar Language the Arabik tongue, and to celebrate their divine Service in the Chaldee, both which agree with Christians of Mozal, but neither of both with those of Armenia, whose Language both in the vulgar and sacred use is knowne to be no other then the Armenian Tongue. As also, because the Indians are knowne to have beene Nestorians, to which Heresie the Armenians were most opposite, as being in a manner Jacobites. But as it seemeth, that Patriarch is said to have beene of Armenia, for the neernesse of Mozal to the Confines of Armenia.

Nestorians, as having the dependance that I related, on the Patriarch of the Nestorians, they could not well be any other. Some specialties of whose Religion I find thus recorded.

1 Osorius de i. That they distributed the Sacrament of the Eucharist rel Emman- j kinds.

uel I i. Bou celebrated it with bread seasoned with rel. p. 3.. 2. J TT- J J r c. delk. Vec- Salt, (pane salato, saith my Historian) and in stead ot cliia Chris- Wine (because

India affordeth none) in the juyce of tianita d' Raisons, softened one night in water and so pressed India. r.1 2 Odoard rorth.

Barbt. p. 3- That they baptized not their Infants till they were

Ramus. Vol. fortie dayes olde, except in danger of death. p- 313 4. That they used not Extreame unction.

I'Navtgat 2X their Priests were married, but excluded int? rrelatione) om the second Matrimony. Osor. de Reb. Emanuel.

novi or bis. c.! 3 134 6. That they had no Images of Saints in their Churches, Joseph. Ind. 1 Qj giy. j g Crosse.

c'."it." 7- That detesting (the Mall of Nestorianisme) Cyrill 5 Osor. loco of Alexandria, they honoured Nestorius and Dioscorus ante citato. as Saints, which yet mee thinkes were strange, beeing

Possev. in q contrary opinions, as they were, the first, for two foiamptri Persons in Christ, as well as two natures: the second, ense Concil. for one nature, as well as one Person; but it may be

Thet. COS. I. that Dioscorus is by the Relater mistaken for Diodoras, 10. ca. 15. Q as indeed a great Nestorian, and for it condemned fi"i!"nt generall Councell.

J Possev. loco 8. That they denyed the Primacie of the Pope. citato. 9. That their New Testament which in their Churches 8 Possev. loco gy formerly read (and still doe) in the Syriak tonge, ' ' was by the Nestorians in sundry places, which are now Jpparz'. sacro altered by the Romanes, corrupted to the advantage iff Nestoriani. of that Heresie, wherein yet, I thinke the Reporter Widmanstad. ig deceived: because the same corruptions objected to tnpraf. Test. (whereof some are no corruptions at all, but- " ' agree rightly with the originall Text, much better then doth the vulgar Latine, by comparing whereof he examines them, and censures them for corruptions) the same I say, are found in the Syriaque Edition that we have, being so farre from being corrupted by the Nestorians that it was brought out of Mesopotamia into Europe (to bee printed by Moses Mardenus, from the Patriarch of the contrary Sect, namely, of the Jacobites. But yet notwithstanding, I am indeed certainly perswaded that the Syriaque Translation of the New Testament (whosoever was the Author of it) is nothing neer of that Antiquitie, which the Syrians (as Bellarmine and others Bellar. de report of them) pretend it to be, namely to have beene ' the work of Saint Marke. First, because Saint Marke rf i 134.1 dyed in the eighth yeere of Nero, as Hierome with Hienn. de others hath certainly recorded, after which time many Scrip. Ecck-parts of the New Testament, were written: as namely jf- '-Saint Johns Gospel, the Acts of the Apostles (for all Junius. the History from the 24. Chapter to the end, relateth in Annot. ad occurrents after Saint Markes death) the Epistles of loc predict. Saint Paul to the Galathians, Ephesians, Philippians, Colossians, to Philemon, and the second to Timothy. Secondly, because that Syriaque Translation is not to be found once mentioned, in any of all those ancient and learned Writers, that lived in those East parts, and diligently sought out and observed the severall Editions and Translations of the holy Scripture. And thirdly, because the Dialect discovereth it to be of a farre later Age, then that of the Apostles: which they will soone find to bee so (to omit some other Evidences) that shall compare the Syriaque words recorded in the

"The Imperfections of the Syriake Edition, consist partly in sundry defects: namely, I. of all the Revelation: 2. of the Epistle of Saint Jude; 3. of the second Epistle of Saint Peter: 4. of the second and third Epistles of Saint John: 5. of the History of the Woman taken in adultery, in the eight Chapter of Saint Johns Gospel, contayning the first eleven Verses: and 6. of the 7. Verse of the 5. Chapter of the first Epistle of Saint John. Of which, the two wants are no lesse found in sundry ancient Greeke Copies, as Erasmus, Beza, Junius and others have observed; And partly, beside these defects, in some (very few) faulty translations.

New Testament by the Evangelists (which all are noted Hieron. I. de by Hieromc and by others) with the Syriaque Booke: nomtmb. Hebr. g example, ixafxixwm. Mat. 6. 25. Mamouno. ya ada loan. 19. 13. Gephiphto. yoxyooa, Mat. 27. 33. Gogoultho. AKexSafxa, Act. I. 19. Chakaldemo, ixapavaqa I. Cor. 16. 22 Moraneto. And to be short, there is not almost any Syriaque word recorded in the New Testament, which varieth not from that ancient pronouncing that was usual in the Apostles time, either in consonants, or vowels, or both: which could not be the alteration of any short course of time.

Of the Jaco- 'T He Jacobites obtained that appellation, as Damascene bites. J Nicephorus have recorded, of one Jacobus

Dal.)'. de surnamed Zanzalus, of Syria, who living about Anno h resi'b. 'post 530. was in his time a mightie inlarger of Eutiches Sect, med. Niceph. and maintayner of his opinion, touching the unitie of hist. Ecclesiast. j ture in our Saviour: And his followers are at this ' 52– great numbers, knowne by the name of Jacobites, in Syria, in Cyprus, in Mesopotamia, in Babylon, and in Palestine, For, the Patriarch of Jerusalem who keepeth his residence still in Jerusalem, (in which City, there

Chitra de ygt remaine ten, or more, Churches of Christians) is stat. Ecclestar. Jacobite. But although in all these forementioned i'j ameh 15. Regions, these Jacobites are found (where they be esteemed

Crus. intur- to make about 160000. Families) or rather ' 50000.

cog.. p. z 7. as Leonard the Bishop of Sidon, the Popes Visiter in 'Bot. reat. recorded, ap. Th. a Jes. 1. 7. p. i. cap.

r Giacobi ' H- Y t chiefly they inhabit in Aleppo of Syria, and in

Brcitenbach. Caramit, and the Mountaine Tur of Mesopotamia: But peregrin, c. de yet their Religion under other Titles, is extended much

Jacobitis. Fit- f j-j-hgr, in SO much that it is recorded to bee spread 'oriettc. je. abroad in some forty Kingdomes.

Pauldiacon. AH which Jacobites of the places before specined, hist. Miscel. have, and long have had, a Patriarch of their owne . 18. Religion (for I find the Patriarch of the Jacobites spoken

T ' 'i Her- o in the Emperour Heraclius his time) to whom they acio render obedience. The Patriarchal! Church of which

Sect, is in the Monasterie of Saphran, neere to the Mh-a-. in Citie of Merdin in the north part of Mesopotamia: "- P'"-But the Patriarch himselfe, keepeth ordinary residence "iot rliatp in the Citie of Caramit, the ancient Metropolis of 3. . 2. c de Mesopotamia, and which at this day, consisteth for the Giaco. greatest part of Christians, for that Caramit is the same Citie, which the ancient Writers called Amida,

Sabellicus, Sabellk. and others have left observed, and Amida to have beene PP "'-" anciently the Metropolis of Mesopotamia, I find in the subscriptions of the ancient Councels plainly recorded.

But till Eutichianisme so mightily prevailed in those parts, as to worke in them a detestation of the Councell Conc. Chal. of Chalcedon, and a departure withall, from their ancient ' "-1 obedience: They belonged till then I say to the Jurisdiction of the Patriarch of Antiochia, as beeing 'Provinces 'Notltia proof the Diocesse of the Orient, which we find in the ' "" ' "second generall Councell, to be the circuit and Conc. Con-limitation of that Patriarchs authoritie, which is the- Z"-reason that the Patriarch of the Jacobites, keeping ever the name of Ignatius, intitleth himselfe Patriarch of Antiochia: And that the ' Patriarch of Jerusalem, who ' f- notlt. is also as I said a Jacobite acknowledgeth him (as some "" " "' ' record) for superiour: Having therein (if it be so) but in some sort returned to the ancient obedience, wherein the Bishops of Jerusalem stood to the Patriarchs of Antiochia, even till the time of the Councell of Chalcedon: for then began Jerusalem, to be erected into a Patriarch-ship: And as we reade in the ""actions of that Councell '"Cone. Chal-with the consent and allowance of the Patriarch of "'-' ' " ' ' Antiochia, the three Provinces of Palestina, which till then (Anno 451.) belonged to Antiochia, were with-drawne from it, and assigned to the Bishop of Jerusalem for his Patriarchall Jurisdiction.

Now as touching the Characters of their Religion. i. 2. 314.

I. They acknowledge but one nature, and but one Jacob, a Fit- will and one operation, ex catechism. Tacobitar. ap. "' ' "-"

- Orienf. c. 76.

Caramit. is Kara Amida, that is (in the Turkish Tongue) blacke Villamont. l. z. Amida, because it was walled with blacke stone. c. 22.

2 Bucebitig. hist. Eccles. part. p. ii. Sahgniac. Itiner. To. 8. c. I. Th. a Jes. I. 7. pa. c. 14.

I. i 135. 4 Bucebing. loco citato. Jlphons. a Castro. I. 4. cont. Heres. Tit. Confessio Baumgar. Iti jer. l.2. c.().

Fitriac. hist. Orient, c. j6.

Th. a Jes. 1. 7. p. i. c. 15. in Christ (as there is but one person) and in token of that, they malce the signe of the Crosse, with one finger onely, which the other Christians of the East doe with two.

2. They signe their Children before Baptisme, many in the Face, some in the Arme, with the signe of the Crosse, imprinted with a burning Iron.

3. They use Circumcision. Saligniac. Itin. Tom. 8. c. I. even of both Sexes. Vitriac. ut ibi.

4. They confesse their sinnes to God onely, not to the Priest, and as others record, but very seldome, so that many communicate without Auricular Confession. Leonard Sidon. ap. a Jes. 1. 7. p. i. c. 14.

5. They admit not of Purgatorie, nor of Prayers for the dead. Th. a Jes. 1. 7. p. i. c. 23.

6. They consecrate the Eucharist in unleavened Bread. Salign. Itin. Hieres. Tom. 8. c. i. They minister the Sacrament of the Eucharist in both kinds.

7. The Priests are married.

8. They beleeve all the soules of just men to remayne in the Earth till the Day of Judgement, expecting Christs second comming, ex Catechism. Jacobit.

9. They affirme the Angels to consist of two substances, fire and light, ex Catechism. Jacobit.

10. They honour Dioscorus and Jacobus Syrus as Saints, but yet condemne Eutyches as an Heretike. Patriarch. Jacobit. ap. Th. a Jes. 1. 7. p. i. c. 14.

These are the Properties (that I find registred) of the Jacobites Rehgion, namely of them, that are properly so called, and still retayne the ancient opinion of Jacobus Syrus. But it seemeth, that their principall errour, and which occasioned their first Schisme and Separation from the Church, Namely, the Heresie of Eutiches touching one nature in Christ, is for the most part, long since abolished: for as Vitriacus hath long agoe recorded, they denied to him (then the Popes Legate in those parts, and demanding the question) that they beeleved one onely nature in Christ: And being further asked, why then making the Crosse, they signed themselves onely with one finger, their answere was, that they did it in acknowledgement of one divine Nature, as also they did it in three severall places, in acknowledgement of three persons in that one nature. And besides of late time, Leonard another Legate of Pope Gregories the Thirteenth in those parts, hath recorded of the Patriarchs profession made to himselfe, that although they held indeed but one personated nature to be in Christ, resulting of the union of two natures not personated, yet they acknow- ledged those two natures to be united in his person, Hoth."ve't without any mixtion or confusion, and that they them- Patrum p. selves differed not in understanding, but onely in tearmes i 5-from the Latine Church. Th. a Jes. 1. 7. p. i. c. 14. ' P dbaron. And although (as it is storied by some Writers of these e Jnnj"'"' times) some there be among them that still retaine that pzag. Zabo. de errour, yet certainly, that it is no generall and received R ig- opinion among them, is most manifest, for we have extant "-the confessions of the "Jacobites of Mesopotamia, and S't'"'"' of those of gypt, and of Ethiopia, and of Armenia, Goes. that is to say, all sorts of Jacobites, out of which it is ' Confess. evident, that that errour of Eutiches, is cleerly re- rmenior. nounced, as articularly acknowledging that the humane 2q"'hc' ' nature of Christ was taken of the Virgin, and of the i v. Cond. same substance with ours, and remayned, after the Chaked. adunation with the Deitie (without any mutation of pro- '- i- perties) distinct from the divine nature ' All which the P "" ' f

T T r T-' 1 1-1 heeres. I. 4. tn

Jtleresie or Eutiches denied. Eutkhe.

THe Sect of Christians named Cophti, are no other Ofthecophti, then the Christians of gypt: And, it is the name Christians of their Nation, rather, then of their Religion (in respect "q whereof they are meerely Jacobites) for as Masius hath Maf."insyror. observed, the Egyptians in some ancient Monuments Pecuiio. are tearmed gophti, whom vulgarly we name Cophti, Baron, in or Copti, and so they also name themselves, as may be f'., seene, in the Confessions of these Egyptians recorded Jdsedapouol in Baronius. And certainly, that the Sigyptians them- Tom. 6. I 369 2 A

Annalinfine. selves, name their Countrey Chibth, Ortelius after Thevet Ortel. tnthe- recorded: As also it is observed by Scaligfer, that sauro tn.,,,,,. a j i t-v

Egyptus. '" the lalmud it is called iridi. And, by Drusius,

Seal, ad out of R. David, and R. Shelomo, that Egypt is by
Eusebii. them named TSij but not without some trajection of
J'Z i letters tt. for ir33 R. David in prsf 1. Radic. R. CXXXIF. helom. in rlxod.
13.

Drus. de But touching their Religion (to omit curiosity about
Trib. sect. the name) they differ not, as I said from the Jacobites. Judceor. l.
z Insomuch that (as Damascen hath observed) the same Phuacter'm Sectaries, that
first were tearmed gyptii, because Damas. I. de among the Egyptians, that Heresie
of one onely nature haresib. post in Christ, found the mightiest patronage, were after
of ' Jacobus Syrus above mentioned, named in Syria, Jaco- bites. And till this day
Severus, Dioscorus and Jacobus, the principall parents and patrons of that Sect, are
by the Egyptians honoured in the memorials of their Lyturgies. Th. a Jes. lib. 7. pag.
i. cap. 5. I hot. rel. p. J Using Circumcision: Yet I am not very certaine Christia
del whether for Religion, or (which I observed it before Egitto. to have beene) as an
ancient custome of that Nation, which custome yet is reported Th. a Jes. 1. 7. p. i.
c. 6. Boter. p. 3. 1. 3, de Christ, de Egitto, to be now abrogated among them, by
the perswasion of the Bishops of Romes Legates in a Synod held at Caire about thirtie
yeeres agoe. Anno 1583.

2. They conferre the inferiour sacred orders (under Priesthood) even to Infants
presently after Baptisme, altogether, their Parents promising for them and performing
in their steads (till they be sixteene yeeres old or thereabout) what they promise in
their behalfes, namely chastitie, and fasting every Wednesday and Friday, and in the
foure Lents of the yeere. Th. Jes. 1. 7. p. I. c. 5. They repute not Baptisme of any
efficacie, except ministred by the Priest and in the Church in what necessitie soever.
Th. Jes. 1. 7. p. I. c. 5.

3. Neither baptize their children afore the fortieth day, though they should die
without Baptisme. Th. a Jes. Ibid.

4. Ministring the Sacrament of the Eucharist in both I. 1. 136. kinds. zthevetin 5.
They minister the Sacrament of the Eucharist in " f 8 leavened bread. Th. a. Jes. ibid.

6. Give the Sacrament of the Eucharist to Infants presently after their Baptisme.
Id. Ibid.

7. To sicke persons they neither minister Extreame Unction, nor the Eucharist. Id.
Ibid.

8. Although they acknowledge the Holy Ghost to proceed from the Father and the
Sonne, yet in relating of the Nicene Creed, they leave out those words (and from the
Sonne) as the Grecians doe. Id. Ibid.

9. They admit not of Purgatorie nor of Prayer for the dead. Th. a Jes. 1. 7. p. i.
23.

10. They contract Marriages even in the second degree of consanguinitie without
any dispensation. Tecla. Abissin. ap. Th. a Jes. 1. 7. p. i. c. 13.

11. They observe not the Lords dayes, nor other Feasts, except in Cities. Tecla.
Abissin. Ibid.

12. In celebrating of the Eucharist, they elevate not the Sacrament. Tecla. Abissin.
Ibid.

13. Reject all the generall Councels after that o Ephesus, expresly condemning the Councell of Chal-cedon. Id. Ibid.

14. Reade the Gospel of Nicodemus in their Lyturgies. Prateol. de Heresib. in Cophti.

15. Repute the Roman Church hereticall, and avoid the communion and conversation of the Latines, no lesse then of Jewes. And although Baron, in fin. Tom. 6, Anal, have registred an Ambassage from Marcus the Patriarch of Alexandria to Pope Clement the Eighth, wherein hee is said to have submitted and reconciled himselfe and the Provinces of gypt to the Pope, yet the matter being after examined was found to bee but a tricke of Imposture, as Th. a Jes. 1. 7. p. i. c. 6. hath recorded.

Thorn, a Jes. i6. Maiiitayning the opinion of one nature in Christ: (ie conv. gent.-xz i sort, that although in the generall position Thorn, a' touching one nature in our Saviour, they follow Euty-Jes. loco citato, ches, yet in the speciall declaration, at this day they differ Bot. loc. cit. very much from him. For they acknowledge him to bee truly, and perfectly both God and man: And, that the Divine and humane natures, are become in him one Nature, not by any confusion or commixtion of them, as Eutyches taught: but onely by coadundation. Wherein although they Catholikely confesse, that there is no mutation of properties in either nature, being united in Christ, from what the divine and humane natures severally obtaine in severall Persons: Yet beeing not well able (as it seemes) to distinguish betweene the nature and the Person, they dare not say there be in Christ two Natures, for feare they should slip into Nestorius Heresie of two Persons. Which Heresie of one onely Nature in our Saviour, beginning with Eutyches, although after dispersing it selfe into many branches, hath ever since the time of the Councell of Chalcedon, by which Eutychianisme was condemned and for it, Conc. Chal- the Patriarch of Alexandria ' Dioscorus deposed, beene ced. Jction 3. nourished and maintayned, as by other Christians of the East, so specially by the Egyptians. Insomuch, that not onely sundry Patriarchs of Alexandria, and Antiochia (but specially of Alexandria) together with many other Bishops of the East parts, their Suffragans, and adherents, are recorded to have maintayned and advanced, that 1: 6 22- o Heresie of Eutyches, but we find moreover, many 33. 1 c. Synods of those parts, registred or remembred in Eva-Leont. de Sect, grius, Leontius, Nicephorus, and the Booke called Jction. 5. ""Sxo' tfov, brought to light by Pappus, c. wherein (in f' l y 5! the behalfe of that Heresie) the Decrees of the Councell y. 18. y of Chalcedon were condemned. In which Councell, sequent. although we reade of the greatest Confluence of Bishops,

""S nod. 97. g gj. j g. about the Establishment of any point in '08 f ii Christian Religion (yet beside the six hundred and 109! ' c. ' thirty Bishops present in that Councell, there are extant in the " Booke of Councels, the Suffrages of about thirtie ' Ad fin. Con-Provinciall Synods, that by their Epistles to the Em- i' ' perour Leo, confirmed it, together with all the Bishops Condl. Binii. of the West, by whom it was likewise received) yet notwithstanding all this, that Heresie so prevailed in the East parts, and specially in Egypt, whereof we now entreate, that from that time to this it was never cleered of it. But as there was never Heresie that so grievously wounded the Church 'of God, as that of Eutyches (except perhaps Arrianisme) so was no part of the Church so deeply and deadly wounded by it, as that of Egypt. So that, even at this day, although the wound be in some sort healed, yet the wemme or skarre still re-mayneth. For it is not many yeeres, since by certaine Jesuites, Agents for the Bishop of Rome, some con- Bot. rekt. par. ferences were had with the Patriarch of Alexandria and ; i"- "'-J his Synod, wherein, although they confessed (if true guto. relation be made of that conference) that Christ is true God and true Man: yet did they purposely refraine from mentioning two natures in Christ, lest they should by little and little slip into the Heresie of two persons.

Now as touching their Ecclesiasticall government they are subject to the Patriarch of Alexandria," whose Patri- Chitra. de archall Seat is at this present translated (and so long hath-Ecclesiar. beene) to the Citie of Caire, in either of which Cities, p jr p-jg. (Caire and Alexandria) there remaine at this day, but ap. Baron. three Christian Temples apiece. Whereas Burchardus Tom. 6. in recordeth of his time (about three hundred and twentie ' " ' yeeres agoe) that in one of them (Caire) there were above fortie, Burch. descr. ter. sanct. par. 2. c. 3. But yet, to the Jurisdiction of this Patriarch belong, not onely the native Christians of Egypt, who are but very few, considering the exceeding populousnesse of that Nation (for they are esteemed as I said before, not to passe fiftie thousand) which in Burchardus his time, are by him I. i. 137. recorded to have beene above 300000. Id. p. 2. c. 3. together with the small remainder of Christians, that are found about the Bay of Arabia, and in Mount Sinai

Alvarez, his-tor. Ethiop. c. 137.

Nicen. Condi. I. 3. f. 36.

Vitriac. hist. Orient, c. 6. Brocard. de-script. Terra. sand.

Eastward, or in Afrike as farre as the greater Syrtis Westward: but the Christians likewise of Ethiopia acknowledge obedience to him. For although Alvarez in his Storie of Ethiopia have related (as he doth also some other matters touching the ancienter condition of the Church, too grossely and boldly) that the Christians of Nubia till their defection from Christianitie, were of the Popes dependance and Jurisdiction, and received their Bishops by his consecration (and say nothing oi the Patriarch of Alexandria) yet certainly, that they were not so, is manifest, for besides that Saligniacus (himselfe the Popes Protonotary, and whose travell had taught him some knowledge of the East parts,) directly denieth the Nubians professing of obedience to the Bishop of Rome, observing, that they were governed by a Prelate of their owne, whome they termed the Priest of the Law. Itiner. Tom. 8. c. 2. Beside that direct testimony of his I say, there bee other Evidences. First, because there cannot be produced any Instance, out of any Ecclesiasti-call Historic, either ancient or moderne (as I am certainly perswaded) to that effect. Secondly, because the Fathers o the Nicene Councell, as we find in " Gelasius Cizicenus, are knowne to have assigned Ethiopia, whereof Nubia is a part, to the Patriarch of Alexandria his Jurisdiction, Thirdly, because the Patriarchship of Alexandria, lyeth directly betweene Nubia and Rome, as beeing immediatly at the backe of Egypt. Fourthly, because the Nubians were in Religion Jacobites, as a Roman Cardinall Vitriacus Brocardus, and others have recorded, and as their baptising with fire remembred by Burchardus and Saligniacus did manifestly import Burch. deser. terr. sanct. p. 2. c. 3. 7. Saligniac. Itin. Tom. 8. c. 2. of which Sect the Patriarch of Alexandria is knowne to be: which, had the Pope the assignement or confirmation of their Prelates, it is utterly unlike they should have bin. Fiftly, because in time of their necessity, being left destitute of Bishops and Ministers, if they had pertained to the Bishop of Rome his Jurisdiction, they would rather have had recourse to him, for repaire of the decayed and ruinous state of their Church who both plentifully could, and no doubt readily would have releeved them, rather, then suffered them to depart as they have done, from the Christian Faith: To him I say, they would rather have resorted for supply, then to the King of Habassia (as they did) beeing of another Patriarchall Alvare. loco Jurisdiction. Certaine therefore it seemeth, that Nubia- "-while it was Christian, belonged not to Rome but to Alexandria: By whom, if the Nubians in their distresses were not releeved, no man can wonder, that knoweth the great want and misery of the Church of Egypt.

NOw touching the Habassines, or mid-land- thi- Ofthehabas-opians, whether they have obtained that name, by '- f-reason of their habitations (in houses) which the Egyptians called Avases, as Strabo hath observed (for Stra. I. z. the ancient Bookes have ava eig not avda-eig) in difference '7-from them, which dwelling neerer the Bay of Arabia, were called Trogloditae (axto rov? rpoxyeov) because they dwelled in Caves, not in Houses, as Plinie and others Pltn-l. z. c. have recorded: whether I say, for that reason they,. " ' ' ' nave obtamed the name or Abassms, or no, let more curious men inquire. But as touching their Religion, they are in manner meere Jacobites: And their King (whom by error we call Prestor John) is sundry times in Histories termed the Prince of the Jacobites. And their leaving out of their memorialls (in their Liturgy) Liturg. the Councell of Chalcedon, by which the heresie main-;-Sr. f tained after by Jacobus Syrus was condemned, whereas patrum'tag. the Councells of Nice, of Constantinople, and of Ephesus 59. y 65. are remembred, doth import so much. And in very deed considering the dependance, that the Church of Zag. Zabo. de Habassia hath of the Patriarke of Alexandria, it is elig. y almost unpossible but they should be so; for as Zaga, V ' Zabo, an Habassine Bishop hath left recorded, although Dammiai they have a Patriarke of their owne, whom they call in Goes.

Liturg. Eth'iop. Tom. 6. Biblioth. Vet. Patruin. p. 62.

Concil. 'Nken. I. 3. can. 36.

Li. 138.

1.2.3.4.5.6. 9. 10. 11.

Zag. Zab. de Reltg. y morib. Etkiop. ap. Dami-anum.

their owne language Abuna, (our Father) and hee chosen by the Habassine Monkes of Saint Antonies Order remaining in Jerusalem, yet are they limited to chuse one of the Jurisdiction of Alexandria, and a Monke of Saint Antonie he must be. And beside that, the confirmation and consecration of him belongeth to the Patriarke of Alexandria, and by him he is sent with Ecclesiasticall charge into Habassia. And (to be short) their prayer in their present Liturgie, for the Patriarke of Alexandria, terming him the Prince of their Archbishops, and remembring him before their owne Patriarke, evidently declareth their dependance and subjection to that Sea. Which supreme Ecclesiasticall power touching Ethiopia, to have belonged very antiently to the Patriarke of Alexandria, may appeare by the Arabike Booke of the Nicene Councell, translated by Pisanus, where that authoritie is found assigned to the Patriarke of Alexandria, touching that Abuna of Ethiopia (by the name of Catholike) and withall, to that Catholike of chiefe Bishop of vethiopia, the seventh place in the Sessions of generall Councells, namely, next after the Bishop of Seleucia (whose Seat was next the Patriarkes of Jerusalem) by the Decree of the same Nicene Fathers was allotted.

But if you desire a register of some speciall points of their Religion; 1. They circumcise their children the eight day, after the manner of the Jewes: Even Females also as well as Males, wherein they differ from the Jewes.

2. They reverence the Sabbath (Saturday) keeping it solemne equally with the Lords day.

You may observe, which I in my reading have done, that all the Patriarkes and other Bishops of the East, are Monkes, of the Orders, either of Saint Basil, or Saint Anthony, for the Patriarkes of Constantinople, of Antiochia, and of Armenia, are Monkes of Saint Basils Order: the Patriarkes of Alexandria, of Ethiopia, of the Jacobites, and of the Maronites, are of Saint Anthonies: And the Patriarke of the Nestorians either of both.

3. They eat not of those beasts, which in the old Law are censured for uncleane.

4. They consecrate the Sacrament of the Eucharist in 4- Alvarez,. unleavened bread: contrary to the custome of all the " ' P-East, the Armenians excepted. Neverthelesse Tecla an Habassine Monke and Priest, saith that they celebrate ordinarily in leavened bread, but on the day of the institution of the Lords Supper (the Thursday before

Easter) they do it in bread unleavened over al Habassia. an. Th. a Jes. 1. 7. p. i. c. 13.

5. And communicate in both kinds, which they receive '-Alvarez. standing. And all of them, as well of the Laity as L ",.,. Clergy at leastwise every weeke, the Priest ministring at. Th. a Jes. the bread, and the Deacon the wine with a spoone. he alleg. Tecla. Abissin. Joel. Zag. Zab. de rel. But yet onely in the Temple; it being not lawfull for any (not the King or Patriarke) elsewhere to communicate. After the receiving whereof, it is not lawfull for them to spit that day till the setting of the Sunne. Zag, Zab. ibid.

7. And that even to their yong Infants, presently after they are baptised: which in their Males is fortie dayes Tecla. Abi-after their birth, and in Females eightie (except in perill "'" P-'-of death, for then they are presently baptised. Tecla. i' Abissin. ib.) till which time be complete, their women y. pa. i. c. i. also enter not into the Temple. Zag. Zab. ibid.

8. They professe but one Nature and one Will in Christ, yet without any mixtion or confusion of the Divine and Humane substances. Tecla. ap. Th. a Jesuit. 1. 7. pa. i. c. 13.

9. Beleeve the reasonable soules of men, to bee traduced from parents by seminall propagation. Zag. Zab. de Relig. thiop. in fine. Th. a Jes. 1. 7. p. i. c. 8.

10. Beleeve the soules of the Infants departing afore Baptisme to bee saved, because they are sprung from faithfull parents, and namely the vertue of the Eucharist, received by the mother after conception to sanctitie the child in her wombe. Zag. Zab. ibid. Th. a Jes. I. 7. p. I. c. 8. Alvar. hist. iethiop. ca. 22.

Alvarez., eod. loco.

Zaga. Zabo.

loco, citato. Jlvarcz. lib. citato, c. 5.

Alvar. f. I 3. Zaga Zabo, ubi supra.

11. They presently upon commission of sinne resort to the Confessour, and at every confession (though it were every day) receive the Sacrament of the Eucharist. Zaga Zabo, ibidem, 12. They have onely painted, not massie Images in their Churches. Tecla. ubi supra.

13. They accept onely the three first generall Coun-cells, rejecting that of Chalcedon, for determining two Natures to be in Christ, and for condemning Dioscorus the Patriarke of Alexandria. Tecla. Abis. ib.

14. Elevate not the Sacrament in celebrating of the Eucharist, but keepe it covered: neither reserve it after the Communion, 15. To excommunicate obstinate sinners, is peculiar to their Patriarke, which yet is not usuall among them, except in case of Murther, Zag. Zab. ibid.

16. Their Priests, and other inferiour Ecclesiasticall Ministers (as also Monkes) live by their labour, having no tithes for their maintenance, nor being suffered to crave Almes, Zag. Zab, loc. citato, 17. But the conferring of Bishoprickes, and other Ecclesiasticall Benefices (except the Patriarchship) be-longeth onely to the King. Zag, Zab. ibid.

18. Use neither confirmation, nor extreame unction.

19. Admit the first marriage in their Bishops and Priests, but not the second, except their Patriarch dispense, 20. Eat flesh every Friday (as on other dayes) betwixt Easter and Whitsunday: as on every Saturday also through the yeere, except in Lent.

21. Baptise themselves every yeere on the day of the Epiphany, in Lakes or Ponds,

Concerning which first and last points, namely, of their Circumcision and annuall Baptismes, I have somewhat to observe: Namely, first, touching their Circumcision, that they observe it, not so much perhaps of Religion, as of an ancient custome of their Nation, For although their circumcising on the eight day, seemeth to imply that they received it from the Jevves, yet their circumcising of both sexes, as certainly argueth that they did not so. And if the Habassines bee of the race of the ancient Ethiopians, the doubt may bee the lesse: because Herodotus and others have recorded it, Herodot. I. z. for an ancient Ceremony of that Nation. Or, if they "–bee not of the Ethiopian race, but of the progeny of the Arabians, as by Uranius in Stephanus Byzantius it Stephanus should appeare, recording them for a Nation of the By ' "f-Arabians, neere to the Sabaans: even m this case also, dictione the occasion and originall of circumcising among the ASditj ot. Abassines will bee discerned well enough: namely, because it is specially storied to have been a very ancient Ceremony among the Arabians: among whom it might have beginning, by reason of the descent of many of I. i. 139. the Arabians, from Ismael, and sonnes of Abraham, by Gc7i. 25. 3. Keturah, planted in Arabia, of which Sheba by name- Skindla: in recorded for one. But yet if the Abassines observe l f-.

'.-.,, Pentaglot. tn

Circumcision, not, as an ancient National Custome, but-.

in any sort for Religion sake, then it may be excused in such manner, as"one of their owne Bishops hath "Z-agazabo professed, namely, that it is done onely in remembrance " ' and love, and imitation of our Saviour, because he was circumcised, and not for any other opinion of holinesse at all.

And secondly, touching their annuall baptisings in the Feast of the Epiphany, which they (with many Ancients of the Church) suppose to be the day of our Saviours Baptisme, it is declared by the "= Ethiopian Bishop above '.- " mentioned to bee practised among them, not as any J" '

Which seemeth to bee true, both because in the Ethiopian Liturg.

Liturgie, they terme their owne Kingdome the Kingdome of Sheba, Ethlop. in and also because the Kings of Habassia deduce lineally their descent, Tom. 6.

from the Queen of Sheba that came to see Salomon: which Sheba Bibuothecte is to the skilfull certainely knowne to be in Arabia: and either the Vet. Pat. p. ().

same that wee call Arabia foelix, or some parts of it. And certainly Zag. Zabo it is observed by learned men, that Arabia fcelix in the Easterne de Morib.

tongue, is named Mnilj, as Arabia deserta "Tip and Arabia Petrasa, Ethiop. apud rqi o y"C Damian.

' Posse fin. de Reb. Moscov. p. 6.

Alvarez, hist. Ethiop.95.

Of the Armenians. Chap. 24.

Vid. Postel. lib. de 12. Linguis. Tit. de Lingua Armenica.

Notitia pro- vinciar.

Orient.

Concil. Chnl-cedon. Can. 28.

Sacrament, or any conceit of sanctification to bee obtained by it, but onely as a memoriall of Christs baptisme, because as on that day he was baptised in Jordan. Even as the Moscovites also do the like on the same day in Rivers, and for the same reason, which appeareth the more evidently to bee so, because this yeerely baptising is no ancient Ceremony of the Habasins, but a fashion of late taken up among them, as Alvarez that lived long in those parts hath related, as being namely the institution of ""his grandfather, that then reigned in Habasia, being about one hundred yeeres agoe.

THe Armenians, for Trafike to which they are exceedingly addicted, are to be found in multitudes, in most Cities of great Trade, specially in those of the Turkish Empire, obtaining more favour and priviledge among the Turkes, and other Mahumetans, "by a patent graunted that Nation under Mahumets owne hand, then any other sect of Christians. Insomuch that no Nation seemeth more given to Merchandize, nor is for that cause more dispersed abroad, then the Armenians, except the Jewes. But yet the native Regions of the Armenians, and where they are still found in the greatest multitude, and their Religion is most supported, are Armenia the Greater (named since the Turkes first possession of it Turcomonia) beyond Euphrates, and Armenia the Lesse on this side Euphrates, and Cilicia, now termed Car-mania.

Now the Armenians touching their Ecclesiasticall government, were anciently of the Jurisdiction of the Patriarke of Constantinople, as being Provinces of the Diocesse called Pontica, which together with the Provinces of the Diocesses Asiana, and of Thrace (three of the thirteen Diocesses, into which the whole Empire was divided) were by the Councel of Chalcedon, assigned or else confirmed to the Patriarke of Constantinople, for his jurisdiction. But at this day, very long since, even before Photius his time (as is evident by his circular

Epistle) the Armenians are departed, both from the government of that Patriarke, from the communion of the Grecians (whom at this present, they have in more detestation then any other Sect of Christians) and that principally, for the very same occasion, for which Photll ep'ist.

the Jacobites of Syria withdrew their obedience from f. T . f v-1 r A-i 1 ITT r baron, lorn.

the Patriarch of Antiochia, namely, the Heresie or one j jj al onely nature in Christ. And ever since that departure, An. 863. they acknowledge obedience, without any further or higher dependance, to two Patriarckes of their owne: whom they terme Catholikes. Namely one of the greater Armenia, the Families under whose jurisdiction exceede the number of 150000. beside very manie Monasteries. Leonard. Sidon episc. ap. Th. a Jes. 1. 7. p. I. c. 19. who at this present 'keepeth residence, in 'Mira-Notit the Monasterie of Ecmeazin, by the Citie, c. Leonard.- Z"- ' " Sidon, episc. ap. Tho. a Jes. loc. citato, by the Citie of " J,." . Ervan in Persia, being translated thither by occasion oi tion. p. x,. l. z. the late warres betwixt the Persians and the Turkes: c. de Dios-but his ancient seate was Sebastia, the Metropolis of ' '"" '-Armenia the greater: And the other Patriarch of Armenia the lesse, the Families of whose jurisdiction are esteemed about 20000. Leonard, Sidon. ubi. supra, who anciently kept at "Melitene, the Metropolis of that Province, but Condi Chal-now is resident in the Citie of Sis, not farre from Tarsus "- ' J- in Cilicia, the middle limit on Interstitium, of those " ' ' two Patriarchs Jurisdictions, being the River Euphrates. Such at this present is the state of the Armenian Church, and the jurisdiction of their Patriarchs. But it should seeme, by that I finde recorded, by Otho Otho. Pkris-Phrisingensis, upon the report of the Legates of Ar- "- 7- menia, sent from the Catholique, to the Bishop of Rome in his time, that the jurisdiction of the Catholique of Armenia was then farre larger, as namely, that he had above a thousand Bishops under his obedience: Except Otho perhaps mistooke, as I verily beleeve he did, obedience for communion: for as touching the communion, which the Arminians maintained with other

Tom. I. Juris Oriental. I. z.

' De Bel. sacro Isovel. 31.(T. I, I. i. i+o.

i. Niceph. hist. Eccle. . i8.

Confes. Armenia. Art. 26.27.28.29.

2 Alfons. a Castro I. 5. cont. Hares. Titul. de Deo. Hceresi. 12. Boem de Morib. gent. I. 2. c. 10.

3 Nicephor. loc. sup. citato Litwgia. Ar-men. apud Cassandrum de Liturgiis.

4 Niceph. loc. citat. Litur. Armenior. ubi supra.

Jacobites, it extended indeede very farre: But the jurisdiction of Armenia, for ought I can finde in any record of antiquitie, contained onely foure Provinces, namely, the two Armeniaes before mentioned, the greater and lesse, and the two Provinces of Cilicia. In which small circuit, that such a multitude of Bishops should be found, is utterly uncredible, especially because we finde registers extant, both of the Bishops of the two Armeniaes, in the Novell of Leo-Sophus the Emperour, touching the precedence of Metropolitans: and likewise the Bishops of Cilicia, in ""Guilielmus Tyrius: and all of them put together, exceede not the number of thirtie. And although I finde that Justinian divided the two Armeniaes into foure Provinces (which yet to have beene after reduced againe into two, the Novell of Leo even now mentioned assureth us) yet were not for that cause, the number of Bishops encreased any whit the more.

Now, touching the properties of their Religion.

1. They are charged with the opinion of one nature in Christ: yet not as Eutyches imagined it one, namely, by a permixtion and confusion of the divine and humane natures, but yet by such a conjunction and coalition of them, that they both together, make but one compounded nature in our Saviour, as the body and soule, but one compound nature in man. But neverthelesse, it seemeth by the confession of the Armenians, which we have extant touching the Trinitie, sent by the mandate of the Catholique of Armenia, to the Patriarch of Constantinople, not fiftie yeeres agoe, that at this present, they have utterly renounced that phantasie.

2. They beleeve the Holy Ghost proceedeth onely from the Father.

3. They celebrate the Sacrament of the Eucharist with unleavened bread (as the Romans doe.) 4. They denie the true body of Christ to be really in the Sacrament of the Eucharist under the Species of Bread and Wine. Guido Sum. de heresib. They mingle not water with wine in the Eucharist. An ancient opinion and propertie of theirs, for I finde it recorded of them (and condemned) in the sixt generall Condi. Con-councell. But they retaine it notwithstanding still. '- 3- '"

5. They receive Infants presently after baptisme to r j,; the communion of the Eucharist; affirming that baptisme Morib. gent. l. cannot be conferred without the Eucharist. Guid. Sum. 2. r. 10.

de heresib. 6 Guido in 6. They denie the vertue of conferring Grace, to belong j j-il to the Sacraments. Guido loc. alleg. They reject Alfons."a Purgatorie, and pray not for the dead. Th. a Jes. 1. 7, Castr. l. 12.

p. I. C. 17. cont. Hceres.

7. They beleeve that the soules of holy men obtaine '. ". not blessednesse till the universall judgement. Th. a 1.

Jes. 1. 7. p. I. c. 17. They admit married Priests, and Boem. loc as Burchardus hath recorded, descr. terr. sanct. pa. 2. " " c. 2.9. admit none to be secular Priests, except they of f"' be married. They rebaptise those that come to their 12. Paste I in communion from the Latine Church. Guid. Sum. de Lingua T er-heresib. but exclude their second marriage. viana.

8. They abstaine from eating uncleane Beasts. Boem. loc.

9. They eate flesh on fridaies betweene Easter and q iv vm Ascension day. Peregr.

10. They fast Lent most strictly, without Egges, Orient. 1. 4. Milke-meats, Flesh, Oyle, Wine, c. onely with Fruits, '9-Herbs, Roots, and Pulse. ' i 11. They celebrate not Christmasse day when other Dioscoriani. Christians doe (Decemb. 25.) but fast on it: and instead 10 Vithac. of it, celebrate the feast of our Saviours Baptisme, " ':-namely, on the day of the Epiphanie. W Fitriac 12. They solemnise the feast of the Annunciation, loc. citato. the sixt day of Aprill. The purification the foureteenth z Boter. kco. of February, c. "-

THe Maronites who were so named, not of an Of the Maro-heretique called Maron, as many falsely write,!, f-Prateol. de Sect. Heretic, in verb. Maronit. But of ' ' a holy man of that name, for wee finde mentioned in

Possevin. Appar. Sacr. in Mafoniiie.

Boier. Relat. p. 3. . 2. r.

de Maroniti. Possevin. loci citato.

Brocard. in Desc. Terr. Sanctis. Tacit, historiar. I. ultimo.

Vitriac. hist. Orient, c. 84. Postell de-script. Sy?-i.

Gerundens. I. I.

Paralipom. Hisparn. ca. de terra Roscilion. Fest. in Diction. Album.

the Booke of Councels the Monasterie of Saint Maron. Concil. Constantinop. sub. Men. act, 5. the Monkes onely whereof at first were termed Maronites: they are found in small numbers, in Aleppo, Damascus, Tripolie of Syria, and in Cyprus: But their maine habitation, is in the Mountaine Libanus. Which although it containe in circuit about seven hundred miles, and is possessed onely in a manner by the Maronites, who for that priviledge, namely to keepe themselves from the mixture of Mahumetans, pay the Turke large tribute: yet of all sects of Christians, they are the least, as being esteemed not to passe in all 12000. houses, (all in scattered Villages) beside a few Monasteries, by reason of the indisposition of Libanus in most places, for frequent habitation. For beside the craggednesse or steepnesse of that Mountaine, which maketh many parts of it in a manner inaccessible, the higher Ridges of it (which by Brocardus his relation are so eminent, that they may be discerned fortie leagues off) are also covered in a manner continually with snow, which it retaineth, as Tacitus with " others, hath left recorded, notwithstanding the heate of that climate, even in the neerest approach of the Sunne. And is scarcely, as hath beene observed by Postell, in one Summer of thirtie to be found cleare of it: for which very cause and no other, that mountaine seemeth to have gotten the name of Lebanon. For-js in the ancient language of those parts (the Phasnician or Hebrew tongue) signifieth White, and Dsb White-nesse: Even as, for the like whitenesse of Snow, Gerundensis hath remembred Canus (the highest part of the Pyrene hills) to have obtained that name. And as Festus supposeth the Alpes, for the same cause, to have gayned theirs, that in the Sabine dialect being

Namely, for every one above 12. yeeres old 17. Sultanines by the yeere (the Sultanine weigheth a dramme of Gold, about seven shillings six pence of our money) and for every space of ground sixteene spans square, one Sultanine yeerely, as is recorded by Possevine, termed (saith hee) Alpum, which the Romans in theirs named Album. For so touching the originall of the name Libanus, had I much rather thinke, then bee led " hidor. by the phantasie of Isidorus and some others, namely, Origin. that Libanus, should purchase that name of Franckin—H– 8. cense which the Grecians call 'Savroi and the Tewes nan-i, ' " '""

T-"-r I 1-1-ri 1 1 j 1- ad Arrian.

Jbor, ir It bee not true, which yet Theophrastus and Periplh.

Plinie write, that Frankincense is gotten onely in Arabia Mar. Ery- foelix, (according with that of Virgil, Solis est Thurea rce. p. i-j.

virga Sabasis) by reason of which propertie of place, to g"i,.

burne incense is termed in Tertullian, aliquid Arabia sanct. in incendere: if that I say bee not true, for indeede, I finde Nepktalim.

in Dioscorides, record of Frankincense gotten in India, ""'- and in Pedro Cieza of the like in some part of America, K t7: ,., r.,. ' hist. Plantar.

yet IS there no mention or remembrance in any historic . n. r. r.

of nature, or other, as I take it, that Frankincense was I. i. 141.

ever gotten in the Hill of Libanus. Plin. I. iz. c.

The Patriarch of the Maronites (to come neerer to.", our purpose) who is noted to bee a Monke of Saint . 2

Antonie, and to have under his jurisdiction eight or Tertul. de nine Bishops, keepeth residence for the most part in ' J'"- Milit.

Libanus, in a Monasterie of Saint Anthonie, and now "-fff fj and then in Tripolie: And is one of them, that Medic mate.

challenge the title of the Patriarch of Antiochia, keep- . c 7.

ing ever the name of Peter as the Patriarch of the Possevin.

Jacobites, the other challenger of the same dignitie, doth 1 "! """

of Ignatius. But touching Religion, the Patriarch of Bot7r. Rel.

the Maronites professeth obedience at this present, to p. 3. . 2. c.

the Bishop of Rome, yet but lately, in Clement the ' Maroniti.

eight his time: And both hee, and all the Maronites, "' '"- '- are become of the Roman Religion (being the onely p j,

Nation of the East, except the Indians, lately brought citat. Boter.

also to the Roman Communion, that acknowledgeth lo:- "(o- that obedience) and have a Seminary in Rome q Mtra: notitte

Gregorie the thirteenth his foundation, for the trayning ol-lff'p up of the youth of their Nation in that Religion. Tho. a Jes. d'e

But before that alteration, these were the Characters of Com: Gent.

their Religion.- 3– 3- 1. That the Holy Ghost proceedeth onely from the Father. Th. a Jes. 1. 7. p. 2. c. 6.

2. That the soules of men were all created together from the beginning. Id. loc. citato.

3. Not to baptise male children together, Interrog. Patriarch. Maronit. ap. Th. a Jes. lib. 7. pa. 2. ca. 5.

4. That Heretiques returning to the Church are to be rebaptised. Th. a Jes. 1. 7. p. i. c. 6.

5. That the childe is made uncleane by the touch of the mother till she be purified, which after a male childe is 40. daies, and 80. after a female, for which reason they baptise not their Infants afore those termes. Th. a Jes. loc. citat.

6. That they celebrated the Sacrament of the Eucharist in both kindes. Possevin. Appar. sac. in Maronitae. Patriarch. Maronit. Interrog. 3. ap. Tho. a Jes. 1. 7. p. 2. c. 5.

7. And in leavened bread. Th. a Jes. 1. 7. p. c. 6.

8. Distributing to all the Communicants each one a peece of the same Bread (which they consecrate in great Masses) together with these words of the Gospell, he blessed, and brake, and gave to his Disciples, saying, take, eate, c. Mat. 26. 26. Id. Patriarch. Interrog. 3. ap. Th. a Jes. loc. citat.

9. To distribute the Sacrament of the Eucharist to children before the use of reason, and first presently after baptisme. Th. a. Jes. 1. 7. p. 2. c. 5. 9. cap. 6.

10. Not to reserve the Sacrament of the Eucharist. Patriarc. Maron. ubi supra.

11. Nor to carry it to any sicke person in danger of death. Th. a Jes. 1. 7. p. 2. c. 5.

12. To omit confirmation by the Bishop. Patr. Maron. Int. 2. ubi supr.

13. To exclude the fourth Matrimonie, in every person as utterly unlawfull. Id. Ibid. Interrog. 5.

14. That marriage is not inferiour to single life. Th. a Jes. 1. 7. p. 2. c. 6.

15. Utterly to dissolve Matrimonle in case of adultery and marry another. Patr. Maronit. Inter. 5. ubi supra.

16. That the Father may dissolve the matrimonie of his Sonne or Daughter if hee mislike it. Th. a Jes. 1. 7. p. 2. c. 6.

17. Not to ordaine yong men Priests or Deacons except they were married. Patriarch. Maronites Inter. 6. ubi supra. Possevin. in Appar. sacr. in Maronitae. But yet to restraine their second marriage. Th. a Jes. Ibid.

18. To create children five or six yeares old Sub-deacons. Patriarch. Maronit. Inter. 5. ubi supra.

19. That no man entreth the Kingdome of heaven before the generall Judgement. Th. a Jes. 1. 7. p. 2. c. 6.

20. Not to fast on the Lords day, nor on the Sabbath. Th. a Jes. loc. citat.

21. In the daies of fasting not to celebrate Masse till the Evening. Patr. Maron. ap, Th. a Jes. 1. 7. p. 2. c. 5.

22. Not to eate of any thing strangled or of bloud. Id. 1. 7. p. 2. c. 6.

23. To exclude women during their monthly issues both from the Eucharist, and from the Church. Patriar. f itriac kistor. Maronit. Interr. 8. ubi supra. O" " '- ' 78-

24. Their maine Errour was, the heresie of the J T, i 1 1-11 1-o"""" sacro. .

Monothehtes, touchmg one onely will and action in 22. c. 8. Christ. Which errour although they renounced about Sallgn'uu. 400. yeeres agoe, and reconciled themselves then to the '- T "'-Roman Church, at what time those parts of Palestine ' ' ' ' and Syria, were in the Christians hands, as Jacobus a Vitriac y Vitriaco, and Guilielmus Tyrius, the one Bishop of '! ' "" " Aeon, and the other of Tyre, have recorded: yet shortly after, when those parts were by Saladin, the King of gypt and Syria, recovered from the Christians, those Maronites relapsed, and forsooke againe the Roman communion, till the late times of Pope Gregorie the XIII. and Clement the VIII. with whom they againe renewed it.

And this heresie of the Monothelites, springing out of that bitter roote of the Jacobites, touching one onely nature in Christ, was the last of that long and wicked traine of heresies, which upon the contempt of the councell of Chalcedon, exceedingly wasted and ruined I. i. 142. the East Church, for after that the detestation of Nestorius heresie, touching two persons in our Saviour (condemned in the third generall Councell) had so inimoderately distempered the phantasies of Eutiches in Constantinople, and the Patriarch of Alexandria, Dio-scorus, with other their adherents, that they thought not themselves safe enough from the heresie of two persons, till they were fallen into the other opposite extremitie of one nature in Christ; the Divine and humane natures in Christ (in their conceits) by permix-tion and confusion of substances, and of properties growing into one, upon their adunation: and withall, that the humane nature of Christ, was not consubstan-tiall to ours, but of another kinde, and condition;

which phantasies the fourth generall Councell condemned. After I say, this heresie of Eutiches and Dioscorus, had growne to that head in JEgypt and Syria, that like a violent and furious streame, whose course would not be staied, it bare downe before it all oppositions, and among the rest, that great and reverend Councell of Chalcedon, that had condemned it, and was contemned by it, it gave occasion for an infinite traine of heresies to follow at the breach, which it had made. Fid'Ntcepkor. For first (to omit infinite extravagant branches that Histor. Eccles. sprang from it, and infinitely deformed the Church, Is'eouent renting with many schismes the unitie, and with as Leont. de many heresies wounding the faith of it.) It drew after ectis. Action, it the heresie of the passiblenesse of the Deitie, because 5. c. j g Deitie of Christ, was become (in their conceits) the same nature with the Humanitie, that was passible. Secondly, (the absurditie of that being discerned) it occasioned another extremelie opposite, namely of the Impassibilitie of the Humanitie of our Saviour (but on the same ground) because namely, it was become one nature with the Deitie, which now wee know to bee unpassible. Thirdly, when the fondnesse of both were discovered, it bred a great device, touching one nature in our Saviour (as the wit of Heretikes will better serve them to devise a thousand shifts to delude the truth, then their pride will suffer them once to yeeld and acknowledge it.) It bred I say a new device, namely, to be one, not by permixtion or confusion of substances, as Eutyches first taught, but onely by composition, the Deitie and Humanitie, by coalition becomming one nature in Christ, as the Bodie and Soule grow into one nature in Man. And fourthly, when this fantasie began also somewhat to abate and relent in many: yet still a fraction, as it were, or rather a consequent of it was retained (for indeed it implieth by neces-sarie consequence the unitie of nature) namely, that there was but one Will, and one Action of both natures in the person of our Saviour. And God knowes what a traine and succession of heresies might have followed these, if that Lord, whom they had infinitely wronged, by their wonton and wandring conceits of him, had not, to stop the course and streame of their wickednesse and follie, brought on them the Sarracens of Arabia. For even while the Church, speciallie that of the Easterne parts, was in a great perplexitie and travell with the heresie of the Monethelites (which I last mentioned) the Mahumetans of Arabia, like a mightie inundation brake forth, and overwhelmed all, and them first, that first and most had wronged the Sonne of God, by fostering the forenamed heresies, and the infinite brood that sprung of them, I meane Egypt and Syria, and to this day both they and the neighbouring Nations, that had beene infected by them, remaine in thraldome. But yet, as in the diseases, and distemper of our bodies, contraries are usually healed by contraries, so seemeth it to have fallen out in the distempers of these mens religions: for as worldly prosperitie and wantonnesse of wit (ordinarie companions)

Biblioth. Vet. Pair. Tom. 4. pa. 1049. 153. " Confess. Arme. de Trinitat. Art. 26. 27. 28. 29. 30. Baron. Tom. 6. Anna I. in fine.

De Relig. ifj Morib. jethiop. ap Domian a Goes. Possevin. Appa. fac. in Nestoriani. Possevin. lib. citat. in Maron. Boter. Rel. p. 3.. 2. c. Maroniti. Michoi'. I. 2. de Sar? natia. c. I. Cius. Turcog. I. 7. pa. i.". l c. Of the several languages zc'herein the Liturgies of Christians in the severall parts of the World are celebrated. Chap. 26.

wherewith these Nations in those times abounded, bred in them their ordinarie children, namely, prosperitie of the world, pride, wantonnesse of wit, error, which couple in matter of Faith and Religion, is wont to produce no better issue then heresie. So on the other side, having now at length their hearts humbled and their wits tamed by that povertie and affliction, wherein the tyrannic and oppression of the Arabians and Turkes hath long holden them, it seemeth the Lord hath taken pittie on them (as it is his propertie not to dispise humble and broken spirits, and to remember mercie in the middest of judgement) and reduced them, or most of them, to the right acknowledgement of his Sonne againe. For certainly, that they and other Christians of the East, have (at least in these later times) disclaimed and abandoned, those hereticall fancies touching our Saviour, wherein by their misleaders they had beene anciently plunged (and which many Christians of these West parts still charge them withall) doth manifestly appeare: First, of the Jacobites, secondly of Nestorians, by their severall confessions, translated out of the Syriacke tongue by Masius, extant in Bibliotheca Veterum patrum. Thirdly, of the Armenians, by their owne confession also, translated by Pretorius. Fourthly, of the Cophti, by the profession of their faith extant in Baronius. Fifthly, of the " Habassines, by the relation of Zaga Zabo, a Bishop of their own. Sixtly, of the Indians, by their reconcilement to the Church of Rome, mentioned by Possevine. And seventhly, of the Maronites, by their like reconcilement, recorded by him and by others.

ANd thus have I related the severall sects of Christians that are abroad in the World, with the places of their habitations, the special characters that are recorded of their Religions. One point notwithstanding of their difference, have I left purposely as yet untouched, both for the amplenesse of the matter, and because I conceive you would have it declared severally.

Namely, touching the different languages, in which all these severall sorts of Christians celebrate their Liturgies or Divine Service.

But first to speake a word or two, of the publique I. i. i43- Service of the Jewes, and of the Mahometans, in their Synagogues, and Meskeds (seeing I intreated before of those Religions.) The Jewes where they obtained libertie for their Synagogues, celebrate theirs in the ancient Hebrew tongue, as Michovius, with many others hath Muhov. . 2. related, and as is manifest by their owne editions of " r"'-their publique Praiers, printed both at Venice and in,. 7-. Polonia, in that language. cogr. I. 7. p.

But the Mahumetans have theirs in the Arabique 487- tongue (the native language of their Prophet) as George-" f. J vitz, Richerius, and sundry others have recorded: So that- ca. 1. not onely in Arabia and T gypt, and Barbaric, and Pales- Rkier. I. 2. tine, and Syria, and Mesopotamia (in which parts the de Morib. S Arabique tongue is become the vulgar language) the ' l ' " ' " ' Alcoran is read, and their publique devotions exercised,-. i. . 7. in Arabique: but also in Greece, and Natolia, and other 87. parts of the Turkish Dominion, where the Greeke, and Turkish, and Slavonique tongues are vulgar, as also in Persia, in Tartaric, in India, where they have other native, and peculiar languages, the Mahumetans reade the Alchoron (which they suppose were profaned if t ' ' j it were translated into vulgar tongues) and performe 2. c a' their publique devotions in that language. Sacerd. Dur-

But Christians in celebrating of their divine Liturgies, and Ration. differ touching the language very much. Indeede I dwinor. 1. 4. finde it recorded in Durandus (but upon what warrant and authoritie I cannot finde) that till the time of Hadrian the Emperour (that is about an hundred and twentie yeeres after Christ) their Liturgies were all celebrated in the Hebrew tongue: And then, the Orientall Church began, first to celebrate them in Greeke. Indeede mee thinkes it is possible, that the Christians of the Gentiles might in honour of the Apostles, retaine the Apostles Liturgies, in the verie tongue wherein by the

Apostles themselves, they have beene first ordayned, Vide Baron, for it is not to bee doubted, but many yeares passing r ' I i I (o t tenne) after our Saviours assention, before the ct ' il' Apostles left Syria, and sundred themselves to preach the Gospell abroad in the world among the Gentile and forraine Nations. It is not to bee doubted I say, but the Apostles, while they remayned in Jurie, ordayned Liturgies in the Jewish tongue, for the use of those Jewes, whom they had converted to Christianitie: which Liturgies by the Christian Disciples of the Jewish Nation, dispersed in many Provinces of the Gentiles, might together with Christian Religion, bee carried abroad, and gladly entertayned among the Gentiles. This is possible I say, but if it bee also true (as I have not observed any thing in antiquitie that may certainly impeach the truth of it) yet that which is spoken by Durandus of those Liturgies in the Hebrew tongue, must bee understood (I doubt not) of the Hebrew, then vulgar and usuall, that is to say the Syriacke tongue: not onely, because in that language wee finde them in these times, celebrated by the Christians of the East: but also because I can conceive no reason, either, why the Liturgies should bee ordayned by the Apostles in that language which the Jewes themselves (the learned excepted) understood not, if it were done for the Jewes: or else why the Gentiles should translate them (or use them so translated) out of the Hebrew into the Syriacke, seeing both were to them alike, vulgarly knowne, and not understood. But howsoever it was in that most ancient and primitive state of the Church, in and immediatly following the Apostles times, the difference certainly among Christians in these present times, in that behalfe is very great, some of them celebrating their Liturgies in their owne native and vulgar, and some other in learned and forraine tongues.

The Christians (to speake first of the first sort) that celebrate them in their owne vulgar languages, are the Armenians, Habassines, Moscovites with Russians, Sclavonians, and Protestantes.

For that the Armenians (howsoever otherwise in their ceremonies belonging to Divine service they approach neerer as Bellonius and others report, to the Rites of Bellonobser.

the Latine Church, then any other sect of Christians)- 3– 12.

„ T u A- ' Vitnac Hist.

that they 1 say exercise their common divine service in q the Armenian tongue, Jacobus a Vitriaco, Brocardus, Brocard. de-

Michovius, Breitenbachius, and many others, some of script. term.

their owne experience, and others of certaine Relation, ' ":- have left recorded. And namely, as touching the trans.

lation of the Holy Scripture, into the Armenian tongue, cap.

which at this present, is in solemne use among them, Breltenbach.

the Armenians themselves as Sixtus Senensis hath re Peregrin. cdc corded, attribute it to no other Author then to Chrysos pl "' tome: who also, out of the historie of George Patriarch Lingua- of Alexandria, written of the life of Chrysostome, Armcnka.

remembreth it specially to have beene Chrysostoms Bellon. loco.

worke after his banishment from Constantinople, while " '. ' ' he lived in those parts of Armenia, to which as we Qrient. 'lib. 4.

reade in "Sozomen, he was by the Emperors decree cap. 19.

confined, and there dyed. And certainly, that the holy VIllamont dc Scriptures were translated into the Armenian tongue J'– ' 2- before Theodorets time, who lived soone after Chrysos g j. Relat.

tome, for he flourished about the yeere 440. Theodoret p. 3. . 2. y himselfe (although he name not the Author of the Alii plures.

Translation) hath left recorded: as I finde also acknow ixt. Senens.

ledged by Angelus Roccha, in his discourse of the– f-

S l7tct itt Lodit-

Vatican Librarie, not onely that Chrysostome is said to Constan- have translated of the Scriptures into the Armenian tlno. polltanus.

tongue, but, that hee is also celebrated among the monu Sozomen.

ments of the same Vatican, as the 'Inventor of the j-8–2 2-

Armenian Characters still in use. de Curand

And touching the Habassines, Alvarez a Portugall, Grecor.

that lived many yeeres among them, hath not onely left Affect, post recorded, that they reade Scriptures in the Tigian tongue,, ' 'f "' which is a dialect of the Habassin, (for Tigia hee noteth; to bee that part of Habassia, which first received Chris. 137.

Fansa de Blblloth. Vaticana pa. 4. dlscors. 21. Alvarez his tor. Etkiop. P S 55- cap. ls. '- I. i. 144.

Idem. c. II. ""P OS tell, de Ling. Indica. Thev. Cos. I. 2. C. z. nlla-mont. l. 2. cap. 24.

Biblioth. Vet. Pat. torn. 6.

M'lchov. I. de Sarmat. z. c. i. Sigism. I. de Rcb. Moscov.). 46. Possc-vin. I. de Rebus Mosc. p. 4. Thev. Cos. I. 19. r. 12.

"Bapt. Palat. de Rat. scribed.

Rocchain Biblioth. Vatican. p. 162. ' Aventin. l. Annal. En. Silt', in Hist. Bohe-mica.13. Aventin. loc. citat. Rocch. loc. citato.

tianitie) into which language Sabellicus Supplem. Histor. lib. 8. recordeth both the Olde and New Testament to have beene translated out of the Chaldee. But "he, with many others, that they celebrate their Liturgie in their owne language, though the Chaldee bee esteemed among them, as their learned tongue, which also the Liturgie it selfe (you may finde it in the new Edition of Bibliotheca veterum Patrum) if you marke the long answers of the People to the Priest, in their prayers doth evidently import.

And no lesse certeine is it also, of the Muscovites and Russians, that their Liturgies are likewise ministred in their vulgar tongue (being a kind of Slavonian) though sometimes intermingling Greeke Hymnes, as Guaguinus hath observed: Descript.

Moscov. ca. 2. as is testified by Mathias Michou, by Sigismund, by Possevine, by Thevet, and sundry others.

And as evident is it of the Illyrians, vhom we commonly call Slavonians that they also exercise their publike Divine Service in their owne language: which to have beene allowed them by the Pope, at the suit of Cyrill their Bishop, or as p others say, of Methodius (but the difference is of no importance, for they both lived in the same time, and were companions in preaching the Gospel to barbarous Nations) veneas Silvius and others have recorded. And in particular of the Liburnians (the more Westerly part of the Slavonians) it is affirmed by Aventine: and of the Dalmatians (the more Easterly part of them) by Angelus Roccha, that they celebrate their Liturgies in their owne language: Which, Roccha saith the Dalmatians are most certainly perswaded to have beene of Hieromes devising. But yet in determining the Antiquitie of that Custome, Roccha that referreth it to Pope Paul the second is greatly mistaken: Because wee find it to have beene much more anciently granted them by Pope John the eighth, that they might both read the Scriptures, and celebrate Masse in their owne tongue, as appeareth by the same 'i Popes Epistle extant to Sfentopulcher. And even "Roccha himselfe (forgetting Epht. 24.7. himselfe) confesseth it in another place, to have beene f' ' ' obtayned of the Pope by Cyrill, who was about six q h p. hundred yeeres ancienter then Paul the second. And ap. Bin. p. certainly (now I am speaking of Popes) of no other 990. Roccha. Judgement touching Divine Service in vulgar Tongues,- " P-seemeth Pope Innocent the third to have beene (and Qg ' n perhaps it was also the Decree of the Councell of Lateran) Lateran. c 9. charging that in Cities, where there was concourse of 13dea-et. I. divers Nations, that differed in Languages and Cere- p-3i–H-monies. Divine Service and Sacraments should be celebrated c- V according to that difference. nacul. kgendo.

But to speake a little in particular of the vulgar Pastel, de Hn-translation of the holy Scriptures used among the Dal- S ' Ulyrka. matians: It is not onely affirmed by sundry Writers to Z' ' " ", be the worke of Hierome, but Hierome himselfe in his censur. theohs-. Epistle to Sophronius, seemeth to some learned men to Paris. Sixt. intimate so much: But yet there is another translation Senens. I. 4. also of the Scriptures into the Slavonicke Tongue, later ' then that of Hieromes, as 'Scaliger hath observed, being Hiet'ommus written in the Servian Character (as the former is in the Stridonensis Dalmatian) used in Rascia, Bosina, Bulgaria, Moldavia, Scalig. Dia-Russia, Moscovia, and other Nations of the Slavonian b. delingms language in the Easterne parts, that celebrate their m;" j Liturgies after the Greeke Ceremonie and professe ixt. Senens. obedience to the Patriarch of Constantinople: Of which o(o " i"- later translation 'Methodius the companion of Cyrill, J'-"' in preaching the Gospel to Gentile Nations, is certainly Lf,". g-Xom, reported to have beene the Author. Which Cyrill (if. Scalig. kc. you question what he was) was neither hee of Alexandria, j' m. citato. nor hee of Jerusalem, as Mutius Pansa hath vainely ' '-J- 4-

J, ir 1 1-1 r-i Annal. Pansa imagined, but another rarre later then either or them, ig lynqth whom in the Slavonicke tongue they call Chivrill, one Vatican, par. that lived about the yeere 860. namely, hee that in the 4. Dzvm-. 23. time of the Emperour Michael the Third, and Pope ""Martyrolog. Nicholas the First, together with Methodius, first brought g J! the Mengrelians, Circassians, and Gazarans, (and after Sarmatia. I. that " many of the Slavonians) to the faith of Christ, as i. c 7.

Pastel de Ling. Dalmatic a. Roccha. B'lb-lioth. Vatican.

p. i6i. y

Alii plurimi.

""Socrat. Hist. Eccles. I. 4. c. 27. Niceph. Hist. Eccles. I. 11, c. 48. Tripart. hist. I. 8. c. 13. Paul. Diacon. Hist. Miscell. l. i2. Soz, ome!. I. 2. c. 37. Socrat. I. 2. f. 32. Vulcan. in pvcef. de Littur. 6 Lingua. Geta-rum. Ins crip. Vet. p. 146. 1. i. 145.

Michovius hath recorded. Neither need wee any other testimony to refell the fantasie of Pansa, touching Cyrill of Jerusalem, then Pansa himselfe, as namely acknowledging that Cyrill was the Inventer of another sort of Illyrian Characters, then by Hierome had beene formerly devised (for of the Dalmatian Characters, that are used in Dalmatia, Liburnia, Istria, Moravia, Silesia, Bohemia, Polonia, c. Hierome is acknowledged to bee the Author.) It could not bee therefore Cyrill of Jerusalem, as being ancienter then Hierome, and by him registred in his Catalogue of Writers. And indeede (to make an end) what reason or occasion might the Bishop of Jerusalem have to divise Characters for the Illyrians But to intreat a little more (on this occasion) of translations of the holy Scripture, made by the ancient Fathers into vulgar languages: Besides those alreadie mentioned, of Hierome and Chrysostome, by the one into the Dalmatian, and by the other into the Armenian tongue: It is also recorded by Socrates and Nicephorus, and sundry "others of Vulphilas, Bishop of the Gothes one more ancient then either of the former, for hee flourished in the time of Constantius the Emperour, and was successour to Theophilus, whose subscription wee find in the first Nicene Councell (being the same man, to whom the Invention of the Gothicke Alphabet is likewise attributed by the same Authors) that hee translated the holy Scriptures into the Gothicke tongue. A Copie of which translation is remembred by Bonaventura Vulcanius, to be yet remaining in some Librarie of Germany: And it may bee that the Gothike translation of the foure Evangelists, mentioned by Gruter in the Booke of ancient Inscriptions, to bee of a thousand yeeres antiquitie, and remaining in the Abbey of Werdin, might bee part of that translation of Vulphilas: But yet, that besides these translations into vulgar Languages, hitherto mentioned of Vulphilas, Chrysostome, and Hierome, the holy Scriptures were likewise anciently translated into the languages of many Nations, is affirmed by Hierome: And in par- ticular (although the translators names bee not recorded) Hieron. in. into the Egyptian, Persian, Indian, Scythian, and Sar- Z'"- 4-matian Tongues, nay into all the Languages of other Nations, as Theodoret, that flourished in the time of the Theodoret. I. Ephesine and Chalcedon Councels (almost 1200. yeeres ' f J' ' ' ' agoe) hath left testified: As also in the following times jjectibuspost (yet ancient) wee read of the like translations of the med. Scriptures, to have beene made by John Archbishop of Vasco. in Sivill into the Arabike, about Ann. 717. which then was ' f' the vulgar speech of that part of Spaine, and some part of it into Saxon or English by Beda about the same time: Into the Slavonike by = Methodius, about An. 860. c. loan. Trevis. Into the Italian by ' Jacobus de Voragine, about An. il' l t. 1290, C. Annal.

And now, to entreate of those sects of Christians that ixt. Senens. celebrate their Liturgies in learned and forraine tongues; Btbl. Sana. which the vulgar people doe not understand: I finde 7f5S-only three languages wherein they are all performed. Genuen-Namely, the Greeke, the Latine, and the Chaldee, or sis. Syriacke Tongues. Vitriac. Hist.

And first, touching the Chaldee or Syriacke, in it are J "-':77-,1,, T r 1 vt TT-Barbos. tn celebrated the Liturgies or the JNestorians, as Vitriacus, y i jg

Barbosa, Villamont, Botero, and others have recorded: Fiag. apud for Genebrard, that pronounceth peremptorily the anius. p.

Hebrew tongue, and not the Syriacke to be the usuall y ' ' ' '"

language, wherein all the Orientall Nations minister Boter. Rel.

their Divine Service, bewrayes but too much, both his par. 3. . 2.

boldnesse and his ignorance, as being not able, I am- Nestoi-i- certainly perswaded, to produce any History or other-j "- lawfull testimony that recordeth the Liturgies of any chronog. 1. 3.

Christians in all the East, to be performed in the Hebrew ad An. Chr.

tongue. But yet it may be observed, that where in 31- sundry Writers we find it mentioned, that the Nestorians exercise their Divine Offices in the Chaldee, we are not to understand them of the pure and ancient, but of the degenerate or Jewish Chaldee, which beside the Chaldee and Hebrew, whereof it is principally tempered and compounded, hath much mixture also both of Greeke

Oser. de Reb. Emmanuel.

Possevin. in Appar. sacr. hi Diamper'iense Concilium. Linschot. I. i. c. 15. Bibl. Vet. Patr. in. Auc-tario. Tom. 2. in fine.

Vitriac. Hist. Orient, c. 76.

and Arabicke, such as the Jewes language was, after our Saviour and his Apostles time, that is (in a word) the Syriake, for the Jewish Chaldee (to declare this point a little better) is of two sorts: One of those that returned not againe after the captivitie to Jerusalem, but setled themselves to inhabite about Babylon, whose language (although somewhat degenerating also from the right Chaldee) is termed the Babylonian tongue, of which sort the Jewes Dialect of Neardea in Mesopotamia (the compilers of the Babylonian Talmud) was: The other of those that returned from the captivitie, whose language is properly termed the Syrian or Jerusalem Chaldee, varying somewhat farther from the native Chaldee then the former, by reason of the mixture of forraine words, Arabicke, Greeke, Roman, and others, which in course of time it contracted: In which Dialect, the Talmud and Targum, both named of Jerusalem, and the bookes of their later Rabbines are written. And in the second sort of Chaldee, is the holy Scripture by the East Christians translated, and their Liturgies at this day celebrated.

Secondly of the Indians, that they in like sort performe their Liturgie (not in the Hebrew, as is confidently affirmed by Genebrard, but) in the Chaldee or Syriacke, is testified by Osorius, Possevine, Linschot, c. and confirmed by their Liturgie extant in Bibliotheca Veterum Patrum, which is there remembred to be translated out of the Syriacke.

And so doe thirdly the Jacobites: Namely, they of Mesopotamia, of Babylon, of Palestine, of Syria, and of Cyprus, which are peculiarly knowne by that appellation. Of whom Vitriacus long since observed, that they read the Divine Scriptures in a language unknowne to the Lay people: And that the language by the New Testament brought from them by Moses Mardenus in Europe to be printed (for the more commodious dispersing of it abroad into their Churches) we now certainely know to bee the Syriacke tongue, even as it is also knowne and ' recorded touching the rest of their i d-

Divine Service, that it is performed in the same Syriacke '" " jf "f 1 1-11 1 i ij A J prafat. iesta- language, which they terme the Chaldee. And it is menti. Syiiaci.

thought, that the Liturgie commonly termed Anaphora Post de lin-

Basilii, which we have by Masius translated out of the gua. Chaldak.

Syriacke into Latine (and is found in Bibliotheca Veterum "'–P-

Patrum) is the Jacobites Liturgie: which language, Qiacobit'i although it be now unknown among them (their Clerkes Blbuoth. Vet.

or learned men excepted) yet that it was vulgarly under Patr. To. 6.

stood, when that Liturgie was first ordained, the long P- V',, answeres or the people to the Priest in their prayers,- which wee finde in it may bee demonstrations. But Admonit.

touching the Old Testament, which they have also (as prefix.

Arrias writes he hath heard from their owne Relations,- ' " f- and Postell, that he hath scene) usuall in all those East 5 parts in the Syriacke tongue, it is specially observed by postel. in

Arias Montanus, to be translated, not out of the Hebrew, Lingua Chal- but out of the Greeke of Origens Emendation. ' '" '

And fourthly, of the Cophti or Christians of Egypt, it is likewise observed, that they celebrate their Liturgies Boter. Rekt.

in the same language: (reading yet the Gospell after it ' i is done in the Chaldee, in the Arabicke tongue, which aVo, is now, and long hath beene the vulgar language of Egypt.) And it may further appeare, beside the testimony of Histories, by the Liturgie of Severus Patriarch of Alexandria in use among them, translated out of Syriake into Latine by Guido Fabritius.

And fifthly, the Maronites in their Liturgies (which I. i. 146. Possevine observeth to be the Liturgies of Peter, of Possemn. in

James, and of Sixtus) use the same Syriacke language Appar. sacro.

(the Arabicke being also their vulgar) as beside Possevine, Maromta.

Postell also, and Villamont, and others have recorded. Chaldaica.

And so doe sixtly and lastly (to make an end of this Villam. I. 2.

reckoning) the poore Christians of the Isle of Zocotora- 24. (an Hand after Barros his dimension of sixtie miles in length, and twenty seven in breadth) without the Bay of Arabia, for although I find it questioned touching the Religion, whether they be Jacobites or Nestorians;

Barros. de Asia. Decad. 2.. I. c. 3.

Anan. Fabric, del. Mondo. Trat. 3. p. 292.

Boter. Relat. par. 3. . '. de Christiani di Socotena.

Jerem. Resp. I. ad Ger-manos.:. 13.

Hieron. in prof, ad Lib. Paralipo.

Juan Barros affirming the first (and it may seeme so for their neerenesse to the Dominions of Habassia) and Ananias, proving the latter because they are uncircumcised, which Jacobites are not, professe obedience to the Patriarch of Mozal, who is known to be Patriarch of the Nestorians: yet in this they both agree, that their Divine Service (such as it is) is performed in the Chaldee tongue. And although Botero relate it to be done in the Hebrew, yet he meaneth (out of doubt) not the ancient and pure Hebrew, but the latter or degenerate language of the Hebrew, that is to say the Syriacke. As the other also that affirme the publike and solemne devotions, either of these Zocotorini, or any other Christians in all the East, or South parts of the world, to be read in the Chaldee, require also the like interpretation: Namely to bee understood, not of the right, and Babylonian, but of the Jewish and corrupted Chaldee.

But now to speake of those Christians, that celebrate their Liturgies in the Greeke tongue: I observe them to be these.

I. The Grecians themselves: Namely, all they whose vulgar speech the Greeke tongue is, inhabiting in Greece, and a great part of Natolia, of Macedon, and of Thrace, together with all the Hands of the jegaean Sea, and the other many scattered Hands, about the Coast of Greece. But yet they doe it, not in the present vulgar, but in the pure and ancient Greeke tongue, whereof as I before observed, the common people understand but little: using namely, on festival! dales the ancient Liturgie of Basil, and on common dayes that of Chrysostome, as Jeremy a late Patriarch of Constantinople hath recorded. And namely, as touching the holy Scriptures, using the Septuagints Greeke translation, and specially that of Lucians Emendation. At least it was so with them in Hieroms time (and I find no mention at all recorded of any alteration) who observeth the Edition of the seventie Interpreters by Lucianus, to have beene re- ceived in use from Constantinople, as farre as Antiochia:

As also that of Origens Emendation, from Antiochia to

Egypt, and in Egypt that of Hesychius. But (howsoever it may bee touching the Edition usuall among them) yet certainly, that the Grecians have not the Scriptures translated into the vulgar Greeke, the 'Grecians them- 'Theodos.

selves have directly recorded. ' utzfcrus 2. The Syrians, namely those, that for distinction i j' Tui-co-' Religion from the Jacobites (who likewise inhabite Syria) T f.. 331. are termed so, that is to say the Melchites, for they having the Arabicke for their vulgar language, as they Z" '- "'- agree in other points of their Religion and Ceremony, f aitho. I de and order of Divine Service with the Grecians, so doe Tartans, c.

they as touching their Liturgie in Language also, as H- is observed by ' Vitriacus, Haitho, Breitenbachius, and Bmtenbach.

, ' Peremn. c. de many others. 5.- 3. The Georgians, who having for their vulgar speech, Baumgart.

a peculiar language of a middle temper (which well Pereg?: I. 2. agreeth with the position of their Countrey) betwixt- 9–Tartarian and Armenian, as Gesner, and Postell, and 2 Boter Roccha, in their bookes of languages have observed, Rel. p.7,. l. exercise notwithstanding their Liturgies in the Greeke c. de Mekhiti. tongue, as 'Jacobus a Vitriaco, Gesner, Postel, Roccha, rtac. hb. and divers others have certainly recorded. Gesner Mith- 4. The Circassians: who yet in such sort celebrate rid. in Lingua their

Divine Service in the Greeke, that their Priests Georgia. themselves, by reason of their grosse ignorance, under- Postelde z. stand not what they read "as Intireano (that lived i ' q' ' among them) hath remembred. Roccha. de 5. And lastly, in the Greeke tongue are celebrated the Dialect, in Liturgies of all the Monasteries, that are of the Greeke Georgiana, y Religion, wheresoever dispersed within the Turkish Do- "S ' '- f-

D ' r li(xuin? art. loc.

minions, in Africke or Asia: As in Mount Sinai, the 7 vilia-Cities of Petra and Eltor in Arabia: in Jerusalem, mont. l. z. c. zt,. Alexandria, Damascus, and in sundry other places, as ""Interian. Bellonius with others hath left recorded. zt7t"

And to come at last to the Nations that celebrate Bella. Obs'er. their Liturgies in the Latine tongue: To speake of. i. e. 35.

them, even this little will bee enough: Namely, that all the Christians, that are found of the Roman Communion in America and in Africa, celebrate their Liturgies in the Roman tongue. As all likewise in Europe (except the Slavonians above mentioned.) And in Asia, except the two new Roman purchases of the Maronites in Syria, and of the Christians of Saint Thomas in India, who retaine still the old accustomed language, which as I observed before, is in the Liturgies of both those Nations, the Syriacke tongue.

I have thought good to adde this note in the conclusion, that Christian Religion may seeme justly to be divided into foure parts, in regard of her professors thorow the World: of which the Grecian Faith pos-sesseth one, reckoning to them the Russian; the Romanists or Papists another; the Protestants (by their adversaries, and by the intemperate zeale of some Lutherans, and other factious persons, made more to disagree then indeed they doe, as by the Harmonie of Confessions appeareth, and by their uniforme acknowledgement of all the maine points of Religion, their differences being about circumstances, rites, manner of presence, and some more abstruse points then whereof the vulgar is capable) these by a generall name called Protestants, may bee reckoned for a third part, perhaps not all so great in I. i. 147. multitudes as either of the former, but more flourishing then the first in splendor of power and learning, onely by an Inquisition inferior to the second; and in numbers as many as all other professions of Christianitie, here reckoned a fourth part.

Chap. XIIII.

Relations of divers Travellers, touching the diversities of Christian Rites and Tenents in divers parts of the World.

Tecla Maria an Abassine, his answeres to questions touching the Religion of the Abassines and Cophti.

Ou have read in Alvares, Bermudez, and the Jesuites Relations, large Relations of the Abassine Faith, and of the Portugalls remaining in Habassia, as also of three Patriarchs sent thither from the Pope, but refused by the Abassine. These Portugalls dwelling there sent one Tecla Maria, an Abassine Priest in their behalfe to Rome, who before the Cardinalls made answere as followeth July i.

1594-

The Reverend Brother Tecla Maria, sonne of Tecla Nebiat, of the Citie Henza Mariam, of the Province of Xena, of the Kingdome of Ethiopia Priest and Monke, of the Order of Saint Antonie, and of the Monastery Libanus of the same Province, aged fortie five yeeres, at the command of the most Illustrious, and most Reverend Lord Cardinall of Saint Severine Protector of the Ethiopian Nation, to certaine interrogatories made in the Arabike to him, thus answered.

Being asked what the Ethiopians beleeve of God and the holy Trinitie, he answered; Wee beleeve in one God and three persons, the Father, Sonne, and Holy Ghost. The Father is unbegotten, the Sonne begotten onely of the Father, the Holy Ghost proceeding from the Father and the Sonne. Being asked, whether the Holy Ghost proceeds from the Father and the Sonne,

Taken out of
Thomas a
Jesu de
Convers. om.
Gent. I. 7. c.
Xena or Sua.
Ofgodb-the Holy Trinity.
A bus sines are
Monothcrtes.
Pictures incensed.
Canonicall bookes 8i.
Gen. Councels.
Sacraments. Tkistecla commeth neerer the Romish Faith in divers things then the Ethiopians, as sup. I. 7. c. 8. perhaps for feare, perhaps of flattery.

as from two beginnings, and two spirations, or as from one beginning and one spiration, he answered, As from one beginning, and one onely spiration. Being asked of the Incarnation, hee answered. That the Person of the Sonne, the Word of God the Father was incarnate by the Holy Ghost of the Virgin Mary.

Being asked how many Natures, Wills, and Operations the Ethiopians professe to be in Christ our Lord, he answered, That the Ethiopians beleeve after the union one Nature, one Wil, one Operation, yet without mixtion and without confusion: in which opinion he confesseth, that the Ethiopians and Cophti, and other Easterne Nations erre from the truth. Being asked whether they hold one Nature in Christ resulting from two, hee answered. The Ethiopians say not so, but simply professe one Nature without mixtion and without confusion, and affirme that to bee Divine,

Being questioned of Images, he answered. That amongst the Ethiopians they are onely painted and not carved or graven, which the Ethiopians have in great veneration, in respect of representation and relation, and incense them. Being asked of the Canonicall Bookes of both Testaments, hee answered. That both the Testaments are divided amongst them into eightie one Bookes, all which are had in Egypt, but without booke he could not remember their names.

Being asked how many Generall Councells they hold, he said. That they hold onely three, the Nicene, Con-stantinopohtan, and Ephesine, which he had read, but could not now recite. Touching the Chalcedon Councel, he said. They condemned it, because it determined two Natures in Christ, and condemned Dioscorus the Patriarke of Alexandria. How many universall Councells were held after, he answered. He knew not.

He acknowledged seven Sacraments instituted by Christ, Baptisme, Confirmation, the Eucharist, Penance, Unction, Order, and Matrimony. Being asked in what formall words the Ethiopians baptised, he answered, That after many prayers they say, I baptise thee in the name Baptisme.

of the Father, and of the Sonne, and of the Holy Ghost:

The matter, hee said, was naturall water; the Minister, a Priest, or in his absence a Deacon, besides whom hee never saw any to baptise: their Males after fortie dayes, and Females after eightie dayes, except in danger of death, and then they baptise presently. Being asked, whether the Ethiopians circumcise their children: hee answered. That from ancientest time to this day in all

Ethiopia, they circumcise their children in their owne houses without any Ceremony, but for a certaine ancient

Custome, cutting away the Prepuce from the Males, the

Nympha from the Females: being asked, whether they beleeve Circumcision necessary to salvation, he answered, Circumcision.

They know that it is now ceased, and that it is no longer necessary. Being asked, why the Ethiopians are said to I. i. 148.

be baptised with fire, and to signe in the forehead: hee answered. That there is none in Ethiopia which is baptised with fire, but in some Provinces onely they No baptwiie marke themselves with a razor in the forehead, either for " hfire.

the health of their eyes and sight; or, as some say, by the command of a certaine King of Ethiopia, to differ from the Mahumetans. Being asked why they baptise themselves every yeere, he answered, That the Ethiopians every yeere for the solemnitie of the Epiphanie goe forth to a River, and there many prayers are said by the Priests, and all are washed in the River; and many stay there all night with great festivitie for devotion of the Baptisme of our Lord Jesus Christ; but no man baptiseth him- selfe as they say.

Being demanded of Confirmation, the Matter, the Seesup. Jlva-Forme, the Minister, he answered. Confirmation with ' 7- 5-us IS conferred by a Priest, together with rsaptisme, and rather beleeve-the Infant is anointed with Chrisme in the forehead, in but this man the name of the Father, Sonne and Holy Ghost: asked d. Zaga of the effect thereof, he said he knew not, but hee be- f J leeveth that it is given, that a Christian may be confirmed published, and in the faith. Being asked, whether Chrisme bee made L. Urreta, dnub over as amongst them every yeere, hee answered; Chrisme is well as they ggj j- fj- j l- g Patriarch of Alexandria, by whom can, divers of.,., i-n- i j the Ethiopian alone it IS made and not by the Bishop, and is sent superstitions, every seventh yeere and seldomer, with the Pilgrimes 6 yet this is which returne from the pilgrimage of the Holy Land, T' rt ' ' ' and the old Chrisme is preserved in all Churches. Being (a very dune;- '" sked whereof it was made, hee said, Of Balsam and hill of lies) Oyle, and of many Flowers and odoriferous things. and then Zaga Being interrogated of the Sacrament of the Eucharist, f- l" '" d matter thereof, hee answered. That the Matter therewith) for ' Bread of Bread-corne, and Wine of the Grape; but which cause I in many Provinces of Ethiopia, in Wine pressed out of have omitted Raisins washed with water, and steeped in the same them: where- y ter the space of certaine houres. Being asked what Ihinzsofmo- words, whereby the Bread is transubstantiated ment saith the into the Body, and the Wine into the Bloud, he answered, truth, hut ex- They are those words when the Priest saith. And he cuseth asfarre tooke Bread in his hands, and lifting up his eyes to 7ome oftheir en unto God his Father, he blessed, saying. Take Rites in Bap- yee and eate yee, this is my Body. And Hkewise taking tisme, Circum- the Chalice, he blessed and sanctified saying. Take yee cision,-C. drinke yee. This is the Chalice of my Blood, which Consecration, y remission of sinnes. The

Minister, he said, is the Priest onely, and the effect

Communion in remission of sinnes. Being asked whether all the Ethio- both kinds. plans are communicated in both kindes he answered,

That all the Ethiopians both Clerkes and Laymen are communicated under both kinds: the Priest ministers the body, and the Deacon the bloud in a spoone. Being asked whether Infants are communicated, hee answered,

Children com- That Infants on the day of their baptisme are communi- mumcated. cated in this manner: The Priest puts his fore-finger in the Chalice, and being dipped in the bloud, he puts it in the Infants mouth. And after baptisme, till they be ten yeeres old, the Priests little finger is put in the childs mouth without the bloud, for devotions sake.

Being asked, whether they celebrate in bread leavened or unleavened, and what they thinke of him, which celebrates in unleavened, he answered, The Ethiopians celebrate in leavened bread, they which celebrate in unleavened make the Sacrament also. And we thorow all Ethiopia, on Mandie Thursday everie yeere, in the Supper of the Lord, in memoriall hereof celebrate in unleavened.

Being asked what the Ethiopians thinke of Purgatory, Purgatory. hee answered, The Ethiopians beleeve that the soules ""'""'"'-after death are detained in a certaine place, called in the Ethiopian tongue Mecan aaraft, that is, the Place of lightning, in which the soules of the penitent are kept, which have departed out of the world, not having finished the satisfaction of their sinnes. Being asked whether the soules of the good presently after death enjoy happinesse, and those of evill men bee punished in Hell, Hee answered. There are some in Ethiopia, which thinke Soule-sleepe. that the soules of the good rest in Paradise terrestriall in which Adam was created, untill the Day of Judgement. There are others which beleeve that the soules of the just, presently after death enjoy their Creator in Paradise.

Also being asked what sinnes, and how many are Mortdl sinne. mortall, he answered. Those are mortall sinnes which are done against the Lords commandements, which are so many that I cannot number. Being asked whether the sinnes of the Will, which passe not into outward act, bee mortall, Hee answered, they are mortall, when a man hath given consent to the desire and concupiscence.

Being asked whether any man can be saved without Un'wersall the faith of Jesus Christ, the Mediator of God and men; "' he answered. None can be saved. Being asked of them which are now in the law of nature, to whom no knowledge of the Gospell hath comne; he answered, I beleeve that God also hath provided for them, that by some meanes they may be saved, when they shall have kept the precepts of Nature. Being asked what the Ethiopians thinke of Indulgences, hee answered, I beleeve they are Indulgences. acceptable amongst all, and they call them Benedictions, Invocation of Saints.

Simony.

Difference twixt Abas-sines and Cophti. I. i. 149.

ivo(f.

but I desire to understand the use of them. Being asked of Invocation of Saints, hee answered, that the Invocation of Saints is very well approved amongst the Ethiopians, and all doe professe their intercession with God.

Being asked of Simony, and of those which by favour or compact are ordained Priests, Bishops, or Patriarch; he answered, that it is forbidden by the holy Canons.

Being asked what difference there is betwixt the Ethiopians and the Cophti, in matters of faith; he answered, that there is no difference betwixt them, and they agree in all things; for they are under the obedience of the same Patriarch. But in some things I have seene them to differ; namely, the Ethiopians contract not in degrees prohibited; But the Cophti contract in the second, and the degrees after it every where with license, and without the license of their Bishop and Patriarch. Also the Cophti in the Country and Villages keepe no Lords daies, nor holy daies, but onely in Cities, which the Ethiopians doe every where. Also the Ethiopians keepe the Sabbath (or Saturday holy) which the Cophti doe not. Also the Ethiopians every where thorow all Ethiopia circumcise their Sonnes and Daughters; but some Cophti, onely at Cairo within these few yeeres circumcise not. Also in the ceremonies of the Masse the Cophti differ much from the Ethiopians, For the Priests of the Cophti celebrate without the Vestments called Planetae, and the Deacons without the Dalmatick Vestments, with their head covered with a wollen Tobalea, and never elevate the Lords body and the Chalice in their Masses; which ceremonies are not amongst the Ethiopians, Being demanded if he knew in what things the Ethiopians and Cophti differ from the faith of the holy Catholike Roman Church; hee answered, they differ principally in these things. They invocate Dioscorus of Alexandria, and James the first his Disciple, and Severus Antiochenus in the Churches with the holy Fathers. They receive not the Chalcedon Councell and Saint Leo Pope. They professe in Christ our Lord one onely Nature, will, and operation. They recite the thrice holy Hymne Holy, holy, with addition of those words, which was crucified for y- us; yet with this exposition that the three sanctifications be applied to the most holy Trinitie, those words, which was crucified for us, onely to our Lord Christ.

The Cophti and Ethiopians use circumcision, and these also observe the Sabbath.

Being asked when, where, of whom and what orders Holy Orders. he had taken: hee answered, when I was fifteene yeeres old, in the Church of Saint Mary in the Monasterie of Denob of the Province Xeva in Ethiopia, I was entered in orders by Joseph a Cophtite, Archbishop Josepkus of Ethiopia, in this manner: The Archbishop before Cophtus. the celebration of Masse shaved my head in five places, in forme of a crosse, and anointed me with Chrisme in the forehead, reciting praiers in the Egyptian tongue, and breathed in my face; and the same houre, in time of the celebration, made me an Ostiarie, and Lector or Psalmist, and Acolyte, and Nescadeaecon or Subdeacon, and Deacon of the Gospell, and gave me the holy Communion: and a long time after, when I was thirty yeeres old, in the Citie Bed in Dembia of Ethiopia, in the Church of Saint George, I was ordered Priest by Archbishop Marke, the successour of the said Joseph. Being asked whether hee heard the Archbishop utter Popish rites of in collating orders, the formall words of each order; g ' g 'd '-he answered. The

Archbishop uttered them, but I heard not, nor understood, because he celebrated in the Egyptian tongue, whereof I was utterly ignorant. Being asked whether any materiall was delivered by the Archbishop in collation of each order, and whether he touched the same with his hands; namely, whether in making him Ostiary the Keyes of the Church, and opened the doore, and sounded the Bell; in the Lector-ship, the Booke of Lessons, or touched the Psalmist, in exorcistship the booke of exorcisme or Missall; in Aco-lythship the Candlesticke, with the candle put out and an emptie pot; in Subdeaconship, the empty Chalice with an empty patene over it, and pots with wine and water, and the basen with a towell, and the Booke of the Epistles, and whether the Amice was by the Archbishop put on his head, and the maniple on his left arme, and whether hee was vested with the Tunicle: and in his Deaconship, whether he touched the Booke of the Gospels, and the stole was put on his shoulder, and he vested with the Dalmatike: and in being ordered Priest whether he touched the Chalice with wine and water, and the patene with the hoste, and whether the Archbishop and Priests imposed hands on his head, and whether the stole was applied to his breast in manner of a crosse, and whether he put on the casule without the planet, and had his hands touched with the Oyle of the Catechumeni: He answered, I certainly know, that I in all the said orders had no materiall or instrument delivered me by the Archbishop in collation of the Orders, nor did I touch any such, nor was I vested with any vestment peculiar to any order, nor did the Archbishop impose hands on me, nor were my hands annointed with holy Oyle. He said also, our Archbishop in Ethiopia giveth orders to 2000. and more at one time, and to each gives six orders together, without examination before, and without enquirie, examination, choise, approbation, writing, or register, and in regard of the multitude, cannot give to each and every of them any materiall to be touched: and in the same manner it is observed in all ordinations by our Archbishops successively; although it be otherwise observed in Egypt, where so great a multitude is not ordered at once together, and some competent matter is delivered to be touched of the ordained. Being asked whether he knew the said Joseph and Marke, Bishops aforesaid, to have beene Schismatickes, and without the communion of the holy Roman Church: he answered, that hee knew not so much. Yea, he rather certainly beleeved at that time, that they were Catholikes, as also all the Ethiopians and Cophti, and that they obeyed the Apostolike See in all things, and held communion with the holy Roman Church; and beleeved that all Christians did agree in matters of Faith; but he learned the things before said, when afterwards hee was at Jerusalem and in Egypt.
. II. I. i. 150.

Relations of the Jacobites and Armenians, written by Leonard Bishop of Sidon, Pope Gregorie the 13. his Nuncio to the Easterne parts.

He Jacobite Nation is dispersed thorow the Cities, Jacobites num-Lands, and Townes of Syria, Mesopotamia and Babylonia, obtaining the number of 50000. houses, most of them poore, and living on daily labour. In Aleppo and Caramit are many rich families which live on Merchandise. Their Patriarchall Church is in Mesopotamia without the Citie of Moradim, in the Monastery Zafram; but the Patri-arch resideth for his greater com-moditie and quiet in the Citie Caramit. This Nation is subject to the Patriarch David, but is governed of the Bishop Thomas, Vicar Generall and brother to the said Patriarch. Under whose obedience live at this time John the

Metropolitan of Jerusalem, by the Thelrbishops. Jacobites stiled the fifth Patriarch: Michael Archbishop of Damasco. James Archbishop of Edessa called Orfa, or Raha. Minas Archbishop of Saur, Effrem Archbishop in the same Province, James Archbishop of Bisuaria, Abraham Bishop of Aatafra. Melchez Bishop of Saint Melchi in Tur, Jesu Bishop of the Monasterie Deiriloemor, Abelmedich in the Province of Tur, Elias Bishop in Salach, Ehas Bishop of the Monasterie Saint Crosse in Zaz, Gazel Bishop in Tarach, David Bishop in Maaden, Pilat Metropolitan in Musal and the East, Gazel Archbishop of Miaferichin, the Archbishop of the Monasterie of Mar Abihai, Ananias Bishop of Saint Bertonias, John Bishop of Hartbert, Isaac

Monasteries and Churches.

Rites.

Jrmenians. Their Patri-arks.

Archbishop of Cyprus, Simeon Archbishop of Caramit, Habib. There are many Monasteries of the same Nation, Churches, Religions, and Deacons, and Clergie men innumerable, which I could not visit, being rejected by the said Vicar Generall Thomas: Yet I visited the Temple of the Jacobites in Tripoli, Aamavin, Damasco, Neph, Jerusalem, Aleppo, Orfa, Orbis, Mar Abihai, Gargar, amongst the Churches of which parts I found those of Jerusalem and Aleppo well furnished, but the rest without Images and ill governed. For the Sacrament was kept in wodden pyxes without light or lampe; and the baptismall Funts wanted water, for at every baptisme they blesse the Funts anew: the ornaments of the Altars also were most vile, and the office of the Masse was performed verie basely and carelesly. Of the holy Oyles, onely Chrisme was kept in Churches: this is called Miron and is blessed of the Patriarch every seventh yeere with many flowers and odoriferous things. They have not the Oile of the Catachumeni, and for the Oile of extreame unction, the Priest blesseth it in lights set on foure parts in manner of a crosse, and therewith anoints the sicke, after many Gospels and Praiers recited. The Sacrament of Confession is rarely frequented, and many communicate without auricular confession. The Patriarch professed that they held the same in substance with the Roman Church, but the Greekes and Latines could not attempt such words and tearmes as the Jacobites in those things had done.

Of the Armenians the said Bishop ot Sidon testifieth, that they are subject to two principall Patriarkes, one of Armenia the Greater, the other of Armenia the lesse. The former resideth in the Monastery and Church of Ecmeazin, neere the Citie Ervan in Persia: the other in the Citie Cis of Cilicia, now called Caramania. Other Patriarkes are sometimes by the favour of the Turks created amongst them, and are exacters of Tributes which the Armenian Families are bound to pay the Turkes. Others also are elected Coadjutors of the same Patriarkes with consent of the Bishops and people. Further there are others, Primates or rather Patriarkes of the same Nation in the remotest parts of Persia in Constantinople, which although legally they are subject to the Patriarke of Armenia major, yet sometimes doe not acknowledge him. The Families subject to the Their num-Patriarke of the Greater Armenia exceed the number ' '" of 150000. besides very many Monasteries, Bishops, Religious persons and Deacons. Their Preachers are Preachers or called Mortabiti, and are obeied by the people, as the " Patriarke himselfe. In the Province Nevuam, in Persia also, in two Cities there live Catholike Armenians subject Romish Ar-to an Archbishop of the Dominican Order, and other "' " Friers of that profession, which observe the Latine Rites, and live under the obedience of the Roman Sea.

The Patriarke of Armenia Minor hath under his Second Patrl-Jurisdiction foure and twentie Prelates, Archbishops and ' ' ' Bishops, and the Election of the Patriarke belongs to 12. Bishops neerer the Patriarchall Church. Yet sometimes the Armenian people by favour and command of the Turkish Officers create their Patriarks, and after obtaine the consent of the Bishops and Archbishops, and by the favour of the principall people, a Coadjutor with future succession is deputed to him, who of a Master and Preacher, after the death of the said predecessor, is received and confirmed by the people for Patriarke. To this Patriarke are subject about 20000. Families, and they live in the Villages, Castles and Cities of Cilicia and Syria: there are twentie Monasteries each contayning 100. Religious, 300. Priests, Deacons and Clerkes many, which live of Almes, and of their owne industry.

. III.

I. i. 151.

. III.

Of Simon Sulaka a Papall Easterne Patriarke amongst the Chaldasans: and of divers others thither sent. Of Abdesu, Aatalla, Donha his Successours.

1 feare the Popish multiplication making great harvests of little come: yet I here recit what I jinde, and wish that all Nesto-rians would abandon those heresies, and in that point be Roman and Catholike. Dry the Patriarch.

I thinke he meaneth Saint Thomas Christians in India. Abdesu or Abilisu.

Mongst the Asian Nestorlans, there have beene some Roman Cathohkes which have exhibited obedience to the Pope. Some of those which professed Simon Sulaka a Monke of Saint Basils Order to be their Superiour, calling themselves Chaldaeans and Assyrians, acknowledged Pope Julius the Third, and rejected the name of Nestorians. Sulaka was by the Pope confirmed Patriarke of that Nation with the Title of Mozal, which Church his adversary possessed. He returned to Caramit, and there ordained certaine Archbishops and Bishops, and rejected the Nestorian Invocation, which at that time was usually made by the Deacon in the Church. He sought to spread the Roman faith, but by the policy of the Antipatriarke Dry he was taken and slaine by the Turkes. The confession of faith by the same Sulaka made at Rome is extant in Bibliotheca Patrum.

The Bishop Ariensis a Dominican was sent by the Pope to visit and confirme this Church, who having reformed some things, was driven with some Assyrians to flee to Ormus and Goa, where hee dyed.

His companion Frier Anthonie, with the Archbishop Ermetes Elias Disciple of Sulaka, visited many Christians in Cochin and India of Saint Thomas, and after his returne was made a Bishop by the Pope. To Sulaka succeeded Abdesu of the same order of Saint Basil, which was at the Councel of Trent under Pope Pius the Fourth, from him carried with him the Title of Muzal, and returning to Caramit and Seert, ordained many Priests, Bishops, and Archbishops, and many Cities of the Chaldees yeelded him obedience, but soone after hee died in the Monastery of the City Seert: and Aatalla a brother of the same Order succeeded, and after him Donha Of these Simon the Archbishop of Gelu and Salamas renounced ' " the Antipatriarke, and was elected Patriarke by the Pre- p lates of that Nation, and confirmed by Gregorie the in To z. l. i. Thirteenth, to whom he sent Archbishop Ermes Elias in Brere-his name to exhibit obedience. Who returned with his '. Patriarchall Pall from Rome 1582, But hitherto they ZJ l g. have nothing of Mozal but the Title, the other Patriarke possessing the See, and they are glad to seeke a place of residence where they can, as at Caramit, and this last at Zeinalbach. The richest and mightiest of that Nation are at Mozal and Gesire, and acknowledge the other Patriarke, lately called Elias, resident in the Patriarchall Monastery of Saint Ermes neere Mozal. He hath under him two and twentie Bishops, above sixe hundred Territories, of which two and twentie are flourishing Cities, each contayn-ing five hundred Nestorian Families, and in Masul 1000. each having about fortie persons: the other Territories have two or three hundred Nestorian Families. They have thirtie Monasteries of Saint Anthonies Order in which fifteene or twentie Monkes live: and in that of the Patriarke seventie. The Patriarke and Bishops must bee Monkes, They extend to Baldach and the East Indies.

. iiii.

Of the Cophti, their Synod at Cairo, the Jesuites being the Popes Agents, and of Stephen Colinzas message to the Georgians, and two Jesuites sent to the Maronites.

Ope Gregorie the Thirteenth sent divers messages Synod at to the Cophti, whereby a Synod was procured at (o-Cairo, in December 1582. which had three Sessions to reconcile them to the Roman Church. At the first were present Bishops and principall men. At the third, the same men, with the Jesuites, especially John J- Bapt. Baptista Romanus. In the first were opened the causes " ' ""-f of their decession in the Conventicle of Ephesus assembled by Dioscorus, whereby Eutyches his Heresie which denied two natures in Christ was begun, condemned after in the Chalcedon Councell. They desired to search their Writings which were few and eaten with Age. And in the second Session was much alteration, and the matter put off to the third. In that third the Law of Circumcision was abrogated first; and after that Anathema was denounced against such as should spoile Christ of either. Yet for all this the Vicar of the Patri-arke then being, resisted the subscribing, and a quarrell was picked by the Turkes against the Popes Agents, as if they sought to subject the East, to the Pope, or the King of Spaine. They were therefore cast into Prison, and their redemption cost 5000. Crownes.

At Cairo is a Librarie in which are kept many Bookes of the ancient Doctors in Arabike, as of Saint Jerome, Gregorie Nazianzene, Saint Basil, c. and the men have I. i. 152. good wits, and some thereby proove learned. In the time of Pope Clement the Eighth, Marke the Patriarke sent a Submission to the Pope, as was pretended; but it prooved to be the Imposture of one Barton.

Paul the Third also sent to the Georgians, Anno 1545. Stephen Colynza elect of Neuvan in Armenia, his Nuncio

King of to the Kings of Georgia and Armenia. The Georgian

Georgia his King writ backe to the Pope, his Letter beginning.

piy ' Miseratione Dei Symeon Rex Cardelii totius Iberise Orientis. Excelse splendissime, sanctissime, beatissime Domine noster, Pater noster Papa, Pastor Pas-torum, Princeps Principum, decime tertie Aposto-lorum, Pater noster Papa Magnas Romas, aurea tuba, organum Dei inflatum, Petre index claviculare Regni coelestis,

Paule Doctor gentium, qui ascendit usque ad tertium coelum, c. Hee proceedeth in swelling Titles of vanitie ascribed to the Pope, and saith so much that all his zeale and profession was spent, as it seemeth, in that Epistle; for little effect hath since appeared.

Pope Clement the Eighth sent two Jesuites with a Bishop to the Maronites in Mount Libanus, Hierom

Dandin a Divine being principall. The cause of sending was, that it might by the eyes be discerned, whether the costs bestowed at Rome on the Seminary of Maronites Sem'marie of were well bestowed. The Pope sent the Patriarch a ' ' ' whole Vestiment of Silke wrought with Gold for a Patri- archall Masse, and many Chists of Bookes in the Chaldaean

Tongue printed in the Citie, contayning the Lyturgies of

Saint James, Saint Peter, and Saint Sixtus, they having no Bookes but written, and those torne or erroneous: with Service-bookes to God and the Blessed Virgin. For they use the Chaldee Tongue as wee doe the Latine.

Out of the Seminary was sent one to bee a Coadjutor to the Patriarch and made Bishop, and another Coadjutor to him in his Bishopricke. Their common language is

Arabike. The Pope sent also silver Chalices, and Iron Instruments to make the Hosts and sacred Vests for other

Priests by the said Dandin. He staid two monethes with his companion a Priest, in the Monasterie of the Patriarke, in which time the old Patriarke died, and the other was substituted by a Synod according to the custome. The

Patriarkes performed all kind Offices to the Jesuites, as did also the Monkes which live sparingly eating little but Rice, Herbs, and Broth. The Priests live single, but Poore Priests.

are addicted to no Studies of Learning, and spend the rest of their time in tilling the ground, or stirring up others thereto, that they may have to live on, and to pay their

Tributes. Their women are very modest and chast, neither have they any mercenary Harlots. They have a place at the entrance of the Church by themselves, and when Service is done they depart first, no man stirring till Their old rites.

they be all gone. Dandin altered divers things amongst them, as to reserve some cases to the Bishop or Patriarke, not to constraine Priests to marrie before they tooke

Orders, that some of the Serviarians should be appointed on some Holy dayes to preach, and write cases for others to learne, where as before they had no Sermons, but sometimes a Homily; to use no other Missals then such g 5 as had beene sent from Rome; that other Bookes should . 9. c. 9.

bee examined; not (as before) to admit Children to the Eucharist, "c.

He which will read more of these Maronites, may read out of themselves and others in this Worke, as also touching them and all other Christians in the East in Master Brerewoods Enquirie hereto annexed: also Thomas a Jesu our Author is farre more ample in these things, then agreeth with our scope. I thought good yet to adde out of a Manuscript above a doozen yeeres since communicated to me by the Right Reverend Father in God Doctor Usher, Lord Bishop of Meath, copied out of a Jesuites written Catalogue of Heresies, these Errours as they are there recited by the Jesuite, and gathered out of the Maronites Bookes.

Errores ex libris Maronitarum excerpti 1580. sunt autem hujusmodi.

1 Hristus caput est divinitatis.

2-J In Christo una tantum est natura.

3 In Christo una tantum est operatio, una voluntas.

4 Natura invisibilis in Christo est passa.

5 Trinitas est passa.

6 Trisagium recitandum est cum ilia additione. Qui crucifixus est pro nobis.

7 Christus non est mortuus ut alii homines.

8 Christus descendens ad inferos omnes filios Adae liberavit.

9 Christus post resurrectionem unam habet naturam.

10 Animae sanctorum patrum deductas sunt a Christo ad

Paradisum terrestrem: animas vero eorum qui nunc moriuntur, aut illuc transount, aut in propriis cor-poribus detinentur vel circa sepulchrum, vel descen-dunt ad locum tenebrosum, pro meritorum vel demeritorum diversitate.

11 In die judicii nova corpora animabus creabuntur.

12 Spiritus sanctus a patre procedit.

13 Baptismus non debet ministrari nisi a Sacerdote.

14 Apostatae, ut haeretici, sunt rebaptizandi.

15 Energumeni non sunt baptisandi, nisi mortis ar- ticulo.

16 Masculus in baptismo non debet suscipero foeminam, nee e contra.

17 Baptismus non debet dari in quadragessima.

18 Parvulus baptizatus non debet tangi a matre quse I. i. 153.

patitur fluxum sanguinis ne eum palluat.

19 Mater non potest lactare suum infantem ratione chrys- matis cum est baptizatus.

20 Angelus custos tribuitur in baptismo homini, 21 Chrysma debet confici ex variis rebus, coqui igne ex 5"- lib' facto.

22 Forma confirmationis haec est. Ungo te hoc chrys- mate in vitam aeternam, ut sis haeres regni cce-lestis in nomine P. F. S. S.

23 Sanguis Christi potest consecrari ex aqua, ex vuis siccis expressa.

24 Summus Episcopus potest consecrare sanguinem sine corpore, 25 Forma con-secrationis base est. Benedixit divisit unicuique discipulorum partem, fecit ut essent, corpus Dominicum, quod datur in vitam mundi in remissionem peccatorum. Item benedixit sancti-ficavit, divisit aequaliter ad bibendum ilium Apos-tolis suis electis, fecit possidere ilium sanguinem viz. novum Testamentum Discipulos suos.

26 Sub speciebus panis vini est corpus sanguis sed non anima Christi.

27 Eucharistia consecranda feria quinta in Coena Domini, debet consecrari per totum annum.

28 Sacerdos qui nunquam celebrat, non peccat.

29 Licet sacrum facere super librum Evangelii.

30 Qui non est dispositus ad communicandum, non debet sacro interesse.

31 Dignius sumit Eucharistiam infans quam adultus.

32 Infantes Christi sanginem sumere debent.

33 Impedit comunionem digitum ori insuisse, aut os abluisse.

34 Absolvere pcenitentes est super ejus caput recitare orationem Dominicam.

35 Impositio manuum Apostolorum super baptizatos erat absolutio a peccatis.

36 Peccata minima sunt aperienda in confessione.

37 Peccata spiritualia ne in mortis articulo dimitti possunt.

38 Mali Sacerdotes non habent usum clavium.

39 Post mortem redditur ratio commissorum peccatorum ab anno 12.

40 Oleum extremae unctionis debet benedici a 7. Sacer- dotibus.

41 Matrimonium in lege veteri erat institutum tantum ob prolem.

42 Matrimonium non est validum sine Sacerdotis bene- dictione.

43 44 Non potest pater filius contrahere cum matre filia, vel duo fratres cum duabus sororibus.

45 Quartas nuptial deinceps sunt illicitae.

46 Ob multas causas licet uxorem dimittere, aliam ducere.

47 Usus Matrimonii in Quadragesima est peccatum irremissibile.

48 Paradisus terrestris fuit creatus ante omnia.

49 Adam fuit formatus ex terra Paradisi.

50 Adam Eva ante peccatum erant circundati pelle, ut non posset cognosci utrum mas vel foemina esset.

51 Sacerdos erat Abel non Cain, ideo Deo placuit illius Sacrificium, non hujus, 52 Noc tempore diluvii in Area sacrificavit.

53 Filii Israel qui adorarunt vitulum, biberunt ejus pulverem, mugiebant ut boves.

54 Judaei in deserto ferebant lapidem secum in quo 12.

fontes manabant. Christus factus est Sacerdos a Johanne Baptista. 56 Mariae apparuit Christus in forma hortulani.

Apostoli usque ad Pentecostem fuerunt in statu peccati.

58 Christus fecit Apostolos Diaconos cum insufflavit iis

Joh. 20. Sacerdotes vero cum ascendit in Coelum.

59 Anima Beatae Virginis fuit primum omnium creata.

60 Omnes credentes, etiam haeretici sunt in statu salutis.

61 Non licet occidere hominem etiam publica authoritate.

62 Deus promisit Mosi visionem divinitatis conjunctam cum anima Christi, quo modo solum est visibilis divinitas.

63 Sancti patres in limbo carebant spe exeundi.

64 Damnati non torquentur die Dominica.

6 Damnatorum poenae minuuntur per sacrificia.

66 Joseph sponsus Beatae Virginis habuit qua tuor filios.

67 Virginitas non est praeponenda matrimonio.

68 Mendacium officiosum licitum est.

69 Judasi coegerunt Beatam Virginem potare aquam amaram propter suspicionem adulterii.

70 Dies Veneris est celebrandus ut Dominicus.

71 Pharao non meretur pcenam, quod Deus cor ejus induraverit.

72 Vestes Sacerdotales si lacerentur id genus alia, amittunt consecrationem.

I have hither also translated some observations of Christopher Angelos a Greeke Monke and Priest, which hath lived many yeeres in England, and some five yeeres since gave mee a Greeke Booke printed by him in-lt waspr'm-London, touching their present Rites, both in their J "' Churches and Monasteries. Many things I could have r l-j added touching the Greekes, and their moderne Language, State and Religion, out of Crusius, Jeremias the Patriarke, and others. But this man being a Traveller, I chose rather to let you heare him in that wherein he hath beene bred. As for dogmaticall differences you have had them before, and the present Greekes are not ordinarily so learned as to give you a perfect account thereof.

I. i. 154- V.

Of the condition of life in which the Greekes now live, and of their rites of Fasts, Feasts, and other observations, gathered out of the Booke of Christopheros Angelos, a Greekish Monke and Priest.

He ancient Graecians heard John the Evangelist speaking in the thirteenth of the Apoc. and first verse. And I saw a beast rise out of the Sea,

Simple silli-nesse either of this Monke or of this Natio?!! Orratherbase courages palliated with Scripture misapplied. The true cause is, that they, weakened by divisions amongst themselves 3 from the Latines; and not assisted from Princes abroad were not able to hold out. An obscure Prophesie ought not to hold mens hands, except they will be treacherous to their state; for Gods will revealed is the rule of our actions; vailed prophesies can but foresigni fie events, being not and power was granted him to make warre with the Saints, and to overcome them, and power was given him over every Kindred and Tongue, and Nation, and all that dwelt upon the Earth worshipped him, whose names are not written in the Booke of Life of the Lambe, who was slaine from the beginning of the World: if any man have an eare let him heare. If any leade into captivity, he shall goe into captivitie: if any kill with a sword hee must be killed with the sword, and that which followeth. The Greekes having this prophesie and many others of this kind of holy men, when they saw the Turkes come, said. This is the Beast, that Saint John speaketh of, and would not fight with the Turke. They fought a httle in the beginning, but afterward yeelded; and for this were not carried away captives. In like manner they carried all their goods with them, and bought all of the King of the Turkes. This thing also did the Monkes, and redeemed their Monasteries, and fields, and houses, and whatsoever they possessed before. Therefore to this day, they retaine all their old Bookes, and observe their Countrey Lawes, and live as the Christians and Monkes in former ages, if the Christians shall at any time get the superi-oritie. But let us returne to our purpose.

Each of the Males pay Tribute to the Turkish King, as likewise the women: that is to say, that the men dwelling in one house from twentie yeeres, and upwards pay yeerely six shillings. But if they be striplings, that terrible till is to say, fifteene yeeres old they pay three only, if J "' '" they are passed fifteene, pay foure or five, till they eligible; as come to the age of twentie yeeres. They will give Gods rule, not this taxe, because the Lord saith, be wise as Serpents, ours, intima-They are mindfull also that John saith, Apoc. 7. 14. f w'jf Those are those which came out of great tribulation, hatweouzht. and washed their garments, and made them white in Deut. 29. the bloud of the Lambe. Moreover, they pay another Divers tri-custome. That is to say, when the Army goeth to warre; they are wont to contribute certaine pieces of monie, to buy bread and flesh, to sustaine the Armie, they doe not yet all equally pay this: but sometimes twentie, sometimes ten shillings in every house, sometimes more having respect to the Armie. But all the houses doe not contribute alike in this as in the former. In that the rich and poore pay the same summe, in this no man gives beyond his abilitie. There is also another dutie: to wit, when the Kings spies are sent to exact Tribute of the Christians, in the journey the Christians which dwel there, allow them victuals. And thus much concerning their Tributes.

The tithing of their children is in this manner. Tithing of When as first the Turke exercised authoritie over the their children. Greeks, in every Citie Province he took an account of the houses, and every fourth yeere, of ten houses took one of their children. There was at that time in one Citie a hundred housholds; of ten times ten hous-hold he chuseth one. Afterwards after that foure yeeres were expired, he took ten other children of the second, that is to say, of the next house, not of that former whereof he tooke before. And so they doe every foure yeeres untill all the houses bee finished. And then againe they beginne to take children at the first house, untill they returne againe to the first. After forty yeeres are past they returne againe to the first house, and after this manner they doe with the other Houses, Cities and Another Provinces. They have another unjust custome of gather- fashion.

ing children, that is to say, when the Janizaries goe from the King to gather Boyes through the Province, that is subject to them, where they ought to gather them: Passing through the Province as many Boyes as they find in the way, they take without tithing, saying, those Boyes are our prey. But if it happen, that any children among them that are unjustly taken, bee of those houses, which are to give a Boy, then they will take no other Boy of those houses, whereof that Boy was, because they may not take two Boyes out of one house in the same yeere; therefore when the Boyes fathers heare that the Janizaries come to gather Boyes, they hide their Boyes before they come, some in Mountaines, some in the houses of the great men that are Turkes, because those Rulers are Citizens, and the Greekes friends, and therefore desire to keepe the Greekes sonnes safe, and after they restore againe their sonnes, sometimes the Boyes flie into the Mountaines, and the Janizaries take the Boyes Father or Mother, and punish them with death. And when the children heare that their parents are punished, they come of their owne accord, and are delivered: sometimes the childrens parents die of the punishment for their sonnes, and thus much concerning their children. Greekishlents Xhe Greekes observe foure Lents every yeere. The foure in every j called the great and holy Lent: this continues eight First Lent. ' forty dayes together before Easter. They fast in that holy Lent eating dry things for the tithing of their soule. On Annuntiation day they eate fish, and feast for joy of the Annuntiation, therefore there remaine only five and thirtie dales for the tithing of the yeere, I. i. 155. which are five times seven, which make five and thirtie daies. Because that for seven weekes together they fast before Easter, five daies in every weeke, that is to say, Monday, Tuesday, Wednesday, Thursday, and Friday: Saturday and they fast not on Saturday and Sunday, because they eate Sunday not Qj g drinke Wine twice in a day, therefore they are j g' j Q called fasting dales, but only after a sort. Some of the Laicks in those five dales of the weeke eate Oile, and drinke Wine, because they respect not the tithing of soules.

The Fasts of the Monkes differ from the Laicks fasts; for the Laicks may sometimes eate Oile, and drinke Wine in those five daies, and have absolution of the spirituall (Priest) when they confesse to him their particular sinnes. But the Monkes may not eate Oile, nor drinke Wine those five daies: for when they confesse, they are punished according to the Canons, unlesse they have some disease, or some other necessitie.

Their second Lent, is called the Lent of dayes, because Second or they fast fortie daies together before Christmasse. They " ' " L "f-fast in those daies, first, in the honour of Christ: Secondly, because Moses fasted forty dayes, and then merited (or obtained) to converse with God: and receive the stonie Tables of the Decalogue. To our example. Moses fasted there forty daies, that he might speake with God and receive the Tables. But we fast so many daies, that wee may meete Christ borne for our sinnes, as the Wisemen did with gifts, and as the shepheards spake with the Angels, and were thought worthy to see an Armie of Angels, and to worship Christ. Wee also confessing our sinnes, and fasting and keeping under our bodie, worship Christ.

The third Lent is called the Lent of the holy Apostles Third Lent. Peter and Paul. It beginnes one weeke after Whitson-tide; and continues to the nine and twentieth day of the month of June, that is to say, to the Feast of Peter and Paul.

Their fourth Lent beginnes from the first day of Fourth Lent. August, and continues to the fourteenth day of the same- "u P io"-month, because on the 15. day they celebrate a great Feast to the Virgin Mary, who on that day ascended from Earth to Heaven, from corruptible things to incorruptible, and went to her Sonne, and to her God and our Lord Jesus Christ and our God, Amen: in her honour they fast fourteene daies.

Difference of fasts in Lent.

Manner of fasting.

O Utinam.

But these fasts differ from the great Lent, for in the Lent of Christmasse, and of Peter and Paul, they eate fish twice in a day: but in our Ladies Lent they eate no fish, yet they eate twice a day.

They beginne to fast after this manner: the tenth Sunday before Easter Sunday, to wit, the ninth weeke before Easter; that Weeke is called, the calling weeke, and the Sunday of the Publican and the Pharisie, for on the tenth Sunday they reade the Gospel of the Publican and the Pharisie, that they may learne humilitie, and abase themselves, and not judge and condemne others, as the Pharisie judged the Publican and was punished; and they sing at Evensong, and the day following before day (that is, the tenth Sunday before Easter) these Songs, with a great and drie voice, and very often melodiously, so that all may heare: Let us avoid the Pharisies boasting, let us learne the Publicans lowlinesse, and others of this kind: and they confesse their sinnes, and pardon the wrongs of their Enemies, that they may be pure in heart when they begin to fast. The following Sunday (which is the ninth Sunday before Easter, and the eighth weeke, that Sunday is called the Sunday of the second comming, and the judgement of our Lord Jesus Christ) wherefore on this day they read the Gospell, then they shall see the Sonne of man comming in the clouds; and the rest that followes. And the Prophesie of Daniel the Prophet, viz. Behold the thrones were set, and the ancient of daies sat downe, and the Bookes were opened to judgement. And they read in the Church these words of Christ, and of the Prophesie of Daniel singing with a drie and great voice, so that all may heare and many tremble, for all heare, that judgement and vengeance is at hand. They feast verie much this Sunday, and give manie almes, and procure friendship with their enemies, and will never judge nor backbite them after they are made friends, nor remember the injurie so long as they live, because

Paul saith, neither thiefe. nor evill speaker, c. shall inherit the Kingdome of God. This is called Shrovesunday, because on this day is an inhibition from flesh; for in the day following (that is) Monday, they begin to fast onely from flesh, and eate Egges, Milke, Cheese, Butter, and such kinde of meates, that come from flesh all the weeke, but on Saturday and Sunday, which is called the eighth Sunday before Easter, and the seventh weeke before Easter.

The eighth Sunday before Easter is called Cheese Sunday, because they eate Cheese and Egges, and all kindes of white meates: and the Greekes doe greatly reject this day, because the day following (that is to say) Monday, they begin to fast. The day is called the fall of Adam, because on that day is read the fall of Adam, that is, how Adam and Eve ate of the Tree of knowledge, and for that unbridled lust of eating, were cast out of Paradise; because they neglected the ordinance of God, therefore they were banished, and because after the fall of Adam they went out of Paradise, and mourned because hee was deceived, by his cursed desire to eate, and was so made the servant of the Divell, therefore they give large almes, and commiserate their enemies (as we said before) and now they doe these things that they may be pure in heart, when they begin to fast: But they begin to fast on Munday, to wit, the i. i. 156. first day of the seventh weeke before Easter, and they fast five daies, viz. Monday, Tuesday, Wednesday, Thursday, and Friday, but they fast eating dry things, that is to say, they eate Beanes, Pease with Vinegar, they boile Herbes in water, and eate them with Vinegar, Raisons, Figges, dried Apples, dried Peares, dried Cherries, and Honie. These they boile altogether in water: they eate the Fruit, but drinke the broth as wine, c. On Saturday and Sunday (which is called the Lords day), they eate Oile, and drinke Wine: and after this manner they live everie weeke untill Easter.,,

They fast also two daies everie weeke throughout r Wednes-the whole yeere, viz. Wednesday and Friday. They day= Friday.

fast on Wednesday, because on that day Judas tooke monle to betray Christ, and they are afflicted with Christ by fasting. But on Friday they fast because Christ was crucified, and they are in heavinesse with Christ, because he saith, when the Bridegroome shall be taken from them, then shall my Disciples fast. Saturdaies, On every Saturday, and other feasts throughout the

Sundaics, and jqqj-q thg Greekes are wont at evening to goe to the dales " Temple. All the Grecian women and children rise very timely, that is to say, the second houre after midnight on every Sunday and Feast day, to goe to the Temple; and leave at home one boy or one girle, to keepe the house, and they continue there singing all the night till morning; when the Sunne riseth, they goe out, and returne home: they sit idlely, and eate not nor drinke, till the ninth houre after midnight. But at the ninth houre the Priest runnes to the Temple, and prepares those things that belong to the liturgie, and takes one loafe which a woman or pure man made the day before (that is, some man which knew not his wife the day before, or a woman which knew not her husband, that is, on Saturday night, or otherwise from the evening of Friday till the morning light of Saturday, lay not together.) That man or that woman, baketh and kneadeth meale, and makes that loafe on Saturday, or another day. Hee must needes be pure which shall make this bread: before they put this Bread into the Oven, they signe it with a certaine peece of wood engraven with letters, viz. Jesus Christ overcomes: and then they put it into the Oven marked with these letters, viz. Jesus Christ overcomes. This Bread signifies the Virgin: as the Virgin was pure, so a pure man must bake that bread: this Bread the Priest takes in his hands, and blesseth, saying. In the memory of our holy unspotted Lady Mother of God, c. and other praiers, and consecrates that Bread to the Virgin, and after this the Priest hath a little speare, in forme of the speare wherewith the Souldiers pierced Christ, and the Priest taketh the little speare, and cuts off some fouresquare peece of the outside of the loafe, which con-taineth those letters, Jesus Christ overcomes, typifying Christ, who was borne of the Virgin Mary; and of this Bread they make their Eucharist: the Eucharist being administred, the Priest or Deacon devides that greater part of bread which was left into verie small peeces, of which bread wee say, that it is the body of the Virgin: and of this bread hee distributes to them which tooke Christs bodie, and to as manie as fasted all that day, who neither eate nor dranke any thing. They call this kinde of bread the reward, because they give it to all those which are, and which are not partakers of the Lords supper as a certaine divine gift. Those things being finished they goe out of the Temple, and again gather themselves to evening Praiers, which custome is observed throughout the whole world.

Moreover, they fast the foureteenth day of September, Cmse Fast. in honour of the crosse, which was found on that day, and they celebrate the feast of the crosse, abstaining from white meates, because on that day they kisse the crosse of Christ, and they desire to kisse it fasting. They fast also the fift of Januarie from all white meates, because Twelfth day the sixt day of that moneth Christ was baptised, according b water. to the Greekish custome. Moreover the Priests that y " day hallow water, whereof the Laickes drinke, and that ceremonies on they may be pure drinking of that holy water, they fast that day in the day before, that is to say, the fift of Januarie. their places.

They observe no fasting the fourth and sixth day of the weeke: for they eate flesh on Wednesdaies and Fridaies, and all white meates which come from flesh, as Egges, Butter, Milke, Cheese, c. from the day of Christs nativitie to the foureteenth day of Januarie, that is, from the 25. of December to the foureteenth of Januarie, they fast not; yet they fast the fift of Januarie that they may drinke holy water the sixt day, whereof we spake before. If the nativitie of Christ happen on a Wednesday, or a Friday, the common people eate flesh, and all white meate: but the Menkes onely whitemeates without flesh, in honour of Christs Nativitie. Also on the sixt day of Januarie, whereon Christ was baptised, the Laicks eate flesh and all kinde of white meates, as we said before: but the Monkes eate onely white meates.

Notwithstanding in the eleventh weeke before Easter, they eate flesh on Wednesday and Friday: the reason

Dog-tale. whereof is this. In times past there were certaine Here-tickes, which had an excellent good Dogge, who were accustomed to tye Letters about his necke, and send him to their friends two or three daies journie from them, who when they had read the Letters, sent backe others to them by the same Dogge, and this they did divers times; At the length the Dog died and returned not, then those Heretickes for griefe fasted Wednesday and Friday, that they might deride the Orthodox Christians, who fasted those daies in honour of Christ: but when the Christians understood this, they decreed in the eleventh weeke not at all to fast with them, but to eate flesh on Wednesday and Friday. They call this weeke Archburch.

I. i. 157. Moreover, throughout Easter weeke, that is, from the resurrection of Christ untill the Sunday following they eate flesh and white meates. The Fathers call it the weeke of renovation. After the same manner, on the day of Penticost they eate flesh, and make merrie, but on the Munday next following that feast, they abstaine from flesh and all white meates, because the Priests on that day after Noone gather the people into the Temple, and all the people kneele in the same place, and the Priests pray, that the holy Ghost would descend upon them, as it did formerly on the Apostles on the day of Penticost. And therefore they fast on that Monday, that is the day following, but on Wednesday and Friday of that weeke, they eate flesh for joy of the holy

Times for Ghost: but the Monkes eate onely white meates.

Orders. The Greekish Bishops have a custome, that at three set times they give the Priests spirituall gifts, as Christ at three times especially gave to his Apostles spirituall gifts, and when they had received this favour thrice, then they were perfit; that is to say, the Apostles received the first gift when he gave them authoritie and power over all divels, and to heale diseases, Luke 9. I. hee gave them the second on the day of his resurrection, when he said to them, John 20. 2 2. Receive the holy Ghost: whose sinnes you remit, they are remitted to them, c. The third gift he gave them in the feast of Penticost, when he sent his holy spirit upon them: which being finished, the Apostles were perfect. After the same manner the Grecian Bishops make other Bishops; first the Bishop makes this or that man a Priest, but no confession, onely to sacrifice and sanctifie. But after that the Bishop understands that that Priest is a Schouer and learned, then on the day following hee gives him power to be a Confessor, and if hee bee unlearned hee onely Sacrificeth. And if hee deserve to bee a Bishop, on the third day two or three Bishops make him a compleate Bishop, and by reason hereof every Priest hath not power to heare Confessions, but hee onely who hath authoritie from the Bishop: the Priests desire, for the most part that the people confesse their sinnes to them in the Confession. Temple, sometimes also in other places, either in a private house, or in the fields, but no man is present besides themselves, whether it be in the Church or out of the Church.

The Greekes pray in the Temple standing upright. Rites ofpmier But they have some high seates in the Temple, such as- ' ' are in many Colledges, and they may sometimes sit in them, and sometimes stand. When the Priests Preach, then the lay people sit in those seates, yet they stand when they sing. But when they come into the Temple, every one takes his proper place, and then standing with his Hat off, bendeth downe the three former fingers of his right hand; which being done, he intimates that there are three persons in one deitie. And these fingers thus bended downe, he first laies on the forepart of his head; signifying thereby that the holy trinitie is in heaven. Then he removes them to his belly, signifying, that the Sonne and the Word of God descended to the earth, and tooke flesh, and was crucified, and buried for our sinnes. Then hee placeth them on his right shoulder, signifying that Christ is risen from the dead, and sits at the right hand of the Father, as David said, Sit at my right hand, till I put thine enemies under thy feete. Then hee laies them on his left shoulder, intimating that Christ should not set us at his left hand at the last day, but deliver us from that, as he hath taught us, deliver us from evill: and againe when he saith. Then will hee place the Sheepe at his right hand, and the Goates at his left: and every one in these severall spaces of time, that is from the first period of time, wherein hee puts those three fingers on his head, untill the laying them on his left shoulder, saith these words; Lord Jesus Christ, Sonne, and Word of God, be merci-full to me a sinner; and he bends his body, and so this figure signifies the signe of the Crosse, that is, putting his fingers first on his head, after on his belly, then on his right shoulder, and lastly on his left: these actions make a Crosse, and signifie the Crosse whereon Christ was crucified for our sinnes. And thus every one makes this figure three or foure times, and then sits downe on his seate.

The Greekes have a custome that the better sort of them receive the Sacrament of the precious body and bloud of Christ, once, twice, thrice, or foure times in the yeere, yet confession of their sinnes must goe before to some spirituall Priest (they call those spirituall Priests, Rites of Con- who have authoritie from the Bishop) And whosoever fesston. j gg l eg which will confesse himselfe to such a kinde of

Priest, ought to come to him. And the Priest asketh him, what he desires? he answereth, saying, I desire to confesse my sinnes. Then the Priest goeth with him to the Temple, and there in some private place he begins to teach him, saying: See, the Angell of God stands before thee to receive thy confession. Take heede therefore, that thou concealest no sinne, neither for shame, nor for any other cause, for I am a sinner like thy selfe. Then the Greeke begins to confesse his sinnes particularly: which being done, the Priest saith againe, take heede that you overslip no sinne through forgetfulnesse. Then more seriously then before hee lookes into himselfe, and whatsoever sinnes he can remember he ingeniously confesseth to the Priest. But if hee can remember no more, he tels him, he hath confest all that hee remembers. Then the Priest im-poseth him penance, that he fast so many daies, and give so many almes: which being finished, hee blesseth him in these words; According to the power which Christ gave his Apostles, saying, whatsoever you shall binde on earth, shall be bound in heaven; and whatsoever yee shall loose on earth, shall be loosed in heaven: Againe, according to the power which the Apostles gave the Bishoppes, and the Bishoppes gave 1.1,158. mee, be blessed of the Father, of the Sonne, and of the holy Ghost, and let thy portion be with the just. Which short benediction being ended, he makes a longer prayer over his head: who ariseth and leaveth some money in the place for the Priest to pray for him afterward. And so hee goes forth and performes whatsoever the Priest enjoynes him. And when the time comes that he must receive the Lords Supper, he must goe to that Priest or some other, who must pray over his head, he in the meane time kneeling.

All the Greekish Temples have a certaine place, dis- Their tinct from the rest of the Temple, wherein Priests, T r JJ'. Deacons, and Subdeacons onely enter, and wherein they performe their holies, and when the Priest will give the holy Sacrament to them that will receive it, hee stands at the doore of that place, and they that desire to receive it come neere the doore, and stand right before I 433 2 E

Communion, it. They come after this manner: when the time drawes neere to receive it, they come before the doore where the Priest celebrates his holies and bend their knees to the East, and worship God. Then they turne to the West, and kneeling, say to the people, Bless us brethren, wee have sinned in word and deede. And the people answere, saying, God pardon you brethren: then they turne to the South side of the Church, and say the same words to them as before, and they answere in the same manner. In like fashion they turne themselves and kneele to the North side of the Church, saying as before, and receiving the same answere. After this they all come neere to doore of the place where the Priest performes his holies, and the Priest comes forth holding the Sacrament in his hands, and stands in the middle of the doore, and gives to every one the body and bloud of our Lord, the Bread and Wine mingled together, saying, N. N. servant of God, receiveth in the name of the Father, and of the Sonne, and of the holy Ghost. And in the very particle of time, wherein they receive the Sacrament every one with a lowe voyce saith to himselfe, Lord I will not kisse thee as Judas, but as the Theefe I confesse thee, remember mee O Lord when thou commest in thy Kingdome: i nd after these words hee takes the Sacrament. And after that holy receiving, presently hee receives of the same Priest, a small portion of the

Holy bread.   Bread, called the divine guift, whereof we spake before, when we mentioned the Greekish praiers of the whole yeere.

Fonts and   The Greekes have certaine small Vessells in the

Baptisme.   Church called Fonts, wherein they baptise Infants in this manner; when the time comes to baptise an Infant, the kindred of the childe heat water with sweet smelling hearbs, and put the water into the foresaid vessell, but whiles the water warmes, the Priest prayes and puts Oyle into the water. After the prayers, the Priest taketh the childe in his armes, and puts the whole Infant thrice quite under the water, saying N. N. the servant of God is baptised in the name of the Father, then hee ducks the Infant, and drawes him out and then addes, and of the Sonne, and then againe ducks him, and drawes him out, and lastly addes in the name of the holy Ghost, and then againe ducks the Infant and pluckes him out, that is three times diving him in the water, and pulling him out of the water, as Christ said to his Disciples, goe forth baptising in the name of the Father and of the Sonne and of the holy Ghost. All which being finished, hee reades certaine prayers, as heere in Great Brittaine, and restores the childe to his Kinsfolke.

It is a custome amongst the Greekes to excommuni- Excommuni-cate those that are grievous offenders (because Saint ' "-Paul saith, when you are assembled together, and my spirit also deliver that man over to Satan; and againe reprove him severely) for example sake. A certaine wicked man hath borne false witnesse, or dealt injuriously with some man, the man wronged, cites this false witnesse before some Priest, or Bishop, and the Bishop asketh the false witnesse whether his testimonie bee true or not: the witnesse affirmes his testimonie to be true; then the Bishop or Priest puts on his Pontificall attire (whether hee be in the Church, or elsewhere) which garments signifie the seamlesse and purple coat of Christ and other things. And at that time the Bishop or Priest is a tipe of Christ, because of those holy Garments, and the grace which he received of the Bishops. Then he commands the false witnesse to stand before him, and begins that Psalme, wherein it is said, O God be not silent of my praise, because the mouth of the sinner and deceitful! was opened against mee, and the rest which followes in that Psalme; then hee addes certaine prayers; and after saith, by the authoritie which Christ gave his Apostles, viz. Whatsoever you shall loose in earth shall bee loosed in heaven, and whatsoever you shall binde in earth, shall bee bound also in heaven: And by the authoritie which the Apostles gave to the Bishops, and the Bishops gave mee, by this authoritie I excommunicate thee; thou shalt not converse with Christians, and shalt be separated from the Father and the Sonne, and the holy Ghost; and from the three hundred and eighteene Fathers, Divines of the Nicene Councell, and from all Saints: and thy portion shall bee with the Divell, and Judas and thou shalt bee indissoluble for ever as stones and Iron for a testimonie, unlesse thou repentest. These things being done, hee dismisseth him. And if the false witnesse doe not afterward repent, but die in his opinion; after a yeere (for the Greekes are wont to digge up the Sepulchres of those, which died in the former yeere, and also the sepulchre of that false witnesse) and they finde him entire, his bodie blacke, his hayre yet remayning and his nayles white, and they cast him out of the Sepulchre, and set him bolt upright against a wall and hee stands firmely of himselfe, as a solid piece of timber: and if you strike his belly it will sound like a drumme, and therefore he is called I. i. 159. Timpaniaeus. Soe also Cassianus an Historian in his histories calls an excommunicate person Timpaniaeum, If you doubt, you may speake to your Merchants to enquire in Palaea-patia, Thessalonica, Alexandria, Constantinople or any where else, you may also enquire of the Greeks that are in England, who will certifie you of the truth.

About threescore yeeres since or somewhat more, the Jewes which inhabited about Cairo, bitterly envied the Christians; for they saw that the Governour was very courteous, and therefore they consulted together to give him a double tribute for the Christians, so that he would destroy them because Christ spake falsely, saying. Whosoever hath Faith as a graine of Mustard seede, shall say to this Mountaine, pass hither or thither, and it shall goe. Math. 17. 20. and if they drinke any deadly thing it shall not hurt them. Mar. 16. 19. Then the furious Governour called the Patriarch, and said, your

Religion is false, because Christ said whosoever believeth Christopher in mee although he drink any deadly thing, it shall " ""f"- . twneth this not hurt him: And presently commanded the Patriarch, patriarch and that he should drinke poison before him, without making his poisoned the signe of the crosse, because the Jewes had enformed Cup. pag. him, that the Christians wrought magically by it, for 1376. "' f when they make the signe of the crosse, then the poison fter An looseth his efficacie, and therefore the Governour com- 1 6.? eing manded the Patriarch, that he should not make the signe then 10 yeers of the crosse, when he drunke the poison. Then the- " f Patriarch calling the people, praied and fasted with them f ountain I three daies, and the third day tooke the Communion doubt Gra: ca with them, and they went all to the Governour. Then fide to have the Governour being present and all the Jewes, one of " "' the Jewes brought a cup full of strong poison, and gave, Vchu it the Patriarch to drinke: Then the Governour said Poio relateth' to the Patriarch, holding the cup in his hand, take heede To. i. pa. jo. you make not the signe of the crosse on the cup; then '"' "' " the Patriarch blessing the cup mistically, asked the f "' . 1-11 1 T J? 1 1 have heard

Lrovernour, saymg, where will you that 1 dnnke, on this s that side, or on this, or on this, or on this? and by this having letters meanes he laid his fingers on the foure sides of the ofcommenda-superficies of the cup, sanctifying the cup mistically. "j' "
""-

A L ' J L J ouths nictittoits

Then the Governour said to the Patriarch, drinke where 7 g j di- you will, not knowing that the Patriarch had blessed the Hon mul- cup with the signe of the crosse; after this the Patriarch tipucation is dranke off the whole cup. And after hee had drunke, he f"' ' "f, J, 1 1 111 1 " ith Miracle- bad them brmg him some water, and they brought some: f ongers.

then he put a little water into the cup, and washed it.

Then he said to the Governour, I have drunke all the poison, let a Jew drinke onely this water that is in the cup, that we may see his faith: then the Patriarch offered the cup to the Jew that first brought it him, that he might drinke it: but the Jew would not. Then the Governour threatned him, saying, drinke, that we may see also thy Religion. And so the Jew dranke the water in the cup, and presently burst in sunder. Then the Jewes gave great quantitie of monie to the Governour, saying that the Patriarch had wrought witchcraft; but Christ saith whosoever hath faith as a graine of mustard seede, shall say to this Mountaine, remove thither, and it shall remove. Now let the Patriarch call that Mountaine which is over against us, and if it come to us, then let the Christians slay us. Then againe the Prince said to the Patriarch, that hee should call the Mountaine, or otherwise the Christians must die. Then the Patriarch besought the Governour to grant him three daies, that the Greekes might take counsell together; but the Patriarch and people praled with teares dale and night, and on the third day, according to their custome, they received the Lords Supper; and after they had done, they all assembled together both Greekes, Turkes, and Jewes, and came to the appointed place, and then the Patriarch stretching out his hand towards the Mountaine, said, In the name of the Father, and of the Sonne, and of the holy Ghost, Mountaine, come hither; and sodainely it clove in peeces, and came to them. But all feard least it should cover them. Then the Governour said to the Patriarch, command that the Mountaine stand still, then againe stretching out his hands, the Patriarch blessed the Mountaine, saying, stand Mountaine, and the Mountaine stood there; and from that time the Mountaine was called Stand-Mountaine unto this day: but in Turkish it is called Dourdag, that is, Stand-Mountaine. Then the Governour said to the Patriarch, that the Graecians should kill the Jewes: but the Patriarch answered the Governour, wee Christians are not accustomed to kill men; but for their punishment let them cause that the water which runs beneath Cairo, may come into Cairo, that all men in the Citie may drinke of it at the Jewes cost, which to this day is done.

The Greekes also have Monkes, but onely of the order of Basil the great. But this order is divided into three orders, the first is called Monasticall, the second is Anachoreticall (which live apart) the third Asceticall, or if you will Exerciticall.

The first Order which is called Monasticall is in this Greehhh manner: there are Monasteries amongst the Greekes,-both great and little; some of them have fiftie Monkes, others a hundred, some one hundred and fiftie, some two hundred, others three hundred, others foure hundred, and others more. But the Monkes of this first

Order live a common life; for they all dine and sup together with their Governor at the same table: And neither the Governors meate nor drinke differs from the rest of the Monks, whether they be illiterate or wise. And whensoever the Governor eates or drinkes, they all eate the same bread and the same meate, and drinke the same drinke. But for decencie, the Governour, Seniors, and Priest, differ in their garments. Most of the Monkes of this first Order labour with their hands: but the Priests and Deacons labour not, but attend to reading and ecclesiasticall functions: but the rest live by the labour of their hands, some make the Monkes shooes, I. i. 160. some spin Sheepes wooll, and Goates haire, some are Brasiers, and make Hatchets of Brasse, others betake Hand labours. themselves to keepe flockes of Sheepe, and hire mer-cenarie Shepheards to serve them: and are conversant with them a yeere, and when a yeere is past, they goe to the Monasterie and tarrie there, others goe to keepe Horses, and remaine out a yeere, and then others are sent out by the Ancients of the Monasteries, and according to this manner the ancients send out Monkes yeerely to keepe Horses, Oxen, Bees, Sheepe, and other businesses, and after a yeere they returne to the Monasterie, and in this manner live the Monkes in the Monasteries: many Priests also are sent by the ancients into Walachia, Moscovia, and Iberia, that whatsoever the Kings give them, they may carrie to the Monasterie, and they abide in the Monasterie, and others are sent forth, and thus live the Monkes of the first Order in their Monasteries.

They weare a hat on their head, which hides their Their habit. eares, signifying that they heare nothing, neither learne mens vices, but are accounted as deafe men: as Paul mlticall.

PURCHAS HIS PILGRIMES saith, bee children in maliciousnesse. They weare also another Hat upon that which represents the figure of a Sepulcher, and hides the head, and hangs downe almost to the girdle, intimating that hee which weares this figure is dead from worldly things, neither ought hee which is cloathed in this habit to be carefull about worldly affaires, that is, about honours, riches, kindred, friends, favour with men, nor cherishing the body, but account himselfe to be dead, not as if hee were really dead, but with a kinde of preoccupated opinion of death, as the Lord saith: Whosoever will come after mee, let him deny himselfe, and take up his crosse and follow mee: And David, Wee are killed all the day long for thy sake.

Monkes Ere- The second Order of Monkes is called Anachoreticall, or Heremeticall, that is, when there is any rich man, that cannot live in the Monasterie, then hee gives as much monie to the Monasterie as will buy a house, and the Monks living in the Monasterie give him some great house, which is distant two or three miles from the Monasterie, wherein hee Hves with two or three poore Monks, as the Monasticall do in Monasteries: but that house hath a Church, Vine-yard, Olive-yard, Nuts, Cherries, Almonds, and other things necessarie to live on abundantly. And this is the second Order of Monkes of Basil the great.

Monkei Asce- The third Order of Monkes is called Asceticall, or ttcall, or Exercit- icall, that is, the Order given to exercise, for vacant to, i i i i t stricter exer- these are exceedingly exercised in vertue: these live a cises. strict and rigid life, they are content only with little houses or Caves, and have neither Vineyards nor Fields; yet some of them have great Vines, but make no Wine of them, but nourish them to eate the

Grapes: they have also Figge trees, and such like things, wherewith they live, namely Beanes, Cherries, Apples, Chesnuts boild on the fire with water. They gather also in the Spring time Apples, Parseley, Figges, Cherries, and cut them in peeces, and dry them in the Sunne: and these thus prepared they eate with bread the rest of the yeere, once in a day, and twice on Feast daies: some eate once onely on Feast daies: these get their living by their sweate and labour: For the Greekish Church doth not suffer Monkes o- or Hermites to begge; because they remember that " J'

Paul saith, Hee which will not worke, let him not eate. ' " " ' " '

But sometimes some rich Grecians send almes to the

Monasteries, and to the Hermites, and these exercised men receive them: but the course of their life is such; some make upper Garments of Goates and Sheepes woou, which the Monks weare upon their Garments: some make Hats of straw, some make wodden Spoones, and some of them write Bookes; and all these hand-wrought things they give to the Monkes dwelling in Monasteries, and they supply the Hermits with all necessaries: and this is the third Order of Hermit Monkes. I write these things, because I am an eye-witnesse, and speake cer- tainely, truely, and boldly. This is the third Order of the Monkes of Basill the great.

The fasting of the first and second Order, that is of Monkes fasts. the Monasticall, and of those who are Governours of two or three Monkes is on this manner: They fast through the whole yeere, everie weeke thrice, Monday, Wednesday, and Friday: they fast on Monday, because on Saturday and Sunday they eate twice in a day, and they eate Fish, and Butter, and Egges, and Milke, and Cheese, and Oyle, and Wine: but that their concupiscence may not be encreased, they fast on Monday: on Tuesday and Thursday, Saturday and Sunday, they eate twice those things which I mentioned before. The fast of the three daies is in this manner: the second houre after noone they pray in the Temple, and going out they goe to the Table, and eate Beanes with broth, without Oyle and Butter, and some Hearbes with Vinegar, or Pease, or other pulse boiled without Oyle or Butter, c. at evening they goe to the Temple, and after praiers going out, they sit neere the Temple, and the Butler is wont to goe round about carrying a Cup full of fragments of Bread, and gives to every one of the Monkes a peece of Bread, and a cup of water: the yonger sort take them, but the elders receive nothing; but after they have sit a while, they goe againe into the Temple, and pray, and sometimes the space of an houre, sometimes halfe an houre; and when they goe forth, the Governour stands in the Church Porch, everie Monke when hee goeth out at the doore prostrates himselfe before him, saying, blesse Lord; but the Governour answers, saying, God grant thee this my Sonne, and so againe they returne to their houses, and it is not lawfull for any, any longer to speake together, and so they I. i. 161. begin to pray in their houses, and performe their private devotions, and kneeling before God, every one to aske pardon for himselfe, and for others a whole houre, and then they goe to sleepe till the clocke sounds midnight, and then they all rise, and goe all to praiers, untill morning, and then going out of the Temple, they goe about their private arts, and worke almost till dinner; and then they goe to the Temple before dinner, and when they are come from thence, they goe to dinner as the day before, and when they rise from dinner the Governour stands in the doore of the dining roome, and everie Monke going forth prostrates himselfe before the Governour, saying, blesse

Lord, and the Governour answereth, saying, God pardon thee my sonne. But in the time of their great Lent, they bow themselves before the Governour, both in dinner time, and after supper in the Temple answering in the same manner: and thus doe they throughout the whole yeere. Moreover, if any of the Monkes chance to sleepe, and not rising at the beginning when they beginne to pray but the first houre of praier, which is called midnight, is past, and hee riseth after midnight; hee on that day dineth not with the other Monkes, but whiles the rest are eating, hee stands at the entrance to the Table before them all, and bowes himselfe before all that are eating, saying. Have mercy on mee O God, according to thy great mercie, c. untill all of them rise from dinner; and when they rise, all would goe forth together, but hee fals on the ground and saith, O holy Fathers, blesse mee an idle person, because I have sinned; and every one of his brethren saith, God pardon thee brother: and when all are gone out, then hee eates: and they doe after this manner both the elder and yonger Monkes: they doe this willingly, that all may have a good example to rise alwayes at the time of the first Prayer.

The third order of Monkes is called the exercised Order, these exercised eate all the yeere once in a day, except on solemne daies, and feast daies, and often then also they eate but once; if they dine they sup not; as we declared before of the fasting of the first and second order of Monkes.

The Monkes also have foure Lents in the yeere as the Their Lent Laickes. The first Lent is called the great and holy Lent, f'-as is said before, because it is the tithing of their soules for the yeere, because in the eighth weeke the Laickes pardon their enemies, and confesse and prepare themselves, that when the holy Lent comes they may be pure in heart, and supplicate God for their sinnes. After the same manner also the Monkes untill the seventh weeke before Easter, forgive one another their trespasses, and prepare themselves that they also may be pure in heart: they beginne to fast from Munday, that is the seventh weeke before Easter: they fast Munday and Tuesday: but one Wednesday they eate: but on the two former daies they eate nothing. But some on Tuesday about the Even eate a morsell of bread with water; and after Wednesday they begin daily to eate once untill Saturday. On Saturday and Sunday, on these two daies untill Easter they eate Oile, and drinke Wine; but on the five other daies of the weeke they eate once, and eat dried Apples, and such like things (whereof we said the exercised eate) they eate, and the Monkes in the great Lent. But some of the Monkes of the two Orders, and of the Exercisers and Heremits, in the great Lent often in three daies eate once. But in the great Even wherein Christ was crucified, all the Monkes Good Friday.

fast all the dales, and neither dine nor sup, but only eate a little bread on Saturday, and drinke Wine moderately, that they may abide in the Church, for they watch all night singing for joy of the Resurrection of Christ.

The Greekish Monkes have an order to rise to pray every night an houre and an halfe after midnight: but on Sundaies one houre after throughout the whole yeere. They watch from the Evening till Morning on Dominicall Feasts, and on the Feasts of great Saints, that is, in the night of the Resurrection of Christ, and of the Ascension: Pentecost and John the Baptist, and the foure and twentieth of the month of June, on the Feast of Peter and Paul, on the sixt day of August: because on that day they celebrate a great Feast for the Transfiguration of Christ on Mount Thabor: And it is called to this day, the day of the transfiguration of Christ. Moreover, rich and poore celebrate a great Feast, and watch all the night the fifteenth day of August; because on that day Mary a Mother and a Virgin was translated from Earth to Heaven: and so on other Feast dales as on Christs Nativitie. Monkes how The Grecian Monkes have a custome, that when a made. Laicke will be made a Monke, he first goeth to the

Monasterie, and there the Governour asketh him what he would have; to whom hee answeres that he would be made a Monke. The Governour replies: it is necessary that you remaine three yeeres in the Monasterie, in which Three yeeres time you may prove and examine your selfe. After the probation. yeeres finished, if he like not to be a Monke, he may goe away and marrie a wife: but if hee like, then the Governour taketh him, and leading him to the Temple thus speaketh to him: Behold, the Angell of the Lord expecteth that he may receive the confession: take heed therefore that thou desirest not to be a Monke because of any affliction (that is lest thou shouldst have killed any, and therefore for feare of death commeth hither; or hast grieved thy parents, or hast desired to have carnall pleasures with some and couldst not, and for easing thy griefe comes to be made a Monke, and not for love to

God, CC.) Then he which is to be a Monke answereth, not so honorable father, but I desire to live a quiet and peacable life, and to abstaine from worldly troubles and tumults, to fast, watch, and in peace to pray unto God. Then the Governour replies againe: therefore doest thou desire to renounce the world, and worldly pleasures for the I. i. 162. love of God? hee that is to be a Monke answereth, yea truly honourable Father, God willing: Will you forsake Father and Mother, Brethren, Marriage, the joyes and delights of this world? (as Christ saith. Whosoever leaveth Father and Mother, c, for the love of Christ) he answeres, yea truly, honourable Father, God willing, and after this manner answeres to everie Interrogatorie. Then the Governour after Praiers attires him in a Monkish Habit; and with a paire of Cissers cuts from his head a few hairesj and fastens them mingled with Bees Waxe in some corner neere the Sacring place, signifying that hee is consecrated to God, nor henceforth hath power over his owne bodie, to marrie a wife: because Christ saith. No man putting his hand to the plough, and looking backe is fit for the Kingdome of God.

The Greekes obey the divine Law verie strictly: when Forgiving one as the Lord saith, Forgive and it shall bee forgiven you, o-they forgive their enemies their offences: every one saith particularly these words, I heartily forgive mine enemies that God may forgive me. Also they obey the lawes obedience. of the holy Apostles for example, where Paul saith. Let every soule bee subject to the higher powers; for there is no power but of God. They obey diligently also the precepts of the Fathers which are according to the Lawes of God.

Moreover, the Greekes celebrate the Feast of Easter Easter zvhy according to the ancient custome for these reasons: first, different from that they may neither keepe it before the Jewes, nor with the Jewes, as it sometimes happens that this new Passeover is observed by the Latines, before the Jewes, and somtimes with the Jewes. Secondly, because the holy Nicene Councell that first and universall one saith, if any celebrate

Easter before the Jewes, or with the Jewes let him bee

See of this accursed. Thirdly, because neere the River Nile, and the

Sandy sup. I. Qj-jg Cairo, is a ffreat wonder the earth casting forth dead ' ' ' " carkasses (that Countrie begins to cast them forth on the great day of Thursday before the Feast in which day

Christ made his mysticall Supper) but it casts forth dead bodies daily till the day of Ascension, that is, the day on which Christ ascended into Heaven, viz. till the fortieth day after Easter, and after that day it ceaseth to cast forth any. This wonder both Graecian and Turkish Merchants mention, as many as come from those places into Greece: as also others testifie, who goe to Jerusalem to worship

Christs Sepulchre, and after they goe to that place, where the bodies are cast out of the Earth, to see the Miracle: but his Miracle is according to the number of the old

Feast. The Greeks did decree twentie yeers since to celebrate the feast according to the new number, but the bodies were neither cast forth according to that time; neither did the holy light shine, as it was wont yeerely to

See Fulcherius shine in the holy Sepulchre of Christ about the ancient sub. I. 8. c. 2. jj g q gaster: then the Greekes staied til the ancient time of Easter, about which time the holy light shined in

Christs Sepulchre, as it was wont yeerely, and the earth neere Nile cast forth dead bodies: and then the Greekes kept the Feast, saying: behold, God sheweth us the true time of Easter, and wee care not for humane wisdome.

The Greekes say, that the Crosse is Christs Scepter, and his two-edged Sword; and as a Souldier fights with his Sword, and overcomes his enemies, so Christ also because hee was crucified, overcame the Devill, he could without the Crosse have saved man, and vanquished the

Devill; but he would not, because it seemed good to him to doe so: but as when a great King goeth to warre, he sends his Scepter before him, and armeth his Souldiers

The weapons with strong weapons, that they may fight with their ofourzvarfare g emies, and that the people may know the King comes: atenotcarnau,. i i i r i t- but spirituall whence it comes to passe that the giorie or the Kmg is z. Cor. 10.4. spread all abroad, before he comes to that place, whither he sent his Scepter before him; after the same manner Christ cruci- also our Lord Jesus Christ doth, he defends us Christians, fi PP '- armed with his Crosse, which Crosse signifies the Passion J ' J-r of Christ, and wheresoever the Crosse appeares, having ing our old this Title written on it, Jesus Christ overcomes, Christ man, and is preached and praysed: but not every Crosse or thing like ff f' ifyt"g our a Crosse is called the Crosse of Christ, but that which is V",, 1 J 1 1 i-r- 1 T r An the spiri- mscnbed with this Title, Jesus Christ overcomes; that is tuall worship called the Crosse of Christ, whether it be of silver or of God would of metall, or of wood, these Letters consecrate that Crosse turned to to Christ: for that Crosse signifies that Christ was cruci " ' f" "f r J r ' l., hodily rites, as ned tor our sinnes, and overcame our enemies: therefore ou see in this David saith. Lord, in thy light we shall see light: the light and almost all of the Father is the Sonne, the light of the Sonne is differmg the Crosse, c. ' f""'

The Patriarke of Constantinople hath now under him Pat'riarke of seventie and foure Metropolitans; but there are more then Constan-thirtie of these, that have not Bishops under them, of i ople. those which have, this hath one, this two, this three, c. " Clcrgte. all the Bishops are seventie two or seventie and three. But all the Bishops and Metropolitans are almost a hundred and fiftie. The Patriarke of Constantinople hath his proper Seate only at Constantinople. Hee hath His main-for his maintenance from that Citie a piece of Gold f "'-at every Marriage. And he hath twelve pence of every house once in three yeeres throughout his whole Province; viz. of every Province of the Metropolitanes that have their Seates subject to him: he hath also a certaine small gift of the Deacons and Priest when he gives them their Orders. Also every Priest in that Citie yeerely gives him a piece of Gold. When rich Christians die, they leave to the Patriarkes of that Church; houses, fields, sheepe, wealth, c. And every Metropohtane and Archbishop when they are consecrated by the Patriarke give him some small gratuitie. And everie Metropohtane yeerely gives the Patriarke, this man twentie pound, that thirtie, another five and twentie pounds for the Kings Tribute. Of which wealth the Patriarke gives i. i. 163.

Tribute.

His Family.

Otherbishops.

Priests livings.

annually 6000. pieces of Gold in name of all the chiefe Priests: that the Turkish King may let the Patriarke remaine in Constantinople, and the Greekish Metropolitanes, Archbishops and Bishops in his whole Kingdome; and observe the Christian Religion, The Patriarkes servants, and of all the chiefe Priests are Monkes. Seven-teene or more Priests and Ministers eate of the Patriarkes bread. Hee hath two Chaplaines, two Deacons, a Steward, Chappell Clearke, two Singers, a Porter, a Horse-keeper, and a Keeper of his great Seale, and another of his Privie Seale.

In like manner every Metropolitane and Archbishop hath a proper Citie: these also receive a small reward for the election of Bishops. Also they receive yeerely of every Bishop, twentie, fifteene, or ten pounds. Moreover, of the Deacons and Priests a small gratuitie for their imposition of hands. Moreover, every Priest yeerely gives to the Metropolitane or Archbishop a piece of Gold: they take also at everie Wedding a piece of Gold; and Almes for burying the dead, as is said of the Patriarke. Moreover, yeerely of everie Family in the Citie a bushell of Corne; and Wine, and Oile, and Silke, and of these things the Metropolitans live

After the same manner the Bishops take a small reward of the Deacons and Priests for Imposition of hands: they also receive yeerely of everie Priest a piece of Gold, and as much for everie Marriage, also as much of everie Family yeerly in his Province, besides a bushell of Corne, Wine, Oile, and Silke.

The Priests live of the superfluitie of the Church, that is to say, some Churches have fields, vineyards, houses and such like: but if the Church had not plentie of those, everie householder gives the Priest yeerely a bushell of Corne (a bushell signifies here the third part of a horse load.) Moreover the Greekes have yeerely six and thirtie feast daies, twelve of them are called Dominican, that is, pertaining to Christ and the blessed Virgin, the other foure and twentie are of Saint John the

Baptist, of the holy Apostles and famous Martyrs: on all these Feast dales the Priest must administer the Communion: and everie Family gives to the Priest two pence, hee prayes particularly for everie donor, before he begins to sacre. Moreover, on these Feast daies, the Greekes entertaine many strangers: and sometimes make five or sixe Feasts in a Village, and the Priest must be present at everie Feast, and blesse the viands; and they give the Priest bread, flesh, wine, monie and other things which will be sufficient for his Family the whole weeke, and thus doe the Priests live.

Moreover, if any living in the Cities or Provinces of the Greekes will be made Deacons, they must first Deacons. marrie: and then the Bishops make them Deacons. But if they will not marrie, they must first be made Monkes, and then the Bishops with their Suflfrages make them Monkish Deacons, and they may not after marrie, because the Bishops have separated them.

Also, the Monkes sleepe alwaies with their Coats girt about them: so also the Laicks sleepe with their wives with their clothes on: because Paul saith; I would have Scripture those that have wives to be as if they had none, and those " ' that have none, as if they had.

Chap. XV.

Collections out of Peter Stroza, Secretary to Pope Paul the Fifth, his Treatise of the Opinions of the Chaldeans, touching the Patriarke of Babylon, and the Nestorians in Asia.

T happened that amongst those poore men, whose feet were on Maundie Thursday, according to the wonted Solemnitie, washed by Pope Paul the Fifth, in the first yeere of his Papacie, there were two Chaldasans, one a Monke, the other a Lay-man, which a little before had made their Pilgrimage to Rome; which I 449 2 F carried some presents to Elias the Patriarke of Babylon from the Pope, and gave him a Booke of the profession of faith, propounded to the men of the East, which came to Rome; whereby and by their extolling the Popes gentle usage, the said Patriarke Elias sent Legates to the Pope to give him thankes and to acknowledge him for their common Father and Lord, with acknowledgement of his subjection profession of the same faith, indeavour-ing to make it appear that the difference betwixt Rome them was only in words not in sense. These Legates fell amongst Theeves; and others were sent, which with much difficultie came to Rome, where hearing how odious the name of Nestorius was, to decline the suspition of Nestorian Heresie, they tooke some pages out of the Bookes of their profession and rites, being perswaded thereto by a Jew lately converted. They returning in this manner, and little being done, Elias consulteth with his Bishops, and sends Adam the Archdeacon of the Patriarchal! Chamber, Abbot of the Chaldaean Monkes, to render account of their faith, and humbly to desire correc-
I. i. 164. tion, if ought therein were erronious. Hee brought a Letter and profession the third yeere after the departure of the former. The Letter is this.

From the Patriarchall Chamber, Prayers and Blessings be given to you.

TAe Letter of TT Rom humble Elias of the East, who by the grace of
Elias Patri- q j serveth the holy See of Babylon, continual!
abflon to the adorations, and perpetuall inclinations everlasting
Pope, kneelings before your holy feet: O blessed Father, and
A. 1610. head of Fathers, Sunne of Christianitie, and Name on which is situated the aedifice of the Church of Churches; my Lord, and my Father the Pope, Lord (and) Father of all the Patriarches which are in the Universe. Your

Charitie towards us may be pleased to take notice, that your Letters have come to us, and your firme Faith, and the blessing which you sent my lowlinesse; and I received a blessing together with my people, and have given thankes to Christ, for that I am made worthy of the blessings of your Holinesse, and of your illustrious memorie, and you have numbred me among the sonnes of your Father-hood besides my merits. I presently sent a thanksgiving and letters, and my Faith. But wicked men met my Legates, and tooke all things from them, and they returned to me emptie: againe I sent others, which came not to your Holinesse, which grieved mee with my Bishops and Archbishops, and I said, What shall I doe? I cannot goe, because the Princes our Oppressors permit mee not; neither can I goe to Jerusalem: they hold us as Slaves, and permit us not to doe our will. At last I sent thy Faith and letters of thy puritie, with my faithful! Sonne and Counsellour Father Adam, to shew them in all our Regions, that we might see what was fitting to bee done of us Orientalls, and he remained in these Regions a whole yeere: and wee all consulted together, and have sent to your Holinesse the same Father Adam; and I have sent with him my Faith and letters, and said that hee should treat with your Holinesse of these things further then is written, because hee is the Head of Fathers and Abbat of the Orientall Monkes, and wee have none of more note, as all the East confesseth. And now, O Father, with bowed head wee adore before thy Seat without fraud and guile, thy Precept is received of me according to his Precept, which delivered thee the Keyes. Nor will I deny that voyce spoken to Peter, I have given thee the keyes, and what thou shalt bind on Earth shall h t y be bound in Heaven, and what thou shalt lose on Earth p pg presence shall be losed in Heaven, And I will not resist as doe can doe with a others, Heretickes against the precept of the holy P ' Patri-Apostles, and orthodoxe Fathers, which affirmed that the See of Great Rome should hold the principalitie, and she is van'm and the Head of all Sees: farre be it from me, but I confesse lies least I that the Roman Church is the Mother of Churches, and be poore and he which doth not confesse it, let him be Anathema. And f our Babylonian See is not elected of it selfe, as of other q j-Heretikes, which have multiplied Patriarches in the world vain, Pro. 30.

without Law, but by the Precept of the Pope, and coun- sell of the Roman Church, was the See ot Babylon chosen, and so it is found written amongst us in the Chronicles, namely that the Orientall Fathers were ordained at Rome.

But afterwards it came to passe, that when they sent men for

Confirmation they were slaine in their journey, and when they did so a long time, all perished. This being told to the Church and Pope, the Pope decreed in a Councell and said. Let us ordaine them a Patriarch, and let us permit them to chuse their Patriarches, that they die not in the way for Confirmation, nor any evills happen to them, and so we should sinne, and they remaine without the Roman fold. And thus wee have received power till this time, and we have done nothing of our selves, as the rest, which have troden under foot the Canons of the Apostles, and

Lawes of the Fathers, and have filled the Earth with

Yea what Patriarches without need. For this cause the See of need, and very Babylon was called the Fifth, for the foure Sees of the need; j onej are f-Q j. Evangelists; and because the Patriarch was elected too, 'which with the Roman Confirmation, and he hath given us makes him tell power to make Pastors, then was the See of Babylon more then called, which doth accompany the foure Sees, and is num-

Romeitselfe f p q Father, behold ever dreamed,.,, t t i i i j of Romes Y t ith hath come to your Holmesse with letters, and greatnes in the you may see if there be fraud in our profession or error,

East, as others or recoiling from our Mother the Roman Church. Ad- thfsouth' " o sh, and we will doe, teach, and we will obey. And if in all things we be true before your See, and there be no fraud in our faith, we desire of your benignitie, that you forget not the poverty of your servants, because many of our profession have undergone dangers when they have

Th' ' h " y- some have dyed, others were slaine by

Easterne enemies, and few have returned. And let this suffice fashion to your Holinesse from our lowlinesse, that from the furthest receive the parts of the East, we beare your Precepts on our heads

Letters g come against all Nations with our bloud,

Mandates of,. jir their Princes sustame calamities that we may adore berore your on their heads. Excellency, and we lowly and subject may receive blessing from the Great Mother Church of Paul Peter. Who urgeth us to do this, but the Christian faith, and your love to our lowlinesse? And let this suffice that we have shewed to your Wisdome. But this whole labour we sustaine for the Roman Church: and your Ministers at Jerusalem hold all that are of my profession, as forrainers and rebells from the Church of Rome, and doe not gratifie us as before, because their Interpreters are of professions which hate us, and those your Ministers enquire not the truth. Wee desire your Holinesse to admonish them, and to hold those of our profession, as of yours, and to bee gentle to them. I have sent Letters to your Teachers, to command those of our profession in Jerusalem, because it was written in our Annalls that our Archbishop, which was in Cyprus, and those of our profession which inhabite Jerusalem, and the Clergie in the Monastery of Saint James in Nisibis, are numbred amongst the sonnes of the Church of Rome for your Fatherhoods love to our lowlinesse. And now who am I, and all mine, and all the Easterne part. f" Wee are lisping before your Holinesse, but as obedient servants, are subject to your Lordship, and with a mind farre from schisme kisse your holy feet, and earnestly desire health to your Holinesse, and flee to your praiers, and the praiers of your fellow servants Peter and Paul, that wee may bee made worthy of the remission I. i. 165. of sinnes in the terrible Judgement Day of God the Word, to whom, and his Father, and the Holy Ghost, bee honour and glorie for ever Amen.

His profession of the Faith followeth, part whereof wee have translated: Wee beleeve in God the Father, who is the Maker of Heaven and Earth, and all things therein visible and invisible. And in the Sonne which is of him, and which is equall with him in Essence, and is not lesse then his Father and Maker of all things. And the Spirit of Sanctitie, which proceedeth from the Father, and is not begetter nor begotten, and hee is a glorious substance, and equall in substance with the Father and the Sonne. The Father is Begetter, and not begotten;

Nestorius." himselfe in an Epistle to Pope Coelestine, hath these words of the blessedvirgtn: Christotocon ausi sunt cum modo quodatn theotocon dicere 3c.

The differences betwixt the Orientals, called l es-torians, y us.

See Fulche-rius, l. J. c. z.

and the Sonne is begotten, not begetter, and the Spirit of Sanctitie proceeding, not begetter nor begotten, c. God the Word descended into the Virgin and was joined with Man, which was compact in her in the power of the Spirit of Sanctitie, and was made one with man, as the conjunction of fire with Iron. And wee beleeve that hee received a body and soule, and understanding, c. And though they say against us, that wee confesse not that the Virgin is the Mother of God but the Mother of Christ, that is, the Mother of Christ God over all: yet this is nothing, for this is set for the confirmation and reprobation of the false opinion of Apollinaris, which said that the Deitie was without Humanitie, and to the confusion of the wickednesse of Semystius, which said, That Christ is a meere Man, to wit, Humanitie without Divinitie, c. Wee in the denomination of Christ comprehend the two Natures, of the Deitie of the Humanitie, and confesse not a simplicitie in Christ as they traduce us, c.

In another Epistle written by the said Elias to the Pope, hee confesseth that the differences acknowledged are brought to these heads. First, The Lord Pope, with all the Fathers of the Great Church of Rome, call the Virgin Saint Mary the Mother of God: but wee of the East call her the Mother of Christ. Secondly, They confesse two Natures of Christ, two Powers, and two Wills: but wee confesse one Power and one Will. Thirdly, They confesse one Person in Christ, and wee confesse two Persons. Fourthly, And they say that the Spirit proceedeth of the Father and the Sonne, and wee confesse that the Spirit proceedeth of the Father. Fifthly, Also the Fathers of Rome say, that that which comes out of our Lords Sepulcher " is not true light, and wee with all ours receive it as true light. Hee saith, hee consulted with Adam aforesaid, and with Gabriel the ancientest Archbishop and chiefe Grammarian in his Jurisdiction: which Gabriel answered. That they had received of their Ancestors, that there is no division twixt us and the Church of Rome, but in Ceremonies, and they in all their Regions observe their owne Ceremonies: and as farre, saith hee, as I can understand, there is none other division but that one understandeth not the other. But touching thy request, behold Father Adam is before thee, which hath beene proved in the desert from his youth. And I said to our Father Adam, What sayest thou of these things? Hee answered, give me three dayes space, and the third day, I will answere as much as my infirmitie is able, and as much as may suffice, and the third day hee brought his writing; and it pleased mee and all mine. And I gave him Letters with my Faith and Thy Epistles and Faith, and sent him to the Countries and our Flocke, writing that if they had any thing to answere, hee should bring it. A yeere after hee returned with Letters, that all of our profession submitted themselves. And now I have sent him, c.

The Treatise of the said Adam in seven Chapiters, is published by the said Stroza the Popes Secretary, in which hee laboureth to reconcile the Roman and Orientall Churches in the differences aforesaid; which by the said Stroza is learnedly discussed, and the truth enucleated and cleared from Nestorian shuffling, which the learned Reader may peruse in Stroza himselfe; the unlearned could hardly doe it, though wee had troubled our selves to trouble him with the Translation. The effect was, Adam was reclaimed in those points aforesaid to the Orthodoxe Faith, and sent with the Popes Breve (published also in the Booke aforesaid) dated on the ve and twentieth of March, 1614. And Adam wrote another Treatise in maintenance of his corrected faith learned at Rome, by him dated, Ann. 1974. Regis Gr corum, Romae. Diebus beatissimi

Patris Petri nostri temporis, Domini Papae Pauli Quinti, cujus oratio nobiscum sit; all published together by the said Stroza.

Godignius and Myraeus say, that John Antonie Maari-erius, and Peter Metoscita two Jesuites, were sent backe with this Adam by the Pope, to make a more full reducing of the Nestorians.

I. i. i66. Chap. XVI.

A briefe survey of the Ecclesiasticall Politie Ancient and Moderne, or of the severall Patriarchs, Archbishops, and Bishops Sees thorow the Christian World: also of the Jesiiites Couedges and numbers, and of other Monasticall Orders.

Rome.

Ubertus Myraeus hath written a Treatise, called Notitia Episcopatuum Orbis Christiani: and another of Ecclesiasticall Politie, or the State of Christian Religion in Europe, Asia, Africa, and the New World divided into foure Bookes; and as many more of Monasticall originalls; out of whom principally, and out of some others I thought fit to collect such things as might serve for our present Historicall purpose; for the Readers knowledge as well of the extension of Christian Religion in these times, as the opinions and differing rites before delivered.

Our Author begins with Italy, as being himself more then enough Itallonated. The Princes now potent in Italy, are the Pope, the Spaniard (which is King of Naples, Sicil and Sardinia, and Duke of Millaine) the Prince of Piemont (which now is the Duke of Savoy) the Great Duke of Tuscaine, the Dukes of Mantua, Mutina, Parma; the Republikes or free States of Venice, Genua, and Luca. Rome is the Seat of our Authors Religion, and by him honoured with that blasphemous title of Urbs Sterna (as for Terrarum domina, urbium Regina, Orbis compendium, they are given too, but too compendious) and was indeed of principall respect in the Church of Christ, ever since the Apostolicall preaching of the Gospell, and the Apostle of the Gentiles testified that their faith was then renowmed thorow the whole Rom. i. 8. world; which was so fattened with the bloud of their Primitive Bishops and Martyrs, that no where was a more fertill harvest then there, during the Raigne of the Ethnike Emperours. Constantine subjecting his Imperiall Scepter to the Crosse, her Bishops also received greater splendor of power and pompe, and being the Imperiall Citie, was therefore reputed the first See or Seat of the Patriarches, which then were three, the Roman, Three Patri-Alexandrian, and Antiochian: which divided the Ecclesi- " astical Jurisdiction of the Roman World (so they called y ar. 2. their Empire) betwixt them: the Constantinopolitan Co istan-being after both added to the number, preferred tlnopk. above the Alexandrian and Antiochian; and equalled also with the Roman, saving his meere primacie of Order (for the same cause that now it was also become New Rome, and the Imperiall Citie) by decree of the Councell of Constantinople, A. 381. and more plainely expressed by the Chalcedon Councell, A. 451.

As for reasons drawne from Scripture, I have prayed for thee, I will give thee the Keyes, feed my Sheepe, c. now adayes alledged as proper causes of Papall preeminence, the ancient Councells knew them not, but alledged meere civill respects of the Imperiall residence and power: which yet so puffed up the Imperious spirits of their successors, that in Gregories dayes the Constantinopolitan would needs be stiled Universall Bishop, which Gregory then withstood as Antichristian; and yet in few dayes after his death, his successor Boniface obtained P-of Phocas the murtherer, that swelling and exorbitant Owa. 5; o. Primacie and Papacie, in Ecclesiasticalls, to the Roman Writers of the See, by Phocas (to make sure of the Romans, in that Popes lives in slippery state of his new gotten Empire by bloud and Bonifac. 3. treason) made the Head of al Churches. Which power could yet, neither by Phocas bee graunted any further then the Roman Empire extended, nor was ever acknowledged in the remoter parts of the world, till in these last times povertie hath made some of the poore Patriarchs (I had almost said Parrats, whom their belly and externall respects have taught their x"' which was never with reall subjection acknowledged) yea the others Patriarches of the Empire to this day gainsay it, and Onuph. ad by long use, the Constantinopolitan is stiled Oecumenicall Plat. inbonif. qj. Universall Patriarch, the Roman universall Pope " (which title of Pope, was in ancient times commonly given to other Bishops, as in Saint Augustines and others Epistles is seene, and the name of Archbishop and Patriarch given as preeminent Titles to the Roman Bishop, yet extant in the Roman Councells) who now having gotten a Spirituall Papacie, Gregory the seventh above 1070. yeeres after Christ, began to turne the same into a Papall Monarchic, which his successours have more fully effected, not onely in the absolute Principalitie of the Churches Patrimonie, but in a wide-mouthed challenge of Supremacie to depose Kings, and dispose Kingdomes in that hypocriticall pretended ordine ad Deum. But this you shall finde in other Authors, and I but touch it and now returne to our Myraeus. The Jerosolimitan Bishop, in honour of that holy Citie was live Paid- dignified with that Patriarchall honor, but later: for arches. vq Councell of Nice left to the Bishop of Caesaria his

Metropolitan right entire: the Councell of Chalcedon give him the Title, which some say Leo the Bishop opposed so much in pretence of the Nicene authoritie, that it was not fully ratified till Justinians time, in the Bellar. 3aln. fifth Councell, A. t. Now for a fifth See at Babylon you have heard EHas (a lye as I conceive) not to be found I thinke ratified by any good History: nor were the most parts of his Jurisdiction ever subject to the Roman Empire. Patrlarkship The Roman or Westerne Patriarch had sixe Dio-ofthe West, cesses, Italy, luyricum, Africa, The Galliae, Spaines, and fl ' 6l Britaine, which were subdivided into severall Provinces, of which Italy is said to have seventeene, luyricum seven, Africa sixe, Galliae seventeene, Hispaniae sixe, and Britaine five, Britannia Prima, Br. Secunda, Maxima Caesariensis, Flavia Caesariensis and Valentia: by Gregory the Great reduced to the two Archbishoprickes of Canterbury and Yorke, and long after Saint Andrewes and Glasco, two other in Scotland, and foure in Ireland, by authoritie of Pope Eugenius, An. 1151. Armach, Dublin, Cassiliensis and Tuamensis. Thus much generally and briefly for the West. Now for the Easterne Easteme World, it was divided into seven Diocesses or Regions, division. Oriens, Egyptus, Asiana, Pontica, Thracia, Macedonia and Dacia. Of the Orientall part (more properly called) Antioch was chiefe Citie, of Egypt Alexandria, of the Asian Ephesus, of the Pontike Caesarea, of Thracia Constantinople, of Macedonia and Dacia Thessalonica, till Justinian made Justiniana Prima the Metropolitan of Dacia. The Constantinopolitan had three Diocesses acknowledged by the Chalcedon Councell, Asiana, Pontica, Thracia. Asiana had eleven Provinces, Pontica as many, Thracia sixe. Macedonia had anciently sixe Provinces, Dacia five. In the time of Leo

Emperour, Pat. ofcon-which began to reigne An. 1386. the Constantinopolitan ("
i op-had eightie one Metropolitans subject to him (and before the Norman Conquest
many more, when Sicilia, Calabria, and many Cities of the Kingdome of Naples were
subject to the Greeke Empire) and eightie three Archbishoprickes in the same Leos
time.

To the Patriarch of Alexandria the Councell of Nice Pat. of Alex-ascribeth Egypt,
Lybia, and Pentapolis: After that there ' ' '-were numbred six Provinces, Egypt,
Thebais, Lybia Superior, Lybia Inferior, or Pentapolis, Arcadia and Augustamnica,
and after ten. The Patriarch of Antioch Pat. ofjnti-had the East Diocesse, in which
were fifteene Provinces, '-Syria prima and secunda; Palestina prima, secunda, Salu-
taris; Phcenicas prima and secunda, Cilicia prima and secunda, Cyprus, Euphratensis,
Mesopotamia, Osrhaena, Arabia, Isauria. When the Frankes had conquered the Holy
land, the Antiochian had six Archbishops onely subject to him, Tarsus, Edessa,

W. Tyr. hist. S.

Pat. of Jerusalem.

Meanerpatri-archates.

Catholici. Aquileia.

See Myr. Notit. Ep. I. I. e. 14. Glos. d. 21. c. I.

verb. Archi-episcopus.

Azarias Fruonius a traveller.

Apamia, Helioplis, Conzensum and Manustrensem: Tyrius reckons thirteene
Metropolitans in the first times, besides nine Cities Metropolitans not Suffragans,
and twelve Archbishoprickes which it seemeth were also autocephali, as the former.
But afterwards Jerusalem was decked with Antiochian spoiles, the three Palestinas
being added to the Jerosolimitan Patriarch. Tyrius addes two other taken from the
Alexandrian Patriarch, Rubensis and Berytensis, in later times stiled Petracensis and
Bostrensis; and under the Frankes, Tyre, Caesarea, Nazareth and Petracensis.

Other Patriarchs there are of lesse note, as of Seleucia, whom Filesacus suspected
to have removed his See to Armenia; of Ethiopia (who is neverthelesse subject to the
Patriarch of Alexandria) of these the Seleucian was to have the sixt place, the Ethiopian
the seventh in Councels, and they both with the Armenian were stiled Catholici. The
Patriarch of Aquileia is mentioned by Paulus Diaconusj and it is probable that when
Aquileia was taken by the Lumbards, the Patriarch removed to Gradus, and was
called the Patriarch of New Aquileia or Gradensis. Friuli also hath had that title,
and Venice hath succeeded in that Aquileian and Gradensian Patriarchate, A. 1450.
by grant of Pope Eugenius. The Pisan Prelate hath beene also stiled Patriarch, and
the Toletane in Spaine, as also the Valentian, and the Archbishop of Goa, and the
Archbishop of Canturbury, Ments, Lions, and Bituricensis, but not so commonly and
constantly. The Jacobites, Nestorians, Maronites, Cophti, and other Easterne Sects
with their Patriarchs wee have alreadie considered. There are also Franc-Armenians
under the Archbishop of Nexivanum, in whose Jurisdiction are the Townes Abbaran,
Abbragon, Carna, Saltach, Hascassen, Meascen, Carsan, Xhabun, Giahug, Caragus,
Chensug, and Artach; in which are Monasteries of Dominicans. Azarias Fridonius
an Armenian, A. 1604. was made Archbishop of Mexivan, in Armenia Major, sixe
dales journey from Tauris. Hee was a Dominican, and came from Armenia in Rome,

and out of his writing this is related. The Georgians were wont to bee subject to the Patriarch of Constantinople, but now are divided. (The Russians also have procured their Metropolitan the title of Patriarch, as wee shall see in D. Fletchers Relations. They tell also of a Patriarch at Damascus, at Mosul, Cairo, and other places which professe the former titles.) But let us looke backe to Rome, where Myraeus next to the Pope the Prince, as he cals him, of all Patriarchs and Bishops placeth the Cardinalls.

The Priests and Deacons of Rome have growne with Cardinalls. the Papacie to a strange Prelacie unknowne in the first ':- Cor. thousand yeeres after Christ, to be not only above r f ' ' J Bishops and Archbishops, and other names or Jicclesias-Onuphriuslib. ticall greatnesse, but to be Peeres to Kings and de Epis. tit. Emperours and conjudices terrarum orbis, (as Pope D. C. l Pius the Second cals them.) Of these sixe are Cardinall ' J C "-Bishops, Ostia, Porto, Savina, Palestina, Frascati, Alba: the Cardinall Priests and Deacons have their names of the Parish Churches in Rome, (all which Cardinals were wont to bee but twelve, and, when a Prelate from any place was chosen, as appeareth in our English Ecclesiasticall Storie, by Wendover, Paris and others, he left his former Prelacie and Residence, and attended the Pope, as one of his Privie Counsell, and another succeeded to his former place: since which time, within these three hundred yeeres, they have not only increased the numbers at pleasure, and chosen the principall Prelates of other Nations; to make themselves strong in each Nation, permitting them there still to reside; but have procured the noblest persons for bloud, and most eminent for power in each Kingdome I. i. i68. to admit of that dignitie, and have heaped greatest preferments in every Countrey on their Cardinals, which only sheare the fleece; and never see the face of their innumerable flockes.)

Besides, this preferring of Priests and Deacons to

Five Patriarchal Churches in Rome.

Where two are joyned with this- stroke, it betokeneth an union of two Bishoprickes.

Ravenna, sometimes competitor zvith Rome.

Fermo.

Naples. Capua.

Patriarkes, in Rome it selfe (as representing the whole Church) they have instituted five Patriarchall Churches, viz. S. John Lateranes, S. Peters, S. Pauls, S. Maries the greater, S. Lawrences. The Church of Laterane hath an Arch-presbyter who is a Cardinall. S. Peters beareth the Title of the Church of Constantinople, and hath an Arch-priest Cardinall. S. Pauls represents the Church of Alexandria, hath an Abbot and Monkes. S. Maries designes the Church of Antioch, hath an Arch-priest, Cardinall and Canons as Lateran and S. Peters. S. Lawrence represents the Church of Jerusalem; it once had an Abbot and Monkes, now is in Commenda, and hath Canons Regulars.

The Bishoprickes of the Romane Province are Sutri-Nepi, Civita-Castellana-Horti, Viterbo-Tuscanella, Bag-narea, Orvieto, Perugia (an Universitie) Citta di Castello, Civita de Plebe, Castro, Arezzo, Spoleto, Terni, Narny, Amelia, Todi, Rieti, Foligno, Assisi (the Countrey of S. Francis) Tivoli, Anagna, Verulo, Terracina, Sezza, Segni, Alatro, Fiorentino, Ancona-Humana, Loretto-Ricanati, Ascoli, Jesi, Osmo, Fano, Camerino. Luca hath the Pall.

The Archbishop of Ravenna hath these Suffraganes, Adri, Comachio, Faenza, Brentinore, Forli Cesena, Sar-sina, (Countrey of Plautus) Rimini, Imola, Cervia,

Fanestria, Ferrara (an Universitie.) The Archbishop of Bologna instituted 1583. hath Bologna (an Universitie) Parma (an Universitie) Placenza, Reggio, Modema, Crema, Borgo di S. Domino. The Archbishop of Fermo erected by Sixtus the Fifth, hath Suffraganes, Macerata (an Universitie) Tolentino, San Severino, Montalto, Ripa, Benevent and Avinion follow in their places.

In the Kingdome of Naples, the Archbishop of Napoli (an Universitie) Pozzuolo, Nola, Cerra, Ischia, Aversa (an exempt) to which are united Cuma and Atella. The Archbishop of Capua hath Suffraganes, Teano, Calvi, Caserta, Gaiazzo, Carinola, Sergna, Sessa, Venafro, Monte

Cassino and Saint Germano, Aquino, Pondi, Gaieta, Sora. The Archbishop of Salerno hath Salerno (an Universitie) Salerno. Capaccio, Pulicastro, Sarno, Acierno, Marsico, Cam-pagna, Nocera delli Pagani, Nusco, Cava. Under the Archbishop of Amalfi are the Bishops of Capri, Scala- Amalfi. Ravello, Minori, Lettre. Under the Archbishop of Sorrento are Vico, Massa, Stabia. The Archbishop of Conza hath Muro, Satriano Cagiano, Lacedogna, S. Angelo di Lombardi-Bisaccia, Monte Verde. The Archbishop of Cirenza and Matera hath the Bishop of Venosa, Tricarico, Potenza, Gravina-Anglona, Monte Peloso. The Archbishop of Tarento his Suffraganes are Motula, Castellaneta, Oria. Under the Archbishop of Brindisi are Hostuni, Nardo, Monopoli. Under Otranto, Lecce, Capo di Leuco, Castro, Gallipoli, Ugento. Under the Archbishop of Bari and Canosa, Bitonto, Giovenazzo, Ruvo, Conversano, Monervino, Pulignano, Laviello, Bitetto, Catzeri, Molfetta an exempt. The Archbishop of Tranni and Salpe hath Bisiglia, Andri. To the Archbishop of Manfredonia and Citta di S. Angelo are subject, Vesti, Melphi-Rappollo. The Theatine Archbishop erected in Civita di Chieti, Anno 1526. hath Suffraganes, Ortona, Citta di Penna-Atri, Valua-Sulmona, Aquila, Marsi, Teramo, Civita di Cali. The Archbishop Lancianensis hath no Saffragane Bishop. Pius the Fourth advanced it. The Bishop of Trivento is an exempt. The Archbishop of Reggio is over the Bishops of Catanzaro, Crotone, Tropea, Oppedo, Bove, Nicastro, Nicotera, Gieraci, Squillaci, Mileto. The Archbishop of Cosenza and Monte alto hath Marterano, S. Marco, Bisignano, Cassano. The Archbishop of Rossano hath no Suffragane. The Archbishop of San Severina hath Umbriato, Belcastro, Isola, Cariati, Strongoli. The Archbishop of Benevento in the Popes Jurisdiction, hath Ascoli, Telese, S. Agatha delli Goti, Alife, Monte Marano, Avellino-Fergiente, Vico della Baronia, Ariano, Boiano Bovino, Vulturara and Monte Corvino, Larino, Termoli, San Severe, Troia, Guardia Alfaena. So that in the Kingdome of Naples, besides the Popes Benevento, there are nineteene Archbishoprickes.

Number of The Jesuites have in the Continent of Italy (besides

Jesuites y he Provinces of Sicilia and Sardinia) foure Provinces, ffli t' " the Roman, Neapolitan, of Millaine, and of Venice.

The Romane Province hath at Rome, Domus professa,

Collegium Romanum, Domus probationis, the Colledge of the Paenitentiarie, the German Colledge, the English

Colledge, the Roman Seminarie, the Colledge of Mar- onites, the Scots Colledge. The Residence at Frascati, the Colledges of Tivoli, Loreto, Perugia, Fiorenza,

Siena, Macerata, Ricanati, Sezza, Ancona, Monte Santo,

Monte Pulciano, Fermo, Citta di Castello, Ascoli, Sora.

In this Province are seven hundred fortie seven of the societie. The Province of Naples hath in Naples Domus professa, the Colledge, the House of Probation, the New House professed. The Colledges of Catanzaro,

Nola, Lecce, Bari, Salerno, Consenza, Barletta, Chieti,

Aquila, Benevento, House of Probation at Atri, Colledges of Bovino, Trepia, Massa, Castell a Mare, Capua, Mol- fetta, the Residences of Monopoli, Taranto, Paula. In this Province are five hundred ninety foure of the societie. In the Province of Millaine, are at Millaine the House professed, and the Colledge Breiden; at

Genua the House professed, the Colledge, and the House of probation; the Colledges of Turino, Como, Vercelli,

Mondevi, Cremona, Bastia, Nizza, Alexandria, the

House of probation at Arona, and the Residence of

Pavia. In this Province are foure hundred and eleven of the Company. The Venetian Province hath the professed House at Venice, the Colledges of Padova, I. i. 169. Ferrara, Balogna, Brescia, Forli, Parma, with another there for the Nobilitie Piacenza, Verona, Mantova,

Mirandola Reggio, Faenza, Castiglione, the houses of probation at Novellara, Imola, Busseto, the Residences of Candia and Vicenza. In this Province are three

Sicilia the hundred seventy three of the Societie.

Bishops. Sicilia hath three Archbishoprickes, first the Panor- mitan, to whom are subject the Bishops of Mazara, Girgenti. Malta is governed by their great Master and Knights Hospitulars. The Archbishop of Messana hath under him the Bishops of Lipari, Patti, Cifalu. The Archbishop of Mons Regalis hath Catania and Siracosa. In it also are Jesuites Couedges, Houses and Residences Jesuites. one and twentie. Fellowes sixe hundred thirtie eight.

The He and Kingdome of Sardinia hath had fourteene Sardinia. Episcopall Cities, and now hath according to Ferrarius, three Archbishoprickes, Calaris, Sassaris, Arborea, and Bishops, Villa Ecclesiae, Bosa, Algarium, Castrum Ara-gonense, and Lassa.

The Archbishop of Calaris or Caglari is Primate of Sardinia and Corsica. His Suffraganes are Doli, Yglesias-Solci. Suel is united to the Archbishop. The Archbishop of Sassaris or Torre Sassari hath Algar, Bosi, Empurias, Terra Nova. The Archbishop of Arborea hath Ussella, Terra Alba, S. Justa. In Sardinia are Houses, Couedges and Seminaries of Jesuites eight, and Jesuites. in them one hundred and ninetie of that Societie and Province.

Millaine is the Seat of the Spanish Viceroy and Millaine. Counsell, and also of an Archbishop, to whom are subject the Bishops of Cremona, Lodi, Novarra, (Birth-place of Peter Lumbard) Alessandria della Paglia, Tortona, Viglevano, Bergamo, Brescia, Vercelli, Aste, Casale di Monferrato, Alba, Acqui, Savona, Vintimiglia, Pavia hath the Pall and is an Universitie.

Etruria is for the most part subject to the Great Toscaine. Duke of the Family of Medices, in which Florentia, Pisa and Siena have beene Free States. Charles the fifth. Anno 1530. created Alexander de Medices his Sonne in Law Duke of Florence, whose Sonne Cosmus by Pope Pius the fifth was created Great Duke of Great Duke. Toscaine, Anno 1569. This Cosmus instituted the Knight Order of Saint Stephen against the Turkes. The Archbishop of Florence or Fiorenza hath Suffragans, Fiezola, Pistoia, Volcerra, Colle, Burgo S. Sepulchro, I 465 2 G

Serzana, Monte Pulciano, where Cardinall Bellarmine was borne, and Cortona are Exempts. The Archbishop of Siena (which is also an Academie) hath Soana, Chiusi, Grosseto, Massa-Populonia, Pientia, Monte Alcino. The Archbishop of Pisa (an Universitie also) hath Suffragans Civitella, Aiazzo, Sagona, Aleria. Mantua. Mantua famous for Virgils birth hath a Duke of the

Family Gonzaga; Duke Vincent, A. 1608. instituted the Military Order of The Redeemer Jesus Christ, in honour of his bloud supposed there kept. Mutina and Rhegium have a Duke of the Este Family, revolved to the Papacie, Anno 1598. Urbinum of the Family Roborea and Parma, and Placentia of the Farnesian. Urbine hath an Archbishop and sixe Bishoprickes subject, the Leopolitan, Pisaurian, Calliensis, Eugubinus, Foro-Semproniensis, and Senogalliensis. Parma and Placentia with Burgo in that Principalitie are Suffragans to the Archbishop of Bologna. Foure Italian Venice, Genua, Luca, and Ragusi are Italian Free Free States. States; the chiefe is Venice, and said to incline to the French, as Genua the next, to the Spaniard: Ragusi supports it selfe by favour of the Turke, paying a yeerely pension to him. Luca hath a Bishop subject to the Ragusi. Pope only, and using a Pall. Ragusi (in times past

Epidaurus) is in Dalmatia, Italionated in language and conditions: it hath an Archbishop, to whom are subject the Bishops Stagnensis, Tribuniensis, Marcatensis, Ro-donensis, Garzalensis, Stephanensis and Curzolensis. Fenice. In the State of Venice are two Patriarkes, one of r f rff ' Venice, which succeeded to Gradus, the other of Aqui-leia: and foure Archbishops, Spalatensis, Jaderensis, Corcyrensis, and Candiensis. The Patriarke of Venice hath Suffragan Bishops, Chioza, Torzello, both Hands. The Patriarke of Aquileia resideth in Udene, and to him are subject the Bishops of Como (Countrey of both Plinies) Verona, Padova, Vicenza, Treoizi, Concordia, Zeneda, Feltre, Civida di Bellun, Pola, Parenzo, Triesti, Petin, Capo d'Istria, Citta Nova, Trento and Mantova arks, i c.

are Exempts, The Archbishop of Spalatro and Salona, Primate of Dalmatia and Croatia, hath Suffragans, Segna, Nona, Faro-Lesina, Tran, Sanadria, Scardona (subject to the Turke) Tina, Almiza. The Archbishop Jaderensis, or of Zara a Venetian Hand, hath Suffraganes, Arbe, Viglia, Ossaro. The Archbishop of Corcyra, or Corfu, hath the Bishops of the Hands Cefalonia and Zante. The Archbishop of Crete or Candie hath under him the Bishops of Canea, Rettimo, Sittia-Hierapetra, Cheronesso, Mellipotamo, Archadias, Sicchimo, Budoa, sometimes subject to the Servian Archbishop. Some adde Catharensem and Curzulensem.

Genua hath in times past extended their Empire to Genua. Caffa in Taurica, Cyprus, Chio and Lesbos, and to Pera. It now commandeth almost all Liguria and Corsica. To the Archbishop of Genua are Suffragans, Albenga, Bobi, Brignale, Noli, Mariana-Accia, Nebio. To the Genuois are thirteene Dioceses subject, but some of the Bishops acknowledge the Archbishops of Millaine and Florence. Sixe Bishopricks are in the Hand and Kingdome of Corsica, subject to that State, Mariana, Aleria, Nebium, Sagonia, Aciensum and Adiacium, Malta hath a Col-ledge of Jesuits.

SPaine first attempted, and one of the last of the Roman I- i- 170- Provinces pacified in the declining of the Empire, P "-was possessed by the Wandals, Sueves, and Alans, whom the Gothes had expelled Gaule, The Gothes expelled thence by the Frankes, chased the Wandals and Alans out of Spaine, and destroyed the Sueves. The Saracens Anno 720. expelled the Gothes, and could not by the Gothicke remnants be quite exterminated till Anno. 1492. at which time the New World also was added to the Spanish Fortunes by Colons Discoverie, and by the Match of the Heire of the Houses of Burgandie and Austria, with the Heire of Arragon and Castile, and since by Conquests c. The Castilan hath in few yeeres from an estate in comparison of some other Kingdomes,

The Manuscript was sometimes presented to Q. Elizabeth: and came to my hand from M. Burrougk Controller of the Navy, not so perfect as I could have wished: yet as it is, not warranting the authoritie, I have transcribed somethings thence, and inserted with Myraus. By fault of the transcriber, many names are so falsly written, that I was loth to give the adventure to prevent the Readers correction. Bertius ascribeth but 200000.

Duckets to the Church of Toledo, and 80000. to the Archbishop. Dam. a Goez 6 Mar. Siculus have poore and almost contemptible growne to the present puissance and almost terrible greatnesse. In Spaine and Portugall are these Archbishoprickes, whose names and revenues out of a Manuscript are thus delivered.

Toledo, his Revenues are said to bee 320000. Duckets, more then of divers Kingdomes. Sivill, 113000. Duckets. Granado, 80000. Duckets. Lisbone, 130000. Duckets. Saragosa, 70000. Duckets. Valentia, 90000. Duckets. Tarragena, 80000. Duckets. Burgos, 90000. Duckets. Santiago, 100000. Duckets. Brago, 90000. Duckets. He omits Evora, which he reckons among the Bishops, being latelier exalted to the Pall. Myraeus reckons them thus, Toledo, Burgis, Compostella, Sivill, Granado, Caesaraugusta, Tarragona, Valentia, Brararensis, Lisbone and Ebora. To the Archbishop of Toledo, Primate of Spaine are Suffragans, the Bishops of Cordova, Segovia Cuenca, Sequenza (an Universitie) Jaen, Cartagena or Murcia, Osma, Valladolid instituted by Clement the Eighth, Anno 1595. made an Universitie also. To the Archbishop of Burgis in olde Castile are subject Pamplona chiefe Citie of Navarre, Calagorra, Palencia. To the Archbishop of Compostella or Santiago in Galaecia, the Bishops of Salamanca an Universitie erected. Anno 1240. Avila, Placenzia, Lugo, Astorga, Zamora, Orense, Tuy, Badajos, Mondonedo, Coria, Civita Rodrigo, Leon exempt, and Oviedo exempt. To the Archbishop of Sivill in Baetica are subject Guadix, Cadiz, and the Bishop of the Canaries. To the Archbishop of Granada, erected by Alexander the sixth, Malaga and America. To the Archbishop of Cassaurau-gusta, or Caragosa in Aragon, Huesca an old Universitie, Jaca, Barbastro, Tarazona, Teroel, Albarazin. To the Arch, of Tarragona in Catalonia, Tortosa, Lerida an Universitie, Barcelona an Universitie, Uicz, Girona, Urgel, Elna, Solsona, Perpinian, by Paulus quintus. To the Arch, of Valencia, Segorve, Orihuela, Mallorca. To the Arch, of Braga in Portugall, Porto, Viseo, Guardia, Lamego, Miranda, Leyra. To the Arch, of Lisbone,

DIOCESES m SPAIN

Coymbra, an Universitie; Portalegre, Ceuta in Africa, Funchal in Madera, Angra in Tercera, Congo in Africa, Cabo Verde, or Sant lago, San Thome, both in the Hands so called, (the Bishop of Brasil) at San Salvador, or the Bay of all Saints (lately taken by the Dutch.) To the Archbishop of Evora, erected 1540. The Bishops of Silves in Faro, Elvas, Tanger in Africa united with Ceuta. Pope Adrian the sixth. Anno 1523. gave the Kings of Spaine power to elect and present their Bishops, as Mariana reporteth.

My Manuscript reckoneth not so many, nor goeth to Africa and the Hands, and perhaps some of the Bishops in that time might be vacant or holden by Commenda, and so the Title drowned. The names differ somewhat, perhaps by false writing, which may be helped by the former Catalogue. For the valuations I thought them not unworthy recitall together as they are in the said Booke expressed, although I must intreate the Readers patience for misse-writing the names by some unlearned transcriber, which yet I present as I found.

Sobrack
Torrossa
Vigue
Alveria
Visio
Astorga
Avela
Badajes
Barcelona
Camora
Callahora
Camaria
Cordova
Cartagena
Cadona
Duckets.

50000. 50000. 45000. 58000. 55000. 50000. 65000. 60000. 5600. 75000. 57000. 65000. 50000. 56000. 50.000 56000.

Rodrigo
Quadripp
Quembra
Quardio
Questarie
Ayne
Lomego
Leon
Lerida
Lugo
Maliga
Osina
Ayda
Placentia
Valentia
Solomonca
Duckets.

65000. 64000. 75000. 47000. 47000. 480000. 53000. 57000. 64000. 50000. 64000. 46000. 48000. 53000. 54000. 65000.

their valuations also but more ancient, QT' much since improved. This Manuscript reciteth the Dukes, Marquessesi Earles of Spain with their severall Revenues, which arefarrefarre lesse then these of the Bishops, the Dukes from 10000. to 70000. which only Braganxa exceedeth, and likewise the Marquesses. The Earles from 8000. to 20000. Bertius saith, the Duke of Infantasgi hath 120000. Duckets, and Medina Sidonia I loooo. Duc. revenue. The rest not under 40000. Marquesses from 10000. Due. to 60000. Earles from 10000 to 40000.

i. i. 171.

Jesuites in Spaine.

Damianus a Goes addeth that the Clergie of Spaine have twice as much Revenues as the Bishops, besides Impropriations of Tithes they granted by the Pope to the King and Grandes: and that besides all this, the Monasteries and Abbeyes Revenues, exceed those of the Clergie.

There are also in Spaine certaine Militarie Orders instituted to free the Countrey from the Moores. Such were the Orders of Saint James, with a long red Crosse, of Alcantara with a square red Crosse, of Calatrava with a square greene Crosse: which were by Pope Adrian appropriated to the King: besides the Orders of Christ and others.

There are also Jesuits divided into five Spanish Provinces: the Province of Toledo hath Colledges, Houses and Residences one and twentie, in them five hundred and seventie Jesuites. The Province of Castile eight and twentie, in them sixe hundred and thirteene. The Province of Aragon fourteene, and Jesuites three hundred and ninetie. The Baetike Province foure and twentie, and sixe hundred Jesuites. The Province of Portugall eighteene, and sixe hundred and eightie of the Societie. The He Majorica hath a Bishop and Universitie. The Canaries have a Bishop also. So have the Hands of Cape Verd with a Colledge of Jesuites. Tercera likewise: and in it and Saint Michaels are Jesuites Colledges. Madera hath a Bishop and Jesuiticall Colledges.

IN France are numbred one hundred and seventeene France. Diocesses, fourteene of which have Archbishoprickes, which are these, with their one hundred and three Suffragans. The Primate Archbishop of Lions hath Austun, Langres, Mascon, Challon Sur Saone. The Archbishop of Rone in Normandie, Baieux, Aurenches Eureux, Sais, Lizieux, Constances. The Archbishop of Tours, hath Mans, Renes, Angers an Universitie, Nantes an Universitie, Cornovaille, Vannes, Leon, Triquier, Saint Brieu, Saint Malo, Dol which weareth a Pall, and is exempt. The Archbishop of Sens, Chartres, Auxerre, Trois, Orleans an Universitie and Dutchie of the Kings second Sonne, Paris an Universitie and seate Royall, Meaux, Nevers. The Archbishop of Rhemes, Duke and Chiefe Peere of France, hath Soissons, Challon, Laon, Senlis, Beauvais, Amiens, Noyon, Bouloigne Surmer. The Archbishop Bituricensis, or of Bourges Primate of Aquitaine an Universitie, hath Suffragans Clermon, Rodes, Albii, Caors, Limoges, Mende, Le Tuy, Castres, Vabres, Tulle, Saint Flour. The Archbishop of Bour-deaux hath Agen, Engoulesme, Santonge, Poitiers an Universitie, Perigeux, Condom, Maillezais, Luzon, Sarlat. The Archbishop of Auch hath Aque, Letoure, Saint Ber-trand de Comenge, S. Legier de Conserans, Aire, Basas, Tarbe de Bigorre,

Oleron on Beam, Lescar, Baionne. The Archbishop of Narbonne, Beziers, Agde, Carcassone, Nismes an Universitie, Lodeue, S. Pont de Tomiers, Alec, Mompelier an Universitie, Uzes. The Archbishop Aquensis, or of Aix in Provence, hath Suffragans the Bishops of Ries, Apt, Freius, Gap, Cisteron. The Archbishop of Vienne, Geneve (now residing at Anessy in Savoy) Grenoble, Viviers, Die-valence, both Universities, S. Jean de Maurienne under the Duke of Savoy. The Archbishop of Embrun hath Digne, Grasse, Vence, Senez, Clandeuez, Nice in Savoy. The Archbishop of Aries, Marseille, S. Paul de Tricastin, Tolon, Orange, the Principalitie of the Prince of Orange, an Universitie and seat of a Parliament. The Archbishop of Tolose

Religious and

Militarie

Orders.

Jesuits in France.

Avinion the Popes County.

Savoy.

(an Universitie) hath Pasmires, Montautban, Mirepoix, La Vaur, Rieux, Lombes, S. Papoul. Foure of the former Bishops, Maurianensis, Genevensis Niceensis and Arau-sionensis are not subject to the French King: in whose roome you may adde Metemsem, Tullensem, Virdum-ensem and Bellicensem to make up the former number.

In France also are the Chiefes or Originals of many Orders, as the Chuniake Order in the Diocese of Matiscon founded Anno 910. by Abbat Berno; Grande-mont founded by Stephen, Anno 1126. Cartusia Major by Bruno 1084. Cistercium 1098. Praemonstratum 1120. In the Diocesse of Laudun. Cervi Frigidi by John Matha 1136. Vallis Scholarium in Champaine by William an Englishman 1218. Fons Ebraldi in the Diocese of Poitiers by Robert Blessels 1117. The Hospitulars of Saint Anthonie in the Diocese of Vienna, by Gasto 1121, Our Ladies Charitie 1300. S. Bernard de poenitentia, or the Reformed Cistercians by John Barrerius 1600. The Willielmites by Saint William Duke of Aquitaine. The Militarie Orders of the Holy Ghost by Henry the Third, and of Saint Michael, and of Saint Mary of Mount Carmel, and of Saint Lazarus approoved by Paul the Fifth.

The Jesuites have five Provinces in France, the Province called of France, hath fourteene Houses, Colledges and Residences; the Province of Aquitaine ten, in which Province are two hundred and eightie Jesuites. The Province of Lions fourteene, in them foure hundred and seventie. The Province of Tolose eleven, in them three hundred and ten. The Province of Champaine ten, and two hundred twentie sixe Jesuites.

In France, though not in the French subjection is the Country of Avinion, in which Citie the Popes resided seventie yeeres together. The Archbishop hath three Suffi-agans, Carpentras, Caballon, Vaison. In Savoy is the Archbishop Tarentasiensis, to whom the Bishops Augustanus and Sedunensis are Suffragans. Piemont is subject to the same Duke, the Metropolitan Citie whereof is Taurinum, Seat of the Dukes and an Universitie, to which are subject the Bishops Eporediensis, Montis Regalis and Fossanensis; Saluzo is an exempt.

The Duke of Savoy is Chiefe of two Military Orders, Two Military Of the Virgins Annuntiation, and of SS. Maurice and O'"' ' "-Lazarus. Loraigne, sometimes a Kingdome, now a Loraine. Dutchie, hath Nancie the Metropolitan Citie, Ponta-mousson an Universitie ruled by Jesuites, S. Nicola is of next note. Loraine is subject to divers Bishops, amongst others, Metensis, Tullensis and Virdunensis Imperiall Cities wonne by Henry the second.

The Principalitie of Orange, hath the B. of Orange Orange. as is said, and an Universitie: it is subject to the house of Nassau, Henry of Nassau marrying the Sister and Heire of Philibertus Cabillonensis Viceroy of Naples, slain at the siege of Florence, A. 1530. Renatus son of Henry was slaine 1544. William his brothers sonne succeeded and was traiterously murthered at Delfe 1584. His Sonne Philip-Gulielmus after long detention in I. i. 172. Spaine, died at Brussels An. 1618. and left his Brother Prince Maurice his Heire by Testament: whose Arts, experience and exploits Militarie have attracted into a stupendious gaze the Eyes of all Europe.

His Name admits us into Gallia Belgica, or the Low The Lozv Countreyes, or seventeene Lands, of which foure are " "'-Dukedomes, Brabant, Limburg, Putuenburg and Gelder-land: seven Counties or Earledomes, Flanders, Artois, Hanalt, Holland, Zeland, Namur and Zutphen: the Marquisate of the Holy Empire, and five Lordships of East Frisland, Mechlin, Utrecht, Overisel, and Gronin-gen. In these are two hundred and ten Cities walled and ditched about. Villages six thousand three hundred, besides Monasteries, Forts, Palaces and Mannor-houses almost innumerable. That part which obeyeth the Arch-dutchesse is Romish, that which acknowledgeth the States government is of the Protestants faith, not without Arminian and other fancies amongst many of them.

In times past there were but foure Belgian Bishop-rickesj of Cambray, Arras, Tournay and Utrick. But King Philip the second (seeking to alter the government, which occasioned the Wars and this Division, whereby about one halfe of the Countrey have not only defended their Liberties, maugre the Austrian Greatnesse, American Treasures, Spanish Ambition and Italian Souldioury, to the Worlds amazement, many hundred thousands of Christians beeing slaine to purchase the Spaniard this losse; but have acquired a Free Estate, with wealth and honour, and by them have beene so acknowledged, whom they would willingly with conservation of their Liberties have obeyed) Philip the second (his losse made me almost lose my selfe) Anno 1559. procured the Pope to constitute three Archbishoprickes, and fifteene Bishop-rickes (his Inquisition shall escape our inquisition) the Archbishop of Mechelen, to whose Jurisdiction are subject the Bishops of Antwerpe, of Bruges, Gant, Iperen, Rurmund, Hertogenbosch: the Archbishop of Cambray, whose Suffraganes are Arras, Tournay, Saint Omer, Namur. The Archbishop of Utrecht hath Deventer, Groeninghen, Harlem, Leeuwarden, Middleborgh. Jesuites. The Jesuites have there two Provinces, Flandro-Belgica which hath eighteene Houses, Colledges and Residences, in which there are of that crue six hundred and seven-teene. And Gallo-Belgica which hath twentie Houses, Colledges, and Residences, and six hundred fiftie two Fellowes of that Order, beside Augustinians, Dominicans, and I know not what others.

GErmanie hath seven Archbishoppes Mentz, Collen, Trier, all three Electors; Mey-dburg Salisburg, Breme, Bessanzon. To the Archbishop of Mentz (an Universitie) are subject Bishops Wormes, Wirtzburg an Universitie, Speir Aichstet, Strasburg, Werden, Chur, Heildesheim, Paderborne, Costnitz, Halberstad, Ausburg. Bamberg is exempt. To Coloigne, are Suffraganes Liege, Munster, Minden, Osenbrug. To Trier, Metz, Toul,

Verdun, all in Loraine and now French. To Meydburg, Meyssen, Merseburg, Brandeburg, Havelburg. To Salisburg (an Universitie) Freysingen, Regenspurg, Passaw, Brixen, Goritz, Lavenmutz, Seckaw Vienna in Austria, is an Universitie and exempt; Newstat and Lesbach are also exempts.

To Breme are subject Lubeck, Rathenburg, Swerin. German To the Archbishop of Vesontionensis or Besanzon (an " P Universitie) are subject Basel an Universitie, Losanne, Bellay en Bresse. All these, as also the Bishop of Trent are Princes of the Empire, and Lords in Temporalibus, except Lavenmuch, Seckaw, Chiemse, and Goritz. Meydburg and Breme, and eight Bishoprickes are Protestants.

The late Warres have since our Authors writing so altered the face of things in Germanie that just account cannot bee given of their Religion and State so unsetled. And how can things be well setled where the Foxes have so many Burrowes. The Jesuites have (as some say) three Jesuites. score Colledges in Germanie, devided into three Provinces.

The Province of Higher Germanie hath thirteene Colledges, two Houses, three Residences, five hundred fortie six Jesuites. The Province of Rhene hath three and twentie, and in them six hundred and one. The Province of Austria five and twentie, and five hundred fiftie three of the Societie.

The Switzers, Cantons are thirteene, Episcopall Cities Switzers. sixe, Lucerna, Uri, Suitz, Underwalden, Zugh, Friburg: Jesuites Colledges two, at Lucerne and Friburg. They are also in great part subject in Spirituals to the Bishops of Constance, and of Basel, whose Seat is now at Brun-tutum. Lausanna hath a Bishop subject to the Archbishop Bezanzon.

The Grisons are divided into three leagues, in which Gtizons. Chur is a Bishop subject to Mentz. The Valesins have seven Communalties, one of which Sedunum hath a Bishop. Pomerland is a Dukedome, and hath foure Cities, Stetin, Caminum sometimes a Bishops See, Griphs-wald an Universitie, and Wolgastum.

Bohemia.

I. i. 173. Hungaria.

Poland.

In Bohemia, Prage is an Archbishopricke, to which are Suffraganes, the Bishops of Olvunctz in Moravia, and Littomssensis in Bohemia. In Silesia, Uratislavia or Preslaw is a Bishopricke.

In Hungaria, Strigonium hath bin the Seat of the Archbishop Primat, which being taken by the Turk, it is removed to Tirnavia, and hath six Suffragans, Nitrich, Raab, Agria under the Turks, Vaccia, Quin-quecclesias under the Turke, as is also Vesprin. Colocia is an Archbishop in Pannonia inferior, under which are the Bishops of Agram, Fairwar in Transilvania, Varadin, Sirmisch, Gonad, Bossina. Transilvania hath an University at Claudiopolis and a Seminary. In Austria Vienna is also an Universitie before mentioned: There and at Oenipont in Triol and at Prage in Bohemia Ferdinand the Emperour founded Jesuites Colledges. Brixina is Suffragan to Salisburg.

Grath hath an University and Colledge of Jesuites, and is a Metropolitan Citie; the Bishop Secouiensis there, and Gurcensis Laventinensis in Carinthia are subject to the Archbishop of Salisburg.

The Kingdome of Poland containeth the Provinces of Lituania, Masovia, Samogitia, Cniavia, Livonia, Varmia, Prussia Regalis, Russia Nigra, Volhima, Podolia, and others. There are two Archbishops of the Latin Church, Gnesnensis the Primat, and Leopoliensis. To the former are subject these Bishops, Krakow, Paznan, Ploczk, Miednikie, Preslaw in Silesia, Lebus, Vladislaw, Chemnicz, Lucko, Vilenzki or Wilde, Wenden, Warmerlant an exempt. Leopolis or Luvow is in Russia Nigra, and hath Suffragans Przemyst, Chmielnick, Kiou, Camienick. All these together with the Bishop Culmensis are Senators or Councellors of the State, except Preslaw and Lebus. There are also eight Russian or Greeke Bishops in Poland, Kiou the Metropolitan, Vlodomir, Luceoriensis, Polo-censis, Praemissiensis or Przemyst, Leopoliensis, Chel-mensis and Pinscensis, which were received into Communion by Pope Clement the eighth. Russia Nigra is subject to the Pole and Russia Alba to the :; ioceSES in Britain

Moscovite. There live also in Poland many Armenians which have a Bishop of their owne, Resident at Leopolis. The Russian Bishops have no Parliament voyce. The Jesuites have two Provinces in these parts, that of Poland containing fifteene Colledges, Houses, and Residences, and 459. Jesuites, that of Lithuania as many, and Jesuites 22. Prussia is divided into Regalis and Ducalis. The Prussia. former hath two Bishops, Varmiensis which resideth at Brunsberg, and Culmensis: the Ducal had two, but extinct with the Order of the Dutch Knights, the one of Kinningsberg, the other at Mariaewerda. The Mar-quesse of Brandenburg possesseth the Countrey.

ENgland hath two Archbishops, Canterbury and Yorke, England. The Archbishop of Canterbury is Primate of all England, and Metropolitan, the other Primate of England and Metropolitan. To the former are subject the Bishops of London, Winchester, Coventree and Lichfield, Salisbury, Bathe and Welles, Lincolne, Excester, Hereford, Norwich, Elie, Rochester, Chichester, Worcester, Saint Davids, Bangor, Landaff, Saint Asse, Peterburrow, Gloster, Oxford and Bristol. To the Archbishop of Yorke, Durham, Chester, Carlile, to which is added Sodorensis, or the Bishop of Man. Scotland also hath Scotland. two Archbishops, one of Saint Andrewes, and the other at Glasco. Suffragans to Saint Andrewes the Primate of Scotland, Myraeus reckoneth the Bishops of Dunckeld, Aberdin (an Universitie) Moraviensis resident in Elgin, Dumblain, Brechin, Rosse, Cathnes, Orcknay: to Glasco, Galloway, Lismor, Colmkil. His Majestie hath beene such a restorer, as he may in some sort bee reckoned the Founder of the present Episcopal, both Sees and Booke of Dis-Government in that Kingdome. At the dissolution of " 56o-the Bishops they erected Superintendents, changing a- p good Greek word for a bad Latin, but reserving to those ceedings at Superintendents the greatest part of Episcopall power; Perth. and after some Changes, his Majestie hath reduced it to the present state.

Ireland. Ireland hath foure Archbishops. To the Archbishop and Primate of Armah are subject, Dunensis, Conner, Derry, Mieth, Clocher, Ardache, Kilmore, Rapho, Dromore, Kiloom, Dundalck. To the Archbishop of Dublin (an Universitie) Kilkenny or Osserriensis, Kildare, Ferus, Leghlin, Glendelagh. To the Archbishop of Cashel, Limricke, Lismor, Rosse, Waterford, Emmelen, Corcke, Lymbricke, Clon. To the Archbishop Tuamen-sis, Galuben, Achade, Alache, Olfin, Roscoman, Clonfert, Killaloe. Thus Myraeus.

Denmarke. Denmarke hath the Archbishop of Lunden erected 1092. Primate of the Kingdome, Suffragans, Roschilt, Odensee, Slezwick, Rype, Wiburg, Arhusen. Norway hath Nidrosia the Metropolitan See, and Suffragans,

Sueden. Bergen, Staffanger, Hammar, Groenlandt, Scalholt, Hola. In Suecia the Archbishop Upsaliensis hath subject to him the B B. of Scar, Lincopen, Stengenes, Abo, Aroesen, Villimen. Thus Myraeus, who addes a little of Russia and Greece, which you shall find more full in the Discourses of those parts, both precedent and following: as likewise touching the Christians of Asia, Maronites, Jacobites, Nestorians, c. handled by Myraeus in his second Booke. The Archbishop of Goa hath subject to him the Bishops of Cochin, Malaca, Macao, Japon, Malahan, Meliaxor or San Thome. The Archbishop of Cranganor (erected by Paul the Fifth, 1608.) is called also the Archbishop of the Christians of San Thome: hee hath no Suffragans. Myraeus reckons Jesuites Houses, Couedges and Residences in the East Indian Province of Goa 15. and 280. of the Societie. In the Province of Malabar 14. in them 150. For China and Japon you shall learne better in our Relations then in Myraeus. In the Philippinas he reckons nine Residences one hundred Jesuites. Neither shall wee need his instructions of Africa in his third Booke, our Relations being farre more full and certaine: as also of the New World handled in his fourth Booke. Hee numbers therein five Archbishops, the first of Mexico, whose Suffragans are the B B. of Tlaxcala in Puebla de I. i. 174. los Angelos, Mechoacan in Valladolid, Guaxara in Ante-quera, Guadalaxara, Guatimala in Saint Iago, Iucatan in Merida, Chiappa, Honduras in Truxillo, Vera Paz, Nicaragua in Leon. This Archbishop, and those of Lima and Domingo were founded by Charles the Fifth, confirmed by Paul the Third, A. 1547. The Archbishop of Saint Domingo hath Suffragans Port Rico, Sant Iago de Cuba, Venezuela, some adde Margarita, To the A. of Lima, Cuzco, Arequipa, Truxillo, Guamanga, Quito. Paul the Fifth erected two Archbishop Sees, Plata or Potosi in Charcas, to whom are subject the Bishops of Baranca, Paz, Santiago in Tucuman, Buenos Ayres, Panama, Santiago in Chili, Imperial, Nuestra Sennora de la Assumpcion, Paraguay: the other Archbishop is of Saint Faith of Bogot in New Granado, to whom are subordinate the Bishops of Popayan, Carthagena, Saint Martha; Manilia is an Archbishopricke in the Philippinas, to which are subject the Bishops of Cagayan, of the Name of Jesus, and Cacerensis. Mexico and Lima are Universities. The Jesuites Dominicans, Franciscans, Carmelites, and the Fathers of our Lady of Pitie are many, besides Priests, Canons, Inquisitors, c. The Jesuites have foure Provinces: that of Peru hath Seminaries, Residences, Colledges and Houses of probation thirteene, and therein 370. of the Societie: that of Paraguay ten, and therein 116. that of New Granado seven and 100. of the Company: that of Mexico fourteene, and therein Jesuits 340. In Brasil they have in nineteen Houses, Colledges, and Residences 180. Jesuites.

And thus have we audited Myraeus his accounts of Bishops and Jesuites, names not otherwise sutable but by Papall Arts. For what concord hath Antiquitie and Noveltie, Jesus and Jesuites, Catholike and Romish, Apostolicall Institutions with Apostaticall? Neither hath the Church wanted Bishops in all ages and places Christian since the Apostles, or knowne Jesuites in any age but this last, or in any Church (except as busie bodies) but the Romish: so that what they object to us, is truely their owne with advantage, to be both Novatores (Loiola being farre later then Luther) and Veteratores Jos. 9. too; like the Gibeonites, which fained themselves Ambassadors, and tooke old Sackes upon their Asses, and old Bottells for Wine both rent and bound up: and old Shooes and clouted upon their feet; also the raiment upon them was old, and all their provision of bread was dried and mouled: Thus pretended they remotenesse being neere neighbours, to delude the Israelites; as these neerer us in time, then those others to Joshua in place and habitation) chant nothing so much as Catholike and Old, when Time knew them not till yesterday, nor doth any Place yet know them but such as are Romish, except in Travells and Treasons: their old, old, old, being but the old Serpent, the old Man, and old refined rubbish to build their new Babel. Nihil mihi antiquius, said one in another case, quam antiquare antiquarios istos. The ancient government of the Church by Bishops, by Papall Monopoly usurped, was set on foot by weakning Episcopall power in exempted Monasteries, that so ail Monasteries might become Papall Forts, and in manner all the learned and leasurely pennes might plead for the Patron of their exemption; furthered by both the one and the others investitures first, and dependance after, with subjection denied to Kings; and when the Wal-denses began to shake downe the Lateran, the Pope dreamed that Dominike, or as the Franciscans will have it, that Francis supported the Lateran, which proved not a dreame in their new devised Orders of Friers, which maintained the Papacy with no lesse reputation of learning and fulnesse of commission in those dangerous daies, then the Jesuites have done since Luther; which all the Devills could not have kept from falling both then and since, if they had not found such old-shooed Ambassadours to travell over the World for their Mother Babylon, and their Father the Pope, palliated with the name of the Catholike Church. I wil not trouble you with recitation of their other orders particularly, but out of Myraeus wil tel you that the Benedictine Order can glory beyond the Jesuiticall in 52000. Monasteries, 15000. Writers, 44000. Saints, 4000. Bishops, 1600. Thus Archbishops, 200. Cardinalls, and 25. Popes, which in f-f succession of times they have had. And if the Jesuite hathabbates pretend his Tarn marte quam mercurio, his mustering eruditione 6 of Armies against the Heretickes, and setting Europe scriptis cele-in the present combustion; the Benedictine can produce-f 15700. Martiall Orders, affixes to his profession, instituted for jr " better purposes against Mahumetans, the Templaries (sometimes as proud as the proudest of Jesuites) the Knights of Calatrava, of Alcantara, Montesia, and Mer-cedis in Spaine, of Christ, of Avise, of Ala in Portugall, of Saint Maurice in Savoy, of Saint Steven in Toscanie, roater.. 21. and others elsewhere. The Augustinians have 555. Monasteries in Italy, and in Europe, as Volatteranus writeth 4000. and besides other subdivided Orders, have also their Military Knights of Rhodes or Malta, the Dutch Knights of our Lady in Germany and Prussia, the Knights of Saint Iago in Spaine; of Saint Lazarus of Jerusalem, of Jesus Christ instituted by Dominike against the Albigenses, of Saint Mary of Mount Carmel and Saint Lazarus (the former Lazarites being united to the Maltases) instituted by Paul the Fifth. But Monastike Religions, notwithstanding their vow of chastitie have so multiplied in the West, (for in the East few Orders are found to this day) that Benedicts Order hath procreated 23, Augustines, 28. and that later of Francis 15. And for the Individuals they are like the Grashoppers of Egypt, Pauperis est numerare pecus. The Pope is not so poore as to bee able to number his Creatures. Of the Franciscans alone Sabellicus numbers in his time at once living 90000. and addes that the Generall to that Order offered to Pope Pius against the Turke, 30000. able warriers of this Seraphicall Family without detriment to their Holies. They have (saith hee) filled the world, being divided into fortie Provinces, each Province into I. i. 175. I 481 2 H

PURCHAS HIS PILGRIMES

Custodiae, Wards or Wardenships, these subdivided abel. En. 9. into Convents and Places, These mortified Minors had in that time found the way, five of them to the Papacy, 26, to the Red Hat: as for inferiour Prelacies who can number them? The Dominicans in the same time (above six score yeeres since 21. Provinces, Convents 4143. in them living 26460. Friers, and of them about 1500. Masters (or Doctors) of Divinity, besides many of them in Armenia and Ethiopia, or Abassia, Constantinople anticipating the Jesuites glory in this kind, the Augustinians also were then numbred 30000. the Carmelites more, not to speake of the rest. This course of life first begun by devouter persons to avoid persecution, Antony and others which made use of Deserts, and a solitary life to escape the Sword, and the Worldes infection by vice together: was after imitated by good men, both for their owne devotions, freed by this meanes from secular interruptions, and fitted for the service of the Church both in Faith by Doctrinal! studies, and exercises in their Monasticke Schooles, and also in charity by beneficence therein to the poore, with the labours of their hands; and lastly, degenerated into smoakie superstition and ambition, of getting the glory of the World; with wealth and ease by seeming denialls thereof; and became a refuge, and sinke-sanctuary to Malecontents, Bankrupts, men in danger of Law, and weary of the crosses which attends each vocation (God having set downe this rule to all men, to eat their bread in the sweat of their browes, which these seeme to illude) that they which cannot bee In negotio sine periculo (to use the Orators words) may bee In otio cum dignitate. A master-piece of hypocrisie, which in another sence, and by another course can say with the Apostle, as having nothing, and yet (even carnally) possessing all things.

But who will hope to number the persons of each Order termed Religious, when the Orders themselves cannot bee reduced to due order or number? All

Historians in manner mention them, but none can name them all, much lesse marshall them. Joannes Wolphius in his Centenaries of Memorable Readings, thus expresseth many of them with the times of their Originall. A. D. 341. Thabenesio-tarum. 366. Ordo Publiae, 384. Order of Saint Basil. 399. Of Saint Augustine. 422. Of Paula Romana. 495. Canonis-sarum Regularium: also Ordo Canonicorum. A. 530. Apostolicorum: also Benedictinorum: also Scholastican-arum Benedicti-narum. 595. Gregorianorum. 610. Ger-undinensium. In the seventh and eighth Centenary none. In the ninth A. 912. Ordo Cluniacensis. 950. Camaldulensium. 977. Canonicorum Secularium. A. 1012. Hospitularii. 1017. Humilitati. 1030. Ordo Jejunantium. 1046. Lazaritarum. 1050. Luceolaniorum. 1076. Grandi-montensium. 1080. Carthusiensium. 1059. S. Antonii de Vienna. 1098. Ordo Cisterciensis. A. D. mo. Templarii. 1113. Bernhardini. 1119. Prasmon-stratenses. 1121. Militiae Calatravae. 1137. Ordo Robertinorum. 1148. Gilbertinorum. 1160.

Carmeli-tarum. 1170. Ordo Militum D. Jacobi de spatha. 1190. Ordo Teutonicorum Morianorum. 1190. Fran-ciscanorum. 1200. Cruciferorum. 1201. Ordo S. Spiritus Hospitaliorum. 1202. Gladiferorum. 1205. Domini-canorum. 1211. Ordo S. Trinitatis, sive Equitum de Redemptione Captivorum. 1214. Ordo Militias Monte-fias. 1215, Ordo Eremitarum S. Pauli. 1217. O. Vallis Scholarium. 1228. O. S. Claras. 1232. Or. Militiae S. Marias. 1250. Ordo de Observantia Minorum Pras-dicatorum. 1252. Ordo Fratriceuorum Beghardorum, Beghinarum, seu Beguttarum. 1257. O. Bethlehemi-tarum 1258. O. Bonorum hominum. 1273. O. Augustinensium Eremitarum Guilhelmitarum. 1282. O. Servorum S. Marias. 1297. Coelestinorum, 1300. Militum Sepulchri Domini. 1303. Sarabitarum. 1323. Militum Jesu Christi. 1326. Alcanthare militum. 1349. Flagellantium. 1350. Charteriorum Equitum. 1360. Equitum Stellas. 1365. O. Jesuatorum. 1366. Ordo

Salvatoris sive Scopetinorum. 1370. S. Brigittae. 1371. Turlupinorum. 1399-Albatorum. 1400. Vallis Um-brosae. 1405. Hieronymitarum. 1407. Canonicorum. S. Georgii in Alga. Also Mendicantium D. Hieronimi. Also S. Spiritus. Also Montolivitensium. 1408. Canonicorum Lateranensium Congregationis Frisonariae. 1409. S. Justinae. Also Mauritianorum Equitum. 1420. O. Equestris Annuntiationis B. Mariae. 1429. O. Eq. Aurei Velleris. 1433. S. Ambrosii ad Nemus 1453. O. Equitum S. Spiritus. I455- S. Catherinas Senensis. 1464. Equitum Lunae. 1469. Equitum S. Michaelis. I499- Ordo poenitentium mulierum seu meretricum. 1500. Ordo peregrinorum pauperum. 1506. Ordo Indianorum. 1529. O. Sodalitatis divini amoris sive Theatinorum. 1537. O. Paulinorum sive Gastali-anorum. 1540. O. Jesuitarum, sive Societatis Jesu. 1549. Capucinorum. 1561. O. militum S. Stephani. 1571. Ordo minorum Jesu Mariae seu Tertiariorum. 1579. O. Eq. S. Spiritus.

Unto these Orders whereof some time is set, may bee added many others of whose Originall no certaine time is delivered. Wolphius hath in Alphabetical! order named these of that kinde, Ord. Ambrosian-orum, Antonianorum, Fratrum de Armenia, Ordo Equestris de Avis. Batutinorum. Bonae voluntatis. Bursfeldensium. Canonicorum Regularium, differing from the former. Capellanorum, Challomerianorum, Cellariorum, Clavigerorum, Constantinopolitanorum militum, Cruciferorum another kind. O. Fratrum Crucis, O. Stellatorum Crucis, O. Forficerorum. O. Genettae Equestris. O. S. Gertrudis Monialium, O. Fratrum Helenas, O. Fratrum de Hispania, Or. Histricis Equestris. O. Hospitalariorum. O. Fratrum D. Jacobi. O. Ignorantias. O. Joannitarum de civitate. Ordo Vallis Josaphati. O. Josephi. Or. militum de Labanda. La-zari seu Magdalenae. Linonchleniorum. Monialium S. Mariae. O. S. Mariae novus. Conceptionis Mariae. O. ex Fratrib. martyrum. Maturinorum. Mensae Orbi- cularis (Knights of the Round Table) O. Pauperum Voluntariorum. O. de Corbuuo S. Petri. O. S. Petri in Schunbach. O. Purgatorialium. Rebaginorum. Re-clusorum sive Inclusorum. O. S. Russi. Ordo Monachae vel Sacerd. liberae. Scalae dei. Sclavonianorum. Fra- I. i. 176. trum ex Scotia. S. Sophias sive Gratiae. Speculariorum. Stellatorum. Militum S. Thomae. Vespillonum. Fratrum de viridi vallo. O. Valetudinario-servientium. Ungarici eq. O. Wenceslaitarum. Zambonitarum. Zupfnonnarum. But it is time to have done, lest such uncouth names make some Reader feare hee shall thereby conjure up some Devills, ordered to disorders. I could also out of History adde others, but these are more then enough, Papall Orders enough to breake all Christian orders and rules of simplicitie and sanctitie, with their superstition and hypocrisie. Of their rules, habits, and other superstitions (understand this of the later, for the ancient were both without vow, and fit Schooles and Seminaries for the Church, as our Universities now) the same Wolfius, Hospinian and other Authors have written at large.

Chap. XVII.

A Discourse of the diversity of Letters used by the divers Nations in the World; the antiquity, manifold use and variety thereof, w ith exemplary descriptions of above threescore severall Alphabets, with other strange Writings.

Od the giver of every good gift, hath endowed Man (created after his owne Image) with divers priviledges above other sensitive Creatures, not onely with dominion over them, but with Reason and Speech, both above their Naturall capacities: By the one he composeth Rationis y naturall syllogismes in himselfe, proposing to his Under-"rationu pri-standing, disposing in it, and by his Will electing what ' S '- seemes best of those things, which the externall Senses, as the Cinque-Port-Intelligencers have brought in, and the Internall, the Common sense, Phantasie, and Memory, as Reasons handmaids have prepared to Discourse. By the other, as a Sociable creature, hee imparteth those Mind-conceptions unto other men, and those which are many persons, are made as it were one body reasonable. God hath added herein a further grace, that as Men by the former exceed Beasts, so hereby one man may excell another; and amongst Men, some are accounted Civill, Manifold and and more both Sociable and Religious, by the Use of excellent me letters and Writing, which others wanting are esteemed oj etters. Brutish, Savage, Barbarous. And indeed much is the litterall advantage; by speech we utter our minds once, at the present, to the present, as present occasions move (and perhaps unadvisedly transport) us: but by writing Man seemes immortall, conferreth and consulteth with the Patriarkes, Prophets, Apostles, Fathers, Philosophers, Historians, and learnes the wisdome of the Sages which have beene in all times before him; yea by translations or learning the Languages, in all places and Regions of the World: and lastly, by his owne writings surviveth himselfe, remaines (litera scripta manet) thorow all ages a Teacher and Counseller to the last of men: yea hereby God holds conference with men, and in his sacred Scriptures, as at first in the Tables of Stone, speakes to all. And whereas speech pierceth the Eare (pierceth in-deede and passeth often, in at the one, and out at the other) Writing also entertaineth the Eyes; and so long, by our owne or others reading, speakes to either of those nobler Senses, as wee will, and whereof wee will our selves; husht and silent at our pleasure; alway free from feare, flattery, and other humane passions. Therefore the dead were esteemed the best companions and faithfullest Counsellors, in Alfonsus his opinion, namely, in their Writings still living to performe those Offices: and want of Letters hath made some so seely as to thinke the Letter it selfe could speake, so much did the Americans herein admire the Spaniards, seeming in comparison of the other as speaking Apes.

Thus excellent is the use of letters: how ancient, un- who first in-certaine. Josephus mentions Writing ancienter then the ventedletters. Floud, by which, knowledge of Astronomy was com- Jos. Ant. I. mended to posteritie in two Fillers, the one of Stone,- 2-the other of Bricke, to outlive those two dismall destructions which Adam had prophecied should befall the World, by Fire and Water: that of Stone remaining to his time. Plinie conceiteth an eternity of Letters, as PUn. l.-j. c. t e. of the World and Mankind: and supposeth that the tj r" Assyrian were such: elsewhere attributing their invention to the Phoenicians, as of Astronomie also, and the Arts of Warr and Navigation, and after others opinion to the Egyptians, after others to the Syrians. It is, I see not how probably by some affirmed, that Moses first received Letters in the Two Tables of the Law written by the finger of God. Master Fuller is of opinion that- '" the Phoenicians themselves learned them of Abraham, + ' ' ' who seemeth to him, as likely in his long stay with the Canaanites to have taught them Letters, as to have instructed the Egyptians in so short a space, in Astronomie and Arithmetike, which Josephus affirmeth. And most probable it seemeth that in blessed Shems posteritie by Heber, Noah had left the best Arts of the former World. Job is by some, upon good reasons, J"- n- 26. holden ancienter then Moses, who yet often speakes of ' ""' Bookes· and writing, as a thing then familiarly used.

Another no lesse controverted question is of the ancientest kind of Letters, which Postellas, Scaliger and I. i. 177- others thinke to be the Phoenician, or as now they are called, the Samaritan, first used by all the Canaanites (of which the Phoenicians were a part) and Hebrewes; f hat Letters but after the deportation to Babylon, the Cuthaeans or j '-Samaritans still continued them (being taught by the j'o. ScaJmot. Israelitish Priest) but the Jewes grew into use of others, in Euseb. which Scaliger saith, are nuperae ac novitiae ex Syriacis Ckron. depravatae; illae autem ex Samaritanis; quod cum luce

See those Coines and Letters at the end of this Chapter.

ler. prof, in I. reg.

G. Posteluing. 12. Alphab.

P. Pilg. I. z. r. 9.

Joh. 4.

clarius sit, tamen quidam semidocti, semitheologi, ut signantius loquar semi-homines, Judaicas literas vere Hebraicas esse priscas audent deierare, c. And after; Visuntur hodie Sicli qui quotidie Jerosolymis effodiuntur, sub regibus Inda in usu fuerunt. In illis nummis easdem literae incusas sunt, quae in scriptis Samaritanorum leguntur; and thinkes it extremae insaniae imperitias to thinke that the elder Hebrewes had any other.

Saint Jerome also affirmeth, that Esdras was Inventer of the present Hebrew Letters after the Captivitie. His words are, viginti duas literas esse apud Hebraeos, Syrorum quoque lingua testatur, quae Hebrasae magna ex parte confinis est. Nam ipsi 22. ele-menta habent, eodem sono, sed diversis characteribus. Samaritani etiam pentateuchum Moysi totidem literis scriptitant, figuris tantum apicibus di screpantes. Certumque est Esdram, post captam Hierosolymam, instaurationem templi sub Zerubabel, alias lit-eras reperisse, quibus nunc utimur, quum ad illud uque tempus, iidem Samaritanorum, Hebraeorum characteres fuerint.

Postellus attributeth the reason of this new Invention to the difference of Religion, which began in Jeroboam, but became worse in those Cuthaeans other strangers which were placed by the Assyrians in the Cities of Samaria, whose irreconciliable hatred I have elsewhere shewed in my Pilgrimage. He alledgeth also such Coines, said to be as old as since Salomons dayes, seene by him (two of which shall follow with their Letters.) Hee addeth that the Jewes affirmed the same, which still hate the Samaritans, but highly prize those Coines as their owne Antiquities; the Inscription whereof being Jerusalem the holy, could not proceed from the Cuthaean Samaritans, which worshipped in their Mountaine, (as the Samaritan woman said to our Saviour) and not in Jerusalem. Postellus saw a Grammar in their Letters, but the Language Hebrew, the Exposition Arabike; the Characters their owne, which now also want the points which in Saint Jeromes dayes they had.

Scaliger sheweth further how the ancient Greeke or Jos. Seal, ubi Ionike Letters (like in forme to the present Latine, f-which seeme thence derived) were by Cadmus carried from Phoenicia, and communicated to the Greekes, of him called by Herodotus Ka t?7ia ypdixfji. ata, which both hee and Pausanias affirme that they had seene; and of which Plinie testifieth, Gentium consensus tacitus primus omnium conspiravit, ut Ionum literis uterentur. Of these anon you shall see an example. Scaliger addeth that the Chaldees fashioned theirs from the Phasnician, now used by the Nestorians and Maronites. These have both Capitall Letters and lesser: from which Chaldee Letters the moderne Jewish and Arabike are derived, the Chaldee being in a meane betwixt the Phoenicians and them.

Our Learned Countreyman Master Fuller, as hee will F"- Miscel-not yeeld that the ancient Hebrew was the Phoenician '" w-' 4-'-4-Language; so neither will subscribe to this opinion, which maketh the moderne Hebrew Letter to be of later devise. But as the Egyptians had two sorts of Letters, one sacred and hieroglyphicall, the other vulgar; and as with us the writing proper to the publike Courts in Court and Chancerie hands differ from the common writing: so the Hebrewes also might have a two fold writing, the one in civill and common affaires, still read in the Samaritans Bookes and Coines; the other Ecclesi-astike or sacred, used by the Priests and Levites, and in which the holy Scriptures are preserved; which then became Secular and Vulgar, when their emulation against the Samaritans admitted nothing common betwixt them, especially in Letters, which it appeareth they learned of one of the Samaritan Priests of Bethel, of Jeroboams institution, and not of Leviticall race. For it is probable that Jeroboams baser Priests either could not, or would i. Reg. iz. i. not write in that Leviticall and Priestly Character, but–retained unto all purposes that which before had beene admitted only to civill affaires. He conceiveth them to bee both of Israeliticall originall; and if either be ancienter, the sacred (still stiled Hebrew) to have the preheminence, Ecclesiasticall things being of more An- Iren. advers. tiquitie then civill; in which sense Irenasus calleth the har. l. z. c. ancient Hebrew Letters, Sacerdotales; these being also ' '" ' ' ' more simple and uniforme then the Samaritan, as is scene in the Iod, which our Saviour citeth as the lest of Letters, which yet in the Samaritan is multiforme and large. How ever the case stands herein, it is evident they are both very ancient, and as it were Mother-letters to the rest of the World: which as wee have noted alreadie of the Chaldee, Ionike and Latine, so may it be observed in the principall of those others which we shall anon present to your view.

Plin. l. j. c. 6. Plinie reporteth that Cadmus brought sixteene Letters into Greece, to which in the Trojan Warre Palamedes added foure others OS X, and after him Simonides other Z H. Aristotle saith there were eighteene ancient ABTAEZIKAMNOnpSTY, to which Epicarmus added O X, or rather Palamedes: veteres Graecas fuisse easdem pene quae nunc sunt latinas, he averreth out of a Brazen Table in the Palace inscribed NAVSIKRATES TISAMENO ATHEN-AI O S (so Scaliger expresseth it) in later Letters Nauo-J-Kpdres TiaajuLTjpov A6f paio9. Scaliger also out of an old Scholy upon Euripides his Orestes, affirmeth that the I. i. 178. old Greekes had seventeene Letters, sixteene of Cadmus his Invention, and V added thereto, and thinkes this to be Aristotles assertion, who would never have reckoned (f) for one, being of later invention. These seventeene are ABTAEHIKAMNOrpSTY. Before 0 X were invented by Simonides, saith Marius Victorinus, they used to place after T, P, K, the aspirate H, as T H E 0 S, HHIAOS, KHPONOS for Oeoy, Xo?, XioOJ09. But let the studious herein read Scaligers whole Discourse or Digression in his Notes upon Eusebius his Chronicle, who also giveth the examples mentioned by Herodotus: AMrhITPVOA: M. ANETHEKEN. EON. At O. TEke AON. in the moderne Letters, kfkpi- pviav fx' aveotjkev ecov airo TiikeSodcov, The like he doth in divers others. But an old Inscription in lonike Letters I could not but transcribe from him. It was ingraven in a Filler in Via Appia, thence removed to the Farnesian Gardens; whereby it appeares that these lonike Letters continued in Italy long after they had ceassed in Greece.

ODEivL EMITON MET KINES I EK. TO. TRIOrlo. HO. ESTIiv. Eri. TO TRITO. EN. TEL HODOI. TEI. Jrr. ly L E7VTOI. HERODO. AROI. O 7 A R LOIOiv: TOI. KIA ESAivTI. MAPTVS. D IMON. EATHODIA. KJl. HOI KIOivES. DEMETROS. K I. KOPES JNA EMJ. KAI 07VI0A. E0A7: KAI.:.

The same Inscription in later Greeke Letters.

ovsevi deixitOV fierakivrjcrai eC TOO TpioTTloV, b TTIV CTTl TOV To'ltOV ev TH 6S(p TU ATTTTia v TU) Upwsov aypw. ov yap Xdol'ov TO) Kivrjcravtf MajoTu? SaijuLcov, evosla, koi ol Kioveg Trjg AijfjLtjtpo?, Kai Koyo?9 a. vd6) fxa, koi- Oovrnv Oewv, Kai."

Plinie saith that the Pelasgi first brought Letters into Pin. ubi sup. Italy: Heurnius cites these Verses out of an old Booke touching the Inventers of Letters.

Moses primus Hebraicas exaravit literas:

Mente Phoenices Sagaci condiderunt Atticas:

Quas Latini scriptamus edidit Nicostrata:

Abraham Syras idem reperit Chaldaicas Isis arte non minore protulit iegyptias:

Gulfila prompsit Getarum quas videmus ultimas,

But who is so literate as to reduce the Letters of each Nation to their first founder? it seeming probable, that as Nations became more civ ill, so some more Heroike Spirit in each Nation devised new of himselfe, or derived the old from some other Nation, or made a mixture of both: besides that the conquered Nations usually have received in some part both Language, and Letters, with their Lawes from the Conquerors.

We see still that those which teach short writing, can and doe devise new Characters daily for that purpose; that others ordaine Cyphres or Characters only knowne to those whom the Authour shall impart the skill unto; and these diversified ad libitum, as any intends to impound or pale in his secrets or mysteries of State, or Art; some of which perhaps in processe of time have beene made vulgar and ordinary Letters. These mys-ticall Writers have also devised other Arts of conceale-ment, as writing with AUume water, not to be read after it is once dried, but laid in water; with an Onyon, to be read at the fire, c. Differing Now for the varietie and differing formes.

Art hath figures of superabounded: both in the subject and instrument, etters, an some writing with Pencils as the Tapenites and Chinois, utvBTSlttc Of ' r ' Instruments Others with Pens, others with Instruments of Iron as and materials, the Malabars, of Gemmes, Brasse also, or other metall, in Table-bookes, Leaves, Barkes, Wood, Stone, Aire, Sand, Dust, Metall, Paper, Cloth, Parchment, and innumerable other materials: in the forme also and manner, with Quippos in Stones or Threads, as in Peru; with Pictures as in Mexico, and the Egyptian Hieroglyphikes; I. i. 179. with Characters, each expressing a word or thing, not a letter, as the Chinois, Japonites, and our Arithmeticians and Astronomers in the figures of their Arts; some Cap. Smith, with fiery Torches, as you may read in Captaine Smiths inf. I. 8. following Relations; the most have used letters, which by Art are disposed to frame all words, and hath beene the most complete kind of writing which ever was. But Babel never had more confusion of languages then Letters have sustained alteration, differenced both by place and time, yea and by the humours of men. Thus not onely divers languages have divers letters, but the same language, as it changeth with time, so the letters also are diversified, as in the Ionike and later Greeke hath beene observed, from both which the Moderne Greekes write much differingly. In this our J hy Saxon Countrey wee have had manifold successions of letters fs ceased. in succeeding ages, as is most easie to be seene in well furnished Libraries, and that especially of the Miracle of industry in this kind. Sir Robert Cotton, both in Bookes, Chartells, and Letters. The Conquerour (as Ingulfus, Edmerus and others then living observe) would not indure the English Language or Letters, whereby the Saxon Letters are now commonly extinct. And both all Records of old, and the divers Courts of this Kingdome, yea every Copy-Booke, and each writing Masters Master-piece hanged forth to publike view, easily manifest the passed and present varietie of Letters Varietle of in common use at the same time. It is impossible "" f-f ,. 1 r 11 1 T with us at this therefore to give an example or all, either J etters or Languages. Yet in this so Generall a History, I thought it would minister some delight to the Reader, to have a taste of that immense varietie, which here out of Thesius Ambrosius, Postellus, Duretus, Scaliger, Gramaye, Lazius, c. we exhibite.

Let the Reader take notice also of the varying in Divers ways of lines, some reading (as the Latines, Greekes, and Z-most of the Europeans) from the left hand to the Right sidewayes; the Hebrewes, Arabikes, and most of the Indians (except the Malabars and Siamites) from the right to the left: the Ingres, Cathayans, Tartars, that is the most of the Easterne and Northeasterne Asians write their lines downeward, and multiply them from the left hand to the right, as you may see in the Japonian charter following. And in Patane they use Japonian three, both languages and sorts of writing: the ' ' 4-Malayan, which I have seene in Arabike characters written from the right hand; that of Siam from the left, and that of China downewardes. The people of Tangut (North neighbours to China) are said to write from the right hand to the left, and to multiply American their lines upwards. The Mexicans had writings in books. forme of a wheele, which were read from the Center

Hiitonin upwards to the Circumference. In Honduras they had Pictures. Bookes of paper made of Cotton-Woou, or the inner ro.2.. 5. C.6. Barke of Trees, or of Metle-leaves, folded like Broad-cloathes, the writing whereof was partly painting (where such things as had forme or figure were therein represented) partly in Hieroglyphicall characters, as Fish-hookes, Starres, Snares, Files, c. In these they Heraldry. kept their Records. And our Heralds Art keepeth Magicall records of pedegrees in a kinde of Hieroglyphikes, not 'diaholiczr much unlike. To let passe Magicall characters, Thesius Ambrosius hath published a confused kind of scroll, the Copie of one (hee saith) written by the Devill, I had rather mention that which Eusebius in the life of Constantine recordeth written by Divine hand, which some say was the Crosse, but by his description appeareth rather to have beene the two first letters of Christs name, x and p combined, with promise of victory to the pious Emperour, not in that signe (of the Crosse) but in Christ himselfe, to whom be glory for ever, Amen.

The Phoenician or Samaritan Letters, which some say were the Mosaicall and first Hebrew, with the Names of the elder and later Syrians, and the Ionike and later Greeke Letters answering them, and answered by the Latine, we have transcribed out of Joseph Scaliger in this forme and order.

I. i. i8o.

By the figure of these Characters it is easie to bee gathered that the Letters (which Herodotus calleth Ka yur; ia ypdxmara seene by him in the Temple of Apollo Ismenius at the Boeotian Thebes ojuoia eovra Toian Iwvikola-i) were devised by Cadmus, with no great alteration in the most from the Phoenician, except in the turning them from the right hand posture to the left, and adding sometimes, sometimes cutting off some particles. The Latine no lesse seemeth derived from the Ionian, and are in the most the very same. Your eyes may easily dis-cerne and judge; and Scaligers Commentary is well worth your consultation hercin, too long to transcribe or translate hither. Of the twenty two all had not the use of I. i. 181. Letters and Elements of writing amongst the Ionians, but sixteene onely: the rest were called ' irla-ijfxa that is notes, to wit, of Spirit or Numbers: and therefore the first note? stands for the numerall VI. F is ETrto-r ijLov TO 13as instead of Wau wherof the ieolians had frequent use, which called EXevr pexeurj and therefore was not reputed a Letter, because it might be taken away without change to the word; it stands also for a note of the spiritus lenis, as in that hexametre avxe? S' Feipv vavro Oeoi. Koi ' wfjioarav Faiiv it is neither Consonant nor Vowell, there being a Synalaephe for ei and no Position in Faleu. H with the old Iones was as H with the Latines, as in that HODOI in the former Inscription is scene: they also used E onely, both long and short syllable, as in the same Inscription KINESANTI sheweth, and T E I for rr. Beda lib. de Indignitatione hath touching those eiria-rnxa these words; Graeci omnibus suis Uteris exprimunt numeros. Verum toto Alphabeti sui charactere in numerorum figuras extenso, tres, qui plus sunt, numeros, notis propriis quae ex Alphabeto non sunt depingunt. Prima est 7 quae dicitur Episimon, est nota numeri VI. Secunda est Q, quae vocatur Kophe, valet in numero X C. Tert ia est 3 quae dicitur Enneacosia quia valent DCCCC. But let the learned read Scaliger himselfe.

The Hebrew Letters and Names thereof now in use are these.

I have also added two Coines of the old Samaritan letters, the higher described from Postellus his Introduction of twelve languages, the lower from Bezas larger An-notations, Matth. 17. His words are Hujus vero numi, id est dimidii Stateris argentei, qui quatuor Drachmarum erat quales ipsi Judas olim signarant, veram imaginem hie exprimendam curavi, expressam ex vero puri puti I 497 argent! numo, mihi a fido illo Christi servo D. Ambrosio Blaurero, donate. Habet autem hie numus Samaritanis I. i. 182. Uteris insignis, una ex parte urnam illam sacram, in qua recondita fuit Manna, superposita litera Aleph, qua declaratur simplex hie fuisse siclus, duarum videlicet drachmarum, cum duplex esset drachmarum quatuor, cum inscriptione S C H E K E L 11 S R A E L id est, Siclus Israel: ex altera vero, Virgam illam Aaronis florentem, cum inscriptione IeRVSCHALAlm KODSCHAH id est Jerusalem Sancta. That of Postellus (of Silver also) differeth somewhat in the figure and the superscription S. B. which (I conceive) signifieth that it was a double Shekel, I have added an Obeliske or Columne inscribed with Egyptian Hieroglyphikes, copied out of Gramaye; and in the basis thereof have added another described out of Laurentius Pignorius his Mensae Isiacae expositio, where the Reader may feast himselfe with Characters of that Inf. pag.() o. kind. I also have elsewhere given some of those Egyptian Socrat. L 5. figures. These I thought good to adde for illustration of that mention of the Crosse in the Ecclesiastical History against the Egyptian figures in the Temple of Sarapis, which occasioned the conversion of many Ethnikes to Christianity.

Soz.. j. c.

The Alphabets following wee have distinguished by figures, for the Readers better understanding of the exposition added. Wherein we have most followed Gramayes.

k? crrqiiilLijhw9. X'ACd p irr5 vvvzv) o 6'LIM CTA v tq: AITlvE r f x ' 5 l'3JttU3t'UC? Z"2.! ' 1 1n."- V'U X nn r UHni P(f)r)a3 rtrhxBn4iu"m" vo"-? O. cat-1,. v V J3a 3o-fsi jm. 1 I, 'nr He first is that of the Alans or Lumbards, set-L forth by Patricius: other have beene published by Bonaventura Vulcanius in his Specimen Variarum linguarum, and others. 2. The old Aleman Alphabet of Trithemius, much different from those of de Bry, Hermannus Hugo, and James Bonaventura. 3, An olde Magicke Alphabet of Honorius Thebanus, of which there are other kinds too many. 4. An Alchymicke of Cid Abdalla, of which the Africans have other sorts. 5. Gramay saith, it is an old English Alphabet sometimes published by Sir Thomas Moore. 6. The ABC. used by the Priests of Jupiter Ammon, devised by Mercurius i gyptius. 7. The Abassine attributed to Salomon; many others by many others are so inscribed, 8. The Assyrian, ascribed to Abraham. 9. The old Apulian, which inverted and read from the bottome is one kind of the Armenian fathered on Saint John Chrysostome.

PFHΛihmxjnf-vqwtXH-rcuihixi· 12 j QVP hvX VilA HV ' X V T 0 j T. t ijjje ss e y Ryz. T T8Al XHVci)0 raS?

4 k vnn YX mwisA Y Y 'HCi m ': tr IT Tij If ts X X-f'gv H YE y 71 j6 ielirmSSnhKXHNOrvCT2S Xl. CJi5? qvl fefiaaf K) a8 4VXVAVX LXvmii; Mf!yvi(: AX? I

The 10. is an old Asian Alphabet ascribed to Peter the Hermit. 11. The old Attike of lamael Megapolius. 12. The old Norman A. B. C. of Rollo. Duret and others have other kindes. 13. The old Alphabet of the Baleares so described by Cid Yabia, 14. The Suevian or old Frisian. 15. The old Cantabrian of Charles the Great. 16. The Bohni-Servian or Slavonian of Saint Cyrill, that also diversified. 17. The Burgundian or Astrologian of Ismael. 18. 19. running or fast hand with Ciceros and Cyprians notes.

H niitiiuAD iit? y 5xtity a'At'Vulxia D'llLipL-? fcf nh

HIT n'nw? Q Emm H m3 p hh 4 1,. B lrl FF3: lr? AB1R (A 6 T Ttf g A D i-e Ya i:? f 20. 21. 22. are Cabalisticall Alphabets attributed, one to the Angell Raphael, the next to Enoch, the third to Abraham: of which sorts Duret, Postellas and others have delivered, with like credit to these. 23. The old Celtike of Doratus. 24. The Carnike or Finnike of Ulphila. 25. The old Saxon of Otfridus Monachus. Lazius, Munster, Theseus, Ambrosius, c. have described others. 26. The Punike. 27. The Cretan or Phrygian of Hercules. 28. The Chaldean of Abraham, that also varied by others.

-.1-.

M ffa H 'KK el) reHftlk Z ih tl

BMW XWtyUB4R Aih r: "Vt fo c vn vwt rtixx avy AF w atmRd

XULA3 i(P A1 0CtcbaMAc

A QbuLrunikLNrnUl'ami vv Y.

2. The old Corsican Alphabet. 30. The old Cim-brian of Hichus. 31. The old Danes. 32. The old Dacian. 33. The old Dalmatike of Methodius. 34. Lumbard notes of Ciceroes Tiro. 35. The East Frankes of Humbald. 36. The old Galles of Wastnaldus. 37. Gallograecian of Rotila. 38. Old German of Faramund.

: z.? msnh2. K ' h'ii Mi imp y hh

RieT Z3 KKUH i OnpfcJ G? X o(e

X J? XVlxIPyltK7Kl 4R H nwiddC

KBT rghhY RTVM NJl nok stTdnvzyi

A BX4)tfFXI F I Jvi BM R FM A cj)

X pir-f i v rff't z: P jf- Atif 1i:Xni o+tt X XX-+'BVK: H T. Air 8 4 iaiiii iridjahiq? gnr4 ftmPaf i9M v W UJWifc - yp 6 tj Z Aocc V Nt 39. The Georgian of Saint James. 40. Old Gotike. 41. Getike or Massagetike. 42. Old Spanish-Gotike of Rodericus. 43. Old Scythian-Hunnike of Attila. 44. Two old Hetrurian. 45. Old Helvetian-Saxon, of Charles the Great. 46. luyrian of Saint Jerome. 47. An African Alphabet in the last page of Gramayes Specimen linguarum literarum universi orbis: which hee thus nameth in their order, the first Aips, A. the word signifieth an Eare. The second Ech, E. and both representeth and signifieth an Eye. The third Ifr. a Nose. I. The fourth Ombr O. The Tongue. 5. Vuld, ahand. V. 6. Lambd. L. The Earth. 7. Mah, the Sea. M. The 8. Nisp. the Aire. N. 9. Rasch, Fire. R. 10. Bap. the Sunne. It is a B. and with a dash P. 11. Cek. The Moone. C. and with a dash K. 12. Dagt, the Sword of Mars D. and T. 13. Gorcq. G. Mercuric. 14. Vaf. Venus, V. and with a dash F. 15. Siach. Saturne. S. and with a dash X. 16. Theue. Jupiter.

It signifieth nothing but is added to the beginnings and ends of periods. They read, as the Hebrewes, from the right hand to the left, and the line should have beene set the other way.

Li. 185.

'.,48. The i thiopike Alphabet, with the Letter A. added thorowout. 49. Syriak. 50. Arabike. They have divers other sorts of Letters, as in Erpennius, Postellus, Megiserus and others which have written of them is seene. The Turkes also use the same Letters and Points, or notes of vowels, howsoever their Language differeth much, being neerer the Persian and Tartarian. 51. Armenian. 52. Dalmatian. 53. Russian. 54. The Jacobites. 55. Egyptian. 56. Indian. 57. Persian. 58. The old Syriake.

In these wee have followed Gramaye, but could have given more complete and exact Alphabets, if the cutting had not beene so exceeding chargeable. This for a taste may serve, and we all know, that in our own other Tongues and Nations (as hath been said) the Letters and kinds of writing are exceedingly diversified: so that for any man to expect all the Letters of all Countries must needs bee impossible, each varying so much in it selfe.

I have added also this Copie of Malabar Writing, read as the Latine from the right hand, written with a needle in a Palme leafe folded up, of which I have two of great length and many folds.

Tom 2 . 2 ' China Characters are seen in our Map of China, c, 7. the Japonian in the Charter of that Emperour to our

Tom. i.. Merchants in Captaine Saris his Journall, as also the Indostan and Arabike; the Mexican Hieroglyphikes in a whole Historie therein written. Wee have ended with our owne ancient Saxon Characters. But first will give you another sort of Ulphilas Gotike Characters set forth by

De Brv.

Tom. 2. I. c. 23.

THE DIVERSITY OF LETTERS

Ulphilas Gotike, and the Saxon Alphabet. A b 1. i. i86.

See of these Gotikeletters, Tom. 2. . 3. c. 23.

END OF VOLUME I.

Lightning Source UK Ltd.
Milton Keynes UK
25 November 2010

163382UK00001B/302/P